ANCIENT CIVILIZATION

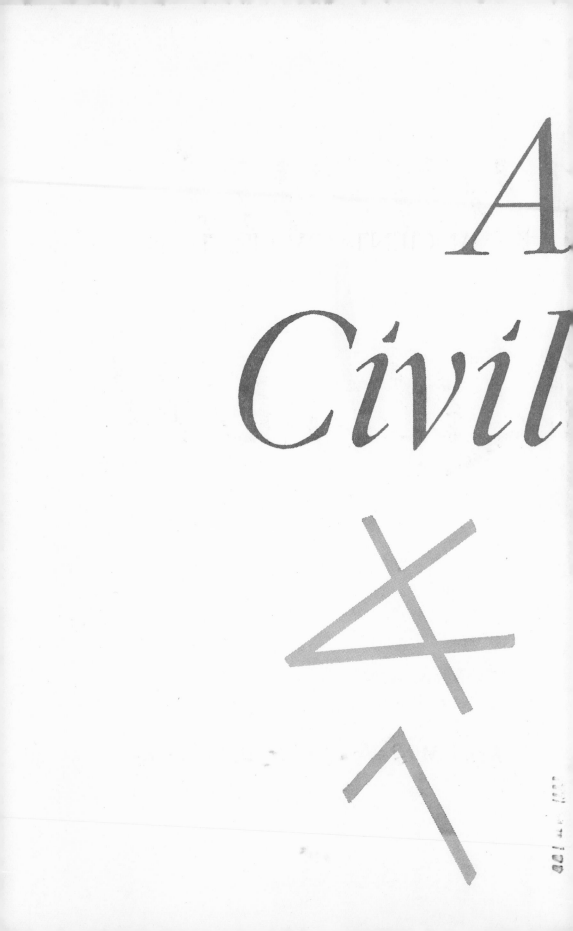

A

Civil

ncient
ization

TOM B. JONES
University of Minnesota

Rand McNally & Company - Chicago

RAND MCNALLY HISTORY SERIES

Fred Harvey Harrington, Advisory Editor

PREFACE

∽ THIS IS NOT an "ancient history"; rather, it is an account of the rise and fall of a civilization which had its origins in the Near East and reached its fullest development in the two Mediterranean peninsulas, Greece and Italy. Although most of the essential factual information required for beginning courses in ancient history will be found in this book, the main emphasis has been placed on the analysis of the causes of certain cultural developments and on the synthesis of the whole story of cultural growth and decline in antiquity. Because this is intended to be a history of ancient civilization, considerable space is devoted to the Near East in order that the beginnings of civilization may be brought under close observation and the subsequent borrowings by the Greeks and Romans more easily identified and understood.

After more than thirty years of study, teaching, and research, one finds that there are innumerable acknowledgements of assistance and encouragement to be made. The burden of debt is heavy, and if this were a more pretentious book, I should try to meet the demands of my principal creditors by an all-inclusive dedication: "To my students and my teachers."

TOM B. JONES

University of Minnesota

Table of Contents

TABLE OF CONTENTS

PART TWO

Greece

PART THREE

Rome

Maps

BY VINCENT G. MAZZUCCHELLI

Charts

ANCIENT CIVILIZATION

INTRODUCTION

MAN IS THE only introspective animal. For countless generations, inspired by curiosity, egotism, or a desire for self-improvement, he has given himself much thought, and it is not too much to assume that this speculation will continue as long as the human ract exists. Man's interest in himself has embraced his past, present, and future; he has sought knowledge of all three, though he has found an understanding of the first two somewhat more accessible than the last.

A large part of modern education is devoted to the study of man. The subject is approached in two ways: through the present, or through the past. One may study man as he is today, observing the physiology or psychology of the living animal or analyzing the political, economic, sociological, and technological aspects of modern civilization and their effects, good and bad, upon man. On the other hand, one may study man as he was in the past, following the course of his physical evolution, making certain deductions about his mental processes from his recorded actions and thoughts, or using material and literary remains to trace the growth of civilization from its beginnings to its present complexity.

Which is the better approach: to study man in the present or in the past? Neither, for they are complementary; one is not complete without the other. So far as we can determine, the physical and mental potentialities of the human race have not changed in any significant way in thousands of years. Consequently, man, the animal, can be most profitably studied as he is today, since contemporary evidence is both direct and abundant. Man can be observed at first hand in what might be called his natural habitat, both physical and cultural. Nevertheless, man is the only animal that possesses a culture; as a result, the human animal can hardly be separated from the civilization which he has created, and the whole matter is further complicated by the fact that, unlike man, civilization *has* changed. The dynamic character of civilization is important because, while it is essential to consider modern civilization and its relation to man, a full understanding of this subject is not possible without a knowledge of the past. Civilization today is not a spontaneous creation of the twentieth century, for we have inherited rather than created a major portion of our contemporary culture. One cannot easily evaluate the importance or comprehend the function of many elements in modern civilization without also knowing something of their origins and the manner of their evolution. The past often explains the present, and to ignore man's past in studying his present state would be like trying to solve a murder without inquiring into the events which led up to the crime.

One of the oldest and most satisfactory approaches to the subject of man and civilization is through the discipline which we call history. The historical method may be used to deal with a period, an area, a society, a set of political institutions, an art form, an economy, or an idea. In treating a subject chronologically, *i.e.,* historically, one may trace its development from simple beginnings to a final complexity, observing how and why changes occurred. The historical method is logical, straightforward, and effective, as the experience of many generations has shown.

The study of history is indispensable as an aid to understanding the complex civilization of our times. The dominant civilization in the world today is Western civilization. This cultural form prevails in Europe and the Americas, and many of its elements are now being adopted by the peoples of Asia and Africa. The traditional division of the history of Western civilization into the ancient, medieval, and modern periods has blurred and obscured an appreciation of the all-important fact that this history is a continuous story from its beginnings to the present time. From its inception in the great river valleys of the Near East about 3000 B.C., through its adoption by the Greeks, Romans, and the inhabitants of western Europe and its diffusion to the New World by European colonists after the time of Columbus, from relatively simple origins through countless elaborations and additions, the story of the growth of Western civilization can be traced through five thousand years of recorded history to our own twentieth century. If one follows through history the building of the imposing edifice which is civilization today, noting how its foundations were laid and the parts of the structure that were added through the centuries, it will often be discovered that the past can clarify many of the obscurities of the present.

The three phases of Western civilization—ancient, medieval, and modern—represent something more than mere chronological divisions. In the ancient period (roughly 3000 B.C.–500 A.D.) civilization began in the Near East, was diffused to the Mediterranean area where it was adopted and elaborated by the Greeks and Romans, and continued to grow in com-

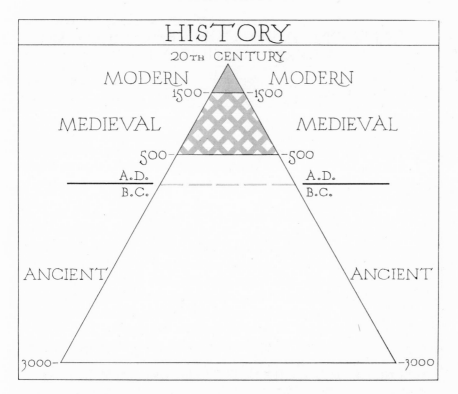

plexity until a climax was reached in the second century A.D.; this was followed by a decline which was paralleled by the fall of Rome. By comparison with the ancient, the medieval period (500–1500 A.D.) in western Europe was not characterized by a robust cultural growth, but the modern period (since 1500 A.D.) has witnessed an extraordinary accumulation of culture which has proceeded at an ever accelerating pace. The chronological relationships of the three periods are shown in the diagram entitled "History," while "The Expansion and Contraction of Western Civilization" is intended to illustrate the relative complexity of culture and its rate of growth in ancient, medieval, and modern times.

"Ancient history," the story of the first phase of Western civilization, is a fascinating and challenging field for study. People have long concerned themselves with this era for a number of reasons: in ancient times, of course, it was current history, but in the modern period "ancient history" has been an object of interest to those who wished to learn more about the Bible, or others who sought to become acquainted with our classical heritage from Greece and Rome, or still others searching for the roots of modern civilization. For the philosophically minded, the ancient period has a special attraction since it affords an opportunity to examine the whole

3

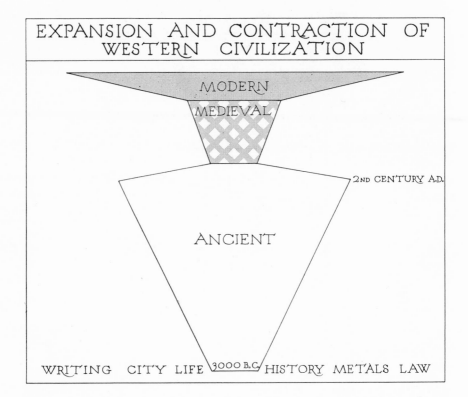

EXPANSION AND CONTRACTION OF WESTERN CIVILIZATION

MODERN

MEDIEVAL

2ND CENTURY A.D.

ANCIENT

WRITING   CITY LIFE   3000 B.C.   HISTORY   METALS   LAW

life cycle of a civilization, to see how it rose and why it fell, and perhaps to draw from the experience of antiquity some conclusions applicable to modern problems. The many parallels between ancient and modern developments make such an approach particularly exciting.

No history is cut and dried; that is to say, there is no period, even the most recent, about which everything worth knowing is already known or which is not subject to reinterpretation. More has been forgotten than is known about the past, and for some periods, not necessarily the most remote, the evidence is anything but abundant. Of all the fields of history, the ancient one is the least static as far as our conception of it is concerned. New discoveries are constantly being made which enlarge the area of knowledge, and the re-examination of old, familiar materials may often lead to new interpretations. Many of our ideas about the past are based on hypotheses which in turn are formed from insufficient information. Often the best that can be done is to take a set of facts and formulate a working hypothesis which is not at variance with the facts themselves. This means that the discovery of a single new item may be enough to destroy a theory which had seemed very well founded.

Research in ancient history is not child's play. In addition to the fact that he must try to piece together the scattered and incomplete parts of a

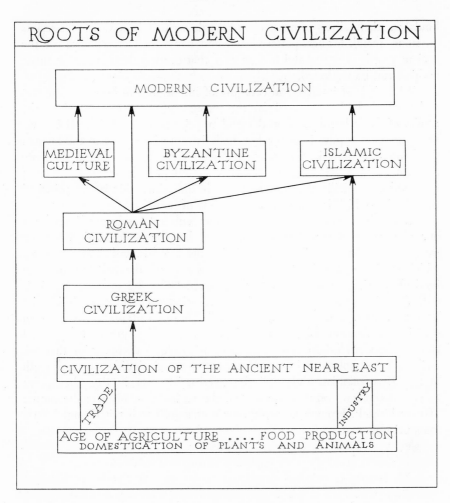

ROOTS OF MODERN CIVILIZATION

MODERN CIVILIZATION

MEDIEVAL CULTURE

BYZANTINE CIVILIZATION

ISLAMIC CIVILIZATION

ROMAN CIVILIZATION

GREEK CIVILIZATION

CIVILIZATION OF THE ANCIENT NEAR EAST

TRADE

INDUSTRY

AGE OF AGRICULTURE .... FOOD PRODUCTION
DOMESTICATION OF PLANTS AND ANIMALS

jigsaw puzzle, the would-be historian must be a jack-of-all-trades: archaeologist, epigrapher, numismatist, statistician, and linguist. A knowledge of languages is absolutely essential in order to deal with the ancient sources and to keep abreast of the research of foreign scholars. The basic language tools are Latin, Greek, French, and German; Italian, Turkish, and Arabic are also desirable, while the Near Eastern specialist needs at least some of the following: Hebrew, Sumerian, Assyrian, Babylonian (Akkadian), Persian, Elamite, Hurrian, Ugaritic, Phoenician, and Aramaic.

The sources employed by the ancient historian fall into three categories: literary records (formal histories—parts of the Bible, Thucydides, Tacitus, and the like—and nearly every kind of poetic or prose composition which has survived from the ancient period); the archaeological remains (towns, graves, buildings, sculpture, painting, tools, weapons, artifacts of all kinds); and, finally, various ancient records written in a variety of scripts on stone, metal, leather, pottery, clay, and papyrus. The evidence for the ancient past is so sparse and fragmentary that every little bit must be used; nothing can be neglected.

While it is of interest and certainly of importance to know the sources and methods which are used for the reconstruction of the past, it is the results of such inquiries that demand a priority of attention. *What* we know about antiquity is in the last analysis more important to the laymen than *how* we know it, yet an account of ancient history should do more than satisfy curiosity about the past; it should provide an explanation of how and why civilization developed as it did, since this is the principal contribution which it can make to the study of man.

In reading history we encounter our cultural, and sometimes even our physical, ancestors. These people can best be understood if we remember that they had the same basic impulses, needs, and desires as those which motivate us today. Four thousand years ago the Babylonians were fond of quoting an already ancient proverb: "The life of yesterday, it is today." This thought is paralleled in Ecclestiastes (1:9) where it is said, "There is no new thing under the sun." The student of history is often surprised to discover the antiquity of customs and ideas popularly supposed to be of modern origin. This occasions the whimsical complaint that the ancients have stolen all our good ideas. The real significance and truth of the Mesopotamian and Biblical proverbs, however, is that they point to one of the few constants among all the variables of history: the nature of man himself. Human nature does not change, nor has it changed since man became man.

PART ONE

The Near East

Chapter 1

BEFORE CIVILIZATION

T HE STORY of man's existence on this planet may be divided into two main periods: historic and prehistoric. The prehistoric period began tens of thousands of years ago and endured until fairly recently. Any account of this first phase of human life must be reconstructed from purely physical remains: bones and stones, tools and weapons, hearths and potsherds. We shall probably never have more than a general idea of what happened in prehistory.

The historic period began about 3000 B.C. with the invention of writing and the consequent production of written records. With the recorded word to supplement the material remains a more detailed reconstruction of the life of the past can be attempted. In general, as we approach our own times, the written records become more abundant, and thus greater certainty is possible.

Writing, which made possible the beginnings of history, was one of the earliest inventions of civilized man. In fact, for practical purposes one may say that civilization and history began simultaneously about five thousand years ago. Since prehistoric man had neither civilization nor writing, the dividing line between history and prehistory is also the boundary between civilization and barbarism.

The word "civilization" will be used many times in the pages that follow, and because people employ the term in several different ways, it is not too early to define its usage in this book. The phrase "modern civilization," for example, is often used in a purely technological sense to refer to great factories with complicated machinery run by steam and electric power, automobiles, jet planes, electronic devices—the products of the "machine age." One person might think of "modern civilization" in terms of a public school system, democratic government, and all the humanitarian interests of the twentieth century; another might think only of contemporary art, music, and literature. For our purposes here, however, civilization may be defined as follows: *A civilization is a culture which has attained a degree of complexity usually characterized by urban life.*

What is a culture? A culture is the sum total of all the culture traits possessed by a given people at a given time. Culture traits or cultural items are (*a*) the material things (tools, weapons, machines, clothing, etc.), (*b*) the political and social institutions, and (*c*) the habits, customs, and ideas, the possession of which differentiates men from animals. "Modern civilization" is an extremely complex culture made up of thousands, even tens of thousands, of culture traits. Television, baseball, atomic bombs, newspapers, comic books, marriage, divorce, communism, capitalism, and countless other things are culture traits or cultural items. In less complex cultures the culture traits are not so numerous. Fifty thousand years ago the habitual use of a few simple tools and weapons, a spoken language, the making of fire, a belief in the supernatural, and certain social customs comprised the meager cultural store of our ancestors.

There was a time, of course, when there was no culture, a time when only their physical appearance and structure served to distinguish our forebears from their near relatives, the great apes. How our ancestors acquired culture, and how culture became increasingly complex until the first civilizations arose are matters of some importance which must be discussed before it is advisable to consider civilization itself.

Today the earth teems with hundreds of millions of animals which we call men. These erect, featherless bipeds are mammals; they fall into the same zoological class as whales, elephants, cows, dogs, and sheep; they belong to the same *order* (primates) as monkeys and apes. "By applying the principle that structural resemblances point to a relationship one is forced to admit that man is an animal whatever else he may be. We have to call him a vertebrate, we cannot avoid calling him a mammal; there is, then, no reason why we should kick at having to call him a primate."[1]

Nevertheless, man is the only animal that possesses a culture, and it is his possession of culture that clearly distinguishes him from the other members of the animal kingdom. Primarily, man's culture is based upon two things: his habitual use of tools and his articulate speech. In building up the material side of his culture as well as in making advances in its non-material or intellectual phases, man found speech invaluable; but just as important was his ability to employ tools.

In order to speak articulately and to become a tool user man had to fulfill certain requirements: he had to have the proper vocal apparatus, a high degree of intelligence, a good memory, manual dexterity, and a special type of vision (stereoscopic). Other creatures are equipped by nature in

---

[1] G. G. MacCurdy, *The Coming of Man* (New York: Univ. Soc., Inc., 1932), p. 11.

such a way as to fulfill some of these requirements—the monkey has manual dexterity, the parrot can talk, the elephant is reputed to have a good memory—but man is the only animal that can fulfill them all. Extremely important, of course, is the fact that man's intelligence is superior to that of any other animal.

All the physical and mental essentials for the creation of culture were provided for man in the course of the evolutionary process by which he became man. Today the idea of evolution is almost universally accepted. Although there are still gaps in our knowledge of the evolutionary chain, the evidence which science has collected is so overwhelming that further proof of the fact of evolution is hardly necessary. How or why evolution occurs is subject to dispute—there are several current theories—but that it has taken place is no longer questioned by informed people.

Our particular variety of man, *homo sapiens,* is one of the most recent animals to appear upon the earth. *Homo sapiens* was not to be found in Europe or the Americas twenty-five thousand years ago; however, recent discoveries indicate that he appeared in Asia and Africa at a much earlier date, and our species *may* be a million years old. In Europe and elsewhere, however, other types of men seem to precede *homo sapiens;* in the Mount Carmel caves in Palestine, for example, Neanderthal men occupied the caves and then intermingled with our species when its representatives arrived in the area. None of the earlier types of men, as known to us today through their fossilized skeletons, can be called our ancestors with any degree of certainty, but somewhere far back in the chain of evolution these fossil men and *homo sapiens* had a common progenitor.

The successive stages through which man evolved need not be followed here. The story of physical evolution is of great interest, but the most important fact about it is that it produced an animal capable of creating culture. Both *homo sapiens* and the fossil men who lived side by side with him possessed culture. Either he or they created it, or perhaps there was an exchange of culture traits. Furthermore, it should be realized that some other creature, not necessarily one known to this planet, might devise a culture. Such a culture need not resemble man's in any way; it would depend entirely on the physical and mental attributes of its creator. In short, and this is a vitally important concept, the form of our culture was predetermined by the course of man's physical evolution. Without manual dexterity, man could not have invented tools; without articulate speech, certain types of communication would be difficult, if not impossible.

After man became man, his physical evolution practically ceased; at least we can see no perceptible difference between *homo sapiens* today and fifty or one hundred thousand years ago. No mental or physical change is apparent, though it might be argued that even a hundred thousand years is only a fleeting moment on the evolutionary time scale. New changes may take place in the future; a few generations of exposure to radiation from atomic explosions might have some significant effects.

It is possible that the evolution of culture tended to arrest and supersede physical evolution. The original aim and primary function of culture was to provide for survival through an artificial adaptation to environment. Perhaps *homo sapiens* would have become as extinct as the fossil men if his superior abilities had not enabled him to create through culture a new and better means of survival.

It is customary to divide the cultural history of man into epochs or ages: the Palaeolithic (Old Stone) Age, the Neolithic (New Stone) Age, the Bronze Age, and the Iron Age. This descriptive system of classification is used by cultural anthropologists, since virtually the only remains of the activities of primitive men are of the material sort (stone artifacts, etc.). In the Old Stone Age flint and obsidian were chipped or flaked into appropriate shapes for use as tools and weapons. In the New Stone Age a new technique for shaping hard and less brittle stones by grinding and polishing was invented. In the Bronze Age many types of stone artifacts gave way to those made of bronze (an alloy of tin and copper); then, in the Iron Age, bronze was in part replaced by iron.

This system is not entirely satisfactory, since the emphasis which it places upon changes in materials and techniques employed in only one phase of man's cultural existence tends to overshadow certain larger developments which were of greater importance than the shift from the use of stone to that of bronze, or bronze to iron. In this book a different terminology will be employed. We shall speak of the Age of Primitive Culture, the Age of Agriculture, and the Age of Civilization.

The Age of Primitive Culture corresponds roughly with the Palaeolithic Age in its time span. It began with the origins of culture and ended about 6000 B.C. when man first began to practice agriculture; it thus includes what is sometimes called the Early Neolithic Age. The Age of Agriculture covers the Full Neolithic Age to the rise of cities. The appearance of cities (about 3000 B.C.) begins the Age of Civilization; the Bronze Age began shortly after this time.

The earliest men lived by hunting, fishing, and gathering. By instinct a herd or pack animal, man roved from place to place with his fellows, gathering roots, nuts, and berries, and preying upon small animals which he ate raw. He himself was hunted by large carnivorous beasts; someone has suggested that man survived because he was tough and stringy and made a very unsatisfactory meal—the carnivores preferred other game and ate man only when there was nothing better to be had. Under such an economy the density of the human population was not likely to exceed one person per square mile even in the best-favored areas. Changes in the environment which affected the flora and fauna also affected man; a change in climate which altered the vegetation might cause a disappearance of the animals providing his food, or a great forest fire might have the same effect. Without culture man was like the plants and animals, a living organism adjusted to a certain environment, though his natural capacity for adjustment was greater than theirs.

Men eventually discovered that sticks and stones were more efficient weapons and tools than hands and teeth. The use of sticks and stones became habitual; from this, it was only a step to the selection of the more suitable sticks and stones. Then came, very naturally, the fashioning of tools and weapons to fit the need at hand. Thus, the use and making of these materials was established on a permanent basis; culture was born.

The effects of habitual tool using were far reaching. The use and manufacture of tools required agile, prehensile fingers; the so-called opposable thumb was also important. Manual dexterity and the constant use of the hands stimulated mental ingenuity and contributed to the growth of the brain in a way that produced a superior capacity for remembrance and imitation. The adoption of tool using was thus extremely important for mental development; it has been well said that man's brain is "hand-made."

It is believed that man began to speak almost simultaneously with the beginning of tool using. Speech made explanation and instruction possible; ideas could be exchanged and experience consolidated. Consolidation of experience has great value; not only can knowledge be perpetuated, but serious pitfalls can be avoided. Let us suppose that a certain root or berry is found to be poisonous. Without speech it would be difficult to warn another person of the danger involved in eating the poisonous food; he would have to learn it by an experience that would be of little value to him if it proved fatal.

The origins of language are obscure and will probably always remain so. No known language, living or extinct, is primitive; nor is the study of language development in children likely to be helpful, because children simply try to imitate what they hear others say. Fundamentally language is a system of communication which employs vocally produced sounds to which arbitrary meanings are assigned. There are various theories about the origin of language: the "bow-wow theory," that language arises out of imitation of sounds in nature; the "ding-dong theory," that language comes as a natural sound-producing response like the warning cries of birds or the mating call of the great bull moose; the "pooh-pooh theory," that language developed from exclamations of pain, wonder, surprise, satisfaction, and the like. More recently it has been suggested that language was preceded as a mode of communication by gestures; various sounds came to be associated with, or to accompany, such gestures, and thus oral communication evolved. Whatever its origin, the subject of language is important to historical research, and we shall return to it later.

Equipped and fortified with tools, weapons, and speech, man was better prepared for survival, and with the passing of time he added slowly to his store of culture. During the long Age of Primitive Culture many new traits or items were discovered or invented. Weapons and tools were manfactured from stone, wood, bone, and horn. Of the weapons, the club and the fist-axe (a stone shaped to fit the hand) came first; the knife, the spear (in principle, a long-hafted knife), and the mace (a hafted fist-axe) followed; at the end of the period (in the Early Neolithic Age) the true axe and the bow were invented. There were numerous implements, among which were scrapers, drills, and needles. Clothes were made of pelts and hides; basketry and wickerwork were begun.

One of the most important of the primitive discoveries or inventions was the making of fire. Fire provided warmth and a means of defense against dangerous animals; food could be cooked, and, as a result, some foods were made more digestible and formerly inedible plants and roots could be added to the diet. The potentialities of fire, however, were of even greater significance, for the chemical changes it could produce later led to the making of pottery and the smelting of metals.

The oldest extant remains of art date from the Ice Age in Europe (fourth glacial period) when people sought warmth and protection in caves. On the walls of these caves their drawings of animals and men may still be seen. The origins of art are obscure, but the development of primitive art was closely connected with a belief in magic. In the beginning men may have amused themselves by making rough sketches in the sand with sharp sticks or by molding figures in mud or clay. But a turning point came when men began to think that by drawing pictures of animals, reciting certain incantations, or following definite rituals they could overcome dangerous animals or increase the numbers of those that were essential as a source of food. Cave art was realistic because men felt that it was necessary to reproduce the subject as accurately as possible in order to gain the maximum magical effect.

Magic and supernaturalism were primitive inventions, and many interesting beliefs and practices were developed. Some men thought themselves the descendants of certain animals; others believed that, for example, by eating deer meat they could run more swiftly or by eating bear meat they could become more powerful. Hence, certain animals came to be associated with various groups of men; this is called *totemism*.

Men also tended to interpret the natural world in terms of their own social relationships, their dealings and contacts with other men. It was not surprising, therefore, that men should believe that other living creatures and even inanimate objects (trees, stones, rivers, etc.) were endowed with "spirits" like men themselves. This is called *animism*.

Death was a great mystery. One wondered what became of the "spirit" when a man died. Perhaps death was like sleep when the "spirit" or "soul" left the body and wandered far afield. In dreams a man often met and talked with people who had died. What further proof did he need that the "spirit" lived on after the body had died? The spirits of the great men who had once aided the tribe might be persuaded to return and help after death; in this manner some of the "gods" were born. It was easy to assume that spectacular natural phenomena were possessed of divine spirits or gods: the wind, the lightning, the sun, moon, and stars.

Evil men should be buried so that their spirits would not walk abroad; perhaps all men should be buried in order that they might find peace after dangerous and trying lives. Naturally, the dead would find solace in having their few poor possessions—their favorite weapons, perhaps—buried with them.

In primitive society tribal organization eventually replaced that of the pack. The chief was very likely the man who was the cleverest hunter and the best warrior. The old men, whose knowledge was the result of accumulated experience, were the advisors of the chief. The elders were also the historians of the tribe; by word of mouth they passed on tribal traditions to the younger men—the great deeds of some long-dead hero, the story of the great drought, of the starving time when game was scarce and only powerful magic had saved the people from extinction. In these early societies, where few lived to the ripe old age of thirty, the elders enjoyed a special respect: it was generally conceded that an old man was very clever, particularly favored by the gods, or just plain lucky. Whatever the reason for his longevity, his experience was useful to the tribe, for he often remembered what had been done in the past when the people had been confronted by unusual problems.

The rhythms of nature—the cycle of growth, the change of the seasons, the never-ending succession of day and night, the beat of the human heart, the act of walking or of breathing—encompassed the life of man. His reaction to these rhythms was subconscious, but powerful: dancing, singing, then poetry were virtually spontaneous in their appearance. Various forms of preliterate (unwritten) prose developed and were transmitted to posterity orally in the form of legend, myth, and folk tale. The story of past events lost nothing in the telling; eventually only a kernel of fact remained, but the legend was, nonetheless, a primitive form of history. People were always asking questions: Where did we come from? Why does the sun rise? Where does it go at night? Plausible answers were provided in the form of stories which told how something began or how it got its present form. These were myths, the primitive substitute for explanations now provided by science. People liked stories; folk tales and fairy tales were devised, some merely for the purpose of amusement and others with a didactic, moralizing end in view. This was a primitive form of fiction.

An elementary division of labor based on sex was common to many primitive societies. While the men hunted and fished, made weapons, and fought the battles of the tribe, the women bore children, gathered roots and berries, and made clothes and baskets. From the food-gathering activities of the women and their basketry came three outstanding discoveries dated at the close of the Age of Primitive Culture: (1) agriculture, (2) pottery making, and (3) textile manufacture.

In the course of their food gathering the women found it profitable to tend or protect young plants, and from this it was only a step to the beginnings of agriculture. It is not known whether root propagation or seed propagation was the first form to be practiced. In the long run the latter was to prove the more significant, but root propagation may have come first. What could be more natural as an act of sympathetic magic (based on the principle that like produces like) than to stick a branch or a root in the ground and expect it to grow? At any rate, we do know that the women began to make small garden plots, though their activity was necessarily sporadic at first because of the migratory habits of the primitive tribes. This first type of cultivation is called garden culture or "hoe culture," and it was begun late in the primitive period. About 6000 B.C. agriculture was established on a more permanent basis, and then, of course, the Age of Agriculture began. ×

The gathering of plant foods made it advisable to provide containers in which to carry and store the food. Baskets were commonly used for this purpose, and it was customary to fill the interstices of the baskets with clay. Ultimately it was noticed that contact with fire transformed the clay into a different and harder, insoluble material: pottery. Though some tribes were to learn to boil food in wooden or stone containers or even the stomachs of animals, in general the boiling of foods began with the invention of pottery. Boiling made available new sources of food; it especially encouraged the use of the cereals, although these could also be parched.

The invention of weaving, of textile manufacture, came as an extension of principles already developed in basketry and wickerwork. While the invention or discovery of pottery was certainly an accident, the application of logical thought is implied in the invention of weaving. These two culture traits provide examples of the way in which man increased his cultural store: the first, pottery, might be called a primary discovery or invention, and the second, weaving, illustrates the growth of culture by elaboration.

The power of the new discoveries and inventions, particularly of plant cultivation, to effect economic changes was potentially very great, but primitive life with its food-gathering economy and all its other culture traits might have continued indefinitely if it had not been for certain developments which took place in the Near East about eight thousand years ago. At that time, as a result of the domestication of plants and animals, man became a food producer and entered upon a new way of life. An important milestone on the road from barbarism to civilization had now been reached.

The transition from food gathering to food producing can be illustrated by a description of the finds made at a succession of sites in the Near East. We may begin with the caves of Mount Carmel in northern Palestine. In these caves, excavated about thirty years ago, debris resulting from many centuries of human occupation was found to reach a depth of about forty feet. The removal of layer after layer of this deposit revealed a long period of human habitation stretching from the so-called Lower Palaeolithic to a time more recent than the end of the Old Stone Age. Thousands of artifacts were removed from the caves; various kinds of weapons and tools were represented all the way from those typical of the Lower Palaeolithic to the microliths (small flints) characteristic of the Mesolithic Age, a post-palaeolithic period.

Many different peoples had occupied the Mount Carmel caves—some of the bones found in the lower (earlier) levels were those of fossil men, not of our species—but all the cave dwellers, from first to last, were food gatherers. The last inhabitants of the caves were "modern" men of the Mediterranean type, slender and short, averaging a little over five feet in height. They buried their dead in the caves, sometimes singly, sometimes in multiple burials. Some of the dead were buried in a flexed position; some were laid on their backs. Elaborate headdresses of shell beads were found in several cases.

The archaeological name for these last cave dwellers at Mount Carmel is the Natufians. They were hunters, fishermen (many bone fishhooks were found), and gatherers of food. They differed from their predecessors, however, in that they appeared to have been on the verge of food production. Although the seeds found in the caves were those of wild grasses and the animal bones those of wild beasts, the Natufians possessed flint sickle blades and built stone walls at the edges of the caves. This suggests that they harvested wild grains or grasses and that the stone walls were used as pens in which young animals were kept either as pets or for food.

Cave dwellings similar to those of Mount Carmel have been found elsewhere in the Near East. It is also of interest that some caves are still occupied on a temporary basis and in a manner somewhat reminiscent of the old way of life. The following paragraph occurs in the body of a report on the excavation of an Iraqi cave, a site rich in palaeolithic material:

Between the colder winter months of November and April, a group of Shirwani Kurds, about 35 people in all, or approximately seven families, inhabit the cave. They maintain small single-roomed winter shelters, constructed of log posts, branches, twigs and straw ranged around the sides of the cave interior. Each of these is warmed by a stone-bordered fire. Completing the scene of communal living are the animal corrals for the goats, and hitching posts and tethering stakes for the larger animals . . . .[2]

After Natufian times (8000–6000 B.C.), the inhabitants of Palestine gave up cave life, preferring instead to occupy temporary open-air shelters. Many of these have been found, but their use was sporadic and did not lead to an accumulation of debris as informative as that of the caves. Therefore, we must look elsewhere to find a site illustrative of the next stage in the change from food gathering to food producing. For this purpose we might select Jarmo, a site thirty miles east of Kirkuk in the hills of Iraq, or Jericho, near the upper end of the Dead Sea.

Not much later than 6000 B.C. Jarmo was the site of a tiny village of thirty houses which sheltered perhaps two hundred persons. The dwellings at Jarmo were made of pressed mud; some of the later ones had stone foundations. Tools and weapons were fashioned from stone and bone. While the flaking and chipping techniques known to the Natufians were also employed at Jarmo, some of the stone was shaped by grinding and polishing, a neolithic technique. Just as at Jericho, pottery was not found in the lower levels. What is more important, however, is that the animal bones are those of domesticated sheep and goats, and that the impressions of seeds found in the pottery fragments are those of domesticated grains: emmer, spelt, and barley.

The people of Jarmo, and possibly the inhabitants of earlier, more primitive sites in the neighborhood, were food producers. In short, the finds at Jarmo suggest three things: (1) that food production began about 6000 B.C. and occurred in the Near East before its appearance in any other area; (2) that the domestication of plants and animals took place concurrently; and (3) that food production began not in the plains or in the river valleys but in the grassy uplands where the wild cereals grew and the herd animals grazed and where the rainfall was sufficient for agriculture without irrigation.

The discoveries at Jarmo are recent; the site was not excavated until after World War II. The evidence from Jarmo casts doubt upon the validity of an older theory that the domestication of plants and animals was forced upon man by environmental changes taking place in the Near East and northern Africa after the close of the Ice Age. This is called the "oasis theory," and it may be outlined as follows:

The European glacial period had had a corresponding period in Africa and southwestern Asia, an age not of extreme cold but of rather heavy

---

[2] A. Solecki, "The Shanidar Cave," *Sumer*, Vol. I (1955), pp. 23–24.

rainfall—a pluvial period. Afterwards the climate became much drier, and gradually the Sahara and Arabian deserts began to increase in size. Arid sandy stretches appeared where formerly a luxuriant vegetation had flourished. As the desert advanced, some tribes crowded together on the oases, and others migrated northward to Europe or (in Africa) eastward to the valley of the Nile. In Asia the enlargement of the Arabian Desert drove people to the banks of the Tigris and Euphrates or westward to Syria and Palestine. As a result of these climatic changes two things happened: (1) man domesticated animals, and (2) agriculture was established on a permanent basis.

1. In the postglacial period animals as well as men sought refuge on the oases. The young animals were often captured and tamed. Some species were found amenable to domestication[3]—cattle, sheep, swine, and goats— but most others man could not tame. Domesticated animals were very useful because they provided a surer food supply than wild game; their hides and wool[4] could be employed for clothing, and later some animals were used for draft purposes.

2. The scarcity of game caused by increasing aridity enhanced the importance of agriculture, and man began to depend more and more upon plants for his food. Primitive "hoe culture" gave way to extensive agriculture. Many species of plants, especially the cereals, were now "domesticated."

The idea that the great river valleys were occupied by man at the beginning of the Age of Agriculture is not in accord with the archaeological evidence, as we shall presently see, but the "oasis theory" cannot be rejected in its entirety until the significance of the finds at Jericho can be properly assessed. Jericho *is* an oasis, and its excavators claim that it is older than Jarmo.

Although Jericho has been an object of archaeological research since 1867, it was not until 1952 that the lower (and older) strata of the mound were reached by the excavators. The lowest levels discovered thus far give evidence of village life presumably based on food production which may date back to 6800 B.C.[5] If the priority of Jericho over Jarmo is established as fact, the hypotheses regarding the beginnings of food production (based on

---

[3] A domesticated animal is one which has become the tame companion or servant of man; it reproduces its kind in captivity. Primitive man had only one domesticated animal, the dog. In the glacial period the dog hung about the outskirts of the camp, and before long it had become man's companion on the hunt. The dog also served primitive man as food.

[4] Textile manufacture and the invention of the true loom would thus come with, or just precede, the domestication of sheep and goats.

[5] This date is derived from a Carbon-14 analysis of limited material from Jericho. The Carbon-14 method measures the radioactivity of organic matter. Living organic matter absorbs radioactivity; after death, radioactivity decreases at a known rate. Thus, the radioactivity of a piece of charcoal or some other organic substance from a site can be tested, and its approximate age computed. The method is not foolproof; it is capable of considerable refinement, and thus the dates which it provides must, at present, be regarded with some skepticism.

the Jarmo finds) must be abandoned. Mature reflection, however, will show that the Jericho materials do not necessarily support the "oasis theory." It is futile to attempt to reach a conclusion on this matter until it is clarified by further research but there is every reason to hope that the problem will be solved within the next ten years.

The domestication of plants and animals was not an invention or a discovery, the work of a moment. It was something that took place gradually, insensibly, without any particular planning. From the harvesting of wild grains people had acquired the habit of watching and tending plants which they hoped to use; ultimately, they went a step further and planted seeds. Wild animals had been captured when young; some were not eaten immediately but lived long enough to reproduce themselves in captivity. The efficiency of raising plants and animals was an obvious thing, once it had been accomplished; thereafter it was adopted as a habitual practice, becoming a culture trait which spread from its center of origin to other areas.

Agriculture is of vital significance in human history. Its adoption augmented and assured the food supply; this allowed an increase in population because it meant that more people could be fed. It has been estimated that even with the most primitive kind of farming any given area may be able to support a population several times the size of that which can exist by hunting and foraging. With "hoe culture" a square mile of territory can support three people, three times the number per square mile in a hunting and gathering economy. With full agriculture (with the plow), a square mile of arable land will support 750 persons, thus allowing for a tremendous increase in population.

The domestication of plants and animals marked the beginning of a great revolution which, though basically economic, was to alter every phase of man's existence and culture. The change involved more than a shift from food gathering to food producing, more than an increase in population; government, society, religion, technology, art, and morality were all affected. In the new age men thought differently and acquired a standard of values different from that which had prevailed during the Age of Primitive Culture.

The tribes that adopted agriculture gave up their nomadic life and became sedentary. Permanent homes were established, since the duties of cultivation and the harvest required man's constant presence. The houses were grouped together in villages because a concentration of the population provided mutual protection; the crowded living quarters also left more land free to be cultivated. Village life automatically increased the complexity of social and political organization. The tribal chief had many new duties; he had to become an administrator and a judge. In time the press of affairs forced him to build up a staff of assistants with specialized functions. The growing importance of land brought a concept of private property; for the protection of property rights and the maintenance of order, regulations were made which ultimately became laws.[6]

Religion, as well as custom and habit, was affected by the adoption of the agricultural way of life. Even in the Age of Primitive Culture man had recognized that nature was more powerful than he; as we have seen, magic and religion were employed by early man in an attempt to coerce nature. Obviously, in the Age of Agriculture man could be threatened by various natural difficulties which endangered his food supply: the rain might fail, destructive floods might ruin the crops, or a cloud of insects might destroy the harvest. Men felt that the gods alone had power to prevent such catastrophes; therefore they sought divine assistance when human skill and knowledge were of no avail.

The new life brought new concepts of the gods. The old hunting gods became the gods of the farmer; they were invested with new powers and functions. Sometimes new gods were created. In order to exercise the proper supernatural controls, man surrounded every simple technological act with ritual and ceremony. The planting of the crops was accompanied by rites which often involved human sacrifice; the ceremonies of the harvest, however, were more cheerful and free from tension. Nevertheless, the gods demanded attention; they must be continually propitiated and made happy with gifts.

It was also possible to bind mysterious powers to do one's bidding if the proper magic spells were recited and magical acts performed. In every community there were certain men who appeared to have potent spells at their command. These were the medicine men, or witch doctors, and they were to become the first professional men of history.

A few of the material cultural items invented during the Age of Agriculture may be mentioned in order to illustrate the advance which was made in this period. Naturally, new implements and tools were developed for agriculture. The neolithic technique of stoneworking was found suitable for the manufacture of the larger weapons and implements: axes, maces, mortars, pestles, hoes, etc. Often bowls and other vessels were made from stone. Nevertheless, it should be emphasized that the palaeolithic methods of flaking and chipping were retained and used side by side with the neolithic technique of grinding and polishing. The true loom, indicative of the growing importance of textiles, and the boat, which revolutionized transportation and symbolized the growth of trade, were both inventions of the Age of Agriculture.

---

[6] Perhaps this point should be elaborated. The first regulations were oral, of course. As they continued to be enforced through the ages, they became sanctified by tradition. In time people began to feel that it was almost sacrilegious to transgress them. In the Age of Civilization, when writing was invented, these regulations were recorded and thus became laws.

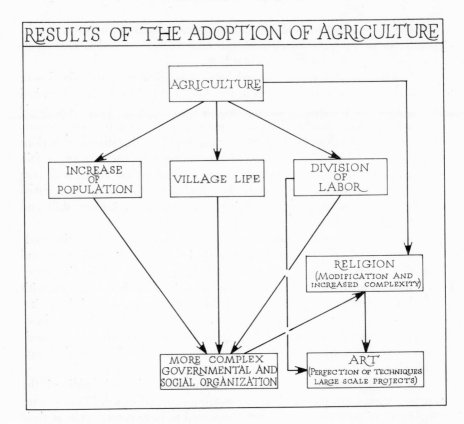

RESULTS OF THE ADOPTION OF AGRICULTURE

AGRICULTURE

INCREASE OF POPULATION

VILLAGE LIFE

DIVISION OF LABOR

RELIGION
(MODIFICATION AND INCREASED COMPLEXITY)

MORE COMPLEX GOVERNMENTAL AND SOCIAL ORGANIZATION

ART
(PERFECTION OF TECHNIQUES LARGE SCALE PROJECTS)

The new life which man began to live in the Age of Agriculture promoted a new psychology. A sedentary existence encouraged a conservative attitude. When everything seemed to be going well, people were inclined to resist innovation and change; they feared any disruption of the *status quo* as a possible danger to the community and its crops. Comparatively recent slogans such as "Don't rock the boat," or "If it was good enough for Grandpa, it's good enough for us," would have been very popular in the peasant village cultures. In the new economy people had to plan ahead— they had to be ready to plow, plant, or harvest at the proper times. This was a new concept, for primitive man had always lived for the day; foresight was not included among his ideals of virtue. Farmers had to live from one harvest to the next; they had to husband their food so that it would last. At certain times of the year they had to work hard and continuously or suffer the consequences of crop failure. They had to help one another in activities which could be accomplished only with co-operative effort. Thus the concepts of thrift, hard work, and neighborliness were born and were identified as virtues. The biblical admonition, "Go to the ant, thou sluggard," and Aesop's fable of the ant and the grasshopper epitomize these attitudes of the Age of Agriculture. It was probably in this period also that a concept of private property first evolved. The land now acquired a value which it had not possessed before; people wanted land for their farms; they wanted to acquire it and to keep it. Plots had to be delineated, and ways had to be found to preserve the boundaries and protect the owners. Traditional methods for the settlement of disputes ultimately became laws.

In the areas in which agriculture was adopted we may assume that there was a relatively sharp and rapid rise in the human population. This increase would continue until an equilibrium was reached when the demand for food caught up with the supply. This situation actually came into existence in some areas, but in others a nice balance between supply and demand proved unattainable because of drought, land exhaustion, or similar reasons. The surplus population then had to move into a more favorable environment.

If it is true that the first farmers lived in the grassy uplands of the Near East in villages like Jarmo, then it was probably overpopulation that forced them out of the hills and onto the plains where they found arable land more abundant and more fertile than in the higher areas. By 4400 B.C. peasant village communities much larger in size and more complex in organization than the early hill towns were in existence on the plains in those areas of the Near East where the rainfall, though less than that of the foothills, was still sufficient for dry farming. Whereas the Mount Carmel caves represent one phase, and Jarmo and early Jericho a second, the third phase in the development from food gathering to food producing can be observed in any one of a large number of peasant villages scattered all the way from the western borders of the Nile Delta in Egypt to various stations in Iran. On sites previously uninhabited, these communities began their existence in the Age of Agriculture.

A good example of the third stage is the site of Hassuna, which is located in northern Iraq near Mosul and not very far from Jarmo. Hassuna was a larger settlement than Jarmo, and its material culture was richer. Houses were still built of beaten mud, but they were larger; Hassuna, like Jarmo, yielded reed mats, clay figurines, mortars and saddle stones for milling grain, but there was a greater variety of tools and less dependence upon chipped flint. Sling pellets from Hassuna hint at new weapons; loom weights or spindle whorls suggest a weaving industry; shells from the Persian Gulf and obsidian from Turkey are evidence of growing trade. Grain was stored in large pottery vessels, and much of the pottery was now decorated by painting or incision. Naturally, the Hassuna people had domesticated plants and animals; the influence which agriculture had upon religious thought and practice is well illustrated by the appearance of female figurines—mother goddesses—modelled in clay: the earliest of these may be dated about 4100 B.C.

Although we can follow the slow development of this peasant village culture in the succeeding levels at Hassuna and other sites, we cannot escape the conclusion that for all practical purposes these people were well satisfied with the adjustment which they had made to their environment. They had achieved a balanced, efficient arrangement. Most of the land that could be farmed by their particular methods had been brought under cultivation. A maximum had been reached, food production leveled off, and the size of the population became more or less fixed. A condition of static well-being prevailed; people felt no challenge and therefore made no response.

This might have been the end of a promising development, but fortunately there were some recently occupied areas where farming, though not so easy at the start, could be far more profitable than in the territory taken over by the early peasant villagers. These seemingly less-favored areas were the great river valleys which man had long avoided. The story can best be followed in southern Mesopotamia, although the pattern of development must have been much the same in the valleys of the Nile and the Indus.

Not long before 4000 B.C. men of the hills to the northeast had begun to move into the swamps at the head of the Persian Gulf. Bringing with them their domesticated plants and animals, these people occupied little islands of dry land which dotted the marshes. Although there was little rain, there was more than enough water available to permit the newcomers to practice in the swamps the same kind of agriculture they had learned in the hills. The lack of wood and stone was overcome by using reeds for building: rush matting was employed for the walls of houses, and arched bundles of reeds provided the framework of the dwellings. Clay cones were made to serve as nails.

At first the venture prospered, but before long the settlers faced serious problems. In order to feed a growing population, more land had to be secured by draining part of the swamps or by moving up river to terra firma. This led to further difficulties: the rainfall in the southern plain was insufficient for dry farming, and thus it was necessary to develop new methods of agricultural production. The land proved to be amazingly fertile if water could be brought to it. This meant utilizing the Tigris and Euphrates; it meant the construction of an intricate system of canals and irrigation ditches; it also meant that the activities of the people must be organized and directed by a central authority, since the irrigation projects now begun and the attainment of full production called for efficient control and direction of the maximum manpower available. For the masses, this meant regimentation.

Unlike the people of the northern plain, those of the south had been faced with a challenge. Their response permitted not only their survival, but also brought a reward of prosperity and an agricultural surplus far beyond that possible in the north. Having learned to live in this different environment, the inhabitants began to expand the cultivated area ever northward in the region between the Tigris and the Euphrates until their progress was finally halted about fifty miles north of modern Baghdad, where the land was less fertile.

By 3000 B.C. the southern plain had become the home of an opulent civilization, the product of agricultural prosperity. An era of flourishing trade and thriving industry was about to dawn, and culture was to grow increasingly complex. It is well to remember, however, that more than a thousand years had elapsed since the first settlers had come down into the swamps. The time span separating the civilization of 3000 B.C. from the earliest communities at the head of the gulf was comparable to that which separates our own civilization from Europe in the days of Charlemagne. Although the period of evolution may be treated as a unit, at least three stages of achievement can be discerned; the archaeological names for these stages or subperiods are Ubaid, Warka, and Proto-Literate.

The Ubaid period takes its name from the type site of al-Ubaid which is located near the more famous site of Ur about 110 miles west and slightly north of Basra. The beginning of the Ubaid period may be as early as 4000 B.C. In its cultural assemblage are found moulded clay bricks of uniform shape, the beginnings of temple architecture, and artifacts of copper. Ubaid culture is thus only a step removed from that of the simpler peasant villages of the north. The finds are concentrated in a small area of the extreme south close to the Persian Gulf; in addition to al-Ubaid itself, remains have been found at Ur, Abu Shahrain, Warka, and Telloh.[7]

The Warka (ancient Uruk) period is characterized by the beginnings of sculpture, the use of gold, evidence for the development of a complex of buildings in the temple enclosures, and the appearance of wheeled carts. In the Warka culture the first ziggurats appear. Beginning in the Warka period with a temple set on a platform, the ziggurat later developed into a large, high tower of several stages crowned by a temple at the top. The memory of such structures survived in later ancient tradition as the "Tower of Babel" or the "Hanging Gardens."

Like the Ubaid, the Warka remains were confined to the south, but in the long Proto-Literate period there was a gradual diffusion to the north

---

[7] General agreement on the chronology for this early age has not been reached. Some would favor the following arrangement: Ubaid, 4000–3900; Warka, 3900–3750; and Proto-Literate, 3750–3100 B.C. These dates are probably too high.

The Ubaid remains are not the earliest known datable materials from the southern area, since at Abu Shahrain (ancient Eridu) just a few miles away the earliest stratum seems to be contemporary with the Halaf period in the northern plain. In the peasant village sequence in the north, the Halaf follows the Hassuna phase, and the various periods of the north and south may be synchronized as follows:

North	South
Hassuna	
Halaf	Abu Shahrain
"northern Ubaid"	Ubaid

beyond Babylon as far as Tell Asmar (Eshnunna). In this last age before the beginning of history in Mesopotamia towns grew into cities, the first examples of primitive writing appeared, wheeled chariots came into fashion, and silver became a common metal in use along with gold and copper.

By 3100 B.C. civilization was incipient if not already established. The trappings of civilization—urban life, class stratification, writing, monumental architecture, and sculpture—were either in existence or developments of the near future. A new revolution had occurred in man's way of life. Compared to the change from food gathering to food producing, this new revolution might be termed one of degree rather than kind, but it was important nonetheless. By building upon the foundations which had thus been provided, the men of the succeeding period were able to create the complex culture which we know as Mesopotamian civilization.

Civilization was soon to begin also in Egypt and the Indus Valley. We shall discuss the prehistory of each of these regions in the chapters devoted to the nature and growth of their civilizations, but first of all it is necessary to make certain generalizations about ancient civilization in its primary stages. This will be the subject of the next chapter.

Chapter 2

THE CHARACTERISTICS
OF THE EARLIEST CIVILIZATIONS

T HE FIRST PHASE in the history of civilization began in the Near
East about 3000 and ended not later than 1500 B.C. During this
period of a millennium and a half three distinct and coexistent
civilizations flourished: one in Egypt, another in Mesopotamia,
and a third in the Indus Valley. Although these primary civilizations were
characterized by cultural differences mostly of environmental origin, they
also possessed certain common features of great importance. All three
civilizations were located in great river valleys and owed their prosperity to
an agriculture based on the cultivation of cereals and the possession of
domesticated herd animals. Furthermore, in each river valley it was found
that the productivity of the soil far exceeded that of the surrounding areas
if irrigation and flood control could be instituted and maintained. These
objectives were assured by the creation of a strong centralized government
and the regimentation of the farmers. Because of the intimate relation between religion and agriculture which had been established before the attainment of civilization and which continued into the civilized period, "church"
and state (temple and palace) were combined, and the government of the
river valleys took a theocratic form; states were headed by men who were
regarded either as gods or the earthly viceroys of gods, and thus these states
were in theory god-ruled. In each of the riverine civilizations one may dis-
cern a planned economy, far-ranging foreign trade, a considerable development of industry particularly in the manufacture of textiles, advanced metallurgy, class stratification, monumental architecture, and distinctive art forms.
All three possessed systems of writing, and we know that Egypt and Mesopotamia developed a mature literature, science, and theology, features which
may well be discovered in the Indus Valley as research proceeds. Finally,

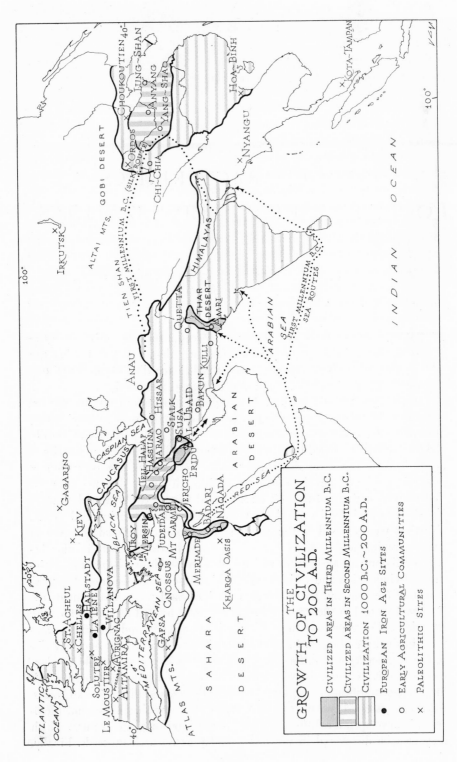

THE
GROWTH OF CIVILIZATION
TO 200 A.D.

		CIVILIZED AREAS IN THIRD MILLENNIUM B.C.
		CIVILIZED AREAS IN SECOND MILLENNIUM B.C.
		CIVILIZATION 1000 B.C.~200 A.D.
●		EUROPEAN IRON AGE SITES
○		EARLY AGRICULTURAL COMMUNITIES
×		PALEOLITHIC SITES

CHOUKOUTIEN 40°
LUNG-SHAN
ORDOS
ANYANG
(SILK ROUTE)
YANG-SHAO
CHI-CHIA
HOA-BÌNH
NYANGU
IOTA-TAMPAN

IRKUTSK

ALTAI MTS.
GOBI DESERT
FIRST MILLENNIUM B.C.
TIEN SHAN
HIMALAYAS

QUETTA
ANAU
THAR DESERT
MARI
ARABIAN SEA
FIRST MILLENNIUM B.C.
SEA ROUTES

CASPIAN SEA
CAUCASUS MTS.
HISSAR
SIALK
SUSA
OBAKUN KULLI
ERIDU AL-'UBAID
TELL HALAF
HASSUNA
JARMO
KEV
GAGARINO

INDIAN OCEAN

BLACK SEA
TROY
MERSIN
JUDEIDAH
JERICHO
Mt CARMEL
RADARI
NAQADA
ARABIAN DESERT
RED SEA

CHELLES
ST. ACHEUL
HALLSTADT
LA TÈNE
VILLANOVA
SOLUTRÉ
Le MOUSTIER
AURIGNAC
ALTAMIRA
MÉDITERRANEAN SEA
GAFSA
CNOSSUS
MERIMDE
KHARGA OASIS
ATLANTIC OCEAN

ATLAS MTS.
SAHARA DESERT

100°
40°
20°
100°

two more points of similarity may be mentioned: (1) these primary civilizations were centers of cultural origin from which there was a diffusion of culture that promoted the rise of civilization in adjacent areas, and (2) the final collapse of the political dominance of the riverine civilizations came as the result of barbarian pressures and invasions which began as folk movements outside the civilized area.

Civilization seems to have begun first in lower Mesopotamia with Egypt a close second and the Indus Valley a poor third. Each of these civilizations will be described in subsequent chapters, but first of all it may prove advantageous to consider early civilization in general rather than in specific terms. It is essential to observe the local individual differences that distinguished the civilizations of the Near East from one another, but it is equally important to recognize the fundamental unity of culture which permits us to speak of *the* civilization of the Ancient Near East.

The overwhelming importance of agriculture in the great river valleys brought a shift in basic human activities. Most men became farmers, and hunting and fishing were transformed into specialized professions in which only a small group of the population participated. As time passed, there was a further specialization or division of labor when some men found it profitable to give up farming and turn to trading and manufacturing. There were two main reasons for the appearance of traders and artisans:

1. Because farming tends to be a full-time occupation, the farmers had little time to make weapons, implements, and utensils. As a result, certain men became artisans and manufactured the articles which the farmers needed; for these articles the artisans received the products of the soil in trade from the farmers. Then, too, there were certain basic necessities of life—flint, salt, etc.—which could be secured only from regions some distance away. The farmers could not leave their fields to procure these necessities, and therefore a class of merchants and traders tended to develop, a group which made its living, like the artisans, by supplying the farmers' wants.

2. Because of the needs of the farmers, trading and manufacturing were bound to develop in any agricultural region on a small scale—such trends were evident early in the Age of Agriculture—but in the great river valleys this development was fostered and enhanced by another factor: the agricultural surplus.

In the river valleys the soil was so fertile that at first, even though the population increased rapidly, it was possible to produce more food than could be consumed. In other words, there was an agricultural surplus. This meant that it was not necessary for all to be farmers—some could turn to trade and manufacturing. We have noted above that with full agriculture with the plow a square mile of arable land can support 750 people, and we may now add that only 600 of these persons need to be employed on the land. The agricultural surplus also supplied buying power that stimulated progressive increases in the volume of trade and industry. It is therefore not surprising that the river valleys soon forged ahead of other areas and became the home of the first civilizations.

The growth of trade, which contributed at the same time to the growth of industry, was a natural outcome of environmental conditions in the Near East. No single area of the Near East was self-sufficient, with the result that an exchange of commodities was essential. Trade also flourished because it was possible to travel from one great river valley to another, especially from Egypt through Syria to Mesopotamia, without encountering impassable natural barriers: high mountain ranges, extensive deserts, or broad seas. Moreover, the easily navigable rivers of the Near East—the Nile, the Tigris, the Euphrates, and the Indus—simplified the problems of communication and transportation.

Villages located at points where trade routes converged began to grow into towns and cities. In the process of urban growth, further specialization of labor occurred. New industries sprang up; middlemen appeared who sold the commodities produced or secured by farmers, traders, and artisans to urban and rural customers. New ways of making a living permitted an additional increase in population, and the growing volume of trade produced an increase in manufacturing which in turn created new opportunities for work. Such economic developments led to a new economic revolution and an increase in population.

It cannot be emphasized too strongly or too often that the agricultural surplus was the foundation of the whole economic structure of the Near Eastern civilizations. The agricultural surplus had made possible the developments already described, but as the population increased as a result of the new opportunities for making a living in the towns, the demand for food tended to catch up with the food supply. A partial solution for this problem was provided by an extension of the cultivated area through the irrigation of marginal desert lands and the reclamation of swampy areas. This necessitated a great effort which was not always justified by the returns; furthermore, the demands of the economic superstructure which had been built up in the towns seem on occasion to have been resented by the farmers—this may have been the origin of the traditional antipathy between the country people and the city folk. The desire for new land also led to interstate warfare and finally to the political unification of the river valleys, as states were welded into kingdoms by conquest.

The growth of larger political units naturally added complexity to a political organization that was already far from simple. It has been mentioned above that theocracy was the prevailing form of government in the early riverine civilizations. In agriculture religion (or magic) and technology had been inseparable from the first. The principal gods of the peasant village masses were agricultural deities, and the main religious ceremonies in the rural areas were those connected with planting, cultivation, and the harvest. The village chief, as representative of his people before the gods, came to be a high priest who presided over these ceremonies. The unity of "church" and state meant that through religion the state gained an additional means of controlling the people. Not only did his priestship give him added authority, but the close connection between religion and agriculture might also allow the village chief to direct agricultural activity when the occasion arose.

Although we can see that the basis for the governmental control of agriculture was established in the Age of Agriculture itself, this function of the government was clearly not of major importance until the growth of cities demanded a great increase of agricultural activity. At this later date the Age of Civilization had begun, and the former village chief, now the ruler of a large city, was in a much better position to exercise sweeping powers. City life had made governmental organization more complex; it had made necessary the growth of a bureaucracy. The growth of a bureaucracy meant that the head of the government became more and more remote from the common man, and the ruler seemed less and less human to those who had no real contact with him. The bureaucracy helped the ruler to take on that "divinity which doth hedge a king." This seeming divinity was enhanced by his high priestship. Some rulers were eventually considered the viceroys of the gods; others even went so far as to claim that they themselves were divine. Nevertheless, the heads of these theocratic states, whether they were viceroys of the gods or gods themselves, would not have great difficulty in ordering and arranging the lives and work of the simple peasants who lived in the country outside the cities. It is also significant that the control of agricultural activity gave the rulers control of labor, and the manpower at their disposal might be employed for projects not even remotely connected with agriculture.

The typical theocratic state of the Near East consisted of a capital city (sacred to the chief god of the region) and the surrounding agricultural area dotted with rural villages and possibly some towns and small cities. The ruler was either a priest-king, the earthly representative of the principal deity, or else he was himself a god, perhaps regarded as the descendant of the deity. The growing complexity of governmental organization was paralleled by a similar development in religious organization, and priest classes came into existence. It is possible that at first the priests were the only administrative officers of the king, but ordinarily in the later period both religious and civil officials existed.

Society was stratified, and class distinctions came to be extremely rigid. There were privileged, less privileged, and underprivileged classes; at the top of the social pyramid were the priests and nobles, then came the commons—traders, artisans, and some free farmers—and at the bottom the serfs and slaves. This is an oversimplification, of course, because in some societies or at certain times slaves as well as free men might be artisans, or at other times the farmers might be mostly free or mostly serfs.

The priest class was supported by the gifts and tribute of the workers; since the priests secured the favor of the gods and protected the people from supernatural enemies, the masses were expected to pay for these valuable services. The nobility formed primarily a warrior class and were also supported by the producing members of society; if pressed, the nobles could justify their position by saying that, just as the priests warded off superhuman enemies, they provided protection from human foes. The origins of the nobility were much more varied and complex than those of the priest class. Appearing on the scene generally later than the priests, the nobles in some cases were invaders who had conquered and subjected a native population; in other cases the nobles were those who owned better land, or who had acquired more land, than their neighbors. Some of the nobility were faithful servants of the king—soldiers or bureaucrats—who had been rewarded with gifts of land or office; others might have been potential enemies whose friendship and allegiance were bought with gifts. Whatever their origins, the nobles were rich: they did not have to do manual labor, and they were warriors because they could afford suitable equipment and had the leisure to learn the art of war.

Serfs and slaves also appeared with the coming of the civilized era. The regimentation of the agricultural masses led directly to serfdom; the farmers, in many cases, became bound to the soil and could be transferred to a new owner when the land changed hands. Slaves were captives of war and debtors. The scramble for a livelihood, which the new age with its complex economic problems had produced, made manpower very important, while man as an individual tended to lose his identity unless he belonged to a privileged class. It was a vicious system. Its growth had been so insidious that it was not perceived until it emerged fully matured. Mankind has fought against it ever since, but without complete success.

The organization of priest classes was important for the growth of culture. In the first place, the priests were essentially a leisure class; that is to say, they were freed from manual labor because they were supported by the economic surplus created by the efforts of the rural and urban workers. Consequently, the priests had time for intellectual pursuits. In the second place, the business of the priests—religion—led almost automatically to new cultural developments. The priests were charged with the duty of ascertaining the correct periods for the sowing and harvesting of the crops; this brought the development of a calendar. The calendar was based upon the observation of astronomical phenomena; its creation and and use led to the science of astronomy, as well as to the invention of the

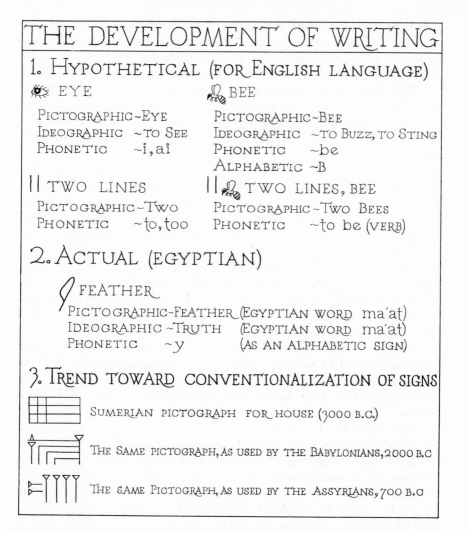

THE DEVELOPMENT OF WRITING

1. HYPOTHETICAL (FOR ENGLISH LANGUAGE)

EYE

BEE

PICTOGRAPHIC ~EYE	PICTOGRAPHIC ~BEE
IDEOGRAPHIC ~TO SEE	IDEOGRAPHIC ~TO BUZZ, TO STING
PHONETIC ~i, ai	PHONETIC ~be
	ALPHABETIC ~B

II TWO LINES

II TWO LINES, BEE

PICTOGRAPHIC ~TWO	PICTOGRAPHIC ~TWO BEES
PHONETIC ~to, too	PHONETIC ~to be (VERB)

2. ACTUAL (EGYPTIAN)

FEATHER

PICTOGRAPHIC ~FEATHER (EGYPTIAN WORD ma'at)
IDEOGRAPHIC ~TRUTH (EGYPTIAN WORD ma'at)
PHONETIC ~y (AS AN ALPHABETIC SIGN)

3. TREND TOWARD CONVENTIONALIZATION OF SIGNS

SUMERIAN PICTOGRAPH FOR HOUSE (3000 B.C.)

THE SAME PICTOGRAPH, AS USED BY THE BABYLONIANS, 2000 B.C

THE SAME PICTOGRAPH, AS USED BY THE ASSYRIANS, 700 B.C

pseudo-science of astrology. The calendar, astronomy, and astrology fostered mathematical studies. The priests were also healers; they relied heavily upon magic and supernatural aid, but through long experience and the necessity of effecting cures, they acquired a vast amount of practical knowledge about medicinal herbs, drugs, and surgery.

In addition to the various mathematical calculations which the priests had to make in connection with their religious duties, the problems of the management of priestly estates and other wealth were their concern. The priests had to keep accounts of the gifts and tribute of the faithful, and their financial transactions had to be recorded. There was also a growing body of rituals, spells, charms, and traditions which was becoming so large that human memory could hardly retain all of it. These demands upon the mind, and particularly upon the memory, led to the invention of writing.

The invention of writing was a potentiality from the very moment that the cave men began to draw pictures on the walls of their caves; but it is a true proverb that "necessity is the mother of invention," and writing was not invented until there was a great need for it at the beginning of the Age of Civilization. The first writing was undoubtedly pictographic: a man drew a picture of a cow; his intention was to convey to the minds of those who saw the picture that this was a particular cow, but later a drawing of this type came to represent not *a* cow, but *any* cow. From this abstraction, it was possible to proceed to others: a man might be represented with his legs bent to convey the idea that he was running; this sign might be used ideographically as a symbol for the verb "to run." From this it was only a step to phonetic writing in which sounds rather than ideas might be attached to signs. To represent the word "manifold," for example, one might draw the figure of a man, an eye, and a folded paper. With phonetic writing established, the use of signs for syllables and, finally, the alphabet (separate signs for separate letters) became potentialities.

Certain trends in early writing are worthy of note. At first, with pictographic and ideographic writing, it was inevitable that hundreds of different signs should be employed; and those who used the signs were always careful to draw their figures as realistically as they could. Later, however, there was a tendency toward simplification; the number of signs was steadily reduced, and the figures themselves became conventionalized. Conventionalization was possible because people were becoming familiar with the signs and necessary because it was desirable to write more rapidly. An example of conventionalization might be provided by a sign for "house." At first the picture of a house would be drawn very carefully; later this same sign might be simplified to a rectangle or even a straight line.

The development of an alphabet was not so easy as one might suppose. The evolution of writing was hampered by man's almost inherent conservatism. Innovation and change were resisted. Moreover, writing was felt to have connections with magic; perhaps the fact that writing was the invention and special province of the priests contributed to this impression. In the systems of writing employed in the Near East, ideographic and phonetic characters were intermingled, and the scribes hesitated to discard the older pictographs. The businessmen, however, who eagerly embraced writing as an aid to their commercial operations, were more progressive—or less inhibited. It was no coincidence that the alphabet first came into use somewhere in the Syria-Palestine area (about 1500 B.C.), where business sometimes took precedence over religion. The question of the alphabet is a complex and interesting one, and we shall give it special consideration at a later time.

The invention of writing meant that more knowledge could be preserved. The human memory had its limits, and written records provided an excellent substitute. Writing also made possible the widening of the horizons of abstract thought. The opportunities for intellectual activity were increased, and "scholarship" came into being. It seems hardly necessary to dwell long upon the unfortunate aspects of the invention of writing. Worthless ideas, as well as good ones, now had a better chance of survival. The magical or supernatural significance attached to writing was full of harmful possibilities. When a man speaks, one is more likely to question his statements than when he writes; even today, many people still feel that the printed word, by some magical process, cannot contain an untruth.

Literature, of course, came into existence with the invention of writing. Legends, myths, folk tales, ballads, and traditional materials were now committed to writing in poetic and prose forms. Religious literature grew apace. The keeping of governmental records eventually led to historical writing.

In the transition from the Age of Agriculture to the Age of Civilization, man first began to use metals. In the Near East copper, gold, and silver were to be found in a free state. At first, these metals were used only for ornamentation and trinkets, but soon copper began to be substituted for stone in the manufacture of some tools and weapons. Then came the discovery, undoubtedly accidental, that when heated in the fire certain ores containing copper and tin produced a hard metallic substance—bronze. Bronze weapons and implements were superior to stone because they were not so brittle and could be reshaped. Bronze became widespread in the Near East about 2500 B.C. The introduction of iron did not come until a thousand years later; this was because iron ores were found mostly outside the civilized area, and also because iron was more difficult to produce than bronze.

Because of their value and their comparative scarcity, the metals became popular as media of exchange. As trade continued to increase, they were employed more and more in this capacity. Traders, and later their governments, adopted the practice of stamping various distinctive devices upon bullion to guarantee its weight and purity. Out of this custom came the invention of coined money—about the eighth century B.C.

Important inventions made early in the Age of Civilization were those of the plow and the wheel. The plow made possible greater agricultural production, and the wheel was important for the development of transportation. Moreover, the invention of the wheel led to new mechanical devices: the pulley, the cog, and the potter's wheel (by means of which more symmetrical pottery could be made).

35

The increase in the power and wealth of the rulers and the priest class and their control of vast labor resources were important for the development of architecture, sculpture, and painting. The greatness of the kings and the deities whom they represented seemed to demand appropriate ostentation. Consequently, large temples and palaces were constructed, and the technical problems which these structures presented to their builders fostered the growth of a knowledge of engineering.

The development of sculpture and painting was closely related to that of architecture. Temples and palaces were decorated with relief sculpture which was often painted with bright colors. While sculpture in the round was encouraged with the production of cult statues for the temples or portraits of the rulers, relief sculpture and painting were often used for essentially decorative purposes in architecture. In Egypt, for example, the early painting and sculpture begin almost as adjuncts of architecture rather than as completely independent arts.

The Age of Civilization with its new way of life naturally encouraged men to think differently and to make changes in their systems of values. Many of the older attitudes of the Age of Agriculture were retained— some are still with us—and people paid lip service to some others which had been identified as good, but there were significant changes. City life allowed a greater freedom to the individual; in the small peasant villages social pressures had enforced conformity, and the group had always seemed more important than any single member, but in the cities individualism was born. In the new age with its larger political units nationalism, merely an exaggerated form of provincialism, developed with imperialism as its companion.

An expanding economy, combined with new ways of making a living, often affords the opportunity to acquire more wealth in less time than is possible in an agrarian age. As a result, although people may continue to mouth the old platitudes about thrift and hard work, they tend to endorse privately such slogans as "get rich quick" and "easy come—easy go"; we may confidently expect to discover the Egyptian or Mesopotamian equivalents of these phrases at any time. Wealth encourages ostentation, patronage, and affectation. The ability to amass riches is equated (by those who accomplish this miracle) with a superior intellectual capacity, and a display of wealth is the obvious proof of the pudding. A wealthy man who lacks creative ability can subsidize a poet or a painter to create for him while he himself can become a connoisseur and critic of their work.

Before leaving the general topic of the rise of civilization to begin a consideration of specific civilizations in the ancient world, it will be instructive to examine some of the laws or principles which seem to govern cultural growth. A few of these laws have already been suggested either

AN IRANIAN MOUND MARKING AN ANCIENT TOWN SITE

Courtesy of the Mary-Helen Warden Schmidt Foundation. Oriental Institute of the University of Chicago

IN SOUTHERN IRAQ TODAY THE MARSH ARABS LIVE LIKE THE FIRST SUMERIANS

Courtesy of Gavin Maxwell

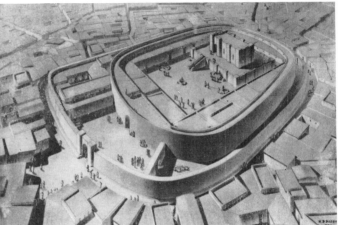

EYE TEMPLE

Courtesy of the Oriental Institute of the University of Chicago

ZIGGURAT

Courtesy of the Trustees of the British Museum and the Museum of the University of Pennsylvania

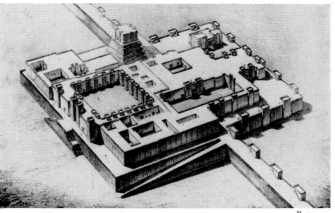

PALACE AND ZIGGURAT

Bettman

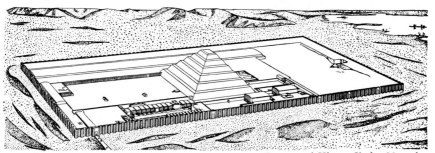

Courtesy of Hirmer Verlag Muenchen

TOMB AND STEP PYRAMID

WHITE TEMPLE AT URUK

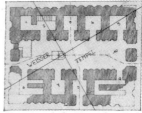

*Courtesy of the Deutsches Archae-
ologisches Institut, Berlin-Dahlem*

EGYPTIAN TOMB OF FIRST DYNASTY

Courtesy of W. B. Emery and Archaeology

Courtesy of the Museum of Science, Boston

Courtesy of the Oriental Institute of the University of Chicago

BUILDING A PYRAMID

ROSETTA STONE—
KEY TO THE HIEROGLYPHS

directly or by inference, and others will now be introduced for the first time. All are contained in the following list:

1. Cultural development has been basically dependent upon the course taken by man's physical evolution, for physical evolution provided man with the mental and physical traits and capabilities which made possible the creation of his peculiar kind of culture.

2. Culture cannot be physically inherited. It is something we acquire after birth. A single example should suffice to illustrate this all-important point: a child born of English-speaking parents if taken from his family in babyhood and brought up in a Chinese household would not know English but would speak Chinese like a native.

3. All culture traits may be traced to very simple origins, to what might be called primary inventions and discoveries. Elaboration and adaptation of these simple traits produce new cultural items; a good example is the spear which is, in principle, a knife with a long handle. Simple traits (and more complex traits) are often combined to produce new items; the combination of the bow with the arrow (another elaboration of the knife) made a more effective weapon; later, of course, there was a further elaboration in the invention of the catapult. Similar developments occurred, and still occur, not only in the case of material culture, but also in social, economic, religious, and intellectual fields.

4. Culture tends to accumulate. In the Age of Agriculture, for example, man retained many of the culture traits developed in the Age of Primitive Culture. Moreover, providing environmental and economic conditions remain favorable, the accumulation and growth of culture tend to be accelerated. The more culture traits a given group possesses, the more will be the opportunites for combination and elaboration. It is an elementary mathematical fact that more combinations and permutations are possible with fifty numbers than with five.

5. Although in modern times man's conquest of nature has somewhat decreased the importance of environmental factors, in antiquity the growth of culture within a given area was greatly dependent upon environment and geographic location. Environment not only encouraged or limited cultural growth, but it also determined largely the course which cultural evolution was to take; Eskimos do not invent iceboxes or fans, nor do the inhabitants of the tropics invent central heating or skis. Climate, soil, natural resources, and topography are factors which must always be taken into consideration. The Near East provides an example of how an environment favorable to primitive agriculture was important for the rise of civilization and how topography and natural resources affected the growth of trade. Culturally, trade was important because it brought the various geographic divisions of the Near East into contact with one another and made

possible a cultural interplay that stimulated the growth of civilization. Culture traits were exchanged; in the countries into which they were introduced they received new adaptations and elaborations.

6. The passage of a culture trait from the area of its origin into a new area is called diffusion. The process of diffusion is important because it makes possible increased cultural complexity in civilized areas and facilitates the growth of culture in regions which might otherwise remain backward because of unfavorable environmental conditions. In ancient times this was especially true of Europe; the Europeans were immeasureably indebted to the Near East for many of the culture traits that later helped to make up "European civilization."

A stone dropped into a quiet pond produces a series of ripples which travel in concentric rings farther and farther from the center of the disturbance until they lap the shore. The action of diffusion is similar to this; a culture trait tends to spread from its center of origin to the far corners of the earth. This point may be illustrated by the story of tobacco:

The use of tobacco, a discovery of the pre-Columbian Indians of the New World, was a culture trait carried back to Europe by the Spaniards about the beginning of the sixteenth century. The trait spread across Europe and Asia and was carried by the Russians (in the eighteenth century) to the Alaskan Eskimos, who had not known of tobacco until that time.

7. The growth of culture is, in a sense, automatic. Given certain conditions, certain developments are likely to take place. The laws of accumulation and acceleration operate without man's conscious knowledge. Man created civilization without being aware of what he was doing. The instincts which drove him in search of food and shelter provided the motivating force for the creation and elaboration of culture. Moreover, stronger than the individual man were the demands of society, the group.

It must be admitted that man was allowed, by the mere force of circumstances, little self-determination—by either his natural or his social environment. Then, too, it is obvious that when culture, especially in its non-material aspects, attained a certain degree of complexity it was no longer the servant of man, but his master. The tail began to wag the dog, and it has done so ever since.

The acquisition of culture and civilization was not an unmixed blessing. It does not take much reflection to realize that a large part of culture controverts nature, and the result is to set up a conflict between man the animal and man the cultured animal. We may pass over the frustrations created by social controls and merely remark in passing that the complexities of modern civilization have burdened us with mental illnesses that never bothered primitive man. The medical knowledge which now permits greater longevity has led only to new social and medical problems; it is difficult to provide for the superannuated members of the community, and while most of us can expect to survive the once-fatal diseases of childhood, it is not a matter of consolation that we shall probably succumb to the horrible illnesses of old age or perish in the wreckage of one of our fine machines. In short, people often confuse evolution with progress. But evolution is not progress, it is change. Change persists. We do not necessarily go up or down, forward or backward, but we do go on.

Civilizations are built upon foundations provided by past cultures. The great indebtedness of our civilization to earlier ages defies complete evaluation. We have borrowed from our ancestors and from peoples not related to us. Fire and funerals are part of our primitive heritage; farming and boats go back to the Age of Agriculture; the ancient Mesopotamians gave us our astronomy, our division of the day into hours and of the circle into 360 degrees; logic we owe to the Greeks, and much of our language stems from Greek and Latin; our numerical notation came to us from the Arabs, firecrackers from the Chinese, and tobacco from the American Indians. More important than mere borrowing is the pyramiding of culture that has occurred through the ages. None of our great inventions or discoveries of the twentieth century could have been made without the support of the knowledge accumulated by our predecessors.

Chapter 3

THE PRIMARY CIVILIZATION
OF MESOPOTAMIA

CIVILIZATION FIRST APPEARED in the lower Tigris-Euphrates Valley. The cultural development which had begun at the head of the Persian Gulf about 4000 B.C. had culminated nearly a thousand years later in the establishment of a civilization which was to contribute more than any other to cultural heirs in the Near East and the Mediterranean area. By the end of the fourth millennium B.C. when the threshold of civilization had been reached in Mesopotamia, there had been a diffusion of culture from the center of origin in the extreme south northward to a point slightly above Baghdad, with the result that the total civilized area comprised about ten thousand square miles.

Some uncertainty still exists regarding the identity of the people responsible for the great advances which had taken place during the Ubaid, Warka, and Proto-Literate periods. It is generally agreed that the bulk of the credit must be given to the Sumerians, a distinct linguistic group believed to have entered the lower valley from the hills which lie to the northeast. Possessing only skeletal remains, we should have assumed that the Sumerians were proto-Arabs, but their language was not Semitic, nor can it be related to any other known language.

Perplexing as this question of identity is, it is even more difficult to determine when the Sumerians arrived. They were certainly present in the Proto-Literate period and probably in the Warka age; it is even possible that they came in the Ubaid period. Regardless of the date of their arrival, the Sumerians do not seem to have been the first people in the valley. It is likely that a few Semitic-speaking nomads from the Arabian Desert had come in very early to huddle on the banks of the Euphrates. Moreover, since the names of certain towns, recognized by the Sumerians themselves

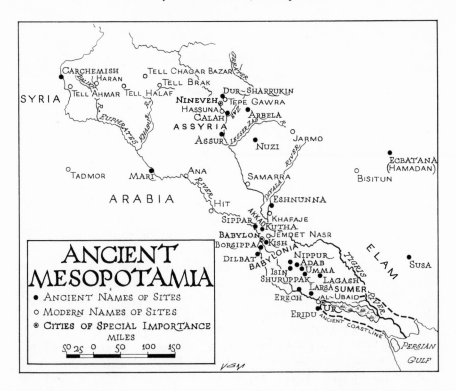

ANCIENT
MESOPOTAMIA
• ANCIENT NAMES OF SITES
○ MODERN NAMES OF SITES
◉ CITIES OF SPECIAL IMPORTANCE
MILES
50 25 0   50   100   150

to have been very ancient, do not have Sumerian etymologies, it is also assumed that the Sumerians were preceded by other people from the hills to the northeast; they may have been hillsmen who spoke an Elamite dialect, or emigrants from farther east in Iran. When the historic period opened, however, the Sumerians were the politically and culturally dominant group, and it is with them and their civilization that we shall be concerned.

By 3100 or 3000 B.C. the Mesopotamian Proto-Literate period ended; it was succeeded by a semihistoric age which archaeologists call the Early Dynastic. During the Early Dynastic period metals became increasingly plentiful, palaces as well as temples began to be built, and there was an increase in foreign trade. The handsome painted scarlet-ware pottery characteristic of the oldest strata on Early Dynastic sites gradually deteriorated as metal vessels became more popular; painted decoration was abandoned for incision, and the pottery lost the artistic qualities which it had once possessed. The famous royal tombs of the First Dynasty at Ur with their rich grave furniture and their evidence of human sacrifice belong to the last phase of the Early Dynastic age (about 2500 B.C.).

In the Proto-Literate and Early Dynastic periods the lower Mesopotamian plain was divided among a number of independent city-states each of which controlled an area averaging about a hundred square miles. In the south were the cities of Eridu, Ur, Lagash, Erech, Shuruppak, and Umma. Farther up the valley were Nippur, Adab, Kish, Babylon, Kutha, and Eshnunna. As time passed and these states increased in population, disputes arose over land and water rights. Sometimes towns defeated in this inter-state warfare became subservient to the victors; thus, tiny kingdoms began to be formed.

It is not possible to write a history of this early period because the records of only a few towns have been recovered. The French excavators of Telloh (ancient Lagash) have brought to light a wealth of epigraphical material which can be used to reconstruct the history of that state, but com-parable sources for other states have not yet been found. The history of Lagash can perhaps be taken as typical of a Sumerian city-state, but it should not be mistaken for the whole history of the Sumerian people in this period.

At Lagash in the so-called Proto-Imperial epoch (2425–2340 B.C.) there was a dynasty of rulers who recorded their acts of piety in building temples and their bravery in fighting their neighbors. The principal opponent of Lagash was the state of Umma located about twenty miles to the west. In a series of boundary disputes the Lagashites at first gained the upper hand. Eannatum, the second ruler of the Lagash dynasty, commemorated his defeat of Umma on a stone stele which was inscribed with an account of the fighting; it was decorated with relief sculpture which showed the army of Lagash advancing in phalanx formation and also depicted a part of the battlefield with decapitated Ummaites lying prostrate on the ground and vultures carrying off their severed heads (Stele of the Vultures). Ean-natum in addition claimed to have controlled Erech and Ur, and he took for himself the title of King of Kish. Later rulers, confident of their supremacy, began to levy burdensome taxes and to increase the landholdings of the palace at the expense of the temples. In reaction to this arrogance a re-former named Urukagina gained control in Lagash. He boasted in his in-scriptions that he set matters to rights again by cutting taxes and returning property to the temples. This champion of justice and protector of the weak may also have promulgated a law code. Unfortunately, the domestic troubles of Lagash encouraged the people of Umma to renew hostilities. Urukagina fell prey to Lugalzaggisi, the ruler of Umma, who sacked Lagash and mastered Ur and Erech as well.

With Lugalzaggisi the first epoch in the history of the southern plain comes to an end. From the beginning of civilization until his reign the dominant people in politics and culture had been the Sumerians whose focus of activity was in the extreme south, but subsequently initiative passed to the Semites who had been increasing in number around Babylon in the north. These Semites, a near-barbarian desert people from Arabia who differed from the Sumerians in language and social organization, had gradually absorbed Sumerian civilization and were now able to contest for supremacy in the plain.

We should like to know much more about the man who led the Semites of the north against the Sumerians of the south, but he is well hidden by the mists of legend. The obscurity of his origin is suggested by the fact that several different stories about his parentage were current in ancient times; one of these stories closely resembled the biblical tale of Moses in the bulrushes. He called himself Sargon, which means "True King." This may not have been his real name, but one which he assumed after gaining the throne; it raises a suspicion that the name concealed the identity of a usurper who was not a true king at all.

Sargon gained control in the north about 2340. As King of Kish he waged a successful war against Lugalzaggisi whom he overthrew and led off in chains. Further vigorous campaigning brought the fall of Ur and Lagash; Elam capitulated to Sargon, as did Mari in the west and towns to the north in Assyria. Sargon boasted that he had overthrown fifty rulers and had penetrated to the "cedar forest and the silver mountains." In later times it was believed that the cedar forest was that of Lebanon and the silver mountains those of Cilicia, but Sargon may have been referring to Elam rather than to the shores of the Mediterranean. As the legend of Sargon grew, it was even said that he had conquered Cyprus; by the fifteenth century B.C. he had become the hero of an epic poem called "The King of Battle" in which he was represented as having campaigned in Asia Minor in order to aid Assyrian traders who did business in that area. This was a serious anachronism, because the Assyrians did not reach Asia Minor until several hundred years after Sargon's death.

While the Sargon of legend was an important figure whom later kings attempted to emulate, the real Sargon of history was no less important. He established his capital in the north not far from Babylon at a place called Akkad. The actual site of Akkad has not been found, but the whole northern area came to be called Akkad while the south continued to be known as Sumer. Moreover, Sargon was the founder of a dynasty of Semitic kings who reigned over Sumer and Akkad until about 2150 B.C.

Although the Akkadian kings inherited a large empire from Sargon which may have attained even wider limits under Naram-Sin (*c.* 2250 B.C.), their control over the subject peoples was anything but secure. Sargon himself had to face serious revolts during his reign and may even have perished in a rebellion, and his successors were plagued by chronic uprisings. We may guess that this internal discord progressively weakened the Akkadian empire, especially after the death of Naram-Sin, though the final collapse came as the result of an invasion of the plain by a tribe of northern barbarians called the Guti (*c.* 2150 B.C.).

43

The Guti did not attempt to rule Sumer and Akkad, but contented themselves with exacting tribute from the cities of the plain. This allowed the Sumerian city-states even more freedom than the semi-independence they had enjoyed during the latter years of Akkadian rule when Lagash, for example, under the leadership of Urbaba and Gudea had regained some of its former brilliance. At length, the defeat of the Guti by Utukhegal of Erech removed any threat of foreign domination.

For over a century after the Gutian danger had passed, the center of power was located once more in Sumer rather than Akkad, and it was Sumerian rather than Semitic kings who ruled the plain. About 2125 Ur-Nammu, the governor of Ur, revolted from Utukhegal of Erech and established at Ur the celebrated Third Dynasty which was to build up an empire rivalling that of Sargon in size.

The two most important kings of the Third Dynasty of Ur were Ur-Nammu, the founder, who reigned eighteen years and his successor, Shulgi, who occupied the throne for nearly half a century. Ur-Nammu incorporated the city-states of Eridu, Lagash, Umma, Adab, and Nippur into his kingdom, beautified the capital, Ur, with many fine structures including a great ziggurat, and promulgated a law code of which portions have been preserved. Shulgi seems to have completed the unification of Sumer and Akkad as well as the extension of the empire to Elam and Assyria. The absence of internal discord during the time of the Third Dynasty suggests that its imperial organization was more efficient than that of the Akkadian kings. The neo-Sumerians, however, did not disdain to follow one precedent established by Naram-Sin: this was the erection of a ruler cult. Ur-Nammu was worshipped as a god after his death, and a cult of the Divine Shulgi was established while Shulgi was still on the throne. Sacrifices were offered to the living ruler, and the seventh month of the year was known as the Festival of the Divine Shulgi. A similar practice was followed by the remaining three kings of the dynasty.

Catastrophe overtook the Third Dynasty about 2000 B.C. during the reign of its fifth king, Ibbi-Sin. Outside pressure from two directions brought the final collapse. A new group of Semites, the Martu (Amorites), advanced from the west along the Euphrates while in Elam a nationalistic revival drove out the Sumerians. Akkad was lost early in Ibbi-Sin's reign; this was possibly due to unrest among the subject Semites encouraged by the impending Amorite invasion. Weakened by this defection in the north and by disloyalty in the army, the Third Dynasty finally succumbed. Invading Elamites sacked the great capital city of Ur, and Ibbi-Sin was carried off into captivity in the twenty-fifth year of his reign.

The Third Dynasty of Ur marked the last period of Sumerian dominance in Mesopotamia. In the succeeding age the Sumerians disappeared; they had been buried in an avalanche of Semites. Yet the Sumerians had put their seal on Mesopotamia forever. Fully a thousand years separated the end of the Proto-Literate Age from the fall of the Third Dynasty. This had been the life span of Sumerian civilization, a period twice as long as that which separates us from Columbus. This was long enough to create and develop a civilization, and the Sumerians made much of their opportunity. They left to posterity in Mesopotamia a number of cultural bequests: a distinctive religion, mythology, architecture, literature, system of writing, and economic organization; in addition, they had developed astronomy, mathematics, a calendar, and a legal system. The people of Mesopotamia and neighboring countries, the Greeks, the Romans, and even our more immediate European ancestors were to adopt and use culture traits discovered or invented by the Sumerians.

This is not to suggest that Mesopotamian civilization was static after the Sumerian period. Mesopotamian history and culture cannot be treated as if nothing was altered from the time of Sumerians to that of Alexander; there were major changes in political and economic organization in several different periods. Furthermore, even during the Sumerian age alterations occurred.

There is some evidence that, before history, Sumerian government had been a kind of "primitive democracy" in which decisions were made by a council of elders or by an assembly of the people. In the historic period, however, the various Sumerian city-states were ruled by kings who functioned as war leaders, administrators, and intermediaries between the people and the gods. In some instances, just before the Sargonid age, the ruling power was exercised by high priests who bore the title of *ensi* (once rendered *patesi;* the Semitic equivalent was *isshaku*). With Sargon and Naram-Sin the normal title was that of king (Sumerian, *lugal;* Semitic, *sharrum*). To match the dignity of his imperial position Naram-Sin called himself King of the Four Quarters (of the World), and since he prefixed the title "Divine" to his own name he may have been officially worshipped as a god. This practice was followed by the later kings of the Third Dynasty of Ur who also called themselves kings of Sumer and Akkad. As far as governmental organization is concerned, we can be definite only about the Third Dynasty of Ur. In this period of empire the king was assisted by a prime minister; the various city-states subservient to Ur were governed by *ensis,* appointed by the king and serving at his pleasure, and a large frontier area on the north was under a viceroy, also appointed by the king. In short, it is not correct to say, as many historians have done, that the early Sumerian states were ruled by *ensis* and that some *ensis* then became *lugals,* or kings. The whole matter is much more complicated than has been thought in the past, and there is still much to learn.

Little is definitely known about the organization of society among the Sumerians. Legally, there were only two classes: free men and slaves, but it is fair to assume that the royal family was set apart when the rulers became god-kings. In an economic sense the priests and officials formed a class, but it may not have been a self-perpetuating one. This is another subject which needs further study, and it is dangerous to project the later and better known social organization of Mesopotamia back into this early period.

X   A widely current historical cliché, one now disproved by the facts, is that a temple state economy prevailed throughout the Sumerian period. The question is somewhat complicated but its solution hinges on the interpretation of fragmentary and scattered evidence. For Lagash in the period before Sargon we have the records of a single temple which possessed more than ten thousand acres of arable land. The cultivation of this land was directed by the priests, but the land itself was divided into three categories: (1) that which supported the temple directly, (2) that designated for the sustenance of the peasants and artisans attached to the temple, and (3) that which was rented or leased. Now this was only one of several temples at Lagash; its land constituted only about one-sixth of the total arable land of Lagash, yet people once assumed that the situation was typical of Sumerian economy throughout Mesopotamia and for all periods. In reality, the documents from the Sargonid period which follows present an entirely different picture, for they show in the north a feudal society with large private holdings in land; there is no suggestion of a temple state economy in Akkadian territory.

The only period of Sumerian history about which we can speak with any certainty with respect to its economy is that of the Third Dynasty of Ur for which we have an abundance of evidence from several sites. This economy can be described but we know that it changed in the succeeding period, and we cannot say that it was representative of any earlier period.

Our information about Mesopotamian economics comes from two types of sources: the archaeological remains and the documents. Archaeologists have discovered tools, implements, buildings (granaries, warehouses, storage pits, etc.). There are also representations in art (relief sculpture, seals, and the like) of boats, wagons, plows, and tools of various kinds. For many periods, however, and particularly for the Third Dynasty the bulk of the information comes from the documents. These documents are mostly records inscribed in the cuneiform script on clay tablets of various sizes. There are huge ledgers, some more than a foot square, ruled in columns and lines on both front and back sides; there are tiny records of receipt or expenditure with faces less than an inch square. The documents of the Third Dynasty which have been unearthed in the last century number in the tens of thousands. In addition to the ledgers and receipts there are contracts, work records, orders, accounts relating to disbursements and inventories, field surveys, budgets, and many other types of records. The details of agriculture, stock raising, trade, manufacturing, transportation, and the employment of labor are all recorded. We should qualify this, however, by noting that these are temple and palace records; they tell us about public rather than private economic life. Moreover, while Sumerian law codes contain economic information, we possess only fragments of these documents, and therefore they are not as useful to the historian as the later and better preserved Babylonian, Assyrian, and Hittite codes.

The principal Sumerian crops were barley, emmer, wheat, sesame, onions, peas, beans, and some minor vegetables; dates, pomegranates, and figs were grown, and various herbs as well. Barley was far more important than any other cereal; it provided food for men and animals, and considerable barley was used for making beer. The work in the fields began in September when the fall plowing commenced; crops were planted in November in time for the winter rains. The harvest time was in May and June, and not much was done in the hot summer months when everything dried up and even the sheep had to be fed barley.

Since agriculture was impossible without irrigation, much work had to be done to keep the canals and irrigation ditches in good condition. Typical also of this kind of agriculture was the prevalence of long, narrow fields on either side of the ditches and the planting of the seed in widely spaced furrows. Seed was used sparingly (less than three pecks of barley per acre), but the average yield was between twenty-five and thirty bushels per acre, depending on the quality of the soil. The cuneiform documents which record the amounts of seed, work by the cultivators and harvest hands, the employment of draft animals, and the amount and disposal of the yield have provided much detailed information which has been supplemented by the discovery of a literary text, the so-called Farmer's Almanac, which describes the kind of work done at various seasons.

The territory of Umma and Lagash constituted the breadbasket of ancient Sumer in the time of the Third Dynasty. At Lagash more than a dozen temples were responsible for the cultivation of about one hundred square miles of arable land which produced two million bushels of barley a year. About a fourth of the yield was paid to the king, and the remainder fed the priests and their laborers, paid the harvest hands, provided food for the animals, and was reserved for seed. By a complicated set of computations it is possible to estimate the population of the territory of Lagash at about sixty thousand on the basis of the available food supply. Similar figures for other states indicate that the total population of Sumer and Akkad cannot have exceeded a million in this period.

Other records from Ur, Umma, and Lagash tell us about wool production, textile manufacturing, leatherwork, and the activities of those who worked in gold, silver, and bronze. The royal palace at Ur and each of the temples had its own staff of artisans; their names, the amount of their

47

rations, and their productivity are recorded in detail. Milling, for example, was done by women and children; various grades of flour were distinguished, and for the coarser grades a remarkable reduction rate of nearly eighty per cent was achieved. Beer making was an art among the Sumerians; many texts relate to brewing and suggest that the varieties of beer were numerous.

In every way the texts having to do with agriculture and industry imply that these activities were virtually monopolized by the state and the temple, and that the crown particularly was using the old temple organization because it was already there and functioning efficiently. Since we have virtually no records from Akkad for this period, it is not safe to assume that its organization paralleled that of the old Sumerian towns.

Trade is more difficult to study than agriculture and industry. Foreign trade objects in Mesopotamia or Sumerian objects found abroad suggest commercial relationships, but the texts are not informative. A functionary called the *damqar* appears in the temple accounts, but although the word is usually translated as trader, the *damqar* was more of a purchasing agent. He took the cloth produced by the temple artisans and amounts of gold, silver, wool, and bronze and exchanged these commodities for other things required by the temple. It is not until the succeeding period (the Old Babylonian), however, that the *damqar,* whose title is now Semitized as *tamkarum,* appears as a full-fledged trader.

A large proportion of the cuneiform texts record the receipt and disbursement of animals, food, drink, and spices for sacrificial purposes: so many lambs received on such and such a day as an offering to this or that deity. As stewards of the gods, the priests had to keep very careful accounts. Daily records were later combined in monthly and annual summaries. The amount of bookkeeping involved was staggering, but it had to be done. It is often claimed that double-entry bookkeeping was an invention of the early modern period, but the Sumerians used it thirty-five hundred years before it was known in the West.

Documents were often validated by means of seals. The Sumerians used a cylinder of stone, a quarter or half an inch in diameter and an inch or two in height, which was engraved with heraldic or other scenes and inscribed with the name and title of the official or scribe who possessed the authority to seal documents. The seal was then rolled over the damp clay of the tablet leaving a cameo impression. Some of the seal impressions are very handsome indeed.

The records make it very clear that Sumer under the kings of the Third Dynasty had a planned economy. Each year, for example, the fields were surveyed; specific persons were assigned as cultivators for specific fields, and the crops to be sown as well as the amounts of seed to be used were predetermined. Budgets were prepared in advance: the total yield was

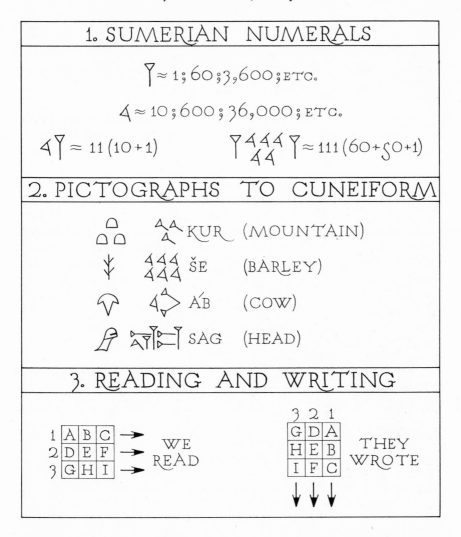

1. SUMERIAN NUMERALS

$\Upsilon \approx 1; 60; 3,600;$ ETC.

$\mathcal{A} \approx 10; 600; 36,000;$ ETC.

$\mathcal{A}\Upsilon \approx 11 (10+1)$ $\Upsilon\mathcal{A}\mathcal{A}\mathcal{A}\mathcal{A}\Upsilon \approx 111 (60+50+1)$

2. PICTOGRAPHS TO CUNEIFORM

KUR (MOUNTAIN)

ŠE (BARLEY)

ÁB (COW)

SAG (HEAD)

3. READING AND WRITING

1	A	B	C
2	D	E	F
3	G	H	I

→ WE READ

3	2	1
G	D	A
H	E	B
I	F	C

THEY WROTE

estimated, and the disposition of the harvest was planned even before the crops were planted. All this necessitated a staff of managers, overseers, archivists, surveyors, and scribes. The crown had its bureaucracy, and each temple had its own personnel for business administration.

All this meant that the Sumerians had to count, figure, and measure; it meant that the planned economy combined with Sumerian activities in building, astronomical observation, and calendar making fostered the development of mathematics. Just how far the Sumerians progressed in mathematics is uncertain, but they undoubtedly laid the foundations for the flowering of mathematics in the Old Babylonian period. The sexagesimal system, in which sixty rather than ten was the basic unit, seems rather strange to us, but it worked very well. In our numerical notation we employ ten figures (0–9) in a place system; the Sumerians used only two figures, a wedge and a crescent, also in a place system (see chart of Sumerian numerals). When we write 111, we are really saying 100 plus 10 plus 1; for 111 the Sumerians would write 60 plus 50 plus 1. Sumerian fractions seem queer until some familiarity with the system is acquired: with 60 as the basic unit, one-third is written 20; one-fourth, 15; and so on.

Although it cannot be proved, the cuneiform system of writing seems to have been a Sumerian invention. It began with pictographs scratched on clay—a fish was drawn in recognizable form, or a bird, a man, and so on. Quite early, ideographs began to be used, and eventually phonetic signs were added. At the same time, familiarity with the characters was leading to conventionalization of their forms. Using a square-tipped stylus, the scribe would sink the tip in the clay and then press the edge of the shaft into the damp surface; the result would be a wedge-shaped impression almost as if someone had put a nail down on the clay on its side instead of the point first. The original pictographic signs were thus transformed into characters composed of a complex of wedges and crescents (made with the stylus tip). This evolution can be seen in the accompanying figure (Pictographs to Cuneiform).

The same character might be used as a pictograph, ideograph, or phonetic sign. Some of the characters were polyphones: a single sign with a number of different phonetic values; others were homophones: two different characters with the same phonetic value. Today we read the lines on the tablets horizontally from left to right, but probably the characters were actually written in columns from top to bottom, and the columns were done from right to left (see chart of Reading and Writing).

The Sumerians measured quantity, space, and also time. Almost all business records and contracts were dated by year, and some by month and even day. The years were named after events: the year when so-and-so became king, the year when the city of X was destroyed, the year when the priest of X uttered the oracle, and so on. The year was divided into twelve months: these were lunar months which would, of course, average between twenty-nine and thirty days. The first appearance of the new moon marked the beginning of the new month. The use of a lunar calendar meant that the Sumerian year did not coincide with a solar year; it was too short by at least a week, and approximately every three years a thirteenth month would be inserted in the calendar. The Sumerians heralded the appearance of the new moon with great ceremony; the half and the full moon as well as the disappearance of that planet were also celebrated by temple services.

Since the Sumerian economy was founded on agriculture, since the government was in theory theocratic, and since the Sumerians had a well-organized priest class which enjoyed a virtual monopoly of thought and education, it is not surprising to discover that Sumerian religion played an important part in Sumerian civilization. The religious beliefs and activities of the Sumerians provided the prime stimulus for the development of architecture, sculpture, literature, astronomy, and cosmology.

The Sumerians appear to have created their gods in their own image, but Sumerian religious beliefs are already well developed by the time we can observe them in any detail. The fundamental concepts appear to have been animistic in that the gods were identified with natural phenomena, but it is possible that there were some totemistic elements present at an early time. Certain trends or characteristics remind us of the Greeks and Romans: local religions existed in an atmosphere of mutual toleration; there were personal, local, national, and universal deities; the Sumerian sky-god was regarded as the chief of the gods as was the Greek Zeus or the Roman Jupiter; the gods were believed to have the tastes and manners of men and to engage in undignified escapades; it was believed that the gods were distinguished from men chiefly by the possession of immortality; there were also legendary figures believed to have been demigods.

The Sumerian priests had a highly developed theology; we know something of *their* speculations, but we do not know whether the people as a whole were aware of, or interested in, what the priests were thinking about. The priests remind us of the scholastics of the medieval period; they had come to the conclusion that they lived in a highly organized cosmos, well balanced, and perhaps one that could be reduced to a mathematical formula.

At the head of the pantheon was the sky-god, An, the father and ruler of the gods. His name was always mentioned first in any series of divine names, but he was believed to be remote and little concerned with the affairs of gods or men. He could be represented by a number as were several of the other important gods; his number was sixty, the perfect or basic number in Sumerian mathematics. The cuneiform character which was used for writing his name was also the character for "god"; this reminds us of the fact that Zeus as a divine name is related to Greek *theos* (god), or Latin *deus.*

A much more important deity and certainly less remote was Enlil, whose number was fifty. Enlil was believed to have brought order out of chaos and to have issued commands that were carried out by the other gods. He was "the lord," and when his worship was taken over by the Semites, they called him Baal (Bêl) which also meant "lord." There is a parallel in usage here between Semitic *bêl,* Greek *kyrios,* and Latin *dominus.* In each case the same word might be used to refer to a god or to address a person as we might say "sir."

The third god in the series (number forty) was Enki (Semitic, Ea), the god of wisdom, medicine, and writing who was believed to have taught civilization to man. Next came Nannar, the moon-god (number thirty), patron of astronomy and astrology; then Utu (number twenty), the sun-god and dispenser of justice, whose Semitic name was Shamash. Number fifteen was Inanna (Semitic, Ishtar), a goddess of the greatest importance identified with the planet Venus. A fertility goddess primarily, she was also called the "Queen of Pleasure" in her role as the patron deity of love, but she was in addition a war-goddess. Among hundreds of other deities might be mentioned Nergal, the god of pestilence and presiding deity of the underworld, the Land of No Return. Nergal was identified with the planet Mars and was much feared.

Although these deities tended to become nationally recognized, they began as local gods. The cult of Enlil centered at Nippur; Enki, at Eridu; Nergal, at Kutha; Nannar, at Ur; and Inanna, at Uruk. The tutelary deity of Lagash was Ningirsu, a deity of war and hunting. Each of the male gods had a consort, or wife, but in many cases they seem to have been conceived as an afterthought: the consort of Enlil was naturally Ninlil (*nin* means lady); of Enki, Ninki; of Nergal, Ninkigal (*ki-gal* was the underworld).

Inanna was generally believed to have a consort named Dumuzi (the Semitic equivalents of the pair were Ishtar and Tammuz). Dumuzi was originally a chthonic deity, perhaps worshipped as a snake. He was the youthful god who died with the vegetation each year and was reborn again —just as the snake was believed to gain a new life by shedding his skin.

Much of Sumerian theology and cosmology was incorporated into works of literature in both poetry and prose. Examples of Sumerian literature have survived, but any study of the subject is beset with problems. Most of the texts are fragmentary and incomplete. The Sumerian language is difficult, and the translations now available are by no means final. Many of the texts in Sumerian actually date from a later period and may not be reproductions of Sumerian originals. It was long assumed that many texts in the Babylonian (Akkadian) language were translations from the Sumerian, but it has now been shown that this is not always the case.

A number of literary types are represented in Sumerian literature. There are magical texts as well as omens and forecasts based on dreams, oracular responses, the examination of the entrails of animals, hepatoscopy (liver divination), aspects of the planets and stars (eclipses, etc.), and the behavior of birds and animals. There are hymns and prayers, proverbs and fables, and various sorts of didactic works. A number of epics and ballads based on legend and myth are also known.

A whole series of short poems deals with the adventures of the hero Gilgamesh, a legendary strong man who, like Heracles, performed many "labors." Other poems are myths of origin which give us some idea of Sumerian cosmological beliefs. The Sumerians thought that the primeval sea had given birth to heaven (*an*) and earth (*ki*); heaven had then become the father, and earth the mother of the gods. The genealogy of the gods was then traced through further pairings: Enlil and Ninlil were the parents of the moon-god; the moon-god in turn was the father of the sun-god and Inanna, etc. There was a flood legend; the Sumerian Noah was Ziusudra who built an ark and floated for seven days and nights on the flood waters. There was a legend about paradise where trouble resulted when Enki ate the plants of the presiding goddess there; the Sumerian paradise was located on an island in the Persian Gulf where, it was thought, there was neither old age nor death.

Sumerian architecture and sculpture were hampered by a lack of easily available stone. Large temples and palaces were constructed, but they had to be made of brick, and this placed limitations on their form and height. The arch, though known and used, did not receive the elaboration that might have been expected. The most impressive creation was the ziggurat which did attain a considerable size and height; however, the theological aspects of the ziggurat are more interesting than its architectural ones, especially if it is true that it was regarded as a place of ascension and the temple at its top was a gateway to heaven. Sumerian sculpture was stiff and hesitant, especially the sculpture in the round, for both the standing and seated types of figures are immobile to say the least. The beautiful work in metal and soft stone (steatite, for example) shows that the Sumerians possessed an appreciation of plastic art even if they lacked facility of execution in the harder stones; if they had had a sufficient quantity of materials to work with, they might have rivalled the Egyptians. One has only to look at the objects from the Early Dynastic period, those from the grave of Queen Shub-ad, to see what magnificence was possible: the little electrum donkey from the pole of the chariot, the "ram caught in the thicket," and the golden bulls' heads are particularly striking. The Sumerians were also skillful with shell inlay, and the excellence of the seal engravings has already been mentioned.

The energy of the Sumerians was spent with the Third Dynasty of Ur. The Sumerians as an identifiable group disappeared, their language ceased to be spoken, and their civilization was adopted and adapted by the Semitic-speaking peoples who were now dominant in Mesopotamia. The basic characteristics of Mesopotamian civilization through the ages continued to be Sumerian, but the Semites made additions and modifications in religion, political and economic organization, and certainly advanced the frontiers of knowledge in mathematics and astronomy. The Sumerian language, though no longer spoken, did survive as a written language very much like Latin in the long centuries after the fall of Rome. Sumerian was studied by the priests, Sumerian religious and literary documents were preserved, and Sumerian words and phrases remained in the vocabulary of law and science; other Sumerian words were Semitized and continued in use for generations.

Mesopotamian unity was disrupted by the fall of Ur. For at least a hundred years the land of Sumer and Akkad was divided into three parts: in the extreme south a kingdom was centered at Larsa just across the Euphrates from Ur; in the north another state had its capital at Babylon; and midway between Larsa and Babylon was the kingdom of Isin founded by Ishbi-Irra, a traitor who had deserted Ibbi-Sin. Of the three states Babylon was destined for greatness by its geographical position. Perhaps because of changes in the channels through the swamps at the head of the Persian Gulf, the older semiseaports of the south had declined in importance, but it is more likely that, with the growth in cultural complexity outside of lower Mesopotamia, the lines of trade had shifted. Babylon was a natural terminus for routes leading into the plain from Iran on the east, Assyria and the country all the way from the Black Sea on the north, and the traffic which came down the Euphrates from Syria and the Mediterranean littoral in the west. Furthermore, Babylon was farthest removed from the menace of Elam, a danger that was clearly demonstrated by an Elamite conquest first of Larsa and then of Isin.

Shortly after 1900 B.C. the Amorites, the Semites from the west who had helped to weaken the Third Dynasty of Ur, took Babylon as their capital. Slowly and carefully they consolidated their position in the north. By the eighteenth century, this Amorite or Old Babylonian dynasty attained full strength under its sixth king, the famous Hammurabi, who enjoyed a long and prosperous reign of forty-three years.

Hammurabi has been an object of interest since the discovery of his law code a half-century ago, but it is only within recent years that it has been possible to place his reign in its proper chronological position or to evaluate his status in the international affairs of his age. A source of new knowledge about Hammurabi has been the discovery by French archaeologists of the site of Mari, an important town on the middle Euphrates. At Mari were found the archives of the local rulers; some twenty thousand cuneiform tablets were recovered which revealed much about the history and diplomatic relations of the Hammurabi period. The tablets disclosed that until the fifth year of Hammurabi's reign, Mari was subject to Assyria. The approximate dates of the Assyrian kings mentioned in the tablets were already known, and thus it was possible to establish a synchronism between Babylonian and Assyrian history and to arrive at a date for Hammurabi. Secondly, letters from spies and emissaries of the kings of Mari contained information about the movements and strategy of Hammurabi until the time when he attacked and destroyed Mari itself late in his reign.

We now know that Hammurabi ascended the throne at a time of crisis. Rim-Sin, the Elamite king, had just added Isin to the possessions of Elam and might be expected to attack Babylon at any moment. To the north was the powerful Assyrian kingdom which now threatened Babylon on the west also through its occupation of Mari. Worst of all, Hammurabi did not possess Eshnunna, an independent state located between Babylon and Assyria; with Eshnunna in Elamite or Assyrian hands or allied with either power, the defense of Babylon would be difficult. When Mari revolted from Assyria and became a Babylonian ally, Hammurabi attacked Rim-Sin and drove him from Uruk and Isin. This temporarily relieved the pressure, and later Hammurabi took the offensive in earnest. In successive campaigns he secured his northern boundary, then turned south and captured Larsa, next attacked Assyria, and followed this with the destruction of Mari which had deserted him for the side of Eshnunna and the Elamites. The final triumph was the capture of Eshnunna. These victories gave Hammurabi an empire approximately the size of that formerly held by the Third Dynasty of Ur.

This great ruler was no less successful as an administrator. His correspondence with royal officials reveals his attention to the details of government and his ability to recognize political and economic problems. Another manifestation of his acumen was his codification of the law. What might be called Hammurabi's propaganda sense was also sound, for he sought to strengthen his position by theological changes aimed at establishing the supremacy of his deity, Marduk, over the Sumerian gods. Religious documents purporting to tell the story of creation and the establishment of order out of chaos were rewritten to give Marduk credit for these achievements; it was suggested in these stories that Marduk (and his earthly representative, Hammurabi) had been especially chosen by the older gods to be responsible for the welfare of mankind. Still another achievement of Hammurabi was the adornment of Babylon which was made handsome with many new buildings suitable for the capital of an empire. For hundreds of years after Hammurabi Babylon remained a political center and a center of culture as well.

Hammurabi was not the "first lawgiver." We now know of four law codes earlier than his; three of them were written in Sumerian, and the earliest dates from the reign of Ur-Nammu, four centuries before Hammurabi. It seems very likely that even earlier Urukagina had promulgated a code of laws. At any rate, there can be no doubt that it was the Sumerians who first codified the law and set the pattern followed by Hammurabi and later lawgivers. Some of the laws found in earlier codes were incorporated without change into the Hammurabi document. Moreover, it was customary to begin the law codes with a prologue which stated that the sun-god, the god of justice, had chosen such and such a ruler to dispense justice, and the laws were always followed by an epilogue which promised blessings to those who obeyed and preserved the laws and called upon the gods to punish those who did not; these features are also found in the Code of Hammurabi.

Although Hammurabi's code was not the first to be devised, it is the most completely preserved document of its kind from this early period, and it is not merely a copy or a translation of the earlier codes. Hammurabi made changes to provide for the altered social and economic situation of his times. The code is concerned with both criminal and civil law; it is "case law" in the sense that it provides penalties for specific circumstances: each "case" begins with the phrase, "If a man . . . etc." Many crimes were punishable by death. In the case of injuries, the law of retaliation was invoked: "If a man destroy the eye of another man, they shall destroy his eye." Many of the laws help to give a picture of social and economic life. Some relate to marriage, divorce, inheritance, wills, and adoption; a number have to do with slavery. Agricultural affairs (tenantry, irrigation, leases), trade, navigation, usury, and contracts are regulated by other laws. There are also provisions having to do with the regulation of wages and prices.

The code implies that Babylonian society was divided into three classes: nobles, commoners, slaves. Women enjoyed an unusual independence; priestesses, for example, could own land, loan money, and engage in business. The laws also disclose the existence of military colonists whose service in the army was repaid by grants of land from the king.

In addition to the Code of Hammurabi a rich source of information about the economic life of the Old Babylonian period is provided by contracts inscribed in cuneiform on clay tablets. Unlike the economic records of the Sumerian period, these are private rather than temple or royal documents, but their evidence is no less valuable.

The Amorite conquest put an end to the temple and royal monopoly of economic activity which had persisted in Sumerian territory until the fall of the Third Dynasty of Ur. The conquerors effected a secularization of land ownership; there was still crown and temple land, but its extent declined as the amount of land in private hands increased. There was also more participation by private persons in trade and industry. In fact, by comparison with the preceding ages in Mesopotamia, this was a period of private enterprise.

Under the early Amorite kings there was much buying and selling of land, mostly of small plots. By the time of Hammurabi and his immediate successors almost no fields were being sold with the exception of very large holdings belonging to high officials. As the volume of selling tapered off, contracts for leases and rentals of fields increased in number. A partial explanation for this phenomenon lies in the inheritance customs of the Amorites. The private landholdings of the earlier period were family plots, the ownership being in the hands of the patriarch, the father, who headed the family. When a patriarch died, his property was divided fairly equally among his sons. In a large family, when the division took place, the inherited plots might be too small to sustain an individual and his family; thus, he would be forced to sell. An astute man, with a little capital, could acquire large holdings by buying up land which came on the market in this way.

Soon he would have more land than he could work, and he could lease plots to the landless members of the community.

It may be inferred that there was an increase in the population of Babylonia during the Amorite period. The contracts often mention new land which is being brought under cultivation, and we hear in the royal records of the construction of many new canals which were designed to bring water to formerly arid land. The possibility of expanding the cultivated area was not unlimited, however, and much of the new land was not as fertile as the old. When the demand for new farms and more food could not be met, the population curve began to level off.

The essentially barter economy of the Sumerian period gave way to a new system in which metals were used more frequently as media of exchange. An expanding foreign trade led to an increase in the supply of the precious metals. This, in turn, caused an apparent rise in prices; in other words, when silver was scarce and therefore high in value, an ounce of silver might buy a measure of grain, but when silver was plentiful and therefore cheap, it might require three ounces of silver to buy a measure of grain. The principal imports of Babylonia in this age were copper, gold, silver, and lead; ivory, precious stones, wood, and building stone were less important.

The *tamkarum,* or trader, functioning as a merchant, broker, and money lender was at the hub of trade. In the big cities these traders were organized in guilds and enjoyed considerable freedom from governmental control until rather late in the Old Babylonian period. Traders might act as creditors, supplying an agent with goods for a trading journey. The agent would then be expected to return the principal to his creditor, and then they would divide the profits of the journey.

The activities of the merchants of Ur are representative of Babylonian foreign trade in the time of Hammurabi. They exported garments, silver, and vegetable oils to Bahrein Island in the Persian Gulf to be exchanged for copper, pearls, ivory, sheep, and wood which may have come from India. People have often assumed that grain was an important Babylonian export, but the weight, bulk, and perishable nature of grain militated against its participation in the foreign trade of this part of the Near East; there was no steady market for it, and there is not a shred of evidence that grain was exported. Textiles, however, were always important. "Akkadian garments" are often mentioned in the trade with the north.

The Old Babylonian period was an age distinguished for its literary and scientific activity. Many of the literary compositions of the time were inspired by Sumerian originals, but their authors managed to invest them with a new spirit and character that secured their recognition as classics in future ages. The great creation epic which told of the struggle of Marduk and the dragon Tiamat was undertaken in a propagandist spirit, but it was an artistic success. An even greater achievement was the composition of the Gilgamesh Epic which involved combining the earlier Sumerian ballads and stories about this great hero into an artistic whole. The careful preservation of the text of the Gilgamesh Epic by copying and recopying for hundreds of years shows the prestige and reverence which this long poem enjoyed.

Most of the cuneiform mathematical texts which have survived were written in the Age of Hammurabi. For this reason, it has been assumed that the proficiency in geometry and algebra demonstrated by these texts was an accomplishment of this period rather than of the Sumerian Age. This may be true, but it may be significant that the Babylonians continued to use the Sumerian words and phrases for addition, subtraction, multiplication, frac-

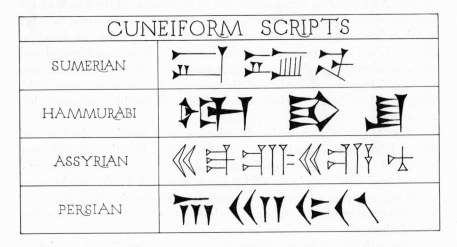

CUNEIFORM SCRIPTS	
SUMERIAN	
HAMMURABI	
ASSYRIAN	
PERSIAN	

tions, squares, cubes, and the like. Tables of multiplication, squares, roots, etc. were compiled and used, but there were also "problem texts" with a practical slant involving the computation of areas of fields and volumes of cisterns or ovens: "How long would it take for x men to clean a canal of such and such dimensions, and how much would it cost if each could excavate so much dirt per day?" In algebra the Babylonians were able to solve quadratic equations in a variety of ways, and problems involving simultaneous linear equations were also common in the problem texts. Still other texts reveal a knowledge and use of the Pythagorean theorem (twelve hundred years before Pythagoras). The Babylonians also calculated the value of pi to about six places, although for ordinary calculation they assumed it to be 3. One text has been found which can only be a table of logarithms.

Similar achievements were registered in the field of astronomy. A very famous cuneiform document records a succession of observations of the planet Venus, the so-called Venus tablets of Ammisadugga. The study of the mathematical and astronomical texts is a difficult and specialized matter; only a handful of contemporary scholars have concerned themselves with these texts. As a result there is still much to be done, and we may anticipate many discoveries in the years to come.

Shortly after 1600 B.C. the Old Babylonian (Amorite) dynasty came to an end. A gradual decline of Amorite power had begun in the seventeenth century with a loss of territory in southern Babylonia, but the final collapse was precipitated by a raiding party of Hittites from Asia Minor who sacked Babylon itself about 1595. This weakened the Amorites so that they fell easy prey to other northern enemies, the Kassites, who had been pressing upon their frontiers for some time. The disappearance of the Amorites may be tentatively dated about 1550. For the next four hundred years Kassite kings occupied the throne of Hammurabi.

The glories of the Old Babylonian kingdom were not forgotten in Babylonia. When Nebuchadnezzar a thousand years later sought to revive the splendor of Babylonian civilization, he took the art and literature of this period as his model. The Old Babylonian language (Akkadian) survived in the Near East throughout the second millennium B.C. as the language of literature and diplomacy; it was used for diplomatic correspondence by the peoples of Syria, the Hittites, and even by the Egyptians.

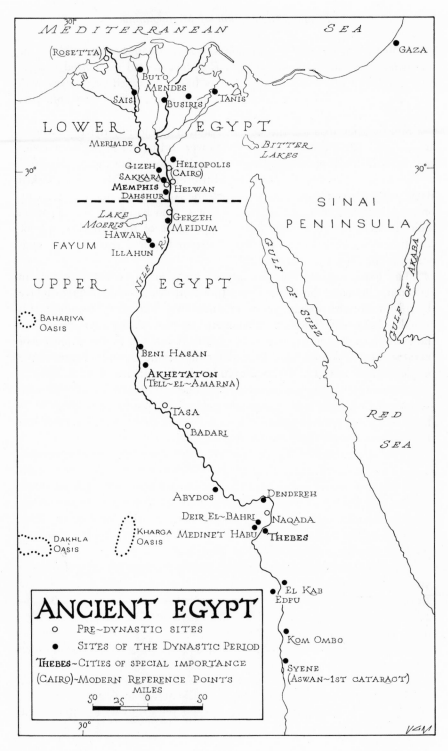

MEDITERRANEAN   SEA

(ROSETTA)   GAZA

BUTO
MENDES
SAIS   BUSIRIS   TANIS

LOWER   EGYPT

MERIMDE   BITTER
LAKES

GIZEH   HELIOPOLIS
SAKKARA   (CAIRO)
MEMPHIS   HELWAN
DAHSHUR

LAKE   GERZEH
MOERIS   MEIDUM
HAWARA
FAYUM   ILLAHUN

UPPER   EGYPT   SINAI
PENINSULA

BAHARIYA
OASIS

BENI HASAN

AKHETATON
(TELL~EL~AMARNA)

TASA
BADARI   RED

SEA

ABYDOS   DENDEREH

DEIR EL~BAHRI   NAQADA
KHARGA   MEDINET HABU THEBES
DAKHLA   OASIS
OASIS

EL KAB
EDFU

ANCIENT EGYPT
  ○   PRE~DYNASTIC SITES
  ●   SITES OF THE DYNASTIC PERIOD
THEBES~CITIES OF SPECIAL IMPORTANCE
(CAIRO)~MODERN REFERENCE POINTS
              MILES
    50   25   0   50

KOM OMBO

SYENE
(ASWAN~1ST CATARACT)

NILE

GULF OF SUEZ

GULF OF AKABA

Chapter 4

EGYPTIAN CIVILIZATION

T HE PHRASE "Ancient Egypt" is likely to evoke three familiar images: the Great Pyramid, the Colossus of Memnon, and the Rosetta Stone, yet it is sometimes forgotten that these well known Egyptian monuments are not of the same period but represent a span of nearly twenty-five hundred years. A thousand years separate the Great Pyramid from the Colossus of Memnon, while there is almost a millennium and a half between the Colossus and the Rosetta Stone. It will be another generation before we can celebrate the five hundredth anniversary of Columbus' first voyage and the two thousandth anniversary of the birth of Christ, yet when the Child was born in Bethlehem, Egyptian civilization was already three thousand years old.

The civilization of Egypt was no older than that of Mesopotamia, ancient and modern impressions to the contrary. Egypt only *seemed* older. This was due to the isolation of the country which encouraged an inbred culture that tended to become comparatively static at an early period and henceforth resisted change. As a parallel we may cite the case of China, regarded by the uninitiated as incredibly old, yet an infant when compared with the riverine civilizations of the Near East.

Egyptian civilization was unique largely because of the peculiar environment in which it was developed. It is important to remember that Egypt was (and is) not the large country ordinarily shown on maps, for only the Nile Valley and the Delta are habitable. Ancient Egypt stretched from the First Cataract in the south to the Mediterranean in the north, a distance of nearly seven hundred miles, but the valley is a narrow ribbon between deserts; it is never more than a few miles wide, while the Delta is an equilateral triangle with an altitude of less than a hundred and fifty miles. Thus, the total habitable area of Egypt measured about ten thousand square miles. It would take weeks to traverse the length of Egypt, but only a few hours to cross it.

Every aspect of life in Egypt centered around the Nile. It was the only source of water, and it was the principal highway. As Herodotus said, Egypt was the gift of the Nile; without the river, the country would have been uninhabitable. Furthermore, each year when the river was in flood, it covered the whole land for weeks; when it receded it deposited fertile mud which renewed the soil of Egypt annually and made the use of fertilizer unnecessary. Even Babylonia, which had little rainfall and owed much to irrigation, was not as dependent on its rivers as Egypt was on the Nile.

A second peculiarity of Egypt was noticed by another ancient writer, Diodorus, who said that Egypt was fortified by nature. Protected by the desert on two sides, the cataracts in the south, and the Mediterranean in the north, Egypt also tended to be isolated by these geographic features. This was to mean that once political unification was achieved in Egypt, invaders rarely penetrated the country, and Egypt seldom knew the pangs of conquest so familiar to Babylonia. On the other hand, it also meant that Egyptian contacts with the outside world were to be limited; it was to be many centuries before foreign trade was of any real significance in the life of the land. Babylonia, by comparison, became a country of merchants, while Egypt remained a country of farmers. Society and culture were thus bound to differ in these two great river valleys. The Egyptians had centuries of peace in which to develop their great civilization, but they paid a penalty for their solitude, since they had to forego many of the advantages of cultural cross-fertilization, a thing essential to continued growth.

Despite its isolation, Egypt was to make its contributions to ancient and even modern civilization. Early Greek painting and sculpture, for example, were indebted to Egyptian models. The Greek system of mathematical notation and arithmetic calculation was derived from the Nile Valley, just as Greek trigonometry and algebra originated on the banks of the Tigris and Euphrates. There are a number of things in the Old Testament that originated from Egypt, and it has even been claimed that our calendar came to us from the land of the pyramids via Julius Caesar and the early church. The Egyptians were the inventors of plywood and the discoverers of castor oil; it is even said that adobe, a familiar word, is of Egyptian origin.

The importance of environmental factors in the development of Egyptian civilization can scarcely be overemphasized. The Nile not only provided Egypt with its fertility, but it was also a factor in unifying the country at an early date. In the prehistoric period a number of independent communities were ranged along the banks of the Nile at the points where the cliffs receded from the river and the valley widened out. Before 3100 B.C. there were forty or more of these separate states in the valley and Delta— the Greeks called them nomes. The Nile as a main highway connected these communities with one another, and it was inevitable that unification should take place. Moreover, the economy of Egypt was dependent upon the fertility of the soil and the nature of its resources. The amazing fertility of the valley made possible the growth of a large population and produced an agricultural surplus which in turn produced a complex economic and social structure. Egypt was more self-sufficient than the Tigris-Euphrates region: it had an abundance of clay and good stone, gold was to be found near Koptos, and copper could be secured from nearby Sinai. What Egypt lacked was timber; as a result, the problem of gaining access to the "cedars of Lebanon" was later to exert a great influence upon Egyptian economic and political policies. The fact that Sinai and Lebanon lay to the northeast was important: Egypt was forced to turn ultimately in the general direction of Mesopotamia. The trade connections which were formed after 2000 B.C. with Sinai, Palestine, and Syria brought the Egyptians into contact and conflict with traders who had come west from Babylonia, but intermittent hostilities throughout the second millennium did not completely inhibit cultural interchange. Environmental influences were also at work in Egyptian political evolution. In Egypt the absolute necessity for irrigation and the conservation of water brought extreme centralization of government and the strict regimentation of the farmers.

Perhaps the development of Egyptian civilization can be clarified if we compare and contrast the situation in Egypt with that in Babylonia. Both regions were fertile, but Egyptian agricultural production was dependent upon getting water to the soil; Babylonia had the same problem and also the additional one of preventing the floods from washing the soil away or destroying the crops. Political unification and governmental centralization were essential for maximum agricultural production in Egypt, whereas in Babylonia, although unification and centralization could be accomplished, they were not as essential as in Egypt since flood control and irrigation could be managed on a local basis. The isolation of Egypt fostered an independent cultural development, but the ease with which Babylonia could be invaded meant that foreign influences were frequently exerted. The central position of Babylonia, as well as its lack of self-sufficiency, paved the way for the growth of trade, while the remoteness of Egypt and the abundance of its resources prevented trade from becoming important as early as it did in Babylonia. The fact that Egypt had good stone virtually predestined a difference between Egyptian and Babylonian architecture: the Egyptians naturally adopted the column and lintel form, while the Babylonians, building with bricks, became the inventors of the true arch. The abundance of stone in Egypt early encouraged a perfection of sculpture that was not possible in Babylonia.

Finally, the relationships between "church" and state were different in Egypt than they were in Babylonia. In Babylonia, the early rulers were considered the viceroys of the gods; in Egypt, the kings themselves were gods. This is easily explained when we remember that the unification of Babylonia came only after a long city-state period during which the theocratic viceroy tradition had become firmly established. In Egypt, on the other hand, the unification of an extensive area came very early; and it was much easier for the ruler of a large area to acquire divine attributes than it was for the ruler whose territory included only a few square miles.

Egyptian prehistory is a morass more treacherous than the swamps of the valley and Delta where prehistoric man used to hunt. The earliest sites known are scattered and difficult to relate to one another in an orderly chronological pattern. Because of violent disagreements among the specialists in prehistoric Egyptian archaeology, a circumstance indicative of the greatest uncertainty with regard to the sequence of cultures, only the most general summary of the prehistoric phases in Egypt can be attempted.

Thirty-one hundred B.C. is roughly the dividing line between prehistory and semihistory in Egypt. The camps of palaeolithic hunters have been found on the cliffs bordering the Nile Valley, but there seems to be no connection between these earlier people and those farmers and herdsmen who began to live in the valley just north of Thebes about 4400 B.C. and possibly on the fringes of the Delta a little later. Cultivating the cereals, herding sheep and goats, and possessing a rough incised pottery, fishhooks, and boomerangs, these people lived in Egypt for half a millennium, gradually increasing their cultural store. Copper beads, figurines, a fine pottery, developed in the south; there is also evidence of trade shown by the presence of shells from the Red Sea, ivory from the south, and turquoise from Sinai. Shortly after 4000 B.C. other sites in the south and north also show further developments: the use of copper tools, better storage facilities for grain, weaving, and particularly in the south, the beginnings of irrigation, (perhaps) slavery, and regular trade with the Red Sea. A final phase after 3500 B.C. is thought to be the result of a Semitic invasion of the valley from across the Red Sea. Stone vases, rectangular houses, cast metal tools and weapons, increasing use of gold and silver, and a painted pottery are among the new traits. Mesopotamian cylinder seals and other foreign objects and art motifs point to outside influences, a subject to which we shall return.

Between 3500 and 3100 a process of unification had been taking place with the result that the various communities in the valley were combined into the Kingdom of Upper Egypt while those in the Delta were joined as the Kingdom of Lower Egypt. Egyptian tradition spoke of warfare between the two kingdoms and a final victory for the southern kingdom (Upper Egypt) about 3100, when the complete unification of Egypt was accomplished by King Menes.

With the success of Menes, the prehistoric period ended. It is customary to divide the succeeding period into dynasties (families of rulers) of which there were twenty-six before the Persian conquest in 525 B.C. The dynastic (or historic) period enjoyed three periods of prosperity: (1) the Old King-dom, Dynasties III–VI, roughly 2700–2200 B.C.; (2) the Middle Kingdom, Dynasties XI–XII, roughly 2000–1800 B.C.; and (3) the New Kingdom, or empire, Dynasties XVIII–XX, roughly 1600–1100 B.C. In time and in de-velopment the Old Kingdom and the Middle Kingdom thus parallel the Sumerian and Amorite periods in Mesopotamia.

The first king of the First Dynasty and probably the first to bear the title Pharaoh was Menes, who is thought to be identical with the king called Narmer who is shown as the conqueror of the north on a ceremonial slate palette. We have no truly historical records for the first two dynasties, though writing began with the First Dynasty, but the archaeological evi-dence bears witness to the wealth and power of the early kings. There is a steady advance which leads to the first great period, the Old Kingdom.

It is now generally believed that Egyptian civilization originated under the stimulus of a cultural diffusion from Mesopotamia which began with the arrival of Semites shortly after 3500 and continued through the First and Second Dynasties. The Egyptians did not imitate Mesopotamian cul-ture slavishly but made significant adaptations and original contributions as well. We have already mentioned the presence of Mesopotamian cylinder seals in the Egyptian predynastic period. The Gilgamesh motif occurs on an ivory knife handle from Gebel el Arak, and on the same artifact as well as on the palette of King Narmer one finds serpent-necked animals with necks interwined in a conventional Mesopotamian style. It may be a coinci-dence that the King of Upper Egypt was called the *insi,* but in the monu-mental architecture of the first two dynasties the use of bricks and an architectural form resembling that of the Proto-Literate period in Meso-potamia can hardly be accidental. The introduction and brief use of the Mesopotamian invention of the arch and vault is also significant. The human sacrifice which accompanied the burial of First Dynasty kings reminds us of the tomb of Queen Shub-ad, while the sudden introduction of writing, the use of a lunar calendar like the Mesopotamian one, and the custom of naming the years by events in the Mesopotamian fashion might also be ascribed to foreign influence.

About the beginning of the Old Kingdom, however, a number of important developments took place. A new calendar intended to approximate the solar year was adopted; the most likely date for the introduction of this calendar is around 2780. The Egyptians began to build with stone in-stead of brick and to develop a new type of architecture, and the old system of dating by events was abandoned for one geared to the regnal years of the kings.

The Old Kingdom was a long period of internal peace and prosperity in which there was an extreme centralization of wealth and power in the person of the king who was a god on earth. In this age the Egyptians began to obtain timber from Syria, copper from Sinai, and frankincense and myrrh from the Somali coast; there was no foreign trade in the ordinary sense, but these commodities were secured by royal military expeditions.

This was the Pyramid Age, and its symbol is the Great Pyramid which was constructed by Khufu (Cheops), the second pharaoh of the Fourth Dynasty. Four hundred eighty-one feet high, measuring 756 feet on each side at its base, covering an area of 13 acres, composed of 2,300,000 blocks of stone averaging $2\frac{1}{2}$ tons each, the Great Pyramid was under construction for 20 years and required an annual labor force of 100,000 men. It was not a temple, not a palace, but a tomb for the god-king.

The implications of the Great Pyramid are staggering. One man had the power and influence sufficient to cause 100,000 men, a large percentage of Egyptian manpower, to work for 20 years to build his tomb. One man possessed sufficient wealth to carry out this stupendous project. Yet we must not disregard the planning, the computation, the measurements that had to precede and accompany the construction of the pyramid. The orientation of the pyramid on the cardinal points—north, south, east, west—is nearly perfect; there is a difference of only 8 inches between the longest and shortest sides of the pyramid; the corners form almost perfect right angles. Without the aid of modern surveying instruments, this represents an almost incredible performance.

Fully as important, however, are the religious implications of the pyramid, complex and difficult as they are to comprehend. The pyramid as an architectural form did not develop overnight. It is possible to trace its evolution from prehistoric times. The predynastic Egyptians were buried in shallow graves lined with matting. Then stone- or brick-lined pits were constructed, and about the beginning of the dynastic period these pits became more elaborate and were covered with a brick superstructure of benchlike form. This is the *mastaba* tomb used for royal and other important burials under the First and Second Dynasties. At the beginning of the Third Dynasty Imhotep, the architect of King Zoser, built a new kind of tomb. By putting a succession of mastabas one on top of another, he constructed a step pyramid of six stages which rose to a total height of 204 feet. The first true pyramid, which added a casing to conceal the steps or platforms beneath, was built by Snefru, first pharaoh of the Fourth Dynasty, about fifty years after the Step Pyramid of Zoser.

An easy solution to the problem of the evolution and significance of the pyramid is to assume that the development from grave to mastaba to step pyramid to true pyramid was perfectly natural and logical, that this was merely a matter of architectural evolution. Unfortunately, this explanation does not take all the evidence into account. The similarity of the tombs of the first two dynasties to Mesopotamian Proto-Literate architecture has already been noted, and one cannot look at a reconstruction of the Step

Pyramid of Zoser with its surrounding wall and complex of buildings without thinking of the Sumerian ziggurat and its temenos. Furthermore, concealed by the outer casing of any true pyramid was a step pyramid. It has been suggested that the change from mastaba to pyramid involved a change in religious thought. If it is true that the mastaba was called the "castle of eternity" and the pyramid was the "place of ascension" mentioned in the Pyramid Texts, then a change in theology is certainly to be inferred. It is also possible that where the step pyramid provided a means for the pharaoh (the earthly sun) to ascend to heaven, the true pyramid may have been primarily a sun symbol like the ben-ben stone at Heliopolis which was in the shape of a pyramid. By the Fifth Dynasty we know that the cult of the sun-god, Re of Heliopolis, had become the official state religion of Egypt.

The Fourth Dynasty represented the greatest achievement in pyramid building as well as the high point of the pharaoh's wealth and power. It was not only the cost of pyramid construction that began to impoverish the kings, but their wealth was also diminished in other ways. Courtiers were allowed to build expensive tombs and were given tracts of land to supply the tombs with provisions. Each time a pyramid or the tomb of a noble was constructed, tax-exempt lands were allocated from the king's estate and the personnel who served the tombs were freed from the responsibility of forced labor on new projects. Simultaneously lands and wealth were passing into the hands of the priests. In addition, the governorships of the nomes, once held by individuals for short terms, now became hereditary, and the families of the nomarchs, or governors, began to acquire large holdings in the nomes. As the wealth and power of the king declined, the nomarchs became increasingly independent until finally, about 2200 B.C., the Old Kingdom disintegrated.

Between about 2200 and 2000 B.C. as a result of feudalism and decentralization disorder reigned supreme in Egypt. At times there seems to have been complete anarchy. According to a lament of the period, "All is ruin . . . the plunderer is everywhere . . . the poor have become the rich . . . ." These two centuries which divide the Old from the Middle Kingdom comprise the so-called First Intermediate Period. It is difficult to outline intelligibly the sequence of events in this age, for its history confused even the ancient Egyptian chroniclers. Their dynastic lists place the Seventh through the Tenth Dynasties in this period, but it is apparent that these families of rulers were neither successive nor nationally recognized. The dynasties overlapped in time, and the authority of the rulers was confined to parts of Egypt. Even the Eleventh Dynasty at Thebes, sometimes considered to begin the Middle Kingdom, overlapped the Ninth and Tenth Dynasties at Heracleopolis. The rulers of the Eleventh Dynasty were really the nomarchs of Thebes who gradually extended their control over a large part of

Egypt. This dynasty was finally overthrown by an internal revolution shortly after 2000 B.C. which brought to the throne Amenemhat I, a Theban like his predecessors, who became the first pharaoh of the Twelfth Dynasty.

The Twelfth Dynasty endured for just over two hundred years (1991–1779). Its rulers never had the security and authority possessed by the pharaohs of the Old Kingdom; they had always to watch and deal carefully with the great families in the nomes, though Sesostris III (1878–1840) seems to have gone a long way toward breaking their power and depriving them of their hereditary wealth. Unlike the Old Kingdom monarchs whose divine mandate to rule was never questioned, the Twelfth Dynasty pharaohs had to maintain position by sheer energy and ability. Succession to the throne was guarded by a system of co-regencies; the pharaoh would appoint the crown prince as co-ruler and divide responsibilities with him. The Twelfth Dynasty also undertook a great deal of military activity outside of Egypt. There was a drive into Nubia in the south below the Second Cataract, and the Libyans to the west as well as the Semites in Sinai and Palestine were driven back from the Egyptian frontiers by punitive expeditions. Trade was reopened with Syria; the ports of Phoenicia came under strong Egyptian cultural influence during this period. One of the great achievements of the Twelfth Dynasty was the reclamation of land in the Fayum area through flood control and the partial draining of Lake Moeris.

After the Twelfth Dynasty a gradual decline of royal power again set in. A lack of able rulers and strong pressure exerted by tribes on the northeastern frontier finally led to a collapse of unity and a second intermediate period. About 1700, or shortly afterwards, the Delta was invaded and conquered by the Hyksos, a Semitic horde which had already acquired considerable territory in Syria and Palestine. In 1570, when the Hyksos were expelled and Egypt was finally reunited by the pharaohs of the Eighteenth Dynasty, a new era in Egyptian history dawned, an age quite different from the formative period of the Old and Middle Kingdoms.

Despite the developments that had taken place in Egypt during the nearly fifteen hundred years separating Menes from the Hyksos, Egypt had not attained the limits of its political or economic potential. It has been estimated that even in the Middle Kingdom, the Egyptian population was less than one million; at the beginning of the Christian era, the figure had risen to seven million. In 1700 B.C. there was still undeveloped arable land in Egypt; some parts of the Delta remained a wilderness, and Egyptian technology was in many respects primitive by comparison with some other parts of the civilized world. On the other hand, in certain cultural areas notable advances had been made, as a survey of Egyptian civilization will show.

Although Egyptian writing and art had begun to develop before the Old Kingdom, the first great advances were made when that age began. Literature, architecture, and sculpture attained their first real importance. Under

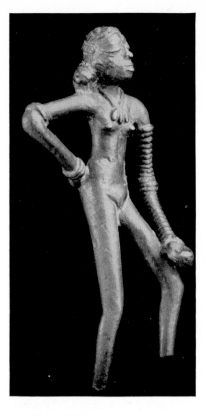

BRONZE DANCER

SCULPTURE IN STONE

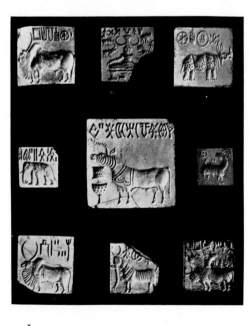

INDUS SEALS

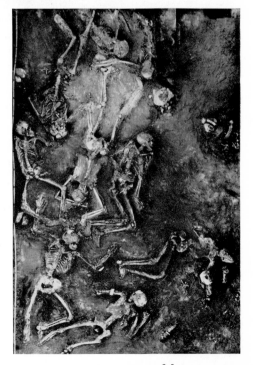

EVIDENCE FOR THE SACK OF MOHENJO-DARO

From The Indus Civilization, by Sir Mortimer Wheeler. Courtesy of the Cambridge University Press

*Courtesy of The Metropolitan Museum of Art, Rogers Fund
and Contribution from Edward S. Harkness, 1926*

Courtesy of Hirmer Verlag Muenchen

HATSHEPSUT

THOTHMES III

*Courtesy of Hirmer Verlag
Muenchen*

Courtesy of Hirmer Verlag Muenchen

IKHNATON

QUEEN NEFERTARI GUARDED BY ISIS—
TWENTIETH DYNASTY

ARMING A SYRO-HITTITE WARRIOR

WARRIORS

ARMING A GREEK WARRIOR—
ATHENIAN VASE, 510 B.C.

Courtesy of The Metropolitan Museum of Art, Gift of John D. Rockefeller, Jr., 1932

PALACE OF ASHURNAZIRPAL

Courtesy of the Cambridge University Press

BLACK OBELISK OF SHALMANESER—JEHU SUBMITS

the Old and Middle Kingdoms the canons of Egyptian art and literature were established. After this no major changes were made except for a brief period when the bonds of convention were temporarily relaxed by a religious reform attempted during the reign of Ikhnaton (Eighteenth Dynasty).

Egyptian architecture, sculpture, and painting are distinctive and impressive. The spectacular results achieved in architecture may be ascribed to the prevalence of good building stone and the wealth of the pharaohs. Moreover, because the Egyptians built in stone, they favored the use of the column and lintel just as the Babylonians, who had to use bricks, were prone to employ the arch. Though the Egyptians knew the true arch as early as the beginning of the dynastic period, the column and lintel technique lent itself naturally to stone construction. The impressiveness of the pyramids is matched by the great temples and palaces of the Middle and New Kingdoms with their gigantic stone columns and labyrinthine rooms. Pylons, courts, and columned halls are characteristic of the Egyptian architectural style which has a massive and monumental quality that dwarfs the architecture of all other ancient civilizations.

Egyptian sculpture, like the architecture, is always on the grand scale. It is a peculiarity of the sculpture that no matter how small a statue may be in actual size, it is large in concept and appears to be a copy of some colossal original. Sculpture began in Egypt largely as an adjunct of architecture, but by the time of the Old Kingdom it had emancipated itself and become an independent art. The Egyptians worked in both hard and soft stones with equal success; they also used bronze, silver, and gold. Although it became customary to adhere quite strictly to certain stylistic conventions, the sculptors were able to rise above mere formalism, particularly in portraiture. Comparisons of royal statues with their corresponding royal mummies show the most accurate delineation of the subject. Whether the portrait is that of a king or a commoner, one is made to feel that a "real person" rather than a mere type is represented. Although Egyptian sculpture in its rigidity and stylized composition frequently gives the impression of being a "three dimensional hieroglyph," the art was never really static, and it is possible even for the untrained eye to catch variations in the styles of succeeding periods.

Painting was even more dependent upon sculpture than sculpture upon architecture. Sculptured figures were usually painted in bright colors to make them appear more lifelike, and Egyptian painting got its start when it was used to decorate relief sculpture in tombs and temples. Not only was the painting closely related to architecture and sculpture, but all three were influenced by the Egyptian environment; in the brilliant sunlight of Egypt, bright colors and sharp contrasts were necessary for effect.

Egyptian painting is often criticized because it ignores perspective and shading, but when one realizes what the art strove to achieve, such criticism is seen to be pointless. The objectives and methods of the Egyptian painters

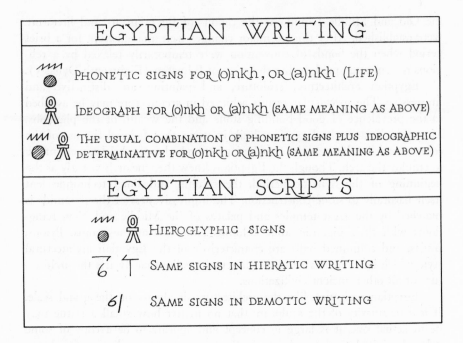

were different from those of painters in the "Western tradition" with which we are familiar. Probably because painting was first used for decorating relief sculpture, it never freed itself from the limitations to which it was first subjected. Furthermore, the art was bound by rules and laws, by canons of proportion mathematically determined, and the result was a kind of painting that simulated descriptive geometry. According to their own peculiar aims, the painters attained technical perfection very early and were satisfied with the results.

Many Egyptian painters were also sculptors and metalworkers. Artists were very carefully trained in schools and workshops; conventional poses and scenes were copied over and over by the apprentices until mastery was achieved. The trained artists often boasted that they knew how to represent all the poses of the body as well as the appropriate magical ceremonies which must accompany the execution of the work, for magic was as inseparable from painting and sculpture as it was from any other phase of ancient technology.

There was little art for art's sake in Egypt; art was utilitarian. One of its purposes was decorative; another was religious or magical. The Egyptians believed that the gods "entered into pictures and statues." They also thought that anything that helped to preserve the identity or remembrance of an individual would provide additional insurance for immortality; mummification, inscribing one's name on stone, and commissioning a sculptured or painted portrait were all means to the same end.

Egyptian painting is tremendously important to the historian because it provides a pictorial record of Egyptian daily life, historical events, religious ceremonies and beliefs, as well as evidence for the introduction of foreign culture and the extension of Egyptian cultural influence abroad. The paintings show costume and the daily round of activities—food preparation, dancing, sports, games, banquets, hunting, and dozens of other things for which other evidence is slight or non-existent.

One of the most distinctive features of Egyptian culture was the system of writing which employed pictographs, ideographs, and phonetic characters. It is sometimes said that the Egyptians developed an alphabet, but this is not strictly true: the "alphabet" was actually a syllabary consisting of twenty-four characters which stood for consonants combined with certain vowels. Like the cuneiform, pictographs, ideographs, and phonetic characters were all used together. A word might be represented very simply by an ideograph or a pictograph, or it might be spelled out phonetically; one commonly finds a word phonetically rendered and followed by the ideograph or pictograph for the word itself. This was in part because there were many Egyptian words with different meanings but identical pronunciations— like English "to," "too," and "two"—and merely spelling the words out would have led to confusion. The Egyptian word *nesh,* for example, meant "pebbles," "to hover (like a bird)," a "plant," or "to drive away."

There were three main varieties of the Egyptian script, the types of writing called hieroglyphic, hieratic, and demotic. The hieroglyphs were carefully drawn pictures developed from early pictographs. Hieratic writing was like the hieroglyphic except that in the former the characters were drawn in a more cursive or running hand. The demotic was an extremely cursive and more simplified type of writing which developed in the first millennium B.C. after the close of the imperial period. The Egyptians carved their writings on stone or inscribed them on metal; where such media were used, the characters were hieroglyphics. More common, however, was the use of a paperlike material made from the pulp of the papyrus plant and also called papyrus. Although hieroglyphs were written on papyrus, it was more convenient to employ the cursive hieratic script for this medium.

Egyptian literature was varied in character. Although magical and religious texts (Pyramid Texts, Coffin Texts, and "Book of the Dead"), hymns, and psalms are common in Egyptian literature, there are also other types of writing. There are narratives of adventure and travel, historical narratives, love songs and banquet songs, accounts of military campaigns, building records, prophecies, proverbs, and technical treatises on medicine, mathematics, and kindred subjects. There is much didactic literature, the work of teachers or wise men who lay down principles of conduct and discuss moral questions. Many of these discourses are addressed to students who are admonished to work hard and become good scribes instead of playing around and going from street to street "where it smelleth of beer." There are copies of model letters written by schoolboys which deal with various subjects. Egyptian poetry is admirable, though much of its excellence is lost in translation because we cannot reproduce its sound or its varied and unfamiliar rhythms. This is also true of the alliteration and the many puns in which the Egyptians indulged.

Egyptian literature and art are inseparable from Egyptian religion. The original stimulus for the development of sculpture, painting, and architecture was largely religious, and this was also the case with writing and literature. Much of the productivity of the Egyptians in these fields continued to be motivated by religious purposes.

In the historic period the cults of Egypt belonged to one of two categories: state and popular. The state cult was a formal religion. Kings were thought to be the sons of certain national gods. In the predynastic period the ruler was considered the son of Horus, the hawk-god, but during the Old Kingdom Horus was replaced by Re, a sun-god. In the time of the Twelfth Dynasty, Re was combined with Amon, the chief god of Thebes, and the national diety was henceforth known as Amon-Re.

The popular cults, of course, were centuries older than that of the state. Totemism played an important role in the most ancient cults. In each of the nomes the chief god had the form of an animal—a crocodile, hippopotamus, jackal, bird, etc. Throughout Egyptian history the old animal gods remained dear to the hearts of the people and were never replaced in popular affection by the state gods. Animism appears also in Egypt, for there were cosmic deities of the water, air, sky, and earth. Neither must one forget the gods of the crafts who came into being with the growing specialization of labor as early as the predynastic age.

Egyptian religion is full of strange and unusual things; much of it is hard to explain, yet it is curious that the Egyptians did not seem to be much given to myth making. They had a creation myth which explained the origin of the world and man and the genealogy of the cosmic deities, but this may have been an importation. Few other myths are known. Perhaps the relatively static and certainly authoritarian environment in which the Egyptians lived did not encourage people to ask questions.

Probably because of the peculiar climatic conditions in Egypt the Egyptians had very early developed a concept of immortality, something unknown to the Babylonians. The dryness of Egypt retarded the decay of organic matter; the fact that the bodies of the dead decomposed fairly slowly heightened the primitive concept of death as a kind of sleep. The Egyptians believed that as long as the body of a dead man was preserved, his soul continued to exist. In the predynastic period when the dead had been buried in contact with the hot sand, decomposition was inhibited, but when the Egyptians began to build underground chambers for the dead, this was no longer true, and the practice of mummification was therefore instituted.

The Egyptians attained great skill in preserving the bodies of the dead, but they were, of course, much aided by the climatic conditions of the country.

It was typical of Egyptian religious thinking, even about immortality, that they were capable of entertaining simultaneously a number of contradictory beliefs without being in the least disturbed by their irreconcilability. They believed, for example, that there was an underworld inhabited by the dead; this was exactly like the Nile Valley—they could not imagine a better environment—and the sun shone there when it was night on earth. The Egyptians also believed that the dead went to a place in the west called the Field of Reeds; this is probably why the pyramids and tombs are all on the west bank of the river. One cult of the dead seems to have been connected with the sun-god of Heliopolis, but the most important was the cult of Osiris.

Osiris, according to legend, had once been a king of Egypt who had been killed and dismembered by his brother, Set. Isis, the wife of Osiris, reassembled her husband after collecting most of the parts scattered about by Set, and Osiris came to life again. He did not, however, return to the earth but became the king of the dead while his mundane throne passed to his son, Horus, the hawk-god and principal deity of the early royal cult. Since Osiris had died and been restored to life, he was also worshipped as a fertility god connected with the Nile, the source of Egypt's fertility. In this aspect of his worship, Osiris resembled the Mesopotamian Dumuzi (or Tammuz), but he was much more important as a symbol of immortality.

A dead person, if properly embalmed, might by special ceremonies become identified with Osiris and so acquire everlasting life. In the early dynastic period only the kings were regarded as eligible for such benefits, but gradually the nobles and ultimately all Egyptians were included. In time it came to be thought that not only must the body be preserved intact and the proper spells be written and recited, but also the morality and uprightness of the dead person must be judged by Osiris in the next world; in the balance scales of judgement, a man's heart must be lighter than the feather of *maat,* or truth.

In the next world, a man was expected to labor as he had in this one. If he was not used to working, he would be well advised to take his servants along with him. This was probably the reason for the human sacrifice under the First Dynasty, but later it was sufficient to put statues of one's servants in the tomb, or still later to employ the little *ushabti* figures, the "answerers," of which as many as 365—one for each day of the year—might be provided.

Then there was also the confusing matter of the *ka* and the *ba* about which students of Egyptian religion do not seem to agree. The *ka* was perhaps the soul or the double of a man which came into existence at his birth and might survive his death and appear at the judgement of Osiris.

The *ba* was a soul or spirit, often represented in the form of a human-headed bird, which appeared at a man's death and continued to inhabit the tomb or commute from the tomb to an effigy of the deceased which might be placed in a temple. At any rate, tombs must be furnished with the possessions and food of this life so that the soul would feel at home. Personal property would be put in the tomb along with regular offerings of food and drink—or else this would be managed at a nearby temple. Scenes from life would be painted on the tomb walls, and little models of buildings, boats, and other objects which had belonged to the deceased would be put into the tomb also.

Clearly, it was just as important to the Egyptians to provide for life after death as it was to provide for life on earth. A great many people in Egypt became engaged in ministering to the dead. In the Old Kingdom this almost promoted a labor shortage among the living. It also meant that many of the great structures of ancient Egypt were mortuary temples devoted to the cults, not of the gods, but of men who had died. As time passed the numbers and wealth of the priests connected with these establishments continued to increase, and this was one of the factors which helped to bring about the final collapse of Egypt at the end of the New Kingdom, or empire. It was no wonder that Herodotus thought the Egyptians the most religious of men.

Religion and government were combined in the full-blown Egyptian theocracy which probably began with the reign of Menes. The god-king of Egypt was an autocrat who headed the administration of justice and economic life, commanded the army and was the chief religious representative of the nation before the gods. Despite the unity of the state which the position of the king expressed, the fact remained that Egypt was a dual kingdom. The king wore a crown that combined the symbols of kingship of Upper and Lower Egypt; he had one name as King of Upper Egypt and another name as King of Lower Egypt. The administration of Egypt was often divided into two parts. Sometimes a king would direct his main attention to either Upper or Lower Egypt, leaving the administration of the other portion to a vizier or to a co-ruler. The latter solution was employed during the Middle Kingdom, while in the New Kingdom there were two viziers, one for the Delta and the other for the valley.

The office of vizier was created in the time of the Fourth Dynasty. At that time the vizier served as Chief Justice, head of the archives, and stood just below the king on the administrative pyramid. Under the vizier were ministers who had charge of the treasury and agricultural affairs. An interesting text from the New Kingdom describes the duties of the vizier in that period: he dispensed justice, received reports daily from the treasury, acted as chief of police for the whole country, was minister of war, of agriculture, and held other portfolios; each day reports of all kinds came to him, and he himself summarized this information in his daily audience with the pharaoh. The pharaoh was the source of law although he delegated judicial authority to the vizier. This virtual monopoly of law by the god-king may explain why Egyptian law was not codified until the eighth century B.C. when the ruler was no longer omnipotent in Egypt. Whatever the reason for the long delay in codifying the law, the situation in Egypt contrasts sharply with that in Mesopotamia where law codes originated in the third millennium B.C.

The once-independent states, the nomes, were made units of administration in the historic period. Under the Old Kingdom royal appointees from among the nobility governed the nomes. When these governorships were allowed to become hereditary, the results were disastrous: the Old Kingdom fell, and a baneful decentralization followed that weakened and impoverished Egypt for two centuries. Though the pharaohs of the Middle Kingdom were able to restore a semblance of unity, it was not until the time of the New Kingdom that the national government was strong enough to remedy fully the fault of disunity and bring the nomes once more under central control.

Egypt remained throughout its history an essentially agricultural country. All the land belonged to the king, and he might give or entrust it to his subjects. The ruler directed agricultural production; this was a consequence of the close connection between agriculture and religion and the position of the pharaoh as god-king. The agricultural population was regimented, and the majority of the peasants had long since been transformed from freeholders into serfs. Egypt was a country of large estates. The land not directly retained by the crown was turned over in large blocks to the nobles and the priests. Every temple possessed vast holdings which contributed to its support; in the latter part of the imperial era, most of the best lands of Egypt were in the hands of the priests.

In order to keep agricultural production at high levels, continuous cooperative work was necessary. Canals and irrigation ditches had to be kept in perfect condition. After the annual floods the whole land had to be resurveyed because the flood waters obliterated the landmarks. A huge bureaucracy was built up to perform these duties, collect the taxes, and take the census of the inhabitants and their possessions. Taxes were paid in kind, and the rural population was subject to forced labor. It has been well said that the economy of Egypt was essentially a plantation economy, but it was also a planned economy like that of the Sumerians. The crops to be grown were specified by government order. Knowing the size of the labor force, the quality of the various plots of land, and knowing also in advance how much of Egypt would be covered in the annual inundation, the government could estimate the yield (and the tax returns) each year even before the crops were planted. Up the Nile at the First Cataract was a gauge, a

Nilometer, by which the annual flood could be measured. Records had been kept of the floods year by year from at least the time of the First Dynasty, and thus it was possible to forecast to what extent the waters would inundate the valley in the coming months.

Industry and trade, particularly the former, were important in Egypt, but they never attained the same place in the economic life of the country that they did in Babylonia. Artisans were to be found in the workshops of the king and the nobles, and there were also independent artisans in the towns. There were metalworkers, potters, weavers, jewelers, brewers, and many other craftsmen of different kinds. Mummification required skilled workers and thus provided employment for many people. The ethics of the mummifiers often left much to be desired in later periods; bodies were not carefully wrapped, and sometime fake mummies were made up—in one case the supposed mummy of a baby "consisted of an old man's skull for bulk and a thigh bone for length."[1]

Egyptian products penetrated equatorial Africa, figured in the commerce of the Red Sea, and made their way into Syria, Palestine, and other lands of the eastern Mediterranean including the Aegean area; some Egyptian products have been found in Italy. The principal exports were pottery, glass, stone and metalwork, textiles and jewelry; Egypt imported wood, copper, pottery, ivory, spices, and slaves.

In Egypt the royal family, nobles, and priests formed an upper class. There was a middle class of traders, artisans, scribes, and other professional men. Most of the farmers were virtually serfs, and there were, of course, slaves. On the other hand, there are numerous examples of persons born in an inferior status who, either as soldiers or scribes, managed to make their way into the higher levels of society. In the so-called wisdom literature of Egypt good advice is often given about careers: the advantages of literacy were great in an essentially illiterate society, so the young men are advised not to be farmers, soldiers, metalworkers, or charioteers, but to become scribes, since a wide-awake scribe could rise to a high post in the bureaucracy.

The life of the nobles was one of culture and refinement. They had fine homes enhanced with gardens and ponds. The labor of their farmers and slaves provided them with adequate incomes and leisure time. Except when a noble served in the army or held some official position, he could devote himself to pleasure. Hunting, fishing, and fowling were popular sports among the nobles. Lions and hippopotami were the game of the more courageous hunters, and one of the most famous accounts in Egyptian literature deals with an elephant hunt in northern Syria. Fish could be

---

[1] W. M. Flinders Petrie, *Social Life in Ancient Egypt* (New York: Houghton Mifflin, 1923), p. 29.

lured with baited hooks or simply speared, while birds were hunted in the papyrus thickets along the Nile and brought down by falcons or sometimes with boomerangs or throwing sticks. Games of chance could be enjoyed at home with a minimum of exertion. Knucklebones were popular, but the Egyptians played other games which required more skill of head or hand; there were several different board games played with gaming pieces moved from square to square.

The Egyptians of the upper classes wore waistcloths, cloaks, and leather sandals. They shaved their heads and wore wigs. It was customary to paint the eyebrows black or green and the nails henna. Both men and women wore jewelry: metal bracelets, rings, and necklaces were common, and much use was made of precious and semiprecious stones. Among the small details of Egyptian life we may note that slate and copper mirrors have been found as well as such beauty aids as curlers for the hair and tweezers. The Egyptian headrest, used instead of a pillow, looks very uncomfortable, but apparently this was not the case since the headrest allowed air to circulate under the neck, a necessity for comfortable sleeping in a hot climate.

Though the common people were desperately poor and anything but free, they seem to have enjoyed life with a happy spirit quite different from the pessimistic attitude often encountered in Mesopotamia. We see them laughing and joking in the tomb paintings, and their remarks to one another are often included in the accompanying hieroglyphs which serve a function like that of "balloons" in our cartoon strips. Perhaps the secret of their happiness and optimism was their assurance of immortality and the confidence which their ruler, a god on earth, inspired. Moreover, the even tenor of nature itself may have been comforting: it almost never rained, the Nile always flooded on schedule, and Egypt was so close to the equator that there were virtually no seasons.

Just as in Mesopotamia, the third millennium and the early part of the second in Egypt had been a formative period during which a distinctive civilization had attained its essential form. The basic cultural features developed in this early age became characteristics or hallmarks which persisted for centuries. If Egypt, rather than Mesopotamia, seemed full of curiosities and marvels to the outsiders who came as traders, invaders, and tourists in later times, it was because the culture of these foreigners was more indebted to Mesopotamia than to Egypt.

Chapter 5

THE INDUS CIVILIZATION

HE THIRD of the great riverine civilizations established at the dawn of history flourished in the Indus Valley in the period 2500–1500 B.C. The Indus civilization may be classed as a primary center for the creation and diffusion of culture even though at present the details of the force and extent of its influence are not fully known; its early date, the complexity of its culture, and the vast area which it covered provide a sufficient guarantee of its importance. Like the civilizations of Egypt and Babylonia, the Indus civilization was situated in a great river valley; its people were faced with major problems of irrigation and flood control which they solved by co-operative effort; and in the Indus Valley we find a familiar cultural assemblage which included city life, cereal culture, domesticated herd animals, metallurgy, writing, monumental architecture, and probably theocracy and class stratification.

On the other hand, there were two major points of difference between the Indus Valley and its civilized neighbors to the west: (1) the Indus civilization sprawled over a huge area with a major axis of a thousand miles running from the upper Indus on the northeast to a point near the Iranian border on the Indian Ocean, and (2) the Indus civilization was completely destroyed and forgotten. The territory in which this civilization flourished was several times larger than that of Egypt and Babylonia, yet the memory of the latter lands and their cultural contributions had a continuous survival while the rediscovery of the Indus culture began only a quarter of a century ago.

The successes of archaeology elsewhere in the Near East almost predestined the excavation of sites in the Indus Valley, for the many large mounds along the river boldly challenged the spade of the archaeologist. Furthermore, seal stones reputed to have come from the mounds were engraved with figures that suggested an Indian rather than a foreign origin and therefore hinted at the existence of a former civilization in the area. The excavations begun in 1923 have been continued almost without interruption until the present; only a major depression and a world war have been causes powerful enough to force a cessation of activity.

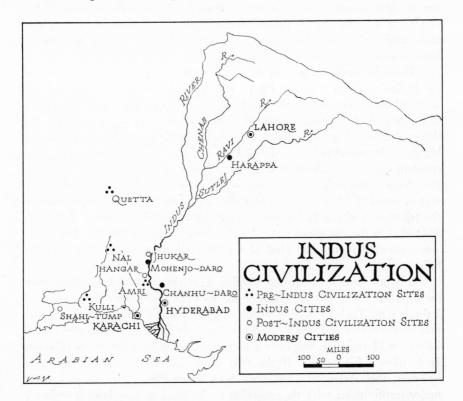

INDUS CIVILIZATION

∴ PRE~INDUS CIVILIZATION SITES
● INDUS CITIES
○ POST~INDUS CIVILIZATION SITES
◉ MODERN CITIES

MILES
100 50 0   100

Although at least sixty Indus civilization sites have been identified, the actual excavation has been largely confined to three: Harappa (near Montgomery) on the Ravi River in the north, Mohenjo-daro (about two hundred miles above Karachi) in the south, and Chanhu-daro across the Indus to the east of Mohenjo-daro. Harappa is the oldest and largest of these sites, but its condition is rather poor due to the fact that it was used as a brick quarry by railroad builders in the nineteenth century. Of the other two sites, Mohenjo-daro is the most important, and it has been excavated far more extensively than Harappa or Chanhu-daro.

One of the most striking features of the Indus civilization is its uniformity. Harappa and Mohenjo-daro are four hundred miles apart, yet the same weights and measures, the same brick sizes, and fundamentally the same city plans are found in each. Towns were laid out on a gridiron pattern with the streets running north and south, east and west, making rectangular-shaped city blocks of a more or less uniform size; the streets were wide by ancient standards with a width of thirty feet not uncommon. Both Harappa and Mohenjo-daro were dominated by huge citadels rising to a height of forty feet and measuring four to five hundred yards in length and two to three hundred yards in width. Fortified with walls and towers, the citadels were crowned by palaces and temples of considerable size. Huge tanks which may have been used for ceremonial bathing were noteworthy features of the temples.

There is much to be said for the theory that theocracy prevailed in the Indus Valley as it did in Egypt and Babylonia. The association of palaces and temples on the citadels and the existence of a civilization like those of Egypt and Mesopotamia founded upon intensive agriculture point toward theocracy. Special quarters for workmen, the milling establishment, and the big granaries associated with the citadel at Harappa may be relics of a government monopoly of flour manufacture. The separate quarters for the workmen suggest the existence of slavery and thus class stratification. Government control of labor may also be indicated by the construction of dams in the tributaries of the Indus which must have served to control the floods and aided in the storage of water for the dry season; possibly the dams were also connected with some kind of terrace cultivation on the slopes of the hills.

It is not known at present whether Harappa and Mohenjo-daro were the capitals of two distinct states or the two chief administrative centers of a single state. Perhaps neither hypothesis is correct; the excavation of other sites might reveal still other centers or "capitals." Mohenjo-daro was settled later than Harappa; it was once a seaport and may have begun its existence as a colony of Harappa. If the two towns belonged to different states, however, their relations must have been extraordinarily peaceful because major fortifications, with the exception of the citadels, have been found only in the hills where stone forts guarded the passes leading into the Indus Valley.

The fact that the valley, particularly the Sind district, was the home of a civilization based upon agriculture gives assurance that the climate in ancient times was less arid than it is today, since the present rainfall is less than six inches a year. Moreover, the favorite motifs in Indus art feature animals which prefer a habitat where water is plentiful; the water buffalo, the rhinoceros, and the elephant are good examples. The extensive use of wood for building and for fuel also presupposes that the climate and vegetation were different in antiquity. Wood was used in architecture far more freely than in Egypt or Babylonia, and where the Babylonians had to content themselves with sun-dried brick for building, the Indus people could afford to employ wood as a fuel to make baked brick in large quantities. It is possible that wood was floated down from the Himalayas, but it is unlikely that the brick kilns of Mohenjo-daro depended on this source. If trees once grew on the hillsides of Sind, deforestation could account at least partially for a climatic change; it is said that similar developments have occurred in modern India.

Many of the mysteries surrounding the Indus civilization might be unravelled if its script could be read, but until this particular riddle is answered it is necessary to depend entirely upon archaeological evidence for our knowledge of this period in India. It is well to remember that while archaeology can provide the basis for a description of material culture and certain inferences can be drawn from the remains, history cannot be written from this evidence alone.

The Indus people were farmers, herdsmen, artisans, and traders. In their fields they grew wheat, barley, sesame, peas, melons, and dates. Fragments of cotton cloth from the excavations indicate that cotton was also a major crop. Naturally the cultivation of cereals was the most important agricultural activity, and along with cereal culture, as in Egypt and Babylonia, went the raising of herd animals: cattle, sheep, and goats. In addition, the Indus people had the water buffalo and the zebu; they may have domesticated the elephant. The presence of granaries on the river banks tells us that grain was transported by boat, while models of two-wheeled oxcarts suggest the common form of land transportation. The ass was another beast of burden with the horse, camel, and elephant (possibly) as his companions.

Textiles, metalwork, and pottery constituted the principal manufactures of the Indus artisans. Ivory and bone were worked along with such metals as copper, gold, silver, electrum, and lead. Bronze was used for tools and weapons; saws, axes, adzes, swords, spear and knife blades, razors, and arrowheads have been found. The artisans knew the art of casting; even the difficult lost-wax (cire perdue) process was employed.

The so-called Harappa style of pottery was characteristic of the Indus civilization. This is a black-on-red ware with designs in black painted on a lustrous red background. Some Harappa patterns were abstract, but naturalistic motifs of plant and animal designs were common. In addition to trees and plants, goats, rabbits, birds, and antelopes, human figures were sometimes portrayed. Many kilns for baking pottery have been found, and the pottery itself bears witness to the use of the potter's wheel.

Finds of artifacts from the Indus in other regions and the discovery of foreign trade objects in the Indus cities give clues to the areas with which the Indus people traded. There was an exchange of goods with Iran and possibly with Turkestan, and there must have been trade eastward into India. It has been thought that Indus traders may have had establishments in the Sumerian cities. At any rate, the presence of Indus seals in southern Mesopotamia indicates that trade contacts began in the Early Dynastic period (before 2350 B.C.) and continued possibly to the Age of Hammurabi.

It is tempting to identify the Indus Valley with the land the Sumerians called Makkan (Ma-gan). From Makkan came gold, ivory, wood, semiprecious stones, beads, and various plants and animals which were exchanged for Mesopotamian garments, wool, oil, and leather. The trade with Makkan was carried on from before the time of Sargon of Akkad until the end of the Third Dynasty of Ur; sometimes even tribute from Makkan is mentioned. After the Ur III period direct contact with Makkan was broken; instead, Telmun (Bahrein Island) served as a point of exchange between east and west.

The location of Makkan, however, is uncertain. Perhaps it was west of the Indus delta in the area now called Makran. A region known as the land of the Maka was part of the Persian Empire in the middle of the first millennium B.C., and it was close to, or part of, India. On the other hand, it is also possible that Makkan was situated in Arabia on the south coast of the Gulf of Oman.

The Indus sites have yielded a profusion of stone weights carefully cut into cubical shapes. An analysis of these stones reveals that a binary system was used for the smaller weights which ran in a series beginning 1-2-4-8-16-32, while for the larger weights a decimal system was employed. Weighing was done with balance and scales as it was in Mesopotamia and Egypt. Although the weight system was unusual, the measures of the ancient Indus were identical with those used in the other riverine civilizations. The dimensions of buildings and the discovery of two measuring instruments, one a graduated bronze rod and the other made of shell, show that the "foot" and the cubit were basic units. The Indus foot ranged from 13 to 13.2 inches, and the cubit measured from 20.3 to 20.8 inches.

If the skeletal remains found to date are at all representative, the inhabitants of Harappa and other towns were a mixed group. A long-headed "Mediterranean" type is thought to have composed the politically dominant class, while bones exhibiting proto-Australoid characteristics may belong to the aborigines who lived in the valley before the coming of civilization and then were subjected to invaders possessing a more advanced culture.

Details of dress shown on sculptured figures indicate that men wore kilts and shawls; the women, skirts. Garments were of cotton, and many ornaments of metal, ivory, shell, bone, and semiprecious stones have been found. Buttons, beads, bracelets, rings, necklaces, and combs are common items uncovered in the course of excavation. People also adorned themselves with nose rings and earplugs. Men wore beards but shaved the upper lip; their long hair was gathered into a bun or knot at the back of the head.

Houses were two-storied structures of wood, brick, and stone with blank walls and flat roofs. Wood was used for doors and rafters; roofs were covered with reed mats and clay. It was customary to build the houses around a courtyard where the cooking was done. There were elaborate provisions for sanitation and drainage: clay pipes connected the houses with channels sunk below the street level and covered with paving slabs. The houses were apparently heated by charcoal braziers which could be carried from room to room; unlike Babylonia where oil lamps were used, Indus illumination was provided by candles.

Indus children did not lack for games and toys. They had miniature carts and toy animals on wheels to pull about; some of the animals bobbed their heads as they moved; even a monkey on a string has been found. Among the animals modelled in clay were bulls, donkeys, dogs, rhinoceroses, elephants, and pigs. It is quite possible that some of the animals were not toys at all, but cult objects belonging to the adults. This is also true of some of the whistles and rattles. Among the games, jacks, marbles, board games, and dice have been found; one fears that knucklebones were of greater interest to the senior members of the community than they were to the toddlers. The children had pets as well as toys and games. Dogs and cats were kept, and like dogs and cats the world over they were not always friends: footprints in a brick from Chanhu-daro bear witness to a chase in which, at the time of crossing the brick, the cat was still in advance of the dog.

The sculptured remains discovered thus far do not give the impression that Indus artists were as competent as those of Egypt and Babylonia. Sculptors worked in metal, stone, and clay. A rather good bronze figurine of a dancing girl far surpasses other figures in sandstone, limestone, alabaster, and steatite, and terra cotta. The general mediocrity of Indus art except for the seals and the painted pottery of the Harappa style has occasioned the criticism that the Indus civilization was dull and bourgeois.

The religion of the Indus civilization can be reconstructed only through inferences made from the material remains, chiefly the sculpture and the seals. A fertility cult dominated by a mother goddess is certainly suggested by clay figurines of women. There was also a male god portrayed on the seals who may have been the prototype of Shiva; at any rate, he was horned and had three faces, and he was often shown in the sitting position of a yogi. Other links between the early Indus religion and Hinduism may be seen in the fact that the fig tree (pipal) was sacred and that certain animals were revered: the humped bull and possibly goats, crocodiles, snakes, and doves. Mythological animals appear on the seals; one of the most striking of these is a creature with the body of a ram and the trunk of an elephant. The figurine of the dancing girl mentioned above may indicate that the dance was included in religious ceremonial.

The dead were buried in large graves with the bodies placed in a north-south position. Pottery vessels in large numbers, ornaments, and toilet articles were placed in the graves. In the case of a female burial it was found that the body was wrapped in a reed shroud and put into a wooden coffin. This is reminiscent of early Sumerian practice, but no conclusions can be drawn from an isolated instance of this kind.

83

The Indus script has not been deciphered for a number of very good reasons. First, the underlying language is not known. Secondly, the available texts are very short; they probably consist only of titles and personal names. Thirdly, the script does not seem to be related to any known system of writing. Examples of the Indus writing have been found on a great many seals, a few pottery vessels, and some inscribed copper objects. The script employed from three to four hundred characters, and the system of writing was probably ideographic and phonetic; it seems to have been read normally from right to left. No long inscriptions have been found. This does not necessarily mean that the Indus people lacked a literature, but rather that they may have written on some perishable material. If it were possible to read the script, the language thus revealed would throw light upon the origin of the people and perhaps upon governmental and economic organization. Unless longer texts or a bilingual come to light, however, the mystery of the Indus script will remain unsolved.

Although there were villages in the hills bordering the Indus Valley long before civilization began, and although there were villages on sites in the valley before the cities grew there, it is not possible to find in the hills or the valley any culture which might have been the parent of the Indus civilization. It is therefore a likely assumption that the creators of civilization were invaders who entered the country from the north and gradually moved southward. The life of the Indus civilization covered a span of about one thousand years, roughly between 2500 and 1500 B.C. Toward the end there is evidence of degeneration: culturally, the people stand still, and the cities decline in size. At last, a new invasion swept down from the north and left destruction and desolation in its wake.

It is thought that the Indus civilization was destroyed by the Aryans who descended upon India at about the same time as their Indo-European-speaking relatives, the Kassites, Mitanni, and Greeks, forced their way into the remainder of the ancient world; the Hittites, too, may be counted as part of this vast migration. The Indus people could offer little resistance. Their cities were sacked, and they themselves were struck down and left lying in the streets where their bones greeted the excavators in the twentieth century.

Despite the fact that its very existence was forgotten, there are reasons for believing that some of the culture of the ancient Indus survived. The addiction to water rites, the tabus regarding certain animals, the binary weight system, the worship of Shiva, and the identification of the pipal as a holy tree may link modern India with the past. It has even been noted that the clay models of carts represent vehicles identical with those of India today; a wheel base of three feet six inches demonstrated by the ruts in the streets of ancient Harappa is still standard for the carts of Sind.

Chapter 6

THE EGYPTIAN EMPIRE

U NTIL FAIRLY RECENTLY a recurrent historical phenomenon has been the mass migration of the human animal from one area to another. Climatic changes and food shortages in more primitive times and, later, economic dislocation provided the principal causes for such movements. The last great migration, of course, was the one that brought the white man to the red man's continents, but perhaps twenty thousand years before that the Indians themselves had migrated to the New World. Europe had known Genghis Khan and earlier the Goths and others whose invasions had helped to destroy the Roman Empire. In the second millennium B.C. there were two great periods of chaos resulting from the mass movements of peoples: the first came in the period between 1800 and 1500, and the second began about 1200. The second series of disturbances is perhaps better known: it brought the Medes and Persians to Iran, the Phrygians to Asia Minor, the Dorian Greeks into Greece; repercussions were felt in Italy, in Syria, in Palestine, and even the frontiers of Egypt were under attack. This second series of movements was more destructive than the first, for it plunged parts of the civilized world into centuries of darkness.

We have already observed some of the effects of the disturbances that preceded 1500. This was the age of the Kassite conquest of Babylonia, the arrival of the Hittites in Asia Minor, the fall of the Indus civilization, and the arrival of the first Greeks in Greece. The Kassites, Hittites, Aryans, and Greeks were all Indo-Europeans who came into the civilized area from the north, but other linguistic groups participated in the movements of this period: from Arabia came the Canaanites and probably the Hyksos, while the Hurrians invaded northern Mesopotamia from Armenia.

These great invasions produced not only political changes, but also significant technological ones. While their immediate effects were disruptive, their long-range results were likely to be more good than bad. The second migration, for example, brought iron users into the ancient civilized world and terminated the Bronze Age in the Near East, Greece, and Italy. The people who came just before 1500 introduced the horse and thereby fostered a revolution in transportation which in turn made possible the creation of the larger political units which were typical of the latter half of the second millennium B.C.

Between the first and second migrations there was a distinct period of ancient history. It was an age of empires, and general conditions in the ancient civilized world were far different from what they had been during the centuries when the great primary civilizations of the river valleys were in the process of formation and growth. Babylonia and the Indus Valley were in eclipse during this new period, while Egypt broke with tradition by expanding beyond its frontiers into Palestine and Syria. Civilization was no longer confined to the river valleys but was diffused into the intermediate areas of the Near East: Syria, Palestine, Asia Minor; it even touched the peripheral region of the Aegean. The truly great powers of the new age were Egypt, the Mitannian kingdom in northern Mesopotamia, the Hittite Empire in Asia Minor, and possibly the Minoan and Mycenaean states in Crete and Greece.

In the Second Intermediate Period, the age of decentralization between the Middle and New Kingdoms, Egypt had been invaded by the Hyksos about the year 1700 B.C. These Semites, whose name is thought to mean "Rulers of Foreign Lands," never really held more of Egypt than the Delta. Although Avaris in the Tanite nome may have been their capital, current opinion holds that the largest part of their empire was in Syria and Palestine rather than in Egypt. The Hyksos are hard to identify. We can recognize their huge fortified camps, their metalwork, and their tombs, but other characteristic culture traits are not plentiful.

Though the Hyksos were anything but popular in Egypt, they did benefit the country with an infusion of new culture. They brought the horse and chariot, the compound bow, and arrowheads of metal. Hyksos horses were small and rarely ridden, and the chariot was a mere skeleton, but Egyptian methods of warfare and transportation were revolutionized. Other innovations attributed to the Hyksos are an improved bellows, better methods of weaving, the branding of cattle, and even a new kind of razor.

During the latter part of the Hyksos period the Egyptian dynasty called the Seventeenth maintained a precarious existence at Thebes. Sekenenre and Kamose, two pharaohs of this dynasty, fought the Hyksos as best they could. Sekenenre was not notably successful; his battered mummy has been found still showing the mortal wounds he received in battle. The groundwork had been laid, however, for the expulsion of the Hyksos. A general named Ahmes, possibly the brother of Kamose, led the Egyptians to victory and became the founder of a new dynasty, the Eighteenth.

Ahmes accomplished the extermination of the Hyksos by heading a national uprising against the hated foreigners which amounted to a crusade. This first pharaoh of the Eighteenth Dynasty, who began to reign in 1570, then found himself at the head of a movement that did not lose its momentum when the Hyksos were overthrown. Instead, the great explosion spilled over the frontiers and was ultimately to result in the establishment of an empire which included Syria and Palestine all the way to the great bend of the Euphrates and the southern mountains of Anatolia. The empire itself was not the creation of Ahmes but of his successors, though during the nearly twenty-five years of his reign he did much to lay the foundations for it. In addition to expelling the Hyksos, Ahmes curbed the power of the feudal lords who had been so troublesome to the Middle Kingdom. He made the army an attractive career for nobles and commons. Military bravery was often rewarded by gifts and appointments to governmental and court posts, and duties were found for the sons of the nobility at the court rather than in the nomes.

After the Hyksos were driven from Egypt, the next step was to pursue them into Palestine. As a result of this pressure, the Hyksos soon disappeared entirely, but the great crusade went on, extended now to all "Asiatics." Amenhotep I (1546-1524) marched all the way to the Euphrates, a feat duplicated by his successor, Thothmes I (1524-1507). The time for the creation of an empire was near, but the actual accomplishment was delayed by two circumstances: (1) invaders called the Mitannians had arrived in northern Mesopotamia and were beginning to make inroads into Syria, and (2) for the next twenty-five years Egypt was ruled by a queen whose imperial interests lay in a different direction.

Hatshepsut, lady pharaoh of Egypt from 1507 to 1482, was the daughter of Thothmes I. Inscriptions tell us of her birth and accession to the throne. Her consorts were first her half-brother, Thothmes II (1507-1491), and then her nephew, Thothmes III (1491-1482). The first was completely dominated by the queen, but Thothmes III was not so pliant and may actually have brought about her death. At any rate, it was a curious period with a queen, called "His Majesty," on the throne. It was a period that saw the aggressive action in Palestine and Syria virtually abandoned for a different policy which sought the establishment of trade relations with the coast of the Red Sea. One wonders whether the drive in this direction was not to compensate for losses to the northeast.

After the death of Hatshepsut in 1482, Thothmes III reigned alone for over thirty years (to 1449). He was a great warrior-pharaoh who renewed the attacks on Syria. His strategy was above reproach. Early in his reign

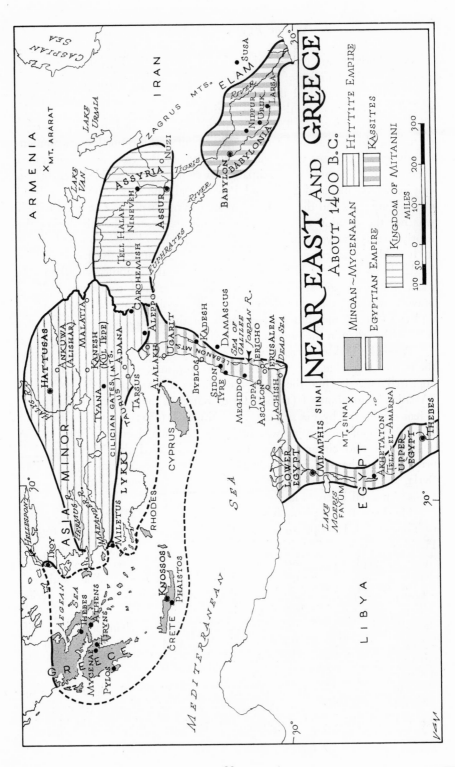

NEAR EAST AND GREECE

ABOUT 1400 B.C.

Legend

Minoan-Mycenaean	Hittite Empire
Egyptian Empire	Kassites
	Kingdom of Mitanni

MILES

100 50 0 100 200 300

ARMENIA
× MT. ARARAT
CASPIAN SEA
LAKE VAN
LAKE URMIA
IRAN
ZAGRUS MTS.
ELAM
SUSA
LARSA
URUK
NIPPUR
BABYLON
BABYLONIA
River
TIGRIS RIVER
ASSYRIA
NUZI
ASSUR
NINEVEH
TELL HALAF
CARCHEMISH
EUPHRATES RIVER
ALEPPO
UGARIT
ALALAKH
KADESH
DAMASCUS
BYBLOS
SIDON
TYRE
LEBANON MTS.
SEA OF GALILEE
JORDAN R.
MEGIDDO
JOPPA
JERICHO
ASCALON
JERUSALEM
LACHISH
DEAD SEA
HATTUSAS
ANKUWA (ALISHAR)
MALATIA
KANESH (KUL TEPE)
IYANA
ASIA MINOR
HALYS R.
HERMUS R.
MAEANDER R.
CILICIAN GATES
TAURUS (MTS.)
TARSUS
ADANA
LYKI
MILETUS
RHODES
CYPRUS
MEDITERRANEAN SEA
AEGEAN SEA
TROY
HELLESPONT
30°
GREECE
THEBES
ATHENS
MYCENAE
TIRYNS
PYLOS
KNOSSOS
PHAISTOS
CRETE
MEMPHIS
LOWER EGYPT
MT. SINAI ×
SINAI
AKHETATON (TELL-EL-AMARNA)
UPPER EGYPT
THEBES
EGYPT
LAKE MOERIS
FAYUM
LIBYA
30°
30°
30°

Thothmes captured Megiddo, the great fortress in northern Palestine which was the key to an invasion of Syria. Later, an unprecedented use of sea-power gave him the Phoenician ports which were then used for a successful drive against Kadesh on the Orontes, another key city. Subsequently, Thothmes carried the standards of Egypt across the Euphrates against the Mitannian kingdom. By 1449 when this great king "rested from life," as the Egyptians put it, an empire was assured.

In the reign of Amenhotep II (1449–1424) although fighting continued in Syria, imperial government had begun. There was a "governor of Asia," garrisons were stationed in important towns, local princes regularly paid tribute, and Egyptian fiscal officers were ubiquitous. The Mitannian problem was solved by Thothmes IV (1424–1411) who made an alliance with the Mitannians and sealed the pact by marrying the king's daughter. Similar alliances, both diplomatic and marital, were made by his successors.

It had been a century and a half of glorious achievement. The Asiatic crusade had broken the traditional isolation of Egypt. Led by warrior-kings who fought hand to hand with the enemy and were always to be found leading the vanguard, the Egyptians had gained new confidence and assurance. They had become consciously imperialistic. The proud boast of Thothmes I that he had made the boundaries of Egypt as wide as the circuit of the sun typified the Egyptian attitude in the new age. Yet much of Egyptian thinking was tempered by a narrow provincialism. Contempt for "those Asiatics" was one aspect of this, but it was only part of the feeling of most Egyptians that Egypt was an earthly paradise in which everything was perfect. They were forced by travel to recognize that Egypt was unique and that Egyptian culture differed from that of the outside world, but from their point of view it was the rest of the world and not Egypt that was strange. Mesopotamia was an incredible country because its rivers flowed backwards! Any self-respecting river would flow northward like the Nile.

The victories of Egypt brought tribute and slaves into the country, and this new wealth and labor could be devoted to vast building programs. Palaces and temples were constructed on a colossal scale. In both the public and private life of Egypt there were luxury and ostentation to a degree not known before. Although pyramids were no longer constructed, their place was taken by the obelisk and the rock-cut tomb. Thothmes I, Hatshepsut, and Thothmes III raised obelisks to commemorate their achievements. The obelisks were made from huge single blocks of stone and may have been sheathed with gold or electrum (a natural alloy of gold and silver). The tendency was to produce bigger and better obelisks. A monolithic block 64 feet high and 7 feet square at the base (weighing 143 tons) was good enough for Thothmes I, but Hatshepsut ordered one 97 feet tall and weighing 323 tons, and a monument of Thothmes III set a new record at 105 feet, 445 tons. An absolute monster had to be left upriver at the quarry: it would have been 137 feet tall with a weight of 1168 tons.

Although mortuary temples for the deceased rulers were built in the vicinity of Thebes, the capital of the New Kingdom, the actual burials took place in a barren valley west of Thebes, the Valley of the Kings, where the pharaohs were laid to rest in elaborate hidden tombs carved out of living rock. These, as it turned out, were no more secure from grave robbers than the pyramids had been; the tomb of Tutankhamen, discovered in 1922 A.D., was the only one to have escaped disastrous plundering.

The pharaoh of Egypt was now the greatest figure on the international scene. The administration of Egypt alone required two viziers, one in the north and the other in the south, and a bureaucracy even larger than before. The influence of Egypt was felt not only within the empire, but also in Cyprus and Cilicia, in Libya, and far south of the First Cataract. Gifts, called tribute by the Egyptians, came from the kings of the Hittites, Babylonia, and Assyria. By the time of Thothmes III the Minoans of Crete were sending embassies to Egypt, too.

The climax of Egyptian power was reached in the reign of Amenhotep III (1411–1380). This was the pharaoh the Greeks called Memnon, at whose order the Colossus (really colossi) was built. Egypt was supreme in the Near East, so strong that none dared to attack her. Amenhotep III was not a great warrior; it was not necessary. He did conduct military operations in Nubia to the south, but these were not of great importance. Amenhotep had a king-size harem from which he could choose a different wife for each day of the year. Many of his women were foreigners: among them were a Hittite princess, a Babylonian princess, and there were two from the Kingdom of Mitanni. Much of the royal correspondence which has survived from the reign of Amenhotep III has to do with his marital entanglements. We find him frequently arranging for new marriages or trying to explain what had happened to some of the old ones. In a big establishment like that of Amenhotep, wives could get misplaced; when he sought to marry the daughter of the Kassite king, Amenhotep was challenged to produce her aunt, the king's sister, whom the pharaoh had married some years before.

Egypt did have a queen, however. This was Ty, Amenhotep's principal wife, a great and powerful lady and a very remarkable woman. She was not of royal blood; her parents were a priestly couple, apparently unrelated to the royal family. This was most unusual, since in Egypt, where descent was reckoned on the distaff side, the heir to the throne tended to marry one of his sisters. Amenhotep and Ty were married fairly early in his reign, and there must have been a considerable scandal. Ty bore the titles "Great Heiress," "Royal Daughter," "Royal Sister," and "Royal Wife," but this can have deceived no one. Ty bore Amenhotep several sons and many daughters, some of whom were to play major roles in the drama that was about to unfold in Egypt.

Just before Amenhotep died, he associated with himself as co-ruler his son and heir, Amenhotep IV, better known as Ikhnaton. From the point of view of imperial welfare this was a very poor choice, since Ikhnaton was not only physically and psychologically unfitted to rule, but he was also a hyper-religious person whose fanaticism was to preclude much attention to routine affairs of state. At this very moment the Egyptian Empire which had seemed so strong and permanent was in grave danger. Amenhotep III had long since lost the vigor of his youth, and the opium of peace had dulled the perception of his generals and ministers. The Egyptians, because of the seemingly static conditions in their own country, had assumed that nothing changed in the rest of the world, either. Once they had counted the Mitannians among their most dangerous enemies, but for many years peace with Mitanni had been assured by a succession of treaties and dynastic intermarriages. Unfortunately, the Assyrians and Hittites who lived on either side of the Mitannians were hungry for conquest. These were the rising powers with which the Egyptians failed to reckon, the great states of the future. The Mitannians were closer to reality than the Egyptians. Appreciating their danger, they could see little hope of protection from faraway Egypt ruled by an uxorious old man and a young visionary. Thus, in Mitanni-land two parties arose: one, pro-Assyrian; the other, pro-Hittite. Old Tushratta, the Mitannian king, recognized the situation and tried to warn Ty in a letter of condolence which he sent to her at the time of Amenhotep's death. Ty did her best to keep Mitannian friendship and confidence. Amenhotep IV (Ikhnaton) was persuaded to marry one of the Mitannian princesses who had formerly been married to Amenhotep III, and while Tushratta lived, Egypt and Mitanni remained allies. After his death civil war broke out in his empire: one claimant for the throne was pro-Assyrian, another was pro-Hittite. Egypt was forgotten. The pro-Hittite party was victorious, and the Mitannian prince who now ascended the throne made a treaty with the Hittites in which he accepted a Hittite princess as his queen and ceded Mitannian sovereignty in such a way that his country became a vassal of the Hittites.

In this manner Mitannian friendship and support were lost to Egypt, and there was no longer any great state in the north to keep Egypt's enemies from her territory in Syria. Troops were needed on the frontiers to impress the Hittites by a demonstration of force, and strong measures were necessary to combat their agents in the courts of the Syrian princes, but Ikhnaton was oblivious to the gravity of the situation. He was completely engrossed in the only thing that mattered to him, a new religion, so dynamic, vital, demanding that he had no time and no desire to concentrate on affairs of state.

What was this new religion and what was its power? It was a form of solar worship. The concept of the sun as a god was not new in Egypt. Egypt had known Amon, the sun-god and king of the gods at Thebes, and it had known Re, the sun-god of Heliopolis. These two gods had been combined into a single deity, Amon-Re, who was served by a rich and powerful priesthood. During the reign of Amenhotep III, however, we begin to hear about a new sun-god named Aton. Aton differed from the other gods in that he was symbolized by the sun disk, and where Amon and Re had been purely Egyptian gods, Aton was a universal god; he was found everywhere and belonged to all mankind.

It is easy to see how the concept of a universal god could arise with the growth of the Egyptian Empire. The sun shone on all lands, not just on Egypt. When the Egyptians left their confined valley and visited far-off countries, this fact was brought home to them in a way they had not experienced before. Earlier Egyptian theology had been all tied up with the narrow land of Egypt, as if there were no other world, but with the empire there was a need for a new god and new thinking.

Much of Atonism is hidden from us now. We have representations of the sun disk in relief sculpture and in painting, and we have a few hymns to the god that tell us that this was an unusually ethical religion that stressed truth and love. We may infer certain other things about Atonism, too. In time the followers of Aton tended to think of him as the one true god; they moved toward monotheism, and as they did so, they became intolerant and iconoclastic. It is interesting that, unlike other Egyptian gods, Aton had no cult statue. Only his symbol was portrayed in art: the sun disk reaching out its kindly rays to touch the true believer. It is also possible that the Atonists believed that they would never die, that Aton would give his followers immortal life.

During the time of Amenhotep IV (Ikhnaton), this new religion attained its full strength and provided inspiration for a movement that rocked conservative Egypt to its very foundations. The chief convert to Atonism was the young pharaoh himself who changed his name to Ikhnaton—"It pleases Aton." The Mitannian princess had died, and Ikhnaton married his sister, Nefertiti—"A beautiful woman comes." When he altered his name, her name was changed, too. She became Nefer-nefru-aton, "Beautiful is the beauty of Aton," and all the six daughters of the royal couple were given names containing the name of Aton; Tutankhamon, the king's younger brother, or perhaps his nephew, was renamed Tutankhaton.

Even this did not satisfy the fervor of Ikhnaton. Everyone must worship his god. The name of Amon-Re was ordered erased from the monuments, and his priesthood was curtailed. A new royal city was built where no city had ever stood before, where no old tradition could inhibit the worship of Aton. Therefore, while the empire crumbled in Syria, and loyal princes wrote frantic letters for aid, Ikhnaton, his queen, his six daughters, and the court withdrew from the world to live in the new town which was named Akhetaton, "The horizon of the Disk."

Today we know the city of Akhetaton as Tell-el-Amarna. In the past seventy-five years a half-dozen archaeological expeditions have found some of its secrets; others will never be found. Tell-el-Amarna is on the east bank of the Nile about two hundred miles north of Thebes. The site extends for five miles along the river in a strip from one-half mile to a mile in width; across the river some land was reserved for farms. The two principal streets of the town ran parallel to the Nile: one was called the King's Way; the other, the High Priest's Street. The city limits were marked by great boundary stelai which proclaimed that the land within belonged to "the Aton."

The buildings within the town included a great temple to Aton, a royal palace, a royal estate, other temples, pleasure palaces, zoological gardens, and a kind of university called the House of Life. There were many private houses, commodious dwellings for the courtiers, with scores of rooms. Akhetaton was a city of mud-brick and wood, built in frantic haste and never completely finished, for it was occupied for only fifteen years and then deserted forever. Workmen were brought to the town and housed in a model village surrounded by a wall and guards, since the workers do not seem to have come willingly. Despite the inferior materials from which it was built, Akhetaton was not unattractive, because paint and plaster covered much of it.

The art of Tell-el-Amarna is unusual because it is naturalistic and in many ways un-Egyptian, although it did incorporate certain tendencies which had been somewhat in evidence during the fourteenth and fifteenth centuries B.C. Atonism called for truth, not convention, and it is interesting to compare the painting of pavements and walls at Tell-el-Amarna with the frescoes of the Palace of Minos in Minoan Crete (see Chapter 12). This Cretan palace had just been destroyed and its people scattered, and one wonders whether Minoan artists might not have found a refuge in Egypt.

At Tell-el-Amarna both sculpture in the round and in relief depart from the earlier conventions of Egypt. Truth was painfully set forth in the sculptured portraits of the royal family. Ikhnaton, Nefertiti, and their daughters are shown riding, at worship, and in other poses. The strange, distorted figure of Ikhnaton himself, already diseased and dying, is displayed in unconcealed ugliness. The workshop of a sculptor named Thothmes has been found in which were life masks of important personages. It was a new, brief, and interesting period in Egyptian art, but its ideas did not survive into the succeeding age.

At Tell-el-Amarna were also found the royal archives. Several hundred clay tablets inscribed in cuneiform in the Akkadian or Old Babylonian language were discovered by a peasant woman in 1887; others were subsequently unearthed. The records constituted the royal correspondence of Amenhotep III and Ikhnaton with Syria, Palestine, and rulers in Babylonia, Assyria, the Mitannian and Hittite kingdoms, Cyprus, and other states. The marital complications of Amenhotep III, the letter of Tushratta, and the appeals from the loyal princes in Syria and Palestine mentioned above were all found in the Tell-el-Amarna letters.

It is said that one thing not found at Akhetaton was the cemetery. If true, this was perhaps because the devotees of Aton were not supposed to die —ever—and no provision was made for backsliders who did.

Yet the beautiful dream of Ikhnaton ended and the awakening was an abrupt one. With the empire falling apart and the pharaoh himself ailing, it is believed that old Queen Ty descended on the court in an attempt to set matters to rights. Nefertiti, who may have been blamed for all the foolishness of Atonism, was forced into retirement. Ikhnaton's brother, Smenkhare, was married to one of Ikhnaton's daughters, made co-regent with the dying king, and sent up to Thebes to make peace with the priests of Amon-Re. But in 1365 Ikhnaton, Smenkhare, and probably Ty died. Tutankhamon, a mere boy, and his child-bride niece (or cousin), one of Ikhnaton's daughters, ascended the throne. Tell-el-Amarna was abandoned at this time, or shortly afterwards, and the capital was transferred to Thebes. Within a few years Tutankhamon was dead, too. Chaos ensued. His widow, the surviving daughter of Ikhnaton, held the key to the throne. We know that she was married briefly to a mysterious personage known as Ay, the Divine Father, who might be suspected of being the high priest of the Aton cult, an Egyptian Rasputin who had brought the fortunes of the Eighteenth Dynasty to their lowest ebb.

Very soon a reaction set in. Ay died or was killed. The army managed a *coup d'état* which brought General Harmhab to the throne (1352–1319). Harmhab restored the old order and rooted out the heresy of Atonism. Akhetaton was destroyed, and people began to speak of poor Ikhnaton as "that criminal of Akhetaton."

The epilogue to the story is provided by two documents found at Boghaz-Köy, the Hittite capital, hundreds of miles away from Egypt in central Asia Minor. One of these documents is a text known as the *Annals* of King Mursilis, who reigned in the generation after Ikhnaton; the other text is a series of incantations and rituals designed to stop the plague which raged in Hittite-land in the reign of Mursilis, a scourge which had already caused the death of his father, a contemporary of Ikhnaton and Harmhab. According to the *Annals,* the widow of Tutankhamon had written to the Hittites proposing that a Hittite prince should be sent to Egypt to be her husband. After some delay the Hittites assented, and one of the royal princes was despatched to Egypt but was murdered on the way, presumably by Egyptian agents hostile to the queen. War then ensued between the Hittites and Egyptians; the latter were defeated, but the Hittites contracted from their Egyptian prisoners a plague which apparently had been severe in Egypt. Thus robbed of a Hittite husband, the Egyptian queen was forced to marry Ay. There is reason to wonder whether the plague which struck the Hittites may not already have been responsible for the reaction against Atonism in Egypt. The plague may have been interpreted as a divine punishment for the heresy of Ikhnaton.

At any rate, we know that Harmhab led a return to orthodoxy. He boasted of his restoration of the temples, and we know that the name of Aton was now expunged from the monuments and the portraits of Ikhnaton defaced. Harmhab also attempted administrative reforms; he claimed to have outlawed graft and instituted a better system of tax collection. He also undertook to win back the lost cities of Syria, but met defeat at the hands of the Hittites.

From the time of Harmhab to the end of the New Kingdom, or empire, more than two centuries elapsed, but the road was downhill most of the way. After the death of Harmhab in 1319, a new dynasty (the Nineteenth) began which endured until about 1200 B.C. The pharaohs of the Nineteenth Dynasty were most greatly concerned with attempts to win back the territory which had been lost to the Hittites. This proved impossible. The great Rameses II, who occupied the throne from 1299 to 1232, made heroic efforts to drive the Hittites back. About 1288 he attacked Kadesh on the Orontes and was ambushed by the Hittite forces. Only the personal bravery of Rameses saved the army from a massacre. The drawn Battle of Kadesh produced a stalemate. About twenty years later the Hittites recognized their inability to win Palestine, just as the Egyptians had already given up hope of reconquering Syria. A treaty was then signed by the two powers in which Syria was recognized as a Hittite sphere of influence and Palestine was left to Egypt. We are fortunate to possess both the Egyptian and Hittite versions of the treaty which included provisions for the exchange or extradition of political offenders and mutual protestations of friendship. The pact was sealed by the marriage of a Hittite princess to Rameses II.

Merneptah, once thought to be the pharaoh of the Exodus, reigned for ten years after Rameses II. His main problem was to repel the attacks of Libyan tribes and the invaders who came from the sea. It was no longer a matter of holding the Hittites at bay—the Hittites now had troubles of their own in Asia Minor—but of protecting Egypt from invasion. Merneptah made futile attempts to hold Palestine and boasted of his "successes" in the famous Israel Stele. In this document Israel is mentioned for the first time in history: Canaan, says Merneptah, has been plundered, and "Israel, his seed is not." The other names in Merneptah's list of victories, including that of Canaan, are those of countries or regions, while the name of Israel alone bears the determinative for "people." Some biblical scholars have taken this to mean that the Israelites had just arrived in Palestine.

After two decades of anarchy at the end of the thirteenth century, a new dynasty, the Twentieth, was established. Its second pharaoh, Rameses

III (1198–1167), is worthy of special mention because he successfully beat off a massive attack from the sea about 1194. The sea raiders, mostly from Asia Minor, were among the participants in a much larger movement which was responsible for the destruction of many cities in Asia Minor, Syria, and Palestine and introduced a new era in the history of the ancient world. It was certainly to the credit of Rameses III that he managed to keep the invaders from Egypt. Other rulers and states had been less fortunate: the Hittites and Mycenaeans disappeared; even such inland towns as Carchemish on the Euphrates were hit, while Ugarit, Alalakh, and the Phoenician seaports were devastated (see Chapter 8).

In repelling the great raid, the pharaoh nearly expended the remnants of his royal strength. Even before this crisis the crown had been close to bankruptcy, because preceding generations had given a large part of the crown patrimony to the priests. The successors of Rameses III continued the alienation of royal wealth by giving more and more of their possessions to the gods in the hope of winning divine favor until very little was left. In 1085 even the throne changed hands as the priests took over the government and set up the Twenty-first Dynasty. The next three hundred years in Egypt comprise a period of weakness and anarchy too dreary for contemplation.

Chapter 7

HURRIANS AND HITTITES

URING THE TIME of the Eighteenth Dynasty in Egypt several major states flourished in other parts of the Near East. The Kassites had succeeded the Amorites in Babylonia, northern Mesopotamia was for a time the territory of the Mitannians, and central Asia Minor was the realm of the Hittites. These three states had one thing in common: they were ruled by Indo-European-speaking minorities. The arrival of these Indo-European overlords signaled the beginning of a new era in the history of civilization, and their invasion of the Near East was related to a general movement of Indo-Europeans which brought the first Greeks into Greece and the Aryans into India where, as we have seen, they destroyed the Indus civilization.

Once a single people, the Indo-Europeans had lived in central or eastern Europe. Although a number of dialects and languages had developed from the parent language before the Indo-Europeans began their wanderings, it is possible to recognize the common roots from which their words evolved and to draw certain conclusions from words which seem to have been in the primitive Indo-European vocabulary. The fact that the Indo-European languages as we know them have related words for many domesticated plants and animals and agricultural tools is enough to tell us that the Indo-Europeans were already herdsmen and farmers before their migrations began. In the same way we know that they had domesticated the horse. Not only did the Indo-Europeans have a common linguistic background but also a common heritage of political and social institutions and religious beliefs.

Familiar Indo-European languages are Greek, Latin, Sanscrit, Persian, Celtic, and the various Germanic tongues (including the Scandinavian). There were, and are, many others. The obvious differences between these languages are due to two things: (1) as the Indo-European groups

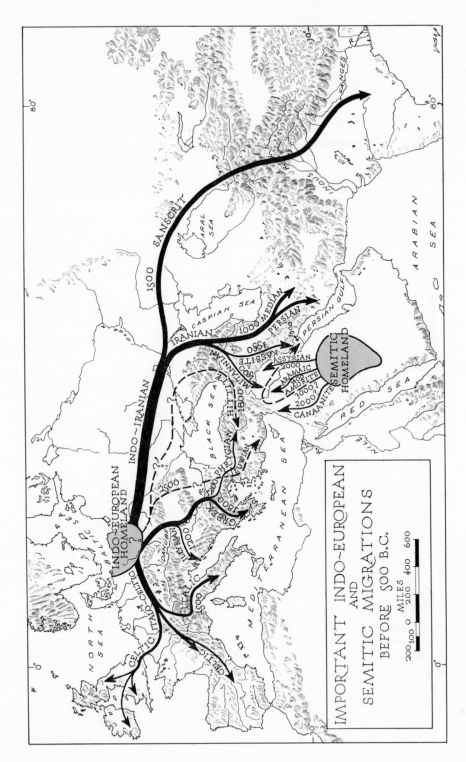

IMPORTANT INDO-EUROPEAN
AND
SEMITIC MIGRATIONS
BEFORE 500 B.C.

MILES
200 100 0 200 400 600

became separated, their speech changed, developing independently both with regard to phonetics and grammar; and (2) the Indo-Europeans came in contact with people who spoke other languages, and from these people they borrowed new words. Many of the borrowed words were the names of objects or processes previously unknown to the Indo-Europeans, anything for which they had no word in their own languages. Apparently unfamiliar with wine before arriving in the Mediterranean area, the Greeks and Romans borrowed the word used by the natives. In the same way, since the people of the Near East had not had the domesticated horse before it was introduced to them by the Indo-Europeans, the Indo-European word for horse was adopted in several Near Eastern languages.

At the time of their appearance in the Near East, the Indo-Europeans were uncivilized. Thus, even though they became the politically dominant group in several areas, they adopted and adapted many culture traits from Oriental (Near Eastern) civilization, integrating these with their own culture as best they could. While something of the primitive culture of the invaders might be retained—and this was to depend upon such factors as environment, proximity to cultural centers, the numerical ratio of the conquerors to the conquered, and so on—virtually every phase of Indo-European culture was altered by contact with civilization.

The Kassites in Babylonia and the overlords of the Kingdom of Mitanni to the north were culturally engulfed by civilization. In Babylonia the coming of the Kassites brought so little alteration to civilization that we should not be able to identify them as Indo-Europeans if it were not for the personal names of the kings, the names of their gods, and a few other words of their language which have survived and can be shown to have Indo-European etymologies. The situation in Mitanni-land was a little more complicated, but again it is the personal and divine names which enable us to identify the rulers. The language of the ruling class in both cases belonged to the eastern family of Indo-European languages of which Sanscrit and Persian are the most familiar examples; thus we know that the Kassites and the Mitannian kings were related to the Aryan invaders of India.

The coming of the Indo-Europeans into northern Mesopotamia, however, had been preceded by the migration of a different linguistic group, the Hurrians. Hurrian, a language which has only recently come to light, is not related to Indo-European or to the Semitic languages. The Hurrians were living in Armenia in the third millennium B.C., and this may have been their homeland. Shortly after 2000, they began to migrate into Assyria; ultimately, they spread westward across northern Mesopotamia into Syria and even Palestine. The Hurrians adopted many elements of Mesopotamian civilization, and we now know that Sumerian and Babylonian myths and

legends were transmitted to the Greeks and Hebrews by Hurrian inter-
mediaries.

One of the best-known Hurrian sites is Nuzi (near Kirkuk in Iran)
which was excavated by an expedition from Harvard University between
1925 and 1931. The site was occupied by Semites in the time of the Akkadian dynasty, then destroyed shortly after 2000 and reoccupied by the
Hurrians. A palace, several temples, and many private houses were found,
but most important was the discovery of several thousand cuneiform tablets
which constitute one of our principal sources of information about the
Hurrian language. The documents are mostly business and family records
which reveal much about property holding, legal practice, trade, and agriculture. In the fifteenth century the people of Nuzi were subjects of the
king of Mitanni.

The Mitannians seem to have followed in the wake of the Kassites.
Some time shortly after 1500 they established themselves as the rulers of
the Semitic and Hurrian population in Assyria and northern Mesopotamia
all the way to the Euphrates. The capital of the Mitannian kingdom was
called Wassukkanni; it has not been found, but it was located somewhere
in the northwest in the territory the Assyrians called Hanigalbat. The
names of about ten kings are known, including Saushsatar (who fought
against Thothmes III), Artadama and Shutarna (whose daughters married
Thothmes IV and Amenhotep III, respectively), and Tushratta, whose
letters to Egypt were found in the Tell-el-Amarna correspondence.

First contesting with Egypt for the possession of north Syria, the Mitannians later became Egyptian allies against the Hittites. In the time of
Ikhnaton, however, the Egyptians failed to support the Mitannians. Tushratta was overthrown and his kingdom cut in half by an Assyrian revolt
which restored the independence of that country. The Mitannians themselves were split into pro-Assyrian, pro-Egyptian, and pro-Hittite factions.
After a powerful Hittite offensive about 1360, the kingdom became a Hittite protectorate but subsequently disappeared about 1345 after an Assyrian
attack.

The Mitannian kingdom was a feudal state with its various parts
ruled by princes who were vassals of the Mitannian king. A number of
social classes within the kingdom have been distinguished. The nobles were
the *maryanni* (chariot warriors); next came the artisans, and finally the
sabe name who were rural retainers and the like. All this is remininiscent
of Aryan class distinctions: warriors, priests, artisans, etc. The Mitannian
deities were Indo-Aryan also: Mitrasil (Mithra), Arunasil (Varuna), Indar
(Indra). Many persons of importance in the kingdom had Hurrian names,
however, and Hurrian deities were also worshipped.

Our information about the third great state in Asia during this period,
that of the Hittites, is somewhat more extensive and definite. The Hittites

Courtesy of the Trustees of the British Museum

ASHURBANIPAL AND QUEEN

ASSYRIANIZING PHOENICIAN BOWL

Courtesy of the Museum Antiker Kleinkunst, Muenchen

HERACLES AND ATHENA—
ATHENIAN VASE, 510 B.C.

Courtesy of Hans G. Güterbock and the American
Journal of Archaeology

Courtesy of the Martin von Wagner Museum, Würzburg

ORIENTALIZING GREEK VASE—SIXTH CENTURY B.C.

Alinari

COLUMN CAPITAL

arrived in Asia Minor about 1800 B.C. They gradually extended their control over central Asia Minor, and then, after 1400, gained hegemony over Syria. During their most flourishing era (roughly 1400–1200) the Hittites were more than a match for Egypt.

The real discovery and identification of the Hittites did not come in modern times until early in the twentieth century, after German archaeologists began to excavate at Boghaz-Köy, the site of the Hittite capital called Hattusas, in modern Turkey some miles east of Ankara. When it became possible to read the thousands of cuneiform tablets inscribed with records in the Hittite language found at Boghaz-Köy, the history of the Hittites was gradually disclosed.

Our knowledge of the prehistory and early history of Asia Minor is somewhat vague and confused. It is perhaps sufficient to say that the area was inhabited from Palaeolithic times and that the Age of Agriculture began there in the fourth millennium. By the historic period Asia Minor had a heterogeneous population. According to a recent theory Indo-European invaders crossed into northwestern Asia Minor as early as 2500 B.C. and gradually occupied the Aegean and Mediterranean coasts. Whether Lugalzaggisi, Sargon of Akkad, or Naram-Sin ever reached Anatolia from Mesopotamia, as later legends claimed, is doubtful, but by 1900 B.C. Assyrian traders were living in many of the towns in central Asia Minor, carrying on business in much the same manner as the Babylonians in the time of Hammurabi. The evidence of these Assyrian activities as revealed by the so-called Cappadocian tablets provides material for a fascinating chapter in economic and social history.

At the beginning of the second millennium B.C. central Asia Minor was divided into a large number of small principalities which were frequently at war with one another. About 1800 the Hittites began to arrive from the east and gradually replaced the native rulers. Interstate warfare continued, but in the seventeenth century a single political unit was formed by Labarnas, the first great Hittite king, and his successor, Hattusilis I, moved the capital from Kussara to Hattusas (Boghaz-Köy). An eastward and southward expansion now began to take place which soon allowed the Hittites to conduct raids into Syria. Aleppo was sacked about 1600, and this success was followed by a raid on Babylon. Conflict with the Hurrians and internal discord now occurred which caused a recession of Hittite influence during the sixteenth century. With a reorganization of the monarchy and the establishment of a stronger central government under King Telepinus (about 1500 B.C.), the way was prepared for a new and greater era in Hittite history.

The period, roughly 1450–1200, of the New Empire was the one in which the Hittites unified central Asia Minor, reduced many surrounding areas to the status of vassal kingdoms, and gained possession of Syria. At

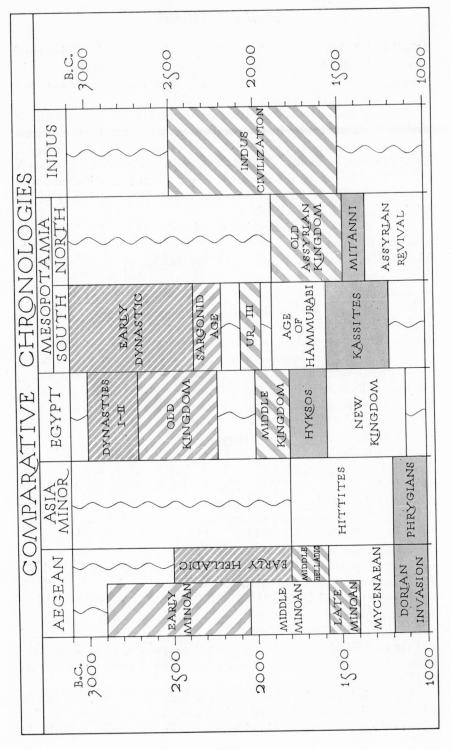

COMPARATIVE CHRONOLOGIES

the beginning of this period the Egyptians and Mitannians were fighting for the control of Syria. The Hittites found it advantageous to ally themselves with Thothmes III, but a later change in Egyptian policy which resulted in an Egyptian-Mitannian alliance left the Hittites without friends. Thus rebuffed, they bided their time, plotting revenge on the allies. In the reign of Ikhnaton, when Egypt had no foreign policy, the Hittites recognized the opportunity for which they had been waiting. Under the greatest of all Hittite kings, Suppiluliumas (1375–1335), Mitanni was attacked and the Syrian princes detached from their Egyptian loyalties. Before his death Suppiluliumas reduced the western half of the Mitannian kingdom to the status of a Hittite dependency and tightened his hold on Syria. He defeated the Egyptians under Harmhab, but a plague carried by the Egyptian prisoners proved equally deadly to Hittites; it carried off Suppiluliumas and the Hittite crown prince and probably prevented the Hittite occupation of Palestine. For the next sixty-five years, Egyptian attempts to regain Syria were beaten off—the famous Battle of Kadesh falls in this period. Finally, harassed by Assyrian attacks and weakened by palace intrigue, the Hittites concluded a treaty of friendship with Egypt (both the Egyptian and Hittite copies of the treaty have been found); the bargain was sealed by the marriage of Rameses II with a Hittite princess (just before 1265). For two more generations the Hittite Empire survived, but it was finally destroyed by the great movement of peoples which occurred about 1200 B.C. It was probably the Phrygians, a new Indo-European group crossing over from Europe to Asia Minor, who overcame the Hittites and succeeded to their hegemony in Asia Minor.

The political institutions of the Hittites upon their arrival in Asia Minor were precisely those found among Indo-Europeans elsewhere at a similar stage of cultural development; this will be observed in the case of the Greeks, Romans, and others. The king was a war chief, high priest, and judge (or rather arbiter). He was assisted and advised by a council of elders (later nobles), and there was a popular assembly (*pankus*, all the warriors) which had the power to ratify succession to the throne. These institutions were modified as the empire evolved and the king's authority naturally increased. A feudal state developed in which the Great King was at the top, ruling over many petty kings. The tendency in the New Empire was to replace the kings by governors and to put members of the royal family in charge of newly conquered areas. The Great King of the Hittites, who was called *Tabarna* and the Sun, became more and more of an Oriental potentate with an elaborate court. At his death, he was deified; people said, "He has become a god."

Various social classes may be distinguished in Asia Minor during the Hittite period: nobles, a middle class of warriors, farmers, and artisans, serfs, and slaves. The main base of the economy was, of course, agriculture and stock raising. Various domesticated animals are mentioned, including pigs. Viniculture was also very important in Hittite-land. The mineral resources of Asia Minor were naturally exploited with the mining of copper, lead, and silver, but the great innovation was the working of iron which had begun as early as 1400 and constituted one of the most important assets of the Hittites. They were able to provide themselves with iron weapons and to profit from the export of iron over which they enjoyed a monopoly; the price of iron could reach fabulous heights: in one of the Tell-el-Amarna letters, the Hittites suggest that the Egyptians should purchase iron with an equal weight of gold. The secret of the development of ironworking was not so much the possession of a superior technology as the availability of wood (charcoal) for smelting and the easy accessibility of iron ores.

Economic documents in the cuneiform script on clay tablets and the fragments of Hittite law codes constitute the principal sources of information about social and economic life. The law codes follow the Mesopotamian pattern; again we encounter case law in the form "if a man" or in another section, "if a vine." The extant passages deal with injuries and penalties, protection of merchants, apprenticeship, prices and wages, return of stolen property, witchcraft, and other subjects. From the law codes innumerable facts of interest may be gleaned: that the Hittites kept bees, branded cattle, crossed rivers by holding to the tails of oxen, and sometimes bit off one another's noses.

The Hittites lived in stone-walled cities. Hattusas, the capital and largest city, covered an area of three hundred acres. It had a strong citadel on top of a hill, and the entire town was encompassed by a thick wall made of huge stones and pierced by five strongly fortified gates of awesome proportions. The prevalence of stone meant that Hittite architecture need not follow Mesopotamian precedents and also that the sculpture might become superior. Hittite stone monuments both in the round and in relief are impressive in size and in their rather forbidding aspect. The principal subjects portrayed are kings and gods and ceremonies. There is no attempt to render historical scenes nor to create realistic portraits nor perhaps even to achieve a decorative effect; the essential purpose of the sculpture is religious or magical with other considerations carrying much less weight than in Mesopotamia or Egypt.

Many texts found at Boghaz-Köy give us an idea of Hittite religious and magical beliefs. Some of these texts prescribe ceremonies and rituals to be performed on specific occasions. Much of "Hittite" religion is not Hittite at all in origin but borrowed from the Hurrians and the predecessors of the Hittites in Asia Minor. A sun-goddess is thought to have ranked high in the "official cult" of the New Empire, but the Hurrian weather-god, Teshub, and his consort, Hepat, were also of prime importance. The Hurrian counterpart of Ishtar, the goddess Shaushka, was the patroness of King Hattusilis III; he tells us that she marked him out for special protection and ultimately placed him on the throne. When people spoke of the "thousand gods of the Hittites" they meant this in a literal sense because of the multiplicity of foreign and local deities recognized and worshipped by the Hittites.

The "official" literature of the Hittites includes royal decrees, treaties, and historical inscriptions (or annals). Numerous examples of these texts are known, but also important are myths and legends found in the archives at Boghaz-Köy. Most of the myths are of Hurrian origin. One of these relates a struggle for supremacy among the gods and bears so remarkable a resemblance to a Greek myth that there can be no doubt that the Greeks borrowed it from the Hurrians (see below, p. 212). Another is the "Epic of Ullikummi," parts of which are reminiscent of both the Typhon myth of the Greeks and of the story of Atlas. It may be assumed that the Greeks acquired their knowledge of Hurrian mythology and literature through trade contacts in Syria at a later date and possibly through Semitic inter-mediaries, but direct contacts of Greeks and Hittites are not out of the question. The problem of the country of Ahhiyawa mentioned in the Hittite texts of about 1330 B.C. and following is difficult and complicated. Ahhiyawa may be the land of the Achaeans, Mycenaean Greece, or it may be a principality on the Aegean coast; certainty is impossible at present.

The cultural indebtedness of the Hittites to the Hurrians and Babylonians was very great. Some instances of this have already been mentioned, but it is nowhere better illustrated than in the written documents from Boghaz-Köy. The Hittites adopted the cuneiform script for writing their own language. Much of their diplomatic correspondence was written in Akkadian (essentially, the Old Babylonian dialect), and Akkadian, Sumerian, and Hurrian religious texts were also studied by the priests at the capital.

Three other languages also occur in the texts at Boghaz-Köy: Hattic, Luwian, and Palaic. Passages in these languages appear in ritual texts where the officiating priest is directed to recite an incantation in one or another of these languages. Hattic appears to be non-Indo-European and may represent the pre-Hittite speech of Asia Minor. Luwian and Palaic are Indo-European and were spoken in distinct sections of the empire. Luwian, for example, may have been the speech of the first Indo-European invaders of Asia Minor who, by the Hittite period, were confined to the south.

While some may dispute whether Hittite was an Indo-European language or a language which shared a common ancestor with Indo-European, the relationship is so close that only a linguist would care to argue about it. When the Czech scholar Hrozny first attempted to show in 1915 that Hittite was an Indo-European language, he made few converts to his theory. People refused to believe that an Indo-European language was likely to have been written in cuneiform. But Hrozny was essentially correct; after a decade other scholars began to come around to his way of thinking. From about 1925 onward the study of Hittite made great strides, and today the grammar is well understood and the vocabulary reasonably well known. From the linguistic point of view Hittite is of great importance because, along with Mycenaean Greek, it provides the earliest example of a written Indo-European language. For the study of Indo-European philology, Hittite is fully as valuable as the traditional guide, Sanscrit.

The discovery of the Hittites and the Hurrians has been important for Old Testament studies for a number of reasons, some of which have already been mentioned. First, we now know that the true Hittites are not the Hittites who appear in the Old Testament; the Hittites of the Bible are the Syro-Hittites (who will be discussed in the next chapter). Secondly, the Hurrians are the people called Horites in the Old Testament. Biblical scholars used to translate both Horite and Hittite as Hittite because the latter term was more familiar to them through Greek literature. From a study of Hurrian personal names, however, we find that many people who are termed "Hittites" in the Bible were really Hurrians. A good example is Uriah "the Hittite" who has a Hurrian name. The Hurrians, we discover, were fairly numerous in Palestine; this was never true of the Hittites. Finally, there are obvious points of similarity between the Mesopotamian and Biblical flood stories, but in the first instance the ark is said to land on Mount Nisir, and in the second on Mount Ararat. These mountains are some distance apart; the Mesopotamians knew the first, but not the second. Mount Ararat lay in Hurrian territory, and, if scholars are correct in thinking that the flood story came to the Hebrews through a Hurrian source, this would account for the change of locale.

Our knowledge of the Hurrians and Hittites is still incomplete, but even in its present state it provides the basic material for a chapter in ancient history which could not have been written a generation ago. This is only one of many areas in which our information about the past has been enriched by archaeology and linguistic research and in which new hypotheses have been necessitated by the discovery of new facts. Moreover, the effects of the Hurrian and Hittite discoveries have been felt outside the realm of history proper, for the new languages have revealed hitherto unsuspected areas for philological research and the new cultures have important implications for classical and biblical studies.

Chapter 8

SYRIA AND PALESTINE

THE REGION of Syria and Palestine is rough and mountainous; among its mountains lie valleys and plains. It is bounded on the north by the Taurus Mountains of Asia Minor, on the northeast by the upper Euphrates, on the east by the Arabian Desert, and on the west by the Mediterranean Sea; it is separated from the Egyptian Delta by a strip of desert country. The character of the terrain naturally fostered the creation of small states, and the poverty of the soil precluded the growth of a large population unless agriculture could be supplemented by trade and industry. The ease with which Syria and Palestine could be invaded from any direction meant that over the centuries many different peoples would enter and occupy the region, bringing a number of cultures and languages. The rough topography of the country which divided it into many small compartments would accentuate cultural and linguistic diversity among invaders who settled in the land, and it would also foster a tendency toward fierce nationalism much like that in Greece in a later period. The Syrian and Palestinian states were too small to conquer one another with the result that political unity, when present at all, would be imposed from the outside. Local patriotism often impeded co-operation against a common enemy and thus left the country at the mercy of the big states of the Near East: Babylonia, Assyria, Egypt, and the Mitannian and Hittite kingdoms. Many people feel that the development of the potent ingroup feeling among the Hebrews which was so important in determining the final form of Hebrew religion was a result of the way the Hebrews were bullied by more powerful neighbors after they came to Palestine.

There were many peasant villages in Syria and Palestine in the fifth millennium B.C., and after 4000 strong cultural influences from Mesopotamia can be discerned, especially in Syria. In the third millennium Akkadians seeking an outlet to the Mediterranean and Egyptians coveting the cedars of Lebanon made their influence felt in the area, just as the Middle Kingdom in Egypt and the Amorite Kingdom in Babylonia were to affect its life on occasion in the period between 2000 and 1700. Later, the Mitannians were to campaign in Syria, and both Syria and Palestine were included in the Egyptian Empire; after Ikhnaton's reign, the Hittites held Syria until 1200 while Egypt maintained possession of Palestine.

The largest single element in the Syro-Palestinian population after 3000 (and possibly before) was Semitic; between 3000 and 1000 B.C. wave after wave of Semites was to sweep in from the Arabian Desert. The Amorites seem to have lived in Syria before 2000 B.C., and only a few Amorites migrated down the Euphrates to found the Old Babylonian Kingdom; the rest stayed in Syria. In the second millennium the Semitic-speaking Canaanites came out of the desert to occupy both Syria and Palestine; they were followed before 1200 by other Semites, principally the Aramaeans and the Hebrews. Other linguistic groups were represented, too, especially in Syria in the second millennium: the Hurrians and their Indo-Aryan overlords, the Mitannians; Luwians and Hittites penetrated Cilicia and north Syria; Minoans and Mycenaeans (see Chapter 12) came to trade; and shortly after 1200 the mysterious Philistines arrived.

In the second millennium B.C. there were many towns of considerable size in Syria and Palestine: seaports, caravan centers, and fortresses. Their names appear in the Tell-el-Amarna letters and were often recorded (at a later time) by the writers of the Old Testament. Ugarit, Aleppo, Hamath, Qatna, Kadesh, Byblos, Beyrut, Sidon, Tyre, Jerusalem, Gaza, Arvad, Damascus, Lachish, Alalakh, and Megiddo (Armageddon) are only a few of these towns. Each town tended to have its own king or prince, often forced into collaboration with Egyptians, Mitannians, or Hittites. Though many different languages were spoken in the area, the Semitic dialects were the most common. Furthermore, for diplomatic correspondence, even with Egypt, the Akkadian cuneiform was used.

The most ubiquitous people in Syria and Palestine down to 1200, at least, were the Canaanites. The term Canaanite is a linguistic one and somewhat awkward because it is frequently used in a cultural sense. Properly speaking, Canaanite is a term for the so-called northwest Semitic dialects which include Hebrew, Phoenician, Moabite, and Ugaritic (explained below), yet Canaanite is used culturally to distinguish the people whom the Hebrews found in Palestine. We shall employ the term in this latter way, ignoring the fact that the Phoenicians sometimes referred to themselves as Canaanites which, of course, they were!

The culture of the Canaanites may have been a single, unified affair while they still lived in the desert, but after they arrived in Syria and Palestine this was no longer true. Some Canaanites became city dwellers, traders, and artisans, while others lived in the country as simple farmers and herdsmen. The Canaanites who lived in Palestine adopted many Egyptian culture traits, but those who lived in Syria were very much under the influence of Mesopotamian culture. Many of the Syro-Palestinian towns occupied by the Canaanites have been excavated. In order to illustrate the regional difference in Canaanite culture, however, we may describe two towns which are typical: Beth-Shan in the south, and Ugarit in the north.

Beth-Shan, on the edge of the Jordan Valley just south of the Sea of Galilee, is represented by a tremendous mound which has not been completely excavated. Remains of the second millennium are found in five different strata, but the excavations have been most informative about the period when Beth-Shan was under Egyptian political domination (1450–1200 B.C.). The five principal temples of the town were constructed from Egyptian models even though they were not used for the worship of Egyptian deities. The principal construction was of brick with walls five feet thick. Within the temples were wooden columns with limestone bases. Walls were covered with white plaster, and the floors were of beaten mud. Cult objects included sacred stones (mazzeboths) and wooden poles (ashera). There were cylindrical flower pots—Gardens of Adonis—in which seeds grew into plants and withered away just as the deity Adonis (Babylonian Tammuz) lived and died with the changing seasons. Model shrines, sacred boxes, clay plaques, and animal figurines were common; the shrines were in the form of two-story houses with figures of people, birds, and snakes, and the clay plaques bore figures of serpents and of Astarte, the fertility goddess. Most figures were modelled in an Egyptian style, and a stele erected by a local ruler was found inscribed with Egyptian hieroglyphs.

The finds at Beth-Shan are paralleled by those made farther south. At Lachish, in a great moat of the Hyksos period, an Egyptian temple was built in the succeeding age. Astarte plaques, libation stands, and kernoi (many-spouted libation vessels) were common at Lachish and Megiddo. Megiddo also had teraphim (pottery figurines) and horned altars. The principal Canaanite deities appear to have been Reshef, the burner, a war- and storm-god; Astarte, the fertility goddess; and Mekal, possibly the Semitic Heracles. Thus we see the southern Canaanites retaining their own religion, echoes of which we hear in the Old Testament with the stone and pillar cult, the ashera, and all the rest. On the other hand, it is clear that in certain areas of culture the Egyptian influence was strong, particularly in traits which the Canaanites had lacked before coming to Palestine.

Turning to the Canaanites of the north, we find a different situation. In a more prosperous location and farther removed from Egyptian influence—and not so powerfully affected by Mesopotamia as the southern Canaanites were by Egypt—the Canaanites of Syria were able to create a spectacular civilization which was complex and influential.

Ras Shamra, called Ugarit in antiquity, is the major site in the north. Almost directly opposite the northeast corner of Cyprus, Ras Shamra is a big mound sixty feet high and a half-mile long situated about a mile inland from the Mediterranean. The port of Ugarit, now called Minet el-Beida, lies a short distance away. The site of Ras Shamra was occupied from about 4000 to 1200 B.C. Sacked and destroyed about 2000 (or slightly later), the town was subsequently rebuilt and populated by the Canaanites. A great temple was constructed for the West Semitic grain-god, Dagan, and another for Baal. While there was trade with Egypt, the principal diplomatic relations of Ugarit before 1500 were with the Semites of Aleppo and Mari. From 1500 to 1350 B.C. Ugarit was the vassal of Egypt. Once the Mitannians and the Egyptians had become friends, Ugarit prospered in the resultant peace. The most flourishing period of the city was in the century between 1450 and 1350. Ugaritic merchants traded with Phoenician ports to the south and Aleppo to the east; merchants came and went from the Mediterranean islands and Egypt. The chief source of Ugaritic wealth was probably its trade with the island of Cyprus from whence came most of the copper ore of the Near East, and Ugarit had a big copper-smelting industry. The town also produced other metalwork, cosmetics, purple dye, and boxwood.

SEMITIC ALPHABETS

RAS SHAMRA	ḫ	r	s	r	b	k	ḥ	n	m
1000 B.C.									
850 B.C.									
KARA TEPE									

Ras Shamra was first excavated by the French beginning in 1928. Shortly after the digging began, clay tablets and other artifacts were found which bore a strange kind of writing, a cuneiform alphabet of about thirty characters. The decipherment of the writing was accomplished by two great scholars, Bauer and Dhorme, who worked independently and completed their work in the spring of 1930. The language of the tablets was Canaanite; its special dialect is called Ugaritic. Once it was possible to read the script, it was found that not all the tablets dealt with economic affairs. A number of texts were religious and literary in content; they not only illuminated the religion of Ugarit but also showed important relationships with the Old Testament.

At the head of the gods at Ugarit was Il, the so-called father of the gods. His consort was Athirat, or Ashera, a sea-goddess, the prototype of the Greek Aphrodite. Then came Dagan, the grain-god, and his son, Aliyan Baal, or Adonis. The consort of the latter was Anat, the equivalent of Artemis. Other deities were Shapsh, a sun-goddess, and Astarte. The gods were believed to live on nearby Mount Casius.

There was a religious literature in the form of mythological poems. Its content and poetic forms show many parallels with Hebrew poetry. The religion of the Canaanites, it is thought, exerted an influence upon the Hebrews in cult practices and forms of sacrifice. Light was also thrown upon Greek mythology and some of its origins. The similarity of Aphrodite and Athirat, Anat and Artemis, Mount Casius and Mount Olympus, has already been suggested. There is little doubt that the Greeks, who traded at Ugarit and other ports along this coast, acquired new ideas which they took home with them. The real question, and one which has yet to be decided, is how much of the religion at Ugarit was truly Canaanite, and how much was Hurrian. Seven different languages were written or spoken in Ugarit; in the temple schools people were trained to read and write many tongues and scripts, and in the archives of Ugarit were found dictionaries for reading Sumerian, Akkadian, and Hurrian.

Sometime between 1375 and 1350 Ugarit was severely damaged by an earthquake, and in its last phase (1350–1200) the city was a Hittite dependency. The end of Ugarit came about 1200 when it, like many other cities in this part of the world, was destroyed in the great raid. When Ugarit perished, its culture did not die, for it was preserved in the Phoenician port towns of the south.

Another important Syrian town was Alalakh (Tell Atchana); it was situated on the Orontes River north and east of Ugarit and about forty miles west of Aleppo. In the eighteenth century B.C. Alalakh was part of the kingdom centered at Aleppo whose king, Hammurabi, was a contemporary of the more famous Hammurabi of Babylon. In this period a large number of people at Alalakh were Hurrians, but the rulers bore West Semitic names. During the time of Hammurabi, Alalakh was destroyed either by the Babylonians, who sacked Mari (its ally), or by the Hyksos, or by an internal revolution. It is attractive as a theory that the raid of Hammurabi of Babylon to the west which caused the fall of Mari and other towns created a vacuum that allowed the Hyksos to come in from the desert. It is shortly after this time that Hyksos camps appear in the south at Hazor, Lachish, and other sites.

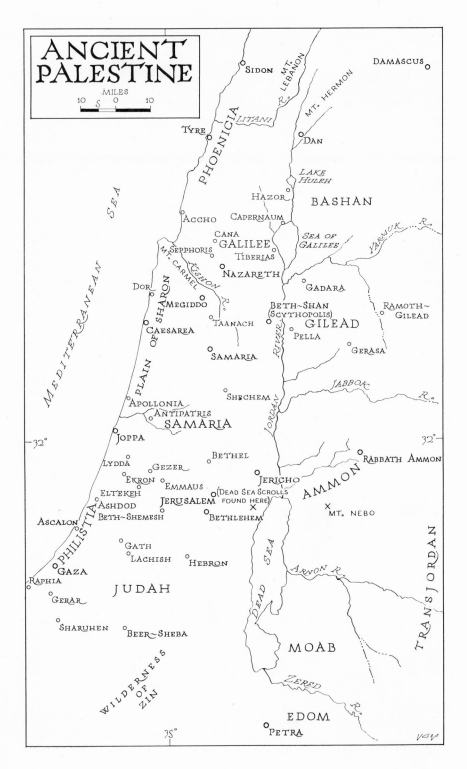

ANCIENT PALESTINE

MILES
10 5 0 10

DAMASCUS

SIDON

PHOENICIA

MT. LEBANON

LITANI

MT. HERMON

TYRE

DAN

LAKE HULEH

HAZOR

BASHAN

ACCHO

CAPERNAUM

CANA

SEA OF GALILEE

GALILEE

SEPPHORIS

TIBERIAS

M. CARMEL

KISHON R.

NAZARETH

YARMUK R.

DOR

GADARA

RAMOTH~ GILEAD

MEGIDDO

BETH~SHAN (SCYTHOPOLIS)

MEDITERRANEAN SEA

PLAIN OF SHARON

CAESAREA

TAANACH

GILEAD

PELLA

GERASA

SAMARIA

JABBOK

SHECHEM

R.

APOLLONIA

JORDAN RIVER

ANTIPATRIS

SAMARIA

32°

JOPPA

BETHEL

RABBATH AMMON

32°

LYDDA

GEZER

JERICHO

EKRON

EMMAUS

(DEAD SEA SCROLLS FOUND HERE)

AMMON

ELTEKEH

JERUSALEM

×

ASHDOD

MT. NEBO

ASCALON

BETH~SHEMESH

BETHLEHEM

PHILISTIA

GATH

DEAD SEA

TRANSJORDAN

LACHISH

HEBRON

GAZA

ARNON R.

RAPHIA

JUDAH

GERAR

SHARUHEN

BEER~SHEBA

MOAB

WILDERNESS OF ZIN

ZERED

R.

EDOM

35°

PETRA

VEM

112

From 1550 down to its destruction in the raid of 1200, Alalakh was subject first to the Mitannians, then to the Egyptians, and finally, after 1370, to the Hittites. Like Ugarit, Alalakh had a port on the coast where Minoan and Mycenaean traders had warehouses, but Alalakh was more of a commercial than a manufacturing center. The palaces of the kings in the earlier period resembled Minoan palaces (see Chapter 12) in architecture and painted decoration, and there is perhaps some connection between Alalakh and Cnossus.

In the period before 1200, probably between 1400 and 1200, the eastern borders of Syria and Palestine had been under attack by Semitic groups coming out of the desert. The Aramaeans had begun to enter the region of the upper Euphrates, and it was probably in the thirteenth century that the Hebrews began to arrive in Palestine. Although the remains of this period at Jericho cannot be found, other towns mentioned in the Old Testament as having been destroyed by Joshua show evidence of devastation.

On the west coast the great raid of which we have so often spoken brought the Philistines to their new homes. Today we tend to think of Palestine as an almost exclusively Semitic land, yet it takes its name from the Philistines, a virtually unknown and certainly non-Semitic group. Before 1200 both Egyptians and Hebrews called Palestine Canaan; after 1200 it appears in both Egyptian and Assyrian records as the land of the Philistines, that is to say, Palestine.

The origin of the Philistines is obscure. Their pottery, tombs, and weapons resemble those of the Mycenaeans, but their costume and what we know of their religion, language, and their companions on the great raid point to Asia Minor. This is not the place to debate the subject or to expose the absurdity of theories that the Philistines were of Minoan or Illyrian origin; it is sufficient merely to say that the most convincing evidence is for the Anatolian origin of the Philistines.

Repulsed from Egypt in the time of Rameses III, the Philistines settled on the Palestinian coast where their superior weapons and military organization enabled them to harass and dominate the Hebrews and Canaanites for many years. The story of the conflict between Hebrews and Philistines is told in Judges and the two books of Samuel. These are the days of Samson, Saul, and David. We hear of the five lords of the Philistines: those of Ashdod, Gaza, Ascalon, Gath, and Ekron. According to tradition, after Samson's one-man campaign was terminated by the wiles of Delilah, Saul (about 1100) began to make real progress in gaining Hebrew independence from the Philistines. David, the giant-killer, and early follower of Saul, was forced to take refuge with the Philistines because of Saul's jealousy. After Saul, Jonathan, and two other sons of the king were killed in battle, David became the leader of the Hebrews; he took possession of the Canaanite fortress of Jerusalem and laid the foundations for the kingdom of Solomon.

After this we hear very little in the Old Testament about the Philistines. The Egyptian records, too, are silent, and we must wait until the eighth and seventh centuries for the Assyrians to lift the veil. In the Assyrian records the Philistines are often mentioned, and the people themselves are portrayed on Assyrian monuments. They still occupy the same area in Palestine, wear the same feathered headdresses, and have the same personal names as when they first appeared on the coast. They have maintained their national identity in an amazing way.

The excavation of Philistine towns has not been very successful, in part because some of them are still occupied. Beth Pelet (modern Tell Fara) has proved the best site for excavation; Philistine tombs, weapons, armor, pottery, and fibulae (safety pins) were found. The Philistine stratum lies on top of a burned layer at both Ascalon and Beth Pelet, all of which confirms the fact of invasion. Archaeology bears witness to an increase of iron with the coming of the Philistines. Their possession of iron weapons was probably the secret of their success, and this may well be why they forbade the Hebrews to possess iron. In other words, the Philistines were very much like the Dorian invaders of Greece who overcame the Bronze Age Mycenaeans by means of superior armament.

With Egypt exhausted, the Hittites destroyed, and the great Assyrian Empire a development of the future, there ensued between 1200 and 750 B.C. an era of local independence in which many small states prospered. The kingdom of Solomon in the tenth century was only one of a number of small principalities arising from such favorable conditions. This is the great age of Phoenicia, and it is during this period that we encounter for the first time people whom we may properly call Phoenicians.

The history of the Phoenicians has yet to be written. Though they constituted a major group in the Syro-Palestinian area and played an important role in the history of civilization, the Phoenicians are hard to get at. Literary sources are not abundant: the Greeks and Romans have left us their opinions of the Phoenicians; there is some information to be gleaned from Egyptian and Assyrian sources; and the Phoenicians are mentioned in the Old Testament. We have, in short, something of the views of other people regarding the Phoenicians, but almost nothing in the way of Phoenician records. Furthermore, archaeological research has not been as rewarding as might have been expected.

Though the Egyptians referred to the traders from the Phoenician area as *Fenkhu* at a fairly early date, this old Egyptian word which means "shipbuilders" may not be the one from which the Greek word that we render as "Phoenician" was derived. *Phoenix* in Greek means red, the deep red or Tyrian purple color which was the stock in trade of the Phoenician merchant. The Phoenician, then, was a "red man" and, to the Greeks, a particularly ignoble one. The Greeks thought of the Phoenicians as sharp traders, often slave traders, frequently kidnappers, and occasionally pirates. The Phoenicians also engaged in a bitter trade rivalry with the Greeks in the Mediterranean, a thing not calculated to foster friendly relations. In the Homeric poems the term Sidonian is more commonly applied to the Phoenicians than Phoenician itself. Sidonian was also the term used by the people of the Near East. The Phoenicians even called themselves Sidonians at one period, although they sometimes used the term Canaanite, too. Actually, the Phoenicians were Canaanites; they were commercial, sea-going Canaanites, the successors of the people of Ugarit whom we have already met; even their language was not far removed from the Ugaritic dialect.

The Phoenicians lived on a narrow strip of coast to the northwest of Palestine. Their territory measured about a hundred miles from north to south, and twenty or thirty miles from east to west. Their principal towns were seaports: the most northerly was Arvad; then came Byblos, Beyrut, Sidon, and Tyre. In front of them was the sea; behind them was the wooded range of Lebanon. The towns lay in tiny pockets of soil backed by hills with terraced slopes. The names of the five principal towns mentioned above all appear in the Tell-el-Amarna letters of the fourteenth century. The princes who rule in Phoenicia in the time of Ikhnaton all have Semitic names, and it is a fair guess that there were Semites living there in the days of the Old Kingdom when trade contact between Egypt and Phoenicia is first reported. Byblos, then called Gebal or Gubla (The Mountain), was certainly in existence in the third millennium. During the Middle Kingdom in Egypt, there were Egyptian governors in Phoenician seaports. Egyptian culture traits were being imported; scarabs and Egyptian inscriptions have been found from this age, and the dead, though entombed in deep underground chambers at Tyre and Sidon, were placed in limestone sarcophagi resembling Egyptian mummy cases. In the days of the New Kingdom Egyptian influence increased as it did elsewhere in Syria and Palestine.

Tyre and Sidon were destroyed in the great raid, and undoubtedly the other towns suffered also. Though there was rebuilding, recovery was not rapid after 1200; nearly two hundred years elapsed before real prosperity was again in evidence. The tenth century which saw the creation of Solomon's kingdom was also the starting point of Phoenician greatness. In these times lived King Hiram of Byblos, whose sarcophagus bears the oldest alphabetic Phoenician inscription, and his contemporary was King Hiram of Tyre, the friend of Solomon.

Both Hiram and Solomon were remembered as builders. It was Hiram who made Tyre into a great city. Tyre had originally been a mainland town with its houses clustered around a big acropolis called Sor, the Rock. In the time of Hiram, however, expansion was necessary: the harbor area was improved, and the main part of the town was built on several islands just off shore. The Greek geographer Strabo describes Tyre as being wholly an island, like the northerly Phoenician city of Arvad. With strong walls enclosing its temples and palaces and many-storied houses, Phoenician Tyre became a great and prosperous city with almost impregnable defenses.

Hiram also aided Solomon in the building of the temple at Jerusalem. Sidonian foresters and thousands of Israelite workmen felled the cedars of Lebanon and rafted the logs by sea to the port of Joppa. Hiram was paid by Solomon in grain and oil, for Phoenicia was not agriculturally self-sufficient. Even this was hardly enough to foot the bill, so Solomon ceded territory to Hiram; this was a parcel of land located in the northeastern part of the Hebrew kingdom.

It does not take careful reading of the Old Testament to discover that Solomon was more than a poser of riddles and the head of a large household. He was a shrewd businessman. As in the case of his marriage to Pharaoh's daughter, many of his seven hundred wives and three hundred concubines represented business connections. A Red Sea fleet, manned by Phoenician "shipmen that had knowledge of the sea," sailed from Solomon's port on the Gulf of Aqaba to Ophir (in Arabia ?) to bring back gold and spices in return for the copper which Solomon was smelting at his "Palestinian Pittsburgh" of Ezion-geber. The Queen of Sheba came to Solomon first of all to talk business and only incidentally to see him in all his glory. In the Mediterranean, sailing from Joppa, Solomon had "at sea a navy of Tarshish with the men of Hiram." This points to trade with Cilicia, for Tarshish is Tarsus beyond a shadow of a doubt. There was also trade by land. The Old Testament says that the horses of Cilicia were exchanged for chariots made in Egypt. Solomon himself was a horse trader, and his "chariot cities" with their forty thousand stalls were scattered throughout his kingdom; one such town was Megiddo where excavators from the Oriental Institute (University of Chicago) found Solomon's stables with accommodations for 460 horses and 160 chariots.

Solomon's kingdom was disrupted soon after his death by political and religious discord in part, but mostly through the machinations of Sheshonk, the Egyptian pharaoh, who invaded Palestine about 930 and captured Lachish, Megiddo, Beth-Shan, and even Jerusalem where he despoiled the temple. The Phoenician towns also apparently submitted to Egypt, for a stele of Sheshonk has been found at Byblos. Shortly afterward, kingdoms once tributary to the Hebrews began to declare their independence. Mesha of Moab, the "sheepmaster" who had paid a tribute of a hundred thousand lambs and an equal number of rams, broke away in the first half of the ninth century. The Old Testament tells us that Mesha was hard pressed and saved himself only by sacrificing his son as a burnt offering, but we also have Mesha's side of the story engraved upon a large stele, the famous

Moabite Stone found in 1868, in which he boasts of his successes against Omri, founder of Samaria, and Omri's son, Ahab.

While the kingdoms of Israel and Judah struggled along as best they could during the ninth century, the Phoenicians prospered. Wasting neither time nor money on idle warfare, the Phoenicians concentrated on trade. Trading posts established on Mediterranean shores began to grow into permanent cities. Cition, in southern Cyprus, became a Phoenician colony in the ninth century. Ultimately, people in Palestine came to refer to the whole island of Cyprus as Chittim.

Late in the ninth century, or perhaps in the eighth, the Phoenicians founded Utica in north Africa, and soon after, Carthage (in Phoenician, Kartihadast, the New Town). The legend of the founding of Carthage was used by Vergil in his *Aeneid* even though he ignored a chronologically impossible situation: it could not have taken Aeneas, fleeing from the sack of Troy in 1194, four hundred years to reach Carthage. Dido, whose Phoenician name was Elissa, was the sister of the Tyrian king, Pygmalion (Pumiaton in Phoenician). She was married to a rich uncle who was killed by Pygmalion for his wealth. Dido managed to escape to Cyprus, where there was another Carthage; afterwards she colonized African Carthage (traditional date, 814 B.C.).

All during the ninth century Palestine and Syria were made increasingly aware of the growing power of Assyria. It was an old story: he who would control Mesopotamia and prosper must have an outlet to the Mediterranean. Furthermore, in that direction lay the cedars of Lebanon, the silver of Cilicia, and the copper of Cyprus. By the eighth century the Assyrians had begun to create an empire; instead of raiding the west for revenue, they organized and held it for tribute. Many rebellions in Phoenicia as well as in other parts of Syria and Palestine were brutally put down time after time. Others suffered more than the Phoenicians, but even they began to decline while increasing competition from the Greeks cost them the eastern Mediterranean markets before the end of the seventh century. As a result, the Phoenicians began to concentrate on the western Mediterranean, though the real prosperity of such ventures accrued to the north African colonies which became independent under the leadership of Carthage. In the second half of the sixth century by the time of the Persian conquest Phoenician glory had materially faded.

Phoenician civilization, if we can call it that, was basically Canaanite tinged with Egyptian, Mesopotamian, and Aegean influences. The Phoenicians were not so much creators as imitators, adaptors, and carriers of civilization. They were responsible more than any other group for the diffusion of Oriental (Near Eastern) ideas to Greece, Italy, Spain, and North Africa; in short, to the classical world. The Greek geographer Strabo was

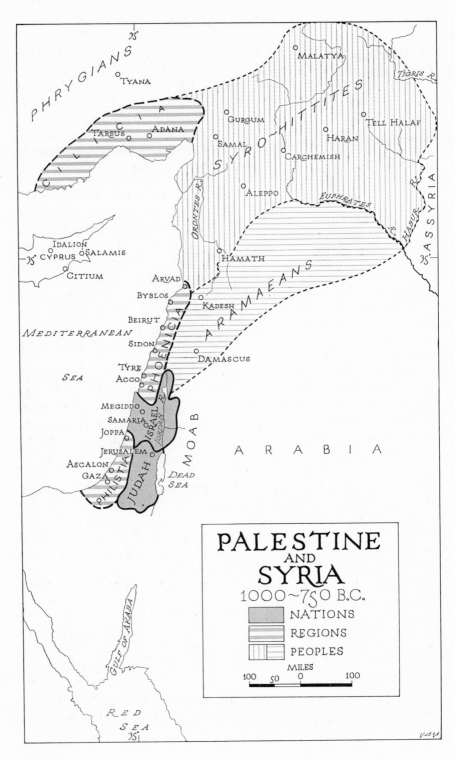

PHRYGIANS

TYANA

CILICIA

TARSUS   ADANA

MALATYA

GURGUM   TELL HALAF

SAMAL   HARAN

CARCHEMISH

SYRO-HITTITES

ALEPPO

TIGRIS R.

EUPHRATES

HABUR R.

ASSYRIA

IDALION   SALAMIS
CYPRUS
CITIUM

MEDITERRANEAN

SEA

ORONTES R.

HAMATH

ARVAD

BYBLOS   KADESH

BEIRUT   PHOENICIA

SIDON   DAMASCUS

TYRE
ACCO

MEGIDDO

SAMARIA

JOPPA   ISRAEL

JERUSALEM

ASCALON   JUDAH

GAZA   PHILISTIA

JORDAN R.

MOAB

DEAD
SEA

ARAMAEANS

ARABIA

GULF OF AKABA

RED
SEA
35

PALESTINE
AND
SYRIA
1000~750 B.C.

NATIONS

REGIONS

PEOPLES

MILES
100   50   0   100

VGV

generous in his praise of the Phoenicians in this role: he said that while the Greeks got their geometry from Egypt, their arithmetic, astronomy, and knowledge of navigation came from the Phoenicians. This was not completely true, nor was it all that might have been said, for the Semitic alphabet, from which the Greek and Roman alphabets were derived, was carried westward by Phoenician traders; moreover, the influence of Phoenician art upon Greeks, Romans, and Spaniards was very great in the period between 750 and 500 B.C.

In the field of religion the Phoenicians do not seem to have had much effect upon the people with whom they traded. The Romans professed to be actively repelled by certain aspects of the Carthaginian cults. In reality, there was little novelty in Phoenician religion. Dagan, Reshef, Ashtart, and Adonis were worshipped; there were also Eshmun-Baal, a god of healing, and Melkart, the principal deity of Tyre. Like the other Canaanites, the Phoenicians worshipped sacred mountains, trees, pillars, and waters.

Primarily, the Phoenicians were businessmen: manufacturers and traders. They were nomads of the sea, just as their Aramaean relatives who lived just over the hills in Damascus were nomads of the desert and occupied with trading on land. Phoenician ships sailed to Cyprus, the ports of southern Asia Minor, to Greece, Italy, Spain, North Africa, and beyond the Pillars of Hercules to the Tin Isles of Britain. Wherever they went, they exchanged their manufactures and slaves for raw materials: metals, ivory, and food. In the *Iliad* and the *Odyssey,* whenever Phoenicians or Sidonians are mentioned it is usually for their metal bowls, textiles, or slave trading. A significant phrase is that of the woman in Eumaeus' story in the *Odyssey:* "I come from Sidon where they deal in bronze." The textiles of Phoenicia were very famous, and along with them went the much-prized Tyrian purple dye made from the shellfish called the murex. Strabo says that the dye factories on the shore at Tyre produced an awful stench; it was probably worse than the cod of Gloucester. The trading activities of the Phoenicians are well described in the section of Ezekiel (26–28) where the destruction of Tyre by Nebuchadnezzar is foretold. Tyre is called "the merchant of the people of many isles," and then follows a list: blue and purple dyes from the Isles of Elishah, fir of Senir, cedar of Lebanon, oak of Bashan, slaves, iron, tin, lead from Tarsus, brass and slaves from Javan, and many other commodities. The Phoenicians were also indispensable as shipwrights. Their ships were copied by the Greeks, and the landlubberly Assyrians and Persians relied upon Phoenician mariners for naval operations.

Phoenician art is known to us from metalwork, ivory carving, and glass. It is a composite art, sometimes Egyptianized, sometimes Mesopotamian, sometimes Aegean. Many of the ivories are beautiful, much of the glass is good, and some of the jewelry is impressive, but a uniform standard of excellence was not maintained. The trade goods exported to the west were often decorated in a style that was garish and vulgar, but this is not surprising since mass production rarely knows self-discipline. People who had seen nothing else were charmed by the wares of the Phoenician peddlers and even strove for a time to imitate the decorative style of these imports; the Greeks, Italians, and Spaniards all went through an "Orientalizing" phase. The distribution of Phoenician ivories, metalwork, and glass is amazing in its geographical breadth; it is, like Greek pottery, an index to the scope of trade.

A group similar to the Phoenicians in several ways was the Aramaeans: both were Semites, and both made their livelihood through trade. The Aramaeans, however, were not seafarers like the Phoenicians but carried their goods over the caravan routes to the east. The Aramaeans were most numerous on the eastern side of Syria from Damascus northward in the area between the Euphrates and the Khabur River. Aramaean princes ruled a number of city-states in the region just described, but the records now available are too scant to permit the history of these states or the people themselves to be written. The importance of the Aramaeans as traders may be inferred from the fact that their language, Aramaic, became widespread in Palestine, Syria, and Mesopotamia. The rulers of these areas from the seventh century onward were forced to employ Aramaic as the chief tongue for communicating with their subjects. The later books of the Old Testament show a strong Aramaic influence on Hebrew, and Aramaic was the spoken language of Jesus and his disciples.

Side by side with the Phoenicians and Aramaeans in north Syria lived the "Hittites." These were not the true Hittites of Asia Minor who flourished in the second millennium B.C., but the so-called Syro-Hittites whose great period fell between 1200 and 750 B.C., a people who inherited and preserved Hittite culture but whose language and background were more Luwian than Hittite. They lived in a rather restricted area of Cilicia, north Syria, and the mountain area just to the north. Among their principal towns were Tarsus, Adana, Tyana, Marash, Milid, Samal, Kunulua, Aleppo, Arpad, Hamath and Carchemish. Each of the cities tended to be the capital of an independent state, ruled by a "Hittite" king, but possessing a diverse population in which the Aramaean element was often predominant.

Although they do not appear in a major role in the Old Testament, the Syro-Hittites constituted a significant group, not quite as mysterious as the Philistines but fully as exotic and interesting. Since the Old Testament fails us as a source, we must turn instead to the records of Assyria in which numerous contacts with the "Hittite" states are described. Particularly from the ninth century onward, the Assyrians were engaged in warfare against the Syro-Hittites. Time and time again the stout resistance of the Syro-Hittites flouted Assyrian aims, especially as the Assyrians strove for an outlet to the Mediterranean; consequently, "wicked Hittite" became a stock Assyrian phrase. The Syro-Hittites held out for a long time against Assyria, but their lack of unity finally caused their downfall. In the second half of the eighth century the Syrian and Cilician states ruled by Syro-Hittites were gradually annexed, one by one, and the Syro-Hittites as a people disappeared forever.

In all the Syro-Hittite cities that have been excavated a fairly uniform culture has been found. A distinctive kind of architecture and sculpture is characteristic of all these sites. Stone was much used for building palaces, temples, and fortifications. The Assyrians greatly admired Hittite palaces and built structures of this type in Assyria. The Syro-Hittite palace, called by the Assyrians a *bit hilani,* or "Hittite palace," had a portico adorned with columns much like the façade of a Greek temple; sometimes, instead of columns, animal and human figures were used. These palaces were also adorned with relief sculptures in the form of orthostats (the lower courses of the wall) which ran around the exterior of the building. Another characteristic of the culture was a peculiar system of writing, known as Hieroglyphic Hittite, which it is now possible to read. Finally, the Syro-Hittites dressed differently from their contemporaries; their warriors with their beards and round shields are always easy to identify in Assyrian and other reliefs.

One of the most important of the Syro-Hittite cities was Carchemish on the upper Euphrates which controlled one of the main fords of the river and thus was able to profit from the trade that passed from the Mediterranean to Mesopotamia. It is easy to understand why the capture of Carchemish was one of the major Assyrian objectives in their drive toward the west. It is also clear why Carchemish was able to hold out for so long against Assyria when we look at the vast mound of the city. Situated on the west bank of the Euphrates, Carchemish was walled on all sides. The town was enclosed, and in addition the citadel which stood next to the river was itself strongly fortified. As a river town, Carchemish controlled the trade that went up and down the Euphrates as well as the commerce that crossed the river.

A Syro-Hittite palace with typical orthostats was found at Carchemish. Some of the reliefs displayed ceremonial and religious subjects while others were devoted to more mundane affairs: one scene, the arming of a warrior, reminds us of similar scenes painted on Greek vases. At Carchemish, too, we get a glimpse of Syro-Hittite religion with its statues of forbidding deities of gigantic proportions.

Carchemish was a rich town. Sangara, its ninth-century king, was a contemporary of Hadadezer (the Ben-Hadad of the Old Testament) and allied with him against Shalmaneser III, the Assyrian king. Sangara paid a handsome tribute to Assyria for his temerity: when Carchemish finally fell to Sargon II in the latter part of the eighth century, its spoil amounted to almost twelve talents of gold and twenty-one hundred talents of silver.

Another river town was located on the site of Tell Halaf on the Khabur, a tributary of the Euphrates. There a big mound covered several hundred acres; in it was found the fortified palace of a prince named Kapara who seems to have reigned in the tenth century. In typical *bit hilani* form, the palace had many orthostats, some of which displayed animals—elephants, pigs, ostriches, camels, and others; there were mythological scenes, and scenes from everyday life with fishermen, hunters, horsemen, charioteers, and warriors. Chariot scenes remind us once more of the Greek area, for similar ones occur on the gravestones of Mycenae. In all, 187 orthostats were found: they averaged three feet high, one and one-half feet wide. Black basalt was alternated with limestone painted with red ochre. There were also statues in the round: birds with curious cylindrical eyes, and a gigantic throned and ugly goddess with a Mona Lisa smile.

In short, the "Hittite" culture revealed at Carchemish and Tell Halaf is the same as that at other sites; the common elements are always present whether at Adana, Malatya, or Samal. For a long time the precise identity of the Syro-Hittites was hidden because their writing, the Hieroglyphic Hittite, could not be read. After World War II, however, a bilingual inscription was found at Karatepe, near Adana, which demonstrated the workings of the strange script: the bilingual was in Phoenician and in Hieroglyphic Hittite. The latter was found to be, as had been long suspected, a syllabary which employed a few ideographic signs. The underlying language was essentially Luwian.

The ancient peoples of Syria and Palestine in the period 1200–750 B.C. did not regard the Hebrews as an important group. It was only under Solomon in the tenth century that the Hebrews played a significant role in Near Eastern political and economic affairs; the later kingdoms of Israel and Judah were little more than satellites of a succession of stronger states. If it were not for the Old Testament, we should know little of the history of the Hebrews and practically nothing about their religion. The Hebrews were either disregarded or misunderstood by their contemporaries, and while archaeology and the records of other Near Eastern peoples may clarify some features of the Old Testament, this great book remains our fundamental and primary source.

These remarks are not intended to disparage the Hebrews and their achievement, for Judaism was a very important development in the cultural history of the Near East. It is possible to theorize about the reasons for the development of monotheism among the Hebrews and about the circumstances which produced the remarkable and exciting Age of the Prophets, but, important as these subjects are, the story of the theological evolution which took place among the Hebrews has no proper place at present in a book of this kind. When the facts have been established beyond the point of argument—and the most cursory perusal of scholarly books about the

Bible or a glance at a periodical devoted to theology will show that such a point has not been reached—then perhaps appropriate chapters can be written.

One of the world's greatest literary works, the Old Testament was centuries in the process of formation; it did not attain its final form until the first century A.D. The individual books are the products of various periods: some of the earliest go back to perhaps 900 B.C., and the latest may be dated about seven hundred years later. In the majesty of its prose, the beauty of its poetry, the compelling force of its moral teachings, and the extent of its influence, the Old Testament has no competitor in the "Western tradition."

Like any other truly great book, the Old Testament is neither obvious nor easy to read with understanding. It cannot be fully appreciated in translation, and a lifetime of serious study will prove insufficient to comprehend its full message. The whole subject is one to be approached with reverence and humility, and it is well to remember that what we do know about the Old Testament is based upon the work of dedicated scholars of many faiths and sects who have worked together in a democracy of learning which scorns the blinding strife of bigotry.

Chapter 9

THE ASSYRIAN EMPIRE

U P THE TIGRIS, northwest of ancient Sumer and Akkad, lay the country of Assyria, a region of rolling hills bounded on the south by the Babylonian plain with rough mountainous country on the east and north and a somewhat arid strip on the west. Comprising an area of less than ten thousand square miles, with moderately fertile land, adequate rainfall, and good stone, Assyria was dotted by peasant villages before 4000 B.C. Quite early it had proved attractive and accessible to tribes from the Arabian Desert with the result that the Assyrians of the historic period were predominantly Semitic and closely related to the Akkadians and Hammurabi's Amorites. On the other hand, the Assyrians, unlike the Semites of the plain, were never subjected to the enervating influence of a hot climate and comparatively easy living. They were a hill folk, chiefly farmers and herdsmen, whose life was not without its difficulties; they had to work hard to eke out an existence, and they were surrounded by enemies who coveted their lands. In their contest with nature and their struggles with their foes, the Assyrians became a hardy and vigorous people.

During the time of Sargon of Akkad and until the fall of the Third Dynasty of Ur, Assyria was under frequent attack from the south and often in a tributary status, but early in the second millennium it became an independent kingdom which exploited the resources of Asia Minor through trade and fought against the Amorites of Babylonia. Between 1450 and 1400 Assyria was part of the Mitannian kingdom, but it regained independence through revolt to enjoy a period of political power and territorial expansion down to about 1100 when struggles with the mountaineers to the north brought a regression between 1100 and 900 B.C. The country emerged from this troubled period as a completely militarized state under kings who were autocratic warlords. Year after year, attacking, raiding, destroying, the

124

Assyrians kept their hostile neighbors on the defensive; Assyrian strength increased as enemy resistance collapsed until at last (after 745) the conquest and occupation of a large territory brought into existence the largest empire the Near East had seen in more than twenty centuries of recorded history.

The Assyrians were almost the first of the great nations of the Near East to be rediscovered in modern times, but even so it is only within the last hundred years that archaeological research has disclosed the ruins of Assyrian palaces and the decipherment of the cuneiform has enabled us to read the texts which provide the details of Assyrian history. Despite frequent mention of Assyrians in the Old Testament and the essentially legendary material relating to Assyria in Greek and Latin authors, we should not know anything definite about the Assyrians if we did not possess the material and epigraphical remains from Assyria itself. More of this material is still being discovered so that gaps in our knowledge are constantly being filled. The bulk of our information about the activity of the Assyrian kings is derived from inscriptions on stone slabs and other monuments, texts which are frequently illustrated by relief sculptures, and other inscriptions on clay cylinders and tablets. The importance of these texts can be illustrated by the following example:

The capital of Assyria had originally been situated at Ashur in the southern part of the country near the junction of the Lesser Zab with the Tigris, but in the ninth century the site of the royal city was moved to Kalakh some miles to the north of Ashur at a point where the Greater Zab enters the Tigris. Kalakh, known as Nimrud in modern times, was excavated about a century ago by Sir Austen Henry Layard, who found there the remains of the palace of Ashurnazirpal II, one of the greatest of the early Assyrian kings, who began to reign about 885 B.C.

Any account of the reign of Ashurnazirpal must come ultimately from the official reports of his exploits which were engraved on limestone blocks and set up as part of the decoration of his palace and some of the other buildings in the capital. Our longest text, arranged in three columns of many lines each, adorned the pavement slabs at the entrance to the temple of Urta (Ninib). This long inscription constitutes the official history of Ashurnazirpal's reign; it is usually called *The Annals*. It must have been put into its final form in the last year of the king's reign (about 858), and it recounts Ashurnazirpal's campaigns year by year. Written in the lofty style that was already characteristic of Assyrian historiography, these annals contain many passages of powerful, if sometimes gruesome, description.

Ashurnazirpal must have been very young at the time of his accession; he was certainly vigorous. In obedience to the great god Ashur, who commanded him to conquer, subdue, and rule, Ashurnazirpal began the first year of his reign with a difficult campaign against the hill tribes to the east.

Passing over steep mountains by difficult roads, Ashurnazirpal tells us, he fell upon the enemy with fire and sword. Some of the vanquished took refuge on a high mountain whose peak "rose like the point of an iron girdle-dagger." No bird of heaven came to it, for it was like the nest of an eagle. Scrambling up the slopes, the Assyrians located the enemy after three days; two hundred of the foe were cut down with the sword, and the mountain was dyed red "like wool" with their blood. Other tribes hastened to submit and to send tribute—horses, mules, cattle, sheep, wine, vessels of copper, silver, gold, and lead. Still more mountain towns were destroyed, devastated, burned. A rebellious governor was brought in chains to nearby Arbela where he was flayed alive and his skin stretched to dry upon the city wall.

On and on, year by year, the account is continued in the annals. Raids to the east, raids to the north, a thrust toward Babylon, campaigns to the west follow in never-ending succession. A city offers resistance; it is stormed and captured. A new batch of captives is carved up, some are broiled, and others are merely disfigured: "from some I cut off their hands and their fingers, from others their noses and their ears, of many I put out the eyes." Cities are rebuilt and populated with Assyrian colonists drawn from the poorer classes.

In a year not mentioned Ashurnazirpal marched westward to the Aramaean state of Bit-Adini on the upper Euphrates where captives and tribute were taken. Subsequently, in an unusual campaign in the autumn, the Assyrians took the road to Carchemish in "Hittite-land." Ashurnazirpal caught the enemy unawares at a season when the yeomen were preparing for the fall sowing and no large forces could be summoned to oppose him. Crossing the flood-swollen Euphrates, filled by the autumnal rains, the Assyrians in bullboats made of skins, landed on the western bank and approached Carchemish from an unexpected direction. Unable to resist, the Hittite overlords of Carchemish paid protection money and provided guides for the roads leading toward the Mediterranean. Kunulua, the capital of the queer northern state of Judah, was entered without resistance, and Lubarna, its Hittite king, gave rich presents to Ashurnazirpal; gold, silver, ivory, boxwood, ten female musicians, a princess, and a *pagutu* (crocodile?) were among the baubles added to Ashurnazirpal's collection. Pressing on, the Assyrians crossed the Orontes and entered the Amq plain, once the territory of Alalakh, and halted for the night in the swamps. Then down along the slopes of Lebanon they went to the Great Sea, the Mediterranean itself, where Ashurnazirpal performed the most sublime of all Assyrian ceremonies of conquest: "In the Great Sea I washed my weapons, and I made offerings to the gods." Tribute now poured in from the frightened Phoenician cities: Tyre, Sidon, Byblos, Arvad, and others. The slopes of Mount Amanus were ascended; cedars, cypresses, junipers, and pines were felled to make great timbers for the palaces and temples of Kalakh.

Ashurnazirpal was no more and no less brutal than other Assyrian kings. The official records served a good propaganda purpose; future rebels and opponents were shown by horrible example what they might expect, and this often prevented trouble. Actually, Ashurnazirpal was also a good administrator who thought about peace as well as war. Towns were rebuilt and improved, colonists were introduced, and the building of Kalakh was a good example on a large scale of what was done elsewhere. Captive peoples were brought in to be drawers of water, hewers of wood, and farmers. At Kalakh an irrigation project was begun with the building of a canal from the Zab to the city, and orchards and vineyards began to line the watercourse. The palace at Kalakh must have been a magnificent thing: "A palace of cedar, cypress, juniper, boxwood, mulberry, pistachio-wood, and tamarisk . . . I founded. Beasts of the mountains and of the seas of white limestone and alabaster I fashioned and set them up within its gates . . . . I made it glorious, and put copper clothes-hooks all around." There were also chairs of maple and boxwood, tables of ivory with inlay, and designs in enamelled brick adorned the walls.

Despite the activity of Ashurnazirpal and similar deeds by his son, Shalmaneser III (858–825/4), no really permanent holdings were created (or, perhaps, even desired) by their victories. Shalmaneser, in his numerous campaigns to the west, encountered and defeated Ahab of Israel, then the ally of Ben-Hadad of Damascus, in 853, and later (842) on the famous Black Obelisk inscription Jehu is shown paying tribute to Shalmaneser. The development of a real empire was perhaps delayed by the fact that Assyria itself was not fully organized. We hear of twenty-seven cities including Nineveh, Ashur, and Arbela joining the crown prince in a revolt against Shalmaneser; this and later occurrences of a similar kind (just after 763) suggest that the kings had much to do at home before they could rule abroad. At any rate, the monarchy seems to have declined during the next seventy-five years. Our information about Assyrian affairs during this period is none too full; there is just enough to whet the appetite. We should like to know more of the regency of Sammuramat, the daughter-in-law of Shalmaneser, which may be dated about 810; it was around the figure of Sammuramat that the legend of Semiramis, the great warrior-queen, grew. Then there is the period of disorder following the plague of 766 and the eclipse of 763 foretold by Amos, when the sun went down at noon and the earth was darkened in the clear day.

After decades of anarchy, order was re-established by Tiglath-Pileser III (745–727). This able king, called Pul (his Babylonian throne name) in the Old Testament, captured Babylon early in his reign and attacked the mysterious and dangerous Urartian kingdom in the north which was centered at Lake Van. Campaigns to the west brought submission and tribute from Damascus, Israel, and Judah. Philistine Gaza was attacked; its king fled to Egypt. Later, Damascus was captured and destroyed (732), and Tiglath-Pileser mentions the assassination of Pekah of Israel and the accession of Hoshea about the same time. In the reign of Shalmaneser V, who succeeded Tiglath-Pileser, Hoshea began to conspire with Egypt against Assyria and so precipitated the siege of Samaria which began about 725. Shalmaneser did not live to see the surrender of Samaria, but the undertaking was successfully concluded by the next king of Assyria, the great Sargon.

Sargon II, who came to the Assyrian throne late in 722, was a self-made man, but he boasted of three hundred fifty kings, his fathers, who had reigned before him. He may possibly have belonged to the junior branch of the royal family, although even this is doubtful because his son and successor, Sennacherib, traced *his* lineage back to Gilgamesh. Esar-haddon, the grandson of Sargon, was more conservative, merely claiming descent from the early kings of Assyria. Obviously, Sargon was not the real name of the new king but rather a name assumed by him to identify himself in the popular mind with that almost mythical personage, Sargon of Akkad, a great conqueror. The fact that Sargon II tried to emulate many of the legendary deeds of Sargon of Akkad suggests what was in his mind. But Sargon (True King) was a good name for a usurper; further-more, it was a name which had been borne with distinction by one of the early kings of Assyria, Sargon I, more than a thousand years before. There is a theory that Sargon was a candidate of the Assyrian priesthood which had been displeased with Shalmaneser V, but he may just as well have been the candidate of one of the still-rebellious cities.

At any rate, Sargon completed the reduction of Samaria. He tells us that he carried off 27,290 people into captivity and refounded the town by bringing in new settlers. Dispersed in small groups throughout the empire which Sargon was now creating, these Israelites were no longer identifiable and became "lost." But the Israelite nation must have numbered more than 27,290. Perhaps the rest were engulfed by the new colonists whom Sargon brought into Israelite territory.

The policy undertaken with regard to the Israelites was typical of Sargon's dealings with other nations. Assyria was creating an empire; wherever the Assyrians went, they meant to stay. In Syria, in Cilicia, in Philistia we find the same pattern under Sargon. His reign was marked by continuous fighting: against Babylon and the wily Merodach-Baladan who is mentioned in the Old Testament; against Urartu (or Haldia) into the cities of which Sargon "cast gloom"; in the northwest against Mita (Midas ?) of Mushki (the Phrygians ?). There was also a journey into the "Sea of the Setting Sun" to Cyprus—an inscription of Sargon has been found on the island—and there was fighting against the Medes in Iran. There was too much fighting; in 705 Sargon died in a battle with the fierce Cimmerians, a horde which had swept down over the Caucasus, devastated the Urartian kingdom, and was to cause more trouble in western Asia Minor.

Sennacherib (704–681) had no easy task to succeed to his father's empire, which soon threatened to disintegrate. Merodach-Baladan, prince of the Chaldean tribes at the head of the Persian Gulf, engineered a Babylonian revolt and plotted with the Elamites, Arabs, Syrians, and Jews to bring about simultaneous uprisings against Sennacherib. Babylon, however, was recaptured by the Assyrians who then turned on the west (702/1). The king of Tyre "fled into the midst of the sea," and Hezekiah of Judah was "shut up like a caged bird" in his royal city of Jerusalem. Punished by a loss of territory, Hezekiah saved his throne by renewing the payment of tribute to Assyria. In 698 the Cypriote Greeks were driven from Cilicia, and their ally, Tarsus, was plundered. Subject Greek and Phoenician shipwrights and sailors were employed a few years later to build vessels for a campaign into the swamps of southern Babylonia. A new revolt in Babylon in 689 was punished by the destruction of the city.

In 681 Sennacherib was the victim of a palace conspiracy, a fact mentioned both in the Old Testament and in the Assyrian records. The murder was avenged by his son, Esarhaddon, whose pious deeds were infinitely pleasing to the god Ashur—the heart of the god rejoiced, "his liver shone." Naturally, this disorder in Assyria was a signal for revolts throughout the empire. These uprisings were methodically put down by Esarhaddon. The king of Sidon literally lost his head as he was caught up "like a fish out of the sea." The Sea Land (southern Babylonia) and the Arabs were "pacified." Then came the turn of the real troublemakers in the west, the Ethiopian rulers of Egypt, who had been tampering with the loyalties of Philistine and Phoenician princes. Egypt was invaded in 671; in a battle at Memphis the enemy were "butchered like sheep." Phoenicia had been organized as an Assyrian province, but the same course was not followed in Egypt; instead, the Assyrians chose to rely upon the somewhat doubtful loyalty of the Delta princes who numbered more than a score and were beset by mutual jealousies. Elsewhere, however, the empire seemed secure. Tribute poured in from many quarters including that from ten Phoenician and Greek kings of Cyprus. A noteworthy achievement of Esarhaddon was the rebuilding of Babylon, the city which had been devastated by his father.

Ashurbanipal, the last of the great Assyrian kings, came to the throne about 668 and reigned (probably) until 631. He claimed to be the eldest son of Esarhaddon, but there is a suspicion that his brother, Shamash-shum-ukin, whom he made governor of Babylon, should properly have been crown prince. The reign of Ashurbanipal began happily enough with the

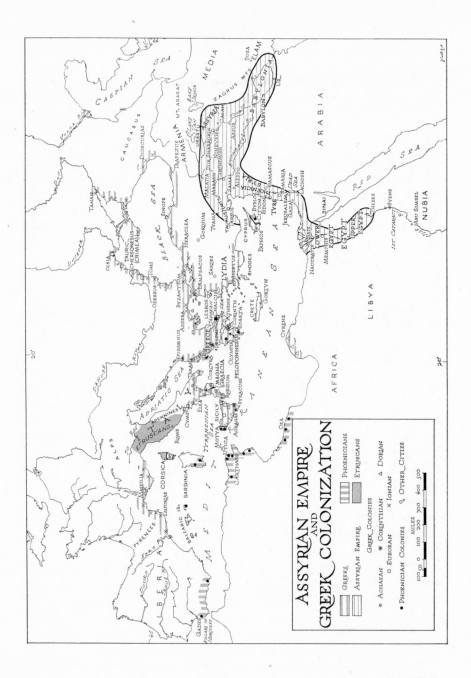

ASSYRIAN EMPIRE AND GREEK COLONIZATION

Assyrians in possession of an empire which had reached its broadest limits. Within a short time, however, disintegration began. Egypt was restless; an initial revolt was put down, but a few years later Egypt was able to become independent because the Assyrians were too busy with uprisings elsewhere. Shamash-shum-ukin apparently resented his inferior position and conspired with the Elamites against Ashurbanipal. This brought on a serious Babylonian war between 652 and 648. The Medes and Arabs ceased to pay their tribute. The Medes were now too strong to be reconquered, but the Arabs were punished by a campaign that netted so many camels as booty that the camel market was ruined by a price drop. By the end of his reign Ashurbanipal tells us that he was in despair; like an Assyrian Job he complains that he has done good to god and man, but that everything has gone wrong: he is old, tired, sick; death is making an end of him, and he spends his days sighing and lamenting.

There was cause for lamentation, for the days of Assyria were numbered. The successors of Ashurbanipal were soon faced by new and more serious revolts which culminated in the invasion of Assyria itself. Nineveh, its last great capital, fell in 612, and the magnificent empire of Assyria ceased to exist.

Although the Assyrians and their empire were soon forgotten, their importance in the history of civilization was immense. Their empire, which stretched from the western borders of Iran to the Delta of the Nile and included Babylonia, Assyria, Syria, Palestine, and part of Egypt, was not only the largest the ancient world had seen, but also it was organized in a more sophisticated fashion than any which had preceded it. The Assyrians were ruthless conquerors and harsh masters, but they were civilized; they preserved and studied the literature and science of Sumer and Babylon; they created fine palaces adorned with handsome relief sculpture; and they recorded their deeds with a completeness and maturity that make possible the writing of a detailed history of the period in which they flourished.

The Assyrians were the cultural heirs of the Sumerians and Babylonians, but a slightly different cultural background, a different environment, and cultural borrowings from their neighbors to the north and west prevented Assyrian civilization from becoming a mere copy of that to the south. This may be illustrated by a few examples: the Assyrian laws, though modelled after south Mesopotamian codes, reflect a different society; the good stone of the Assyrians enabled them to surpass the Sumerians and Babylonians in sculpture, while contacts with the Urartians, Phoenicians, and Hittites led to the introduction of features in architecture, metalwork, and ivory carving that were not Mesopotamian in origin at all.

Assyrian civilization is of special interest because it was one of three varieties of Oriental culture with which the Greeks became acquainted during the formative period of their civilization in the years right after 750 B.C.; in addition to the Assyrian, the Egyptian and Phoenician influences upon the Greeks were strong. Certain techniques of Greek sculpture have been compared with Assyrian ones, and in both sculpture and (vase) painting the borrowing of scenes common to Assyrian relief sculptures may be demonstrated. Other matters in which the Greeks were indebted to the Assyrians will be mentioned subsequently.

The whole subject of Assyrian governmental organization is one which needs detailed examination. We know something of the palace hierarchy and the elaborate court ceremonial, but municipal organization, which seems to have been very important in Assyria, and the details of the imperial government have yet to be studied. The king who stood at the head of the state held his position by virtue of divine nomination. In cases where orderly dynastic succession was possible, the crown prince would be designated early and carefully educated for the task of government. In his inscriptions Ashurbanipal relates some of the history of his education for the throne; he studied mathematics, astronomy, divination, various cuneiform scripts—"taking pleasure in reading stones coming from before the flood." He was also trained as a warrior, learning to use different types of weapons, and he was allowed to practice the art of ruling in the presence of his father, the king. Superiority, perfection in every endeavor was the ideal.

High officials in the Assyrian government were the prime minister, the commander-in-chief of the army, the city governors, and the governors of provinces. At the court were a master of ceremonies, cupbearers, stewards, chamberlains, and so on. Although the king was the national high priest, each temple had its organized priesthood. Scribes were necessary and important in many activities; some were specialists in the various languages written in the cuneiform script, some wrote Egyptian hieroglyphs, and others wrote Aramaic in an alphabetic script.

The affairs of empire involved defense and conquest, diplomacy, the collection of revenue through tribute and tolls, and various projects to improve the economy. Defense and conquest constituted the province of the army which was versatile, well equipped, and well trained. Cavalry in chariots, heavy-armed infantry, lancers, light-armed troops, archers, slingers, and engineers are well attested. Assyrian success was due in large part to the national militia, which fought for the greater glory of the king and the god Ashur, and to Assyrian artillery and siege machinery. Strong-walled enemy cities could be taken by undermining or by battering down the walls with huge armored machines; movable towers raised the Assyrian archers to heights equal to that of the enemy on their city parapets. The details of military organization and equipment are provided by the royal inscriptions and their accompanying relief sculptures which show the arms and

GOLD AND IVORY SNAKE GODDESS

Courtesy of the Museum of Fine Arts, Boston

IVORY LID OF BOX FROM RAS SHAMRA
SHOWING MINOAN INFLUENCE

*Copyright by Professor Claude F. A. Schaeffer,
Director of the French Archaeological Expedition*

GORGON COIN FROM SOUTHERN ASIA MINOR

FACE OF HUMBABA DRAWN IN A CONTINUOUS LINE—
THIRD MILLENIUM B.C.

LABYRINTH ON A CNOSSIAN COIN

MYCENAEAN LABYRINTH FROM PYLOS

FROM A

SIMPLE CROSS

SWASTIKA ON A
CNOSSIAN COIN

TRISKELES FROM A LYCIAN COIN

TRISKELES COIN FROM SOUTHERN ASIA MINOR

MINOTAUR ON A CNOSSIAN COIN

GORGON FROM A SICILIAN TEMPLE

A PROBLEM IN CULTURAL DIFFUSION

The Sumerian legend of Gilgamesh and his friend Enkidu who slew the bull-demon Humbaba is very old, and it was borrowed from Mesopotamia by the Hittites. The story of the Minotaur, the bull-man slain by Theseus in the Labyrinth, was connected with the Minoans who may have come from southern Asia Minor. Perseus was supposed to have slain the Gorgon in or near Asia Minor also.

Mycenaean Labyrinth courtesy of Mabel Lang and the
American Journal of Archaeology. *Photo Alison Frantz*
Coins courtesy of the American Numismatic Society
Gorgon courtesy of the Syracuse Museum
Face of Humbaba courtesy of the Trustees of the British
Museum

BULL-MEN FROM A MESOPOTAMIAN SEAL

Courtesy of the Musée du Louvre

GILGAMESH AND ENKIDU
KILL HUMBABA—SYRO-HITTITE

*From Tell Halaf, Band III, courtesy of Walter
de Gruyter & Co. and the Oriental Institute
of the University of Chicago*

GILGAMESH AND ENKIDU SLAY HUMBABA—
ASSYRIAN

Courtesy of the Staatliche Museen zu Berlin

XIII   *Gilgamesh, Theseus, Perseus?*

LYDIAN RELIEF—THESEUS KILLING
THE MINOTAUR

*Courtesy of The Metropolitan Museum of Art, Gift of
the American Society for the Exploration of Sardis, 1926*

PERSEUS AND HERMES
SLAY THE GORGON—ATTIC VASE

Courtesy of the Trustees of the British Museum

SLAYING THE GORGON—
SICILIAN TEMPLE   *Alinari*

GOLD SEAL

AMETHYST SEAL

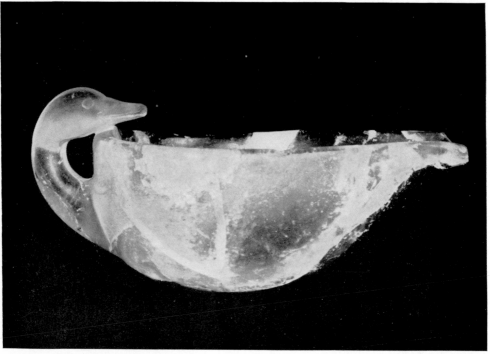

ROCK CRYSTAL BOWL

armor of the Assyrians and their enemies and display the siege machines at work. We also learn from the reliefs that the Assyrians, like the Romans, constructed fortified camps. As time went on, the Assyrians seem to have used more and more troops drawn as levies from the subject peoples; it is clear that they began to employ mercenaries, too. These non-Assyrian troops played an increasingly important role in the army as a chronological survey of the reliefs will show. In addition to the fighting men, credit for Assyrian success must be given also to a well-organized intelligence service; reports of enemy activities form a substantial section in the Assyrian royal correspondence.

This royal correspondence, a body of material still increasing by virtue of contemporary finds, consists of hundreds of letters in the cuneiform script on clay tablets. Layard's finds of a hundred years ago included documents from the time of Sargon to that of Ashurbanipal, but recent discoveries push the date back to Tiglath-Pileser III. These are letters to and from the kings dealing with a host of subjects: petitions, decisions, diplomatic correspondence, reports of the royal astrologers, military affairs, the work of the palace artisans, medical diagnoses and prescriptions, materials for the building of palaces, plans for economic improvements, and many others. From the letters we learn how Ashurbanipal issued a "white paper" in an attempt to wean the Babylonians away from his rebellious brother, how the priests cured the king's fever by pulling his infected teeth, how Sargon ordered a travelling coach with a sleeping compartment in it.

There is still much to be learned about the Assyrians. We know something of their religion, literature, and magic; much about their architecture, sculpture, and military exploits; but we must inquire about the Assyrians themselves to discover what was behind their brazen façade of arrogant imperialism and what sort of people wore the borrowed coat of Babylonian culture.

We may take it for granted that few Assyrians, exclusive of nobles, professional scribes, and priests, were as cultured as Ashurbanipal, who made a great parade of his education. The rank and file of Assyrians were not city dwellers, but farmers and shepherds. Assyria was for a long time an agriculturally self-sufficient country; where there was not farmland, there was pasture. Cattle were rare. We get a glimpse of lonely shepherds moving across the land with sizable flocks guarded by huge dogs. Assyria produced barley and wheat, and also onions, garlic, lettuce, dill, radishes, and cucumbers. Many of the words we still use for herbs are Assyrian words which have come to us through Greek or Arabic: coriander, cumin, saffron, and others. Poppies were raised for opium; cotton and indigo, imported from farther east, were also produced. There were fruit trees and grape vines. We have a big census report from the west around Harran enumerating the households of a certain district together with the number of vines possessed by each family; some of the vineyards contained as many as thirty thousand vines.

Some farms were cultivated by small landholders, some by tenants, and others by captives from the empire. There were also military holdings possessed by professional soldiers of many nations who received land in partial payment for their services. There was an interest in colonization for economic reasons. One of the letters in the Assyrian royal correspondence is from an official who proposes the establishment of a settlement at an intersection of roads so that a collector of customs and a scribe may be stationed there. In the ninth and particularly in the eighth and seventh centuries, we may infer a growth in the population of Assyria from the fact that new land was being made arable through the construction of irrigation canals.

It is fair to ask whether the construction of palaces and temples which went on apace under the empire may not have served some purpose besides royal ostentation and glorification of the gods. It is true that labor and material were provided by the subject peoples, but the structures were not put up without cost; so much building must have meant a profit for someone. Sargon built a palace and temples and a town at Dur-Sharrukin (Khorsabad). Sennacherib made Nineveh his capital. He not only built a new palace, the "Palace without a Rival," but also he laid out new streets, widened the squares, dug a canal, and made other improvements. Babylonians, Aramaeans, Cilicians, and various subject peoples labored on this project. A huge terrace was built to serve as a foundation for the palace constructed of ivory, ebony, cedar, cypress, and boxwood with its great doors of cypress bound with bronze. On the river bank, with adjacent temples and a ziggurat, this was an imposing pile.

The Assyrians were zealous in their efforts to preserve the older Mesopotamian culture. In the great library of Ashurbanipal all manner of religious, historical, literary, and scientific texts were collected. Older texts were recopied; some were translated; dictionaries for the extinct languages and dialects were compiled. The extent of scientific and technological knowledge revealed by texts from this library is astonishing. The medical and chemical texts, for example, have shown how much the Assyrians knew about drugs, minerals, and glassmaking.

It may perhaps be helpful to think of the Assyrians as a people who might be called the "Romans of the Ancient Near East." They were, like the Romans, a hardy rural people surrounded by enemies who threatened their national existence. Both the Romans and the Assyrians adopted an aggressive policy of defense by means of which they conquered their neighbors and created empires. Both were not so much creators as adapters, elaborators, and carriers of culture. Both were, in their national traditions, practical rather than theoretical in their approach to life; they tended to be builders rather than dreamers. Their preoccupation with warfare, moreover, encouraged technological developments.

The creation of the Assyrian Empire was not the result of a preconceived plan but rather of an historical accident. The real Assyrian interest in the west came with the growth of the strong Urartian kingdom which cut the Assyrians off from the sources of copper and silver in the north which they had exploited since the second millennium B.C. This forced the Assyrians to turn to the copper of Cyprus and the silver of Cilicia. To assure themselves of these resources, they were obliged to conquer and hold Syria and Phoenicia, and this, in itself, had further consequences: it presented the prospect of great wealth if the trade routes from Iran and the Persian Gulf to the Mediterranean could be included within the territory of a single political unit. This may have been a deciding factor in the drive toward the Sea Land at the head of the Persian Gulf.

How much the Assyrians themselves were to profit from the economic prosperity which their empire created is unknown, but the Near East as a whole now entered upon the most flourishing economic era which it had ever enjoyed. If history shows nothing else, it has demonstrated time and again that the Near East is most prosperous when it is politically unified. In this particular instance, though Assyrian rule may have been universally hated, the subject peoples as a whole benefited in an economic way from the existence of the empire. The new prosperity, which would have been out of the question in the preceding period of disorganization (1200–750 B.C.), was extended to peoples without, as well as within, the Assyrian Empire. It is one of the keys to the revival of Greece which took place between 750 and 500 B.C. when the foundations for classical Greek civilization were laid.

The decline and fall of Assyria can perhaps be explained by the failure of the Assyrians to find a prominent place for themselves in the economic structure of their empire. They were content to feed upon their subjects through the tribute which they demanded, and we have no real evidence that the Assyrian people ever entered wholeheartedly into trade and industry. The Assyrians seem, for the most part, to have remained farmers who left trade and industry to their subjects. The immediate cause of the collapse of the empire was provided by nationalistic revolts in areas in which the economy had attained a flourishing condition. This collapse could not be prevented because the Assyrians themselves had greatly declined in numbers. The sturdy peasantry which had fought irresistably in the earlier campaigns had been wiped out, exterminated by success, as they perished winning their country's battles. The Assyrian ruling class, having exhausted this valuable reservoir of military power, could not get the same results with subject levies and mercenaries. Undoubtedly, Assyria itself was as populous as ever at the death of Ashurbanipal, but its inhabitants were foreigners who had been transplanted thither as captives of war, and they did not have the vigor, the loyalty, or the military training of the old peasant stock. For all practical purposes, the Assyrians disappeared before, not after, the fall of Nineveh in 612.

Chapter 10

THE AGE OF THE
FOUR KINGDOMS

ETWEEN THE FALL of Assyria at the end of the seventh century B.C.
and the rise of Persia about 550 a strange situation prevailed in
the Near East. The major part of the area was divided among
four kingdoms of about equal strength. When, after several contests, it became clear to the rulers of these states that a real balance of
power existed, they were content to become friends and settle down to live
peaceably together, enjoying the prosperity which the late Assyrian Empire
had provided for them. The four kingdoms of the new era were (1) the
Neo-Babylonian kingdom which included Babylonia, Assyria, Syria, and
Palestine; (2) the Median kingdom which controlled western Iran, Armenia,
and Asia Minor to its midway point at the Halys River where the Hittite
Empire had once been centered; (3) the Kingdom of Lydia in western
Asia Minor from the Halys River to the Aegean Sea; and (4) the Saite
Kingdom (Twenty-Sixth Dynasty) in Egypt. All four states were the product of the nationalism which characterized this new period, and three of these
states—Babylonia, Egypt, and Media—had gained their independence from
Assyria through nationalist uprisings within them. Nationalism, prosperity,
balance of power are the key words or phrases which describe this new
age, but a fourth one might be added: archaism, for in the older civilized
areas, principally Babylonia and Egypt, there was a conscious effort to
recreate the glories of the ancient past.

The Assyrian Empire had begun to crumble even before the death of
Ashurbanipal, and his successors were powerless to halt its disintegration.
In 626 an Assyrian official in Babylonia, Nabopolassar, headed a revolt and
was crowned king in Babylon. Ten years of serious fighting ensued in
which the Assyrians were gradually driven from Babylonia and confined

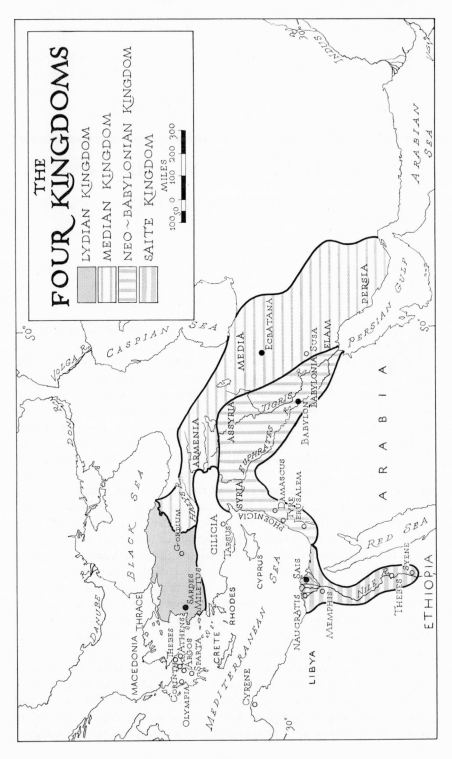

THE
FOUR KINGDOMS

LYDIAN KINGDOM
MEDIAN KINGDOM
NEO~BABYLONIAN KINGDOM
SAITE KINGDOM

MILES
100 50 0 100 200 300

to their own country. Nabopolassar invaded Assyria in 615 and attempted to capture the old capital city of Ashur but was repulsed. In the following year the Medes crossed over from Iran, sacked Ashur, and allied themselves with Nabopolassar for a final assault on Nineveh. At last, in the summer of 612, its walls weakened by a Tigris flood, Nineveh fell to the Medes and Babylonians; the Assyrian king, Sin-shar-ishkun, perished in the sack of the town. The surviving Assyrians were pursued westward into Harran where, despite Egyptian support, the Babylonians gained a final victory at Carchemish in 605. The Babylonian crown prince, Nebuchadnezzar, planned to invade Egypt, but he was forced to return to Babylon because of the death of his father, Nabopolassar.

Nebuchadnezzar, the most famous of the Neo-Babylonian kings, ascended the throne in September 605 and reigned until 562. The early part of his reign was occupied in a vain struggle with Egypt, whose kings constantly intrigued with the Jews, Philistines, and Phoenicians against him. On several occasions Nebuchadnezzar was on the verge of invading Egypt, but although he often defeated the Egyptian forces, the conquest of the country never eventuated. At last, about 568 he made an enduring peace with the Egyptians.

Nebuchadnezzar was able to deal decisively with his rebellious subjects, however. Jerusalem was twice captured by the Babylonians. The city was first taken in March 597; Jehoiachin was carried off a prisoner to Babylon where he remained as a "guest" of the crown—cuneiform ration texts have been found which enumerate the food supplied for his subsistence—and Zedekiah was chosen by Nebuchadnezzar to reign in Jerusalem. Although Zedekiah had promised not to intrigue with Egypt, he was not true to his word. About 588 both Tyre and Jerusalem rose in revolt, hoping for Egyptian aid which never came. Tyre managed to withstand a Babylonian siege, but Jerusalem fell in July 586, and the Jews were led off into the Babylonian Captivity.

The long and brilliant reign of Nebuchadnezzar was not entirely taken up with military campaigning. His building inscriptions are numerous and list the names of many temples in Babylon and other Mesopotamian cities which he built or restored. Babylon was strongly fortified and made the show place of the Near East. A large city for the times, its population may have reached eighty thousand. A great ziggurat was erected in Babylon by Nebuchadnezzar; this structure, the purpose of which was sometimes misunderstood by foreigners, was remembered in tradition as the "Hanging Gardens," one of the Seven Wonders of the Ancient World. The building activities of the reign kept the captive peoples busy at the brick kilns, and it was probably from this circumstance that the story of Shadrach, Meshak, and Abednego originated. The herbivorous proclivities of Nebuchadnezzar, evinced at the end of his reign, may have been the result of senility, although a number of other explanations have been offered from time to time.

Little need be said of the immediate successors of Nebuchadnezzar: Amel-Marduk (562–560), Neriglissar (560–556), and Labashi-Marduk (556), but the last of the Neo-Babylonian kings, Nabonidus (556–539), deserves some attention. Nabonidus may have been a distant relative of Nebuchadnezzar, but he was not a native of Babylon. His father had been a priest in Harran, and the fact that Nabonidus was not connected with Babylon or its local priesthoods did not increase his popularity. In addition to his unpopularity at home, Nabonidus had other problems to contend with. The Medes were no longer friendly, and there is more than a suspicion that Nabonidus aided the Persian revolt against the Medes which took place about 550 and resulted in the overthrow of the Median kingdom. Whether or not this was the case, Nabonidus soon had a quarrel with the Persians. They invaded Assyria and annexed territory all the way to Cilicia. This was serious enough, but it may be guessed that the real pinch was not in the Persian aggression in the north but rather that they had closed trade routes to the east through the Persian Gulf. This would afford an explanation for the long absences of Nabonidus in the Arabian Desert at the Oasis of Tema, where he was attempting to open a caravan route across Arabia to the Red Sea. While Nabonidus was absent from Babylon, Belshazzar, his son, acted as regent; Belshazzar was on no occasion, however, the king, for the dated cuneiform contracts continue to bear the name of Nabonidus right to the end of the kingdom and its annexation by Persia. The end came in 539 when, aided by a priestly fifth column within Babylon itself, the Persians won an easy victory. The jubilant priests composed a poem to celebrate the deposition of Nabonidus whom they had come to hate.

If it were not for a number of fragmentary Babylonian cuneiform chronicles which have been discovered for this period, we should know few of the details of its history. These chronicles cover the reigns of Nabopolassar and Nebuchadnezzar to 595, a fragment exists for a portion of Neriglissar's reign in 556, and there is material for the long reign of Nabonidus. The official inscriptions, however, contain very little historical information although they are numerous; most of them deal with building operations. Economic texts, on the other hand, have been found in a great abundance rivalled only by similar documents from the Third Dynasty of Ur.

Our information about the second of the great kingdoms of this age, that of the Medes, is even more scanty than that which we possess for Babylonia. The Medes were an Indo-European people who had come into Armenia during the great invasions at the end of the second millennium B.C. Gradually they had worked their way into western Iran where, in the eighth century, they had fought the Assyrians and been made tributary. About the middle of the seventh century the Medes regained their independence, and under the great king Cyaxares, who began to reign about 633, they began a series of attacks upon Assyria itself. Allying with the Babylonians, they had brought about the fall of Nineveh in 612. Subsequently, the Medes began to expand across Armenia and into central Asia Minor where in 585 they encountered Lydian forces pushing eastward. A battle between Medes and Lydians was averted by an eclipse of the sun (foretold, it was said, by Thales, the Greek philosopher). Interpreting the eclipse as a divine prohibition against further hostilities, the Medes and Lydians became allies, and a Lydian princess married the Median crown prince, Astyages, who succeeded Cyaxares on the throne probably in 584. In addition to holding Media, with its capital at Ecbatana (Hamadan), and the northern territory all the way to the Halys, the Medes also controlled the Persian tribes living in southwestern Iran. It was these tribes, possibly supported by Nabonidus, which revolted against Astyages about 550 and brought the Median kingdom to an end.

Before we can discuss the third of the great kingdoms, that of Lydia in western Asia Minor, we must go back a bit in time and review what had happened in Asia Minor after the fall of the Hittite Empire in 1200. The Hittites had been overcome by a new set of Indo-European invaders, the Phrygians, who had crossed over from what is now European Turkey. The Phrygians, probably to be identified with the people the Assyrians called the Mushki, had established a state in central Asia Minor with its capital at Gordium, some distance to the west of modern Ankara. The Phrygian kingdom remained in existence until about 700 B.C. when it was overrun by the Cimmerians, the same people against whom Sargon of Assyria had died in battle in 705.

Until recently the Phrygians were a little-known people. Some of their tombs had been excavated, and some of their alphabetic inscriptions had been found. There were also some traditions about the Phrygians preserved in Greek literature—stories about King Gordios who tied the Gordian Knot that Alexander cut, and King Midas with the golden touch and ears like a donkey—but this was all. Excavations begun by the University of Pennsylvania at Gordium in 1950, however, have yielded important results, and more may be expected in the future. It is now possible to distinguish Phrygian remains elsewhere in Asia Minor. It is clear, for example, that the Phrygians reoccupied and refortified many old Hittite sites. It is also clear that Gordium, as well as other sites, was devastated by the Cimmerian raids, and that later there was some destruction when the Persians and Lydians met in combat in 548–547 B.C. Contrary to expectations, it has been shown that there was little contact between the Greeks and the Phrygian area until about 650 B.C., in a period after the Phrygian kingdom had been destroyed. The trade relations of the Phrygians were eastward with the Urartian peoples and southward over the Taurus with Syria and Cilicia.

In building the Phrygians used much wood. Their houses and some other structures were bedded on wooden beams. Houses employed the megaron form (see Chapter 12), and they had gabled roofs. The façades of some Phrygian buildings closely resembled those of Greek temples. Phrygian royal burials took place in tumuli: first a tomb of wooden timbers was constructed; this was then protected by a log and then a stone wall, while after this a mound of rubble and clay was heaped up. The largest of the Phrygian tombs was enclosed in a mound 150 feet high and nearly 900 feet in diameter. This monument contained a single body, presumably that of a great king. The dead man was placed on his back upon a wooden bed overlaid with a coverlet of no less than 20 layers of cloth. The tomb contained inlaid three-legged tables and inlaid wooden screens; there were also 170 bronze vessels, including three handsome large cauldrons, a large number of bronze fibulae (safety pins), and some pottery. The date of the tomb was apparently between 725 and 700 B.C., just before the Cimmerian invasion.

After destroying the Phrygian kingdom, the Cimmerians swept on across Asia Minor to the west, reaching the coast of the Aegean where they attacked even the Greek cities there. The Greeks resisted, but the chief brunt of the fighting was borne by the Lydians, a native people, whose territory lay back from the coast some distance up the Hermus River. It was the Lydians who helped to stem the Cimmerian tide; in so doing, they themselves gained national strength and unity with the result that they were able to replace the now weakened Phrygians as the principal political power in western Asia Minor.

The Greek tradition regarding the origin of the dynasty which now occupied the Lydian throne at Sardes and the subsequent history of its kings is reasonably correct in broad outline, but untrustworthy in detail. The first Lydian king, who fought the Cimmerians and finally died in battle against them, was called Gyges by the Greeks. He is undoubtedly the king called Gu-gu in the inscriptions of Ashurbanipal. The Assyrian king related that when Gyges (or Gu-gu) was hard pressed by the Cimmerians, he was advised in a dream to seek Assyrian aid. Becoming an Assyrian vassal and thus gaining the invaluable aid of the gods of Assyria, Gyges was able to prevail against the Cimmerians. Later, however, Gyges no longer felt the need of Assyrian help and disavowed his allegiance by joining in an alliance with the rebellious people of Egypt. Without the help of Ashur, Ishtar, and the other Assyrian deities Gyges could not hope to prosper. He was, of course, killed by the Cimmerians—as Ashurbanipal notes with satisfaction—and his son, realizing the error of his father's ways, sought to renew the Assyrian alliance. The death of Gyges at the hands of the Cimmerians was also a fact known to the Greeks, but the synchronism with Ashurbanipal tells us that the reign of Gyges must be dated roughly in the period 675–650 B.C., somewhat later than the Greeks supposed.

The successors of Gyges acquired holdings in western Asia Minor that included many of the Greek states on the coast and the old Phrygian territory as well. An eastward expansion of Lydia was halted by the Medes at the Halys River in 585 as we have seen. Astyages, heir to the Median throne, then married the daughter of Alyattes, king of Lydia. The famous Croesus, son of Alyattes and the last of the Lydian kings, ascended the throne about 560 B.C.

Once again, the Greek tradition cannot be trusted. Herodotus, our main source, turned Croesus from a man into a myth and distorted history to belabor a moral point: that pride goeth before a fall. Perhaps Croesus did have a bad case of *hybris* (the Greek word for pride), but it could hardly have been Solon, the Athenian wise man, who diagnosed it. Solon, well over seventy, enfeebled, and involved with political strife in Athens, died the year after Croesus became king; his earlier travels in Egypt and Asia Minor would have brought him to Lydia in the time when Alyattes, rather than Croesus, was king. Plutarch, in his *Life of Solon,* is scarcely more helpful than Herodotus, for he says:

> That Solon should discourse with Croesus, some think not agreeable with chronology, but I cannot reject so famous and well attested a narrative, and what is more so agreeable to Solon's temper, and so worthy of his wisdom and greatness of mind simply because it does not agree with some chronological canons which thousands have endeavored to regulate and yet to this day could never bring their differing opinions to any agreement.

There is no doubt that the reign of Croesus constituted the most prosperous period of Lydian history and that his kingdom fell when it was attacked in 548–547 by the Persians. Croesus' brother-in-law was the king of Media and the ally of Lydia. When the Persians revolted against the Medes and overthrew Astyages, Croesus made war against the Persians and was defeated. Whether, as related by Herodotus, Croesus consulted the Delphic oracle before going to war is not known, but he did send gifts to Delphi; they were on display there in the fifth century. Croesus seems to have allied himself with the Spartans before undertaking the Persian war. The connections between Sparta and Lydia were very close, and we shall have occasion to refer to them in Chapter 13.

Sardes, capital of the Lydian kingdom, was excavated by an American expedition just before World War I, and new excavations have been started since World War II. Sardes was a big town, even in the Lydian period. Its acropolis was higher and larger than the Acropolis at Athens

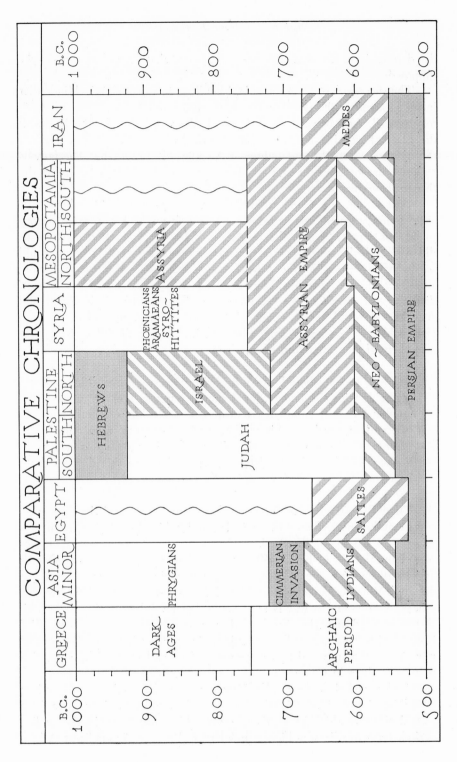

COMPARATIVE CHRONOLOGIES

144

and much more strongly fortified. The Lydian finds of the first expedition were somewhat disappointing: they consisted of a sixth-century temple, some richly furnished graves, and, most important of all, about two score Lydian inscriptions including an Aramaic bilingual and six panels of marble inscribed with what seemed to be poetry. It has not been possible to read the Lydian inscriptions; the meanings of some words have been established, and some idea of the grammar has been formulated. There are obvious similarities in vocabulary and grammar between Lydian and Etruscan (which cannot be read, either), but it is hoped that the new excavations will reveal more about the Lydians and their language.

The Greeks had a high regard for the Lydians. They credited them with the invention of coined money, and there is great likelihood that the Greeks were culturally indebted to the Lydians in several other ways, most particularly in music and poetry. Sardes, in the time of Croesus, may well have been a culture center from which Near Eastern traits were diffused to the Greeks. There are reasons for thinking that the fall of Sardes in 547 shocked the Greeks just as much as the fall of Constantinople to the Turks shocked the Europeans of 1453 A.D.

The first of the great national states to gain its freedom from the Assyrian Empire and the last to fall before the Persians was the Saite Kingdom in Egypt, where the Twenty-Sixth Dynasty reigned for nearly a century and a half. The Saite period is an interesting one in Egypt because of various internal developments, but no less interesting are the contacts which the Saites had with many Greek states. Furthermore, the Saites had intimate connections with the Jews, although these are not so familiar as the relations between the Jews and the Neo-Babylonians.

From the end of the Twentieth Dynasty in 1085 B.C. to the middle of the eighth century, Egypt had been in eclipse; for three long centuries the country had been overrun by foreigners—Libyans from the west and Nubians from the south—and in brief periods of freedom from foreign domination there had been internal disorder as kings in Upper Egypt fought the many princes of the Delta. There is still confusion enough in 750 B.C., when it is possible to see once more the general shape of affairs in Egypt. The south, Upper Egypt, was under the control of Nubian kings whose capital was far up the Nile by the Fourth Cataract at Napata. These negro kings, who had adopted all the trappings of pharaonic Egypt including the hieroglyphic script, reigned in the old Egyptian style and were buried in brick pyramids. The north, Lower Egypt, was the realm of a score of quarreling princes; of these, the rulers of Sais were the most important. Just to add to the general confusion, we might note that the Egyptian chronographers called the Nubian kings who began to reign in Upper Egypt about 742 the Twenty-Fifth Dynasty, while the princes of Sais, Tefnakte and Bocchoris, who reigned from about 726–712, constituted the kings of the Twenty-Fourth Dynasty!

Tefnakte controlled not only Sais but also Memphis, and before the end of his reign he also managed to subject most of the Delta princes to his authority. After a Nubian invasion Tefnakte submitted to the southern rulers, but turned disloyal and was replaced by Bocchoris about 718. Bocchoris was known to the Greeks who were beginning to come to the Delta to trade; in Greek tradition he was remembered as a great and civilized ruler who codified Egyptian law. Nevertheless, Bocchoris came to a bad end: he was burned alive (*c.* 712) by the Nubians who now added the Delta to their kingdom in Upper Egypt.

The possession of the Delta encouraged the Nubians to look toward Palestine where they entered into intrigue with the Philistines and Jews against Assyria. This led to a series of wars against Sargon, Sennacherib, and Esarhaddon in which the Assyrians had rather the best of it. Esarhaddon invaded and annexed the Delta about 671, but the country was not organized as a province; instead, Esarhaddon tried to use the Delta princes as vassals. This policy proved notably unsuccessful because of continued intrigue from the south. Necho, possibly the grandson of Bocchoris, was now the prince of Sais and presumably the chief vassal of Assyria, but he was so untrustworthy that the Assyrians had to carry him off to Nineveh to improve his manners. Later returned to Sais, Necho got involved in a war against Nubia and was killed by the southerners. His son, Psammetichus (Psamtik), then fled to Assyria but was later restored to Sais when Ashurbanipal invaded Egypt and sacked Thebes. Within a year or two, certainly before 660, Psammetichus was well on his way toward independence. Holding the Delta and gaining control of Upper Egypt, he threw off the Assyrian yoke about 655 while Ashurbanipal was busy with the Babylonian revolt.

Psammetichus, who reigned until 610, was the first pharaoh of the Saite or Twenty-Sixth Dynasty. He built up friendships with the Greek states of the Aegean and allied himself with the Lydian king, Gyges. He also began a policy or hiring Greek and Carian mercenaries; these well-disciplined heavy-armed infantrymen came to form the backbone of the Egyptian army. Psammetichus' establishment of a unified government and his introduction of the heavy-armed foot soldiers terminated a century of internal strife in Egypt. The period before Psammetichus had been a heroic age in Egyptian history, an era immortalized in the popular literature of the country as an epoch of chivalry, bravery, and individual combats of great warriors.

The three successors of Psammetichus, who reigned during the next forty years, were the archenemies of Nebuchadnezzar. Necho II (609–593), the assassin of Josiah, vainly tried to aid the Assyrians against the Babylonians but was driven back into Egypt by Nebuchadnezzar, then crown prince. It was also Necho who attempted to build up Egyptian trade with India and Arabia by constructing a canal from the Nile to the Red Sea (finished by the Persians a century later); he also hired Phoenician navigators to attempt the circumnavigation of Africa. Psammetichus II (593–588) was faced with an internal revolt in the course of which the revolutionists withdrew into Nubia. The pursuing loyalist force contained Greek and Carian mercenaries who carved their names on the legs of the Ramessid colossi at Abu Simbel; these graffiti are the earliest Greek inscriptions in Egypt. Apries (588–569) supported the Jews in their last revolt against Nebuchadnezzar. After the capture of Jerusalem and the beginning of the Babylonian Captivity many Jews took refuge in Egypt. Some lived at Daphne in the eastern Delta where a large mercenary garrison was stationed, and it was perhaps at this time that the first Jews began to inhabit the colony at Elephantine in upper Egypt; Aramaic papyri, mainly of the fifth century, have been found at Elephantine which provide considerable information about the life and customs of these exiles.

Apries was deposed by an army revolt in 569 led by the next pharaoh, Amasis (Ahmes). The overthrow of Apries, who was finally put to death in 566, came on the heels of an Egyptian defeat in Cyrene and on the eve of a threatened Babylonian invasion. Amasis, who reigned from 569 to 526, was able to restore order in Egypt, make an alliance with Babylonia, and provide Egypt with its greatest prosperity under the Twenty-Sixth Dynasty. Amasis was a friend and ally of the Samian tyrant, Polycrates, and also of the great Lydian king, Croesus. He is said to have married a Greek woman. His reign saw great changes in the Near East brought about principally by the rise of Persia and the growing strength of the Greek states, Sparta and Athens. By the time Amasis died Media, Lydia, and Babylonia had already been conquered by Persia, and the Persians certainly had Egypt high on their list of unfinished business. When Psammetichus III succeeded Amasis in 526, the Persians attacked. Egypt was added to the Persian Empire in 525 without much difficulty.

In the Saite period there was a definite attempt to revive the glories of ancient Egypt. Old temples were restored, and many new structures were built. The art of the period, while lacking in originality—the whole tendency is an archaizing one—nevertheless displays technical proficiency. An abundance of contracts on papyrus and pottery fragments (*ostraka*), if exhaustively studied, might yield important information about the economic state of the country. Incidentally, these documents are written in the demotic script which was henceforth extensively used for ordinary writing. The growth of a popular literature is another interesting aspect of the period; older tales long transmitted orally were committed to writing, and new stories also made their appearance.

Greek contacts with Egypt in the time of the Saites also deserve special attention. We have seen that the Greeks were already coming to the Delta in the time of Bocchoris. By the seventh century mercenaries and traders were settled at various points in the Delta. Amasis, however, decided to concentrate the Greek traders in a single trading colony, Naucratis, in the western Delta. The site of Naucratis was discovered and excavated in the latter part of the nineteenth century; although the high water level in the Delta hindered excavation, a number of interesting finds were made. The earliest Greek pottery represented was mostly from towns on the east Aegean islands or the west coast of Asia Minor, and it seems likely that the Greeks of Miletus were the first to trade at Naucratis. Just after his accession Amasis ordered all Greeks to settle at Naucratis. From the town where the various states had warehouses the traders would set out across the countryside by boat during the inundation season to trade with villagers immobilized by the flood. Naucratis was a kind of Shanghai or Hong Kong where the foreigners mingled with the natives to some extent but preserved their national identities. Some of the important states represented at Naucratis had their own temples: there were the temples of the Milesian Apollo, Samian Hera, and Aeginetan Zeus. There was also the Hellenion, a temple constructed jointly by Greeks of Ionian, Dorian, and Aeolian cities. Much inscribed Greek pottery was found; the vases had been dedicated in the temples by Greek travelers to Naucratis during the centuries, and among the familiar names on the pottery were Herodotus, possibly the historian, Rhoecus and Theodorus, famous early sculptors, and Phanes, a disloyal mercenary who led the Persians into Egypt in 525. There was also a scarab factory which made tourist souvenirs.

The Egyptians did not forget the Saite Age for a long time. It had been a period of independence and prosperity which they treasured in memory. Dissatisfied with Persian rule and longing to renew their profitable contacts with the Greeks, they rose in revolt against the Persians several times in the fifth and fourth centuries B.C. As a result there were actually a few fairly long periods during this time when Egypt was free of Persia and ruled once more by native kings. This, too, is an epoch of Egyptian history which needs further study.

Chapter 11

THE PERSIAN EMPIRE

D URING A PERIOD of nearly two centuries which began before 500 B.C. and ended after 350, the ancient civilized world was dominated by a single major power, that of Achaemenid Persia. The Persian Empire was the most extensive political unit the world had ever seen. The borders of the Assyrian Empire had been Elam and the Taurus range, and Egypt had never been included among the possessions of Assyria except in the hopes of the royal propagandists at Nineveh, but the territory of the Persians, stretching from India to the Aegean and enveloping Egypt as well, was many times larger than the realm of Assyria. Westward of the Persian domain the area which might be called civilized was inconsiderable: it consisted of parts of Greece and a narrow ribbon of coast around the Mediterranean where the Greek and Phoenician colonies were located. Carthage, the Phoenician power in the west, was frequently a Persian ally, while the mainland Greeks, divided and weak, were independent of Persia largely because the Persians had better things to do than subject the obstreperous Hellenes. The Greeks were justly proud of their victories at Marathon, Salamis, and Plataea, but they continued to fear the might of Persia, and in their soberer moments they were never quite sure that their earlier successes could be duplicated if the Persians chose to attack in earnest.

Not only did the Persians have a great empire, but also they had a virtual monopoly of ancient civilization. The Greeks, even in the fifth century B.C., possessed only a smattering of the accumulated knowledge stored up in the lands of the Persian Empire, for it was not until Alexander conquered the Persians that the full impact of Oriental civilization was felt by the Greeks. Without minimizing the impact of the Greek achievement and its vast importance for the subsequent history of Europe, it is reasonable to insist that the role of the Persians was also a significant one. Looking at the history of civilization as a whole, the possibility suggests itself that the Greeks and Persians might be viewed as one group rather than two. They had much in common, a fact which even the Greeks admitted. Both Greeks and Persians were Indo-Europeans: this meant that they had the same ultimate origin, that not only were their languages similar, but also their political and social organization stemmed from a common source; moreover, they had once worshipped the same gods. Both Greeks and Persians had come from the outside into the orbit of the civilized world, the Greeks in the second millennium and the Persians early in the first; both had come into contact with an advanced civilization, that of the Near East. The Persians rapidly adopted and absorbed this civilization, the Greeks not so rapidly because they were more remote from its center. Because they lived in the Near East the Persians were overwhelmed by its culture; the Greeks, farther away and in a different environment, had an opportunity to develop a distinctive culture since they could take what they wanted from the Near East and adapt parts of its culture to their own peculiar needs. Furthermore, while the Persians had their first and foremost contacts with Mesopotamian civilization, the Greeks were most affected by contact with Egypt and got their knowledge of Mesopotamian culture secondhand in Asia Minor, Syria, and Palestine. But we may well ask what might have happened if the geographical position of the Greeks and Persians had been reversed. Would the Greeks have become the powerful, sophisticated rulers of an Oriental empire and the Persians our cultural ancestors in Europe? Were the physical environment and the geographical position of these two groups of Indo-Europeans more important in determining the outcome than the people themselves?

In the early sixth century B.C. the Persians were a scattered and disunited group living in southwestern Iran as vassals of the Medes, but their fortunes began to mend about 559 when Cyrus, an able and ambitious prince, ascended the throne of Anshan as leader of the tribe called the Pasargadae. It is possible that this Cyrus, who founded the Persian Empire and whom we call the Great, was indeed the son of a Persian prince and a Median princess as Herodotus relates, although the details of the legend as he gives them cannot be accepted as historical fact. At any rate, Cyrus managed to unite all the scattered Persian tribes, and then, backed by Nabonidus of Babylonia, he began a revolt against the Medes which culminated with the capture of Ecbatana and the overthrow of the Median kingdom about 550 B.C.

This Persian victory set in motion a chain of events which made it possible for Cyrus to acquire territory in addition to Persia and Media. Croesus, the Lydian king, seeking either to avenge his brother-in-law the king of Media or to profit from the fall of the Medes, soon crossed the Halys River into Median territory. After an indecisive campaign, Croesus returned to Lydia for the winter, but early the following year Cyrus invaded Lydia in a surprise attack and laid siege to Sardes. The town was soon captured and Croesus killed (547); Lydia with its Greek dependencies was then joined to the Persian Empire. The next few years were devoted to campaigns in the east which carried the Persians almost to the borders of India and into Bactria, north of the Hindu Kush, but this was merely an interlude, since the rise of Persia had upset the balance of power in the Near East and an early trial of strength with Babylonia was inevitable. Nabonidus could no more afford to have a strong Persia than a strong Media as his neighbor; furthermore, he had been an ally and friend of Croesus, though the most pressing reason for Babylonian hostility may well have been that the rise of Persia had cut the lines of trade between Babylon and markets to the east. The brief contest which began in 539 was soon over; dissatisfied Babylonian priests betrayed their country to Cyrus, and not only was Nabonidus deposed but Cyrus also annexed Babylonia and its possessions in Syria, Phoenicia, and Palestine. Thus, of the four great kingdoms which had risen out of the fall of Assyria, only Egypt remained. Cyrus might have attacked Egypt, too, but instead he turned his attention once more to the east where he died campaigning in Bactria in 530.

Cyrus' successor was his son, Cambyses, who had served for eight years as governor of Babylon. In 526 when the death of the Pharaoh Amasis seemed to create a situation favorable to invasion, Cambyses launched a successful attack upon Egypt and occupied the country (525). Additional plans for the conquest of Ethiopia and Carthage had to be abandoned as impractical, but Egypt was securely held by Persian garrisons, and the Greeks of Cyrene were accepted as Persian vassals.

While Cambyses was still in Egypt reports came to him that his brother had raised the standard of revolt at home. Cambyses knew this could not be entirely correct since he had secretly killed his brother before setting out on the Egyptian campaign. The revolt, however, was a fact, but Cambyses died before he could deal with it. The circumstances and place of his death are uncertain; he may have committed suicide, or he may have met with an accident, and we do not know whether he died in Syria or in Media.

The causes of the revolt seem to have been both political and religious. Cambyses was not a popular ruler; his assassination of his brother suggests that he feared palace intrigue or even the rise of a political faction hostile to his reign. An additional complication was provided by the religious struggle then taking place in Persia, a contest between the converts to the new Zoroastrian religion and the adherents of the older worship headed by a priestly caste called the Magi. The Persian royal house had embraced Zoroastrianism, and Cambyses may have become a fanatic. The upshot of the matter was that the Magi took advantage of Cambyses' long absence to revolt and put an impostor on the throne who masqueraded as the brother

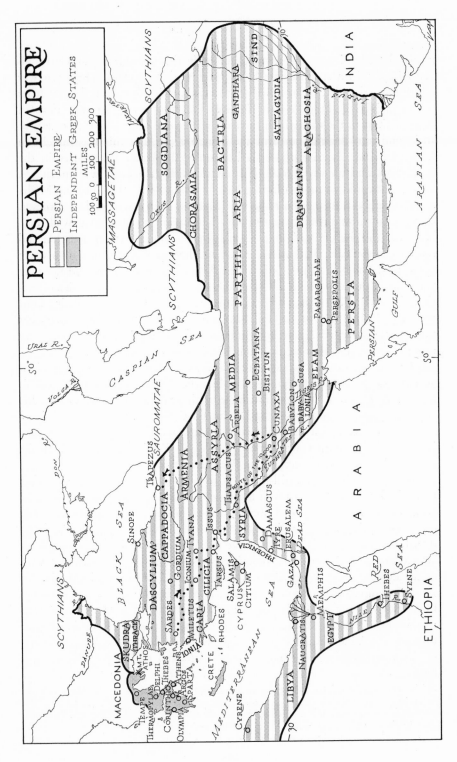

PERSIAN EMPIRE

PERSIAN EMPIRE
INDEPENDENT GREEK STATES

MILES
100 50 0 100 200 300

152

of Cambyses. The deception was successful until the army returned from Egypt to disclose the truth. The usurper was then overthrown at the end of 522, and the Persian nobles chose Darius, a distant cousin of Cambyses, as their king.

Darius the Great, the real organizer of the Persian Empire and the founder of a dynasty which ruled until 330 B.C., was, like Cyrus and Cambyses, the descendant of a Persian prince named Achaemenes who had flourished in the early part of the seventh century B.C.; this explains why we refer to all these Persian kings as Achaemenids. Darius was to enjoy a long reign from the end of 522 until the autumn of 486. After putting down a dozen revolts which, encouraged by the magian conspiracy, had broken out in Media, Babylon, Armenia, and elsewhere, Darius devoted his attention to consolidating the empire.[1] One of his problems was to establish the logical boundaries of his realm, to discover the limits to which the Persians might expand. A series of campaigns finally resulted in the conquest of Sind, the upper Indus Valley, while in the west Darius crossed from Asia Minor into Europe (513 B.C.) where he acquired a large part of what is now European Turkey and a partial protectorate over Macedonia. An expedition against the Scythian nomads north of the Danube was a dismal failure; the equally unsuccessful dealings of Darius with the mainland Greeks will be discussed in a later chapter. Nevertheless, Darius did come to appreciate the importance of using natural defensible frontiers, and by trial and error he found how much territory the Persians could garrison and hold. During his reign the empire attained its maximum extent.

Other achievements of Darius, in addition to the expansion and organization of the empire, included the promulgation of a law code, the establishment of uniform weights and measures, the issuance of an imperial currency, and the construction of a number of important buildings and other public works. The law code, which has not been found, seems to have been called the Ordinance of Good Regulations; it is believed to have followed the time-honored pattern of Mesopotamian codes of which the Code of Hammurabi is a good example. The obvious economic advantages of providing the empire with uniform weights, measures, and currency were perfectly clear to Darius, for he seems to have had the economic welfare of the empire constantly in mind. Three examples suggest his acumen. First, he finished the canal (begun by Necho) which connected the Nile with the Red Sea. An inscription found along the route of the canal celebrates the completion of the work, and Darius adds the meaningful words: ". . . after this canal was dug . . . as I had ordered . . . ships went from

---

[1] The official account of his rise to power and his victories over the rebels is to be found in the great Bisitun inscription which included identical texts in Persian, Elamite, and Babylonian and provided, through its decipherment in 1846 A.D., the key for the modern knowledge of the cuneiform scripts. See below, p. 157.

Egypt . . . to Persia as was my desire." A second project, less successful, was the expedition against the Scythians. During the reign of Cyrus the Persians had acquired territory in Bactria (Turkestan) where the trade routes from China terminated, but westward from Bactria there was a choice of routes, either through Iran to the Near East or a northern route around the Caspian and Black seas and up the Danube into central Europe. The northern route was in the hands of the Scythians, nomadic tribes spread all the way from Bactria through southern Russia to Rumania. The Persians had fought the Scythians in Bactria, and apparently Darius had thought that he could destroy the Scythians and gain control of the northern route by crossing the Danube and driving all the way eastward to the Persian province of Bactria. On paper, or perhaps we should say on leather, clay, or papyrus, this was a good idea, but if Darius had had any knowledge of the distance he must traverse or the terrain he would encounter, he would never have embarked on the Scythian expedition. Some people have thought that his objective was merely south Russia and the control of the Pontic grain trade. This seems unlikely, however, since the aim of such a maneuver would have been to hurt the mainland Greeks, something that would have seemed more desirable to Darius about fifteen years later after the Ionian Revolt of 499. It is more credible to suppose that he wished to get control of the routes by which gold was being brought out of the Urals. A third project of Darius was the exploration of a sea route from India to Egypt. A fleet was constructed on the Indus which sailed down the river to the Indian Ocean and two and a half years later arrived in Egypt. A noteworthy feature of this expedition was that the admiral of the fleet was one of the Greek subjects of Darius, Scylax of Caryanda in Asia Minor.

In the reign of Darius there was much building under royal auspices in Babylon, Susa, and Ecbatana, but the major project was the construction of a new imperial capital at Persepolis in Persia itself. Under Darius and his successors, Xerxes and Artaxerxes, Persepolis became a real show place with its complex of palaces and other buildings situated on a great terrace built on the spur of a hill. The structures either completed or begun by Darius included a palace, a council hall, a treasury, and a building called the Apadana, or audience hall. Because of an abundance of stone the architects at Persepolis used the column and lintel technique; the great halls contained literally a forest of tall slender columns topped by sculptured capitals in the form of lions and horses. Enamelled bricks in bright colors and much handsome relief sculpture were used for decoration. The Apadana was approached by a great double staircase embellished with reliefs which portrayed Persian nobles, soldiers, and subjects. Today the ruins of Persepolis are impressive enough; in the fifth century B.C. these buildings must have been magnificent. The so-called Persepolis treasury tablets, cuneiform texts in the Elamite language, record the rations and pay of the workers at Persepolis in the period 492–460 B.C. From these texts and from Persian inscriptions we learn that the splendor of Persepolis was created by Egyptian, Babylonian, Syrian, Greek, and Carian artisans, skilled workers in stone, wood, and metal. There is no mention of Persian artisans, and one should, therefore, be cautious about referring to Persepolis as an example of "Persian art."

The Persians were the cultural heirs of Babylonia and Assyria. They adapted the Assyrian imperial system to their own needs; they borrowed and adapted the cuneiform system of writing; and in many other respects their civilization was "Oriental." On the other hand, the Persians did make contributions to civilization, and the mingling of new and old which became typical of Persian culture can be observed in Persian government, religion, and writing.

The Persian monarch, who bore the title of Great King, ruled by divine right. At first advised by the nobles, he later became remote even from them, surrounded and enveloped by elaborate court ritual. The empire was divided into about thirty provinces or satrapies. Each province was administered by a governor called the satrap; princes of the royal house and prominent nobles were appointed satraps. Certain areas were administered by native rulers; this was a convenient arrangement where there was no problem of defense or danger of revolt and where subject minorities could be more easily handled through the local authorities who would be responsible to the satrap. Key points, areas, and cities were garrisoned by Persian troops, and a good system of roads provided rapid communication and easy access to the remote parts of the empire. The army was well organized and versatile with a nucleus of Persian troops supplemented with mercenary soldiers and contingents levied from the subject peoples. The weaknesses of the empire were its huge extent, the numerical inferiority of the Persians themselves, and the mixed character of the subject population. The Persians may have been outnumbered by their subjects as much as sixty to one, and there was nothing to hold the empire together except the loyalty, often rather dubious, of the subject people to the Great King. For some of the subjects membership in the empire offered advantages, but others were restless and dissatisfied. The Phoenicians were happy enough because the empire brought them prosperity and its strength aided them in their rivalry with the Greeks. The Egyptians and the Asiatic Greeks, however, resented Persian rule and did not benefit greatly from Persian economic policies. The Persians possessed all the territory they could possibly hold by the time of Darius; in matters of offense and defense they encountered problems of manpower: the Persians were too few, there was a limit to the number of mercenaries who could be hired, and it was not safe to arm or mobilize large contingents of subjects from any one area. It was really a tribute to the ability of the Persians as rulers that their empire survived as long as it did.

By ancient standards the Persian Empire was wealthy. Revenues in gold, silver, and commodities provided an income perhaps fifty per cent greater than that of the Roman Republic in the time of Cicero. The Persian budget was unbalanced in a comfortable sort of way: income always exceeded expenditures. Year after year ingots of gold and silver continued to accumulate in the Persian treasuries at Persepolis and Pasargadae. Much of this wealth in the precious metals came from outside the empire through trade. The Mediterranean area, Greece especially, suffered from an unfavorable balance of trade with the subjects of the Great King. As a result Greece was progressively drained of her supplies of gold and silver, a fact which produced economic stresses and strains in Greece by the fourth century B.C.

One of the assets of the Persians in creating and holding their empire was their policy of religious toleration. They had found it advantageous to make friends with religious factions; the alliance of Cyrus and the Babylonian priests, for example, had been useful in bringing about the defeat of Nabonidus. The Persians also won friends by restoring the Jews to Jerusalem and allowing them to have a semi-independent local theocracy. The key to this tolerance on the part of the Persians is to be found in their adherence to the new (and exclusively Iranian) religion of Zoroastrianism.

The old Persian religion had been a highly polytheistic, animistic kind of worship largely concerned with natural phenomena. Mithra, the sun-god, and Anahita, a mother goddess, had been important deities. No temples were constructed; much of the ritual centered on fire altars built in the open. Even by the standards of antiquity, early Persian religion seems to have been riddled with crude superstition.

About 550 B.C. a great preacher appeared in Iran. This was Zoroaster, an uncompromising critic of the older religion who offered a new faith far more reasonable and compelling than the ancestral beliefs of the Persians. Despite the bitter opposition of the Magi, Zoroaster made many converts, particularly among the nobility; it was especially important for the future that the father of Darius and Darius himself espoused the new religion.

It is difficult to ascertain the truth about Zoroaster and his original teachings. The Zoroastrian writings which have survived belong to a later age and the theology which they contain has been contaminated by accretions from other religions and by additions made by Zoroaster's followers. Many attempts, none of them successful, have been made to separate the primitive from the later Zoroastrian beliefs, but this may never be accomplished.

One may guess that Zoroaster was born about 580 B.C. He began his preaching, according to tradition, when he was about thirty years old after having spent ten years in meditation. This tradition is worthless; in the Near East no prophet was considered worth his salt until he was thirty and had spent some time meditating in a solitary place. Another tradition, probably equally worthless, was that Zoroaster suffered martyrdom. It would have been exceedingly unmystical of him to have died of old age.

Despite the uncertainties which plague the subject, the general outlines are clear. Zoroastrianism was a highly ethical, essentially monotheistic religion. It centered on the adoration of Ahuramazda, the god of light, who also symbolized truth and goodness. Zoroaster seems to have stressed purity: "good thoughts of the mind, good deeds of the hand, and good words of the tongue." The worship of idols was forbidden, though Ahuramazda was often represented on Persian monuments as a tiny winged figure with the head and body of a man. Ahuramazda was a creator god who also bestowed the power to rule upon the king of his choice. There was more than an element of dualism in Zoroastrian thought. The enemy of Ahuramazda was a demon or devil named Ahriman, and the forces of the contestants were in perpetual conflict. The opposites represented by Ahuramazda and Ahriman were frequently contrasted: the truth and the lie, good and evil, light and darkness, living and not-living. It is possible that Zoroaster included among his aphorisms a Golden Rule: "That nature alone is good which shall not do unto another whatever is not good for itself."

The conversion of Darius and the adoption of Zoroastrianism as the religion of the royal family are illustrated by such phrases as, "Thus saith Darius . . . may Ahuramazda protect the country from a hostile army, from famine, from the lie." On the other hand, the majority of the followers of Zoroaster did not attempt to proselytize or to make Zoroastrianism the official religion of the Persian Empire. Perhaps the case of Cambyses was an exception, but on the whole the Persian government was unusually tolerant. For political reasons, within Persia itself even Darius did not deny the existence of other deities besides Ahuramazda; he speaks of the "other gods" of the royal house, and his later successors departed more and more from the monotheism of Zoroaster.

The Persians made no more attempt to spread the use of their language than they did to popularize Zoroastrianism. Persian was not a familiar language in the Near East, and the mixed character of the subject population made it expedient to employ a variety of languages for communication. From the frequency of trilingual inscriptions in Persia itself, one might suspect that Persian, Elamite, and Babylonian were the "official" languages of the empire; these were the three employed for the great Bisitun inscription of Darius, but an Aramaic copy of this same text was found on papyrus in Egypt, and there can be little doubt that Aramaic was used or understood by the majority of people in the western half of the empire all the way from Babylonia to Egypt.

The Persians might have used the cuneiform script for writing Persian as many of their predecessors had done, but instead they devised an essentially syllabic script of forty-three *cuneiform-shaped* characters; this was a purely arbitrary system of writing which did not use the characters of the cuneiform script but merely copied their general form. The efficient thing would have been to adapt the Semitic alphabet for writing Persian, but this was not what the Persians had in mind. They wanted a handsome script for display inscriptions which would resemble Assyrian and Babylonian; something that would look respectable and important. The script was never used except for official documents on metal and stone, and it is doubtful whether many persons, except the Persian scribes, could or did read it.

The rapid rise of the Persian Empire was due to two things: (1) the aggressive nationalism of the Persians, and (2) the exhaustion of the peoples of the civilized Near East. Nowhere did Cyrus, Cambyses, or Darius have to face the determined opposition of men who were fighting for their homes—except in Greece and Scythia where the Persians failed. The independent spirit of the Near East had been broken by generations of imperialism. The Persians had only to defeat ruling minorities whose armies consisted largely of mercenaries—professionals who hastened to take service with the enemy when they could not defeat him. If the Persians could conquer the Near East, so could the Greeks. And ultimately they did.

EPILOGUE TO PART ONE

Between 3000 and 500 B.C. civilization had developed from simple beginnings in the great river valleys of the Near East to a complex structure that sprawled over a very considerable geographic area. In 500 B.C. cultural unity did not exist in every detail throughout this area, for there were many obvious regional differences in culture, but it is just as important to be aware of the cultural features which the individual areas had in common as it is to note the variations. There was an appreciable community of culture traits; we can speak of *the* civilization of the Ancient Near East.

While many of the similarities and even identities in material culture and the realm of ideas that might be found from region to region in the Near East were the result of borrowing and exchange, this explanation does not fully account for the remarkable uniformity which prevailed in social thought. In the literature of the Egyptians, Sumerians, Babylonians, Assyrians, Hebrews, and Persians one finds a unanimity of opinion with respect to what was considered proper and improper social behavior. Most of these precepts of conduct were identical with those to which we subscribe today. This is partly because society in the modern Western world derives its moral code from the Old Testament, and partly because these precepts are based on good common sense and would be practical for any society.

The didactic writers of the Ancient Near East urge their fellow men to avoid boasting, lying, drunkenness, and overbearing manners, to keep from injuring others by either word or deed. Humility, guarded speech, truthfulness, temperance, moderation, self-control, and kindness are virtues to be cultivated. Men are told to honor their parents, to be kind to their social inferiors, and to succor the weak and unfortunate. Murder, robbery, sharp dealing, and sexual abnormality are condemned in all societies. Very early in Egypt and Babylonia, the idea developed that the gods will punish the sinner—either in this life (according to the Babylonians) or in the next (according to the Egyptians). Everywhere the virtuous woman, the good wife, is extolled.

Among the common people, there was a universal feeling that hard work was a virtue and idleness a vice. Honest toil, though unproductive of great wealth, was preferable to ill-gotten gains. On the other hand, we often find writings that express a deep pessimism regarding the uncertainties of life. Wealth may easily be lost, life and work are futile, and so on. More than once the cynic advises his contemporaries "to eat, drink, and be merry."

Few questioned the value of education as a means of gaining worldly success. An Egyptian teacher said: "Be not a foolish man, that hath no instruction." The point was a good one, for an educated man who came from the lower classes might hope to better himself by becoming a scribe, a priest, or an official. Some even valued knowledge for its own sake—like Ashurbanipal, who had "a large ear for learning."

There was a morality for the royalty and the nobility, too. Their responsibilities to society lay in providing justice and good government. Often, a ruler left behind a testament in which he listed his accomplishments—his upright administration of justice, his piety, his solicitude for the common people and for economic welfare. In Egypt and Persia there were also didactic writings on the duties of the rulers. Frequently, there is evidence that the nobles possessed a social conscience. In an inscription erected by a nomarch of the Old Kingdom in Egypt we find:

"I gave bread to the hungry. . . . I clothed him who was naked. . . . I never oppressed one in possession of his property. . . . I was a benefactor to the nome."

Philosophy was a Greek "invention," but the peoples of the Ancient Near East had long before constructed organized theologies and instituted cosmological speculation. In fact, the earliest Greek philosophers began where the Oriental theologians left off. Some of the best known Near Eastern explanations of the origin of man and the universe may be summarized as follows:

In both Babylonia and Egypt, men believed that originally there was no dry land—only water. According to one Babylonian myth, it was the gods who first created dry land and brought man into existence. In another myth from Babylonia, the primeval waters were envisioned as the dwelling place of the dragon Tiamat (chaos). Tiamat was slain in a battle with the gods. Her body was cut in half; one half became the earth which floated upon the waters beneath it, and the other half was elevated to form the sky and support the waters above which occasionally seeped through in the form of rain. After heaven and earth were thus created, plants and animals were devised by the gods. In Egyptian mythology, the grandchildren of the sun-god, Keb and Nut, formed the earth and the sky. Nut rested both hands and feet upon the earth (her brother, Keb) and her torso constituted the heavens. A similar Egyptian belief postulated the sky as a cow-goddess whose hooves rested upon the earth.

The Babylonians believed man to be half animal and half divine; his intelligence differentiated him from the animals, and his inability to attain immortality separated him from the gods. Once, they said, man lived like the animals, but the gods taught him how to domesticate plants and animals, and thus man was able to become civilized.

By 500 B.C. civilization was no longer confined to the Near East but had spread beyond its boundaries. The European lands bordering the Mediterranean were especially affected by this diffusion, and in Greece and Italy whole new chapters in the history of civilization were now to be written. The Greeks combined with their own culture the traits which they borrowed from the Near East, and they made additions and elaborations that produced the great Hellenic civilization from which the Romans and later European peoples borrowed in turn.

For the history of Western civilization, however, the most important single fact disclosed by the last fifty years of archaeological and linguistic research is that we can no longer treat separately Greek and Near Eastern civilizations. They do not belong in separate compartments.

PART TWO

Greece

From a replica, courtesy of William A. McDonald

Courtesy of the British School of Archaeology in Egypt

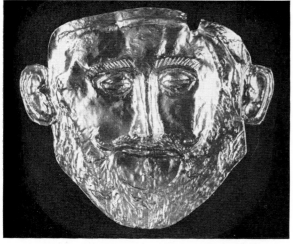

MYCENAEAN FACE MASK

PHILISTINE POTTERY COFFIN

GRAVE STELE FROM MYCENAE

From Mycenae, *by Heinrich Schliemann*

Courtesy of the Staatliche Museen zu Berlin

SYRO-HITTITE ORTHOSTATS

EGYPTIAN—FOURTH DYNASTY   KOUROS   KORE

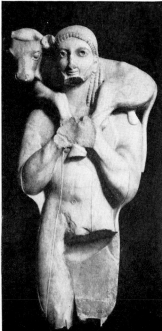

MOSCHOPHORUS FROM ATHENS   SYRO-HITTITE   SEATED FIGURE

Chapter 12

MINOANS AND MYCENAEANS

T HE FALL of the Assyrian Empire was symbolic. It marked the end of a chapter in the history of civilization, for the Assyrian was the last of the essentially Oriental empires of the pre-Christian era. The period of the Four Kingdoms was only an interlude between the fall of Assyria and the rise of Persia, and both the Persian Empire and that of Alexander the Great which succeeded it were to be created and ruled by Indo-Europeans. Moreover, it was not only political, but also cultural, leadership that passed from the hands of the ancient Oriental peoples to their Persian and Greek conquerors.

In 600 B.C. cultural progress in the Ancient Near East was beginning to slacken its pace. One obstacle to further advance was the dead weight of tradition, of reverence for past glories. There was a tendency to look backward to the "good old days," and it is highly significant that archaism was most clearly manifested in Egypt and Babylonia, the oldest centers of culture; the Saites and Neo-Babylonians were almost pathetic in their efforts to recreate the glories of the past, especially by reviving the old forms of art and literature. Perhaps archaism, however, was only a symptom of creative bankruptcy, and the real cause was rooted in the senility of the old theocratic system in all its aspects: religious, political, economic, and social. Theocracy had not been well adapted for conditions outside the great river valleys, and by 600 B.C. it may have lost much of its reality even in Egypt and Babylonia. Certainly, its ancient power to stimulate achievement had vanished.

But the culture of the Egyptians, Babylonians, and their neighbors did not become extinct. It was adopted and preserved by the Persians in their empire in the Near East, and it passed by a process of diffusion into an adjacent region to the west, a region which we may call the eastern Mediterranean, where it provided basic ingredients for a new civilization,

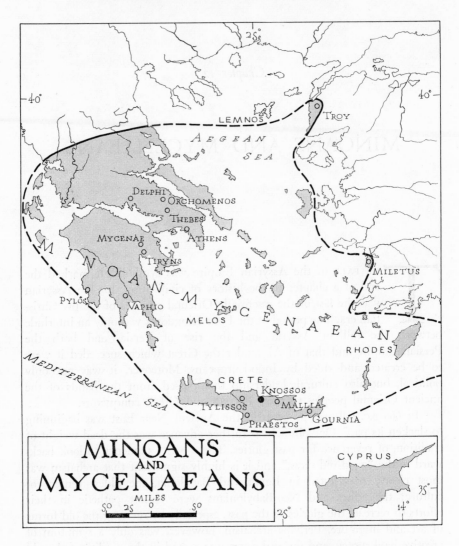

MINOANS
AND
MYCENAEANS

MILES

CYPRUS

that of the Greeks. The Persians and Greeks entered the ancient civilized world as barbarians. Culturally youthful and vigorous, these Indo-Europeans were able to conquer their elders of the Near East while at the same time the novelty of the ancient civilization with which they came in contact had a power to stimulate them, a force that was no longer felt by its creators. Where the potential creativity of the Persians was blunted by a contact with the Near East that was too intimate and prolonged, the Greeks were situated at a convenient distance from the center of civilization. They could pick and choose, adapt and elaborate, and so had an ideal opportunity to build a new civilization. It was also to the advantage of the Greeks that the tide of diffusion from the Near East intermittently advanced and receded; this gave them a chance to absorb and consolidate this culture, and thus they were able to avoid the inundation suffered by the Persians.

The eastern Mediterranean, where the Greeks came to be concentrated, may be defined as a region including Crete, Cyprus, the islands of the Aegean Sea, the western coast of Asia Minor, and the southeastern portion of Europe (Greece, Macedonia, and Thrace). The Greeks were invaders, rather than aborigines, of this area. They did not make their appearance in any part of it before 2500 B.C. and certainly did not arrive in Greece itself until 1800 B.C. But the eastern Mediterranean had been occupied by man many centuries before the Greeks invaded it. Moreover, prior to the arrival of the Greeks, their predecessors had created a Bronze Age civilization which had its center on the island of Crete.

The pre-Greek phase of civilization in the eastern Mediterranean provides a cultural and historical link connecting the Greeks with the peoples of the Near East. The foundations of the early Cretan civilization were derived from the Near East. As a matter of fact, Crete became almost as much a part of the ancient Oriental cultural province in the second millennium B.C. as did any one of the intermediate and peripheral areas regarded as primarily Near Eastern: Syria, Palestine, or central Asia Minor under the Hittites. The Cretan was the first Oriental realm to be conquered by the Greeks, but their victory did not come until they had learned from Crete their first lessons in civilization.

The first inhabitants of Crete seem to have been migrants from Asia Minor. Skeletal remains indicate that most of the prehistoric Cretans were representative of the Mediterranean branch of the white race—short, slender, dark people of the same physical type found in North Africa, Spain, Italy, and Greece. Crete was first occupied in the Neolithic Age, certainly as early as 4000 B.C. In the centuries that followed, other Aegean islands were settled and Greece as well, but Crete was closest to the Near East and therefore had the earliest opportunities for cultural advance. The Bronze Age began in Crete about 2500 B.C.; between 2000 and 1400 B.C. Crete was the cultural center of the eastern Mediterranean, and from it civilization was diffused to Greece, the Aegean islands, and even to the western Mediterranean.

Despite the importance of the Cretans in the second millennium B.C.—as diplomatic and commercial associates of the Levant and Egypt and as teachers of the Greeks—they and their civilization were virtually forgotten except for a few vague memories well hidden in classical Greek legend and myth. It is only within the last one hundred years that the prehistory of the eastern Mediterranean has been detected and reconstructed by archaeological and linguistic research. Some of the most important discoveries are of very recent date, and the whole subject illustrates in a highly dramatic way that the study of "ancient history" is anything but static.

A century ago it was commonly thought that the history of Greece before the date of the First Olympiad (776 B.C.) could never be freed from the realm of legend. The events connected with the siege of Troy, dated by tradition about 1200 B.C. and commemorated in the Homeric poems, were regarded as unhistorical, and the culture described in the *Iliad* and the *Odyssey* was so unlike classical civilization that it was suspected of being a product of Homer's imagination. As for legendary events of the period before the Trojan War, these were dismissed as being even more fanciful.

At least one man, however, did not share the skepticism of his age. This was the fabulous Heinrich Schliemann, amateur archaeologist and Homeric fundamentalist, who believed in the literal truth of the Homeric story. Beginning in 1870, Schliemann dug in the great mound of Hissarlik, the citadel of the classical town of New Ilium in northwestern Asia Minor. This was the site which the ancients had identified as Troy, and in the lower strata at Hissarlik Schliemann found evidence of a preclassical civilization which he insisted was Homeric. Encouraged by his discoveries at "Troy," Schliemann turned his attention to the site of Mycenae in Greece, the legendary home of Agamemnon. At Mycenae and other sites in Greece there was soon revealed a civilization more spectacular and seemingly more "Homeric" than anything Schliemann had yet found at Troy. Heinrich Schliemann had a real flair for publicity. His finds were soon known far and wide, and his own faith and enthusiasm were so contagious that both public and scholarly opinion shifted from disbelief to an acceptance of the historicity of the Homeric legends. Other archaeologists, more careful and more objective than Schliemann, now joined in the search for prehistoric Greek remains and began to gather materials for a new chapter in ancient history.

As credence in the Homeric legends increased, the pre-Homeric traditions were also brought under scrutiny. Many of the older legends and myths seemed to center in the island of Crete and especially at Cretan Cnossus where the hero Theseus had killed the Minotaur in the Labyrinth of King Minos. The site of Cnossus was known. Schliemann had considered digging there, but he was dissuaded by political disturbances in Crete. It was not until the close of the nineteenth century, just a few years after Schliemann died, that Sir Arthur Evans began the work at Cnossus which was to continue for several decades. Almost immediately the efforts of Evans were rewarded by the discovery of a civilization different and older than that of Troy and Mycenae. Since Cnossus was the legendary capital of King Minos, the new culture unearthed there was called Minoan.

At Cnossus Sir Arthur Evans found a site which had been occupied for a long time. A number of layers or strata of occupation could be distinguished: at the bottom was a neolithic stratum twenty-three to twenty-six feet in depth characterized by a rather crude unpainted pottery, some of which was decorated by incision; on top of the neolithic stratum rested nineteen more feet of debris in which three layers could be distinguished, and these in turn could be subdivided into eight substrata easily identified by pottery which changed either in shape or decoration from level to level. The first main stratum on top of the neolithic layer Evans called Early Minoan; the second, Middle Minoan; and the third, Late Minoan. The Early Minoan had three substrata as did Middle Minoan, while Late Minoan at Cnossus had only two. These were then called Early Minoan I, II, and III, Middle Minoan I, II, and III, and Late Minoan I and II. In the Middle Minoan II layer, for example, the characteristic pottery was a polychrome painted ware with highly conventionalized floral motifs painted on clay of eggshell thinness; since this pottery had already been found in a cave at a place in Crete called Kamares, the pottery was known as Kamares ware. This meant, of course, that the use of the Kamares cave was contemporary with the occupation of the Middle Minoan II layer at Cnossus. Other layers at Cnossus could be similarly associated with finds elsewhere in Crete. This provided archaeologists with what is known as a *relative chronology*.

A relative chronology which established a cultural sequence and aided in tying together scattered finds at other sites was extremely useful, but an *absolute chronology* was also needed. This would provide dates—so many years B.C.—for the various strata. The absolute chronology for the Minoan strata was made possible by (1) the discovery of datable foreign objects in certain layers and (2) the finding of Minoan objects in datable contexts outside of Crete. Kamares pottery, for example, was found in Egypt on a site which could be dated in the Middle Kingdom; moreover, a Babylonian cylinder seal of the Amorite period was found in a Middle Minoan layer at Cnossus. To cite another example, in Egyptian tombs of the Eighteenth Dynasty there were discovered paintings of men in Minoan costume carrying pottery vessels characteristic of Late Minoan I. Or again, the scarab of one of the Hyksos kings turned up in the Middle Minoan III layer in Cnossus. As a result of these and other correlations, it is now possible to estimate that Early Minoan endured from perhaps 3000–2100; Middle Minoan, 2100–1600; Late Minoan I, 1600–1450; Late Minoan II, 1450–1400.

The stratification at Cnossus and the related material from other sites demonstrated that Minoan civilization had begun a spectacular growth in the Middle Minoan I which reached its highest point in Middle Minoan III and Late Minoan I. The first palaces appeared at the beginning of Middle Minoan not only at Cnossus but also at other sites in north and south central Crete. Caves began to be used as sanctuaries, and there was evidence of the beginnings of a pictographic script. By Middle Minoan III, great palaces were being constructed; writing had advanced to a syllabic stage. At the end of Late Minoan I, however, destruction was evident at many sites, while Cnossus seemed to emerge the victor over what might have

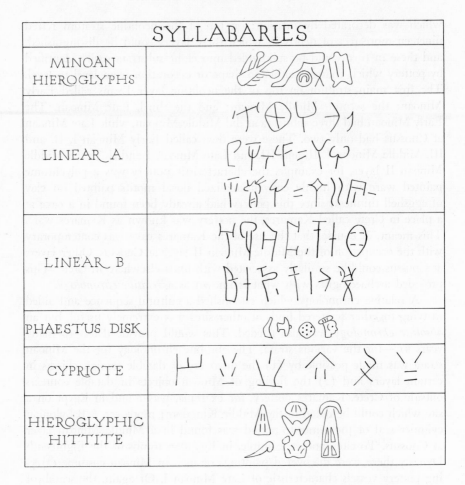

SYLLABARIES	
MINOAN HIEROGLYPHS	
LINEAR A	
LINEAR B	
PHAESTUS DISK	
CYPRIOTE	
HIEROGLYPHIC HITTITE	

been other states or principalities in Crete. Cnossus itself, however, was destroyed at the end of Late Minoan II. After this time Minoan culture seemed to wither away, and on many sites were found artifacts and pottery which had come from the Greek mainland. Between 2000 and 1450, then, there had been a steady expansion in Crete. The Minoans had exercised a cultural influence in Greece; they had colonized some of the Aegean islands, and they had traded with Syria and Egypt. After 1450 influences from the Greek mainland had become stronger and stronger; there was evidence also that there had been a migration from Greece to Asia Minor, Rhodes, Cyprus, and ultimately to Crete itself. In addition, Minoan trade in the eastern Mediterranean had fallen into the hands of these people from the Greek mainland.

So much could be gleaned from purely archaeological evidence, but archaeology could not answer two vital questions: (1) Who were the

Minoans? and (2) Who were the people from the Greek mainland? These problems could be solved only by the decipherment of the writing which had been found in Crete and on certain Greek mainland sites of this period.

During the Minoan period a succession of scripts was employed. The first script, called Hieroglyphic, had developed in the Middle Minoan period; the principal examples of this type of writing were found inscribed on clay at a number of Cretan sites. The second script, essentially syllabic, was developed in Middle Minoan III; it was found principally at two sites in the south, Phaistos and Hagia Triada, and it was called Linear A. The third script was dated in Late Minoan II in Crete; called Linear B, it was found in Crete *only* at Cnossus, although examples of the script were also found at Pylos, Thebes, and Mycenae in Greece. The three scripts seemed to be related in so far as Linear A appeared to derive its form from the Hieroglyphic and Linear B seemed to be a development from Linear A.

The Linear B script was deciphered by the late Michael Ventris in 1952. The underlying language is an early form of Greek, very much like the language of the *Iliad* and *Odyssey*. This meant that the inhabitants of Greece, the people who had supplanted the Minoans in Mediterranean trade and who occupied the Palace of Minos in 1450 and destroyed other Cretan towns, were Greeks. Whether the final destruction of the Palace of Minos in 1400 was the result of a new raid from Greece or a native uprising in Crete is unknown.

The Linear A script has not been deciphered to the extent that the underlying language can be identified. The presence of Semitic words in Linear A texts has been demonstrated beyond a shadow of a doubt, but these may be borrowed or "loan" words. The possibility that the Minoans of the Middle Minoan and Late Minoan I periods were Semites cannot be ruled out, especially in view of the fact that Cretan palaces and their frescoes strongly resemble palaces and paintings in Syria during the same period. Nevertheless, the Hieroglyphic script, the parent of Linear A, is very much like Hieroglyphic Hittite. We do not know the language underlying the Minoan Hieroglyphic script, though it may well be shown that both it and the language of Linear A are Luwian, as it is in Hieroglyphic Hittite. This would mean that the people in Crete in the Middle Minoan and Late Minoan I periods were migrants from Asia Minor forced out of their homes in Anatolia by the coming of the Hittites.

Minoan civilization, as revealed by archaeology, was complex and included many unique features. Building upon an agricultural base, the early settlers had developed an industry and trade which assumed their greatest proportions in the second millennium b.c. Cereals, legumes, and flax were grown, and there were olive orchards and vineyards. For domestic use the Minoans manufactured clothes and other necessities; their chief exports were wine, olive oil, metal products, and their magnificent pottery which has been found in Egypt, Syria, Greece, and Italy. During the first half of the second millennium a large share of Mediterranean trade was carried in Minoan ships, and it has been guessed that the Minoans had a navy so powerful that it was not deemed necessary to fortify the Cretan cities against foreign attack.

During its great period Crete was a populous island, especially in the center and east. The fresco paintings of the palaces depict a vivid and colorful people. Following well-established Egyptian conventions of painting, the men are represented as deeply tanned, while the women of the paintings have white skins. The small, wiry men have amazingly slender waists. Their costume is usually a waistcloth and sandals, but the women wear elaborate low-necked dresses with full skirts adorned with flounces and ruffles. The impression which we gain from their art is one of gaiety and lightheartedness; the bright colors employed and the freshness and life of the frescoes and vase paintings suggest that these people were observant, sensitive, and close to nature.

Perhaps, however, the Cretan religion gives a truer picture of the temperament of the people than does the art, for in the religion the joyousness of some festivals and ceremonies was contrasted with other, more sinister, rites that demanded human sacrifice; there were gods of the underworld, the serpent was a sacred creature, and the Cretans undoubtedly believed in ghosts. The bull played an important part in their religion; representations of bulls' horns have been found in numerous shrines, and the dark legend of the Minotaur (a beast half-human and half-taurine) was connected with Cnossus. Then there was the ritual of bull leaping: athletic young men and women would enter an enclosure in which was kept a ferocious untamed bull; when the bull charged at them the athletes would seize his horns and vault over his back. It was a dangerous trick; often the vaulter was impaled upon the horns or trampled under the animal's hoofs. One can imagine the savage thrill which the watching holiday crowd received when such an accident occured. The Minoans seem to have worshipped an agricultural deity, the so-called Great Mother, whose devotees were also found in Asia Minor and other parts of the Near East. Trees, pillars, and stones were often considered sacred.

Minoan art did not follow the colossal tendencies of Egypt and Mesopotamia; neither was it hampered by the traditionalism which exerted such an influence upon the art of the Near East. Environmental conditions in Crete perhaps did not necessitate extreme governmental centralization and regimentation, nor was there an opportunity for the growth of a powerful priest class. Minoan artists were able to take advantage of the knowledge of technique which Egyptian and Mesopotamian artists possessed, but they were not bound by the conventions that were imposed upon mainland artists.

Minoan palaces were rambling structures with many rooms and corridors oriented about numerous open courts. The famous Palace of

Minos at Cnossus covered an area of approximately six acres; it was the result of the combination of several separate buildings which had stood facing a large plaza. Stone, brick, and wood were the materials used by Minoan architects; pavements, foundations, and some walls were built of stone; the upper courses of the walls were of brick, and wood was employed for columns and lintels. The Minoan column was unusual in shape because it tapered downward instead of upward. The walls of the rooms and corridors in the palaces were often decorated with fresco paintings. Domestic architecture was not pretentious in the Minoan period. The houses were one- or two-story buildings with no windows on the ground floor; the roofs were probably flat. The houses were huddled close together and faced upon very narrow streets. The Minoans built carefully with a view to permanence; remains of their paved streets and roads may still be seen in Crete.

Minoan sculpture was not monumental. The examples of Minoan work which have survived are small and rather delicate. Stone, metal, terra cotta, and ivory were the principal materials. Jewelry was made of hard stones, bronze, copper, gold, and silver; rings, seals, bracelets, necklaces, and a few other trinkets have been found. The pottery was superbly made, and its decoration excelled that of the pottery of the Near East. The fine clay at the disposal of the Minoan potters made possible the manufacture of vases of fine smooth texture and eggshell thinness. The style of decoration varied in different periods from monochrome to polychrome, from geometric to naturalistic and finally to conventionalized patterns. Marine and floral motifs were very popular. Some vases were made of stone by a technique borrowed from Egypt; both hard and soft stone were employed. A favorite material was a soft, soapy stone called steatite which could be easily carved in fairly high relief. It is possible that steatite vases were often covered with thin sheets of gold.

Painting was less dependent upon sculpture than had been the case in Egypt. The frescoes of the Minoan period were painted upon wet mortar, and the work had to be completed before the mortar dried. The amazing results which the Minoan painters obtained in executing a whole painting within the space of a few hours is sufficient proof of their skill. When the painter made mistakes, however, he could not erase them, and the results were sometimes amusing; for example, there are paintings of bulls with several heads and numerous tails.

The economic situation in Crete was apparently such that rigid class distinctions did not develop. Wealth and property were probably distributed much more evenly among the population than in Egypt or Mesopotamia. Farmers, artisans, and traders seem to have formed a middle class; though there must have been nobles and priests, they never gained the predominance which similar classes acquired in the Near East.

All things considered, the Minoans, in the period of their greatness, must have been a happy and prosperous people. They were inveterate sportsmen, fond of boxing, wrestling, fencing, and hunting; singing and dancing were common; the discovery of a gaming board in the ruins at Cnossus indicates an interest in less strenuous amusements. The Minoans had most of the common domesticated animals; moreover, the horse was introduced into Crete about 1600 B.C., and the cat seems to have been imported from Egypt. Wild bulls were caught with nets, a hazardous undertaking.

The cultural indebtedness of the Minoans to the ancient Near East was considerable. Many of their art motifs and techniques were derived from Egypt, as were some of their religious practices; the system of weights and measures was Mesopotamian in origin; Mesopotamian cylinder seals were common in Crete. Minoan gems often bear representations of mythological animals—winged quadrupeds, creatures with human bodies and animal or bird heads, etc. These also represent borrowings from the East; as a matter of fact, the Minotaur appears on Babylonian seals. Nevertheless, Minoan civilization was important because it foreshadowed future cultural developments; it provided the first illustration of what might happen when the civilization of the Near East was transplanted into a European environment and released from the baneful influence of traditionalism.

The discovery of the Minoans and the gradual growth of information about their civilization in turn shed light on the civilization which Schliemann and his successors had found in Greece. Piece by piece the story of the Greek mainland was put together. Even today there is some uncertainty about the details, but the general outlines of Greek prehistory seem to be reasonably clear.

No palaeolithic remains have been found in Greece. It is possible that the country was devoid of human habitation before perhaps 4000 B.C., when peasant villagers, probably from Asia Minor, began to filter into Greece. The neolithic period begun by their arrival ended shortly after 2500 B.C., when new immigrants from Asia Minor arrived on the east coast and spread into the Peloponnesus, the southern peninsula. Though the use of bronze gradually increased and villages were somewhat larger than in the succeeding period, there was really no major change in the life of Greece until about 1800 B.C. when a devastating invasion occurred. The new invaders were the Greeks who were now to start on the long road toward civilization by adopting slowly many elements of Minoan culture. According to a recent and rather attractive theory,[1] the Greeks had followed the Luwians from Europe into Asia Minor about 2300 B.C. Subsequently, the Hittite movement into central Anatolia pushed tribes westward, in turn forcing the Greeks out of northwestern Asia Minor to the eastern coast of Greece and the Peloponnesus.

---

[1] J. Mellaart, "The End of the Early Bronze Age in Anatolia and the Aegean," *American Journal of Archaeology,* Vol. 62 (1958), pp. 8–33.

Quite naturally, the Greeks who settled in the southern part of Greece were most vitally affected by Minoan civilization. As a consequence, it was primarily in the Peloponnesus that a complex culture began to develop. This development occurred rather slowly in the period 1800–1550 B.C. but more rapidly during the next one hundred years with the result that by 1450 the Greeks could wrest political supremacy from the Minoans and dominate the Aegean area until they themselves succumbed to a new invasion from the north about 1200 B.C.

From the end of the neolithic period in Greece down to 1200 (or possibly 1100) B.C. in east-central and southern Greece, archaeologists distinguish three main cultural periods which are characterized by ceramic changes and other cultural developments. The first period is called Early Helladic—Hellas was the ancient name for Greece—and the age includes roughly the years 2500–1800 B.C. This, like the neolithic, was a pre-Greek period. Next comes the Middle Helladic Age (1800–1600/1550 B.C.), the period in which the first Greeks arrived. Finally, there is the Late Helladic (1600/1550–1200/1100 B.C.), also called the Mycenaean Age.

The Mycenaean Age takes its name from the great site of Mycenae in the Argolid, the traditional home of Agamemnon, leader of the Greeks in the Trojan War. Mycenae is typical of the political centers of the age: situated on a strongly fortified hilltop, it contained within its great walls the palace of the king. Similar citadels are known at Athens, Tiryns, Thebes, and Pylos; the palaces within the walls are best preserved at Pylos and Tiryns.

Huge stones weighing several tons each were employed in Mycenaean fortifications. This type of masonry is called Cyclopean because the later Greeks believed that only the Cyclopes, a race of giants, could have raised these huge blocks into position. The walls were high and very thick; at Tiryns, for example, there were even arched passageways running through the walls. The Mycenaeans did not know the true arch with its keystone; their arch was of the false, or corbelled, type of which a notable example may be seen over the great lintel block of the Lion Gate at Mycenae.

Mycenaean palaces were complexes of rooms built around open courtyards. At Pylos more than sixty rooms and chambers have been found in the "Palace of Nestor." The largest rooms were of the megaron type, consisting of a vestibule or antechamber opening into a pillared hall. In the center of the hall was a large circular hearth that provided heat for the entire room; the central hearth at Pylos had a diameter of thirteen feet, and the smoke was drawn up through a terra cotta chimney placed over the hearth. A single palace would contain several megarons, but in the main one the king's throne was placed. Stuccoed floors were laid out in colored checkerboard squares, and the walls were adorned with frescoes in the Minoan style. Palaces were at least two stories in height, but it is not known whether the roofs were gabled or flat although, considering the Greek climate, the former seems most likely. The palace rooms provided ceremonial halls, living quarters, workshops, and storage space. Presumably the king, his family, retainers, and slave workers inhabited the palace, while the subjects of the king lived in their own houses outside the fortifications.

Associated with the palaces were royal tombs. At Mycenae, just inside the Lion Gate, there was found a circular area within which were shaft graves containing rich grave furniture with the individual graves marked by sculptured slabs or tombstones. This "grave circle" belonged to the beginning of the Mycenaean Age, the sixteenth century B.C. An earlier grave circle dating from the end of the Middle Helladic period has recently been found outside the walls. After 1500 great tholoi, or beehive tombs, were built in the surrounding hillsides. Constructed underground, these tombs were circular in cross-section and shaped like a beehive; their domed roofs were corbelled like the Mycenaean arch. An inclined shaft, or dromos, sloped down to the entrance of the tomb and afforded easy access. Large numbers of tholos tombs have been found at Mycenae, Pylos, and elsewhere in Greece, but it might also be mentioned that a different type of chamber tomb, resembling those found at Ras Shamra, was recently discovered at Mycenae associated with the earlier grave circle outside the walls.

Mycenaean culture might be described as basically Minoan with the addition of certain northern or Indo-European elements introduced by the Greeks. Minoan art and technology were adopted, but climatic conditions in Greece encouraged a different kind of architecture and dress, while the invaders tended to retain their own political, social, and religious customs. Mycenaean clothes were heavier and more voluminous than those of the Minoans, and the men are represented in the frescoes as bearded. Warriors employed chariots heavier than the Minoan ones; they wore bronze helmets and greaves, and their weapons were heavy swords in contrast to the Minoan rapier.

Gold, silver, copper, and bronze were common in the Mycenaean period. There was an abundance of jewelry made of metal and semiprecious stones, and gold masks were placed over the faces of the dead in the shaft graves. Innumerable examples of fine Mycenaean workmanship in metal, stone, and ivory have been found. Among recent discoveries might be mentioned two from the early grave circle at Mycenae: an amethyst bead with the portrait of a "Mycenaean" and a beautiful rock crystal bowl in the form of a duck. Many handsome ivories are known, including a wonderful little box found in the tomb of a princess at Athens.

The clay tablets inscribed in the Minoan Linear B (now called Mycenaean) writing found at Pylos and Mycenae as well as at Cnossus have revealed much about Mycenaean political, social, and religious life. It had been assumed that it was Mycenaean life and customs that Homer described in the *Iliad* and *Odyssey;* the Mycenaean was often called the

Homeric Age, and the archaeological discoveries and the material from the tablets have demonstrated that there is much in the Homeric epics which is descriptive of the Mycenaean period.

The king in Mycenaean times was called the *wanax;* second to him was the *lawagetas* or war leader. Other titles or class names found in the tablets suggest that there was a feudal system in which land was set aside for fief holders. Occupations and professions included those of shepherds, goatherds, huntsmen, woodcutters, masons, carpenters, shipwrights, bronzesmiths, potters, and bowmakers. Women were employed in carding, spinning, and weaving as well as grinding grain. Captives of war were made slaves.

Lands were assigned to the king for the support of himself and his household; there were feudal holdings for which certain duties were performed by the recipients, and there was also private and communal land. Wheat, barley, olives, and grapes were raised, and the domesticated animals were cattle, sheep, goats, and pigs.

The Mycenaeans traded with Syria, Egypt, and the islands of the eastern Mediterranean. They colonized Rhodes, Miletus in Asia Minor, and the island of Cyprus; they maintained warehouses in Tarsus, Ugarit, and al Mina, the port of Alalakh. Their exports were wine, olive oil, and pottery, while they imported metals, metalwork, spices, drugs, textiles, and ivory. Amber came all the way from the Baltic through central Europe to the Adriatic and then by sea to the Peloponnesus.

Though priests and priestesses are mentioned in the tablets, no Mycenaean temples are known. The gods whose names appear are Zeus, Hera, Poseidon, and Athena. No other deities can be identified with certainty, although it may be expected that additions to the list will be made in the future.

It should not be forgotten that the Mycenaeans were contemporaries of the Hittite Empire, and it is well to remember the many parallels or similarities between the two peoples. Both were Indo-Europeans; both arrived in the civilized area about 1800. Their institutions, both political and social, were similar in many ways, and parallels can be drawn between Hittite and Mycenaean systems of land tenure. Certain aspects of Mycenaean fortifications resemble those of Boghaz-Köy. In view of the fact that the Mycenaeans colonized Miletus and Cyprus and that there were Mycenaean traders in Tarsus, Ugarit, and al Mina, towns under Hittite rule during the Mycenaean period, it is hard to believe that the two peoples did not meet. We do not know what or where Ahhiyawa was, but we may some day discover that it was the kingdom of the Achaeans with its capital at Mycenae.

In Greek folk memory the major event of the Mycenaean period was the siege and sack of Troy, a city traditionally located in northwestern Asia Minor. Since the time of Schliemann, it has been generally assumed that Hissarlik marks the site of Troy. The mound at Hissarlik, however, consisted of nine major occupation levels; the earliest was a neolithic town, and the latest was of Greco-Roman date. The problem, then, was to identify Homeric Troy, the town destroyed by the Greeks. Schliemann at first called the "second city" Troy, but this was the next oldest level of occupation in the mound, and its culture was utterly unlike that found at Mycenae. It was not until the very end of his life that Schliemann began to uncover the remains of the sixth and seventh "cities" where he found pottery and other artifacts of Mycenaean date. After Schliemann's death his collaborator, Wilhelm Dörpfeld, identified the "sixth city" with Homeric Troy; this identification was based on its Mycenaean date and on evidence of violent destruction of the town. The later excavations (1932–38) of Carl Blegen, however, showed that "City VII-*a*" had been destroyed by military activity about 1200 B.C., the traditional date of the Trojan War, while the "sixth city" had suffered a disastrous earthquake about a century and a half earlier. It is now customary, therefore, to speak of the town of level VII-*a* as the Troy of the *Iliad*.

"Troy" was an important town in the second millennium B.C. because it was located at a site which had both strategic and economic significance; today it is a very important archaeological site which is useful for the study of early culture in Asia Minor and for connections with the Aegean area. On the other hand, one should bear in mind that there is a difference between assumption and proof. "Troy" was destroyed about 1200 B.C., but there is no proof that its destroyers were Mycenaeans. The Phrygians, who invaded Asia Minor about this time, are much more likely candidates, and we cannot be sure that our "Troy" was the site that Homer had in mind.

Just as the Greek invasion of 1800 B.C. had destroyed the villages of the Early Helladic period in Greece and ultimately led to the downfall of the Minoans in 1450, so a new movement of Greek peoples into the Greek peninsulas caused the overthrow of the Mycenaeans. This new wave of invaders produced a series of disturbances more extensive and prolonged than the first Greek invasion of 1800, probably because a larger group of people was involved. The principal group which now (1200–1000 B.C.) came into central and southern Greece was the one that spoke the Dorian Greek dialect, and hence the whole movement is called the Dorian invasion. It should be borne in mind, however, that groups speaking other Greek dialects also arrived at this time and settled in the west-central and northwestern portions of Greece. These movements continued for about two hundred years, and the confusion which they caused brought about an economic and cultural regression. This was a transitional epoch bridging the gap between the Mycenaean period and the succeeding Greek Dark Ages (1000–750 B.C.).

The Dorian invasion was paralleled in time and character by other movements elsewhere in the ancient world at the end of the second millennium B.C. The coming of the Dorians coincided with the overthrow of the Hittites by the Phrygians, the attacks of the sea raiders upon Egypt, the settlement of the Philistines in Palestine, the arrival of the Medes and Persians in Armenia, and the invasion of Italy by iron-using tribes. It was a time of widespread catastrophe and change, the end of an era in ancient history.

Though the Mycenaeans disappeared from Greece, their colonists in Cyprus maintained the old way of life for many generations. The ancient language and many of the early institutions persisted in Cyprus well into the classical period. A derivative of the Minoan script was used for writing Greek long after the Greeks elsewhere had adopted the alphabet. Though the Dorians overran Crete and Rhodes and even the area of southwestern Asia Minor where the Mycenaeans had once colonized, Cyprus remained independent, the last stronghold of the Mycenaeans.

In Greece itself the Mycenaeans were gone but not forgotten, for the memory of their deeds and culture lived on in song and legend. Theirs was thought to be an age of heroes, an age of chivalry and daring, and it was greatly revered. The Mycenaean Age was to provide inspiration for later Greek poetry and drama, and people often sought to gain prestige by tracing their ancestry back to Achilles, Agamemnon, or Aegeus.

Chapter 13

FROM DARKNESS INTO LIGHT
(GREECE: 1000–500 B.C.)

T HE SO-CALLED DORIAN invasion brought to an end the Mycenaean period in Greece. The Dorians were a migratory pastoral
people whose culture was far less complex than that of the
Mycenaeans. When large groups of these barbarians poured into
Greece within a short space of time, there was no opportunity for a cultural
assimilation like that which had taken place when the earlier Greeks had
come in contact with Minoan civilization; the Dorians by sheer weight of
numbers dragged the other inhabitants of Greece down to their cultural
level. Thus, the coming of the Dorians had an effect upon Greece similar to
that which the barbarian invasions of the Christian era had upon the Roman
Empire.

Moreover, at this time the Greek world was isolated from the civilization of the Near East. The Hittite civilization had been eclipsed by the invading Phrygian hordes, while Egypt and Syria were harassed and weakened by the attacks of the sea raiders. As a result, the commercial and cultural interplay which might have fostered an immediate revival of civilization in Greece was not possible. Mycenaean trade relations were disrupted
by invasion, piracy, and local warfare; the towns dwindled to villages, and
political separatism was the order of the day. From trade and industry men
were forced to turn back to agricultural and pastoral pursuits. Conditions
were made more chaotic by the fact that the invasions displaced large sections of the pre-Dorian population; many groups may have deserted Greece
for the coast of Asia Minor. Southern Greece (the Peloponnesus) became
a Dorian stronghold, and most of the non-Dorians who remained there were
reduced to agricultural serfdom by their Dorian conquerors.

With the Dorian invasion Greece reverted to an Age of Agriculture, but in the period between 1000 and 750 B.C. (the Greek Dark Ages) cultural evolution began anew, and the first steps were taken toward the creation of classical Greek civilization. Although certain technological and religious traits developed in the Minoan-Mycenaean period were retained by the Dorians and their contemporaries, and although the Dorians enriched the culture of Greece by introducing iron weapons and implements, the general trend in the early part of the Dark Ages was one of cultural regression, a decline in complexity. Even when the decline halted and the slow climb toward civilization began, the Greeks were without the important stimulation for cultural growth which contact with the Near East had provided in Minoan and Mycenaean times. This isolation from the Near East continued until about 750 B.C., and as a result, during most of the Dark Ages the most powerful force guiding the evolution of the new Greek culture was the environment of Greece itself.

Greece is a rugged, mountainous country; nestled among its mountains are small valleys and plains. Nature has divided the land into a number of small compartments, and in the Dark Ages each of these compartments tended to become the home of a distinct group of people who set up a tiny independent state. In other words, political separatism is inherent in the Greek environment, and the disturbed conditions produced by the Dorian invasion aggravated this situation. In many cases, at the beginning of the Dark Ages, there were political divisions even within the tiny valleys and plains themselves; but when more peaceful times began to prevail, naturally unified areas were consolidated. Ordinarily, in each valley or plain there was one town whose location was more favorable than that of the neighboring towns and villages. A harbor town, or one which had good natural defenses, was likely to become the capital of the surrounding territory. Athens and Corinth were good examples of this latter type: each had a natural citadel—the Acropolis at Athens and the Acrocorinthus at Corinth—where the people might take refuge in time of danger.

The small size of the Greek states was important for future developments, because in the early period no one state was powerful enough to conquer the others. Moreover, the divine or theocratic monarchy of the Near East was a type of government which could not flourish in a small country where the population was not large. The fact that everyone tended to know everyone else rather intimately made it quite unlikely that a man's contemporaries, who had grown up with him from childhood, would ever think him eligible for divine honors. This situation thus led political evolution in the opposite direction from autocracy and favored the growth of more democratic governmental forms.

The common political unit in Greece was the city-state, just as it was in the early history of the Near East; but the *polis* (the Greek term for city-state) continued to be the unit of government throughout the classical period in Greece, whereas in the Near East the city-states were consolidated into kingdoms and empires. Here again we may see the influence of environment, for the various large regions of the Near East were geographic units, but in Greece there was no unity of this kind. Repeated attempts were made to consolidate the city-states and to create empires in Greece, but none of these efforts met with more than temporary success before the whole peninsula was conquered by the Romans. ›

Since Greece is a peninsula, it has a long coast line, and no region is far removed from the sea. It is not surprising, therefore, that the Greeks became sailors. Everything favored this development: the Mediterranean and the Aegean have no tides; during the summer months the winds are steady and dependable; the Aegean is crowded with so many islands that not even the most timid seafarer need worry about getting out of sight of land. Also important was the fact that the Greek rivers are small, shallow, and usually swift, and therefore not suitable for navigation; as a result, the Greeks were forced to learn how to sail on the sea. This was fortunate because it might otherwise have been difficult for them to make the transition from river navigation to that in open water—certainly this difficulty beset the Egyptians and Mesopotamians who never became good sailors.

The seaward outlook of Greece was necessarily toward the east and south, for in the north the peninsula joined the European continent, and much of the west coast bordered on the Adriatic Sea which, because of its winds and currents, was avoided by most Greek navigators. To the east was the Aegean, easy to sail; the Aegean became a kind of Greek lake, and it acted as a unifying force in welding the east coast of Greece and the west coast of Asia Minor into a single cultural province. To the south, the Mediterranean afforded access to Crete, Syria, and Egypt. Consequently, when there was a revival of cultural influence from the Near East in the time of the Assyrian Empire, Greece was immediately affected because of its geographic relation to the Aegean and Mediterranean. This was very important for the cultural and political history of Greece; the point can be emphasized by comparing the positions of the Italian and Greek peninsulas. Italy faced the west (because of its inhospitable Adriatic coast on the east), and the Italian peninsula was not especially open to influences emanating from the east. The situation was exactly reversed in Greece, and Greece was able to forge ahead culturally under stimulus from the Near East, whereas the cultural growth of Italy was long delayed.

Other factors in the Greek environment were the climate, soil, and natural resources. The cold, rainy winters influenced architectural developments even in the Mycenaean Age; the megaron with its sloping roof and "central heating" was better adapted to the Greek climate than was the drafty, flat-roofed Minoan house. The soil of Greece was moderately fertile, although not more than one-fourth of the total land area was cultivatable.

The middle slopes of the hills were covered with valuable forests, but the hilltops were mostly bare rock. In the beginning it had been possible to raise crops on the lower slopes as well as in the valleys, but when the Greeks began to cut off the timber for wood or to make more land available, serious erosion occurred, and in the end only the valleys and plains could be cultivated. On the middle slopes grazed the cattle, sheep, and goats. The goat, "man's worst servant," contributed much to the deforestation of Greece because its nibbling destroyed the second growth which might have replaced the virgin timber cut down by its masters. The Greeks had an abundance of fish and game to supplement their cereals and vegetables. They were also blessed with a climate and soil suitable for the vine and olive culture. As in Egypt, good stone was available; without Greek marble and limestone classical architecture would have been impossible. Greece, moreover, had what Egypt sadly lacked—good timber. The Greek clay was excellent and permitted the making of fine pottery, tile, and terra cottas. Last of all, the peninsula contained silver, copper, iron, and gold. The Greeks were fortunate in their possession of timber, stone, clay, and metals, for when agricultural production began to decline—as the result of erosion and soil exhaustion—they were able to develop trade and manufacturing in order to buy food from abroad.

When the Greeks came to Greece their government was monarchical. It was, in fact, the traditional primitive Indo-European monarchy found also among the early Persians, Romans, and Celts. In the Dark Ages each Greek state was headed by a king (*basileus*) who was chosen from a hereditary royal family. The king was commander-in-chief of the army, high priest, and arbitrator of disputes. Except in time of war when his power was slightly greater, he was limited in his actions by public opinion and by the *gerousia* (council of the old men) which he was supposed to consult on all occasions. In reality, the king enjoyed just as much authority as the forcefulness of his personality could gain for him. There was a popular assembly, the *ecclesia,* which consisted of all men able to serve in the army. The ecclesia could vote in the affirmative or the negative on questions submitted to it by the king, and when a candidate for the monarchy was selected by the gerousia, the choice could be accepted or rejected by the ecclesia.

The social organization of the Greeks was arranged upon a patriarchal basis. The smallest social unit was the family, which consisted of all the male and unmarried female descendants of a common living male ancestor. Thus a family might be headed by a great-grandfather, and the group would include his wife, all his sons and their wives and children, his unmarried daughters, his grandsons, and so on. When the patriarch died, the family would split up into several parts, and the patriarch's sons would become the heads of new families of their own. Groups of families which traced their descent from a common (but long-deceased) male ancestor formed a social unit much larger than the family: this was the *genos,* or clan.

After the invasions were over and the Greeks settled down upon the land, the adoption of the agricultural way of life began to have its effect. The population increased, and specialization of labor gradually appeared. At the same time certain families, or even whole clans, became more and more influential in governmental affairs. These people were those who possessed more land, or better land, than others. In some cases they might have inherited plots of land at the bottom of a valley; land thus located became more and more valuable as the hillsides began to erode (as a result of deforestation) and much soil was washed down into the valleys leaving the slopes uncultivatable. In the Dark Ages land was the chief form of wealth in Greece, and the possession of this wealth meant political power. Thus the large landholders came to have more and more influence; they became the nobles or aristocrats (the "best" people).

The holders of small or unprofitable plots of land sometimes sought the protection of the aristocrats; they might even abandon their lands to become tenant farmers on the estates of the great landholders. The aristocrats, backed by their clients (those who had sought their protection) and their tenants, were then able to exert pressure upon the kings. Military and executive powers were taken from the kings and given to elected magistrates drawn from the aristocratic faction. Eventually, the functions of the king were reduced to those connected with his high priestship, and even this in many cases became elective. The gerousia was transformed into a council of the nobles and wielded most of the real political power; the councillors were usually representatives of the most powerful clans. While the gerousia gained power, the ecclesia declined because fewer and fewer of the common people could afford to equip themselves for the army; the few independent commoners still in the assembly could scarcely outvote the aristocrats and their clients. Greek government thus changed from a limited monarchy to an oligarchy, a type of government in which only *the few* participate.

This brief description of developments in Greece between 1200 and 750 B.C. is sufficient to show that the overdependence upon agriculture and grazing which characterized the Greek economy for four and one-half centuries was productive of dire results. It should be emphasized, however, that these developments were confined to the eastern coast of Greece, southward from the borders of Thessaly. On the west, especially north of the Corinthian gulf, the rainfall was three times that of the east coast. The dense forests on the west coast discouraged agricultural development. Even in the classical period the people remained largely pastoral with virtually no development of city life. If all Greece had been like the west coast, there might never have been any Greek civilization in the ancient period.

At any rate, conditions on the east coast had changed during the Dark Ages. As the forests were cut down and erosion set in, pasture land for cattle and horses became so scarce that the numbers of the animals greatly declined, and they were replaced by sheep and goats. Beef practically went out of the Greek diet, and horses became prohibitively expensive; the ultimate military and political consequences of the latter will be discussed presently. A growing scarcity of wood was also to affect metalworking by creating a shortage of fuel for smelting, and it may have been a decisive factor in encouraging the use of stone for building and sculpture. Once again the importance of environmental factors is brought to our attention. The Greeks had actually changed the environment in which they lived; in so doing, they had created serious problems which they must somehow try to solve.

With the steady decline in the fertility of the soil and the concentration of the land in the hands of a few people, the Greeks on the east coast were faced first of all with a problem of overpopulation. The landless had no means of making a living, and the tenants were becoming little better than serfs. An even more serious result of the economic developments was that the very group that had profited by the changes in land tenure, the nobles, was also in control of the government and the administration of justice. Naturally, the oligarchic aristocrats did not concern themselves with the problems of the masses until the latter became desperate and threatened revolution. Then, and then only, did the governing class begin to consider possible reforms.

For the Greek reformers of the eighth century B.C. there were three possible solutions: (1) a redistribution of the land in order that the common people might be able to support themselves, (2) conquest of neighboring territory and division of land among the conquerors, or (3) a program of colonization in foreign lands to relieve overpopulation in Greece. In most states the poverty of the soil made redistribution impractical, nor did the aristocracy seriously contemplate sharing its wealth with the masses. Conquest was likewise impractical because of the comparative equality of strength of the Greek states and their small size. One Greek state, Sparta, did resort to both redistribution of land and conquest, as we shall see, but the Spartan case was a very special one. Most of the Greek states which were plagued by overpopulation therefore resorted to colonization, since it was really the only choice open to them.

Thus far we have considered only the history of the mainland Greeks; but before we can carry this account further and discuss the great age of Greek colonization, we must see what had been happening in the Aegean islands and Asia Minor. It used to be thought that the west coast of Asia Minor had been occupied shortly after 1200 B.C. by Greeks who had been driven from their homes in Greece by the Dorian invasion. A familiar older theory explained very nicely and neatly that the Greeks who spoke the

Aeolic dialect of Greek had been pushed from their homes in northeastern Greece to the northwestern shores of Asia Minor; that the Greeks who used the Ionic dialect had fled from east-central Greece to a position just south of that occupied by the Aeolians, and that some Dorians had spilled over from the Peloponnesus into southwestern Asia Minor. The theory was correct as far as the Greek origin of the various dialects in Asia Minor was concerned —Dorians were opposite Dorians, and the speech of Attica and Euboea was essentially Ionic like that of the settlers opposite them in Asia Minor—but the date of their migration eastward from Greece was wrong: it was not 1200, but probably about 850 B.C. In other words, the first tentative efforts of the Greeks at colonization occurred in Asia Minor even before the Dark Ages had ended. City-states were established by these Greek migrants in Asia Minor and on the islands; among the important foundations along the Asiatic coast were Ephesus, Miletus, and Halicarnassus, and in the islands were Mytilene (in Lesbos), Chios, and Samos. After 800 B.C. these states engaged in increasing trade with the hinterland of Asia Minor and with Syria. When the rise of Assyria in the eighth century began to interfere with the commercial activities of the Phoenician cities, the Asiatic Greeks fell heir to the carrying trade that had been monopolized by the Phoenicians. Even before this temporary decline of Phoenicia trade had brought prosperity to the Asiatic Greeks. The growth of business encouraged the adoption of writing; an alphabet was borrowed from the Phoenicians and adapted to the Greek language in the middle of the eighth century. Increasing contacts with the Near East led to the borrowing of many other culture traits; the art, religion, and intellectual life of the Asiatic Greeks were greatly enriched by these new acquisitions. Naturally, the growth of culture among the Greeks in Asia Minor soon began to have an effect upon the people of mainland Greece. We shall return to this point later, only noting here that archaeological research has shown that trade between Asia Minor and mainland Greece was beginning to develop before the end of the Dark Ages.

One aspect of the commercial activity of the Asiatic Greeks was particularly significant: they began to follow the Phoenician custom of establishing trading posts. These were located on the coasts of backward cultural regions inhabited by non-Greeks, especially in the northeastern Aegean and later in the Black Sea area. Some of the mainland Greek states on the eastern coast of Greece or on islands near that coast began to find similar ventures profitable. From the idea of the trading post or trading colony it was only a step to the idea of the colony as a means of relief from overpopulation. Within a short time after the first colonial trading ventures began, the hard-pressed Greek mainland states commenced to send their surplus populations to new homes outside of Greece.

The great age of Greek colonization extended from 750 to 550 B.C. As we have seen, there were two main motives for colonization: (1) the establishment of commercial connections, and (2) the relief of overpopulation. The first motive was more common among the Asiatic Greeks and the states of the Greek mainland which had close connections with Asia Minor, whereas the second was characteristic of the colonizing activities of the majority of mainland Greeks. Colonies were established all around the Black Sea, along the passage between the Black Sea and the Aegean, on the northern Aegean coast, in Cyrene in Africa, in southern Italy, in Sicily, and in what is now southern France and northeastern Spain. Northern Africa (west of Cyrene) and southern Spain constituted a Phoenician sphere of influence which the Greeks were not allowed to penetrate. In central and northern Italy the powerful Etruscans prevented the establishment of Greek colonies.

Ordinarily, the Greek colonies were harbor towns; few of the settlements were located at any distance from the coast. Plots of land were distributed among the colonists for cultivation, and trade was built up with the interior. The fact that the Greeks did not attempt to settle the back country made relations with the natives more cordial than they might have been if extensive conquests had been attempted. The colonists rarely had close political connections with their mother city (the metropolis); instead, the settlers governed themselves. At first, their governments tended to be democratic rather than oligarchic; this is typical of a frontier society. Later, however, when the colonies became older and more mature, an unequal distribution of land and other forms of wealth paved the way for oligarchies, and there were bitter struggles between the rich and the poor.

The chief relations of a colony with its metropolis were of a commercial nature; naturally, there was also a close bond of religion, custom, and sentiment between the colony and the homeland. When the Greeks left the Aegean and came in contact with non-Greeks, obvious differences between Greek culture and language and those of the natives led to a feeling of "racial" unity among all Greeks no matter from what city they came. The Greeks called themselves Hellenes (Hellas was the Greek term for Greece itself); all non-Greeks were classed as barbarians, people whose language had a strange sound.

Through colonization the overpopulation of the Greek mainland was somewhat relieved. Moreover, the planting of colonies had far-reaching economic effects. It was natural that trade should be stimulated, but, in addition, many of the mainland states turned to manufacturing; this was also true of the Asiatic Greeks. Textiles, pottery, and metalwork were manufactured for the colonial market, and there was an increased demand for Greek wine and olive oil.

No facile generalizations, however, will suffice to tell the story of Greek colonization and its results. Earlier research on the subject was confined to the purely literary sources, but archaeological discoveries have already produced enough new evidence to show that traditional accounts must be modified. Moreover, there were variations in motive and procedure from city to city. This may be illustrated by a few specific examples:

Miletus, which colonized for commercial reasons, had taken advantage of the great pastoral industries of Asia Minor to become a manufacturer of textiles; pottery and wine were soon added to the list. Before 700 the Milesians had begun to trade with Egypt, but this trade was a triangular affair. The Milesians sold their manufactures through trading posts in the north Aegean (later in the Black Sea area), taking in return gold and silver which could be used to buy Egyptian products.

In Greece, or just off the Greek coast, the first ventures of this kind began on the prosperous island of Euboea, well provided with forests, mines, grainfields, and pasturage. The city of Chalcis in Euboea specialized in metalwork and pottery. In search of mineral resources, principally copper, iron, and silver, the Chalcidians established trading posts in the mid-eighth century in the three-fingered peninsula of the Chalcidice in the north Aegean and also around the Bay of Naples in Italy. At the same time the growing scarcity of horses in Greece encouraged the great land-holders of Euboea to abandon cereal culture for horse raising. This led to an enclosure movement, like that in early modern England when sheep raising became important, and the peasants were forced off the land. This caused, in effect, overpopulation, and the trading colonies became settlements where the surplus population of Euboea found new homes.

One index to the contacts of the Greeks abroad is provided by the distribution of datable Greek pottery in foreign lands. It is instructive that the earliest Greek pottery found in the western Mediterranean is in Etruria and Latium, from the region around Rome northward along the west coast of Tuscany. The presence of this pottery in territory then controlled by the Etruscans indicates not colonization, but trade. Since this pottery belongs to the first half of the eighth century B.C., it is clear that trade preceded colonization in the western Mediterranean by about a generation. The earliest colony in Sicily or south Italy was the Chalcidian foundation at Cumae, near the Bay of Naples, which obviously grew out of the trade between the Chalcidians and the mining area controlled by the Etruscans; this was as close as the Greeks could get to the source of supply, and the traditional date of the Cumaean colony was 750 B.C. Other colonies founded by the Chalcidians (or Euboeans) before the end of the century included Zancle and Rhegium, situated so as to control the straits between Sicily and Italy.

Early Corinthian colonization was primarily commercial in intent, although it also contributed to the relief of overpopulation. Just before 730 the Corinthians simultaneously founded Corcyra (Corfu) and Syracuse in Sicily, and during the seventh century the predominance of Corinthian pottery in Sicily and south Italy shows that Corinth dominated western trade. The founding of many Corinthian colonies along the east coast of the Adriatic during the period 625–585 B.C. is an indication that Corinthian trade with the west was entering a new phase. The Adriatic colonization aimed at establishing the third corner for a new triangular trade between Corinth, the Adriatic, and Sicily. This development was promoted by two circumstances: (1) Sicily and south Italy were now suffering a shortage of silver caused by Carthaginian (or Phoenician) seizure of the Spanish silver mines, and (2) the growth of the Corinthian population at home and the parallel increase in the size of other Greek mainland cities had created a grain shortage which made the import of grain a truly profitable venture. Mints in the Corinthian Adriatic colonies produced silver coins which were exchanged for Corinthian manufactures; the coins were used to buy grain in Sicily which was in turn sold in Greece.

Much more might be said about the circumstances attending the founding of the Greek colonies, and much more will be added in the future when further research has extended our knowledge, but we may end this section with two observations. The foundation of Taras (or Tarentum) about 700 B.C. by Laconians was predominantly a measure to relieve over-population; Taras was orginally a kind of Spartan Australia to which un-desirables were sent, but in time it grew into a great and prosperous city. Finally, in the second half of the sixth century B.C. the fall of Lydia and the coming of the Persians to the Aegean coast of Asia Minor caused a migra-tion of Greeks from the Asiatic cities; these Greeks settled as colonists in the north Aegean and also in the western Mediterranean.

As for Greece itself, the great development of trade and manufactur-ing which resulted from the creation of colonial markets led also to the adoption of two new culture traits: writing (the alphabet) and coined money.

The metals had been used as media of exchange for two thousand years, but coins were a late development. A coin may be defined as a piece of metal of definite shape and weight which has been stamped or sealed by its issuing authority as a guarantee of its weight and purity. The Greeks believed that the Lydians were the inventors of coined money, and it is true that the earliest coins known (eighth century B.C.) were made in Lydia. However, sealed ingots of gold and silver were used by the old Assyrian traders as early as 1900 B.C. Later, Sargon II of Assyria (722–705 B.C.) mentioned the casting of gold half-shekel pieces bearing the effigy of the goddess Ishtar.

In the seventh century the Greeks began to coin gold, silver, electrum, and bronze. The main coinage of the Greeks was in silver and bronze, and the denominations of the coins were geared to the Babylonian system of weights and measures which the Greeks had adopted. The basic silver coin was the *drachma;* in general, sixty drachmae equalled the weight of one mina, and sixty minas, of course, equalled one talent. Drachmae were minted in multiples of two, four, and ten; there were also silver half-drachmae. The bronze coins were based on a unit called the *obol;* six obols equalled one drachma. The word obol comes from a word also used for a cylindrical spit or rod, and drachma means "handful"; this suggests that the Greeks may have used iron rods as currency before they adopted coinage.

The smaller coins circulated locally and could be used for making change, but the larger denominations were used for foreign trade. The didrachm, tetradrachm, and decadrachm were convenient divisions of the mina which made the shipment and weighing of bullion easier and facilitated business transactions. Larger coins were cast, while the smaller ones were struck with dies. The devices or types which appeared on the coins symbolized or suggested the issuing authorities. The coins of Corinth bore on the obverse (heads) side the portrait of Athena in a Corinthian helmet; on the reverse (tails) side was the winged horse, the pegasus. Athenian coins bore the head of Athena, patron goddess of Attica—the Athena (Athene) also suggested a pun on the name Athens (Athenai)—and on the reverse was the owl, Athena's symbol.

Coined money was an important invention. Coins were a great convenience for both seaborne and overland trade, and the adoption of a money economy in the ancient world was to usher in a new era in economic history. Money, however, was soon found to have both advantages and disadvantages.

The great landholders were pleased with the new economic developments. They began to concentrate on the production of wine and olive oil; they sold these commodities abroad and bought foreign wheat and other foodstuffs at prices lower than the cost of growing the same products at home. Then they invested their profits in trading and manufacturing ventures, acquired more land, or else lent money to the poor farmers and then gained control of their land and labor when the farmers could not pay off their mortgages.

On the other hand, the small farmer found himself in an increasingly unfavorable position. He could not compete with the low prices of foreign foodstuffs, and he did not have the capital to convert to olives and grapes—that is, he had not the resources to tide him over until the vineyards and olive trees began to bear. Furthermore, the small farmer had little or no legal defense against the encroachment of the politically powerful large landholder, and the new money economy also wrought hardships. Interest rates were high; 12 per cent interest was considered moderate in this period, and usually the rate was in excess of that figure. There is little question that the large landholders took advantage of the ignorance of the poor peasants and indulged in sharp practices when they lent money. The only security that the farmer could give for a loan was his labor or the use of his land—the land itself was family property and could not be transferred except by a false adoption procedure in which the owner might adopt another person as his son and make him an heir to the property. The debtor could mortgage himself or the members of his family; in this case, failure to repay a loan might mean slavery. Many farmers became bound to their own lands by debt, forced to work and produce for their creditors until their debts were repaid; the repayment of the debt was difficult, virtually impossible, because the interest kept piling up and the principal could not be reduced.

The farmers could not give up agriculture and become artisans because they had had no training as metalworkers, potters, and the like. In many states of mainland Greece the majority of the artisans were Asiatic Greeks or foreign non-Greeks who had settled in the towns or who had been brought in as slaves to work in the shops. Few people realize how much of the pottery, metalwork, and sculpture of the period before 500 B.C. which is called representative of "Greek art," was actually made by non-Greeks of Oriental origin.

As one might expect, the growth of trade and industry was accompanied by an increase in the size of the Greek towns some of which became cities. In the towns and cities a class of businessmen and artisans began to appear. Many of the traders and manufacturers were wealthy; the introduction of a money economy had meant that land ceased to be the only source of wealth in Greece. The newly rich began to demand a voice in the government, and it was undoubtedly the businessmen who agitated for the codification of the law. Greek tradition has it that the common people wanted the law set down in writing, but it was the literate merchant and industrial group rather than the agricultural masses which would profit most from the codification of the law. The first Greek law codes date from the second half of the seventh century B.C.

The codification of the law was not enough, for the new middle class wanted to be able to determine governmental policies. A way had to be found to break the governmental monopoly of the landed oligarchs so that the new class could share in the government. Quite unexpectedly, a solution was provided by a new military development.

It has already been mentioned that the denudation of Greece by over-cropping had resulted in a decline in the amount of arable land and a consequent decrease in the number of horses and cattle. The scarcity and high price of horses militated against the older type of chariot warfare, the kind described in the Homeric poems, and about 680 B.C. armies of heavy-armed foot soldiers (hoplites) which fought in the close, or phalanx, formation began to appear. Individual combats on the field of battle gave way to masses of armored infantry moving with great co-ordination, blocks of troops meeting on a plain and pushing against opposing blocks in an attempt to break the enemy's ranks and so win the day. The word phalanx itself is an Asianic word; it has no Greek etymology, and so it appears that the new style of fighting had been introduced into Greece from Asia Minor.

Sheer manpower suddenly became of the utmost importance in military operations when the phalanx was adopted. The landed aristocrats, the traditional warrior group, were too few in number to man the new formation, and reinforcements had to be found. The middle class, with its expanding sources of wealth, could afford to purchase the heavy armor worn by the infantry. Thus, the services of this class became valuable to the state, and since these people could serve in the army, they were also eligible according to long-established custom to participate in the assembly and to take part in governmental affairs. The result was that oligarchy gradually gave way to timocracy, a type of government in which the participation of the individual varies in proportion to his wealth.

There were few instances in which timocracies were established without revolution and bloodshed. In many cities there arose popular leaders who led the middle class, or in some cases the masses, in rebellion against the aristocrats. Often these popular leaders themselves gained and held political control; these were the "tyrants." In those days the word tyrant did not have the harsh connotation that it now has. A tyrant was usually a kind of political boss who adhered strictly to the constitutional forms of his city-state; the tyrant rarely held any state office; he remained behind the scenes and directed operations through the duly elected magistrates who, he was careful to see, were his own henchmen. The general policy of the tyrants was to break the power of the aristocrats through confiscation and banishment, to foster trade by founding colonies and by making alliances with other states, and to alleviate the suffering of the masses by creating opportunities for work through large state building programs and by dividing the lands of the aristocrats among the poor agricultural population. The businessmen and small farmers acquiesced in the rule of the tyrants because of the numerous benefits which tyranny had to offer. Often when a tyrant seemed to have outlived his usefulness to the state, he would be overthrown by revolution, and a timocracy would be established.

Tyrannies were common in Greece and Asia Minor during the seventh and sixth centuries B.C. Among the most famous tyrants were Periander of Corinth and Cleisthenes of Sicyon, who did much to enlarge the trade of their respective cities and played major roles in international affairs in the early part of the sixth century. Polycrates of Samos was important enough to be a valued ally of Amasis, the Egyptian pharaoh, in the third quarter of the sixth century, while his contemporary was the great Peisistratus, tyrant of Athens (see below, p. 197). Many of the tyrants were famous as patrons of art, literature, and learning. The financial inducements which they could offer attracted noted sculptors, poets, and philosophers to their cities, and the patronage afforded by the tyrants was a major factor in promoting the so-called Greek Renaissance which took place during this period.

Our information about Greek political and military history between 750 and 500 B.C. is more extensive than for the Dark Ages; Greek history may be said to begin with 750. In Greece the city-states which were most important were Argos, Aegina, Corinth, Megara, Sicyon, Chalcis, Thebes, Sparta, and Athens. Argos was strong in the eighth and seventh centuries; probably this was partly due to a survival of Mycenaean prestige; the rise of Corinth and Sparta in the sixth century brought a decline of Argive power. Aegina, Corinth, Megara, Sicyon, and Chalcis were great trading cities; their rise more or less paralleled that of the Asiatic Greek cities. The importance of Thebes was due to her hegemony of the cities of the Boeotian plain which made her a power in central Greece. The states about which we have the most information, however, are Sparta and Athens, whose influence, though not felt strongly in Greece until the sixth century, was to determine the course of Greek history in the classical period (the fifth and early fourth centuries). The rise of Athens and Sparta will therefore be considered in some detail.

Archaeological investigation has disclosed that, although Athens was one of the more important centers of the Mycenaean civilization, the city lost much of her early prestige after the Dorian invasion and the coming of the Dark Ages. At the opening of the historic period (750 B.C.) Athens was almost completely out of the main current of events in the Greek world. She did not take part in the great movement of colonization, nor were her people greatly affected by the numerous foreign influences that produced such radical changes in the more progressive Greek states at the beginning of the Greek Renaissance.

Although the geographic location of Athens would not have prohibited her early participation in the trade and commerce of the Aegean, it is certain that several other Greek cities were in a much more favorable position. The island city of Aegina, for example, commanded the entrance to the Saronic Gulf and acted as a middleman for trade which might have gone directly to Athens. Corinth in the Peloponnesus, later a bitter rival of Athens, was situated so as to control the western trade route through the Corinthian gulf and also serve as a terminus for goods from the east. Moreover, Corinth had many colonies that naturally preferred to trade with their mother city. As a result, Athens remained for centuries a backward little country town, and the land of Attica was devoted to agricultural pursuits. The indifference of the Athenians to trade and commerce was shown by the fact that they continued to use the open Bay of Phalerum as a harbor until the fifth century, overlooking completely the advantages of the Peiraeus, their natural seaport.

Attica was not a particularly rich agricultural region, but it was not without other resources. Silver, for example, was to be found at Laurium. Moreover, there was an abundance of good stone. The limestone of the Acropolis was used early for building purposes; at a later date the Peiraic limestone (poros) was quarried for the foundations of almost all the great temples, and the marble of Mount Pentelicus was popular in the classical period. Nevertheless, before 550 B.C. the only natural resource extensively exploited by the Athenians was the excellent clay of Cape Kolias, far superior to any other in Greece. Most of the early pottery, however, was made for the home market; it did not play any considerable role in foreign trade until the Athenians fell into step with the rest of the Greek world. Until the middle of the sixth century B.C. the Athenian resources of stone, silver, and clay were only potential factors in the development of Athenian commerce and art.

At the opening of the sixth century B.C. the Athenians were faced with a situation which necessitated a radical departure from their traditional agricultural economy. Most of the arable land had become concentrated in the hands of a few families who by virtue of their wealth monopolized the government. A large majority of the once free population of Attica had been reduced to serfdom, and many of those who had escaped that harsh fate were without any means of sustenance. The soil had lost much of its former fertility, so that even if it had been distributed equally it could not have supported the entire population of Attica.

The evolution of Athenian government had been typical of a mainland Greek state. The original limited monarchy had been transformed into an oligarchy in which the aristocratic council (called the Areopagus) was all-powerful. The kingship had been abolished, and the functions of the king had been divided among annually elected magistrates who were, of course, members of the aristocratic group. In the last quarter of the seventh century Athenian law had been codified. The provisions of the code of Draco were so harsh they were said to have been written in blood, but merely putting the law in writing afforded little relief for the economic situation.

By the early sixth century affairs in Athens had reached the breaking point. The prospect of a civil war between the landless and the landed forced the upper class to seek a compromise. Solon, an aristocrat whom the common people trusted, was given power to make reforms that would relieve the tension, and a really serious outbreak was avoided.

The precise date of the Solonian reforms at Athens is unknown, and there is also some uncertainty as to the extent of the reforms and their effectiveness. We know that Solon held the archonship (chief magistracy) at Athens in 594 B.C., but there is reason to believe that his reforms should be dated about 570. This is because certain datable events in the life of Solon before he became a reformer fall in the period after 594. We may suppose, then, that about 570 the constitution was suspended, and Solon was named *nomothete,* or sole archon and lawgiver, and given the authority to make sweeping changes.

Solon's first step was to provide relief for the debt-ridden small farmers of Attica; this reform was known as the *seisachtheia,* the "shaking off of burdens." Debt slavery was forbidden in the future, and people who had become slaves through debt were freed. Athenian citizens who had been sold abroad as slaves were redeemed at government expense and emancipated. Moreover, Athenians who had been bound by debt to labor on their own farms for their creditors were freed by a cancellation of mortgages. This latter kind of "enslavement" had arisen because inherited family lands could not be sold or transferred, and thus the debtor could mortgage only his labor and not his land. This had created a difficult situation, yet public opinion would not have sanctioned a law permitting the alienation of family holdings. Solon therefore seems to have done the next best thing by legalizing false adoption which made possible a disguised sale of family holdings when the buyer was adopted into a family and thereby became heir to the land. Solon also helped the debtor class by instituting inflation of the currency. He is said to have minted a lightweight drachma which was coined at one hundred to the mina instead of the former ratio of sixty (or possibly seventy) to one.

Other economic reforms of Solon more than justified his reputation for sagacity and farsightedness. The *seisachtheia* reduced tension and prevented an immediate revolution, but Solon wished to do more than treat the economic ills of Attica; he felt that the cause of the disease must be removed. Therefore, he took other steps for the rehabilitation of the country. Mere subsistence agriculture was no longer practical; Attica could not be agriculturally self-sufficient, and thus it was necessary to find a way to purchase food from abroad. To this end, Solon tried to build up exports that could be traded to foreign countries in return for grain and other agricultural products. He saw that the land of Attica was one of the few regions in Greece in which olive trees grew well. Therefore, he forbade the export of any farm products except olive oil. When the citizens realized that they would be allowed to export only olive oil, they concentrated upon olive culture with the result that Attica soon became a leading producer, and those who possessed olive orchards enjoyed considerable prosperity. In addition, Solon encouraged the Athenians to turn from farming to the more profitable fields of commerce and industry. A law was enacted that no son who had not been taught a trade should be compelled to support his father, and Solon further stimulated the development of industry by offering citizenship to foreign artisans on condition that they settle permanently at Athens to ply their trades. The introduction of foreign artisans was helpful to the native Athenians because it enabled them to study the methods of the newcomers. The first major industry to develop at Athens was pottery making; the growth in the manufacture of pottery paralleled the rise of Athenian exports of olive oil, for the oil was shipped in pottery containers.

In addition to his economic measures, Solon is credited with political and judicial reforms, but we cannot be sure that the tradition about these matters is reliable. It is a fair guess that before Solon the Athenian citizen body had been divided into three main classes on the basis of ability to perform military service. The lowest class were the *thetes* who were free men but too poor to provide themselves with weapons and armor. Since they could not serve in the army, the *thetes* had been excluded from office holding and participation in the ecclesia, or popular assembly. The next class were the *zeugitai,* those who could equip themselves as *hoplites,* or heavy-armed foot soldiers, and who were allowed to vote in the ecclesia and possibly to hold minor offices. At the top were the *hippeis* (knights) who were also hoplites but in addition could afford to maintain horses which they rode to the battlefield. The *hippeis* could participate in the assembly, hold the highest offices, and attain membership in the Council of the Areopagus.

Apparently for purposes of taxation, Solon defined the three classes of citizens as census classes and added a fourth class called the *pentecosiomedimni* (five-hundred-bushel-men). The *pentecosiomedimni* were those persons whose income was equal to 500 *medimni* (approximately seven hundred and fifty bushels) of grain per year. The rate for the *hippeis* was set at 300 and that of the *zeugitai* at 200; a citizen with a lower income would belong to the class of the *thetes*. As far as political privileges were concerned, the *pentecosiomedimni* did not differ from the *hippeis,* nor were the privileges of the *hippeis* and *zeugitai* changed, but the *thetes* were now admitted to the assembly. Thus oligarchy was exchanged for timocracy, and all citizens could participate in the government, though the degree of their participation varied with their wealth. Contrary to tradition, current opinion holds that Solon did *not* create a new council (the so-called Council of the Four Hundred).

The judicial reforms of Solon seem to have included (1) a new codification of the law which modified the harsh Draconian code of the seventh century and (2) the creation of a mode of appeal from sentences involving the death penalty, exile, or a heavy fine. It seems likely that such sentences could henceforth be appealed to the assembly, for the *heliaia* (the name given by the ancient authors to Solon's court of appeal) was a term used to denote the assembly in some Greek states.

Solon claimed to be impartial in his reforms; he said that he wished to be fair to both sides and to favor neither the rich nor the poor. Some people thought him simple-minded for not making himself a tyrant when he might easily have done so. Solon, they said, had his net full of fish and did not draw it up. But Solon was not a self-seeking politician. A businessman, a public-spirited citizen, he was to be numbered among the Seven Sages of Greece, and he was in addition a well-known poet. From his poems it is quite clear that he did not favor democracy: timocracy was as far as he cared to go.

No one at Athens was satisfied with what Solon had done. The aristocrats thought that he had gone too far, while the common people felt that he had not gone far enough. A period of political instability and perhaps even anarchy ensued. By 560 B.C. three factions were engaged in a battle for the control of the Athenian government: the landed aristocrats continued to form a powerful group; opposed to them were the owners of small unproductive farms and those citizens who were still without land; a third party, composed of the new group of artisans and traders brought into existence by the commercial expansion of Athens, was also making a strong bid for a share in the government. The second faction—the poor citizens—was by far the largest, and it secured the most able leader, Peisistratus, son of Hippocrates.

Three times between 560 and 546 B.C. Peisistratus attempted to overthrow the government. When his third attempt met with success, he became the virtual head of the Athenian state, although he held no office except the unofficial one of tyrant. This position of supremacy Peisistratus retained until his death in 527, after which his sons, Hippias and Hipparchus, succeeded him. Hipparchus was assassinated in 514 B.C., and Hippias was finally driven from Athens by a popular uprising about 510 which brought the tyranny to an end and paved the way for the establishment of democratic government.

It must not be thought that the period from 546 to 510 B.C. in Athens—the Age of the Tyrants—was characterized by repression and brutality. On the contrary, Peisistratus himself proved to be a benevolent despot who was able to solve most of the economic problems that beset Attica. By giving the Athenians a stable government and freedom from internal strife he made it possible for them to follow along the lines of commercial and industrial development already marked out by Solon. Peisistratus continued to encourage the production of olive oil (and also wine) which could be traded abroad for wheat, and he reformed the Solonian currency so that it was even better adapted for foreign trade. There is little doubt that the businessmen, many of whom were foreign-born, soon came to support Peisistratus when they saw that he was breaking down the traditional Athenian policy of isolation by making political alliances with foreign powers which were proving decidedly helpful to foreign trade. Peisistratus performed another valuable service to Athens when he broke the power of the landed aristocrats by wholesale banishments and confiscations; by giving many of the confiscated lands to poor citizens, he retained the enthusiastic support of his proletarian followers.

In the second half of the sixth century B.C. Athens was more prosperous than she had been for seven hundred years. Athenian olive oil, wine, and honey were exported to all parts of the ancient Mediterranean world. Since these products were, as we have seen, shipped in Athenian pottery containers, the distribution and quantity of this pottery in foreign lands serves as an index to the volume of Athenian trade. The quality of the Athenian pottery was so superior to that of other cities that it was soon in great demand, and the Athenian potters capitalized upon the popularity of their wares by producing many different types of vases for this new foreign market.

We are better informed about the Athenian potters and their work than we are about any of the other craftsmen of Athens. The products of the metal and textile workers have long since disappeared, but the pottery provides evidence which was not so easily destroyed. Moreover, it was in their pottery that the Athenians first developed a style of art that could be called distinctive of their city. This Attic black-figured style of vase painting was contemporary with the Age of the Tyrants and was a reflection of the great prosperity and commercial expansion of Athens.

The sixth century also saw the beginning of an interest in the major arts at Athens. In order to divert the minds of the citizen body from his tyranny Peisistratus embarked upon an extensive program of public works; as a result, the appearance of Athens was greatly improved. An aqueduct and a public fountain were built; a propylon, or gateway, was constructed at the entrance to the Acropolis. Down in the southeastern part of the city work was begun on a gigantic temple of Zeus which was not completed until seven centuries later. These artistic projects were carried out under the supervision of foreigners, principally Ionians from Asia Minor and the Aegean islands. Sculptors from the island of Chios dominated the scene at Athens in the Age of the Tyrants; there was no real native school of sculpture, and those who aspired to become sculptors copied the Chian style.

The tyranny of Peisistratus and his sons gave Athens her start on the road to political, economic, and artistic greatness. Patterns of thought and activity were established that had great persistence. The idea of alliance with Thessaly and Argos coupled with hostility toward Thebes and Sparta was one which was to seem attractive on other occasions at a later date. We should like to know, too, what Peisistratus thought about the advance of Persia; his son Hippias became a pensioner of the Great King, and this suggests that Hippias' cordial relations with Persia were based on more ancient ties.

Peisistratus also built up the Panathenaic festival in honor of Athena in such a way that it bade fair to rival the great Hellenic celebrations at Olympia, Delphi, Nemea, and Corinth. This was not an innovation, for other tyrants had promoted festivals, too. In the seventh century Pheidon of Argos had helped to make the Olympic games internationally important; early in the sixth century Periander of Corinth had established the Isthmian festival in honor of Poseidon, while Cleisthenes of Sicyon had had a hand in promoting both the Pythian games at Delphi and the Nemean games. In theory, these celebrations were primarily religious, but they were also good for business: people came from various parts of Greece to be edified and entertained, but they also spent freely. The festival of Dionysus at Athens, accompanied by a literary competition very important in the development of the drama at Athens, was also enlarged and invigorated by Peisistratus.

When Peisistratus died in 527, the tyranny was continued by two of his sons, Hippias and Hipparchus. As the years passed, however, the hold of the tyrants upon Athens was weakened by a series of developments. Hippias and Hipparchus faced growing opposition at home: other men coveted their power, and the Athenians as a whole began to long for greater freedom. The advance of the Persians into Europe meant the loss of revenue from mines owned by the Peisistratids in the north Aegean. Political exiles from Athens, particularly the powerful clan of the Alcmaeonidae, began to intrigue with Sparta and Thebes and bought the important support of the oracle of Apollo at Delphi. In 514 revolution broke out in Athens. Hipparchus was killed, but Hippias quelled the uprising with great severity, thereby increasing the unpopularity of the regime. A new revolt in 510, aided by Sparta, finally drove Hippias from Athens, and the Age of the Tyrants was terminated.

Factional strife at Athens, which had been held in abeyance under the tyranny, now revived. Conservatives and liberals struggled for political control while the friends of Hippias who had not followed their leader into exile conspired to bring about his return. The liberals wished to democratize the government, but the conservatives wanted to go in the opposite direction and perhaps even deprive of citizenship those who had been included in the body of citizens by the reforms of Solon and the generosity of Peisistratus. Supported by the Spartans, the conservatives at first had the upper hand, but by 508 (possibly 507) the liberals overcame their opponents and forced the withdrawal of the Spartans. Led by Cleisthenes, one of the Alcmaeonidae, the liberal faction instituted reforms which paved the way for the Athenian democracy of the fifth century.

Cleisthenes, like Solon, was credited by later writers of antiquity with more reforms than he actually instituted. His principal achievement was the creation of a new council, or *boule,* known as the Council of the Five Hundred. The old Council of the Areopagus, if it was indeed composed of former archons, cannot have been a very representative body or sympathetic to a liberalization of the government, since most of its members must have been the wealthier (and more conservative) citizens. The new boule, however, was composed of five hundred citizens chosen annually from the upper three census classes. The boule had the responsibility for state finance, the conduct of foreign affairs, and the supervision of the magistrates; it also decided what business was to be brought before the assembly. The Council of the Areopagus was not abolished: it continued to have jurisdiction as a court in certain homicide cases, but its more important function was the "Guardianship of the Laws," which suggests that it may have been a kind of supreme court that passed on the constitutionality of legislation.

The composition of the Council of the Five Hundred was based upon and connected with other changes made by Cleisthenes. Formerly the Athenian citizen body, like that of many other Greek states, had been divided into four groups called *phylai,* or tribes. These tribes were used as a basis for religious, military, and political organization. Perhaps to provide for a military reorganization, but certainly for political purposes, Cleisthenes now organized ten new tribes to replace the four traditional ones. In each tribe citizens from the demes, or wards, of the three main geographical divisions of Attica (city, coast, interior) were represented in about equal numbers; this seems to have had the effect of breaking up old geographic and party groupings. From each of the ten tribes were chosen fifty councillors; all together they made up the five hundred members of the new boule. Cleisthenes also made citizenship dependent on membership in a deme. Having one's name on the rolls of the deme became a badge of citizenship, and this was an improvement over the older system which had required membership in a clan or brotherhood (artificial clan), something much more difficult to obtain because of objections on religious or kinship grounds which might be raised by the in-group.

Each of the ten tribes furnished a contingent for the Athenian army, and by 501 B.C., if not before, each tribe elected its own general, or *strategos.* The office of general was to become the most important post in the Athenian constitution in the next century, but we do not know whether the generalship itself was an innovation of Cleisthenes or a development stemming from his reforms.

By 500 B.C. Athens had become a city-state of the first importance in Greece. Her trade and industry, her growing fame as a cultural center, and her increased military strength had all developed during the sixth century. Athenian government, through the work of Solon, Peisistratus, and Cleisthenes, had followed a course which was to lead to democracy in the fifth century. Solon had substituted timocracy for oligarchy; Peisistratus had provided political stability and had strengthened the middle class by attacking the aristocrats and fostering Athenian trade and industry; Cleisthenes had weakened old traditions and factions and in general had liberalized the constitution by making the government more representative and more responsive to the popular will.[1]

Sparta, which was to become the principal state in the Peloponnesus in the sixth century, boasted an unusual history. Down to the last half of the seventh century, the growth of Sparta was much like that of other mainland states. The region of Laconia, in which Sparta was located, had been fairly prominent in Mycenaean times. Probably even before the Dorian invasion much of the pre-Greek population had been reduced to a status of agricultural serfdom, a process which the Dorians completed. Sparta was a town formed by a union of five villages in the Dark Ages. It was the center of a fertile agricultural region; nature had also provided iron deposits, good clay, and an abundance of building stone. The people of Laconia exported their iron and their pottery; the Laconian pottery was popular with the Greeks in Cyrene who traded their silphium and other products in return for it.

Early Spartan political and economic evolution was typical. The landed aristocracy became very powerful and dominated the council. The kingship was not abolished, but possibly as a compromise measure to satisfy one particularly powerful clan, a second royal family was added to the one already in existence. Thus Sparta had two kings, one from each of these families, and in this way a kind of collegiate magistracy came into being. One king acted as a check upon the other.

Just before the extension of Spartan commercial relations took place at the end of the eighth century B.C., the Spartan aristocrats invaded the country of Messenia which lay to the west, divided up the agricultural land, and made serfs of the inhabitants. Clearly, this move was inspired by land hunger, but conquest was not the complete answer to the problem since only the large landholders profited from this addition of territory. The Laconian colonization of Taras, or Tarentum, in southern Italy at the very end of the eighth century demonstrates how the Spartans experimented with still another solution to the problem of overpopulation.

About 630, or possibly later, the Messenians revolted, drove out their Spartan overlords, and invaded Laconia itself. The Messenian revolt precipitated a crisis in which the very existence of Sparta was at stake. Complete destruction was averted only when the Spartan aristocrats called upon the

---

[1] Cleisthenes was believed to have introduced another great innovation called ostracism, but since the first ostracism was not earlier than 488 B.C., we shall discuss this matter in Chapter 15. It might be added that some think Cleisthenes also provided for the direct election of the archons, but this is extremely doubtful. This is another matter reserved for Chapter 15.

common people for aid. The Messenians were then defeated and reduced to their former position of servitude. Nevertheless, the Spartan nobles paid dearly for their victory, for the commons demanded sweeping reforms which included a redistribution of wealth and increased popular participation in the government.

Accordingly, a settlement was made, and a new system was gradually instituted at Sparta. We do not know the details of its evolution but only the form which the system had achieved by the end of the sixth century. Traditionally, all the reforms are ascribed to a great lawgiver, Lycurgus, but there is evidence that changes were still being made in the sixth century and that Chilon, a younger contemporary of Solon and also one of the Seven Sages of Greece, had something to do with the final arrangements.

The object of the Spartan system was to preserve the *status quo* once the wealth had been redistributed and the machinery set up to make the government responsive to the popular will. To attain the first end, private ownership of land was abolished; the land belonged to the state, but each Spartan citizen was given land for the support of himself and his family. This land was worked by serfs, and the citizen was thus free to devote himself to his civic duties.

These civic duties were largely military. The serfs in Laconia and Messenia may have outnumbered the Spartans as much as ten to one, and to keep them in subjection it was necessary for Sparta to become an armed camp. Beginning at age seven Spartan males were trained as soldiers; strict standards of discipline and physical perfection were maintained. Newborn children in any way deformed were destroyed. The Spartan girls as well as the boys were given physical training in order that they might bear healthy children. Comfort and luxury were forbidden. The Spartan boys were not allowed to wear shoes; they had only one garment for both winter and summer so that their powers of endurance would be developed; they were deprived of sufficient food and expected to steal from the serfs to learn resourcefulness. Dancing and sports were emphasized because they fostered muscular and group co-ordination. The Spartans thus became the best soldiers in Greece, but their intellectual and cultural development ceased.

Not only were the serfs, who were called helots, held in check by the military machine, but there was also a secret police force that spied upon them continually. Any helot who showed a spirit of independence might be assassinated. Every year a declaration of war was issued against the helots so that any Spartan could slay an obstreperous serf without incurring blood guilt. The helots could not escape, for around the territory in which they lived was a ring of communities inhabited by a population known as the *perioeci* which was also subject to the Spartans. The perioeci had their own local governments and were allowed to engage in trade, but their foreign relations were controlled by Sparta, and they were required to furnish contingents for the army.

Control of the internal situation in Laconia and Messenia was not enough, however, to preserve the *status quo* in Sparta. Some of the other states of the Peloponnesus feared the growth of Spartan power. It was essential that Sparta dominate the Peloponnesus because an attack upon Sparta by a hostile state might precipitate a helot revolt. Argos was Sparta's principal rival, and in order to prevent the Argives from becoming dangerous, the Spartans (in the sixth century) built up a confederation called the Peloponnesian League which included all the states of the Peloponnesus except Argos and a few cities along the Corinthian gulf. The rich and powerful city of Corinth, of course, was only too glad to find an ally to side with her against Argos.

The member states of the Peloponnesian League were bound to Sparta by separate treaties which were for a term of one hundred years. These treaties were purely defensive: if a member state was attacked, the others were bound to come to its aid. Any other action was preceded by the deliberation of the league members at a council to which all sent representatives. With her own fine military organization as a nucleus, Sparta could put into the field a force of forty to fifty thousand men when joined by her allies, and this was more than enough to make Sparta the great power in Greece in the sixth century. It was no wonder that Croesus sought the Spartans as allies against Persia, and it was fortunate for the Greeks that Sparta was not imperialistic but bent only on protecting what she had.

The governmental organization of Sparta in its final form was unique. The two kings were retained, and the council (gerousia) continued to be the monopoly of the old aristocratic clans. The popular assembly (*apella*), however, in addition to possessing the usual powers of making a declaration of war and ratifying the choice of a new king, was the body which elected five magistrates called *ephors* (overseers) who exercised the real power in the state. The ephors kept close watch over the kings; when a king conducted a military campaign outside the borders of the country, two ephors accompanied him; the ephors could also fine the kings or force them to abdicate. In addition, the ephors conducted the foreign relations of Sparta, watched over public morals, proclaimed the laws, presided at meetings of the council and assembly, and acted as judges. It was their function to safeguard the interests of the people and to see that the system, once established, remained unchanged.

It is easy to see why progressive Athens and reactionary Sparta were to become rivals in the fifth century. The Spartans always favored oligarchic governments, while the Athenians, menaced by oligarchic jealousy, were anxious to aid in the establishment of more democratic governments in Greece. The trade rivalry between Athens and the Spartan ally, Corinth, was another source of discord. Thus the seeds were sown for the bitter struggle that was to ruin Athens, Sparta, many of the other Greek states, and finally bring an end to Greek independence.

Chapter 14

THE GREEK RENAISSANCE

THE INCREASING COMPLEXITY of Greek economic and social life which was evident from the late Dark Ages (850 B.C.) on was accompanied by the rise of Greek art, literature, and philosophy. The art of the Greek Renaissance (750–500 B.C.) is often called archaic, and there is no reason why we cannot apply the same term to all the cultural aspects of the period. Thus, we may refer to the Greek Renaissance as the Archaic Period of Greek history.

No thinking person would ever insist that "history repeats itself"; yet it is clear that there are certain parallels between the rise of civilization in the Near East and that in Greece. If we call the Dark Ages the Greek Age of Agriculture, we see that the rise of trade and industry at the end of the Dark Ages brought Greece into an Age of Civilization which began with the Archaic Period. The growth of cities, the introduction of slavery, the adoption of writing (which led to the development of literature), and the rapid evolution of architecture, sculpture, and painting in Greece were developments identical with those which occured in the Near East about 3000 B.C.

It is also necessary to emphasize the extent to which the Greeks were indebted to the Near East. We shall observe many instances in which cultural items borrowed from the Near East played an important part in the foundation of Greek art, religion, philosophy, science, and literature. The cultural effects of the unification of the Near East by Assyria were certainly felt in Greece as well as in the Near East. Moreover, cultural diffusion was one of the important results of the commercial activities of the Phoenicians; and the Greeks themselves, through their indirect overland trade with Mesopotamia and their direct sea trade with Egypt and Syria, were able to learn much from the inhabitants of those lands.

In our discussion of the culture of the Archaic Period we may well

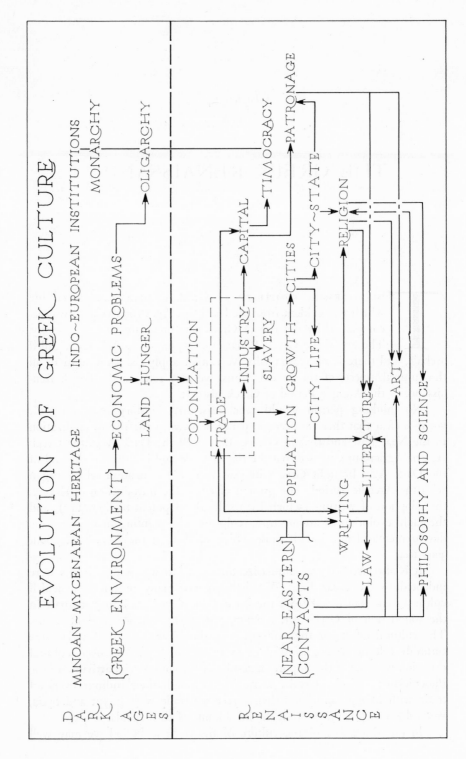

EVOLUTION OF GREEK CULTURE

DARK AGES

MINOAN~MYCENAEAN HERITAGE   INDO~EUROPEAN INSTITUTIONS
                                                    MONARCHY

[GREEK ENVIRONMENT]——ECONOMIC PROBLEMS——OLIGARCHY
                          LAND HUNGER

RENAISSANCE

                          COLONIZATION
                          TRADE——INDUSTRY——CAPITAL——TIMOCRACY
                                  SLAVERY
                          POPULATION GROWTH——CITIES——PATRONAGE
                                  CITY LIFE——CITY~STATE
                                              RELIGION
NEAR EASTERN
CONTACTS
          WRITING——LITERATURE——ART
          LAW
                          PHILOSOPHY AND SCIENCE

206

begin with Greek religion, since that particular phase of Greek life was closely connected with (and provided a stimulus or starting point for) art, literature, and philosophy.

It is difficult to present a simple picture of Greek religion; the whole subject is tremendously complicated because of the many elements which the Greeks borrowed from other peoples and because there were innumerable variations of worship and religious practice among the several Greek states. In the Dark Ages Greek religion was a combination of elements imported into Greece by the Greeks themselves and of various features of the religion of the Neolithic inhabitants and the Minoans. In the period of the Greek Renaissance there were borrowings from the religions of the Near East. In Greek religion there was an ancient and underlying substratum of totemism, animism, and magic which the anthropomorphism of the later Dark Ages failed to conceal. Undoubtedly the owl of Athena, the eagle of Zeus, and the other companions of the classic Greek deities had once been worshipped as divinities. Early animistic beliefs, to quote only a few examples, would account for the sacred groves, springs, and rivers to which many references are made in Greek literature. Anthropomorphism, however, had produced a goddess, Athena, whose familiar was an owl; it was responsible for the river gods, the nymphs, and the dryads. Sympathetic magic pervaded Greek ritual and ceremony. The Greeks believed that man might coerce or supplicate the gods; he might also make a contract with them, and if he kept his part of the bargain, the gods must do likewise. Sacrifices were pleasing to the Olympians; to them were dedicated the first fruits of the harvest. The gods also looked with favor upon athletic contests and upon literary competitions.

The Greeks seem to have carried polytheism to extremes. The individual had his own personal gods; the farmer, the herdsman, the artisan, and the sailor looked to certain deities for aid. The family had its protecting spirits of the hearth and the doorway; births, marriages, and funerals were accompanied by domestic rituals. There was also the state religion; each city had its own peculiar god or gods whose worship was the subject of public festivals and ceremonies. Although the Greeks never questioned the power or the existence of foreign gods (the gods of the barbarians), certain deities were nevertheless recognized as belonging especially to all the Hellenes or Greeks. Zeus, Apollo, Hera, Artemis, Athena, and the other Olympians were thought of as Greek gods. The festivals and games in honor of Zeus at Olympia, Apollo at Delphi, and Poseidon at Corinth were attended by Greeks from every state; in other words, they were Panhellenic.

The Greeks practiced divination. They sought to interpret dreams and the flight of birds. A favorite means of foretelling the future was to examine the entrails of animals and fowls; this custom the Greeks had borrowed from the people of the ancient Near East. There were also centers of prophecy where oracles inspired by the gods gave answers to those who sought advice regarding future conduct. Most famous and least fallible was the oracle of Apollo at Delphi. There the priestess, the Pythia, transmitted the god's messages to Greeks and non-Greeks who came from far and wide to obtain a glimpse into the future.

The Greeks, like other people, sought immortality. Their ancient cults—those of the state, the crafts, or the home—did not offer them hope of everlasting life, and therefore they turned to a new cult which was imported from the Near East. The wine and fertility god, Dionysus, became the Greek counterpart of the Mesopotamian Tammuz and the Egyptian Osiris. According to legend, Dionysus had been slain, yet he had risen from the dead and had gained immortality. The rites of the Dionysiac worship were wild revels that took place at night deep in the forests. Dancing to the accompaniment of drums and cymbals, the devotees of the god worked themselves into a frenzy. In their emotional intoxication they seemed to gain the immortality of the god himself. The worship of Dionysus was transformed into a disciplined religion by the followers of the legendary poet and musician, Orpheus. They devised sacred writings, prophecies, and hymns which were transmitted to their converts after impressive rites of initiation. The Orphic theology was based on the idea that a man's body was the prison of his soul, that the soul was being punished for sin in a previous existence. By pure living after initiation, the soul might be cleansed and liberated for eternal happiness.

Religion in Greece, as in every other ancient land, was all-pervasive. Certain conditions in Greece, as we shall see, made religion the source of the artistic and intellectual activities for which the Greeks became famous.

Along with the religion of the Greeks went their mythology. The primary purpose of a myth is to offer an explanation to questions that naturally arise concerning the gods, the universe as a whole, and even man himself. We have already observed the comprehensive supernaturalism which pervaded primitive society everywhere. When a question admitted of no obvious answer, the reply which one received usually involved an explanation in terms of the supernatural. A myth is a hypothesis; in ancient times it occupied the place now held by modern scientific explanations and theories. Each of the Greek states, as might be expected, had its own collection of local myths; but a "national" mythology for all Greeks was provided by the Homeric poems and the works of Hesiod.

The making of myths was the first intellectual occupation of the Greeks, and Greek philosophy was the descendant of mythology. In its first stages Greek philosophy was an attempt to explain the universe without recourse to supernaturalism. It cannot be emphasized too strongly that this early philosophy was not an independent development; it drew its inspiration from ideas and theories already present in Greek mythology and from hypotheses of the same nature as those which were part of the religions of the Near East. It was no coincidence that Greek philosophy arose in Asia Minor at a time when there were increasing contacts with Egypt, Syria, and Mesopotamia. Then, too, the adoption of writing which had occurred only a century before (*c.* 750 B.C.) now made it possible to express abstract ideas that could not have been adequately developed through oral intercourse.

The first of the Greek philosophers was Thales of Miletus, who lived at the beginning of the sixth century B.C. Thales was interested in mathematics, astronomy, and physics; he owed the fundamentals of his knowledge to the Egyptians and Babylonians with whose scientific learning he was well acquainted. He tried to explain the universe in terms of a basic element, water, by expounding the theory that water was the source of all other matter. Thales envisioned the earth as a flat disk floating on water, and he also thought that the sky was enveloped by water. There is marked similarity between this concept of the universe and that of the Babylonians, who thought that the earth and the sky were composed of the two halves of the body of Tiamat and that there was water both below the earth and above the sky (see above, p. 160). The hypothesis of Thales was likewise very close to the explanation of the universe offered in the theology of the Orphic cult:

> In the beginning there was a primal undifferentiated unity, called by the Orphics "Night." Within this unity the World Egg was generated, or, according to some accounts, fashioned by Ageless Time (*Chronos*). The Egg divided into two halves, Heaven and Earth. . . . In physical terms, the upper half of the Egg forms the dome of the sky, the lower contains the moisture or slime from which the dry land (Earth) arose.[1]

Anaximander, the successor of Thales, denied that water was the prime element; instead, he postulated some undefined material which he called "the unlimited." The universe evolved out of the separation of opposites in which "the Hot" moved outward away from, and "the Cold" moved inward toward, a central nucleus. Since, under this theory, the points farthest from the earth possessed the hightest temperatures, it was natural to suppose that the sky was surrounded by a sphere of flame. A second pair of opposites was produced when the fires of heaven dried the earth; thus,

---

[1] *Cambridge Ancient History* (Cambridge, Eng.: Cambridge University Press, 1923–39), Vol. IV, p. 536.

land and water, "Dry" and "Wet," came into being. Anaximander believed that:

> The elements . . . encroach and prey upon one another. The Hot draws up moisture to feed the heavenly fires, and the cold earth, in its turn, claims warmth and rain. . . . The first living things were generated out of moisture evaporated by the sun. Man, like the other animals, must have been a fish-like creature, which later took to the land. This traffic of the elements was to Anaximander the work of "injustice," of encroachment and self-assertion on the part of hostile "opposites."[2]

Again it is possible to see the parallels between the Orphic cosmogony and philosophical speculation. Night, Chaos, and the Unlimited are the same in principle; Tiamat, the World Egg, and Hot and Cold all form heaven and earth by the process of separation; and the sundered opposites then reunite to generate life. Moreover, all this dualism reminds one strongly of the contemporary theology of the Persian Zoroaster with its emphasis upon the war between light and darkness, truth and falsehood, and good and evil (see above p. 156).

A third philosopher, also like Thales and Anaximander an inhabitant of Miletus, was Anaximenes. He identified the Unlimited with air, and he held that the thinning or thickening of the air produced all visible forms. This was really the starting point in the evolution of an atomic theory which became popular at a later time.

A school of philosophy more religious and mystical than that of the Milesians was founded by Pythagoras of Samos, who established himself in southern Italy in the latter half of the sixth century B.C. Pythagoras was a mathematician who came to believe in the divinity of numbers and the transmigration of souls. The members of the cult-society which he established ate only certain foods and wore only linen. Through purification and contemplation, "by following God," man might free his soul from his body, and his soul would become immortal.

It is easy to see the similarity of Pythagorean and Orphic beliefs. The Pythagoreans also stressed the conflict of good and evil, and light and darkness, just as Zoroaster had done. These tendencies toward ethics and religiosity are more marked and more readily discernible in Pythagoreanism than in the thinking of the other philosophers whom we have mentioned. But it has been said that, despite its concern with science, all the early Greek philosophy was partly theological and not truly scientific, since the philosophers tended to rely somewhat on traditional wisdom which in turn was

[2] *Ibid.*, pp. 540–41.

confirmed by inward conviction. One suspects that the characteristic Greek interest in nature (physics), man (ethics), and method (logic) was present at least in embryonic form from the very beginning. Certainly the terminology of the Ionian philosophers of the sixth century was filled with words that had ethical connotations, but Pythagoras (or his followers) represented almost a lunatic fringe of the early science with their asceticism, divine mathematics, and vegetarianism. Other contemporary philosophers had a low opinion of Pythagoras, saying that he made a wisdom of his own with "much learning and bad science."

The early philosophers often expressed their ideas in poetic form, and this was true not only of philosophers but also of people in public life: Solon, for example, used poetry to advocate his reforms while others used it for political invective or to arouse patriotism. In fact, in the Archaic Period, which is very important in the history of Greek literature, the most significant productions were poetic; virtually no prose has survived from this age.

The earliest literature of the Greeks was in the form of epics and sagas dealing with the deeds of the Achaeans, the great heroes of the Mycenaean Age. These sagas were transmitted orally by the *rhapsodes,* the singers of the Dark Ages. It was probably in the eighth century that the great poet Homer composed the famous *Iliad*. The *Iliad,* like many of the early sagas and many of the later epics, had as its background the siege of Troy, but the principal subject of Homer's poem was the "Wrath of Achilles." Homer may also have been the author of the *Odyssey,* the story of the wanderings of Odysseus after the fall of Troy, although there are many indications that the *Odyssey* was composed about half a century after the *Iliad*. The *Iliad* and *Odyssey,* like other epics of the Archaic Period, were couched in the dactylic hexameter. They were composed and transmitted orally; it was only at a later date that they were committed to writing. The "Homeric Question," which involves the authorship and date of these poems, has been debated for many years; it comprises a complex and fascinating set of problems on which scholars have expended a vast amount of time and ingenuity without arriving at a universally acceptable solution. The *Iliad* and *Odyssey* are difficult to employ as historical evidence. The *Iliad,* for example, contains material descriptive of political organization and economic life in the Dark Ages, but since it is based on the earlier sagas, it also describes in part the culture of the Mycenaean period. The *Odyssey,* being later in date, contains not only the same elements as the *Iliad* but also refers to culture and events in the Age of Colonization. Contact with the Near East is shown in the case of the *Odyssey* by the inclusion of a number of Oriental folk tales; this is one of the best arguments for dating the *Odyssey* later than the *Iliad*.

Both the *Iliad* and the *Odyssey* are sophisticated compositions, on a much higher literary level than the sagas from which they derived their inspiration. The *Iliad,* particularly, was recognized by both Greeks and

Romans as the supreme achievement in Greek literature, and no sensible Roman ever claimed to have done anything better. The Greeks admitted that there was a difference between the *Iliad* and the *Odyssey,* even though they believed that Homer was the author of both; their explanation was that the *Odyssey* was the product of Homer's old age after he had passed his prime.

Another great poet of the early Archaic Period was Hesiod, reputedly a farmer in Boeotia. Two long poems in the epic hexameter are attributed to him: the *Works and Days* and the *Theogony.* Both are didactic in purpose. The *Works and Days* is the better poem, though somewhat lacking in unity. Definitely moral in purpose, it expounds the virtues of justice, thrift, industry, and neighborliness and recommends farming as the best possible occupation. Hesiod gives detailed instructions for the successful management of a farm as well as certain precepts for conduct and then ends his poem with a list of tabus and lucky and unlucky days.

The *Theogony* aimed at providing a genealogy of the gods. Hesiod's account of the creation of the world has a familiar ring: "First was created Chaos . . . then broad-bosomed Earth . . . and Earth first bore the starry Heaven . . . that he might cover her." Like Thales, Hesiod imagined that the earth floated on the surface of the sea. It should be noted also that a part of the *Theogony* parallels the Hurrian "Song of Ullikummi."

The interests of Hesiod are ethical and, in a sense, "scientific." He wants to set up moral standards, to improve farming, and to explain the world and its origins by organizing and systematizing Greek mythology. In short, Hesiod, not Thales, was the first Greek philosopher. Like the sixth-century philosophers, Hesiod was indebted to ideas from the Near East. In both the *Works and Days* and the *Theogony* the Oriental influence is apparent: in the former, the list of lucky and unlucky days resembles similar lists from Assyria, the advice to farmers is reminiscent of the Sumerian "Farmer's Almanac," and the subject and treatment of his moral apothegms recall a number of the biblical proverbs; in the *Theogony* there are other Oriental parallels in addition to those already mentioned, and one of the most convincing examples is provided in the story of the emasculation of Ouranos where the operation is said to be performed with a *harpe*—a Semitic, not a Greek, word for sickle.

More consistently than the *Iliad* and the *Odyssey,* the *Works and Days* portrays life in Greece at the end of the Dark Ages. We can see the specialization of labor that has taken place in backward Boeotia and how the landed nobility have risen to a position of political power where they can control the administration of justice. At the same time, Hesiod gives the impression that trade by sea, as a sporadic activity, has developed.

The date of Hesiod is subject to dispute, but the traditional ninth-century date for his work is too early. Since he quotes a verse from the *Iliad,* he must have lived after Homer (that is, the poet of the *Iliad*); since

Hesiod himself was quoted by poets as early as the middle of the seventh century, he must have lived before that time. There was a legend of a poetic contest between Homer and Hesiod; known historical events mentioned in connection with the contest occurred about 700 B.C. If Hesiod lived at the end of the eighth century, the conditions that he described in Boeotia would very likely have still prevailed there, yet this date would not be too early for him to have acquired his smattering of Oriental ideas.

The Greeks of the historic period held Homer and Hesiod in high esteem. Their poems were committed to memory by educated people and were quoted when questions concerning theology or morality arose. It has been well said that Homer and Hesiod provided the Greeks with a bible, for these two poets formulated concepts of the gods and set up standards of behavior which were accepted by the Greeks of every city.

After 700 B.C. there was a quickening of the tempo of Greek life and an increasing complexity of political, social, and economic organization. These developments, together with the introduction of writing, produced changes in Greek literature. The epic style of Homer and Hesiod and their simple hexameter verse were largely replaced by new forms and meters. The poets turned to the elegy, the iambic, and the personal and choral lyric.

The recitation of an elegy was often made to the accompaniment of a reed pipe or a flute, and the elegaic form was employed for many purposes. In the seventh century B.C. Callinus of Ephesus wrote martial elegies to inspire the Asiatic Greeks in their struggle with the invading Cimmerians; Tyrtaeus likewise roused the Spartans who participated in putting down the Messenian revolt. Solon's elegies embodied his ideas for reforms at Athens, whereas Theognis of Megara used similar forms to vent his political hatred upon tyrants and the proletariat; Mimnermus of Ionia wrote love elegies. The sharper iambic verse was well suited to satire; it was employed by the famous soldier of fortune Archilochus of Paros, and the later and more philosophic Simonides of Amorgos.

The lyric was sung to the accompaniment of a lyre or cithara. Alcaeus and Sappho of Lesbos, who lived in the sixth century, were two of the foremost exponents of the personal lyric. The lyric was well suited to the expression of emotional states, especially love. Another Ionian, Anacreon of Teos, was famous for odes which dealt chiefly with the themes of love and wine.

The choral lyric was employed for religious purposes when groups of trained singers sang marriage, processional, or victory hymns; there were also funeral dirges. An Asiatic Greek named Alcman was famous in the seventh century for the choral works he composed at Sparta.

The earliest prose writers appeared in the sixth century. Many composed genealogies of the gods and men, the first form of historical writing in which the Greeks engaged; these writers were called the *logographoi*.

ALPHABETS

	A	B	C (G)	D	E	F	(Z)H	I	K	L M N	O P	Q R S	T (Y)	V	X	8	≠(f)
ROMAN	A	B	C (G)	D	E	F	(Z)H	I K	L M N	O P	Q R S	T (Y)	V	X		
ETRUSCAN	A	B	C	D	E	F	I ⊕	I K	L M N	⊞	O ⊓ M Ϙ Φ D S Ϻ	X V Ϙ V	X			8	≠(f)
WEST GREEK	A	B	C	D	F F	I ⊕	I K	L M N	K Ψ X	O P	Ϙ R Ε T Y	Φ Χ V	+ Ψ Ϻ			
CORINTH	A	Ͷ C	D	B F	⊕	I K	L M N	Μ Ϥ Θ ⊦	O Γ	Ϙ Φ P M T V	Φ + Y				
ATHENS	A	B	D	F	I ⊕	I K	L M N	Κ O Γ	Ϻ	P S T V	Θ Χ V	Γ Ϻ			
IONIC (EAST GREEK)	A	B	Γ	E	H ⊞	Z H ⊙	I	I K Λ M N	Ε O Γ	Ϻ	P Σ T Y	Φ Χ V	Γ Ϻ		
PHOENICIAN	∀	9	1	Δ	∃	Y	I ⊗	ℸ	⊗	⩚ Ϲ 9 Ϥ ʒ	ℸ O 7	⧻ O ̵ Ϥ Φ	۹ W X				

214

Hecataeus of Miletus wrote the first Greek treatise on geography in which he described the world as he knew it.

From this brief survey of the philosophy and literature of the Archaic Period, it will be seen that the Asiatic Greeks surpassed all others in numbers and activity in these fields. This was due partly to their proximity to the Near East and partly to the favorable economic conditions which existed in Asia Minor during the eighth, seventh, and early sixth centuries. The conquest of Lydia and the Greek coastal cities by Persia, however, forced many Greeks to migrate to the Greek mainland and the western Mediterranean. They naturally carried their culture and their ideas with them, with the result that they stimulated cultural activity among the Greeks of the mainland and the West. Thus, in the fifth and fourth centuries, Greece, southern Italy, and Sicily became the centers of cultural growth.

Finally, the new poetry of the seventh and sixth centuries may have derived its form from non-Greek sources. Elegy, iambic, and dithyramb are words which lack satisfactory Greek etymologies. We hear of Phrygian and Lydian modes of music. The names of musical instruments are also non-Greek in some cases: phorminx (lyre), salpinx (trumpet), syrinx (flute). *Sambuca* and *iambuke,* names of lyres, remind us of Assyrian *pagu,* a word for a stringed instrument. The discovery of poetic inscriptions in the Lydian language at Sardes, the predominance of the Asiatic Greeks in the production of the new poetry, and the actual association of poets, especially Alcman, with Sardes suggest a Lydian inspiration for at least part of the new developments.

Regardless of the cogency of these particular suggestions, it is essential to realize that Greek literature was not born, nor did it ever exist, in a vacuum. Throughout its whole history it was subjected to all kinds of influences which were economic, social, religious, political, and environmental —even technological. City life, country life, hard times, good times, local conditions, foreign ideas, the Greek language, foreign languages, and innumerable things less tangible made Greek literature what it was at any special time, but one of the great turning points in the development of Greek literature came near the beginning when the Greeks adopted the alphabet.

The Greeks were more or less literate in the Mycenaean Age when the Linear B script was used for writing Greek. Syllabaries derived from the Minoan script continued to be used by some Greeks right down to the first century B.C., but none of these syllabaries was devised for writing Greek— only adapted for it—and as a result they were not satisfactory. If they had been used exclusively, Greek literature as we know it might never have come into existence.

When civilization began to develop in Greece after 750 B.C., there was a growing need for a simple and manageable system of writing primarily for the conduct of business and for general communication. The Semitic alpha-bet was then borrowed and adapted by the Greeks from the Phoenicians. The determining factor, the reason that the Greeks took over the alphabet instead of Egyptian hieroglyphics or the Mesopotamian cuneiform, was that the Greeks were doing business with the Phoenicians.

The Semitic, and primarily Phoenician, origin of the Greek alphabet is easy enough to establish. The Greek names of the letters are Helleniza-tions of Semitic words: alpha comes from Semitic aleph (ox), beta from Semitic beth (house), and so on. The Greeks also retained the traditional Semitic order of the letters: aleph (alpha) came first, beth (beta) second, gimel (gamma) third, etc. The earliest Greek inscriptions use the forms of the Phoenician letters of about 800 B.C., and the earliest Greek texts are read, like the Semitic ones, from right to left.

One of the problems of the Greeks in taking over the Semitic alphabet was that this script, like the earlier syllabaries, had not been devised for writing Greek. There were sounds in Phoenician that did not exist in Greek and sounds in Greek that had no counterpart in Phoenician. There-fore, some changes had to be made in the original phonetic characters. Moreover, the Semitic alphabet was really a stenographic system which con-tained only the characters for the consonants, and we may credit the Greeks with a significant invention because they supplied signs for the vowels which transformed the alphabet into a truly phonetic system of writing.

The adoption of the alphabet instead of a more complicated form of writing increased the potential literacy of the Greeks. If a man wished to learn to read and write, it was no longer necessary for him to spend years in training as a scribe. As the Greeks learned to write they could not only keep records and perpetuate their growing knowledge in writing, but also the introduction of writing was to affect the form of Greek literature. The old dactylic hexameter had been easy to memorize; it was eminently suitable for oral transmission. Now, however, that poetry could be written down, more varied meters could be employed, and experimentation was possible. In addition, prose, which had not been amenable to oral transmission, at last had a chance to develop.

The spread of literacy and the extensive use of writing by the Greeks, however, came rather slowly. The fact that the sixth-century philosophers often used the old hexameter instead of prose suggests that they wrote very little. The brevity of the new-style poems was not entirely due to their subject matter. It is significant that the Greeks did not soon develop a cursive script but continued to write in capitals. The reason for this was probably technological, for the Greeks lacked sufficient quantities of suitable materials on which to write. Papyrus and leather were expensive and hard to come by. In the fifth century a Herodotus or a Thucydides might write a long history in prose, but the duplication of the author's manuscript for distribution to a reading public was not feasible on a large scale. Therefore, even prose was written to be read aloud, or recited, to a group; this meant that the arrangement and style of a prose work were severely limited. There had to be convenient stopping places at which the performer and his audience could rest, and when an author had to write as he would speak, his literary style would be subject to the influence of oratory, poetry, and the drama.

Since the Greeks were not inhibited by theocracy, they were free to create a secular culture. There was no priestly caste to monopolize intellectual and literary activity, but it would be incorrect to say that religion failed to provide the Greeks with inspiration in literature, philosophy, and the arts. In fact, the religious life of the Greeks provided the main stimulus for the development of their architecture and sculpture. The temple was the first and most important type of building to be devised by the Greeks of the Archaic Period, and their first efforts in sculpture were devoted to cult statues. Thus, in a general way, the history of the development of art in Greece begins as it did in the Near East.

The first Greek temples were wood and mud-brick structures erected to shelter cult statues from the elements. Their plan resembled very closely that of the Mycenaean megaron with its portico leading into a square or rectangular chamber. From these simple origins more complex arrangements were developed. Columns could be added to the façade of the portico, the portico duplicated at the rear of the temple, the inner chamber subdivided into a number of rooms, and the temple enclosed by a colonnade. In the seventh century stone began to supplant the earlier wood and mud-brick materials; limestone, and finally marble, came into use. The Greeks, who like the Egyptians had plenty of good stone, preferred to use the column and lintel rather than the arch. Nevertheless, the wooden origins of Greek architecture were important for the development of their architectural styles, because various features of a functional nature in the wooden buildings were retained for decorative purposes when stone became popular. The triglyphs and metopes of the Doric style, and the column capitals and dentils of the Ionic represent survivals from the period when wood was used instead of stone.

Two of the three Greek orders of architecture, the Doric and the Ionic, were developed in the Archaic Period. The Doric order was the product of the mainland Greeks and their fellows in the western Mediterranean, whereas the Ionic order had its origin on the shores of Asia Minor. The distinguishing features of the Doric order were its columns and its entablature. The Doric column had no base, and its capital consisted of two simple blocks: the curved echinus and the flat abacus. The principal feature of the entablature was the frieze which consisted of two alternating parts, triglyphs and metopes. The triglyphs were blocks marked by three projections;

in the old wooden buildings the triglyphs were the sheathing for the ends of the ceiling beams of the cella (inner chamber). The metopes were blocks inserted between the triglyphs; sometimes the metopes were undecorated, but often they bore figured reliefs. In the Ionic order the column was provided with a base, and its capital was a volute or scroll. The Ionic frieze was a plain band of stone which might be decorated with a continuous pattern of reliefs.

The roofs of the Greek temples were sloping, and they were covered with terra cotta tiles. Bright colors, principally red and blue, were often applied to the exteriors to make a contrast with the white marble. Beneath the gabled roof of the façade of the Greek temple was a triangular space formed by the two raking cornices (the lines of the roof) and the horizontal cornice; this was the pediment which, in the Doric order, was often embellished with sculpture in the round.

In the Archaic Period somt rather large temples were constructed. The Ionic temple of Artemis at Ephesus was especially impressive, and in Sicily and southern Italy a number of huge Doric temples were built. The temple of Olympian Zeus which Peisistratus planned to construct at Athens would have equalled these in size.

The Greek sculptors employed wood, limestone, marble, ivory, and various metals, principally bronze. Both solid and hollow casting of metals became common in the Archaic Period; a technique for hollow casting was developed in the sixth century. Decorative sculpture advanced with the evolution of temple architecture, whereas substantive sculpture (sculpture in the round) evolved from the demands for cult statues and for statues of victorious athletes. Three main types of figures were produced over and over again by the early artists: the *kouros,* a nude standing male figure which might represent a god or an athlete; the *kore,* a draped standing female figure representing a goddess; and, finally, draped seated male or female figures which represented gods or goddesses. This repetition of types was important, because continuous practice with a limited number of subjects made for mastery of material and gradual improvement of technique. The first statues were crude and stiff; the use of the law of frontality was reminiscent of Egyptian practice, for undoubtedly the Greek sculptors owed much to the Egyptians. Eventually, the Greek artists broke the bonds of convention; their work began to show close observation of anatomy, and they began to portray drapery in a more realistic fashion.

The Asiatic Greeks were most proficient in the making of female figures. A distinctive style, characterized by a careful attention to detail, was developed by the sculptors of Chios; their female figures had oblique eyes, and the lips were curved in a pleasant but vacuous smile. The artists of the Peloponnesus specialized in athletic figures which were generally short and stocky.

Stone sculpture was colored with red, blue, brown, and black. Bronze statues were often given eyes of paste or colored stone to make their appearance more lifelike. Sometimes the bronze figures were gilded.

We do not know much about early Greek painting because no examples of it have survived. There seems to have been a continuation or a revival of the Minoan-Mycenaean tradition of mural frescoes, and the literary sources tell us that a certain Kimon of Kleonai (*c.* 500 B.C.) invented foreshortening and paid much attention to the portrayal of anatomy and drapery. It is possible to gain some idea of the progress of painting by observing the advances that were made in contemporary vase painting, for here an absorbing interest in anatomy and drapery is evident during the last quarter of the sixth century.

It would not be entirely inaccurate to say that vase painting was one of the major arts of Archaic Greece. A number of cities developed distinctive styles of decoration, but the best work, from about 550 onward, was done at Athens. The Attic black-figured style consisted of black silhouettes painted against the natural red background of the baked clay; interior details were-indicated by incised lines filled with white. After about 520 B.C. the Attic red-figured style became popular; in this the background was covered with a black glaze and the figures were produced by an outline technique in which brownish lines were applied to the red clay. Many of the potters and vase painters signed their names to vases which they considered especially fine work. The names of more than fifty artists who made the black-figured ware are known, and the names of the red-figured artists are even more numerous.

Amazing as the developments in Archaic philosophy, literature, and art may seem, they constituted only a promise of the things that the Greeks were to accomplish later.

Chapter 15

THE FIFTH CENTURY

I N THE PERIOD between 500 and 362 B.C. the city-state civilization of Greece attained its fullest development. The Athenians of the fifth century were able to create the democracy for which the sixth-century reforms of Solon, Peisistratus, and Cleisthenes had paved the way; Greek art, literature, and philosophy rose to new heights. Nevertheless, by 362 B.C. the city-state, as a dominant political institution, was on the decline, although the civilization which it had made possible was facing an even more brilliant future.

The fifth century opened with an invasion of Greece by the Persians. For two decades the independence of Greece hung in the balance, but the Greeks, united under the leadership of Sparta and Athens, finally managed to repel the invaders. After the great victories which removed the Persian threat to mainland Greece, the Spartans, whose domestic situation did not permit an aggressive foreign policy, resigned their hegemony in favor of the Athenians. The latter then formed a league of maritime Greek states with the object of carrying the war into Asia Minor and freeing the Asiatic Greeks from the Persian yoke. Shortly before the middle of the fifth century, the Athenians took steps to reduce their allies to the position of subjects. The result was the creation of a fairly large Aegean empire with its capital at Athens; the economic benefits that accrued from the empire made possible Athenian democracy and the flowering of Athenian culture. The Spartans, however, were drawn once more into Greek politics by the demands of their more commercially minded allies whose prosperity was being undermined by Athenian economic imperialism. Sparta and her allies on the one side, and Athens and her empire on the other, engaged in a series of conflicts which were brought to a conclusion with the complete collapse of Athens at the end of the fifth century. After this the Spartans, partly because they had become imperialists and partly as an extension of their sixth-century

Peloponnesian policy, began to force their rule upon all of Greece. The movement of reaction against Sparta was led by Athens and Thebes; by 370 B.C. Spartan power had been broken, and during the next eight years a Theban imperialist movement also rose and collapsed. By 362 B.C. all traces of Greek unity had vanished, and there was no Greek state powerful enough to force unification upon the others. As a result, the exhausted Greeks fell easy prey to the newly risen Macedonian kingdom of the north.

The numerous conflicts of the period summarized above were caused partly by the traditional separatism and desire for local independence that were the heritage of the Dark Ages, but more fundamental issues were involved. The capitalist system had produced within each city-state an antagonism between the wealthy minority which held most of the agricultural and industrial property and the poverty-stricken masses who agitated for a redistribution of land and other forms of wealth. Overlying this economic conflict was a corresponding battle between two political philosophies: oligarchy and democracy. The rich naturally favored a restriction of the franchise, whereas the poor desired greater participation in the government in order that they might gain their economic ends. These party struggles disrupted domestic peace and often cut across city-state lines, for the oligarchs or the democrats of one city often aided the members of the corresponding party in another city. Thus, civil wars frequently led to "international conflicts." Then, too, the policy of the Persians, after their failure to subjugate the mainland Greeks, involved continual interference; the Persians wished to keep the Greeks divided and weak, for if the Greeks united they were sure to attack the Persian holdings in Asia Minor. Therefore, if any one Greek state threatened to become too strong, the Persians were always ready to give financial and military support to the other Greek cities.

We have already traced the rise of the Persian Empire from its beginnings under Cyrus the Great about 550 B.C. through the European conquests of Darius in the two decades preceding 500 B.C. After the fall of the Lydian kingdom of Croesus the Asiatic Greeks had become Persian subjects; in most of the Greek cities of Asia Minor, local tyrants were set up to rule as representatives of the Persian king. The Persians also gained a foothold in Thrace, and they undoubtedly hoped to extend their rule over the Aegean islands.

Where was the Persian advance to end? Although the Persians already possessed more territory than their small ruling caste could hold conveniently, it was felt that further conquests were necessary. As long as the malcontents of Asiatic Greece could flee across the Aegean to a safe refuge in Greece proper—where they could make plans for organizing rebellions in Asia Minor—the Persian control of the Asiatic Greeks would be uncertain. Therefore, the next logical step for the Persian government appeared to be the conquest of Greece itself. Moreover, the Persians felt that there were certain scores with Athens and Sparta which ought to be settled. Hippias, the Athenian tyrant, had fled to Asia Minor and had asked the Persians to reinstate him at Athens. A Persian request to the Athenians to take Hippias again as their ruler had been refused in a manner which was far from polite. In addition, the Spartans had been the allies of Croesus; even though they had not sent aid to Croesus when Cyrus attacked him, the Persians bore them a grudge.

The immediate cause for war between the Persians and the Greeks was provided by the so-called Ionian Revolt, an uprising of the Asiatic Greeks which began about 499 B.C. The Ionians were dissatisfied with their tyrants, they disliked the high Persian taxes, and they had suffered economic reverses; in the closing years of the sixth century the prosperity of Ionia had declined because of the competition provided by Phoenician, Carthaginian, and mainland Greek traders. The revolt began at Miletus and spread to other Asiatic towns. Aristagoras, tyrant of Miletus and leader of the revolt, came to Greece to seek aid; he secured help at Athens and at Eretria (in Euboea), but the Spartans, though nearly persuaded, finally decided to remain aloof. Since the Persians were caught unawares by the uprising, the rebels at first met with success: Sardes, the old Lydian capital which was now a Persian administrative center, was sacked and burned. As the Persians regained their composure and were able to bring in reinforcements, the tide of battle turned. The Athenians and Eretrians became afraid and deserted the Ionians; by 494 the last embers of the rebellion had been stamped out. Persian control over Asia Minor was tightened, heavier taxes were imposed, and the Persians began to consider measures of retribution against Eretria and Athens.

Darius the Great, who now occupied the Persian throne, despatched two expeditions against Greece, one in 492 and the other in 490. His objective was primarily punitive. Persian prestige had suffered, and if the Athenians and Eretrians were made to feel the might of the Great King, then perhaps the mainland Greeks would be dissuaded from further meddling. The first Persian expedition got no farther than Macedonia, for it had to turn back when its fleet was destroyed by a storm off Mount Athos. The second attack was made directly across the Aegean to Euboea; Eretria was besieged, and a Persian force was landed on the Plain of Marathon in Attica about twenty miles northeast of Athens. The Athenians planned to go to the relief of Eretria, but the occupation of Marathon pinned down their forces in Attica, for the Persian plan was first to reduce Eretria and then attack Athens. The Athenians, realizing their danger, appealed to Sparta; before help arrived from that quarter, Eretria fell, and the whole Persian force was freed for the move on Athens. The Athenian army at Marathon was thus placed in something of a predicament: if they remained where they were, holding the road from Marathon to Athens, the Persians at Eretria could

sail to Athens and attack the virtually undefended city, and if they re-
treated from Marathon, the Persian force there could advance unmolested.
Time was of the essence; the Spartans had not come, and something must be
done at once. The Athenians descended to the Plain of Marathon, drove
the Persians into the sea, and then proceeded back to Athens by a forced
march where they prepared to fight again the following morning when the
Persian fleet appeared in the Bay of Phalerum. This discouraged the Persians, who had had enough at Marathon, and they sailed away. Shortly after,
the Spartans arrived, but they could only view the slaughter at Marathon
and listen to Athenian boasting of victory. Although the Battle of Marathon
was no great thing from the military point of view, it gave the Greeks the
confidence they needed to oppose the Great King in the future.

Before another invasion could be organized, Darius died. His successor,
Xerxes, was too busy with revolts within the empire to bother about the
Greeks for several years, but at last he was persuaded by his advisors that
the Greek problem could be solved only by the conquest of Greece itself. We
should like to know more about those around Xerxes who promoted the new
action against the Greeks. One of them was Mardonius, the general in 492,
who had been forced to turn back at Athos; another was Hippias, still alive
and still anxious to return to Athens—Hippias had accompanied the expedition of 490 but had been disappointed of restoration by the events of Marathon—another was Demaratus, former king of Sparta, who had been recently deposed by his colleague, crusty old Cleomenes; and still another seems
to have been a mysterious soothsayer named Onomacritus who had lived at
Athens under the Peisistratid regime.

Careful plans were laid for the invasion. A huge army and fleet were to
proceed along the coast of Thrace and Macedonia into Greece. Stores and
provisions were accumulated in neutral territory along the projected line of
march, and two pontoon bridges were built across the Hellespont; a canal
was dug through the isthmus behind Mount Athos so that the fleet might
avoid another disaster. In the autumn of 481 Xerxes himself came to Sardes
where his forces were being mustered; he reviewed the preparations and
made ready for an invasion in the following spring.

The Greeks could not be unaware of the impending danger. Athens
and the Peloponnesian League were determined to resist, but the Thes-
salians, Thebans, and Argives decided to remain neutral: the first could see
no possibility of stopping the Persians, the Thebans hoped that the
Athenians would be punished and humiliated, and the Argives were hoping
for the destruction of Sparta. The Delphic oracle, perhaps fearing that its
treasures would be plundered, counseled submission. To make matters
worse, Cleomenes, the fiery old Spartan king, had become insane, and the
Greeks in the west in Sicily could send no aid because they were momentarily expecting a Carthaginian invasion (prearranged by Persia).

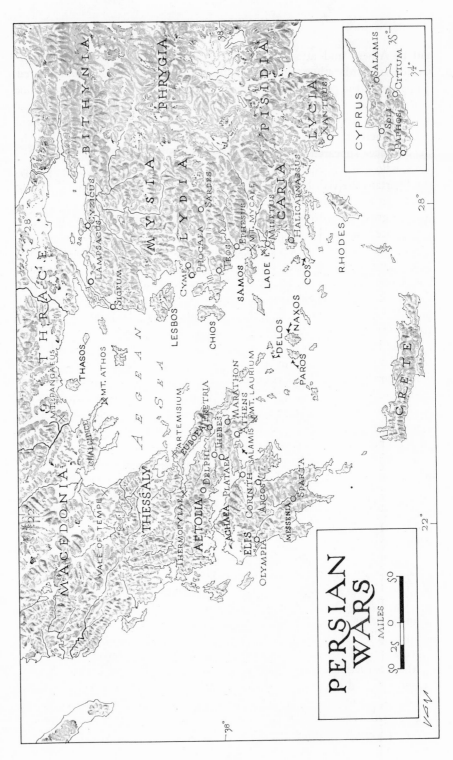

PERSIAN WARS

MILES

CYPRUS

224

Athens, though determined to resist, was torn by party strife. In order to understand the situation, it is necessary to go back to the beginning of the century. Three parties at least can be discerned in Athens around the year 500: the partisans of Hippias who hoped for the restoration of tyranny, the Alcmaeonidae who were tending toward conservatism, and a popular party which soon found a leader in Themistocles, who held the archonship in 493. The identity of the fire-eaters who got Athens into the Ionian affair in 499–498 is uncertain, but it is clear that the Athenians repented of their audacity and tried to appease Persia by electing Peisistratids to office in 496 and possibly 497. Then the tide turned, and anti-Persian leaders were chosen: Themistocles was one of these, and Miltiades, the hero of Marathon, was another. Miltiades, whose father had been put to death by the tyrants, had been living in a colony in Thrace. He had accompanied Darius on the Scythian expedition and had incurred Persian enmity when he attempted to sabotage Darius by suggesting to the other Greeks in the Persian entourage that they destroy Darius' bridge across the Danube while he was still on the northern bank chasing the Scythians. When the Persians under Mardonius had planned their first invasion of Greece, Miltiades had returned to Athens. In 490 Miltiades was one of the ten generals, and it was he who engineered the attack which drove the Persians into the sea at Marathon. After Marathon Miltiades was placed in charge of a fleet detailed to pursue the Persians, but he turned aside for some reason to attack the island of Paros. If the attack had been successful, no questions would have been asked, but the Athenians were defeated with severe losses. Miltiades was prosecuted by the conservatives; although he died before the trial ended, he was nevertheless fined fifty talents. Ironically enough, Miltiades' fine was paid by his son, Cimon, who later married into the clan of the Alcmaeonidae and became a conservative leader, while Miltiades' prosecutor was Xanthippus, already allied by marriage with the Alcmaeonidae, whose son was Pericles, the great democratic leader of the future who became the rival of Cimon.

Opposition to Persia grew after the success at Marathon. Both conservatives and liberals included anti-Persian planks in their campaign platforms, but Themistocles was able to outmaneuver the conservatives. While they insisted that Athens must build a big army to combat the impending Persian invasion, Themistocles argued that the Greeks as a whole lacked ships, that the Spartans and their allies could supply sufficient land forces, and that the Athenians would be wise to build a fleet. The resources were at hand. Through the discovery of a rich new vein of silver at Laurium in Attica, ships could be financed, and the common people of Attica, who could not be armed and trained as infantrymen, could be utilized as rowers for the ships.

A new political weapon was available which enabled Themistocles to silence his adversaries. This was ostracism, an ingenious device which gave the people as a whole a means of controlling state policies. Ostracism, traditionally attributed to Cleisthenes, was probably a brain child of the resourceful Themistocles. It was instituted in 488, and its procedure was as follows:

In any year, if it seemed advisable, the Athenians might go to the polls to cast their ballots for the man considered "most dangerous to the state." The winner of this—we might say—unpopularity contest had to leave Athens and go into exile for ten years. The Athenian ostracism, which is so called because the voters scratched the names of the candidates on broken pieces of pottery (*ostraka*), was the reverse of the modern vote of confidence, but it served its end equally well. An ostracism ordinarily occurred when there were two leaders who advocated opposite policies; the people thus cast their votes for the man whose policies they disliked, and he would be removed from the scene by exile, thus leaving his opponent to carry out the alternative program undisturbed.

The first person to be ostracized (487) was a Peisistratid partisan, but in the next four years prominent members of the Alcmaeonid party were eliminated by the same route. The last to go was the pro-Alcmaeonid Aristides who had strenuously opposed the big-navy policy of Themistocles. Thus, Themistocles rid himself of his rivals and could at last make the necessary preparations to resist the invasion of Xerxes.

When Xerxes in the spring of 480 began to move through Thrace and Macedonia, his army supported by a big fleet, the Greeks had worked out a scheme of defense: they would use their small forces to best advantage by trying to hold the passes along the route which the Persians must travel. The first stand, at Tempe on the northern border of Thessaly, failed because the Persian fleet was able to sail in behind the defenders and turn their position. At Thermopylae, however, there was a more defensible position: the pass was narrower, and the Greek fleet could hold the straits between Euboea and the mainland in order to prevent the Persian fleet from repeating the maneuver which had been so successful at Tempe. The small Greek force, commanded by the young Spartan king, Leonidas, held out at Thermopylae for several days, but when a traitor showed the Persians another route over the mountains, Leonidas was surrounded, his troops annihilated, and the way was open for the Persians into central Greece. Thebes and Boeotia offered no resistance; Athens was easily taken.

The position of the Greeks was now truly desperate. The Spartans, with their usual ingenuity, proposed to fortify the Isthmus of Corinth to prevent the invasion of the Peloponnesus, but Themistocles demonstrated the futility of this plan by pointing out that the Persian fleet could land troops at any place in the Peloponnesus and repeat the strategy of Tempe.

The best chance of the Greeks, he said, was in forcing a naval encounter. Thus, the decisive sea battle of Salamis was precipitated; the Persian fleet was lured into the narrow strait between the Island of Salamis and the mainland of Attica, virtually ambushed, and certainly destroyed by the small, swift Greek warships. Without a fleet the Persian advance was stalled and their communications with Asia in jeopardy; furthermore, the campaigning season was nearly over. Xerxes went back to Persia, and Mardonius withdrew the army into Boeotia for the winter. In the spring of 479 hostilities were renewed. A final contest took place at Plataea in Boeotia, just over the border from Attica. Once again the Persians were beaten, Mardonius was killed, and as the remnants of the Grand Army of the Great King withdrew from Greece, the Greeks rejoiced in a well-earned victory.

It was not enough, however, to have driven the Persians from Greece. Encouraged by a victory over the Persians at Mycale in Asia Minor—tradition placed the battle on the same day as the Battle of Plataea—the Greeks planned to follow up their advantage by carrying the war across the Aegean for the purpose of liberating the Ionian cities. A combined Greek fleet began to operate in the Aegean, and many island and mainland states were freed.

At the same time Greek unity began to disappear. The Spartans proposed that structures ruined by the vandalism of the Persians should not be rebuilt but left as they were to remind posterity of what the Persians had done. The sentiment was a laudable one. The Spartans had nothing to lose by such a policy because Sparta had been untouched by the war, but at Athens this would have meant that not only the temples and other structures would have been left in ruins but also the walls of the town; Athens would be an open, undefended city at the mercy of any attacker—and this might some day include the Spartans. Themistocles realized the implications of the Spartan proposal, tricked the Spartans into believing that the Athenians were in agreement, and then refortified Athens before the Spartans found out what was happening. Henceforth, Themistocles was rather unpopular in Sparta, especially so after he fortified the Peiraeus, the natural harbor of Athens, for use as a naval base.

But this was not all that Themistocles accomplished. Throughout the war military leadership had been given without much question to the Spartans, but after 479 the overbearing attitude of their generals in the field —especially in the case of Pausanias, the hero of Plataea—antagonized Greek contingents from the other states while the Athenians had cultivated popularity. Moreover, the home government at Sparta was not in sympathy with the aggressive policy advocated by Pausanias. The traditional Spartan sentiment for isolation began to reassert itself, and when the other Greeks intimated that they preferred to be led by Athenians rather than Spartans, the

Spartan government withdrew its troops and commanders with little protest. In 477 B.C. when the leadership thus devolved upon Athens, Themistocles proposed a naval confederation known to history as the Delian League.

The fundamental idea behind the Delian League was that the states interested in carrying on hostilities against Persia would ally themselves with Athens. Each state would contribute a definite quota of ships and men (or a money equivalent), and operations would be conducted each year under Athenian leadership. The league treasury and its administrative center would be located on the island of Delos. The object of the league was to free the Greeks still subject to Persia, prevent a renewal of Persian imperialism directed at Greece, and acquire enough loot from Persian territory to pay the expenses of the war. The quotas due from the member states were determined by Aristides, whose reputation for probity was universally accepted; he did not disappoint the Greeks on this occasion, for he apportioned the contributions in such a way that he earned for himself the title of "the Just." The league, once organized, met with continued success down to 468 B.C., when its forces climaxed their operations with a great naval victory which swept the Persians from the seas and completed the liberation of most of the Asiatic Greeks.

In 468 it seemed to many people that the Delian League had served its purpose and might well be disbanded. The Athenians, on the other hand, argued that the setback suffered by the Persians was only temporary; peace had not been concluded and the Persians had not acknowledged the independence of the Ionian cities. As a matter of fact, the Persians had continued to assess the Ionian tribute even though they were not able to collect it, and the assumption was that at some time in the future an accounting would be demanded. The Athenians protested that it would be unfair for the allies to withdraw from the league, thus leaving Athens to provide protection for all at her own expense.

The real basis for the Athenian desire that the league should continue, however, was that the league had been a profitable venture for Athens. Many of the allies had preferred to pay money into the league treasury at Delos rather than risk ships and men. As a result, it was the Athenian navy which had borne the brunt of the fighting. Money from the treasury had been used to finance the Athenian operations, and much had been spent in improving and enlarging the Athenian navy which had become the most powerful in Greece.

Moreover, the whole situation was closely tied up with domestic politics in Athens itself. Whereas in the Athenian army the fighting was done by those who could afford to buy armor and weapons—the upper and middle classes—in the navy the rowers were ordinarily recruited from the citizen proletariat. The fact that Athens had become a naval rather than a land power meant that the proletariat had become very useful in military oper-

ations. The Athenian proletariat capitalized on its important position to demand an increasing share in the government with the result that Athenian democracy came into existence. The navy, which was essential to the continued political predominance of the lower classes and to their financial support, could not be maintained at full strength without the funds which the league provided; and therefore, the league, in one form or another, must be continued.

As early as 468 a movement of secession from the league was on foot among the allies. The Athenians, however, argued that the treaties of alliance that had been made in 477 were eternally binding and might not be abrogated. When various states attempted to secede, they were attacked and overpowered by Athens; once in control, the Athenians made subjects of their rebellious allies. Control of their foreign relations was vested in the Athenian government; usually the states were forced to accept new constitutions which set up democratic forms of government similar to those of Athens. Athenian garrisons might be stationed in the chief cities; desirable lands might be given to colonists sent out from Attica, and tribute was imposed upon the subject states. Eventually nearly two hundred cities were made subject and tributary to the Athenian government, and only a handful of the former allies retained their original status. Athenian imperialism reached its peak in the period between 461 and 445 when the democratic party at Athens was in the ascendant under the leadership of Pericles. Before we can consider the developments of this era, however, we shall have to see something of the internal politics in Athens after 477.

The popular party and Themistocles were definitely in the saddle after the Battle of Salamis, but the conservatives slowly began to gather strength and at last found an able and popular leader in Cimon, son of Miltiades, who had directed the naval operations of the Delian League with great success. Themistocles, of course, was committed to an anti-Spartan policy for both personal and political reasons; his domestic policy called for an extension of democracy, or at least a continued liberalization of the constitution, but it was on his attitude toward Persia that he finally came to grief. Themistocles came to feel that the war against Persia had gone far enough, that peace should be concluded in order that the Athenians might open up trade with Persian territory. Cimon and the conservatives, on the other hand, began to advocate friendship with Sparta and continued attacks on Persia; their domestic policy, which they may not have emphasized, was naturally opposed to any further liberalization of the Athenian government. By 471 the contest between the parties represented by Themistocles and Cimon had reached a point where an ostracism was in order; Themistocles was the loser and went into exile as the conservatives came into power for the next nine years.

Cimon attained the zenith of his popularity with the great victory over the Persians at the Eurymedon in 468. After this an anti-Persian program held little meaning, while the antidemocratic and pro-Spartan sentiments of the conservatives came in for more attention. These were issues the popular party could use to undermine Cimon's popularity with the majority of the voters. A turning point was reached in 464 when a bloody helot revolt began in Laconia. The Spartans were hard pressed, for some of the helots dug themselves in on Mount Ithome and could not be subdued. When the Spartans finally appealed to Athens for aid, Cimon persuaded the Athenians to send a force to Laconia. This was a mistake: even with Cimon's help the helots could not be recaptured, and finally the Spartans with scant courtesy told the Athenians to go back home. Cimon had thus exposed

Athens to insult by Sparta; he paid the penalty for poor judgment by incurring ostracism in 462.

The opponent of Cimon in 462 was a popular leader named Ephialtes who advocated democratic reforms, but he was assassinated the following year, and the leadership of his party, which was now in the majority, passed to Pericles, son of Xanthippus. Elected to the generalship every year except one from 461 to his death in 429, Pericles was to head his party and direct the foreign and domestic affairs of Athens for a whole generation. His influence on every phase of Athenian history was so great that the whole period is called the Age of Pericles.

The policies of Pericles may be considered under two general headings: foreign and domestic. The foreign policy of Pericles from 461 to 445 was aggressively imperialistic as he tried to build up a land empire in central Greece to match the maritime empire the Athenians already possessed. The whole attempt was a dismal failure, for Pericles was unrealistic and certainly no strategist. The over-all plan was attractive in theory, but it had the distinct disadvantage of being unworkable.

As a liberal and the opponent of Cimon, Pericles was committed to an anti-Spartan policy, and his success in antagonizing the Spartans, the Peloponnesians, and the Thebans was outstanding. He was seduced by the attractiveness of the old Peisistratid idea of an alliance with Argos and Thessaly; the Argive alliance would theoretically drive a wedge between Sparta and Corinth (depending, of course, on the strength of Argos), while the Thessalian alliance would be a knife in the back of Thebes. The next step was to gain control of Megara, the state which lay on the Isthmus of Corinth between Athens and Corinth. Megara was persuaded to join the Athenian Empire in 459. As a matter of fact, the poor Megarians had to join Athens to keep from being gobbled up by Corinth. From the Athenian point of view, the adherence of Megara was a fine thing: the two harbors of Megara provided Athens with ports on either side of the Isthmus of Corinth, while Athenian possession of Megara would keep the Peloponnesians from marching up the isthmus to join the Thebans.

The alliances with Argos, Thessaly, and Megara alarmed the Peloponnesians and annoyed the Spartans, but Pericles now outdid himself: in 458 the unsubdued helots on Mount Ithome were allowed by the Spartans to leave Laconia. They were promptly befriended by Athens and settled at Naupactus on the Gulf of Corinth in a position where they could prevent a Peloponnesian crossing to central Greece and possibly close the outlet to the gulf in time of war. By 458 also the Athenians had attacked Aegina, the Dorian island state in the Saronic Gulf, which would make a fine Athenian naval base. Corinth came to the aid of Aegina, and before long Thebes and Sparta had joined in the war against Athens. At first, things went well for the Athenians. Most of central Greece, including Boeotia, was overrun, and in 456 Aegina surrendered. Athenian holdings on land and sea had now reached their greatest extent.

Simultaneously with the war in Greece, Pericles had managed to get involved in a war with the Persians. Revolts had broken out in Cyprus and Egypt against Persia, and Athens sent aid to both areas. In Egypt a large Athenian expeditionary force was cut off and destroyed along with another smaller force which had been sent to supplement the first. In a short time Athens had lost 250 ships and their crews, and as a result had lost control of the sea as well; the situation was so grave in 454 that the treasury of the Delian League had to be removed from Delos to Athens for safekeeping.

Matters continued to go from bad to worse. Pericles found that he could not fight on two fronts at once, so he enlisted the aid of Cimon, now returned from exile, with the object of making friends with Sparta. Cimon (about 451) patched up a five-year truce with Sparta; the Spartans withdrew from the war in Greece leaving their allies to fight on alone. Then Cimon was sent to Cyprus in 449 to battle the Persians. He died there, and Pericles immediately made an informal peace with Persia, for without Cimon's military leadership the Athenians could not go on with confidence.

Back in Greece, Thebes, Megara, and Euboea revolted in 447. In the following year the truce with Sparta ended, and the Peloponnesian armies invaded Attica itself, although a bribe of ten talents of silver provided from the Athenian treasury dissuaded the Spartans from doing any real damage to the country. The Athenians were able to recapture Euboea, but Thebes and Megara were lost forever. In 445 Athens and Sparta came to terms with the arrangement of a thirty-year truce which left Sparta's allies with no choice except to end hostilities, too. The Athenians had lost their temporary land empire in central Greece, but their maritime holdings were still intact.

The period from 445 to 431 B.C. was one of armed peace. Both Athenians and Peloponnesians realized that the first war had decided nothing and that a continuation of the struggle was inevitable. Athenian imperialism was by no means dead, although it had been somewhat chastened. The Peloponnesians and Thebans felt that only the complete destruction of Athens would remove the threat to their political and commercial independence. The grand strategy of Pericles had come to nothing; all that he had accomplished was to weaken Athens and gain the undying enmity and suspicion of the other Greek states. With her great navy Athens could hold a maritime empire, but she lacked the army and the transportation and communication facilities to maintain an empire on land. Anyone but an armchair strategist should have been able to realize this; it was the true measure of the military genius of Pericles. Foolish as it might appear at first glance, the attempt to aid Cyprus and Egypt to gain independence made more sense than the grandiose plan for an empire on the mainland of Greece. Cyprus was an important source of copper, and the trade of Egypt would have enriched Athens and given her a surplus of grain. The naval operations which aid to Cyprus and Egypt entailed were feasible except that the Athenians were unable to employ their full strength because of the war in Greece.

Pericles was a better politician than general. His domestic policies bore rich fruit, and by comparison with his foreign policy which withered on the vine, his management of affairs at home could be called successful. Under Pericles the maritime empire provided Athens with great prosperity, the city of Athens was made beautiful with handsome buildings, and the Athenian democracy flourished. We shall review the story of political evolution at Athens and then examine the details of the Periclean democracy itself.

One of the most important cultural contributions of Athens was the creation of a democratic form of government. This was not the work of a moment, but the result of a long evolution which reached its climax in the fifth century in the years between 461 and 429 B.C., the so-called Periclean Age. The Athenian democracy was largely the product of Greek economic developments, the Persian wars, and the creation of the Athenian navy and empire. Without the Athenian navy, which gave the proletariat a political lever, and the Athenian Empire, which provided the means to pay Athenian citizens for their participation in the government, the democracy could not have been brought into existence. Before we consider the operation of the full-blown democracy, it will be necessary to review briefly its evolution in the pre-Periclean period.

In the Dark Ages the monarchical form of government had existed in Athens. There was a king, a council (called the Areopagus), and the assembly (ecclesia). Between about 750 B.C. and the time of Cleisthenes the Areopagus had become the stronghold of the landed aristocrats who had abolished the kingship and reduced the power of the ecclesia. The powers of the king were divided among elected aristocratic magistrates called archons. One archon was a general administrative officer for Attica, another was commander-in-chief of the army, and another was high priest. About 620 B.C. the threat of sedition forced the nobles to allow the codification of the law; it is probable that at the same time six junior archons, the *thesmothetae* (or keepers of the laws), were added to the original three magistrates.

About 570 B.C. an economic and political crisis brought the reforms of Solon, and the Athenian government was transformed from an aristocratic oligarchy into a timocracy. The citizen population was divided into census classes according to its wealth; the members of the two upper classes were eligible for election to the major magistracies, and those of the third class could hold minor offices; all citizens were allowed to participate in the ecclesia and the *heliaia* (the great court of appeal).

The tyranny of Peisistratus produced no constitutional changes, but the persecution of the landed aristocrats made it possible for the businessmen to gain increased participation in the government. Those who fulfilled the financial qualifications for office were able to step into positions formerly held by the aristocrats. Under Cleisthenes the creation of the ten new tribes, the Council of the Five Hundred, and possibly the board of ten generals had the effect of disrupting old traditions and breaking down prejudices. The introduction of ostracism early in the fifth century enabled the masses to eliminate political leaders who were oligarchically inclined.

The period of the Persian wars was notable for conditions favoring the development of the democracy. The almost continuous state of war which existed during the first three decades of the fifth century made the ten generals the most important officials of Athens. To save themselves from the Persian conquest, the Athenians were forced to elect the best and most capable men available without regard to financial standing. The archonships, mere civic offices, paled into insignificance before the predominance of the generals. After the wars the creation of the empire and the difficulty of holding it increased the importance of the generals. The ancient authors tell us that even as early as 487 B.C. the archonship was filled by lot (sortition); in other words, the duties of the archons were routine matters, and it made little difference who filled these posts as long as the incumbents satisfied the financial qualifications stipulated by law.

Moreover, when the Athenians built up a strong fleet in the period of the Persian wars, the proletarians, who could not afford to equip themselves for the army, suddenly became valuable to the state as rowers for the ships. Naturally, the new significance of the proletarians gave them a lever with which they could pry concessions from the government. Last of all, the creation of the empire brought revenue to Athens which could be used to pay public servants. As a result, persons who could not have afforded to take time from the business of earning a living to participate in governmental affairs now found it worth while to do so.

The final steps in the creation of the democracy came at the opening of the Periclean Age when the leaders of the popular party, Ephialtes and Pericles, secured the passage of laws which deprived the Areopagus of most of its power (462 B.C.). The Areopagus had already declined with the archonship, for it was composed of former archons, but in 462 the ancient council lost its guardianship of the laws and its other functions, except its judicial ones, and the bulk of its powers passed to the Council of the Five Hundred, the ecclesia, and the *heliaia*. The introduction of the method of choosing the archons by lot, probably masterminded by Themistocles, had automatically lowered the caliber of the personnel of the Areopagus so

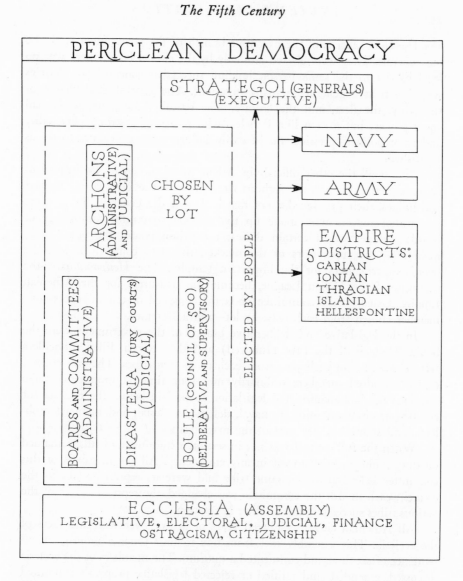

PERICLEAN DEMOCRACY

STRATEGOI (GENERALS)
(EXECUTIVE)

NAVY

ARMY

EMPIRE
5 DISTRICTS:
CARIAN
IONIAN
THRACIAN
ISLAND
HELLESPONTINE

ARCHONS (ADMINISTRATIVE AND JUDICIAL)

CHOSEN BY LOT

ELECTED BY PEOPLE

BOARDS AND COMMITTEES (ADMINISTRATIVE)

DIKASTERIA (JURY COURTS) (JUDICIAL)

BOULE (COUNCIL OF 500) (DELIBERATIVE AND SUPERVISORY)

ECCLESIA (ASSEMBLY)
LEGISLATIVE, ELECTORAL, JUDICIAL, FINANCE
OSTRACISM, CITIZENSHIP

that its prestige must have been lessened. Even so, the composition of the court must have been conservative, if not reactionary, and we may suspect that it may have rejected some liberal legislation as unconstitutional. As an obstacle in the path of the growing democracy, the Areopagus had to be removed.

✓In the Periclean Age the Athenian democracy attained its fullest development and its most efficient operation. The governmental machinery of the democracy as well as its aims and accomplishments merit detailed description and careful consideration.

The chief officials of the executive branch of the government were the ten generals. They were elected annually by the citizen body; there was no legal barrier to the same person holding successive generalships—Pericles was chosen as a general on many occasions. The generals had charge of the army, the fleet, and the empire. Theoretically, the generals all had equal power; but a man like Pericles, who possessed a strong personality and great political prestige, might easily influence his colleagues to do as he wished.

Almost all the other officials in Athens were chosen by lot instead of being elected. Although the archons were important as civic administrators and judges, their prestige did not match that of the generals. There were also minor officers who made up the various governing committees or boards and performed certain duties: the prison board, the police commissioners, the supervisors of the market, the state contractors, and the boards of treasurers for the important temples. The *Hellenotamiae,* the treasures of the Delian League, became the treasurers for the Athenian Empire. Usually each committee or board consisted of ten members—one member chosen from each tribe by lot—and a secretary.

In the legislative and deliberative branch of the government were the boule (Council of the Five Hundred) and the ecclesia. Fifty councillors were chosen by lot each year from each of the ten tribes. The full council of five hundred members ordinarily met four times a month; at these meetings the boule considered legislation to be laid before the ecclesia for enactment, discussed military, naval, defense, imperial, and financial problems, and scrutinized the acts of the magistrates.

When the full council was not in session a committee of fifty remained on duty night and day to act in any emergency. All the members of this committee belonged to the same tribe and were its representatives in the council; each month the committee was changed, the representatives of the various tribes succeeding one another in rotation.

All Athenian citizens eighteen years of age or over were members of the ecclesia. This assembly met from one to four times a month; an attendance of six thousand constituted a quorum. The members of the ecclesia discussed, amended, and ratified or rejected legislative proposals submitted to it by the boule. The ecclesia received foreign emissaries, elected the generals, and alone had the power to grant citizenship. It was also the body that voted on ostracism.

During the Periclean Age the Areopagus (as a court for homicide) and other special courts continued to function, but more important were the jury courts, the *dikasteria.* The growth of the empire had increased the judicial business which had to be transacted at Athens, for the Athenians required all major cases arising in the subject states to be tried there. Each year a panel of six thousand jurors was drawn from the Athenian citizen body. This panel was called the *heliaia,* though by the mid-fifth century the old Solonian court of appeal had probably ceased to function. The jurors, thus selected, were divided daily into groups of 201, 501, or similarly large numbers and assigned to try individual cases. The archons were usually the presiding magistrates; trials began at sunrise and had to be completed by sunset; the defendant had to plead his own case, although he might hire someone to write his defense for him.

The *dikasteria* were a more significant factor in the government than one might suppose. The introduction of pay for jury service during the Periclean Age meant that the poor of the city of Athens were provided with some means of support. The daily wage was small, and rich men or small farmers outside the city would not be much attracted by it; but the unemployed of Athens were naturally anxious to offer themselves for jury duty. Through the courts the proletariat gained considerable political power. "The courts were in almost perpetual session; their jurisdiction extended to every aspect and department of public life; and from their decision there was no appeal."[1]

As a result of the transformation of the Delian League into the Athenian Empire, nearly two hundred states were reduced from the position of allies to that of subjects. The "contribution" that the allies had paid for the support of military operations against Persia became the "tribute" which was now paid to Athens. A few of the original allies remained faithful to Athens and managed to retain their freedom, but the other states were forced to turn over to Athens the conduct of their foreign relations and to submit to the establishment of democratic constitutions drawn up by the Athenians. As we have seen, the subject states had to bring many lawsuits to Athens for trial; they were also bound by Athenian commercial regulations. In some cases, Athenian garrisons were sent to the subject cities; often, fertile lands in the subject states were given to Athenian military colonists, the *cleruchs*. From this it is clear that, although the empire was productive of certain economic benefits to the subject states (the suppression of piracy and the adoption of a uniform currency), there were many just reasons for dissatisfaction.

With the details of Athenian domestic and imperial government in mind, we may now attempt an evaluation of it. A major aim of the Periclean democracy was to secure the participation of all the citizens in the government. This was accomplished by throwing open the various branches of service to the entire citizen body; the three upper census classes could hold any office, and the only office not open to the fourth class was the archonship. The use of the lot was based on the theory that any man was capable of filling any position. The practice of rotation in office—forbidding successive terms in the same position—made it possible for a greater proportion of the citizens to engage in public service; the use of the committee

---

[1] *Cambridge Ancient History*, Vol. V, p. 112.

—to perform certain tasks which might have been performed by one official—was another method of gaining the end sought by rotation. The introduction of payment for service in the *dikasteria* and the boule enabled even the poorest citizens to participate.

There was some attempt to insure honest and efficient government and to fix responsibility. The personal qualifications of candidates were considered; auditors examined the accounts of officials and committees; officials were liable to impeachment; and the general conduct of the government was carefully scrutinized. Maladministration might be punished by fines, exile, or execution.

The greatest benefits of the democracy were enjoyed by the masses—it might even be said that this was the main purpose of the whole system. The tremendous power of the ecclesia in which the masses secured preponderance by mere weight of numbers, the composition of the juries, and the use which was made of imperial revenues—the tribute was used to pay the rowers in the fleet, the court fines to pay the jurors—all tended to benefit the common people more than any other group. The military cleruchies scattered throughout the empire helped to relieve overpopulation at Athens, and Pericles also sponsored a colonization project at Thurii in Italy. Finally, the state expenses that could not be met by the imperial revenues were provided for by revenue extracted from the metics (resident aliens) and the rich citizens. The rich citizens were liable for the *liturgies,* the expensive public services which were financed by individuals. A wealthy man might be requested to build and equip a warship, to pay for the training of a chorus for one of the Dionysiac plays, or to provide a feast for all the members of his tribe. It would not be fair to subject these features of the Athenian system to criticism, for they were the methods by which the chief end of a democracy might be gained—that is, the greatest good to the greatest number.

On the other hand, the Athenian democracy in operation displayed certain features which outrage modern notions of the ideal democracy.

First, the Athenian citizen body was a very limited group. Only about half of the inhabitants of Attica were citizens; the rest were metics and slaves. The Athenians of the Periclean Age had no idea of extending citizenship to others; instead, they tried to reduce the numbers of those eligible for its privileges and exemptions.

Second, the democracy was dependent upon imperialism and economic exploitation. The Athenian citizens were really a group of 150,000 oligarchs who derived their financial support from 2,000,000 subjects. The enjoyment of democracy by each Athenian citizen was made possible by the labor of a dozen subjects of his government.

Last of all, although the point cannot be pressed, one might question whether the Athenian democracy in the Age of Pericles was actually a democracy. It is very doubtful whether the Athenian people had much to do with the formulation of fundamental governmental policies. Pericles was not a dictator, but he and his clique certainly directed the government. The masses seem to have exercised their own initiative only when they wanted something that was of special benefit to them; and as long as Pericles kept them happy and satisfied, he could propose and secure ratification for other projects which he himself favored. It might even be said that the democracy functioned most efficiently when it was under the partial dictatorship of Pericles; for after his death, when less able leaders were at the helm, the proletariat took the bit in its teeth and was responsible for many ghastly mistakes.

These criticisms should not be construed as an indictment of democracy as a system. Democracy never received a fair trial at Athens, for one very necessary element for the success of democratic government was lacking: an intelligent, well-educated citizen body. Contrary to a belief which is widespread today, the Athenian citizen body was neither unusually intelligent nor well educated; at least, it was not educated for the task that it had to fulfill. We know that only a small group of Athenians ever received any formal education; only a minority knew how to read and write. Furthermore, it may well be asked whether the system of formal education in vogue at Athens would have helped the citizens to operate their government even if education had been available to all. It is often said that the opportunity for the actual participation of large groups of citizens in the government was an education in itself. It is true that most of the citizens well understood the workings of their governmental machinery, but it is perfectly possible to understand how a machine works yet not to know what to do with it. The real point is that the Athenians were not sound judges of policy, although Pericles claimed that they were. Socrates later demonstrated clearly that none of his contemporaries understood, or were able to think clearly about, matters of ethics, society, and economics. Precise, or even general, knowledge of these things was not available to the Periclean Greeks.

The subsequent history of Athenian government need not concern us here. The oligarchic government which the Spartans forced upon the Athenians at the end of the Peloponnesian War was overthrown when Athens regained her independence. Democracy was restored, and it was retained during the fourth century with only minor modifications.

Elsewhere in Greece government varied from extreme oligarchy to moderate democracy. There were frequent revolutions in the city-states during the fourth century, and the government of individual states was altered when the oligarchs or democrats rose or fell in power. The most common governmental form was the timocracy, although some of the Greek states in the west fell into the hands of tyrants who occasionally established monarchies.

Fathered by war and nurtured by imperialism, the power of Athens was to be destroyed by the same means. The great Peloponnesian War

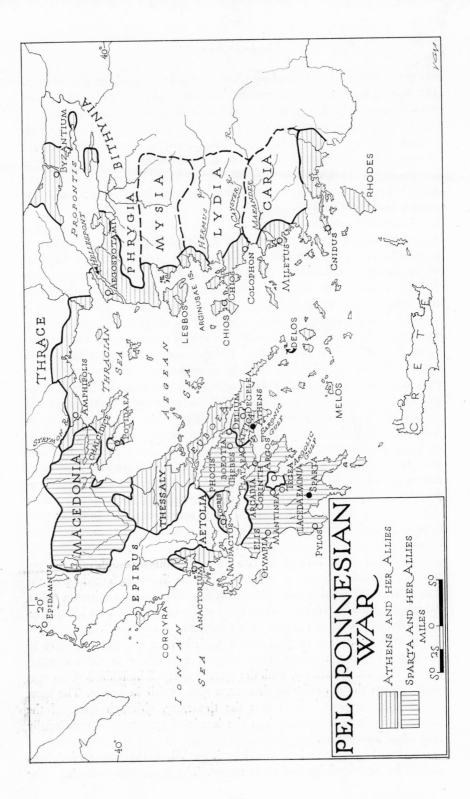

PELOPONNESIAN WAR

ATHENS AND HER ALLIES

SPARTA AND HER ALLIES

MILES

50   25   0   50

which began in 431 and ended in 404 terminated both the Athenian Empire and the economic prosperity of Athens. This famous conflict, immortalized in the history of Thucydides, found Athens on one side with the Peloponnesians and the Thebans on the other. Idealized and glorified as a titanic struggle between two systems, democracy and its opposite, the true nature of this inglorious strife has been somewhat obscured.

Like all wars, this one had two kinds of causes: underlying and immediate. The underlying or fundamental causes were those which made the conflict inevitable, while the immediate causes were those which precipitated the hostilities at a particular time. The bitterness engendered by the earlier war between Athens and the Peloponnesians and the fear of Athenian imperialism must be listed as underlying causes, but most important was the trade rivalry between Athens and Corinth. The commercial prosperity which accrued to Athens through the empire had ruined the trade of Corinth, Megara, and Sicyon; it mattered little that these latter states were in a better natural position for trade, for Athenian predominance in trade was an artificial thing created by the empire, and as long as the empire existed Athens would have the advantage. The Spartans were not the villains of the piece; they tried to remain aloof as long as possible, but they were drawn into the situation by the insistence of the Corinthians. The war was fought on an ideological plane: the Athenians were told they were fighting for democracy, and the Peloponnesians were told they were fighting to free the world from Athenian imperialism, but thinking people must have understood the real issues. These had little propaganda value, and therefore it was not polite to mention them.

Many people living at Athens at the beginning of the war said that Pericles precipitated the conflict because his party was losing popularity and he wished to divert the minds of the Athenian voters from domestic to foreign issues. There does not seem to be much doubt that Pericles welcomed the war at this particular time, not for political reasons, but because he recognized the inevitability of the struggle and felt that the situation in 431 was favorable to Athens. The immediate causes of the war, however, were a series of crises or incidents that led up to the outbreak of hostilities.

First came the affair of Epidamnus. Epidamnus was a colony of Corcyra, as Corcyra was in turn a colony of Corinth. The site of Epidamnus was far removed from Athens, Corinth, and Sparta; it lay on the eastern coast of the Adriatic some distance above Corcyra (modern Corfu). About 436 *stasis* (civil war) between oligarchs and democrats had broken out in Epidamnus; the oligarchs were expelled from the town, whereupon they joined with the fierce natives of the surrounding countryside and returned to invest Epidamnus with a vigor that promised success. The alarmed democrats within the town appealed to Corcyra for aid; when their request was refused, they appealed to Corinth and received a promise of aid. Corcyra then sided with the oligarchs. The Corinthian relief expedition was beaten off, and the town fell to the oligarchs and their Corcyrean allies. One thing continued to lead to another: the Corinthians prepared an even larger expedition, and the alarmed Corcyreans decided to seek help from Athens.

The Athenians were interested in an alliance with Corcyra despite a Corinthian warning that such an action would be regarded as a breach of the treaty of 445 which had ended the previous war. There were three main reasons why a Corcyrean entanglement appealed to Athens: (1) Corcyra had a large navy which would constitute a valuable addition to Athenian imperial forces; (2) the Corcyreans could seal off the Corinthian gulf in time of war and prevent the Corinthian fleet from sailing out to the west, just as the Athenian navy could bottle up the Corinthians on the east in the Saronic Gulf; and (3) Corcyra and Epidamnus had formed parts of the third leg in the triangular trade between Corinth, Magna Graecia (Sicily and south Italy), and the Adriatic, and the alienation of Corcyra from Corinth would be just as damaging in peace as in war. Ideological considerations seemed unimportant; expediency outweighed the fact that the Athenians would be giving support to an antidemocratic faction and opposing the Corinthians who were helping the liberals of Epidamnus!

The Athenians did not want an open break with Corinth, yet they hated to pass up such an opportunity. They wanted to have their cake and eat it, too, so, hoping for the best, they made a *defensive* alliance with Corcyra. The Corinthians sent 150 ships to the Adriatic, worsted the smaller Corcyrean fleet, and set off in hot pursuit of the survivors. At this point, a small Athenian squadron interposed itself between Corcyreans and Corinthians. The Corinthians stopped short and begged the Athenians to withdraw. The latter refused, and the Corinthians, hesitating to attack without orders from home, bitterly sailed off. This incident alone might have begun a "hot war," but instead the cold war continued.

The second incident occurred in another remote place. A former Corinthian colony in the north Aegean, Potidaea, was subject to Athens. Fearing that the Potidaeans were on the verge of revolt, the Athenians ordered them to tear down their walls and provide hostages (432). The Potidaeans were thus driven into revolt, and before the Athenians arrived to besiege the town, a Corinthian force was sent to aid Potidaea. War had not been declared, yet within besieged Potidaea there were Corinthian soldiers.

War was already imminent when the third incident took place. Pericles issued the so-called Megarian Decree which banned Megarian traders from the ports of the Athenian Empire. The object of this move was to force Megara to join Athens as it had in the previous war instead of continuing its adherence to the Peloponnesian League. The whole economy of Megara was dependent on trade, and the plight of the country was soon desperate.

At the insistence of Corinth, a congress of the Peloponnesians was now called, and the Athenians were accused of having broken the peace of 445. The Spartan king, Archidamus, warned the assembly of the horrors of war, but the ephors were more sympathetic to the plight of the allies. An ultimatum was despatched to Athens: in order to avoid war the Athenians were told they must free Aegina, raise the siege of Potidaea, and rescind the Megarian Decree. They could do none of these things without loss of prestige; they were not really expected to comply with the ultimatum, for its purpose was to force the Athenians into war and make them appear the aggressors. The ultimatum was rejected by Athens, and so at last the long-awaited explosion occurred.

The naval power of Athens was to be pitted against the land power of Sparta and her allies. There was no common battlefield on which they could meet without great risk to one or the other of the combatants; like the war between the British and Napoleon, it was a struggle between a whale and an elephant. Pericles had laid his plans and was confident of success. Athens would fight a long war, a war of exhaustion. The Athenians had a war fund of six thousand talents; their opponents had no reserves. The Athenians would withdraw within their walls; the Peloponnesians could ravage the fields of Attica, but they could not capture the strongly fortified cities of Athens and the Peiraeus which were connected by the famous Long Walls. In the meantime, the Athenian fleet could sail out and ravage the coasts of the Peloponnesus, destroy enemy trade, and protect the grain ships from the Black Sea which would bring food to Athens. Year after year this would go on until the enemy was forced to his knees by economic exhaustion.

Pericles, with his keen intellect, would have made a very good chess player. He was probably adept at whatever similar board game it was the Athenians played; but war is not a game, and the beautiful academic strategy of Pericles was full of defects. To begin with, few wars have been won by purely defensive tactics. Furthermore, the whole concept of defensive war is bad for morale. Secondly, the Athenians needed to possess Megara for the same reason that they had needed it in the previous war: to prevent the Peloponnesians and Thebans from joining hands. Thirdly, without Pericles to enforce the consistent application of his plan, it could hardly succeed, and he, unfortunately, died in 429 when the war had scarcely begun.

The Great Peloponnesian War lasted twenty-seven years. It had two phases: the first covered the decade 431–421, and was called the War of Archidamus (after the Spartan king); then there was an uneasy truce to 414 when the second phase began: this was the Decelean War which ended in 404. The first phase began with a sneak attack by the Thebans on Plataea, the Boeotian border town allied with Athens. Plataea was a strategic point which controlled the roads leading from Boeotia into Attica and also southward to the Isthmus of Corinth. The town was not captured by surprise, as intended, but withstood a siege of several years which hampered Spartan-Theban co-operation.

The first year of the war went much as Pericles had anticipated. The Athenians withdrew within the Long Walls, and the enemy occupied the countryside; the Athenian fleet sailed out on forays. There were few losses on either side, and when winter came on, or it was time for the fall plowing, hostilities were largely suspended until the next campaigning season rolled around. In 430 matters did not go according to schedule because Athens was ravaged by a horrible plague; the only redeeming feature was that the enemy went home to escape contagion. Public sentiment in Athens rose high against Pericles; he was not re-elected to the generalship in the summer of 430, the first time he had failed of election since his rise to power in 461. In 429 Pericles was again chosen general, but he contracted the plague and died in office.

It is scarcely worth while to follow the course of the Archidamian War. It seesawed back and forth with victories first on one side and then on the other. The conflict might have stopped at any time since each side was ready to desist at one phase or another. At Athens the mantle of Pericles had fallen upon the demagogue Cleon, a bloodthirsty rabble-rouser who inflamed the passions of the Athenian mob while the brain trust which had once been the guiding force of the Periclean democracy became a minority group without political influence. The conservatives, on the other hand, managed to remain united. They were able to take advantage of the split in the popular faction to gain control after the death of Cleon in 422. At the same time the brilliant Spartan general, Brasidas, was killed in battle, and without his inspiration the Spartans were willing to cease hostilities. In 421 Nicias, the Athenian conservative leader, arranged for a peace between Athens and Sparta. With Sparta out of the conflict, her allies could not continue the war.

The Peace of Nicias, as it was called, was hailed with joy on both sides, although it pleased some people more than others. Definitely unhappy about this turn of events was the young Alcibiades, Pericles' nephew, who could see no political future for himself under a conservative, peaceful regime. Clever, ambitious, and unscrupulous, Alcibiades began to scheme for a renewal of the war which would bring the popular party and himself into power. He persuaded the Athenians to renew their old friendship with Argos and talked the Argives into organizing a league with Elis, Mantinea, and Tegea. The alliance of these four Peloponnesian towns would draw a line right across the Peloponnesus, cutting off the Spartans from their allies to the north. The members of the new quadruple alliance were given to understand that Athens would support them if they were attacked by Sparta. Sparta did attack, of course, in 418. No Athenian help was forthcoming.

The allies were beaten and bitter; the Spartans were bitter toward Athens, too, because, even though the Athenians had abstained from hostilities, there had been no doubt of their inimical intentions.

With Nicias advocating friendship with Sparta and Alcibiades the opposite, there was bound to be an ostracism after this affair. For seventy years ostracism had worked wonderfully for the Athenians. No one had been able to discover a loophole in it, but Alcibiades was cleverer than most. Knowing full well that the contest of 417 would be between himself and Nicias, he proposed to the conservative leader that they should pool their resources, that their respective followers should combine to vote for a third candidate. The choice fell upon poor, simple Hyperbolus, a soap box agitator who was loud but harmless. Hyperbolus was honored with ostracism, and Nicias and Alcibiades remained in Athens to continue their feud. Ostracism was soon discarded by the Athenians.

The drift toward war now became pronounced. In 416 the Athenians demanded that the Dorian inhabitants of the island of Melos, who had observed a strict neutrality in the early phase of the war, should join the Athenian Empire. Melos, of course, would make a fine naval base for operations against the Peloponnesus. The Melians begged to be allowed to retain their neutrality: they wished to remain friendly with Athens, and they did not want to offend their kinsmen of Sparta. The Athenians, however, were brutally insistent. Might was right, they said, and the Melians should submit to Athens and save their skins. The Melians retorted that they had preserved their freedom for centuries and would not give up without a struggle. The Athenians attacked and overwhelmed Melos; the men were put to the sword, the women and children sold into slavery, and the island was repopulated with Athenian colonists. A few people at Athens were shocked by this unprovoked act of barbarism; Euripides, at least, was brave enough to treat the atrocity in a great play, *The Trojan Women,* in such a way that there could be no doubt of the events to which he referred.

Then came the Sicilian fiasco. In 415 there arrived in Athens an embassy from the town of Segesta in Sicily. The Segestans were being bullied by the powerful city of Syracuse (Dorian, of course), and they wanted Athenian protection. They told the Athenians how easy the conquest of the rich island of Sicily would be. The possibilities seemed enormous, and the Athenians voted to send a great expedition to aid Segesta and take over Sicily. Outstanding in his support of the idea was Alcibiades, who was the natural leader of the expedition and might have carried it off successfully. But the Athenians managed to find a way to muddle the whole affair: they chose three commanders, including Alcibiades, who believed in the project, Nicias, who did not, and Lamachus, a professional soldier with no definite opinion. To cap the climax, after the Sicilian expedition set sail, Alcibiades was accused of impiety by his enemies at home who secured an order for his arrest. He managed to escape, but the expedition proceeded to Sicily without him where it gained some preliminary successes and laid siege to Syracuse. Blundering by Nicias, however, led to a dismal failure in 413 when the Syracusans, aided by Sparta, destroyed the whole Athenian force.

The Sicilian disaster came at a time when affairs were grim enough at home. Alcibiades had fled to Sparta where he had encouraged the Spartans to resume the Peloponnesian War (414). He even pointed out to them the error of their tactics in the first phase of the conflict; he suggested that they should occupy Attica all year round so that the Athenians would never be able to come out from behind the Long Walls. As a result, the Spartans occupied the Attic fortress of Decelea as a permanent base, and Athenian morale slid to a new low. By 411 the conservatives, hoping for peace, overthrew the democracy by revolution and began negotiations with the enemy. Their plan was foiled by Alcibiades, who had worn out his welcome at Sparta and had now gone to Asia Minor, where he made friends with one of the Persian satraps named Tissaphernes. Alcibiades persuaded Tissaphernes that a Spartan victory was not in the Persian interest: the Spartans had been talking about liberating the Greeks (from Athens), but the next step would be the liberation of the Greeks from Persia, too. The best Persian policy was to keep the Greeks fighting among themselves. Therefore, Persia should intervene to help the Athenians. When Alcibiades, with a promise of Persian aid, turned up at Samos, where the Athenian fleet was mustered in force and where sentiment was against the oligarchic revolution at home, he was warmly welcomed. Word was sent to Athens, and a counterrevolution overthrew the oligarchs and secured the pardon of Alcibiades.

The war went on. For three years (410-407) the tide ran in favor of Athens under the leadership of Alcibiades, but in 407 a naval defeat by one of his subordinates brought censure upon him. When he went into exile to escape execution, the end was in sight. The Persians had taken the advice of Alcibiades to heart; as Athens had begun to win battles under Alcibiades, the Persians threw their support to Sparta. After the fall of Alcibiades, hysteria gripped the Athenians. Part of the fleet was lost in a storm in 406; the remainder was destroyed by a blunder at Aegospotami in 405. In 404, Athens surrendered to the Spartans. As the price of peace, the Athenians were deprived of their empire, the walls of Athens were torn down, and the democracy was superseded by an oligarchy supported by a Spartan garrison.

No comment on the fall of Athens seems necessary; the Athenians richly deserved their fate. A single footnote, however, is in order: of all their follies the Athenians least merit criticism regarding the Sicilian expedition. Success (which was not at all impossible under Alcibiades) would have given the Athenians control of the grain supply of Corinth and the possession of the triangular trade in the west. The Sicilian venture was no harebrained scheme, for Alcibiades was a better strategist than his uncle.

Chapter 16

CLASSICAL GREEK CIVILIZATION

IN THE FIFTH CENTURY B.C. the Greeks of the mainland reached the peak of their military and naval effectiveness, and their characteristic political unit, the *polis,* attained its fullest development. During roughly the same period Greek art, literature, and philosophy evolved into the forms which the world has come to regard as typically Greek. In this chapter we shall describe certain aspects of what is considered "classical Greek civilization." How the Greeks lived—their economic and social life, and what they accomplished; their art, literature, and philosophy—are the main subjects to be considered. Although Greek civilization in its classical form developed in the fifth century, the evolution of certain phases was not completed until the first half of the fourth century; this was true of painting, sculpture, oratory, and philosophy. We shall therefore include not only the fifth century developments but also those of the period between 400 and 350 B.C.

The Persian conquest of the Asiatic Greeks resulted in a shift of the economic, political, and cultural center of the Greek world to mainland Greece. This development took place in the closing years of the sixth century B.C. In the fifth century, after the unsuccessful attempts of the Persians to conquer Greece, the rise of Athens and the creation of the Athenian Empire made that city the commercial and cultural capital of the Greek world. As Athens rose, there was a corresponding decline of her economic competitors—Corinth, Chalcis, Megara, and Aegina. On the whole, however, the economic life of the Aegean was stimulated because of certain benefits conferred upon it by the creation of the Athenian Empire: (1) the Athenian navy was able to suppress piracy, and (2) the cities of the empire were forced to use a uniform currency, that of Athens. Both the suppression of piracy and the introduction of a uniform currency were most helpful to the growth of trade. Thus, although it was certainly the Athenians who gained the

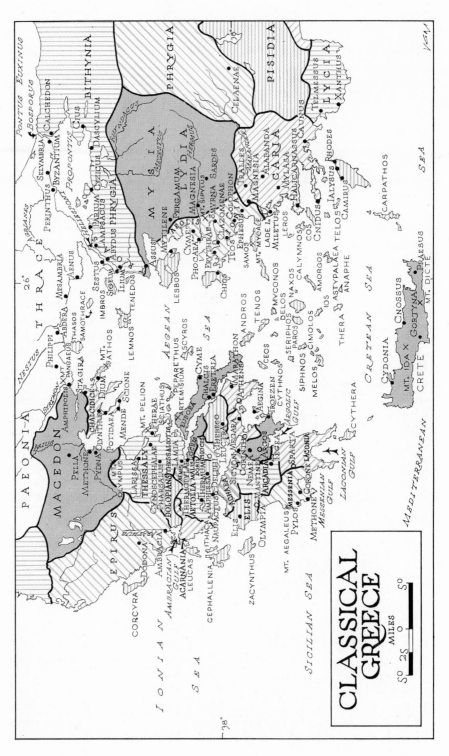

CLASSICAL GREECE

MILES
50   25   0   50

greatest economic advantage from their empire, other states in the Aegean area also enjoyed an increased prosperity.

The long Peloponnesian War undoubtedly injured agriculture, especially in Attica where the fields were ravaged and the vines and olive trees cut down; moreover, trade and commerce were seriously disrupted while the war was in progress. Nevertheless, the fourth century witnessed recovery in all fields of economic activity, even though mainland Greece had to face increased commercial and industrial competition from the Greeks in Sicily and southern Italy. The fourth century was also characterized by a number of new developments. The Greek city-states had more and more difficulty in managing their public finances; this was partly an aftermath of the Peloponnesian War, partly the result of the numerous interstate conflicts of the first half of the fourth century, and partly due to the frequent civil wars which broke out in many of the states. Apparently the division between the small group of the very rich and the increasing multitude of the very poor was becoming more marked; the struggles between the oligarchs and the democrats were, as we have seen, the political expression of economic discontent. Another result of the Peloponnesian War and the subsequent Greek conflicts of the fourth century was the appearance of large numbers of professional (or mercenary) soldiers, men who lacked the opportunity, or did not wish, to return to peaceful occupations. During the fifth century there had been evident an increasing specialization of labor, and this tendency was even more marked in the fourth century. Last of all, after 400 B.C. private banking first assumed considerable significance, and financial operations of all kinds became more complex.

The importance of agriculture varied in different areas of Greece. In Boeotia and the Peloponnesus, where the soil was fertile and a fair amount of good land was available, the inhabitants were not compelled to import large quantities of food stuffs—if, indeed, it was necessary to import any. But where the industrial population was large and the land was not rich, as at Athens, Corinth, and Megara, self-sufficiency was out of the question. The small farmers of Attica could supply their own needs, and there were truck gardens around Athens that produced vegetables for the city market; but wheat and barley had to be brought in from southern Russia to supply the city population. This was probably also true at Corinth and other large cities.

Greek agricultural methods were rather primitive in the fifth century. The use of fertilizer was not common; usually the fields were allowed to lie fallow in order to recuperate. In the fourth century the soil was renewed by planting leguminous crops at intervals.

There was some specialization of agricultural production, particularly in areas where certain products were intended for export. In Attica, for example, there was great emphasis on the production of wine and olive oil, with the result that much land was devoted to vineyards and orchards. On the island of Thasos, to cite a similar case, there was considerable concentration on viniculture, for Thasian wines were popular.

Along with agriculture went grazing. The sparse vegetation made the raising of sheep and goats more practical than cattle raising. The sheep were kept for food and for their wool, whereas goats' milk and cheese were universal Greek foods. In many regions of Greece cattle were so scarce that hides became important imports. Horses were raised in Thessaly and on the island of Euboea. Occupations of minor importance in areas outside the urban centers were charcoal burning and bee keeping.

Trade and industry were the most significant features of Greek economic life. Metalwork, textiles, weapons, armor, pottery, lamps, marble, furniture, olive oil, wine, and honey were exported from the Greek manufacturing cities in return for foodstuffs, some Oriental luxuries, and great quantities of raw materials from all the corners of the ancient world. Wheat and barley came from Russia, Cyrene, and Sicily; timber and hides came from Macedonia and Thrace; fish was brought from the Black Sea, dates from Phoenicia, and papyrus from Egypt. The Phoenicians secured tin from the British Isles; metals came from Cyprus, Asia Minor, and Thrace. Wool was imported from Asia Minor; flax, from Egypt and Cyrene. Phoenicia sold to the Greeks its metalwork, glass, and textiles; Egypt, its ivory and perfumes.

Much industry and trade were carried on with borrowed capital. Rich landowners might invest capital in some industrial or commercial venture; in the fourth century the bankers lent the depositors' money for similar purposes. A shipowner might trade on his own initiative, but more often he leased his ship to carry cargoes. A rich man frequently set up one of his slaves or freedmen in a shop to manufacture some product. It was not considered proper for a gentleman to engage in manufacturing or trading. It is amusing to read about a Greek who complained that he had to carry on his own business because he was too poor to own a slave. The result of this reluctance of the citizens to sully their hands with any business other than farming was that in many states a large proportion of the trade and industry was dominated by slaves, freedmen, or aliens (free non-citizens).

The ancestor of the Greek banker was the money-changer. In a world where there were many different coinage systems, the money-changer, who sat at his table in the market place and exchanged the coin of the realm for foreign currency (at a nice profit), was essential to the conduct of trade. About 500 B.C. the Athenian money-changers became pawnbrokers as well; they lent money when valuables were deposited with them as security. They also received deposits of money which were then invested in industrial or commercial ventures in the form of loans. Before these private bankers appeared on the scene, the temples made loans to governments and private individuals, just as they did in the Near East. The ordinary rate of interest was about 12 per cent.

Although it was customary for the Greek family to make its clothing and some of its coarse domestic pottery in the home, by the sixth century B.C. industrial shops and even factories had appeared in the cities. These establishments grew larger and the work of their employees became more specialized in the fifth and fourth centuries. In the shop of average size would be found the master craftsman and perhaps a dozen slaves and free workers; the largest establishment about which we have any information was a shield factory which had 120 slaves. In the large cities all the shops devoted to one craft would be concentrated in a certain quarter. The same thing was true of those which sold food or other commodities; fish, vegetables, flowers, fowls, etc., would be sold at different stations in the market place. In the small manufacturing establishments goods manufactured at the rear of the shop would be sold by the proprietor at the front entrance. In well ordered factories specialization produced an ancient version of the modern assembly line; in the production of pottery, for example, certain men prepared the clay, others molded the vases, still others made the bases, rims, and handles, and a separate crew watched over the oven; specialists, of course, applied the painted decoration.

The Greek governments often concerned themselves with business and other economic affairs. In the fourth century, for example, the government of Thasos sought to regulate its wine trade. Speculators were discouraged by a law which forbade them to buy up the harvest of a whole vineyard in advance. State inspectors saw to it that wine jars contained the specified amount, and Thasian ships were not encouraged to carry foreign wines. We have already seen something of the activities of Solon and Peisistratus at Athens—how they made reforms and issued regulations to improve the condition of agriculture, industry, and trade. Commercial treaties were often negotiated, and frequently two governments were able to improve the trade relations of their subjects by the adoption of identical systems of currency.

The Greek laborer may best be discussed in connection with the general topic of Greek social organization. The Greek nobility and the commons were never, after the close of the Dark Ages, divided by a rigid caste system such as one finds in the ancient Near East. The principal social divisions in Greece were rather those of the citizens, the aliens (metics), slaves, agricultural serfs (like the helots), and special groups like the Spartan perioeci; there was no priest class.

The citizens were the full-fledged members of the city-state who could vote and hold office; they also enjoyed special privileges and exemptions. Citizenship was highly prized, and it was rarely given to outsiders. Sometimes foreign rulers or foreigners who assisted the state in some way were given civic rights; occasionally an alien might be adopted into a citizen family, or a government might, like Athens in the time of Solon, offer citizenship to alien artisans. In 451 B.C., however, the Athenians restricted citizenship to those who could prove that both parents had been Athenian citizens.

In Athens, and in other industrial and commercial centers, there were large alien populations. Each alien or metic had to have a citizen sponsor (*prostates*) who could represent him in the law courts. Aliens were required to pay a head tax and to render military service. They had no political rights, and they could not acquire land.

Captives of war, the victims of slave raids, and some criminals provided the slaves of the fifth and fourth centuries. Slaves were used in domestic service, mining, and industry, but not much in agriculture. The most intractable slaves were relegated to the mines where the unspeakable conditions under which they worked soon brought their lives to an end. The Athenian aristocrat Nicias had a thousand slaves whom he rented out for mining; from them he derived an income exceeding ten thousand dollars a year. Slaves might hope for manumission at the death of their masters; sometimes slaves were set up in business by their owners and managed to make enough money to buy their freedom. An emancipated slave became a freedman whose former master was his patron; the patron was the legal protector of the freedman, and the freedman owed certain obligations to his patron.

Most Athenians and some other Greeks felt that the only respectable form of manual labor was farming. In the country citizens, slaves, and serfs worked together. In the city, on the other hand, the artisan and the trader were mostly recruited from the slave class and the alien group. Some citizens did engage in these activities, but they were looked down upon by others. Sculptors, architects, and painters were generally classed as manual laborers in the fifth century, and only a few very famous artists were thought to be socially above shoemakers or potters. As far as we can determine, architects at Athens received the same wages as the laborers whom they supervised. Building inscriptions from Athens and Eleusis show that citizens, slaves, and metics all worked together; the combined numbers of slaves and metics exceeded those of the citizens in the proportion of five to two.

Most of the Greeks, except perhaps a few wealthy citizens or metics, lived in what we should consider extreme poverty. Their food was simple: wheat and barley were made into porridge or loaves of bread: they ate vegetables, cheese, onions, figs, olives, and fruit; they had fish more often than mutton, pork, and beef. Wine was almost always diluted with water. Greek private houses were built of mud brick; they were not large, and they did not contain much furniture. In cold weather, individual rooms might be heated, most inadequately, with braziers filled with coals. In the fourth century people with more than average incomes began to build larger and more permanent houses and to live in comparative luxury. In fifth-century Athens, however, a display of wealth in any form was considered bad taste.

In Greek society men occupied a favored position. They had complete freedom, whereas the women had almost no freedom at all. While the men engaged in politics, lounged about the market place, or exercised at the wrestling ground, or *palaestra,* the women were confined to their houses. The one major event in a woman's life was her marriage, and even that was arranged for her by her prospective husband and her father; ordinarily she would not be consulted. After marriage, the woman was supposed to keep her house in order and bear children. She usually left the house only to attend some religious festival.

There were, of course, "other women." These were the *hetaerae,* the courtesans, mostly aliens. The hetaerae were usually skilled entertainers; some of them were well educated and able to meet the men on equal intellectual terms. Men found them much more interesting than their wives, many of whom did not even know how to read or write.

In addition to the entertainment that the hetaerae were able to provide, the men found pleasure in banquets, drinking bouts, and simple games. The chief sports were boxing, wrestling, running, jumping, cockfighting, and chariot racing. There were professional athletes who participated in the national games. The mention of them calls to mind certain epigrams concerning their abilities: the one about the boxer whose competitors erected a statue to him because he never hurt any of them, and numerous others about runners who were mistaken for statues. There was also the runner who started in a race in one year, continued on around the course until the race was run in the second year, and still came in last.

Greek children, outside of Sparta, led fairly happy and normal lives. One must not forget, however, that the exposure of infants was practiced by all Greeks. Above all, the Greek wanted sons; daughters were a burden, and if a husband could not be secured for them, they became liabilities. Thus female babies were more likely to be discarded by their parents than the males.

Girls, if allowed to live, were rarely formally educated. They were taught to cook and sew and to perform other domestic duties. Boys, on the other hand, were given more attention. The son of poor parents might be apprenticed to a master craftsman. A boy who came from a rich family would be sent to a private school. His education would begin when he was six or seven years old and would continue until his fourteenth year. Reading, writing, and arithmetic were taught, of course. The best literature was read and memorized—the works of Homer, Hesiod, Solon, Theognis, and Pindar. Vocal and instrumental music was included, and the boys learned to play the lyre and the flute. There was also much emphasis upon physical exercise. The aims of Greek education were to produce good citizens who

253

were well grounded in national traditions (and thus patriotic), who sub-scribed to a high standard of morality, and who possessed certain social graces. Boys who were just emerging into manhood were given military training by the state; they were taught military formations and the use of weapons.

A more advanced kind of education than that offered by the private schools might be gained by attending the lectures of the itinerant teachers known as the Sophists who appeared in large numbers in the fifth century. The activities of the Sophists will be discussed below (p. 266).

In turning from daily life to a description of Greek intellectual and cultural accomplishments, a word of caution is in order. Modern admirers of the Greeks have done them a great disservice by proclaiming each and every ancient Greek to have been a genius. A modicum of sober thought will cast some doubt on the validity of the thesis that the Greeks were a race of supermen. There is no reason to believe that the average Greek of the fifth century differed very much from the "man in the street" today. No one would seriously maintain that the achievements of the twentieth cen-tury A.D. can be attributed to the genius of our population as a whole, for it is painfully obvious that many people are indifferent to, or unaware of, many accomplishments of our age. It detracts nothing from an appreciation of the Greek achievement to accept it for what it was—the work of a few talented individuals. Plato, Phidias, Pericles, and Polygnotos were not typical Greeks.

The century and a half from 500 to 350 B.C. constitutes the classic period of Greek art. In this century and a half the Doric and Ionic styles of Greek architecture reached their highest development. The peak of Greek achieve-ment in sculpture was attained by Phidias and Praxiteles, and advances in painting were made which paved the way for the perfection of that art be-fore the end of the fourth century.

In the fifth century it was still the temple that received the major atten-tion of the architects, but there was a growing interest in city planning and the construction of public buildings other than temples, a trend which be-came more marked in the next hundred years. In the fifth century, for ex-ample, the famous Hippodamus of Miletus revised the plan of the Peiraeus and later laid out the streets of the Periclean colony of Thurii in Italy. Council chambers, city halls, and stoae (colonnaded porches) began to make their appearance. In the fourth century gymnasia, stadia, and theaters with stone seats were built in a number of cities.

In discussing Greek architecture of the classic period our interest natu-rally centers on Athens, where Pericles inaugurated the great building pro-gram that made his city the most beautiful in the ancient world. The empire had placed huge economic resources at the disposal of the Athenians. The position of Athens as an imperial capital seemed to Pericles and his followers to necessitate a certain degree of ostentation in order that the subjects as well as the enemies of Athens might be suitably impressed. At the beginning of the Periclean Age few of the buildings which had been destroyed by the Persians in 480 B.C. had been restored; most of them had been purposely left in ruins as a reminder of Persian barbarity. The Periclean generation, however, was less bitter than its predecessors, and the unsightly ruins offended civic pride. Moreover, both contractors and workmen must have enthusiastically supported a building program that had obvious financial possibilities for them.

The principal structures erected during the Periclean Age were the Parthenon, the Propylaea, the temple of Athena Nike, the Odeum (music hall) of Pericles, and the temple of Hephaestus; the Erechtheum was built shortly after Pericles' death. The Parthenon and the temple of Hephaestus were in the Doric style; this style reached its fullest development in the Parthenon. High above the city on the Acropolis, with its magnificent sculptural decoration planned by Phidias, the Parthenon in all its glory impressed the Greeks with its beauty and dignity; it was a monument to the greatness of Periclean Athens, and even today its majestic ruins conjure up visions of a mighty past. It was constructed of Pentelic marble; its pediment groups dealt with two famous Athenian legends, the birth of Athena (the eastern façade) and the contest between Athena and Poseidon for the possession of Attica (the western façade). Around the cella ran an Ionic frieze showing the Panathenaic procession, the annual parade which culminated in the presentation of a new garment to the statue of Athena. Inside the temple was the gigantic gold and ivory statue of Athena, the work of Phidias.

The temple of Hephaestus was down in the agora, or market place north of the Areopagus. This temple is sometimes erroneously called the Theseum because its metopes depict episodes in the life of that hero. It is important today because it is one of the best preserved temples in the Doric style.

The Propylaea (Gates) constituted the monumental entrance to the Acropolis; both Doric and Ionic columns were employed in its construction. The ceilings were richly coffered; in one wing was a famous gallery of paintings. The temple of Athena Nike was a small but very handsome Ionic temple situated on a bastion adjoining the Propylaea. The Erechtheum was another Ionic temple sacred to Athena and Erechtheus (a legendary Athenian king); in its south porch figures of maidens (caryatids) were substituted for columns; under the north porch were three depressions in the limestone rock which were supposed to be the marks of Poseidon's trident. The Odeum of Pericles was located at the southeastern foot of the Acropolis; it had a conical wooden roof, "like the tent of Xerxes," or, as some people unkindly said, "like onion-headed Pericles."

After the Persian wars Athens included in its building program the massive fortifications that rendered the city impregnable—the Greeks of the

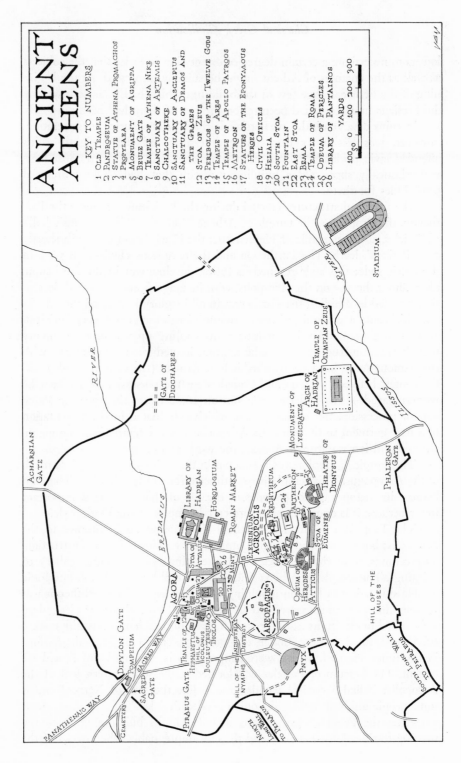

ANCIENT ATHENS

KEY TO NUMBERS

1 Old Temple
2 Pandroseum
3 Statue of Athena Promachos
4 Propylaea
5 Monument of Agrippa
6 Beule Gate
7 Temple of Athena Nike
8 Sanctuary of Artemis
9 Chalcotheke
10 Sanctuary of Asclepius
11 Sanctuary of Demos and
    The Graces
12 Stoa of Zeus
13 Peribolos of the Twelve Gods
14 Temple of Ares
15 Temple of Apollo Patroos
16 Metroon
17 Statues of the Eponymous
    Heroes
18 Civil Offices
19 Heliaia
20 South Stoa
21 Fountain
22 East Stoa
23 Bema
24 Temple of Roma
25 Odeum of Pericles
26 Library of Pantainos

YARDS

100 50 0   100   200   300

STADIUM

RIVER

ILISSUS

ARCH OF HADRIAN

TEMPLE OF OLYMPIAN ZEUS

MONUMENT OF LYSICRATES

THEATRE OF DIONYSUS

GATE OF DIOCHARES

RIVER ERIDANUS

ACHARNIAN GATE

LIBRARY OF HADRIAN

HOROLOGIUM

ROMAN MARKET

ELEUSINIUM

ACROPOLIS

ERECHTHEUM

PARTHENON

STOA OF EUMENES

ODEUM OF HERODES ATTICUS

AREOPAGUS

HILL OF THE MUSES

PHALERON GATE

DIPYLON GATE

POMPEIUM

CEMETERY

SACRED WAY

SACRED GATE

PIRAEUS GATE

TEMPLE OF HEPHAESTUS

HILL OF COLONUS

BOULEUTERION THOLOS

HILL OF THE NYMPHS

PNYX

STOA OF ATTALUS

MINT

INDUSTRIAL DISTRICT

PANATHENAIC WAY

TO PEIRAEUS

NORTH LONG WALL

SOUTH LONG WALL

TO PEIRAEUS

AGORA

fifth century were notably unskilled in siegecraft. The Peiraeus was also fortified, and Cimon (471–462 B.C.) superintended the building of the famous Long Walls which connected Athens with the Peiraeus and made the two cities into a compact defensible unit.

At the opening of the fifth century there were distinctive schools of sculpture in the Peloponnesus, Athens, and south Italy. At Argos, Sicyon, and Aegina Peloponnesian sculptors and their pupils created mostly statues of victorious athletes distinguished by short, stocky figures. Calamis at Athens was famous for his statues of horses; either he or his contemporary, Pythagoras of Rhegium, may have made the famous bronze charioteer which was found at Delphi.

The sculptured works of the fifth century are characterized by their dignity, simplicity, and grace; the archaic stiffness of the earlier figures was gradually overcome, and the representation of men and animals in both stone and bronze was considerably improved. Solutions were found for problems connected with the representation of drapery. The statues of divinities produced by fifth-century artists, particularly Phidias, influenced all future thinking about the actual appearance of the gods and goddesses. After Phidias created his Athena and his Olympian Zeus, few people could conceive of these divinities in any other form.

Three sculptors of the fifth century deserve special mention: Myron, Phidias, and Polyclitus. Myron, an Athenian who flourished about 475 B.C., was especially famous for his statues of athletes and animals. His Discus Thrower is well known to us today; he also made a statue of a runner in full career and a statue of a heifer so true to life that it "deceived cattle in the fields."

We have already mentioned the Athena and the Zeus of Phidias. Phidias was another Athenian; his work was done between 450 and 425 B.C. He and his pupils were distinguished for their *ethos,* dignity and simplicity, a characteristic which may well have had its inspiration from the majesty of Pericles and the Athenian Empire. Idealism was the keynote of Phidian sculpture; even his figures of men and women seem to represent people who are something more than human.

Polyclitus lived at Argos at the end of the fifth century. He devoted himself chiefly to the statues of athletes, although he did produce a gold and ivory statue of the goddess Hera. Polyclitus evolved mathematical formulae for the ideal proportions of the human body, and his statue the Doryphorus (Spear Bearer) exemplified his theories in practice.

Technically, the sculptors of the fourth century were superior to those of the fifth; but in many cases this very facility of execution proved their undoing, for many of these later artists were concerned with displaying their own cleverness, and they lacked the sincerity and personal modesty that had contributed so much to the success of their predecessors. Some artists, how-

Contributors to Greek Civilization

Roman numerals indicate century B.C. *in which individual flourished*

ABDERA
Philosophy
Democritus V
Sophistry
Protagoras V

ACRAGAS
Philosophy
Empedocles V

ALEXANDRIA
Literature
Zenodotus III
Aristarchus II
Aristophanes of
Byzantium II
Mathematics
Apollonius III
Medicine
Herophilus III
Science
Euclid III

ARGOS
Sculpture
Polyclitus V

ASCRA
Poetry
Hesiod VIII

ATHENS
History
Thucydides V
Xenophon IV
Oratory
Lysias V
Demetrius IV
Demosthenes IV
Isaeus IV
Isocrates IV
Painting
Apollodorus V
Parrhasios V
Polygnotos V
Philosophy
Socrates V
Plato V–IV
Antisthenes IV
Heracleides IV
Strato III
Poetry and Drama
Solon VI
Aeschylus V
Aristophanes V
Euripides V
Sophocles V
Menander IV
Science
Meton V
Sculpture
Alcamenes V
Calamis V
Myron V
Phidias V
Praxiteles IV

CARDIA
History
Hieronymus III

CEOS
Medicine
Erasistratus III
Sophistry
Prodicus V

CHIOS
History
Theopompus IV

Poetry
Homer ?

CLAZOMENAE
Sophistry
Anaxagoras V

CNIDUS
Science
Eudoxus IV

COLOPHON
Painting
Apelles IV
Philosophy
Xenophanes VI
Poetry
Mimnermus VII
Antimachus IV

COS
Medicine
Hippocrates V

CYPRUS
Philosophy
Zeno IV

CYRENE
Geography
Eratosthenes III
Philosophy
Aristippus IV
Poetry
Callimachus III

ELEA
Philosophy
Leucippus V
Sophistry
Parmenides V
Zeno V

ELIS
Philosophy
Pyrron III

EPHESUS
Painting
Zeuxis V
Philosophy
Heraclitus VI
Poetry
Callinus VII

HALICARNASSUS
History
Herodotus V

LEONTINI
Sophistry
Gorgias V

LESBOS
Philosophy
Theophrastus IV
Poetry
Alcaeus VI
Sappho VI

MEGALOPOLIS
History
Polybius II

MEGARA
Poetry
Theognis VI

MILETUS
Architecture
Hippodamus V
Geography
Hecataeus VI

Philosophy
Anaximander VI
Anaximenes VI
Thales VI

NICAEA
Astronomy
Hipparchus II

OLYNTHUS
History
Callisthenes IV

PAROS
Poetry
Archilochus VII
Sculpture
Scopas IV

RHEGIUM
Sculpture
Pythagoras V

RHODES
Philosophy
Poseidonius I
Poetry
Apollonius III
Sculpture
Chares III

SAMOS
Astronomy
Aristarchus III
Philosophy
Pythagoras VI
Epicurus IV
Poetry
Simonides VII
Choerilus V

SICYON
Sculpture
Lysippus IV

SMYRNA
Poetry
Homer ?

SPARTA
Poetry
Alcman VII
Tyrtaeus VII

STAGIRA
Philosophy
Aristotle IV

SYRACUSE
Poetry
Theocritus III
Bion III–II
Moschus II
Science
Archimedes III

TARENTUM
Medicine
Heracleides III
Philosophy
Aristoxenus IV

TAUROMENIUM
History
Timaeus IV

TEOS
Poetry
Anacreon VI

THEBES
Poetry
Pindar V

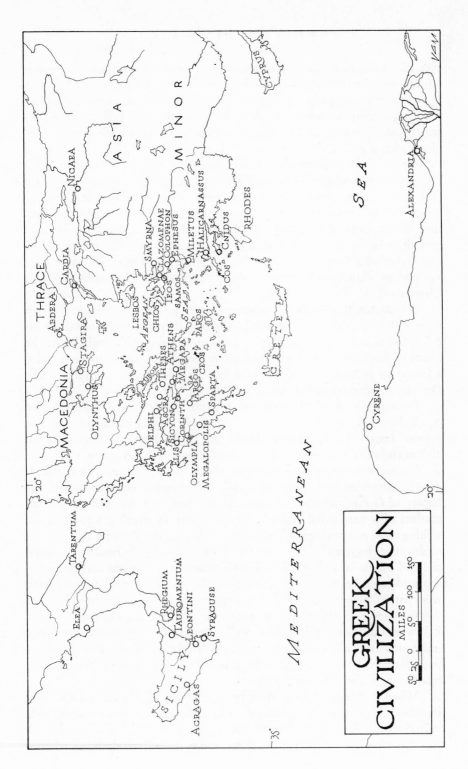

GREEK CIVILIZATION

MILES

ever, like Praxiteles and Scopas, managed to escape this pitfall. The fourth century saw the rise of portraiture in sculpture, the development of devices to express emotion, and some improvements in the representation of drapery.

Two famous names in Greek sculpture in the first half of the fourth century are Praxiteles and Scopas. Praxiteles combined a perfection of technique with a greatness of concept which make his work, in the opinion of many people, the greatest of ancient times. His Cnidian Aphrodite and his Hermes and Dionysus are too well known to require comment. The grace of his figures and his rendition of drapery were never excelled by later artists. Scopas gained recognition when he discovered a way to express emotion in the faces of his statues by parting the lips and setting the eyes very deep in the head. Another artist, Lysippos, is generally mentioned in connection with Scopas and Praxiteles, but most of his work was done after 350, and we shall include him with the sculptors of the Hellenistic Age (see Chapter 18).

Polygnotos, the Phidias of painting, came to Athens after the Persian wars at the invitation of Cimon. Like Phidias, Polygnotos was noted for his *ethos*. He was also the first to give his murals perspective and depth; the colors he employed were white, red, ochre, and black, and thus he is called a four-color painter. Two of his most famous paintings were entitled "The Descent of Odysseus to the Lower World" and "Troy Taken."

Painters who worked in the late fifth and early fourth centuries were Apollodorus, Zeuxis, and Parrhasios. Apollodorus was called the "shadow painter" because of his mastery of light and shade; Zeuxis was noted for his violent contrasts of color, and Parrhasios for lightness and gaiety.

It should never be forgotten that literature is a cultural form that is greatly influenced by its political, social, and economic environment. In the history of Greek literature we have already seen how the epic, the natural product of a patriarchal and aristocratic society in which a knowledge of writing was not widespread, was superseded in the Archaic Age by the iambic, the elegy, and the personal and choral lyric. In a bustling commercial and industrial milieu where individualism was rampant and there was a considerable knowledge of writing, the iambic, elegy, and personal lyric were naturally popular. Thus it is not surprising that we find these forms in Asiatic Greece in the period between 750 B.C. and the Persian conquest. Likewise, the choral lyric, a form well suited to the expression of national unity, was especially popular in mainland Greece where the state was more important than the individual; the choral lyric, for example, flourished at Sparta where the state was dominant.

When the Asiatic Greeks were brought under the Persian yoke and the mainland Greeks were threatened with conquest by the Persians, individualism was subordinated to the group (or the state). The natural result was that after 500 B.C. the iambic, elegy, and personal lyric declined, whereas

CORINTHIAN KRATER

ATHENIAN BLACK FIGURE—EXEKIAS

ATHENIAN RED FIGURE—EUPHRONIUS

ATHENIAN RED FIGURE—EUTHYMIDES

Bettman

TEMPLE OF APOLLO AT DELPHI

*Courtesy of the American School of Classical Studies
at Athens. Photo Alison Frantz*

OSTRAKA BEARING THE NAME OF THEMISTOCLES

DIOLKOS—
SHIP ROAD ACROSS THE ISTHMUS OF CORINTH

*Courtesy of Eugene Vanderpool and
the* American Journal of Archaeology

RECONSTRUCTION OF THE AGORA

RECONSTRUCTION OF THE ACROPOLIS

the choral lyric reached its highest point in the first half of the fifth century in the skillful hands of Pindar of Boeotia, and the Greek drama, which had evolved as a special form of the choral lyric, became important.

Another feature of the development of literature after 500 B.C. was the increasing use of prose. Whereas philosophy, political propaganda, and history previously had been couched in poetry, in the fifth century writers turned to prose as a more suitable medium for conveying their ideas. All this certainly indicates a wider use of writing and a growing reading public. Moreover, the development of prose was undoubtedly influenced by the greater attention paid to oratory which helped to lead people away from poetry toward prose as a means of expression.

This is not to say that the Greeks no longer composed poetry, but we know little about poets who wrote in the period between 450 B.C. and the age of Alexander the Great, for contemporaries rarely mentioned them, and only fragments of their works have survived. The principal exception was Pindar, who brought the choral lyric to perfection. Pindar was born in Boeotia in the latter part of the sixth century and died shortly after 450 B.C. Of aristocratic extraction and sympathies, he had little feeling for democracy. He was inspired by the glorious victories of the Greeks over the Persians, but most of his poetry which has survived consists of victory odes written for the various Panhellenic games.

The most significant literary development of the fifth century was that of the drama. Unfortunately, this subject can be discussed only in connection with the drama at Athens, since we know little of the Greek drama elsewhere. The drama owed much to two earlier literary forms, the epic and the choral lyric. It took its subject matter from the former, and it evolved out of the latter.

Greek tragedy originated with the choral songs honoring the wine-god, Dionysus. These songs dealt with episodes in the life of Dionysus, and they were sung by choruses of men dressed in goatskins (to represent satyrs). It became customary for the leader of the chorus to punctuate the songs of the chorus with what might be called dramatic recitatives; thus, he eventually became an "actor." The tragedy or "goat singing" of the Athenians was given great encouragement by Peisistratus in 534 B.C. when he established annual dramatic contests in honor of Dionysus. This custom continued, and by the time the drama reached its more or less completed form in the fifth century, the usual procedure was to select the works of three tragic and three comic writers for performance. The dramatists were much limited at first by having to deal only with subjects which related to Dionysus, but they evaded this restriction by composing trilogies (sets of three related plays) on other mythological subjects and attaching a fourth play—a satyr play—which established a connection with Dionysus. In a sense, each part of a trilogy would correspond to one act in a modern play.

Athens produced three great writers of tragedy: Aeschylus, Sophocles, and Euripides. Aeschylus (525–456 B.C.) was the first of this group. To the bare choral lyric with its recitative form he added a second actor and reduced the chorus to a subordinate position. His plays became a series of episodes in which the action of the piece took place, and these episodes were separated by choral songs; it might be said that the choral songs were like the triglyphs separating the episodic metopes of a Doric frieze. The plays of Aeschylus were majestic in concept; their theme was usually the struggle of human endeavor against the irresistible force of fate or the will of the gods. Aeschylus seems to have preached that sin is always punished by suffering. He repeats the gloomy Greek warning of Solon to Croesus, "Count no man fortunate until his death."

The works of Sophocles (496–406) are more sophisticated artistically than those of Aeschylus. Sophocles added a third actor, inaugurated the use of painted scenery, and devised plots which were more complex than those of his predecessors. Sophocles was a product of the Periclean Age; his tragedies partook of the same spirit, or *ethos,* that characterized the sculpture of Phidias and the painting of Polygnotos. His characters are idealized and, like those of Aeschylus, drawn larger than life, but there is more humanity in them. Sophocles did not believe that immutable laws arranged man's life but rather that, although the gods often intervened in human affairs, a man might shape his own destiny through moderation and self-control.

Euripides (480–406) was clearly affected by the changed conditions which prevailed in Athens after the death of Pericles when the irresponsible citizen masses held sway. He was a realist in that he depicted human beings as they are in everyday life, but he also bowed to popular demands for sensationalism by presenting striking scenes and brilliant speeches. Euripides had little respect for the traditional Athenian attitudes toward the gods and society, and he was distinguished for his skepticism and his rational approach to human problems. Undoubtedly, he was much influenced by the contemporary sophistic teaching.

Athenian comedy sprang from the Dionysiac revels with which the country folk honored the wine-god. From the rustic mummers and their leader, the comic poets developed the chorus and the actors of the fifth-century comedy. Attic comedy concerned itself with the present rather than with the legendary past and consisted of satire leveled at individuals prominent in public life or well known groups—philosophers, tragedians, jurymen—whose behavior or characteristics might be ridiculed.

The greatest of the comic poets was Aristophanes (446–388). During the Peloponnesian War he wrote many comedies dealing with contemporary affairs, and, on occasion, he openly made fun of prominent people in

Athens—Pericles, Socrates, Cleon, Euripides, and others. His attitude was generally conservative; he did not hesitate to express his dislike of democratic leaders and institutions and the Sophists by caricaturing them in his plays. After the Peloponnesian War, public sentiment was opposed to free speech on political matters, and Aristophanes turned his attention to more general subjects; parodies of myths and the works of the tragic poets and satires on social institutions and the foibles of mankind became popular.

In the fifth century two great historians appeared: Herodotus of Halicarnassus and Thucydides of Athens. Herodotus (*fl.* 440 B.C.) was the author of a history of the Persian Wars. He saw in the struggles of the Greeks and the Persians a mighty conflict between the East and the West, and he tried not only to describe the actual military operations of the period 499–479 B.C. but also to provide a background by considering the earlier history of the seventh and sixth centuries. Therefore, he devoted considerable space to a description of the customs and origins of the inhabitants of the ancient world, with the result that his work contains geographic and anthropological information which makes it much more than a conventional history. Herodotus has been severely criticized for his credulity and his ignorance of military strategy, but his ability to tell a story is unrivaled, and it must be admitted that it would be difficult to reconstruct the early history of Greece without the information with which he alone supplies us.

Thucydides (460–395 B.C.) wrote the history of the Peloponnesian War. His impartiality and his careful analysis of situations and events have won for him the title of "the first scientific historian"; he was undoubtedly the greatest historian the ancient world ever produced. Thucydides' remarkable insight into human nature may be illustrated by a few quotations:

> The way that most men deal with traditions, even traditions of their own country, is to receive them all alike as they are delivered, without applying any critical test whatever. . . . So little pains do the vulgar take in the investigation of the truth, accepting readily the first story that comes to hand. . . . The absence of romance in my history will, I fear, detract somewhat from its interest. . . . I have written my work, not as an essay which is to win the applause of the moment, but as a possession for all time.

In spite of his scientific approach, Thucydides did not neglect the dramatic possibilities of his narrative. His description of the plague at Athens is one of the most famous passages in his history, but it is surpassed by the memorable account of the Sicilian expedition. Excellent as his narrative style is, Thucydides' substitution of dialogue for narrative in presenting the "Melian affair" of 416 was a stroke of genius. Finally, the often-quoted "Funeral Oration" of Pericles, a Gettysburg Address delivered at the end of the first year of the Peloponnesian War, ranks with the greatest works of Greek literature.

The inclusion of speeches in the narrative is characteristic of both Herodotus and Thucydides, but while Herodotus inserts them incidentally, almost accidentally, in Thucydides they are an integral device which always provides a dramatic method of exposition and in which the historian sometimes expresses his own opinions. Thucydides' speeches also reflect the contemporary art of oratory that was just beginning to flourish at Athens.

Even as early as the time of Homer oratory had been highly regarded by the Greeks, but until the closing years of the fifth century B.C. the ability to speak well was considered to be a gift; it did not occur to people that oratory might be studied and cultivated. The rise of democratic government and the increasing importance of the law courts, however, brought home to the Greeks the necessity of learning to express themselves in a creditable manner. Thus, rhetoric and oratory became important features of the sophistic training, the object of which was to enhance the pupil's chances of success in public life. Style, diction, and ultimately grammar and syntax were carefully studied; in fact, so much attention was paid to the externals of oratory that fluency and style and diction were considered more essential to a good speech than any ideas which it might contain.

Nevertheless, it was discovered that while some people could be trained to speak well, others could not master the art. Therefore, about 400 B.C. professional speechwriters began to appear; these were skillful men who could not only write good speeches but also adapt them to the personalities of the people who were to deliver them. Lysias and Isaeus were two of the most prominent and successful men in this field at Athens.

After 500 B.C. Greek intellectual activity had been diverted into many new channels. In the preceding age the early philosophers had been chiefly mathematicians, astronomers, and physicists, but the fifth and fourth centuries brought important new developments. There was a continuation of the work in plane and solid geometry; there were astronomical and calendrical studies; some thinkers advanced the theory of the sphericity of the earth, and others attacked the geocentric conception of the universe. Anaxagoras, the friend of Pericles, shocked religious conservatives when he claimed that the sun was a huge mass of blazing metal. The fifth century also saw great progress in the science of medicine through the work of Hippocrates, a priest of Asclepius (the god of healing) at Cos. Hippocrates owed much to studies he had made in Egypt, but he was able to free himself from the traditions of magic in medical treatment and to see disease as a natural evil that might be combatted by natural methods. He stressed hygiene and maintained that nature is the best physician. The crudeness of his methods, however, was well expressed in his maxim: "Where drugs fail, steel will cure; where steel fails, fire will cure; where fire fails, there is no cure."

✗ Despite these manifestations of a continued interest in science, the main trends of Greek thought in the fifth and early fourth centuries led in a different direction. In the century and a half after 500 B.C., Greek philosophy passed through three stages.

1. Roughly speaking, between 500 and 450 B.C., various philosophical schools elaborated, adapted, and altered the ideas that had been advanced in the sixth century. The increasingly abstract and purely speculative character of this thought ultimately led this type of philosophy into a cul-de-sac, with the result that in the second half of the fifth century it was largely abandoned and speculation proceeded along new lines.

2. Between 450 and 400 B.C. there was a growing tendency for men to think more about the problems of society, economics, and government and to pay less attention to the problems of the universe and nature. This new thinking, it was felt, was more "practical." Certainly, the popular mind was attracted by it; it is understandable that a man is most interested in things which relate directly to himself.

3. After 400 B.C. ethics, the formulation of "personal" philosophies, speculation concerning ideal forms of society and government, and the systematization of knowledge dominated philosophical thought.

Although the work of the philosophers who were the immediate successors of the sixth-century Ionian school and Pythagoras is important in the history of philosophy, it is not absolutely essential to our purpose here. After Anaximenes the Greek thinkers struggled with several problems. The motion and change postulated by Anaximander in his theory of the separation of opposites was upheld by Heraclitus of Ephesus, who considered fire to be the prime element and maintained that the universe and all it contains are in a constant state of flux, and that there are continuous generation and decay. The opposite point of view was taken by Parmenides of Elea and his school, who said that change and motion are illusions: what is, always was, and always will be; something cannot be created from nothing, nor can Being become nothing, or not-Being. The Sicilian Empedocles (495–430 B.C.) combined these divergent views by postulating four elements (fire, water, earth, and air) which united or separated to form all other types of matter; the elements themselves were constant and changeless, and it was their combination or disintegration which gave the impression of change. About the middle of the fifth century Leucippus and his successor, Democritus, elaborated the atomic theory that was the logical outgrowth of the philosophy of Anaximenes (see above, p. 210). Leucippus considered all material forms to be composed of an infinite number of tiny particles (atoms), continually in motion, uniform in substance, which unite temporarily to form visible objects. In addition, Heraclitus, the Eleatic school,

Anaxagoras, and others spoke variously of a single divine wisdom, a God, or a universal mind (nous) that was the supreme guiding force in the universe. The materialistic interpretation advocated by the atomists, however, left no room for such ideas.

The main result of this speculation was the growth of a feeling that no satisfactory conclusion could be reached. Many people took the practical attitude that even if the philosophers did arrive at a really demonstrable theory, nothing could be done about it. Therefore, men began to turn from their meditations upon "divine" affairs to "human" problems.

The leaders in the new intellectual movement were the Sophists, the itinerant teachers and lecturers, the professional "wise men," who went from city to city giving lecture courses on society, political science, grammar, rhetoric, argumentation, and other subjects. The students of the Sophists were men who wanted a "practical" and "useful" education that would help them in politics and the law courts; for this they were willing to pay their teachers considerable sums of money. In general, the attitude of the Sophists toward established customs and beliefs was one of skepticism, and they regarded the efforts of the philosophers as rather futile and meaningless. The famous Protagoras (*fl. c.* 450 B.C.), for example, preached the relativity of knowledge and said that truth was neither absolute nor eternal; the reality or unreality of anything depended upon its reality or unreality to each individual, and "man is the measure of all things." The Sophists tried to take all knowledge as their province; they had some information on almost every subject, but each Sophist had his own special field for which he was famous.

The Sophists were not well liked by the conservatives in the Greek city-states; the skepticism which sophistic teaching fostered undermined religion, and the individualism encouraged by the Sophists ran counter to the principles upon which the city-state was founded. As a result, the Sophists were frequently driven from cities where the elements in control were hostile to their unconventional ideas. There is a story that the books of Protagoras were burned at Athens about 411 B.C., and the very word "Sophist" came to have an unfavorable connotation.

The Sophists were the first to emphasize "education for life," a phrase that was just as meaningless in antiquity as it is today. Their success in gaining popular interest was due at least partly to the fact that the Greeks had been bewitched by the idea of "thought." Logic in the fifth century, like mathematics in the sixth, seemed to offer great opportunities for power and accomplishment. The influence of contemporary political and court oratory can be seen, too, for what the Sophists really tried to do was to convince or persuade rather than prove. Despite all their pyrotechnics, the Sophists were intellectually lazy. When a Protagoras said, "Man is the measure of all things," or when a Gorgias proclaimed, "There is no truth;

if there were, it could not be known; if known, it could not be communicated," it is clear that he chose to take the easy way out. Unfortunately, the elements of charlatanry in sophism were more often sensed than seen by its opponents, and attacks on the Sophists inspired by emotion rather than thought did little to counteract the widespread effects of the sophistic educational philosophy and method.

The greatest teacher of the fifth century was not a Sophist. He was Socrates (469–399 B.C.), the Athenian who stands at the beginning of a new era in Greek philosophy. The real Socrates will probably never be known. None of his writings has been preserved—if, indeed, he ever wrote anything —and we see him today chiefly through the eyes of his follower Plato, who in his dialogues gives us an idealized picture of the master. The Socrates of Plato is unlike the Socrates of Xenophon's *Memorabilia,* and neither Plato nor Xenophon would subscribe to the unfavorable view of Socrates which Aristophanes seems to have had. Moreover, the biography of Socrates by Diogenes Laertius is a miserable hodgepodge in which fact and fiction cannot easily be distinguished.

In spite of conflicting testimony, however, it is possible to present some general impressions of Socrates' life and work. Socrates was an Athenian who came from a "middle-class" family. He was plain in his tastes, moderate in all things, and extremely healthy; his pale face, flat nose, bulging eyes, and thick lips made his physical appearance anything but prepossessing. Nevertheless, his conviviality, his homely wit, and his ability as a teacher attracted many people to him, especially the young men of Athens who sought the intellectual stimulation that he was able to provide.

Socrates had studied physical science under Anaxagoras, but he came to the conclusion that it was impossible to learn about natural phenomena; therefore he turned to a field that he hoped might prove to be more profitable: the study of society and human relationships. Socrates himself did not profess to have definite knowledge of anything; instead, he pretended to seek information from others. It was his practice to interview people in all walks of life—statesmen, poets, craftsmen, and the like—in order to ascertain their ideas about certain general subjects: justice, truth, courage, piety, democracy, and law.

On these subjects "every man fancied that he could give a confident opinion, and even wondered that any other person should feel a difficulty. When Socrates, professing ignorance, put any such questions, he found no difficulty in obtaining an answer, given off-hand, and with very little reflection. The answer purported to be the explanation or definition of a term—familiar, indeed, but of wide and comprehensive import—given by one who had never before tried to render to himself an account of what it meant. Having got this answer, Socrates put fresh questions, applying it to specific cases, to which the respondent was compelled to give answers inconsistent with the first. . . . The respondent then amended his answer; but this was a prelude to other questions—and the respondent, after many attempts to disentangle himself, was obliged to plead guilty to the inconsistencies, with an admission that he could make no satisfactory answer to the original query, which had at first appeared so easy and familiar."[1]

This type of discourse showed clearly the ignorance of mankind in general regarding certain human problems that were of prime importance. Socrates found that definite knowledge was confined to the crafts where the craftsmen knew precisely what they were doing and were able to transmit a knowledge of their work to others; this was in direct contrast to the situation with regard to man and society where exact knowledge, even if it existed, would be difficult to pass on to other people.

Socrates' great contributions to philosophy were the stress which he put upon ethics and his invention of inductive discourse (dialectic). His successors, from Plato onward, followed in his footsteps. Moreover, although Socrates was not himself interested in science, his methods were employed by Aristotle and later scientists with great profit, for his use of general definitions followed by logical classification proved ideal for marshalling scientific facts into clear and concise forms.

It is not surprising to learn that Socrates was not universally popular in Athens. He was thought by many to be a Sophist and dangerous to the state. Those who had been subjected to one of his cross-examinations and shown to be hopelessly ignorant naturally became his bitterest enemies. For many years his influential friends were able to protect him, but finally he fell a victim to the unsettlement and hysteria which prevailed in Athens after the Peloponnesian War. In 399 B.C. he was indicted for religious nonconformity and for corrupting the youth of Athens. Although at his trial Socrates was able to refute his accusers, the jury voted for his conviction by a narrow margin, and he was sentenced to death. Two famous works of Plato are well worth reading in connection with Socrates' trial and execution: the *Apology of Socrates,* which describes the trial, and the *Phaedo,* which is an account of his death.

We have now completed our survey of classical Greek civilization. During the Archaic Period and to a lesser extent in the fifth century, elements from the Near East were borrowed, adapted, elaborated, and combined with new elements in a new environment. This was the process by which the civilization of classical Greece was formed. Subsequently, this civilization was spread to non-Greeks. It was transformed by its new contacts, and there was created a world civilization, the Hellenistic, which combined culture traits from the Near East, classical Greece, and (eventually) new elements from the western Mediterranean.

---

[1] George Grote, *History of Greece* (revised edition; London, 1869), Vol. VIII, p. 235.

To the world civilization of the Hellenistic and Roman periods and to medieval and modern civilization, the Greeks of the classical age contributed directly. Their language influenced Latin and all the Indo-European and Semitic languages spoken by the people who became their cultural heirs—our English vocabulary today is rich in Greek roots. Greek literature was read, translated, copied, and imitated, and through the ages the influence of Greek art is apparent even to the casual observer. The science and philosophy of the Hellenistic peoples and the Romans were predominantly an outgrowth of the classical period; this was also true of ideas in the fields of religion, politics, and aesthetics—to cite only a few examples. Even the city-state, although it was no longer the largest of the political units of the new Hellenistic world, was retained and put to good use, for in the empires of the Hellenistic period and in the Roman Empire the polis became a basic element of imperial organization. In the last analysis, the great empires of the period after 362 B.C. were federations of allied communities (mainly city-states) bound in varying degrees of subjection to a central authority.

We cannot dismiss classical Greek civilization without a reference to the so-called Greek view of life, which tended to become an integral part of later thinking. The "Greek view of life" is made up of several elements: the ideal of moderation, and the love of freedom, justice, beauty, and wisdom. Moderation was epitomized by a Greek phrase, "Nothing too much," and a word, *sophrosyne,* which signified sanity, balance, and self-control. The democratic city-state fostered the ideals of freedom and justice; Greek art, because of its sincere attempt to imitate or reproduce nature, stimulated a love of beauty; and Greek philosophy, by divorcing itself from the supernatural, opened the gates to wisdom. The concepts of freedom, justice, beauty, moderation, and (in part) wisdom were not unfamiliar to the peoples of the ancient Near East, as we can see from a perusal of Babylonian, Egyptian, Persian, and other literature; but it was the Greek statement of these concepts that made them known to western Europe.

It is something of a paradox that classical civilization was less familiar to the majority of the Greeks in the classical period than to their successors, for before 362 B.C. civilization was not widely diffused among the Greeks. Even at Athens, the cultural center of classical Greek civilization, the country people and many of the city proletarians may never have been much affected culturally, and there must have been numerous outlying geographic areas (Aetolia, Arcadia, etc.) where civilization was unknown.

Chapter 17

A PERIOD OF TRANSITION

(404-336 B.C.)

F ROM 404 TO 372 B.C. Sparta was the dominant state in Greece. Her autocratic policies and her friendship with Persia became more and more irritating to the rest of the Greeks, until Thebes, Athens, and some of the other states combined forces against her. After a number of military reverses the power of Sparta began to wane, and in 371 B.C. the Thebans inflicted a crushing defeat upon the Spartans at Leuctra in Boeotia which brought an end to Spartan dominance. The Thebans, however, were unable to demolish Sparta completely; nine years later the imperialistic ambitions of the Thebans themselves were shattered, and Theban power collapsed after a tremendous effort that produced only a Pyrrhic victory over the Spartans at Mantinea.

Sadder, but not much wiser, after nearly a century of fighting among themselves, the Greek city-states now found themselves second-rate powers whose future was uncertain. Within a few years when their independence was menaced by the growth of the Macedonian kingdom in the north, they lacked the strength to escape the almost complete political eclipse which, it is to be feared, they richly deserved.

The period from 404 to 336 B.C. which may conveniently, though in-accurately, be called the fourth century was one of transition from the classical (fifth century) or Hellenic Age to the succeeding epoch known as the Hellenistic. It was a period of gradual change and was marked, like all ages of transition, by a mingling of the old and the new.

A fact of prime importance was that the city-state had failed. It could not be adapted for the government of the larger political units which were in the process of formation. The collapse of the polis brought political, social, and intellectual changes and left many men of the older generation in hopeless confusion because they had lost their traditional frame of reference. The city-state had demanded intense loyalty and the subservience of the individual to the welfare of the state as a whole; in return it gave the individual a feeling of security and provided him with a vicarious importance which was based on the fact of his membership in an organization. Yet as the cities themselves grew in size, the complexities of urban life fostered a trend toward individualism which undermined loyalty to the state and even encouraged a resentment toward governmental authority.

This was one reason for the decline of the city-state, but there were others which were economic rather than social or political. External and internal warfare damaged the Greek cities beyond repair in the late fifth and early fourth centuries. These incessant extra- and intramural struggles were economic in origin. The expansion of trade had brought trade rivalries that often culminated in wars between states, while the accumulation of wealth by those individuals engaged in trade and industry had widened the gap between rich and poor and promoted class warfare (stasis) within states. While the rise of large-scale banking, the growth of international trade, and increased specialization of labor were characteristic of the fourth century, these developments were found throughout the Mediterranean world as a whole and occurred in Greece only because they formed part of the pattern of Mediterranean economic life. In comparison with other regions, Greece declined; its mineral resources failed, the landholding class had suffered from wars and revolutions, and Greece had lost markets in the East to the Phoenicians and in the West to their former colonies which had now become self-sufficient. Worse than this, the lifeblood of the economy —the actual coin in circulation—had been thinned by the decline of gold and silver production and drained off by trade with the Persian Empire which demanded cash in return for its products. The Persian Fort Knox at Persepolis was helping to suffocate the Greek economy.

The fourth century was the age in which Plato, Aristotle, Demosthenes, Isocrates, and Xenophon flourished. Their thinking and their activities can be employed to illustrate the old and new elements in this period. Plato and Aristotle, the two giants of Greek philosophy, exerted an influence upon their contemporaries exceeded only by the influence which they had over later Greek, Roman, and medieval thinkers. In ethics, politics, science, aesthetics, and nearly every conceivable field the effort of subsequent philosophers was conditioned by ideas first put into recognizable form by either Plato or Aristotle.

Plato (428–347 B.C.) had sat at the feet of Socrates. After the death of his master he traveled to Egypt, Cyrene, Italy, and Sicily. About 387 B.C. he returned to his native Athens where he founded a school in the Grove of Academus, an institution which was afterward known as the Academy. Plato employed the discussion methods developed by Socrates, and he continued the search for universal ethical truths. His writings were mostly in the form of dialogues in which Socrates played the part of an interrogator. One of Plato's greatest works is his famous *Republic* in which he set forth his ideas on the ideal form of government. Plato's dream was a utopian city-state in which the citizens (numbering about five thousand) were divided into three classes: workers, warriors, and rulers. The rulers were men of special intellectual abilities who were trained for their task from childhood. This ideal state was, of course, to be economically self-sufficient. Toward the end of his life Plato produced his *Laws,* a work which described a more practical city-state government and organization than the one proposed in the *Republic.*

Plato was not only a magnificent and stimulating philosopher, but he also possessed a fine literary style. Perhaps the most serious criticism which might be made of him is that he looked backward rather than forward. In his political thinking he was not entirely in touch with the trend of his times, and he could not see that the day of the independent city-state was nearly ended. In many ways Plato belongs to the fifth rather than the fourth century; the fact that most of his work was done in the fourth century helps to demonstrate how much that century constituted a transitional period in which there was a mingling of classical Greek culture with the new elements that were to be characteristic of the Hellenistic Age.

Aristotle (384–322 B.C.) spent twenty years as a student in Plato's Academy; then he was appointed tutor to Alexander the Great, and finally, about 335 he returned to Athens to open a school of his own in the grove known as the Lyceum. In large part, Aristotle emancipated himself from Plato; his main interest was in studying and organizing in logical form all the knowledge then available to mankind. But Aristotle was more than a compiler of facts or an encyclopaedist; through his own observation and thought he was able to add much to the sum total of information available in his own day. His writings on logic (he was the inventor of formal logic), metaphysics, natural history, ethics, rhetoric, and aesthetics help to give some idea of the broadness of his interests and his intellectual power. Aristotle also dealt with political science; he made a careful study of the constitutions of about one hundred and fifty of the Greek states, and he began a philosophical work, the *Politics,* which was not completed when he died. For Aristotle as well as Plato, the city-state was the chief form of government, but Aristotle's views were more realistic than those of his predecessor.

The philosophical schools of both Plato and Aristotle, the Academy and the Lyceum, continued to exist after the deaths of their founders. Naturally, both men had followers and imitators who founded schools of their own.

We have been accustomed to thinking of the Greek city-state as synonymous with democracy. This was not the Greek view of it. Plato and Aristotle believed in the city-state, but they, like many of their contemporaries, mistrusted democracy. They regarded the democracy of Periclean Athens as a hopeless failure, a fruitless experiment never to be repeated. The best state, in the minds of educated Greeks, was an aristocracy in which the "best" people (variously defined) should rule. Plato, one suspects, with his belief in censorship, eugenics, and euthanasia, secretly admired the Spartan system. Aristotle called democracy a perversion of constitutional government, and he said, "Some men are by nature free and others slaves, and for these latter slavery is both expedient and right." He also said, "Democracy is a tyrant."

For all their thought and wisdom these Greek philosophers missed the real point: that democracy might be possible—not under the conditions of life and technology in an ancient world—but in another world. Plato and Aristotle, perhaps because they were Greeks, never envisioned an improvement of technology which would free the manual laborer and make communication possible over wide areas; they failed to realize that succeeding generations might profit by their lesson of failure, might come into the possession of knowledge of society, economics, and human nature that would make democracy at least a potentiality.

Just as the fourth century was a period of great developments in philosophy, it was also significant in the history of oratory. Now a carefully developed study, oratory was so highly regarded that professional teachers and speechwriters were influential enough to take an active part in Greek politics. In the fourth century, as a matter of fact, Greek oratory reached its peak under two major political figures who earned their living from the art of speaking: Isocrates and Demosthenes.

Isocrates (436–338 B.C.) was an Athenian who conducted a school for training in rhetoric in his native city. As an orator, Isocrates is considered to have perfected a florid, periodic style notable for its figures of speech and varied rhythms. In his political views he was Panhellenic rather than Athenian. He favored a confederation of Greek states for the purpose of ending intercity warfare and protecting Greece from outside enemies; particularly, he thought that the Greeks ought to unite in an attack upon Persia. When his proposals for confederation were ignored, Isocrates turned to Philip II of Macedon and urged him to unite the Greeks by force.

Where Isocrates was representative of the new age in that he could look ahead into the future enough to see that the city-state had failed and was doomed, Demosthenes was equally representative in that he looked backward and retained his faith in the polis. Born in Athens in 384 B.C., Demosthenes was the greatest of all Greek orators. A professional speech-writer, he rose high in Athenian politics and became the principal opponent of Philip at Athens (see below, p. 281). Demosthenes was much more than a rhetorician and maker of fine speeches, for his orations displayed great intellectual ability and high ideals. Ranked by the Romans as the equal of Cicero, Demosthenes had a powerful style which was inimitable; like a "whirlwind or a thunderbolt," it was said, Demosthenes swept away or consumed the obstacles in his path.

Another man truly representative of the fourth century was the Athenian Xenophon (430–350 B.C.), whose activities, interests, and attitudes illustrate both the traditional and the novel in this period. Like many other young men of good family in Athens, Xenophon was attracted in his adolescence and early manhood to the great teacher, Socrates. Like Plato, after Socrates' martyrdom Xenophon tried to perpetuate the memory of the master by writing an *Apology* and a *Symposium;* both were inferior to Plato's famous works. One wonders whether Xenophon really understood what Socrates was talking about, but his *Memorabilia* is valuable because it presents a different view of the philosopher than one finds in Plato and also contains many anecdotal details not found in other sources.

Xenophon is best known as the author of the *Anabasis,* the story of the march of the ten thousand Greeks. The tale is a familiar one:

In the closing years of the fifth century the Persian king, Darius II, died, leaving his throne to an elder son named Artaxerxes. This embittered a younger son, Cyrus, who thought *he* should have been king. His reasoning was rather curious; he claimed that Artaxerxes had been born before Darius became king, and therefore Artaxerxes was not "born to the purple" like Cyrus himself, whose birth had occurred after Darius ascended the throne. This was a poor argument from any point of view and convincing only to Cyrus himself.

Cyrus had been one of the satraps in Asia Minor during the last years of the Peloponnesian War. He had favored throwing the support of Persia to the Spartans rather than to the Athenians as Alcibiades had hoped and nearly persuaded Tissaphernes, the other satrap, to do. Cyrus had also been a party to the assassination of Alcibiades (about 403).

The Peloponnesian War over, Cyrus turned his attention to the internal politics of Persia and began to plot the overthrow of his brother, Artaxerxes. A preliminary scheme was discovered; Cyrus was imprisoned and would have been executed if the queen mother had not intervened in his behalf. He then returned to his province in Asia Minor and renewed his plots, but with greater caution and finesse. At the same time he revived his feud with Tissaphernes, satrap of southwestern Asia Minor, a staunch supporter of Artaxerxes. Cyrus began to collect a large force of Persian and native troops in Sardes, his provincial capital, and he also recruited Greek mercenaries. The excuse which Cyrus gave for gathering such a large force was that he was going to campaign against various tribes which had not fully submitted to Persia, but Tissaphernes began to fear that he was about to be the object of a private vendetta.

The news of the recruiting came to the mainland Greek states. Many Spartans and other veterans of the Peloponnesian War had acquired a real taste for soldiering and decided to enlist with Cyrus. At Athens Xenophon heard of Cyrus' activities and thought they promised adventure. He consulted Socrates, who advised against enlisting with Cyrus, but Xenophon ultimately set off with other friends to join the expedition. About ten thousand Greeks hired themselves out as soldiers of Cyrus, though Xenophon did not; he merely attached himself to Cyrus as a sort of military observer with no official status.

In 401 the army left Sardes. None except Cyrus and a few confidential friends knew the object of the expedition, but Tissaphernes suspected the truth at last and fled hastily from his province to warn Artaxerxes. In the meantime, the army of Cyrus marched across Asia Minor to its central point and then turned southward through the Cilician Gates to the plain of Tarsus. Here the real objective of the expedition, the overthrow of the Great King, was revealed to the men. The Greek mercenaries balked; it was not that they cared who ruled Persia, but they wanted more pay—and got it. The march was resumed across northern Syria to the Euphrates and down toward Babylon. At Cunaxa the army of Artaxerxes was encountered and beaten, but Cyrus, pursuing his brother, lost touch with his troops and was killed. Suddenly, the ten thousand Greeks found themselves alone in the very heart of the Persian Empire, for Cyrus' Persian and native troops just melted away into the desert. Artaxerxes and Tissaphernes appeared and called for a parley; they professed themselves desirous of peace (for they feared the Greek phalanx) and invited the Greek officers to a conference. The officers were wined, dined, and butchered; the ten thousand Greeks were left leaderless. Undaunted, they held a general assembly at which new commanders were chosen; among the elected leaders was Xenophon who, encouraged by a propitious sneeze, had made an inspiring speech—it was also long, but he gives the quotation in full. It was resolved to turn northward through Assyria in an attempt to reach the Greek settlements on the shores of the Black Sea; it would also be difficult for the Persian cavalry to follow the Greeks through the rough mountain country of Armenia. At this point the *Anabasis,* the going up, ends, and the *Katabasis,* the real story, begins. Through the winter the Greeks struggled northward, fighting bitter engagements in the snow with hostile Kurdish tribes which hated any invader, Greek or Persian. In the spring the Greeks felt they must be nearing the Black Sea and the end of their seemingly endless journey. Then came that famous day, immortalized by one of the best-known passages in all Greek literature, when the sea was sighted from the top of the last mountain range. A year later (399) Xenophon saw Athens again; he had arrived home just after the execution of his friend and teacher, Socrates.

The *Anabasis* is not, strictly speaking, history; it is journalism. Xenophon was one of the first war correspondents in history, and his book has been popular for over twenty-three hundred years. The *Anabasis* has many good narrative passages, but it bogs down often in the speeches, many of which were delivered by Xenophon himself and are exceedingly dull. Foreshadowing the birth of biographical writing are the fascinating sketches of the Greek leaders which Xenophon gives in the *Anabasis;* it is significant that though these men were all young, they were already hard-bitten veterans and could never be converted to peaceful lives.

Embittered by the death of Socrates and hating the Athenian democracy, Xenophon left Athens and went to Sparta where he took service with the Spartan king, Agesilaus. When he fought by the side of Agesilaus against Athens in 394, Xenophon was formally exiled from his native city, but his Spartan friends took good care of him. They gave him an estate in Elis near Olympia, where he lived until the fall of Sparta in 371. Subsequently, the country was so anti-Spartan that he had to leave Elis and return to Athens, where he was forgiven for his political and ideological sins. One of his twin sons was killed in 362 in the Battle of Mantinea. The story of Xenophon's reception of this sad news is a familar one: in keeping with his self-imposed dual role of philosopher and Spartan-by-adoption, he merely remarked, "I knew my son was mortal."

From 399 until his death about 350, Xenophon devoted most of his leisure to writing; all of his works date from this period. We have already seen that Xenophon was not much of a philosopher, and his *Hellenica* (a history of the period 404–362 which was to supply a continuation of Thucydides) was a poor thing compared with the great work that it was intended to supplement. Nevertheless, he was a prolific writer and important because his work is representative of new trends in prose composition. Xenophon was essentially a pamphleteer, a new species of literary animal that had begun to appear during the Peloponnesian War. Xenophon also produced a rudimentary biography, really a panegyric, in his *Life of Agesilaus,* and he wrote a monograph, *The Constitution of the Lacedaemonians,* a political treatise which was both analytical and descriptive, the sort of thing that Aristotle and his students were to turn out by the dozens within a few years. In Xenophon's *Cyropaedia (Education of Cyrus)* we have an educational romance. What Xenophon pretends to do is to describe the upbringing of Cyrus the Great; it is pure fable, with Cyrus represented as a minor Socrates who favors Spartan fascism. Equally fanciful was the *Hiero,* a dialogue between a Syracusan tyrant and the poet Simonides in which each was portrayed as envious of the other's station in life. Other essays by Xenophon included one on *Horsemanship,* another on *Hunting,* and still another entitled the *Hipparchicus* (*Cavalry Officer*). All were intended as manuals for practical use. A treatise called *On the Revenues of Athens* is ascribed to Xenophon but may not be from his hand. Unintentionally amusing is another essay on domestic economy, the subject of which seems to be how to wear the chiton in your own home.

The growing individualism of the fourth century had its effect upon politics and literature, but it was also displayed in other fields. Individualism in thinking had encouraged man to think about man rather than nature; it was to lead through Socrates, the Sophists, Plato, and Aristotle to the "personal" philosophies of the Hellenistic Age. Individualism also weakened the old religious faiths and aided the rise in popularity of the mystery religions. Its influence was paramount, too, in the art of the fourth century. The effects of technical facility and individualism upon the sculptors of the fourth century and the development of portraiture were other manifestations of individualism (see above, p. 257).

In still another field, architecture, there were new developments during the fourth century with a trend toward the construction of larger buildings; the temple was no longer the only type of structure on which the Greeks lavished their money and attention. Magnificent theaters were built at Athens and Epidaurus, and the big assembly hall (Thersilion) at Megalopolis, a new and carefully planned town in the Peloponnesus, exemplified new trends. Two of the Seven Wonders of the Ancient World were constructed in Asia Minor about 350 B.C. These were the Mausoleum and the temple of Artemis at Ephesus. The latter was erected after a fire had destroyed another temple on the same site (some said that Alexander was born on the night of the fire). The new temple was in the Ionic style, and its size was extraordinary, for it covered an area 340 by 160 feet. The Mausoleum was a funeral monument to Mausolus, the king of Halicarnassus. The structure was at least 150 feet high and had four main elements: (1) a base or podium which supported (2) an Ionic peristyle on which was (3) a pyramid crowned by (4) a quadriga, or four-horse chariot. The first three elements had equal altitudes.

The cultural advances of the fourth century took place in the midst of, and almost in spite of, the disturbed conditions of an age which saw the political fall of the civilized Greeks and the rise of the barbarous Macedonians.

The almost unbelievable strategic ineptitude of the Athenians at Aegospotami in 405 raises a suspicion of treachery. The oligarchic revolution at Athens a few years earlier had demonstrated that many Athenians were heartily sick of the Peloponnesian War and of the democratic tyranny at home, though it was clear that the conservatives only wished to exchange one tyranny for another. On this earlier occasion, however, the return of Alcibiades had thwarted the oligarchs who were forced to bide their time until he was out of the way and the democracy discredited in the final phases of the Peloponnesian War.

After the Athenians had outmaneuvered themselves at Aegospotami, preparations were made for the surrender of Athens. Exiles returned to the city and joined the extreme oligarchs in an interim government—the Thirty —which was set up to revise the constitution and to treat with the Spartan admiral, Lysander. During 404–403 the Thirty, led by Critias and Theramenes, made peace with Sparta and organized a new government. Democratic leaders were arrested and put to death, while others whose wealth was greater than their political guilt also perished in the reign of terror that ensued.

Critias and Theramenes, however, had only their treachery in common. Theramenes, of course, had been mixed up in the revolution of 411, and he had also been loud in the denunciation of the generals in 406. Nevertheless, his views were more moderate than those of Critias, the atheistic, power-loving disciple of Socrates, who would have preferred to keep the Thirty in power forever. The paths of the two leaders soon parted: Theramenes was condemned to death, torn from the sanctuary of the Sacred Hearth, haled off to prison, and promptly poisoned early in 403. Presently, democratic exiles under Thrasybulus invaded Attica, and even the Spartan garrison could not withstand them. Critias fell in battle against the democrats at Munychia; the Spartans were withdrawn and the democracy restored.

Undoubtedly, the Spartans could have supported the Athenian oligarchs more strongly, but there was dissension at Sparta, too. Pausanias, the more powerful of the Spartan kings, hated Lysander. He persuaded the government to recall the ambitious admiral. This left the oligarchs at Athens without support, and the democrats were victorious.

Very shortly the troubles of the Spartans multiplied. Their boast that they meant to procure the freedom of the Greeks was hardly compatible with their alliance with Persia. They could not emancipate the Greeks in Asia Minor without going to war with the Great King. Moreover, the Spartans preferred to support the oligarchs in Greece itself, a policy not easily reconciled with freedom as far as most Greeks were concerned. The Spartans, in reality, were aiming at empire, and when this fact became clear, they lost their friends in Greece and Persian aid as well.

The unofficial approval which Sparta had given the plot of Cyrus to unseat Artaxerxes angered the Persians. Then the Spartans tried to prevent Tissaphernes from recovering the Greek cities that had been subject to Cyrus and supported a new Ionian Revolt in 398. Despite some successes on land which were due to the efforts of the new Spartan king, Agesilaus, the Spartan fleet was demolished in 394 by Persian forces commanded by the exiled Athenian admiral, Conon.

Not content to fight the Spartans in Asia Minor, the Persians had been intriguing against them in Greece, too. Thebes, weaned away from Spartan friendship, went to war in 395 and was soon joined by Athens, Corinth, and Argos. As soon as the Spartans were on the defensive and Asia Minor was safe from their depredations, the Persians changed sides and renewed their co-operation with Sparta. The result was a stalemate in Greece which provided an opportunity for the Great King to dictate the terms of peace that ended Greek hostilities in 387. Under the terms of the so-called King's Peace of that year, all Greeks were declared "free," Sparta and Persia pledged themselves to maintain this freedom, and it was agreed that all political leagues and alliances should be terminated. Athens repudiated her allies, Thebes was separated from the Boeotian League, and the union of Corinth and Argos was dissolved.

It was all a trick. The Spartans now had the upper hand in Greece and began to interpret the "King's Peace" in very broad terms, attacking cities that were potentially their enemies and breaking up even religious confederacies. They seized Thebes in 382 as a "precautionary measure." This exceeded the limits of Greek endurance: in 379 a counterrevolution occurred in Thebes which accomplished the slaughter of the pro-Spartans and the withdrawal of the Spartan garrison. In the following year the failure of a sneak attack by Spartan forces on Athens brought the Athenians and Thebans together. The Athenians (377) organized a new naval league, a cautious modification of the Delian Confederacy of a century before, and set about "liberating" maritime states from Sparta and Persia.

By 371 the Spartans were willing to sue for peace. A congress of the warring powers met in that year to draw up a treaty to end hostilities, but the deliberations ended in failure when the Thebans insisted upon signing the treaty in the name of Thebes *and* the Boeotian League. When the Spartans invaded Boeotia, they were beaten at Leuctra (371).

Nine dreary years ensued while the Thebans tried to take up where the Spartans had left off. Under the leadership of the two heroes who had liberated Thebes in 379, Pelopidas and Epaminondas, the Thebans built up an empire in central Greece, gained control of Thessaly, brought a Macedonian prince, Philip (the father of Alexander), as hostage to Thebes, and tried to weaken Sparta in the Peloponnesus by creating the Arcadian League which was composed of anti-Spartan states. Pelopidas died fighting in northern Greece, and the whole bubble burst in 362 when the Thebans made their final attack on Sparta. At the Battle of Mantinea the Thebans were victorious, but Epaminondas was mortally wounded. As he lay dying, he advised his countrymen to make peace.

The events of the century between the beginning of the Periclean Age and the Battle of Mantinea had shown that the Greeks could not, and would not, unite. Topography and technology were against unification. Athens could create and hold an empire, at least briefly, as long as it was a maritime union, but the failure of Pericles to control the states of central Greece should have been an object lesson to the Spartans and Thebans. Transportation and communication by land were too primitive to permit Greek unification by relatively small states like Athens, Sparta, and Thebes which lacked the manpower and rapidity of movement to hold what they might conquer. Even a stronger, outside, non-Greek power could succeed in uniting the Greeks by force only after they had exhausted themselves by fighting one another.

The mainland Greeks, during the bitter years of the early fourth century, had failed to keep pace with the rest of the Mediterranean world; but few Hellenic statesmen who took the trouble to examine the international situation in the period of comparative peace that followed the Battle of Mantinea were sufficiently acute to recognize this vital fact. The intense desire for local independence which had been one of the virtues of the pre-Persian and Periclean Ages had become a vice that was shortly to bring about the complete destruction of any sort of political freedom in Greece. This narrow provincial attitude, long a tradition in the city-states of Hellas and now so out of date, precluded the attainment of the political unity necessary to keep the Greeks predominant in the affairs of the Aegean, for in the new era the nation and not the polis was to play the leading role.

The development of national groups in southern Europe at this time was due largely to the diffusion into the hinterland of the Greco-Oriental culture of the Mediterranean littoral. Macedonia and Rome, the two most important states thus affected, were destined to figure prominently in the subsequent history of the Greeks and to carry Greek culture to the far corners of the ancient world. More favorably situated, nearer to what was then the center of cultural diffusion, Macedonia reached the high point of her career long before the Romans became interested in affairs outside of Italy; when Rome finally attained the status of a world power, Macedonia was declining.

Before 350 B.C. Macedonia was a very primitive country; her inhabitants, cut off from the seacoast by the Greek settlements in the northern Aegean, were largely a pastoral people. Although the Macedonians were probably distantly related to the Hellenes, they were classed as barbarians by their more civilized neighbors who lived to the south; only the Macedonian royal family, which traced its descent from Heracles, was accepted in Greek society. The despised Macedonians, however, had many excellent qualities. They were hardy, fond of war, and devoted to their kings; these national characteristics enabled their first great king, Philip II, to transform his people into highly efficient soldiers for whom the Greeks were no match.

Philip II was a man who well understood the Greeks and their politics. With a genius for organization and a great capacity for intrigue, he soon had the disunited and mutually jealous city-states of Greece at his mercy; step by step, he moved relentlessly toward his goal—the establishment of Macedonian supremacy in Greek lands. As a hostage in Thebes during the days of Pelopidas and Epaminondas Philip had been able to observe at first hand the new military tactics which had been more than a match for the older system as exemplified by Sparta; the greater use of cavalry and light-armed troops and a generally more versatile army had been the answer to the Spartan phalanx. Philip also learned the ways of diplomacy; he learned, too, that the Greeks were divided among themselves and that Greek politicians could be bribed.

The brother of the late king of Macedonia, Philip served first as regent, and then in 359 at the age of twenty-three he ascended the throne as king. After centralizing the government, building up a new national army, and cowing the barbarians on the eastern, northern, and western frontiers, Philip was ready to move against the Greeks. The first step was to get access to the coast. Taking advantage of the rivalries of Amphipolis, Olynthus, Potidaea, and other states, he cleverly played one against another until he possessed them all. In the process he got control of gold mines in Thrace which paid his expenses at home, allowed him to build up trade, and also provided the means to buy good friends at Athens, Thebes, and elsewhere. Athens, which might have opposed his operations in the Chalcidice, had been occupied by a revolt of her allies who were aided and abetted by Mausolus, the king of Halicarnassus. By 351, when the fall of Olynthus was imminent and Demosthenes delivered the First Philippic, it was almost too late to stop Philip in the north.

In the meantime, a conflict in Greece known as the Sacred War had begun in 356. This originated in a quarrel between Thebans and Phocians. Bullied and threatened by Thebes, the Phocians had seized the treasury at Delphi and purchased a fine army for their national defense. After years of fighting, the Thebans, who had had much the worst of it, invited Philip to intervene against the Phocians, while the Athenians, who had the impression that Philip was going to attack Thebes, stood idly by and let him enter central Greece. The hapless Phocians were beaten (346), and Philip came into the possession of their two votes in the Delphic Amphictyony (religious league). Nor was this the end of his successes: in 344 Philip became the warlord of Thessaly and two years later made Epirus a vassal state.

In vain Demosthenes thundered against the wily Macedonian in successive Philippics (344 and 341). There were other orators in Athens, secretly in the pay of Philip, who were ready to reply to Demosthenes' accusations. Furthermore, there was a growing sentiment in many Greek states that Philip could provide the strength to bring about a cessation of intercity warfare and stasis. They were willing to sacrifice a little freedom for stability. The situation was further complicated by the Persians, who had now begun to fear that Philip would turn his attentions to Asia Minor; Persian money poured into Greece in an attempt to arouse anti-Macedonian sentiments.

Though Philip failed to cut the Athenian lifeline to the grain of south Russia by attacks in the Chersonese which would have closed the outlet of the Black Sea, he met with better luck in Greece itself. A new Sacred War broke out in 339 when the Delphic Amphictyony accused Locrian Amphissa of offenses against Delphi. Philip was entrusted with the leadership of the war, and his presence in Phocis encouraged the Thebans and Athenians to try conclusions with him. In the ensuing battle at Chaeronea (338) a Macedonian victory was clinched by the brilliant charge led by Philip's eighteen-year-old son who was soon to be known as Alexander the Great.

After he had dealt harshly with the Thebans, Philip had little difficulty in bringing the rest of the Greeks to terms. All the important city-states (except Sparta) made haste to attend the Hellenic Congress which he now called at Corinth. From Philip's point of view the congress was an unqualified success. At his suggestion the Greeks entered into an alliance which was to devote itself to maintaining peace in Hellas; the league members were to support all existing constitutions and to punish any state which became an aggressor against another. The league became Philip's ally; he was its commander-in-chief, pledged to lead a combined Greek and Macedonian army in an invasion of Persian territory in Asia Minor. A venture of this sort was traditionally popular; hence the project inspired temporarily a good feeling toward Philip in Greece.

Philip, who had seen his great plans succeed with amazing perfection up to this point, was not destined to witness their culmination. In 336, with his advance guard already in Asia, Philip was himself on the instant of departure when he was assassinated by one of his own Macedonians. The ultimate responsibility for Philip's death was never fixed. Whether the Persians, the Greeks, or Olympias (Alexander's mother) engineered the plot that brought Philip's career to this premature end will never be known.

The abrupt conclusion of the life of Philip marked also the termination of an era in history. Within a few years after the accession of Alexander the Great, the next Macedonian king, the shape of the whole world and things to come had been altered by his exploits.

Chapter 18

ALEXANDER
AND THE HELLENISTIC AGE

THERE ARE THREE Alexanders: the legendary Alexander, the historical Alexander, and the real Alexander. The first was born in men's minds soon after the death of the last, and he still lives in the East as Iskander. He has been many things: a saint and a devil, a defender of civilization and a barbarian, a perfect knight and a worthless debauchee. The historical Alexander is dead, but he is frequently revived in the pages of histories and biographies that fashion him in the image that each particular age admires; in one age he may be "a greater than Napoleon," and in another he may be the man who first dreamed of "one world." The real Alexander died in Babylon on the thirteenth of June, 323 B.C. We know a little of what he did, but we shall never know what he thought or what he was like. The real Alexander is gone forever.

With the exception of a few inscriptions, the coins, and the sculptural representations of the great conqueror which have survived, it is necessary to depend almost entirely upon rather late historical and biographical works for our information about Alexander. Plutarch's *Life of Alexander* was written in the second century A.D. It is one of our best sources, but it is brief and selective. About the same time another Greek, Arrian, wrote his *Anabasis of Alexander* which is quite long but is concerned mainly with military affairs; factually, the work is considered generally reliable. Diodorus (first century B.C.) deals rather fully with Alexander in his *Universal History* and includes material not to be found in Plutarch or Arrian. Quintus Curtius Rufus (first century A.D.) is copious enough in detail but credulous, biassed, and inaccurate. Justin's condensation (date unknown) of the longer work of Pompeius Trogus (about the beginning of the Christian era) leaves much to be desired. Thus, these main sources are removed from

Alexander by several centuries, and even though they were in part based upon primary sources not available to us—the daily journals written in Alexander's camp by two officers assigned to the task, the polished but unfinished history written by Callisthenes (Aristotle's nephew) who accompanied Alexander until 327 B.C., the memoirs of Alexander's generals, etc.— we should be happier if Thucydides or Polybius had been with Alexander.

Alexander was born in 356 B.C., the son of Philip of Macedon and an Epirote princess named Olympias. He was tutored by Aristotle, who is supposed to have exercised a great influence upon his thinking. It is an understatement to say that Philip and Olympias were incompatible. They were both difficult people, and Alexander cannot have had a very happy childhood, since he was devoted to his mother and seems to have engaged in a continuous rivalry with his father. If Alexander had a mother fixation and resented his father, it would be easy to understand many of the motivations of his adult life; a number of the things which he is reputed to have done would tend to support this interpretation. Supposedly precocious in childhood, Alexander was certainly a great leader, a brilliant general, possessed of a quick and resourceful mind; there was a strong romantic strain in his nature, and he had a real flair for the dramatic.

A king at twenty by virtue of strong army support, Alexander was an unknown quantity to the Greeks. While he campaigned along the frontiers of Macedon against barbarian invaders in 335, a rumor of his death circulated in Greece. Thebes revolted and then barred its gates in consternation two weeks later when a very live Alexander appeared to demand submission. The city was taken and destroyed; the people were sold into slavery, and no structures were left standing except the temples and the house of Pindar. The other Greeks now hastened to assure Alexander of their loyalty and to promise ships and men for the renewal of Philip's plan for the invasion of Asia Minor.

In the spring of 334 B.C. Alexander began the ten-year campaign that was to make him the ruler of the eastern Mediterranean and the old Persian Empire. With thirty-five thousand men and an empty treasury he boldly crossed into Asia and defeated the Persian satraps at the Granicus River near Lampsacus. Enemy resistance in Asia Minor collapsed; the cities along the Aegean coast opened their gates to the liberator. Only Miletus and Halicarnassus, garrisoned and supplied by elements of the Persian fleet, offered opposition. In 333 Alexander pressed on into central Asia Minor as far as the old Phrygian capital of Gordium and then turned south along the road which led through the Cilician Gates to Tarsus. From Tarsus he made his way to Issus on the Gulf of Alexandretta, where he left the sick and wounded in camp while he went southward in Syria to discover the whereabouts of a big Persian army led by King Darius himself. A ludicrous game of hide-and-seek in a labyrinth of mountains ended when Darius got behind Alexander and cut Macedonian communications with the north by capturing the camp at Issus. Persian ineptitude lost the ensuing battle for the Great King; the superior numbers of the Persians were no match for the skill and bravery of Alexander. Darius fled ignominiously from the field of battle, leaving his harem and his bathtub behind; he also lost the war chest which he had thought safe in Damascus, for troops of Alexander soon occupied that town.

Issus was one of the greatest of Alexander's battles. His generalship was never better, and he never had more at stake. With his safety line to the north cut off, defeat at Issus would have meant the end of the expedition and possibly of his life, but victory restored the morale of his troops while the capture of the Persian treasure allowed Alexander to pay his men for the first time in months.

After Issus Alexander had a choice to make: he might pursue Darius into Mesopotamia, or he might proceed southward along the Mediterranean coast toward Egypt. The latter course was wisely adopted. The Persian fleet was still at large in the Aegean, but its ships and men were Phoenician. When Alexander took the Phoenician towns one by one, the Phoenicians deserted to him, and the fleet melted away. The mighty fortresses of Phoenician Tyre and Philistine Gaza capitulated after prolonged sieges, and in 332 B.C. Alexander entered Egypt, where he encountered no resistance.

In Egypt Alexander reorganized the country, founded Alexandria (which soon became the greatest city in the eastern Mediterranean), and made the expedition across the western desert to the fabulous oasis of Siwah, where he was recognized by the priests of Amon as the son of the god and thus legitimate ruler of Egypt. In 331 the army retraced its steps to Syria. Darius had offered to make peace on the basis of the *status quo,* but Alexander resolved to follow up his advantage by pushing the attack into Mesopotamia. Crossing the Euphrates and the Tigris and passing into what had once been Assyria, Alexander won another victory over Darius at Gaugamela (October, 331). Darius fled across the mountains to faraway Media while Alexander within four months gained possession of the three vital cities of Babylon, Susa, and Persepolis.

In the spring of 330 after the great palace at Persepolis had been burned, probably by accident, the invaders moved northward toward Median Ecbatana where Darius was hiding. The Persian king did not dare to await Alexander's arrival; instead, he tried to escape to Bactria, a remote province in the northeast. In swift pursuit of his quarry, Alexander covered four hundred miles in eleven days. The chase ended when the Macedonians came upon the corpse of Darius; the Persian king had been slain by his satrap, Bessus, who planned to seize Bactria for himself.

By right of conquest and by virtue of the death of Darius, Alexander was now King of Persia, but rather than turn back to consolidate his con-

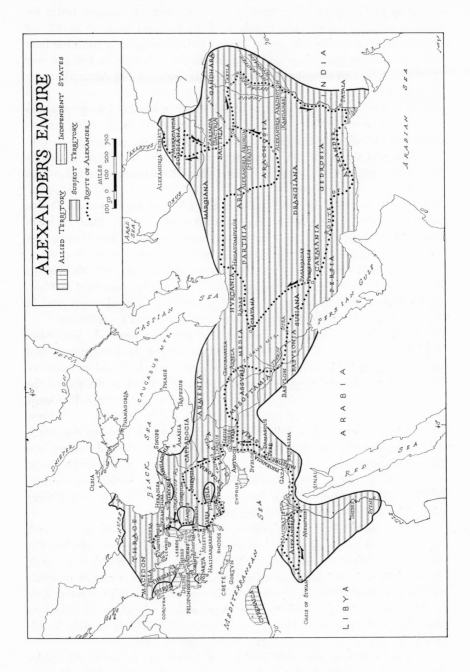

quests, he resolved to push on toward the east to punish Bessus for the murder of Darius. This plan resulted in the reduction of the eastern Persian provinces and the invasion of India (330–326). These later years were packed with drama: the crossing of the mighty, snow-clogged Hindu Kush range into Bactria; the pursuit and capture of Bessus, who was torn apart by having his arms and legs tied to four young trees which were bent down for the purpose and then allowed to spring back; Alexander's marriage to the beautiful princess, Roxane; and the encounters with the gigantic Indian king, Porus, and his war elephants, terrible machines of war which the Greeks and Macedonians had never before had to face.

Alexander wished to proceed farther to the east than the Indus Valley, but his troops mutinied; the men, tired of many years of campaigning, wanted to go home. Alexander followed the Indus to its mouth and then turned back toward Babylon. While most of the troops marched across the southern deserts, a fleet under the command of the Greek admiral, Nearchus, made the return journey by sea through the Indian Ocean and the Persian Gulf. Alexander himself reached Susa in 324 B.C.

The later years had not been happy ones. Strife and suspicion among the Macedonians and a growing arrogance on the part of Alexander had alienated even men who had been his friends since childhood. A number of prominent generals were executed on the charge of disloyalty. Alexander killed with his own hand the friend who had saved his life at the Granicus, and Callisthenes (Aristotle's nephew and official historian of the expedition) sealed his own death warrant by boasting that no one would have heard of Alexander if he had not had Callisthenes to publicize his exploits.

Worst of all, from the Macedonian point of view, Alexander was fraternizing with the Persians and was putting on airs, dressing like a Persian ruler, demanding that everyone observe the degrading Persian court ceremonial to the extent of crawling on hands and knees to kiss the hem of his garment. This was all very well for Persians and other foreigners and even Greeks, but it was definitely not suitable for men, *i.e.,* Macedonians. They began to compare Philip and Alexander and to say that it was really Philip who had laid the foundations for Alexander's success.

No one imagines that the original intention of Alexander had been the conquest of the whole Persian Empire. At first he had meant to free the coast of Asia Minor—if he could—but one success had led to another. Even the possession of Asia Minor, Syria, Palestine, and Egypt might have been sufficient for most ambitious men. There is a story that when Darius offered to cede this territory, Alexander was approached by one of Philip's old generals, Parmenion, who said that if he were Alexander, he would accept. Alexander tartly replied that if he were Parmenion, he probably would. After Gaugamela or after the murder of Darius at the Caspian Gates, Alexander might have turned from conquest to organization, but he chose to carry the conquest to its logical conclusion, and we shall never know whether his military genius was matched by a talent for administration.

Alexander planned further conquests, but he died at Babylon in June, 323. It was not the sword of an enemy in battle, nor the dagger of an assassin that brought an end to Alexander's career, but a fever (malaria?) that carried him off after a brief illness. Although his empire soon broke up into several parts, his conquests shattered ancient traditions and paved the way for a new period, the Hellenistic Age (323-146 B.C.).

There is little to be gained from a recital of the complex details of political and military history in the Hellenistic Age. The cultural developments of the period are far more important. Therefore, after outlining briefly the struggles of Alexander's successors, we shall concentrate our attention on Hellenistic civilization.

Alexander's empire was his own creation; its various parts were bound together only by the connections which each had with Alexander—no ties bound them to each other or with Macedonia. Thus, when Alexander died, the empire soon disintegrated, for he had made no careful provision for a successor, nor was there any man strong enough to step into his place. Alexander's logical heirs within the Macedonian royal family were his half-witted half brother, Philip, and his posthumous son, the young Alexander. Since in 323 B.C. neither of these heirs was in any way fitted to participate actively in the government, a regency was set up; by 316 B.C. Philip had been assassinated, the young Alexander was held a prisoner by his most implacable enemy, and Alexander's generals had begun to fight one another for possession of all, or parts, of the empire.

The struggle for supremacy among Alexander's would-be successors continued for the next thirty-five or forty years. Eventually, his empire was divided into three large states and a number of smaller ones. The origin of the three major states was as follows:

1. Ptolemy, son of Lagus, one of Alexander's younger officers, had become governor of Egypt in 323 B.C. Ptolemy was able to defend his territory against all claimants, and about 306 B.C. he took the title of king. His kingdom came to include Egypt, Cyrene, Cyprus, and southern Syria. His descendants ruled Egypt until 30 B.C.; the famous Cleopatra was the last of the Ptolemaic Dynasty in Egypt.

2. Seleucus, another of Alexander's companions, after many trials and tribulations founded a dynasty at Babylon in 312 B.C. His descendants, the Seleucids, in their heyday controlled most of the old Persian Empire (except Egypt), but dynastic quarrels and the increasing power of neighboring states weakened their kingdom. By 63 B.C. when the Seleucids finally fell before Rome, they held little more than northern Syria.

3. Two of the most aggressive claimants for the empire of Alexander were Antigonos Monophthalmos (a general) and his son, Demetrius Polior-

cetes. Antigonos (between 316 and 301 B.C.) and Demetrius (between 301 and 285 B.C.) made almost superhuman efforts to gain control of a major portion of the territory once held by Alexander. They built up a strong navy which commanded the Aegean, they made friends in Greece, and they held Macedon for brief periods; but their opponents—Seleucus, Ptolemy, and others—finally overcame them; Antigonos was killed at Ipsus in Asia Minor in 301 B.C., and Demetrius was captured by Seleucus in 285.

This did not terminate the activities of the Antigonids, however, for Antigonos Gonatas, the son of Demetrius, still held the fleet and was in possession of parts of Greece. When Greece, Macedonia, and Thrace were invaded by bands of Gallic marauders (280–277 B.C.), Antigonos Gonatas gained such popularity by defeating and driving out these invaders that he was able to ascend the Macedonian throne without much opposition. The dynasty he established, that of the Antigonids, ruled Macedon until the last king, Perseus, was conquered by the Romans in 167 B.C.

The great period of these three large Hellenistic kingdoms was between 277 and 200 B.C. During this age the Seleucids, Ptolemies, and Antigonids engaged in numerous wars in which, generally speaking, the Seleucids and Antigonids opposed the Ptolemies. Their actions were dictated by certain fundamental policies.

1. The Ptolemies needed a fleet to hold their territories outside of Egypt. Therefore it was necessary for them to have access to the naval supplies of Asia Minor and the cedars of Lebanon. This brought the Ptolemies into conflict with the Seleucids because (*a*) the Seleucids wanted access to the Mediterranean through Syria, and (*b*) they claimed Asia Minor as their territory. As a result, the Ptolemies hotly contested the possession of Syria with the Seleucids and encouraged the growth of the native kingdom of Pergamum in Asia Minor as a state independent of the Seleucids.

To prevent the effective co-operation of the Seleucids and the Antigonids, the Ptolemies stirred up revolts in Greece and fostered movements for Greek independence so that the Antigonids would be kept too busy in Europe to join the Seleucids in Asia Minor. Toward the end of the third century B.C., however, the struggle began to turn in favor of the Seleucids and Antigonids, with the result that the Ptolemies and their Pergamene allies were forced to call upon Rome, the rising state in the west, for aid.

2. The Antigonid control of Greece was in no sense complete. The Antigonids were never strong enough to conquer all the Greeks, yet it was necessary for the Macedonian monarchs to prevent the rise of any powerful Greek movement hostile to Macedon. There were Macedonian garrisons in Athens, Chalcis, and Corinth, but in the Peloponnesus and in central Greece there were strong and independent Hellenic groups. These were the leagues: the Achaean confederation of city-states in the Peloponnesus, and the league of the hill tribes of Aetolia. During the first part of the third

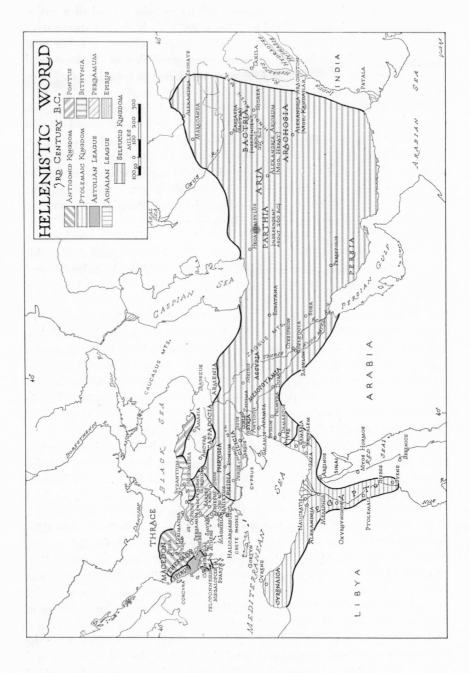

century B.C. the Aetolians were friendly with the Antigonids, and the Achaeans were not. The situation was reversed about 230 B.C., when there was a temporary revival of Spartan power which menaced the Achaeans. In desperation, the Achaeans made an alliance with Macedonia, and the Spartan power was broken. This action of the Achaeans in calling in the Macedonians angered the Aetolians, who felt that it would increase Macedonian predominance in Greece and endanger Aetolian independence. The situation became much more complicated when Philip V, the Macedonian king, became the ally of Carthage during the Second Punic War (218–201 B.C.) in which Rome and Carthage struggled for control of the western Mediterranean. The Aetolians sided with the Romans; they fought Philip in Greece and thus prevented him from aiding the Carthaginians. After the Second Punic War, the Romans drove Philip from Greece (200–197 B.C.), and in 196 B.C. a Roman general attended the Olympic games to make a political address in which he proclaimed that Rome had established and would maintain the "freedom of the Greeks."

The Aetolians, Achaeans, Pergamenes, and Ptolemies soon discovered that they had made a mistake in inviting the Romans to "help" them, for the Romans began to meddle in the affairs of the eastern Mediterranean. The Aetolians were the first to regret their friendship with Rome. In the first decade of the second century B.C. they invited Antiochus III, the Seleucid king, to invade Greece and free them from the Romans. In a brief war (192–188 B.C.) the Romans punished both the Seleucids and the Aetolians; the Seleucids were forced to relinquish all claim to Asia Minor, and the Aetolians were made subordinate allies of Rome. Later, when there was a temporary revival of Macedonian influence, the Achaeans sided with the Antigonids against Rome, but once again the Romans were victorious; the Macedonian kingship was abolished, and the Achaeans were severely punished (167 B.C.). Finally, a combined Greek and Macedonian revolt (149–146 B.C.) was crushed by the Romans; Macedonia was made a Roman province, Corinth was destroyed, and the Roman governor of Macedonia was given power to supervise Greece very closely.

As the second century wore on, the increasing strength of the Romans in the eastern Mediterranean reduced the Seleucids to impotence, and the Ptolemaic kingdom became little more than a Roman protectorate. In 133 B.C. Attalus III, the Pergamene king, recognized the inevitable; he willed his kingdom to Rome, and it was organized as the Roman province of Asia in 129 B.C.

3. It has been said that trade was the lifeblood of the Seleucid Empire. This statement provides a key to Seleucid policies; the Seleucids were like their predecessors, the Babylonians, who were the middlemen in the trade that passed north and south, east and west, through the Tigris-Euphrates Valley. The Seleucids desired a western outlet through Syria and Asia

Minor; in like manner, Bactria, India, and the Persian Gulf were important to them as eastern outlets.

Unfortunately, in the west the Seleucids had to contend with the Ptolemies and their Pergamene allies. The conflict between the Seleucids and the Ptolemies over the possession of Syria was probably the feature of this struggle that produced the greatest trouble for the Seleucids. While a succession of "Syrian" wars was fought, the Pergamenes were able to consolidate their independent position in Asia Minor, and the eastern Seleucid provinces began to break away after 250 B.C.

Alexander had brought most of the Indus Valley under his sovereignty, but in the time of the first Seleucid a native north Indian dynasty, the Mauryas, occupied this territory. The Seleucids, because of their troubles in Syria and Asia Minor, could not actively oppose the Mauryan advance; instead, they followed a policy of appeasement which resulted in the establishment of friendly relations. In this manner, trade with India was assured, and a profitable peace endured for over a century.

Seleucid affairs in the northeast were less favorable. About 250 B.C. the Parthians, a native group located in the territory between the Caspian Sea and Bactria, declared their independence from Seleucid rule. The Parthian kings claimed descent from the Persian dynasty which Alexander had overthrown. This nationalistic appeal was not in vain, and ultimately (in the second century B.C.) the Parthians were able to build up a state which controlled the Iranian plateau and drove a wedge between the central Seleucid possessions in Babylonia and the provinces in the east. In the reign of Mithridates I (171–138 B.C.), the first really great Parthian king, the Parthians extended their rule over Media and Babylonia.

The rise of the Parthians in 250 B.C. was very important for the history of Bactria, the northeastern territory of the Seleucid Empire. Before the end of the century Bactria had become an independent state. Its Greek kings, whose dynasty was connected with the Seleucid royal family on the distaff side, ruled over a mixed population of Greek settlers and natives. One ruler, Demetrius (189–167 B.C.), invaded India about 183 B.C. and gained possession of the territory once held by the Mauryas. After his death his kingdom was divided into two independent parts: Bactria and northern India.

The Greek states in Bactria and northern India continued to exist until shortly after 130 B.C., when barbarians (the Scythians or Sacae) who had formerly lived on the northern borders of Bactria were displaced by pressure from Chinese tribes. The Sacae swept over Bactria and into India and destroyed the Greek kingdoms. At the same time, as we have seen, the Parthians came into the possession of most of the Seleucid Empire; the Seleucids had little left but northern Syria.

In the Hellenistic Age there were, in addition to Pergamum, three other native kingdoms in Asia Minor: Armenia, Bithynia, and Pontus. Each

LEMNIAN ATHENA

Alinari

PARTHENON FROM THE PROPYLAEA

J. Lane Miller

PHILIP

Courtesy of the American Philosophical Society

OLYMPIAS

Courtesy of the American Philosophical Society

ALEXANDER

Alinari

MAUSOLEUM AT HALICARNASSUS

Two others dating from the Hellenistic period, the Temple of Artemis at Ephesus and the Colossus of Rhodes, are not shown.

PHAROS AT ALEXANDRIA

Courtesy of B. T. Batsford, Ltd.

Courtesy of The Metropolitan Museum of Art, Kennedy Fund, 1921

of these owed its independence to its remoteness and comparative inaccessibility. Bithynia and Pontus were located on the Black Sea and had at least a veneer of Greek culture, but Armenia was closer to the old Near East in its outlook. In the first century B.C. these native kingdoms came into conflict with Rome.

The Hellenistic Age is sometimes defined as a period in which Greek culture was widely extended over Greeks and non-Greeks alike, whereas in the preceding Hellenic (or classical) Age this culture had been almost exclusively a Greek possession. Such a definition is useful, but it may also be misleading. It is true that in the Hellenistic Age Greek culture was diffused in some degree throughout the old Persian Empire and into India—some Greek influences even penetrated China—the western Mediterranean region was also affected. On the other hand, it should not be forgotten that both the Near East (and India) and the western Mediterranean had cultural contributions to make. Hellenistic civilization was by no means an unadulterated Greek civilization; it was rather a compound of Greek, Oriental, and Western elements. Unquestionably the Greek element was the major one, but the westward flow of culture from the Near East was almost as strong as it had been during the early years of the Greek Renaissance in the seventh century B.C. Moreover, with the eastward advance of the Romans, the West began to make its contribution.

Strictly speaking—in terms of military and political history—the Hellenistic Age began with the death of Alexander (323 B.C.) and ended in 146 or 133 B.C. If, however, we consider the Hellenistic Age as a cultural epoch, it is more difficult to establish its chronological limits. Many developments characteristic of the period were in evidence at the close of the fifth century B.C., although we might think of the years from the end of the Peloponnesian War to the death of Alexander as forming a period of transition in which the change from Hellenic to Hellenistic culture was taking place. Moreover, it is even harder to find a satisfactory date for the end of the Hellenistic Age. What is usually called Roman civilization was, after all, basically and essentially Hellenistic; the really original contributions of the Romans were relatively few in number. For the most part, the Romans played the role of adapters, elaborators, and carriers of Hellenistic culture. It might be maintained that the Hellenistic Age came to an end only with the fall of Rome and the beginning of the medieval period.

The most satisfactory solution for this problem is to divide this large cultural epoch into two parts: the Hellenistic Age proper and the Roman phase. The Hellenistic Age coincided with the great period of the Hellenistic monarchies when Hellenistic civilization was centered in the eastern Mediterranean region. The Roman phase began with the gradual expansion of Rome's political power into the eastern Mediterranean. At the same time the Romans were adopting more and more of Hellenistic civilization. The high point of the Roman phase came in the first two centuries of the Christian era when the ancient world was politically unified by the Roman Empire and civilization was diffused into Rome's western provinces.

The decline of the city-state and the rise of empires, related political developments, were partly responsible for two characteristics typical of the Hellenistic Age: universalism and individualism. The separatism fostered by the Greek city-states in their desire for local independence had been an outstanding characteristic of the classical period, but in the new age the empire of Alexander helped give rise to the concept of *oecumene,* the unity of the inhabited world. The world was considered the common possession of all human beings; the old distinction between Greek and non-Greek (barbarian) no longer seemed valid. Culture was internationalized: there was a common speech (the *Koine,* an adaptation of Attic Greek), people read the same literature and enjoyed the same art, and commerce disregarded political boundaries. The great Hellenistic kingdoms of Alexander's successors brought vast areas under single governments, while the city-states were reduced to subordinate political units. Nationalism could not flourish in the new kingdoms with their diverse populations; the people of the various parts of these kingdoms were bound to their rulers by personal ties, but they had no strong feeling of kinship with the other subjects of the same ruler. Individualism, like universalism, increased as the importance and significance of the city-state declined. In the classical period the individual had subordinated himself to the state; but under the autocracies of the Hellenistic Age this was no longer necessary, since people were merely expected to obey the commands of the ruler rather than to devote all their efforts to the common good. Freed from the obligations of citizenship in the classical polis, personal energies and ambitions were allowed a freer scope, though within a more limited area of possible achievement.

The feeling of world unity, the broadening of political horizons, the innumerable contacts furnished by international trade, and the great movement of peoples (the settlement of Greek colonists in the Near East, the introduction of Oriental slaves into the West, and the journeys of travelers and traders) were all productive of a tendency toward syncretism and also eclecticism. People were exposed to a host of new ideas in religion, art, philosophy, and other fields. In order to avoid the mental confusion and chaos which the impact of these new ideas might create, men were forced to turn to syncretism and eclecticism. The widespread concept of universalism (*oecumene*) impelled people to search for common denominators for seemingly diverse things. Thus—to cite an obvious example from the field of religion—the Egyptian Amon, the Hebrew Jahweh, the Persian Ahuramazda, and the Roman Jupiter were all recognized as the foreign counterparts of the Greek Zeus. This led to assimilation and combination (syncretism); in Egypt, for example, the ancient gods might be worshipped under

Greek names: Horus became Apollo; Thoth, Hermes; Hathor, Aphrodite.

Syncretism was obviously very limited in scope; complete combination or reconciliation of the ideas and materials available even in a small field was not possible. The next step was eclecticism, picking and choosing desirable elements or parts from separate organisms and systems. In philosophy or religion, for example, a man might choose individual ideas or practices from a number of systems or beliefs and combine them in a new pattern. This was also done in art and numerous other fields.

The Hellenistic Age was notable for its specialization of activity. It was no longer possible for one person to take all knowledge for his field. The common fund of knowledge had increased so greatly that it was difficult enough to master a single division of it. This was likewise true of other phases of human endeavor; in industry, trade, art, and even politics, one had to limit oneself.

Finally, in the five centuries between 300 B.C. and 200 A.D. the ancient world reached the high point of its urbanization. There were more and larger cities than had ever existed before, a situation not duplicated until the modern era (after 1500 A.D.).

In its universalism, individualism, syncretism, eclecticism, specialization of activity, and high degree of urbanization, the Hellenistic Age bears some superficial resemblance to the modern era. Other parallels might be suggested. In the Hellenistic Age there were republics, democracies, federal states, and divine-right monarchies; arbitration and mediation were employed to settle international disputes; capitalism, imperialism, militarism, and communism were to be found; class struggles were not unknown; city life bred romanticism and primitivism in literature; realism, impressionism, and archaism appeared in art.

The Hellenistic world, however, differed from our modern world in that it was almost empty of machines. It is usually said that the place which is today filled by the machine was then occupied by the slave. This is not strictly true, for in the Hellenistic Age the number of free laborers in industry increased. But because slavery did exist, the free laborer had to compete with it; he had no bargaining power and had to work for the equivalent of slave wages (or less) or not at all. Thus, labor was cheap. The interesting result was that although the scientists of the Hellenistic Age made a number of important discoveries and inventions, their work was not turned to any practical use because cheap labor discouraged the development of labor-saving devices.

With the Hellenistic Age ancient civilization reached its climax; the highest point was attained during the Roman phase in the first two centuries of the Christian era. The conquests of Alexander helped to pave the way for a cultural unity which followed upon the heels of an economic unity that had been in the process of formation even before his time; last of all came the Romans who imposed political unity upon a major portion of the ancient world. The cultural interplay which these unities made possible brought ancient civilization into its most complex form. Although it may be argued that the Hellenistic Age was decadent because it produced no Pindar, no Sophocles, no Phidias, and no Plato, the fact remains that civilization (as we have defined it in this book) reached the highest development which it was to attain in ancient times. In the vast number of its culture traits, the complexity of its culture, and the extent of its urbanization, the age was the most civilized in the history of this planet before our own epoch.

The Hellenistic Age was notable for its variety of governmental forms. Athens, Rhodes, and Corinth, as well as many other Greek cities, continued to exist as more or less independent, but politically unimportant, city-states. The monarchy of the Antigonids in Macedonia was only a slightly more sophisticated version of the old Macedonian form of government, not far removed from the primitive Greek monarchy of the Dark Ages. Two new governmental developments of the Hellenistic Age were the great Greco-Oriental monarchy and the federal state.

The Greco-Oriental (or Hellenistic) monarchy was a combination of Macedonian, Egyptian, and Persian forms. Alexander himself had recognized the problems involved in ruling a large territory containing diverse national elements in its population. The powers of the ruler, the basis of these powers, the form of governmental organization, and the sources of imperial revenues had to be established. If possible, the various national elements must be fused into a unified whole.

Alexander apparently decided that the ruler of an empire must be an autocrat who governed through an efficient bureaucracy. This was the way of the Near East; it had been followed successfully by his immediate predecessors, the Persian kings and the pharaohs of Egypt. Furthermore, the ruler must be a god or else hold his place by divine right. The continuation of the ancient theocracy solved Alexander's problems in the Near East; he became a god-king in Egypt and a divine-right ruler in Persia. There still remained, however, the difficulty of finding an absolutist basis for ruling the Greeks and Macedonians. This obstacle Alexander proposed to overcome by requesting the westerners to recognize him as a god. He did not consider himself a god, nor did the Greeks and Macedonians have any illusions about his divinity. His apotheosis was simply a political device. The westerners would not be ruled by a man, but they could salve their consciences by pretending that a man was a god; as a god, he would be above mortal laws and also free to make autocratic demands upon his human subjects.

We do not know whether Alexander planned to unify the governmental organization of his empire. He had begun to build up a bureaucracy before his death, but he retained the existing forms of government in most areas as well as the systems of taxation then in force.

There was, however, one other problem which Alexander did attack: that of creating loyal elements in the imperial population. Throughout the empire, especially in the eastern provinces, he established city-states of the Greek type which were settled by his veterans and Greek and Macedonian colonists. These city-states were intended to serve as garrisons in the conquered regions. It is often said that these settlements were also meant to be centers of diffusion for Greek culture so that the native populations might become Hellenized. Another part of Alexander's program was to conciliate the Persians by appointing them to responsible governmental posts and by encouraging intermarriage between Persians, Greeks, and Macedonians. Alexander rightly recognized the close linguistic and institutional kinship of the three Indo-European-speaking groups as opposed to the masses of Semites who formed the subject population of the Near East, especially Mesopotamia and Syria. By fusing Persians and westerners he hoped to build up a loyal and substantial ruling class.

Many of Alexander's policies were followed by his Seleucid and Ptolemaic successors. The Ptolemies became pharaohs, god-kings, following the Egyptian custom. The Seleucids were divine-right monarchs after the custom of the Persians; when a Seleucid king died, however, he was deified, and thus his successor was invested with a semidivinity as the son or brother of a god. At the courts of the Ptolemies and Seleucids there developed a hierachy of palace dignitaries; there was also in each of the two kingdoms a fully developed bureaucracy, a pyramid of officials that began at the top with a prime minister and other high officials (military, financial, judicial, etc.) and descended in a horde of minor agents who discharged civil, military, and financial duties.

The imperial armies were composed of Greek and Macedonian mercenaries. These hired soldiers were rewarded with good lands within the empires, and their descendants formed a national militia. Moreover, the Seleucids continued Alexander's policy of colonization by Europeans; traders, craftsmen, and farmers, as well as soldiers, were settled in many newly created city-states. For a few generations the newcomers retained their identity and also their loyalty to their imperial benefactors, but ultimately they became fused with the native populations and their usefulness to the government decreased.

The problems of the Seleucids were different and more difficult than those of the Ptolemies. Whereas the Ptolemies centered their power in Egypt which was geographically unified and possessed a homogeneous native population and had an empire which could be easily reached by sea, the Seleucid Empire was a far-flung land empire inhabited by peoples of diverse

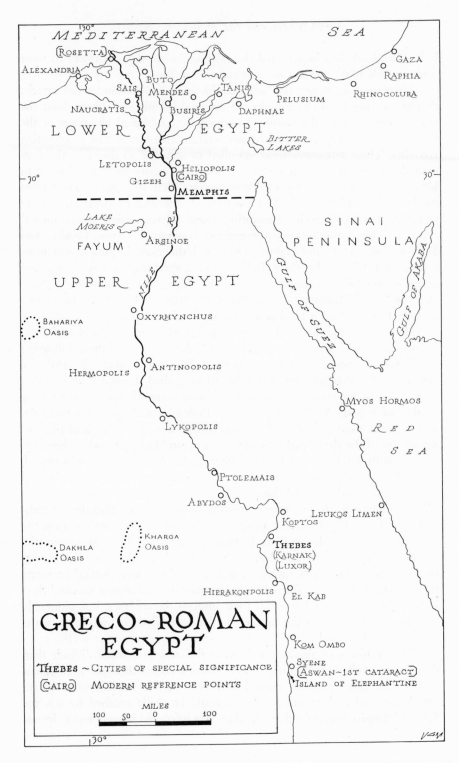

GRECO~ROMAN EGYPT

THEBES ~ CITIES OF SPECIAL SIGNIFICANCE
(CAIRO) MODERN REFERENCE POINTS

MILES
100 50 0 100

298

nationalities. The Seleucids could not win the loyalty of all their subjects; neither could they afford an army large enough to hold effectively the extensive regions which they claimed. Consequently, when the Parthians fostered a nationalist revival on the Iranian plateau, the Seleucids had to give way, mainly because they had failed to complete Alexander's plan to fuse the Persians and the Europeans into a ruling class.

The Ptolemies made no attempt to unite the Greeks and Macedonians with the Egyptians. The Greeks and Macedonians were introduced as mercenaries; they formed a caste superior in rank and privilege to the native Egyptians. It is interesting to see how, at the close of the third century B.C., when the Ptolemies had been weakened by their struggles for a Syrian empire, the native Egyptians of the old warrior class were able to win many concessions from their Macedonian rulers. Thus, in a way, Egyptian nationalism proved almost as trying and disastrous to the Ptolemies as the nationalism of Iran to the Seleucids.

The governmental philosophies of the Seleucids and Ptolemies present marked contrasts. The Seleucid government was an agency which provided law, order, and defense; these advantages offered by the Seleucids to their subjects were given in return for value received (revenues in the form of taxes). Trade was probably the greatest source of wealth in the Seleucid Empire. Therefore, the governmental policy of the Seleucids was to encourage and protect trade; the larger its volume, the larger the royal revenues which might be derived from commercial taxes. Industry and agriculture were also important. The land of the empire was distributed in various ways: the land owned by the king was called the royal land, and was worked by royal serfs; much land was given to Seleucid nobles who held their estates as feudal lords; temple lands were administered by the priests of various cults and worked by slaves; the city-states founded by the rulers were also granted land, and the mercenaries possessed agricultural holdings (cleruch land). Taxes on agricultural produce were paid both in money and in kind.

The attitude of the Ptolemaic rulers was far different. Egypt, for example, was regarded as the private estate of the king, and the whole economic life of the country was organized in such a way as to provide the greatest possible revenue for the government. The land was the chief source of wealth. In theory, all the land belonged to the king; some of it he kept as royal land and rented it out for cultivation by the royal serfs; land given to the nobles was taxed as was the Egyptian cleruch land; there was also temple land as in the Seleucid Empire. External trade was a state monopoly, and internal trade was taxed. Other state monopolies were salt, the manufacture of papyrus, oils, and linens, the mines, and banking. With the Ptolemies state capitalism first appeared on a large scale. The government was a trading company that also controlled the production at home of the things which it sold abroad. Not only did the Ptolemies possess the agricultural surplus of Egypt, but they also operated factories that made papyrus, oils, and linens. Ptolemaic practices of state capitalism and mass production were followed by the kings of Pergamum, their allies.

While the great Hellenistic monarchies were developing in the Near East, the growth of federal representative government reached its climax in Greece in the Aetolian and Achaean Leagues. The Aetolian League was originally a federation of rural cantons in central Greece. Its governmental organization consisted of (1) a popular assembly of all citizens of the league, (2) a federal council in which each community was represented according to the size of the military contingent it furnished the league, and (3) an inner council elected from the federal council which sat as a permanent committee with the league officials. The league officials were a general, a secretary, a board of treasurers, and other minor officers; all were elected by the assembly. The individual communities of the league were independent as far as their local governmental affairs were concerned, but foreign relations were in the hands of the federal government. The federation also had a uniform system of weights, measures, and coinage.

The Achaean League was a federation of city-states. It, too, had a popular assembly with legislative and electoral powers, but general discussions of policy were sometimes decided by another body (the synod), a representative group in which each individual city-state had one vote. The federal council was composed of delegates from the cities; the number sent by each city was based on the size of its population. The Achaean League had as its executive a general; there were other elected officials whose duties were similar to those of corresponding officials in the Aetolian League.

From this brief description of the league governments it is clear that democracy, federation, and proportional representation were not novelties twenty-two hundred years ago.

It cannot be emphasized too strongly that the early Hellenistic Age was for the Greeks a new era of colonization. The growth of a small group of very rich men and a large group of very poor ones in the Greek city-states during the fourth century was a warning that Greece, as far as its economic organization was concerned, had once more become overpopulated; the same thing seems to have been true of the Greek states in Asia Minor. This situation was relieved when Alexander and his successors settled thousands of Greeks as colonists in what had once been the Persian Empire. The Ptolemies rewarded their Greek mercenaries with Egyptian lands, and the Seleucids planted military garrison colonies and organized Greek city-states throughout their empire.

The Hellenistic period brought many other new economic developments. During the early fourth century wages and prices had risen, and the price rise was accentuated when Alexander came into possession of the Persian treasuries from which he released vast quantities of gold and silver long hoarded by the Persian kings. The increase of the actual coin in circulation may have doubled or even tripled within a few years. This had the effect of stimulating trade and business enterprise and of reducing interest rates; new areas of the ancient world passed from a barter to a money economy. The creation of the Hellenistic kingdoms broke down old trade and customs barriers; the number of coin standards was reduced, a fact which alone greatly aided the expansion of trade.

Trade was carried on by both land and sea. There was an exchange of goods even with India and (indirectly) with China; in the west the commerce with Spain, Gaul, and Britain increased. Ships were improved and made larger; harbors, lighthouses, and new roads were constructed. Agricultural products, pottery, metalwork, textiles, slaves, books, and hundreds of other items were exchanged in international trade. Alexandria, the city founded by Alexander, soon became the main port of Egypt; from it were exported textiles, perfumes, glass, and papyrus. Parchment, silk, manufactured goods, and agricultural and pastoral products came from Asia Minor. Spanish silver, British tin, Italian cattle and wine, Sicilian grain, Greek olive oil, Sudanese ivory, Russian wheat, and fish from the Black Sea were only a few of the manufactured and raw products drawn from all corners of the ancient world. Key trading cities were Antioch in Syria, Sardes and Ephesus in Asia Minor, Seleucia on the Tigris (near modern Baghdad), Rhodes in the Aegean, Alexandria in Egypt, Tarentum in Italy, Syracuse in Sicily, Carthage in Africa, Gades (Cadiz) in Spain, and Massilia in Gaul.

About 300 B.C. the center of industry and commerce began to shift from Greece to western Asia Minor, Rhodes, and Syria. Greece (except Corinth) had little part in the revived east-west trade through the Mediterranean, and the Asiatic and Syrian cities built up their manufactures to such an extent that the mainland Greeks could not compete with them. In the western Mediterranean the old Greek colonies had, of course, been increasing their industrial output for many years, and this market was lost to the mainland Greeks in the fourth century.

The industry of the Hellenistic Age was more inclined to mass production and worldwide distribution than that of the classical period. Shops were larger and specialization was more pronounced. State-owned factories for the production of oil, wine, beer, linen, and papyrus in Egypt under the Ptolemies, and similar state-production monopolies in Pergamum illustrate the trend toward mass production for the world trade.

Ancient capitalism now reached its fullest development. Financial operations became more complicated. Banks received deposits, honored checks, and issued drafts, loans, and letters of credit. Rich men had multiple investments in commercial and industrial ventures. Speculation was rife; frequent attempts were made to corner the market on certain commodities.

The operations of Cleomenes, the Egyptian governor appointed by Alexander, disrupted the wheat market in such a way that a near famine resulted in Athens.

In some areas agricultural production was improved and better organized than ever before. The conquests of Alexander had resulted in a new knowledge of and a new interest in plants and herbs; scientific studies in these fields were carried on by the pupils of Aristotle. Reclamation and irrigation projects were common. The use of fertilizer, the rotation of crops, and attention to stockbreeding were outstanding developments.

By and large it was the Greeks who reaped the benefits of the new age, not the Greeks who stayed at home but those who went to the Near East. A horde of Greek carpetbaggers descended upon Egypt, Alexander's richest province, and stayed to exploit it when the Ptolemies made it the center of their empire. The story of two such adventurers has emerged from the so-called Zenon papyri, the private archives of a Carian Greek from which more than a thousand documents have been published.

Zenon was the righthand man of Apollonius, an important bureaucrat in the reign of Ptolemy II. Apollonius was *dioecetes* (secretary of the treasury) in Egypt and seems to have used his high office to feather his own nest. In addition to serving his royal master, Apollonius built up his own enterprises: he was a merchant, landowner, industrialist, importer, and promoter; he even had his own merchant fleet. In Alexandria itself he maintained a huge establishment which must have rivalled the palace in size, splendor, and organization.

For a time Zenon travelled in Syria, Palestine, and southern Asia Minor doing errands for Apollonius, but he came back to Alexandria about 258 B.C. to be a kind of private secretary for his master. Two years later, perhaps after an illness, Zenon was sent up river to a place called Philadelphia in the Fayum region, where his duties were to organize a large estate which Apollonius had just acquired. This was to be a big development; not only was there to be a model farm, but also a new town (Philadelphia) was to be built and Greco-Macedonian settlers had to be found to live there. Zenon laid out the town, built the houses, temples, and other public edifices, and found the colonists. The farm was developed and new land brought under cultivation. Novel crops (for Egypt) were introduced— grapes, olives, fruits of many kinds—there was a project to plant pine trees and groves of other trees; experiments with stockbreeding were carried on. Zenon ran the farm, dickered with the local Egyptian peasants to till the grain land, policed the town, and collected the taxes. All the time he was badgered by letters and notes and orders from Apollonius who had innumerable ideas, good and bad, about what should be done next. Zenon had so much to remember that he got into the habit of writing memoranda to himself.

Apollonius lost the favor of the king and disappeared sometime after 250, but Zenon lived on in Philadelphia for a decade, raising sheep and goats, renting out the public baths which he had built, and acting as a money-lender. His was a real success story.

In the thriving economic milieu of the Hellenistic world it was only natural that the bourgeoisie should dominate the social scene, whereas the nobles and the priest class receded into the background. The elaborate houses, extravagant dress, and luxurious appointments of the bourgeoisie were the outward signs of their opulence and power. Undoubtedly their influence upon government and the determination of governmental policy was much stronger than we suspect. The kings of Pergamum, for example, prided themselves on being bourgeois monarchs and intermarried with the daughters of wealthy commoners.

The position of the masses, both agricultural and urban, was anything but enviable, and it did not improve as time went on. Slave labor kept wages low. Moreover, although prices continued to rise after 300 B.C., wages did not; inadequate wages and the increase of unemployment in the urban centers produced discontent. Typical of the Hellenistic Age was the large city with its proletarian masses living from hand to mouth, housed in wooden tenements where the dangers of fire and plague were ever present. Long before similar problems became acute at Rome, the Hellenistic cities knew proletarian unrest and resorted to the policy of "bread and circuses."

The growth of large cities intensified three problems that had not been solved in the classical age: the water supply, the food supply, and the maintenance of order. Wells and springs would not provide enough water for cities whose populations ran into the hundreds of thousands; aqueducts had to be built. In many instances, food for the new cities could not be produced locally in the countryside but had to be imported from great distances; separate departments of the city government came into being to deal with the food problem and to insure that the supply and price of food were adequate at all times. A police force had to be created to quell riots; not much was done or could be done about crime unless the offender was caught in the act or could be readily identified—at any rate, it was not a matter of crime prevention, but punishment.

Although the conditions of urban life were fairly uniform throughout the Hellenistic world, great regional variation characterized rural life. In Egypt, for example, most of the Egyptian peasants were serfs, bound to the soil and seldom allowed to leave their native village districts. In addition to the peasants there were the Greek mercenaries and their descendants, free men who enjoyed privileges denied to the peasants. In the Seleucid territories there were serfs on large crown and private estates, slaves on the estates of the temples, and free farmers elsewhere. Greek and Macedonian colonists, settled in small city-states throughout the empire, also farmed the land as free men. In Greece the small farmer seems to have held his own, and perhaps he even gained ground during the Hellenistic Age.

Everywhere, however, whether in the city or the country, the masses were restless and dissatisfied. The rise of the bourgeoisie worsened rather than bettered the lot of the masses. The gap between the very rich and the very poor widened, and in widening it increased social bitterness. Slave, serf, and proletarian revolts were frequent. In the cities the more vigorous proletarians agitated for the redistribution of wealth and dreamed of setting up communist utopias. In the country the serfs often deserted their fields, took refuge in the temples, and from their places of sanctuary bargained with the government or the landholders. For the most part, however, the masses succumbed to a feeling of hopelessness. No advance, no reform seemed possible. They sought comfort in religions that promised them an afterlife in which they would live in prosperity and happiness, in which the humble would be exalted and the proud brought low.

The old city-state of the classical Greek period had served an important social purpose by uniting its citizens into a compact social group with common interests. To the individual, the opportunity to identify himself with a large group of his fellows had afforded great personal satisfaction. An ordinary person, whose mediocrity would never have allowed him to attain any distinction, took great pride in being a member of a distinct society—the same psychology partly explains tendencies toward extreme nationalism today.

In the large new cities of the Hellenistic Age—Alexandria, Antioch, and the rest—the group unity of the old city-state was lacking. Citizenship in the new cities had neither the duties nor the privileges that it had in the old city-state. The inhabitants of the new cities were drawn from many nations and races: there were Greeks, Macedonians, Syrians, Jews, Phoenicians, Persians, and many others. Each national group retained its traditions, religion, and in many cases its language, with the result that each city was composed of irreconcilable factions. "Race" riots were common; the Jews especially were the victims of persecution.

The instinctive gregariousness of mankind was not to be denied, however. Craft guilds, religious societies, political clubs, and national organizations began to appear in the large cities. These organizations satisfied in some measure the desire for human companionship and membership in a group.

With the decline of the city-state, the state cults of the Greek *poleis* likewise waned in influence and degenerated into formalism. The individualism of the age encouraged men to seek personal rather than national or civic gods. Mystery religions and the worship of various eastern mother goddesses (Isis of Egypt and Cybele of Asia Minor) gained swift popularity; in some cases their appeal was based upon their promise of a future life, and in others their devotees were satisfied by the emotional stimulation these cults had to offer.

Other influences besides individualism were at work in the field of religion. We have already noted something of the syncretism and eclecticism which were so widespread at this time. It was inevitable, too, that universalism should ultimately encourage beliefs in the existence of one supreme and unique god. Monotheism was already present, of course, in Judaism, and we shall see that Christianity was undoubtedly the product of the conditions which prevailed in the Hellenistic Age.

Another result of the decline of the old order and the impact of the new era was the growth of uncertainty and skepticism. One of the most popular divinities of the Hellenistic Age was Tyche (Fortune or Chance). Uncertainty, skepticism, and the increase of scientific knowledge led also to agnosticism and complete atheism. At the same time, it is not surprising to find that in an Age of Science people should be attracted by the pseudo science of the Near East, astrology.

Philosophy, as well as religion, was vitally affected by the new conditions of life in the Hellenistic Age. Personal problems of existence assumed such importance in human thinking that the majority of the philosophers abandoned their search for "knowledge" and set themselves to the task of finding bases upon which practical "ways of life" might be built. In general, the new philosophic systems that developed sought one or the other of two seemingly possible goals: happiness or freedom from unhappiness. Resignation, withdrawal, or conformity were conceded to be the best means of attaining these ends.

Between Socrates and the great Hellenistic schools of philosophy were the transitional philosophies of the Cynics and the Cyrenaics, founded by two of Socrates' disciples. The Cynic school had its origin with Antisthenes, who carried on his teachings at the gymnasium of Cynosarges at Athens. For Antisthenes, virtue was the sole good, and vice the sole evil. Pleasure, comfort, convention, and all externals were to be discarded; man's attention should be focused upon the exercise of virtue, and the inner satisfaction that virtue afforded should be sufficient compensation for anyone.

Aristippus of Cyrene taught that pleasure rather than virtue was the ultimate goal. All pleasures were considered equally good, for they would contribute to happiness. Overindulgence, however, must be restrained by reason.

The philosophy of Skepticism founded by Alexander's contemporary Pyrrhon was another interpretation of the teachings of Socrates and Plato. The Skeptics denied the possibilty of real knowledge; for every argument an equally valid counterargument could be advanced. Such a philosophy fostered nihilism in many cases; its alternative effect was agnosticism, as in the case of the later Platonic Academy which became predominantly Skeptic in its thinking.

The transitional schools of the fourth century pointed the way for the two great Hellenistic philosophies that appeared about 300 B.C. at Athens: Stoicism and Epicureanism. Although neither the Stoics nor the Epicureans were completely successful in solving the difficult problems of human existence, they did much to help thinking people who could not accept or gain comfort from the religions of the age. The widespread and enduring popularity of Stoicism and Epicureanism is convincing testimony that they met, at least partially, the needs of the men of the ancient world for the next five hundred years.

The founder of the Stoic school was Zeno of Cyprus, who came to Athens about 314 B.C. Zeno met with his disciples at the Stoa Poikile, the Painted Porch, in the Athenian Agora (market place); hence, the origin of the term Stoic. The Stoics sought happiness, but their search was not an active one. They said, in essence, "To be happy is to want what you get." Happiness is attained by conforming to the will of God (*i.e.,* the laws of nature). Everything in nature is rational and good. All evils that befall man are necessary evils since they are intended for his education. It is his duty to discover what the laws of nature are; these laws are not necessarily man-made statutes or conventions; even suicide, incest, and cannibalism may be justified in some cases. Inasmuch as the Stoics accepted the existence of a supreme god, albeit an impersonal one, their philosophy tended to take on the aspect of a religion. Moreover, their universalism encouraged them to believe in the brotherhood of man; race, nationality, class, and sex were discarded as criteria for distinguishing one human being from another.

Epicurus of Samos came to Athens about 306 B.C. He maintained that the supreme good was happiness, which he defined as freedom from fear and pain; thus, pleasure is good, and pain is evil. The Epicureans did not deny the existence of gods, but they did maintain that the gods were not concerned with human affairs, and therefore man need not fear them. One primary aim of the philosophy was to emancipate man from superstition and the fear of death. The atomistic theory of Democritus was employed to prove that birth is simply the result of a combination of atoms, and death nothing more than their separation. Death, therefore, entails no succeeding pain; it merely brings the end of sensation and resembles "eternal sleep," In its purest form, Epicureanism did not exclude sensual pleasures, but it emphasized that such pleasures entail more pain than those of the intellect.

Looking back upon all these philosophies, one gets the impression that the men of the ancient world had reached a turning point in their attitudes toward life. They were able to see, though dimly, that they were fighting against irresistible forces which they could not hope to harness to their control. One force had been present since the beginning of time: this was nature, the physical world and its unalterable laws of life and death. Another force was culture, the social and economic forms created by man himself. Socrates, Plato, and Aristotle had felt that man could manipulate culture, but the Hellenistic philosophers possessed no such confidence. "Make the best of it," they said; or else "Withdraw." Individualism was a solution—self-sufficiency. Best of all, create a solitude and call it peace.

From the time of Thales to the end of the fifth century B.C., Greek science went hand in hand with philosophy. Then came Socrates, who turned away from the study of natural phenomena to concentrate upon ethics and pointed the way for Aristotle, who finally effected the separation of science and philosophy. In the Hellenistic Age the greatest scientists were not philosophers, although they continued to work in mathematics, physics, and astronomy, fields which had formerly been subject to philosophical study. In addition to the older fields of research, however, the Hellenistic scientists found new worlds to conquer. Aristotle's study of animals created the foundations for the science of zoology, and those who came after him followed paths which led to botany, physiology, anatomy, geology, geography, and many other fields.

The majority of the outstanding Hellenistic scientists lived in the third century B.C., or early in the succeeding century. Euclid (*fl.* 300 B.C.) organized the study of geometry in his treatise, the *Elements,* which is still used in our schools today. Many students have been forced to recognize the truth of his dictum, "There is no royal road to geometry." This great geometrician also wrote on perspective and music.

Conic sections were exhaustively studied by Apollonius of Perga (*fl.* 230 B.C.). It was he who originated the terms hyperbola, parabola, and ellipse; and if he had pursued his work to its logical conclusion, he would have been the founder of analytic geometry. Apollonius was likewise a devotee of astronomy and seems to have advanced the theory that the planets move in eccentric circles.

Aristarchus of Samos (*fl.* 280 B.C.) believed that the earth revolves about the sun; he also attempted to ascertain the relative diameters of the earth, the moon, and the sun. His heliocentric theory, however, did not gain wide acceptance. His ideas were attacked by the second-century astronomer, Hipparchus of Nicaea, and the geocentric theory of the universe was restored to its former preeminence.

Other important scientists were Eratosthenes, the geographer, and the astronomers Heracleides of Pontus and Poseidonius. Eratosthenes (*fl.* 250 B.C.) produced a map of the world using lines of longitude and latitude; he likewise measured the circumference of the earth and by a happy accident came within two hundred miles of the correct figure. Heracleides, who lived in the fourth century B.C., proved that the earth rotates on its axis every twenty-four hours, and Poseidonius (*fl.* 100 B.C.) believed that tides were affected by the moon.

Most brilliant and versatile of the Hellenistic scientists was Archimedes of Syracuse (*d.* 212 B.C.). His discovery of specific gravity and his wide knowledge of mechanics are well known. He invented a planetarium which demonstrated the movements of the heavenly bodies and explained eclipses. He also computed the value of pi by inscribing and circumscribing a circle with regular polygons of 96 sides. Thus he anticipated the invention of the calculus, which has been called (by a phrase which must contain a *double-entendre*) the "mathematics of exhaustion."

Extremely interesting work was done by Strato (*fl.* 300 B.C.), who advanced the theory of the vacuum, experimented with magnets, and investigated the "electric fish," the *narke*.

It was the conquest of the Persian Empire that provided the impetus for studies in geography and botany at the beginning of the Hellenistic Age. Alexander derived from his tutor, Aristotle, an interest in the collection of data relating to these two fields, and he took with him on his campaigns men whose duty it was to describe the country through which they passed. The *History of Plants* by Theophrastus, Aristotle's pupil and successor, was based largely upon the observations made by Alexander's scientists. Theophrastus became the founder of botany, just as Aristotle had been the founder of zoology. In the field of geography, the work of Eratosthenes has already been mentioned. The astronomer Hipparchus also worked in geography, and Poseidonius was the author of a treatise on the ocean. It was perhaps Poseidonius who first suggested that it might be possible to reach India by sailing westward from Spain.

It was also the conquest of Persia that brought the Greeks into direct contact with the mathematicians and astronomers of Babylon. We have seen how important the indirect contacts of the period of the Greek Renaissance had been in giving Greek philosophy its start in mathematics and astronomy. Now the ability to get at the material first hand provided a great stimulus for new work among the Greeks. Futhermore, the Babylonians had made some advances since the time of Thales and Pythagoras. Although the Greeks adopted as much of Babylonian mathematics as they could absorb and made some progress during the Hellenistic and Roman periods, they never surpassed the Babylonians as mathematicians.

In view of the extraordinary activity in science during the Hellenistic Age, it is surprising that few scientific discoveries were put to any practical use. This was partly because people felt no pressing need for labor-saving devices, and partly because the scientists still followed the philosophic tradition that ennobled pure science—science for science's sake—and regarded applied science as beneath their dignity. Archimedes, extremely clever in mechanics, made numerous machines for his own amusement, but he thought of them simply as "gadgets" or toys and was usually annoyed when other people suggested that they might be employed for practical purposes.

It was only in the field of medical science that the results of research were turned to the advantage of humanity. In the first half of the third century B.C. three great doctors lived and worked: Herophilus, Erasistratus, and Heracleides of Tarentum. Herophilus and Erasistratus were chiefly interested in the causes of disease, whereas Heracleides concerned himself with its cure. Herophilus was an anatomist who studied the brain and the nervous system. He also discovered the function of the arteries in the circulation of the blood and conducted research on the action of the pulse. Erasistratus founded the science of physiology; his work on the nervous and circulatory systems widened the horizons of the knowledge made available by Herophilus. Whereas Herophilus and Erasistratus opposed the excessive use of drugs, Heracleides took an opposite point of view. Perhaps as early as his time the juice of the mandragora plant was used as an anaesthetic.

Scholarship came into its own during the Hellenistic Age. As early as the fifth century the Sophists had begun the scientific study of grammar, rhetoric, and oratory; later, Plato had concerned himself with etymology, and Aristotle's *Poetics* had laid the foundations for literary criticism. As time went on, these interests continued to gain ground. Demetrius of Phalerum (*fl.* 315 B.C.), himself an able orator, wrote a history of oratory. The philosophers of the Aristotelian school wrote scholarly tracts on history, music, art, and literature. The Stoic philosophers studied grammar. The Ptolemaic rulers of Egypt, at the suggestion of Demetrius of Phalerum, founded a great library; the long succession of Ptolemaic librarians at Alexandria were scholars and scientists of the first rank. Zenodotus of Ephesus, the first librarian, made a scientific edition of Homer based upon a study of the available manuscripts. Advances in textual criticism were made by later librarians, Aristophanes of Byzantium (*fl.* 240 B.C.) and Aristarchus of Samothrace (*fl.* 180 B.C.). At one period the scientist Eratosthenes served as chief librarian at Alexandria; the post was also held by the great literary figures Apollonius of Rhodes and Callimachus (see below).

Connected with the library at Alexandria was the Museum, the "place of the Muses," where numerous scholars and scientists lived and worked, supported by the bounty of the Ptolemies. The Museum was a truly utopian university, where there were many professors but practically no students, and where the professors received a living wage for engaging in scholarly pursuits.

The Alexandrian library was the largest of its day, although other large libraries existed at Pergamum, Rhodes, and Antioch. The library at Alexandria contained more than half a million books, or more properly speaking, papyrus rolls. One of the big tasks of the early librarians was to catalogue the contents of the establishment; from the fragment of a list that has survived we learn that, among other things, the library contained a number of treatises on how to bake a cake, but this was not surprising since the library was designed to include among its holdings practically everything that had ever been written in Greek.

A very important undertaking of the Alexandrian scholars was the creation of standard editions of the great works of Greek literature. The manuscripts of Homer, for example, were found to contain many divergent readings and extraneous lines, and it was something of a problem to separate the verses of Homer from those which later poets had added; it was even a problem to decide what poems were to be attributed to Homer, since a number of epics in addition to the *Iliad* and the *Odyssey* were popularly supposed to have been composed by him. The Alexandrians also ventured into the field of literary criticism and attempted to set up canons of taste by selecting for special preservation the works of certain authors whom they judged to be superior: the ten best Attic orators, the best lyric poets, the best writers of tragedy, and so on. The authority of Alexandrian scholarship was such that many works that did not gain their commendation failed to survive; thus, we today may or may not have what was best in Greek literature, for we cannot be sure that Alexandrian judgment was infallible.

In the popular mind the denizens of the Museum and library were regarded as more than a little peculiar. These scholars were often eccentrics, and in true scholarly fashion, they feuded bitterly among themselves. The somewhat rarified atmosphere of the Museum was soon lampooned in verse as follows:

> *Egypt has its mad recluses,*
> *Book bewildered anchorites,*
> *In the hencoop of the Muses*
> *Keeping up their endless fights.*

Compared with its predecessors, the Hellenistic Age was an age of literacy. More people than ever before knew how to read and write, and, moreover, were not averse to employing this knowledge. Writing became a profession which was not unprofitable. A small group of readers constituted a market for literature of high quality and for works on specialized subjects. There was also a much larger reading public that enjoyed light reading and read without much discrimination fables, moralizing tales, dialogues, paradoxes, mythological stories, travel books, and novels.

The writing of comedy reached its greatest height since the time of Aristophanes in the skillful hands of the Athenian Menander (*fl.* 310 B.C.), the principal exponent of the New Comedy, the comedy of manners. Menander enjoyed the reputation of being able to portray life accurately, but on the basis of his works which have survived, the praise of antiquity seems more than a little extravagant. While he could create humorous situations, he wrote tragicomedy rather than the rollicking comedy of the older period. But perhaps it is unfair to render a judgment on the basis of parts of three plays and one complete one (all found in the papyri), adaptations of his plays in Latin, and scattered verses quoted by later writers. Certainly the works of Menander were very popular in the Hellenistic and Roman periods; even Saint Paul quoted a line from one of Menander's plays in I Corinthians 15:33.

The poetry of the Hellenistic Age was affected by three influences: the extreme urbanization of the age, its individualism, and a tendency to look backward (which led to archaism). Furthermore, the Hellenistic Age posed certain problems for its poets. What might be called the "classic" forms of Greek poetry had been thoroughly exploited and brought to perfection long before: the epic, the lyric, the elegy, the dramatic poem (tragedy), all had run a certain course and achieved a level of development which discouraged imitation. One could scarcely hope to improve on Homer, Sappho, or Pindar. Besides this earlier poetry was "dated." It was the spontaneous product of a society that no longer existed. No poet of the Hellenistic Age could hope to command much attention by slavishly imitating the earlier poets, just as one today would hesitate to compose sonnets in the style and language of Shakespeare. Thus the Hellenistic poets were led into experimentation in an attempt to develop new forms, particularly those which might provide a true expression of the complex, highly urbanized culture in which they lived. One solution to the problem was found in a kind of escapist primitivism, a "back-to-nature" movement, a reaction against city life in which the poets dreamed of simple bucolic scenes with shepherds and shepherdesses, bees and butterflies, and what not. Theocritus of Sicily with his idylls, "little pictures," of rural life was representative of this school; other noted writers of pastoral poetry were Bion and Moschus. The individualism of the age also encouraged a revival of such forms of personal poetry as the elegy and the lyric. The third-century Alexandrian poet Callimachus employed these forms skillfully and also wrote a number of hymns. This involved Callimachus in a kind of scholarly archaism, as he took the older forms and combined them with new material.

The mention of Callimachus reminds us once more of the Alexandrian Museum and library which were rocked by the bitter quarrel between Callimachus and Apollonius of Rhodes. The feud raged about the middle of the third century and was precipitated by a difference of opinion about the writing of epic poetry.

The epic was the oldest of the Greek literary forms. It had been perfected by Homer, and it was generally agreed that Homer was the supreme poet, regardless of form. His influence had pervaded all subsequent Greek poetry, and although the literary "advance guard" and the disciples of "new directions" had for centuries looked upon the epic as outmoded, it had not become extinct. In the middle of the fifth century B.C. a relative of Herodotus had written an epic on the exploits of Heracles, and about the year 400 B.C. Antimachus of Colophon, regarded by some as nearly the equal of Homer, had composed an epic dealing with the legends of the Theban cycle. A historical epic by Choerilus of Samos had appeared about the same time. A real revival of epic, however, came in the Hellenistic Age, and it provides a good example of literary archaism and experimentation combined.

Callimachus admired Homer, but he felt that imitation of the great poet would be unprofitable. Therefore he experimented with something new: a short epic, or epyllion. In this new-style epic Callimachus insisted that the subject matter must not be taken from the sagas which had been used over and over by the Homeric or cyclic school; rather, new, untouched material from the Greek legends must be employed. Secondly, the epic must be short in order to attain a complete unity and compactness which was lacking in the longer epics. Thirdly, the subject must be treated in a "modern" manner, for much of Homer which had seemed real enough to the earlier Greeks had no reality for the city dwellers of the Hellenistic Age. To prove his point Callimachus composed a little epic entitled the *Hecale,* which dealt with a single episode from the adventures of the Athenian hero Theseus. The *Hecale* was much admired, and the epyllion was adopted as a genuine form by later poets, both Greek and Latin.

Apollonius, on the other hand, believed that it was possible to write a long epic which would command attention. Therefore he selected the story of Jason and the Golden Fleece to which he gave the title *Argonautica.* The tale of Jason and the heroes who sailed in the good ship Argo was an old one, familiar to Homer. It had been touched upon by Pindar, a sequel had been written by Euripides in the *Medea,* and there was also in existence at least one prose version of the story, but it had never before been the subject of an epic. By selecting material outside the Trojan cycle, Apollonius was in harmony with the beliefs of Callimachus, but in writing a long epic (about six thousand lines) and by writing in the traditional epic style, he acted in direct opposition to what Callimachus had been preaching. This was asking for trouble, especially if the tradition is correct that Apollonius was very young when he wrote the *Argonautica* and that he was the pupil of Callimachus. Callimachus had already said, "I hate the cyclic epic," and after reading the *Argonautica* he snarled, "A big book, a big evil"; or, freely translated, "The bigger they are, the sooner they pall." Apollonius retorted by calling Callimachus "the idle singer of an empty day," while Callimachus' rebuttal was a poem called the *Ibis.* This was understood to refer directly to Apollonius, since an ibis in Egypt was a bird which performed the functions of a buzzard or vulture, going about eating up all the garbage thrown in the streets, just as Apollonius (in the opinion of Callimachus) was snatching up crumbs from the banquet of Homer.

According to tradition, the immediate victory in the battle went to Callimachus: Apollonius lost his job. Later, however, Apollonius was recalled, became librarian (as one of the successors of Callimachus), and—the final blow—was buried beside his rival. Furthermore, the *Argonautica* has survived intact to the present day and was tremendously popular and influential in antiquity, while the *Hecale* has long since disappeared.

Prose works of the Hellenistic Age dealt with oratory, rhetoric, grammar, and geography and the other sciences, as well as history and biography. Regional histories were popular; well known works of this type are Timaeus' history of Sicily which used Carthaginian sources, Manetho's history of Egypt which was compiled with the aid of Egyptian records, and Berosus' history of Babylon which was based on cuneiform texts. The two greatest historians of the period were Hieronymus of Cardia and Polybius the Achaean. Hieronymus (*fl.* 275 B.C.) wrote a history of the period 323–266 B.C. with special reference to the successors of Alexander and their deeds. Polybius (198–117 B.C.) took as his subject the rise of Rome and the Roman conquest of the Greeks. Large portions of his history are still extant and are more than enough to convince us that Polybius was a much greater historian than the ancients thought.

A citizen of the Achaean League—his father was president of the league in 184, and he himself served as hipparch (second in authority) in 169—Polybius was not only well educated but also mature in political and military experience. Accused of pro-Macedonian sympathies in the conflict between Rome and Macedonia (171–167 B.C.), Polybius and a thousand other Achaeans were carried off to Rome as hostages. There he stayed in Rome for the next quarter of a century, not behind bars, but having the run of the city, cultivating old friendships already formed with prominent Romans and making new acquaintances. About 150 B.C. Polybius returned to Greece where he earned the gratitude of his countrymen by his efforts to alleviate their sufferings when they became involved in a new war with Rome (149–146 B.C.). Inscribed bases for statues erected to Polybius by his admirers have been found in Greece.

As a historian Polybius may be called the most eminent successor of Thucydides; he was more of a professional historian than any of the great historians who wrote in Latin, and none of the later Greeks could equal his competence. Polybius was an intellectual and a man of affairs, not a pedant loaded with book learning. He based his writings on literary sources and documents, interviews, and personal experiences. He lacked the literary ability of Thucydides, but he did have something essential to any great work of history—a message for his generation. His aim was to explain to the Greeks, who were not well informed, how and why the Romans had been able to "conquer the world." The main subject of his history, about one-third of which is still extant, was the period 218–146 B.C., from the beginning of the Second Punic War to the destruction of Corinth. He described not only the military campaigns of the age, but also the constitutions of Rome, Carthage, and the two Greek leagues. There is, in addition, much about tactics and strategy and much about the craft of the historian. Polybius stressed the importance of practical experience in military and political affairs and a knowledge of geography. He was also an exponent of a broad historical point of view, for he said:

> No one, as far as I am aware, has even attempted to inquire critically when and whence the general and comprehensive scheme of events originated and how it led up to the end. . . . We can no more hope to perceive this from histories dealing with particular events than to get at once a notion of the form of the whole world, its disposition and order, by visiting, each in turn, the most famous cities, or indeed by looking at separate plans of each. . . . He indeed who believes that by studying isolated histories he can acquire a fairly just view of history as a whole, is, as it seems to me, much in the case of one, who, after having looked at the dissevered limbs of an animal once alive and beautiful, fancies he has been as good an eyewitness of the creature itself in all its action and grace.[1]

In addition to the prose types already mentioned, short essays were also popular. The *Characters* of Theophrastus, a series of descriptions of human personality types—the miser, the boaster, the garrulous man, etc.—and the essay on the *Art of Shopping* by Lynceus of Samos are good examples of this kind of writing. Finally, there were travellers' tales, collections of myths, and paradoxes (descriptions of the wonders of nature—an ancient version of our "Believe It or Not").

In the Hellenistic period tendencies that had been present in fourth-century art became more pronounced. The decline of the city-state in Greece meant that artists became dependent for their commissions upon the new Hellenistic monarchies and upon private persons who possessed great wealth. As a result, Greece ceased to be the center of artistic production. Moreover, the new patrons of art—the monarchies and the rich—naturally exerted an influence upon the character of the work that the artists produced. The inspiration and the idealism which the city-state, as a patron of art, had fostered were replaced by individualism and other personalistic features typical of the new era. Art became "Art"; and although

---

[1] Book I, Chapter IV.

technical knowledge increased, the inspiration and *ethos* of the fifth century disappeared.

In Hellenistic architecture the favorite styles were the Ionic and Corinthian; experiments were made with composite styles, and the arch was used more frequently. The new structures were larger and more elaborate than those of the classical period. Moreover, although new temples were erected, the number of secular public buildings constructed was much greater. Stadia, gymnasia, colonnades (stoae), theaters, council chambers, and office buildings appeared in every city. The construction of fortifications became a science. Last of all, domestic architecture entered a new era. Houses were larger, contained more rooms, and were built with a view to permanence.

In sculpture, the individualism of the fourth century and the popularity of portraiture continued into the Hellenistic period. Other characteristics of Hellenistic sculpture were symbolism, realism, and, to some extent, impressionism. The eclecticism of the age is also to be seen in its sculpture. In other words, a Hellenistic sculptor might borrow ideas from a number of his predecessors and combine them into a style of his own. The Pergamene sculptors, for example, were greatly indebted to both Praxiteles and Scopas.

Lysippos, the official portrait sculptor to Alexander the Great, was the best of the Hellenistic artists in this field. Lysippos' favorite medium was bronze. He was especially well known for his athletic figures, for he excelled in portraying motion. His Apoxyomenos, the statue of an athlete scraping oil from his body, is familiar to everyone. Lysippos, together with Scopas and Praxiteles, exerted a tremendous influence upon Hellenistic sculpture.

The three main schools of sculpture in the third century were those of Alexandria, Antioch, and Pergamum. The Alexandrian school, which was influenced by Praxiteles, showed impressionistic trends, with its emphasis upon sharp major details and its practice of merely suggesting other less important features. The Alexandrian sculptors were fond of the grotesque and caricature, but they reached their greatest heights with their *genre* subjects in which old people and children were realistically portrayed. Pergamene sculpture is best known through the famous Great Altar and the series of statues dealing with the Gauls. Everyone is familiar with the Dying Gaul (sometimes erroneously called the Dying Gladiator). The schools of Antioch and Rhodes were influenced by Lysippos. The great Colossus of Rhodes, the work of Chares of Lindus, was one of the Seven Wonders of the Ancient World.

Greek painting reached its climax late in the fourth century with Apelles. This painter was famous for his *charis* (grace), and his portraits were unrivalled in the accuracy and fidelity with which they depicted their subjects. He painted the portrait of Antigonos Monophthalmos (the One-Eyed), a picture of Aphrodite rising from the sea, and many others. A great art critic of the Roman period said of Apelles: "All have profited by his innovations, though one of them could never be imitated; he used to give his pictures when finished a black glazing so thin that by sending back the light it could call forth a whitish color, while at the same time it afforded a protection from dust and dirt, only becoming visible itself on the closest inspection. In using this glazing one main purpose was to prevent the brilliance of the colors from offending the eyes. . . ."[2]

With the exception of the developments in painting, the Hellenistic Age may perhaps be said to have made its greatest advances in the minor rather than the major arts. The coins of Alexander and many of his successors, for example, were triumphs of engraving, and one should not neglect to mention the graceful, bright-colored terra cotta figurines produced by the craftsmen of Tanagra and Myrina. Although painted vases were no longer important except in Italy, the potters of the Greek East were able to find a market for their fine table ware, a glazed pottery decorated with reliefs.

In retrospect, Hellenistic art seems in several ways symbolic of the age as a whole. The construction of larger and more varied types of buildings suggests the political change from the city-state to the great kingdom with its diverse ethnic groups. The beginnings of portraiture in sculpture and painting reflect the individualism rampant in philosophy and politics, while the achievements in the minor arts remind us that an age without a Pindar or a Plato might nevertheless produce a Theocritus or a Theophrastus.

---

[2] Pliny, *Natural History*, XXXV, 15, 97.

PART THREE

Rome

Chapter 19

THE WESTERN MEDITERRANEAN

THUS FAR we have been concerned mainly with the history of civilization in the Near East and the eastern Mediterranean. We have seen how civilization had its origins in the Near East, how it spread to Greece where it received considerable alteration and elaboration, and how, in the Hellenistic Age proper, a composite civilization was built up in the combined areas of the Near East and the eastern Mediterranean.

We have yet to consider the climax of these developments, the Roman phase of Hellenistic civilization. This phase began about the middle of the second century B.C., when a new area, the western Mediterranean, was gradually added to the already existing cultural unit formed by the Near East and the eastern Mediterranean. The Roman phase reached its climax, its cultural developments attained maturity, in the first two centuries of the Christian era at the time when the whole Mediterranean basin became a political unit, the Roman Empire.

Before we can discuss this climax of ancient civilization, however, it will be necessary for us to consider the earlier history of culture in the western Mediterranean. We must trace the westward diffusion of culture from the Near East and Greece and see how and why the western Mediterranean area passed from an Age of Primitive Culture to an Age of Agriculture and finally to an Age of Civilization. In addition, we must pay considerable attention to the phenomenon of the rise of Rome and the development of its institutions. How and why the Romans became the rulers of the ancient world are important questions which necessitate detailed explanation.

The region which we shall call the western Mediterranean includes Italy, present-day southern France and eastern Spain, the coast of Africa west of ancient Cyrene, and the western Mediterranean islands, especially

Sicily. At the opening of the Age of Agriculture, which may be dated about 4000 B.C. in the western Mediterranean, this area was populated by Mediterranean man, just as in the case of Crete and Greece; in the post-glacial period the increasing aridity of north Africa may have driven this Mediterranean type into Italy and Spain. Between 4000 and 2000 B.C. the inhabitants of the western Mediterranean led a quiet agricultural and pastoral existence which underwent no significant alterations. While civilizations arose in the Near East and Crete, and a stream of culture began to flow up the Danube to penetrate central Europe, the western Mediterranean remained unaffected, for the African desert, the sea itself, and the Alps provided serious obstacles to cultural diffusion.

It was not until the close of the third millennium B.C. that the isolation of the western Mediterranean began to break down. About 2000 B.C. some Swiss groups moved across the Alps into the Po Valley, and Minoan traders began to come occasionally to south Italy and Sicily. Two hundred years later bronze-using tribes from central Europe penetrated Italy from the north; by 1500 B.C. Italy had passed into a Full Bronze Age, although "civilization" as we have used the term in this book was not yet established.

The bronze-using peoples who came into Italy during the middle centuries of the second millennium B.C. spoke Indo-European languages. As a matter of fact, their coming was closely connected with the same general movement that brought the Mycenaeans (or Achaeans) into Greece. In like manner, the next wave of migration among the Indo-Europeans (about 1200 B.C.) which brought the Dorians into Greece and the Phrygians into Asia Minor was also felt in Italy. Moreover, after 1200 B.C. tribes from western Greece displaced by the Dorian invasion crossed the Adriatic and settled along the eastern coast of Italy and in Venetia. These last arrivals were not Greeks, but they were iron users, and most of them spoke Indo-European languages.

Slightly later than these Indo-Europeans from the north, the first civilized invaders of the western Mediterranean arrived from the east. These were: (1) the Etruscans, (2) the Greeks, and (3) the Phoenicians.

1. Before 850 the Etruscans, a people related to the Lydians, left (or were driven out of) their home which was probably in Asia Minor. They came to Italy and settled on the western coast north of the Tiber River in the region which is still called Tuscany.

2. Just after 800 B.C. the first Greek traders began to make their appearance in the western Mediterranean. They were closely followed by colonists from many Greek cities; colonies were established in southern Italy, Sicily, southern France, and northwestern Spain. The areas of Greek colonization were limited by the Etruscans, who were powerful in northern Italy, and by the Phoenicians, who had established a sphere of economic influence in northern Africa and southern Spain.

3. It is difficult to determine when the Phoenicians arrived. There was a tradition that Gades (Cadiz) in Spain was founded by Phoenician traders as early as 1100 B.C., but certainly the real power of the Phoenicians dated from the foundation of Carthage in north Africa. The traditional date of 814 B.C. for the founding of Carthage may be too early, but the true date cannot be later than the first half of the eighth century.

All the groups which have been mentioned, from the early Mediterranean men to the last Greek and Phoenician invaders, contributed something to the subsequent history of the western Mediterranean. The Mediterranean men who founded the Age of Agriculture in the West were also important because their descendants continued to form the bulk of its population. Although they intermarried with later invaders, it was usually the Mediterranean physical characteristics that predominated, and the Mediterranean physical type continued to be the prevailing one throughout the historic period just as it did in Greece. The Indo-European invaders of the second millennium were important in Italy especially because it was their languages and social and political institutions that survived and were most significant during the epoch when the West became civilized. The Etruscans, Phoenicians, and Greeks were important in the history of the western Mediterranean because they carried their versions of the civilization of the ancient Near East to the barbarians of the West. For the development of culture in Italy, credit must be given to the Greeks and Etruscans; in Spain both Greeks and Phoenicians were contributors; for the rest of the western Mediterranean, the Greeks were important in Sicily and southern France, and the Phoenicians left their stamp upon northern Africa.

The Etruscans were not a large group, but they were able by virtue of their better weapons and military organization to conquer the natives of the region in which they settled. They established themselves in stone-walled towns throughout Tuscany; each town became a city-state which was independent of all others. The various Etruscan cities often fought one another; their only real bond was a religious league which held an annual festival and elected a high priest. The Etruscans traded with the Phoenicians and the Greeks, and even with the Egyptians. They brought about an increase of agricultural production by forcing the conquered population to labor for them in the fields. The Etruscans also manufactured pottery, terra cottas, and metal products, although their techniques seemed to have been derived from Greek sources. Their alphabet of twenty-seven letters was adopted and adapted from the Greeks to meet the phonetic needs of their language.

Etruscan religion seems to have been rather gloomy. There was a belief in demons and in human sacrifice; gladiatorial combats were staged as part of certain religious ceremonies. Divination was practiced by observing various signs and portents and examining the entrails of animals; hepatoscopy (liver divination) represents an indisputable contact with the Near East.

Etruscan gods were often grouped in threes, or triads; each city had its own particular god, and there were divinities that were considered the patrons of special crafts. Around each city a sacred boundary, the pomerium, was drawn by magical ceremonies. The Romans were greatly influenced by Etruscan religion: they built their temples in the Etruscan fashion, took over many Etruscan religious ceremonies, and borrowed Etruscan gods: Uni (Juno), Velchan (Vulcan), Maris (Mars), Nethun (Neptune), and others.

A large part of Etruscan culture is known to us either through Roman survivals or by finds made in Etruscan tombs. In the latter the fine metal-work, strong portrait sculpture on the sarcophagi, and the lively painting on the walls can tell us much about daily life and religious beliefs. Despite strong Greek and Orientalizing influences, the Etruscans managed to create a distinctive art rather than a pale copy of the originals that stimulated them.

Although the phonetic values of the letters in the Etruscan alphabet are known, it is not possible to read Etruscan beyond recognizing the personal names, titles, a few words, and some of the grammatical constructions. About twelve thousand Etruscan inscriptions have been found, but they are short, dedications or sepulchral texts, and contain little more than personal names, place names, titles, and a few words which are used over and over. Thus it is difficult to build up vocabulary knowledge or to make much progress with the grammar. The longest Etruscan text was found on the wrappings of a mummy in Egypt, but unfortunately it is a magical text; such documents are difficult enough to understand when they are couched in a known language, and in an unknown tongue they are next to hopeless. It is worth noting, however, that the language most like Etruscan, as regards vocabulary and grammar, is Lydian, although it, too, cannot be read.

The origin of the mysterious Etruscans is a matter which has been argued for over two thousand years. Since the dispute began, there have been three theories: (1) that the Etruscans were indigenous; (2) that they came from central Europe; and (3) that they came from western Asia Minor. In modern times German scholars have tended to favor the second theory and Italian scholars the first—both for painfully obvious reasons—but leaving considerations of nationalism or patriotism aside, the weight of the evidence definitely favors the third theory. There are many elements in Etruscan culture, in addition to their language, that point to a connection with Lydia.

After 700 B.C. the Etruscans began to extend their political influence outside of Tuscany. To the south they advanced as far as Campania, where they reached the Greek frontier; to the north they reached the Po Valley. Wars were fought with the Greeks, the Samnites (a powerful group of tribes in central Italy), and the Gauls, who began to invade the Po Valley just after 500 B.C. The Etruscans were defeated in a great battle with the Greeks in the south about 475, but the main reason for their withdrawal north of the Tiber was that they were forced to concentrate on the defense of their northern frontier against the Gauls.

As we have seen, the Greek colonies of the western Mediterranean became very prosperous. The principal Greek cities in Italy were Tarentum, Cumae, Sybaris, Croton, Neapolis (Naples), Locri, and Rhegium; in Sicily were Syracuse, Acragas, Gela, Leontini, Himera, and Selinus; in southern France (Gaul) was Massilia (Marseilles). Trade, industry, and agriculture flourished. The Greeks introduced their culture to the natives with the result that Greek architecture, sculpture, pottery, and metalwork influenced the native arts and crafts. The western form of the Greek alphabet was adopted by the natives. This was the form borrowed by the Romans and passed on to us; the western alphabet was already quite different in many respects from the East Greek, or Ionic, form that evolved into what we call *the* Greek alphabet today. The introduction of Greek coinage brought important changes in the economy of the western Mediterranean. Moreover, the olive and possibly the vine were imported from Greece and planted on Western soil.

The Phoenicians continued their commercial activities in the western Mediterranean until the sixth century, when the Persian conquest of their country caused a break in their Western connections. Carthage, the greatest of the Phoenician colonies in the West, then asserted its independence and gained control over the other Western Phoenician settlements as well as founding new colonies of its own. Carthage was a city-state like Tyre and Sidon and was at first ruled by kings, but it later became a republic. The chief magistrates were called *suffetes,* or judges, and there was an aristocratic senate, another council, and possibly a popular assembly. Most of the power was concentrated in the hands of an oligarchy of merchant princes and large landholders. The interests of the traders and landholders were often conflicting, however. As a consequence, the policies of Carthage might shift and change as those interested in trade and industry or the agricultural bloc gained the upper hand.

Carthaginian religion was like Phoenician religion, of course. The chief deities were Baal Hammon, Melqart, Eshmoun, Reshef, and Tanit (Asherat). Many Carthaginian personal names were theophorous compounds: Hannibal (Baal) or Hamilcar (Melqart). The Carthaginian language was naturally Phoenician, and the Phoenician alphabet was employed; most of the "Phoenician" inscriptions which have survived are of Carthaginian provenience and date. At Carthage the dead were buried in chamber tombs and sarcophagi as in ancient Tyre, Sidon, and Byblos. Carthaginian art was, if anything, less inspiring than Phoenician. There is no doubt that the Carthaginians had a literature, but none of it has survived.

From the middle of the sixth century onward the Carthaginians and Etruscans combined forces in an attempt to halt the political and economic

advances of the Greeks in the West. In this they were able to take advantage of the frequent quarrels among the Greeks themselves. The Etruscans formed a barrier to the Greek advance in Italy, while the Carthaginians were able to confine the Greeks to northeastern Spain as they themselves occupied the rich southland. The wealth of Sicily and its proximity to Italy and Africa made the island a natural battleground for Greeks and Carthaginians, but it should be remembered also that events in the western Mediterranean were often connected with developments in the East. The warfare of Greeks and Persians, or the struggles of the mainland Greeks with one another, had their repercussions in the West. The Carthaginian attack on Sicily in 480 was timed to coincide with the Persian invasion of Greece. In both cases the Greeks managed to repel the enemy, but this was not the end of the story. When the Athenians met disaster in Sicily in 413

324

AN OPPIDUM

Alinari

Alinari

Etruscan orator

Augustus

The Nile—Alexandrian

Alinari

The Tiber—Roman imperial

Courtesy of the Deutsches Archaeologisches Institut, Rome

CAESAR   CICERO

CATO   POMPEY

LIVIA

Courtesy of the Ny Carlsberg Glyptothek

AUGUSTUS

Courtesy of the Ny Carlsberg Glyptothek

AGRIPPA

Alinari

MARK ANTONY

*Courtesy of Cornelius C. Vermeule, III,
and the* American Journal of Archaeology

and the irate Sicilians planned to send aid to Sparta in the second phase of the Peloponnesian War, the Athenians made a treaty with Carthage, and a Carthaginian attack on Syracuse kept the Sicilians at home.

The earlier Carthaginian attack on Sicily in 480 had encouraged the rise of tyranny among the Sicilian Greeks. Gelon, tyrant of Gela, beat off the Carthaginians and got control of Syracuse, while his brother Hieron, who succeeded him, centered his power at Syracuse and even campaigned against the Etruscans in Italy. Partly as result of these activities, Syracuse became the political center of Sicily and a natural target for Carthaginian attacks. During the fifth century the Carthaginians did manage to gain a foothold in western Sicily. Thus they were able to advance more easily on Syracuse when they formed their alliance with Athens during the Peloponnesian War. By 405 almost all of Sicily was in Carthaginian hands except Syracuse. There a young officer named Dionysius persuaded the Greeks to make him sole general, and he utilized his power to make himself tyrant. Yet Dionysius managed to save Syracuse from Carthage; he then brought most of Sicily under his sway, and after his death his sons were able to maintain the tyranny for about ten years (to 357 B.C.).

By this time Sicilian history had begun to follow a frightening pattern. The Carthaginians would threaten, the Greeks would unite under a strong leader; once the danger was past, disunity would prevail, and the whole process would be repeated. This happened after the fall of the Dionysian tyranny, and it happened again at the end of the fourth century when a new tyrant, Agathocles, came into power in much the same manner as Dionysius. By 311 Syracuse was under siege by the Carthaginians. Agathocles conceived the brilliant plan of invading Africa and attacking Carthage in order to relieve the pressure on Syracuse. His military operations in north Africa were not successful, but he did frighten the Carthaginians sufficiently to gain a cessation of hostilities. Subsequently Agathocles made his tyranny into a monarchy, and before his death in 289 he had come to exercise some influence in southern Italy as well as Sicily.

After the death of Agathocles a group of his mercenary soldiers seized the city of Messana which controlled the straits between Sicily and Italy. By means of this strategic position these former mercenaries (the Mamertini) were able to prey upon the commerce passing through the straits. The piratical activities of the Mamertini soon became so obnoxious that the Syracusans undertook to dislodge them from Messana. Besieged and in danger of capture, the Mamertini appealed for aid both to Carthage and to Rome, the rising state in Italy (265 B.C.). The Carthaginians were only too happy to have an excuse to gain a foothold at Messana, and they quickly sent troops to the city. The Romans, on the other hand, had not been interested in the appeal of the Mamertini; but when the Carthaginians entered Messana, the Romans became alarmed, for they feared that Messana might serve as a stepping stone for Carthaginian expansion into southern Italy. Consequently, a Roman expeditionary force was dispatched to Sicily for the purpose of driving the Carthaginians from their new position.

Thus it was that the affair of the Mamertini—in itself a minor incident in history—brought Rome and Carthage face to face and precipitated a series of wars in which Rome eventually overcame the Carthaginians and gained control of the western Mediterranean. Before we can carry this narrative further, however, we must retrace our steps to consider the early history of Italy and of Rome, the city-state which by 265 B.C. controlled all of peninsular Italy.

The influence of environment upon history is well demonstrated in the case of Italy. Italy, like Greece, is a peninsula jutting out into the Mediterranean. The topography is rugged; there are many mountains, valleys, and plains; but on the whole, Italy is less rugged than Greece. Although Italian topography fostered separatism, the possibility of building up a united state was greater in the Italian peninsula than in Greece. The Adriatic coast of Italy was forbidding, and thus cultural contact with the Eastern civilizations was long delayed. On the other hand, it was possible to invade Italy from the south, as was done by Mediterranean man in the prehistoric period. The country could also be penetrated from the north. Many of the Bronze and Iron Age peoples came down over the Alps, and this route was also followed by the Gauls after 400 B.C. The plains and valleys of Italy were better adapted to agriculture than were those of Greece; vines, olive trees, and grains grew well on Italian soil. There was an abundance of good timber. In early times the country was best known for its flocks and herds, but it was especially important for the later development of Italian culture that copper, tin, clay, and much good stone were available in the peninsula; moreover, iron could be secured from the nearby island of Elba.

Like the Greeks, the Italian peoples of the historic period were largely the product of a fusion of the Mediterranean stock with the early Indo-European-speaking invaders. The elements provided by the Etruscans, Greeks, and the later Gauls were also of some importance in determining the physical appearance of the Italians. The significant point to be noted, however, is that the Italians of the historic period were a mixed people, and no particular "race" was responsible for what they later achieved.

When the Greeks came to Italy they found many nations and tribes of barbarians living in much the same manner that they themselves had lived in Greece in the Dark Ages. Agriculture and grazing were the chief occupations; there was little trade and practically no manufacturing. The formation of city-states had begun; the *oppidum,* a town clustered about a fortified citadel, was becoming the political center of its surrounding agricultural territory. The primitive monarchy was being replaced by aristocratic, oligarchic governments; the great landlords dominated the political life of their communities, and the subordination of the peasants was taking place. It should be emphasized that there were many of these nascent city-states in Italy. Those in the central part of the peninsula were stronger than the others, and the Greek colonization of the south had brought commercial and cultural contacts that accelerated their growth.

Some distance from the sea, located at a ford of the Tiber River was a little town called Rome, a town destined to become the capital of the ancient world. There was nothing about Rome in 750 B.C. that seemed to mark it out for greatness. Its population was not large, and its economic life was not thriving. There was little trade or contact with the outside world; most of the people were either farmers or herdsmen. A number of other city-states in Italy were more populous and more prosperous than Rome. If it had been suggested to a contemporary observer that a single city-state might some day unify Italy, he probably would not have selected Rome as a possible candidate for that honor. Nor did Rome emerge rapidly from its obscurity. After more than three and one-half centuries (about 390 B.C.) the town, now grown to a small city, achieved its first international recognition when it was sacked by the Gauls. Even then, civilized people in Greece were not exactly sure where or what Rome was. One author referred to it vaguely as a Greek city in Italy.

It is almost impossible to reconstruct Roman history before 390 B.C. The city was too insignificant to merit the attention of the Greek historical writers, and the Romans had no literature of their own worthy of the name until the late third century. Tradition had it that Rome was founded in 753 B.C., but archaeological excavation has disclosed that the site was occupied shortly after 1000. In the seventh century B.C. Rome became the stronghold of Etruscan robber chiefs who used the city as a base for expansion toward the south. Etruscan kings ruled over the native population; stone fortifications, streets, and sewers were built; the countryside was made agriculturally more productive by drainage projects and the governmental direction of native labor.

About 500 B.C., or possibly even later (the traditional date, however, is 509), there was a revolution at Rome, and the Etruscan overlords were expelled. At the same time, apparently, the monarchy was abolished; it was replaced by a republican form of government which resembled very closely that of the early Greek oligarchies. The landed aristocrats, the patricians, were now in control. Their political stronghold was the Roman council of the elders, called the senate. Each year there were elected two chief magistrates, the consuls, who had military, executive, administrative, judicial, and religious functions. The Romans felt that with two magistrates, each enjoying equal power, autocracy was not to be feared. There was an assembly of people, the *comitia curiata,* which, like the Greek ecclesia, was composed of that portion of the citizen body available for military service.

The regal government at Rome had been almost identical with that of a Greek state in the Dark Ages. The Roman king, *rex,* had the same functions and powers as a Greek *basileus;* the Roman *senate* paralleled the Greek *gerousia;* the *comitia curiata* was like the early *ecclesia.* The only essential difference between the new Roman republic and the primitive monarchy was that the king was replaced by the two consuls, executives chosen from the ranks of the aristocrats and limited in their actions by the senate. A remarkable continuity of governmental theory was evidenced by the retention of the concept of the *imperium.* This was the power or authority to rule which included the right to command troops, dispense justice, and perform administrative and religious functions. The comitia curiata, the assembly of the people, alone had the right to bestow the imperium. In the regal period when the assembly elected a new king, it gave him the imperium, the right to rule; under the republic, when the assembly each year elected the consuls, it also conferred the imperium upon them.

At the beginning of the republic the Romans were not numerous, nor was their army particularly efficient. Like the Assyrians, they were menaced by enemies on almost every side, and they were forced to adopt an aggressive policy in order to defend themselves. This was the real secret of Roman success. They had to conquer or be conquered. When they were victorious, they could not allow their defeated enemies to go free; they had to make them Roman subjects or inferior allies. For over two centuries (500–265 B.C.) the Romans doggedly followed this policy, and when they finally stopped to take stock of their position at the end of the period, they found themselves in control of the whole Italian peninsula.

Between the time of the establishment of the Roman Republic and the beginning of the First Punic War, a period of something over two hundred years, three phases may be distinguished in the history of Roman foreign relations: (1) from the fall of the kings to about 334 the Romans fought innumerable wars of survival against their immediate neighbors and gradually secured their position as the dominant group in west-central Italy; (2) from 334 to 290 B.C. there was a struggle between the Romans and the Samnites and others for supremacy in peninsular Italy (except the extreme south); and (3) between 290 and 265 the Romans completed their conquest of the whole peninsula from its southern tip to the Po Valley.

The traditional date, 509 B.C., for the expulsion of the kings and the establishment of the republic is too early: it may have been 500, 475, or even as late as 450. The fall of the monarchy is not likely to have occurred before the defeat of the Etruscans by the Greeks about 475, however. Whenever it was that Rome became independent, the situation of the Romans was anything but secure: they must fight off the Etruscans who were lurking north of the Tiber, and they must be prepared to repel the attacks of the surrounding Italic tribes. Thus shortly after independence the Romans concluded an alliance with a confederation of their neighbors known as the Latin League. The allies agreed to live at peace with one another, to render mutual aid in time of war, to divide their booty equally, and probably to alternate the command of the allied forces; it was also agreed that citizens of the contracting parties could intermarry and acquire property as well as trade freely with one another. For over a century the alliance proved beneficial to both sides; enemy attacks were repelled, and there was a gradual expansion of holdings outside of Latium itself.

Just after 400 B.C. the Romans advanced across the Tiber and overcame the Etruscan town of Veii. This was always remembered as a great achievement; the Romans of later times tried to compare the siege of Veii with the Greek capture of Troy—both legends were good for morale. Historically, however, both were unimportant.

About 390 B.C. the Gauls, who had ravaged Etruria, also sacked Rome; the invaders evacuated the ruined city only after they were paid a ransom in gold valued at about a quarter of a million dollars. Impoverished but undaunted by this reverse, the Romans rebuilt their city and improved their army. Shortly after 340 B.C. a war broke out between the Romans and the Latin League. The members of the league felt that Rome was becoming too strong and was taking an unfair proportion of the plunder from their joint conquests. The Latins were defeated in the war, and the territory and people of the Latin League were incorporated into the Roman state.

The conquest of the Latin League was the beginning of really important Roman expansion in Italy. Within the next generation great strides were made. The Greeks around the Bay of Naples were being harassed by the Samnites, a powerful and warlike group of tribes that lived in the Apennines. The Samnites did not want to conquer the Greeks but enjoyed raiding their territory for plunder and military glory. When the Greeks sought the aid of Rome, the Samnites took the field in earnest, and a long series of wars ensued. After several humiliating defeats the Romans pulled themselves together and broke the power of the Samnites. The experience of the Samnite Wars taught the Romans much: they learned something of the logistical problems of campaigning far from home, and they built their first great road, the Appian Way, which ran southward from Rome into Campania and then across into the center of the peninsula. Ultimately the road was to be extended to its terminus at the harbor of Brundisium on the heel of the boot of Italy. The last phase of the Samnite Wars came in the first decade of the third century, when the Samnites allied with Gauls and Etruscans to make the Romans fight simultaneously on several fronts, but by 290 the Romans had won again.

The protection against the Samnites which the Romans had provided for the Greeks of Campania now induced the Greeks farther south to seek Roman aid against the wild Lucanian tribes. This led to unforeseen complications. During the later Samnite Wars the Romans had enjoyed the co-operation of the great Greek city of Tarentum; the Tarentines had attacked the Samnites from the rear while the Romans pressed upon their front. The Tarentines, however, did not want the Romans coming into what they considered their sphere of influence in south Italy, and the Romans had agreed not to send any vessels into the Gulf of Taranto. When, however, the Thurians asked for Roman aid against the Lucanians, the Romans conveniently forgot their agreement with Tarentum and sent transports into the gulf. These were promptly attacked and sunk by the Tarentine navy (282). Rome protested, but the Tarentines not only refused to apologize but also insulted Roman emissaries, and a cause for war was provided.

Tarentum could not hope to withstand the Roman attack unaided, but the city was rich enough to buy the services of the most famous and skillful general then alive. This was Pyrrhus, King of Epirus, whose prowess approached that of Alexander and Demetrius Poliorcetes. Pyrrhus was a professional soldier with a professional army. At the moment he was unemployed; therefore he accepted the Tarentine offer and arrived in Italy in 281 with twenty-five thousand mercenaries, a herd of war elephants, and a tame philosopher. The first battle between Pyrrhus and the Romans was fought in 280 at Heraclea near Tarentum. Pyrrhus won, but his losses were so heavy that he could not follow up his advantage; it was a victory almost as costly as a defeat: this is the origin of the phrase "Pyrrhic victory." In 279 at Asculum, farther north, Pyrrhus "won" again, but the Romans would neither acknowledge defeat nor enter into negotiations despite the arguments of Cineas, the tame philosopher.

At this point the services of Pyrrhus were needed elsewhere. Agathocles, the Syracusan king, had died in 289, and the Carthaginians had renewed their depredations in Sicily. During the Tarentine War, and probably even before, the Romans and Carthaginians were in alliance. With the Romans pressing the Greeks in Italy and the Carthaginians those in Sicily, the Greeks could not aid one another. After Pyrrhus had stalled the Roman advance toward Tarentum, his help was required against the Carthaginians in Sicily, and he spent three years fighting there. By 275, however, the Romans were on the march again. Pyrrhus returned to Italy to be defeated in the Battle of Beneventum. After this, with his army badly depleted, Pyrrhus abandoned the Tarentines to their fate; he went home to enter the employ of the Ptolemies against the Antigonids in the Peloponnesus. In 272 B.C., the same year in which Tarentum surrendered to Rome, Pyrrhus was killed ignobly in street fighting in Argos when a woman dropped a roof tile on his head.

Supreme in Italy, and with an established reputation as protectors of the Greeks, the Romans could scarcely avoid being drawn into the quarrels of the Greeks and Carthaginians in Sicily. In this sense, the Punic Wars were inevitable.

By 265 B.C. the Romans had completed their conquest of the Italian peninsula. About one-seventh of the land south of the Rubicon River was held by the Romans themselves, and the rest belonged to Italian allies bound to Rome by treaties that made the Romans the commanders of a powerful military machine fully a match for the might of Carthage.

Of equal importance with the external history of Rome is the story of the internal developments that took place in the period between the establishment of the republic and 265 B.C. Perhaps the clearest perspective of Roman economic and political history may be gained if one considers Rome as a city-state of the type we have already observed in Greece. The original monarchical government of Rome was very similar to that which one might have found in almost any Greek state during the Dark Ages, and Rome's subsequent internal economic and political evolution followed the familiar path from oligarchy to timocracy and finally a kind of democracy. The details of this story are not essential to our study, but the general trends ought to be considered. Although some of the events of the early period—the fifth century especially—cannot be determined with certainty, a tentative reconstruction might be made as follows:

At the time of the abolition of the monarchy and the establishment of the republic (about 500 B.C.), the Roman people were divided into two classes: patricians (nobles) and plebeians (commons). These divisions were political and economic as well as social. The patricians were the great landholders; only patricians could be members of the senate or hold the consulship or important religious offices. The plebeians were, for the most part, small farmers. Ineligible for the senate or the consulship, lacking the right of intermarriage with the patricians, the plebeians had little voice in the government. If a plebeian could equip himself for military service, he could participate in the meetings of the comitia curiata, the popular assembly; but, as we shall see, this privilege was of little significance at this time.

Between 500 and 450 B.C. the power of the patricians increased. Naturally, the administration of justice was in their hands, and a combination of circumstances allowed the upper class to build up the prestige of the senate at the expense of the popular assembly. As in Greece in the Dark Ages, so in fifth-century Rome declining returns from agriculture impoverished the small farmer and made it difficult for him to equip himself for the army; consequently, the popular assembly declined. In addition, some of the small farmers gave up their unproductive lands and became tenants on patrician estates; other free men with small holdings found it wise to seek the legal protection (become the clients) of patricians. As a result, the plebeians in the popular assembly became divided into two groups—the tenants and the clients of the patricians on the one hand, and the remaining plebeians on the other. With the plebeian ranks split in this manner, concerted action through constitutional channels was difficult. The patricians with the support of their tenants and clients were probably able to outvote the independent plebeians in the comitia curiata.

What happened next is uncertain, but apparently the independent plebeians, excluded from any real participation in the oligarchic republican government, resolved to build up a government of their own, a state within a state. Some time after 500 B.C. the plebeians[1] began to meet together to discuss matters pertaining to the welfare of their class. When patrician oppression became unbearable, this unofficial assembly of the plebeians elected four officers called *tribunes of the people,* one from each of the four Roman tribes.[2] A sacred oath, sworn by all the plebeians, declared the tribunes to be sacrosanct—anyone who harmed or disobeyed a tribune was guilty of sacrilege and could be put to death without trial. The tribunes, thus protected, became in turn the protectors of the plebeians against the patrician magistrates, for a tribune could veto (forbid) any official action that endangered a plebeian. The tribunes were the presiding officers of the unofficial plebeian assembly. The assembly itself, which had begun as a deliberative body and had added electoral powers when the tribunes were chosen, soon entered the legislative field also; the assembly began to pass measures—*plebiscites*—which were binding upon plebeians.

We do not know whether the patricians took much interest in the plebeian efforts at organization, but the situation was soon altered. About 450 B.C. there seems to have been a crisis in the external affairs of Rome which forced the patricians to seek plebeian aid; Rome may have been threatened by Etruscan reconquest, or her other neighbors may have endangered her independence. At any rate, the patricians, with plebeian help, were able to weather the storm. Afterward, however, the plebeians demanded increased civic rights as payment for their assistance, and the patricians had little choice but to accede to their requests.

The series of reforms which were now inaugurated gave the plebeians a number of advantages and transformed the Roman government from an oligarchy into a timocracy. Plebeians were henceforth allowed to hold the consulship and intermarry with the patricians. The law was codified; this initial codification was known as the Law of the Twelve Tables. The patricians formally recognized the veto power of the tribunes, and it was

---

[1] Henceforth, unless otherwise specified, the term plebeian will refer to the independent plebeians—not to plebeians who were tenants or clients of the patricians.

[2] At first, as in the case of many Greek communities, the entire citizen body of Rome was divided into four tribes; in this case, the division was probably based upon the four wards that comprised the city in the Etruscan period.

probably at this time that the board of tribunes was increased in number from four to ten. Moreover, the patricians agreed that the plebeian plebiscites, if ratified by the senate, were to become laws binding upon the whole Roman citizen body, patricians as well as plebeians.

One outcome of the crisis of 450 B.C. was the reorganization of the army; the new army became the basis for a new popular assembly—the *comitia centuriata*—which paved the way for timocratic government. In the comitia centuriata the citizens were assigned to property classes, and the vote of each class was given a weight proportionate to the wealth of its members. The new assembly elected the consuls and other officials; it was a legislative body, and it also functioned as a court of appeal to which sentences involving the death penalty or a heavy fine might be referred for final decisions. One feature of the comitia centuriata was particularly notable: even the poorest citizens, those who could not equip themselves for military service, were allowed a place in the assembly. Thus, in this innovation and in the establishment of the principle of appeal, we are reminded of the Solonian reforms which also, of course, established a timocracy.

The general military and political reorganization of the mid-fifth century was accompanied by the creation of new offices of state. The business of government had now increased to a point where it could not be handled by the consuls alone. They needed the help of deputies and assistants in order to discharge the various duties which had devolved upon them. Each consul was given an assistant called a quaestor, who acted as a treasurer in Rome and as a quartermaster when the army took the field. The two quaestors were annually elected by the comitia centuriata.

In addition, the institution of the comitia centuriata itself, a body in which the citizens were assigned to census groups according to their wealth, created a new task to be performed. Two officials, called censors, were therefore elected from the ranks of the former consuls every five years. The censors assigned the citizens to the appropriate census classes, revised the rolls of the senate, and ultimately became responsible for letting public works contracts. The censorship was an important post; it not only carried great prestige, but also the censors could exert political influence through their performance of the *lectio senatus* (formerly the prerogative of the consuls) because they could appoint and remove the senators and so control the membership of the senate.

These settlements made about the middle of the fifth century only temporarily relieved the discontent of the plebeians. After the sack of Rome by the Gauls in 390 B.C. a critical economic situation caused by property losses, financial unsettlement, and the burden of heavy taxes for the rebuilding of the city culminated in new agitation for reform. Shortly after 370 B.C. the patricians were forced to make new concessions. It was agreed

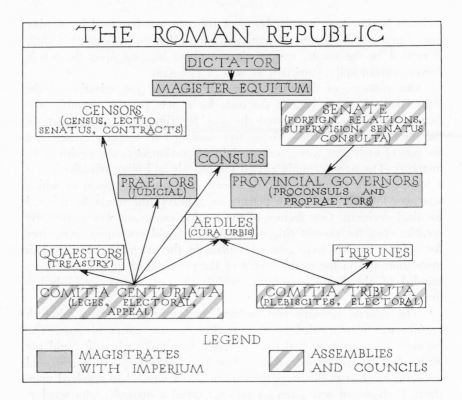

THE ROMAN REPUBLIC

DICTATOR

MAGISTER EQUITUM

CENSORS
(CENSUS, LECTIO
SENATUS, CONTRACTS)

SENATE
(FOREIGN RELATIONS,
SUPERVISION, SENATUS
CONSULTA)

CONSULS

PRAETORS
(JUDICIAL)

PROVINCIAL GOVERNORS
(PROCONSULS AND
PROPRAETORS)

AEDILES
(CURA URBIS)

QUAESTORS
(TREASURY)

TRIBUNES

COMITIA CENTURIATA
(LEGES, ELECTORAL,
APPEAL)

COMITIA TRIBUTA
(PLEBISCITES, ELECTORAL)

LEGEND

MAGISTRATES
WITH IMPERIUM

ASSEMBLIES
AND COUNCILS

that at least one of the two consuls elected each year must be a plebeian. Some relief was provided for plebeian debtors whose difficulties were probably the result of the transition to a money economy that was slowly taking place in Italy at this time. In addition, land hunger seems to have been a serious question. Since 500 B.C. the Romans had acquired new land by conquest, but the major portion of this new territory had been gobbled up by the patricians. Therefore, an attempt was made to limit the amount of land that an individual might obtain.

The reforms of this era were again accompanied by the establishment of new offices. Judicial business had so increased that once more the consuls needed help. This was provided by the creation of the post of *praetor urbanus,* city praetor. This official, like the consuls and unlike the censors or quaestors, possessed the imperium. He served primarily as a judge, but he could also take over the municipal administration when both consuls were absent from the city, and the imperium also gave him the right to command troops. The praetor was annually elected by the comitia centuriata.

Another innovation was the establishment of the aedileship. The post of aedile was not new to the Romans. The unofficial plebeian assembly had been choosing for some time two assistants to the tribunes of the people who bore the title of aedile. About 370, however, four aedileships were added to the offices of the regular government. Each year two patrician and two plebeian aediles were elected. As a board of four, they were given the responsibility for the *cura urbis,* the care of the city (of Rome). They supervised the grain supply, the markets, the various festivals and games, and the upkeep of public buildings and streets. The division of two patrician and two plebeian aediles clearly represented a compromise between the warring factions.

It is possible to interpret the subsequent expansion of Rome in the fourth century B.C. as an effort to find a solution for the land problem. It will be remembered that in the case of the majority of the Greek states, overpopulation and land hunger had been solved by colonization. This course was not practical in Italy at this late date; hence the Romans were forced to resort to the alternative policy of conquest.

Nevertheless, dissatisfaction over the debt situation and the land question continued to grow until 287 B.C. (immediately after the close of the Samnite Wars), when the most serious of the plebeian revolts occurred. On this occasion the plebeians banded together and threatened to secede from the state unless the patricians yielded to their demands. Once again the patricians were forced to make concessions. A debt moratorium was declared, and new governmental reforms of great significance were instituted.

The settlement of 287 B.C. made the Roman government a democracy. All former constitutional distinctions between patricians and plebeians were wiped out. The old unofficial plebeian assembly was reorganized and set up beside the comitia curiata and the comitia centuriata as a third official assembly. It was called the *comitia tributa* because its organization was based upon the tribe.[3] Both plebeians and patricians were eligible to participate in the comitia tributa; this body elected the tribunes and could make laws. The legislative measures passed by it were still called plebiscites, but the senatorial power to reject these measures was abolished. The important fact about the comitia tributa, however, was that it was a democratic body; each man's vote, regardless of his wealth or social position, was equal in weight to that of any other citizen.

In 287 B.C. the tribunes were given new powers. They were allowed to attend the meetings of the senate, and they could interpose a veto to halt any legislative action in the senate or any of the three assemblies. The tribunes were thus included in the Roman constitutional machinery.

The Roman government of 287 B.C. was a democracy—at least in theory. The constitutional distinction between patrician and plebeian had been

---

[3] As a result of Roman expansion in Italy, new tribes had been created. In 287 there were twenty-seven tribes in addition to the four original ones. The maximum number of tribes, thirty-five, was reached about 240 B.C. Each citizen was assigned to a particular tribe, and membership in a tribe became a badge of citizenship.

eliminated. There was no legal barrier to prevent any man from holding any office, and in the comitia tributa the vote of a poor man carried as much weight as that of a rich one. For the second time in the history of the world a large and important state had traveled the rough road from oligarchy to democracy; Athens, of course, had been the first. It is interesting to note, too, that at Rome, as at Athens, the democracy could support itself upon an imperialistic base.

Nevertheless, the theoretical Roman democracy never materialized into actuality, and the Roman government did not advance beyond the timocratic stage. Subsequent developments, both internal and external, were responsible for this rather surprising outcome, and we shall consider them in some detail in the next chapter.

Chapter 20

THE ROMAN CONQUEST
OF THE MEDITERRANEAN
(264-133 B.C.)

B Y 265 B.C. the successes of the Romans in Italy had given rise to a spirit of imperialism which grew increasingly strong as the years passed. Rome's only rival in the west was Carthage, and it was almost inevitable that the two states should become enemies. The Romans seemed to think that Carthage constituted a threat to their independence, but their feelings of mistrust and enmity toward the Carthaginians were certainly encouraged by the Greeks of southern Italy who were now the subjects and allies of Rome. These Greeks had long desired the destruction of Carthage in order to further their own commercial expansion. Moreover, the Greeks in Sicily whose freedom was menaced by Carthage had begun to regard Rome as a potential protector.

The immediate cause for the first contest between Rome and Carthage was provided by the affair of the Mamertini, the former mercenaries of Agathocles who had taken up piracy in the straits between Sicily and Italy. The Mamertini had sought Carthaginian aid in repelling a punitive attack emanating from the Sicilian Greeks, but the cure had proved worse than the disease, for the Mamertini then had to ask Rome to rid them of the Carthaginians. By acceding to this request, the Romans precipitated the First Punic War (264–241 B.C.).

The Romans became involved in the First Punic War with little thought of the implications or consequences of their action. The senate had balked at accepting an alliance with the Mamertini, but the comitia centuriata voted for war. The Romans had always prided themselves on their devotion to *fides,* fidelity or integrity, but they were the aggressors in this

337

war, and they broke a treaty of alliance with Carthage to join people who had recently been judged the common enemy of Carthage and Rome. Later Romans who wrote the history of their country had to disregard a number of facts and perform violent literary gymnastics to explain how the war guilt should rest on the shoulders of the Carthaginians.

In 264 Rome managed to get a relieving force across the straits from Italy to Messana in spite of the Carthaginian navy. The enemy was driven from Messana, but then the Romans found themselves under a double siege which was conducted independently by the Syracusans and Carthaginians. Another Roman expeditionary force had to be sent to rescue the first one. Messana was saved, and the Romans chased the Syracusans back home. Then Hieron, the Syracusan king, decided it would be more advantageous to fight Carthaginians than Romans, so he made an alliance with Rome.

The events of the First Punic War are interesting enough but not sufficiently important to engage lengthy attention here. The war was long because the combatants had no common battleground. At the beginning of the war the Romans had a big army and the Carthaginians a big navy. In order to beat the Carthaginians the Romans had to build and man ships. This took several years, but it took even longer before the Romans learned to sail the new vessels. They could win battles at sea against the Carthaginians, but Neptune beat the Romans in every encounter. The Carthaginians began the war with 120 "battleships," while the Romans built 150 as a starter. Before the war was over, the Romans had lost 600 vessels: about 450 in storms and the rest in battle. At one point the Romans tried to end the war by invading Africa in imitation of Agathocles, but they lost their whole force. Due to the efforts of Hamilcar Barca, the father of Hannibal, the Romans never fully drove the enemy from Sicily. The final victory came at sea only after a last violent effort which exhausted the Romans; fortunately, the Carthaginians were more exhausted than they and sued for peace.

Under the terms of a treaty signed in 241, Carthage ceded Sicily and its surrounding islands to Rome and agreed to pay an indemnity in installments over a period of twenty years. The Romans had won, but the war had cost them seven times the indemnity imposed upon the Carthaginians; at least 30,000 Roman citizens had lost their lives along with perhaps 200,000 allies. Old noble families were wiped out by the war, for they had provided officers for the army and navy in the long struggle.

Between 240 and 238 Carthage was concerned with a revolt of her mercenary troops. While she was thus engaged, the Romans seized Sardinia. The Carthaginians protested. The Romans declared war anew, and the Carthaginians were forced to purchase a new peace at the price of the cession of Sardinia and Corsica and the payment of another indemnity.

As in the case of the wars of the Athenians and the Peloponnesians in the middle of the fifth century, the First Punic War was not conclusive. The Carthaginians were bitter and revengeful, and the question of supremacy in the western Mediterranean was still undecided. While the Romans busied themselves during the next twenty years fighting pirates in the Adriatic, repelling a new Gallic invasion, and conquering the Po Valley, the Carthaginians quietly prepared for the next war. Hamilcar, the hero of the first war who had also put down the revolt of the mercenaries, went to Spain where he extended Carthaginian territory and trained the hardy Spanish natives for disciplined warfare. After his death the work was continued by Hasdrubal, his son-in-law, and later by his own son, Hannibal.

As the years passed, the Greeks in southern France and northeastern Spain became alarmed at the steady advance of Carthage up the east coast of Spain. They raised a clamor in Rome which moved the Romans to a kind of action. Because their armies were busy elsewhere, the Romans decided to use diplomacy and about 226 signed a treaty which divided eastern Spain into Roman and Carthaginian spheres of influence; the Romans pledged themselves to remain north of the Ebro River, while Carthage promised not to advance above this line.

When Hannibal, the brilliant son of Hamilcar Barca, succeeded to the command in Spain in 221 B.C., he began to move against the Spanish town of Saguntum south of the Ebro. He besieged and captured Saguntum in 219 in spite of strong Roman protests, for it was now disclosed that the Romans had secretly broken the treaty of 226 by allying themselves with Saguntum. A cause for hostilities, in Roman eyes, was thus provided; war was declared against Carthage in 218.

The Second Punic War (218–201 B.C.) was more bitterly contested than the first; it was to be fought, not on the sea, but in Italy, Sicily, Spain, and Africa, and a Roman victory was by no means a foregone conclusion, because of the brilliant generalship of Hannibal. The Roman strategists, with the foresight often characteristic of the military, had planned to fight the Second Punic War very much as they had fought the first one. Rome now ruled the seas; it was to be merely a matter of sending a force to hold Hannibal in Spain while troops were massed in Sicily for an invasion of Africa. Hannibal, however, refused to remain where he was. He passed the Roman army on its way through Gaul from Italy to Spain, crossed the Alps, and entered the Po Valley in 218, where he defeated a superior Roman force sent to oppose him; it is said that the Romans lost three men out of every four in the Battle of the Trebia.

Unfortunately, Hannibal's knowledge of strategy exceeded his skill in diplomacy or his understanding of the situation in Italy. He seems to have had the impression that the Italian allies would welcome him as a deliverer and join him against the Romans. This might have happened, but when Hannibal allied himself with the Gauls, he was regarded as a barbarian, since the Italians hated and feared the Gauls as much as the Romans did; therefore, the Italians remained on the Roman side.

In 217 Hannibal out-generalled the Romans again at Lake Trasimene.

In this crisis the Romans chose Quintus Fabius Maximus as dictator.[1] Fabius instituted a new strategy: he cautiously followed Hannibal around Italy, picking off the stragglers and laying waste the land so that Hannibal found it difficult to provision his army. At one point Fabius trapped Hannibal and might have destroyed him, but in an excess of caution he allowed Hannibal to slip away. As the Romans regained their confidence, the policy of Fabius was severely criticized. For 216 two consuls, real fire-eaters, were elected who promised to take the offensive and destroy the enemy. The result was the Battle of Cannae in which the Roman army, as usual, was annihilated by Hannibal.

This, for the Romans, was the low point of the war. The Italian towns now began to surrender to Hannibal; Tarentum fell, and Rome might have been taken by Hannibal if he had been aware of its weakness; Roman losses in Spain had been appalling; in Sicily the great city of Syracuse abandoned its alliance with Rome and went over to Carthage in 213. *If* Philip V, King of Macedon, who had become the ally of Hannibal in 215, had not been detained by fighting in Greece and had been able to aid Hannibal in Italy, and *if* the Carthaginian fleet, which remained intact during the war, had been willing to risk bringing reinforcements to Hannibal at Tarentum, the Carthaginians could have won the Second Punic War and the whole course of Western history to the present would have been quite different.

But none of these things happened. Syracuse was taken in 212 B.C. in spite of the infernal machines for its defense provided by the great scientist Archimedes. By 210 the Romans had discovered a great commander, Scipio, later called Africanus, who began to win battles in Spain. Without reinforcements Hannibal had been reduced to impotence in Italy. In 207 the remnants of the Carthaginian army in Spain made a desperate attempt to join forces with Hannibal in Italy, but one Roman force held Hannibal in the south while another met and defeated the Carthaginian invasion of the Po Valley. Then Scipio led an invasion of Africa. Carthage sued for peace, but with the return of Hannibal from Italy, the fighting in Africa was renewed. A final decisive battle was fought at Zama in 202 in which Hannibal and Scipio, two great generals, opposed one another for the first time. Though Hannibal fought with his customary skill, his troops were not equal to those of the Romans. The defeat of Carthage was at last a fact.

Under the harsh terms of the peace concluded in 201, the Carthaginian navy ceased to exist, Carthage was assessed a huge indemnity, and the Carthaginians were forbidden to go to war without the consent of Rome; all territory was lost to Carthage except that in its immediate vicinity in

---

[1] Under the Roman system, when the state was in great peril, governmental affairs might be placed in the hands of an official called the dictator. The dictator outranked even the consuls, and the appointment of such an official meant the declaration of martial law. The dictator was supposed to resign as soon as the crisis had passed; under any circumstances, his term expired within six months.

Africa. Yet while the Carthaginians had lost the war and their empire, there were compensations: no longer did they have to bear the expense and trouble of defending and governing an empire; now they could devote themselves wholeheartedly to trade, and the Romans could assume all the responsibilities of empire while the Carthaginians made money, their primary objective from the very beginning.

Rome, the winner, was supreme in the West; she had acquired an empire outside of Italy which must be governed and protected. The Punic Wars had extremely important effects upon Roman political, social, economic, and cultural life; few of these effects were beneficial, as we shall see. Perhaps the most serious result of all was that the Romans came out of the Punic Wars with a belligerent imperialistic attitude, and the idea soon became well established that an empire could be a source of profit to individuals. It seemed to follow from this that the larger the empire became, the greater the profits that could be made.

No sooner had the Second Punic War ended than the Romans received an appeal from the Ptolemies and Pergamenes for aid against the impending coalition of Philip V of Macedon and Antiochus the Great, the Seleucid king. The Romans did not wish to fight Antiochus and Philip simultaneously, so they sent a message of friendship to the former and an ultimatum to Philip ordering him to leave the Greeks alone and submit his differences with them to arbitration. Philip, who had no love for the Romans, of course refused and was promptly beaten in a short campaign (200–197). The freedom with which the Romans now promised to provide the Greeks was disagreeable to the Aetolians who soon invited Antiochus to dispense a different variety of liberty—freedom from the Romans. The Romans did not take kindly to Antiochus' invasion of Greece, nor were they complacent about the fact that Hannibal had fled from Carthage to join the Seleucids. Either because there was jealousy on the Seleucid general staff or because someone thought that Hannibal, being a Carthaginian, could manage the Phoenicians who provided the backbone of the Seleucid fleet, the great ability of Hannibal was not utilized in the new war: he was made an admiral and did very poorly. Antiochus and his generals, however, did not outshine Hannibal; the Seleucids were driven from Greece, beaten in Asia Minor, and forced to conclude a humiliating peace (187). A new Macedonian War (171–167) resulted in the defeat of Perseus, Philip's son, by the Romans; Macedonia was split up into four independent republics. At the same time the Seleucids under Antiochus IV were cowed by the mere appearance of a Roman ambassador, and the Achaeans were forced to give hostages to Rome.

A final revolt in Macedonia and Greece (149–146) was put down with great severity. Macedonia was made a Roman province, Corinth was destroyed, and Greece lost all but a nominal independence. When Attalus III of Pergamum bequeathed his kingdom to Rome in 133 B.C., a base

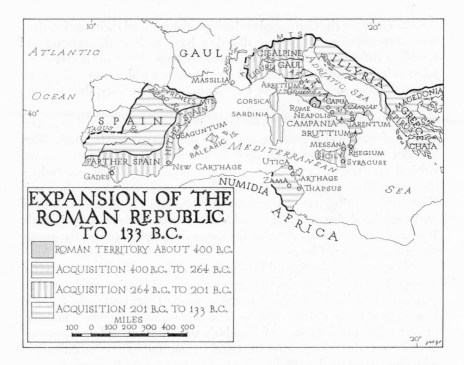

EXPANSION OF THE
ROMAN REPUBLIC
TO 133 B.C.

ROMAN TERRITORY ABOUT 400 B.C.
ACQUISITION 400 B.C. TO 264 B.C.
ACQUISITION 264 B.C. TO 201 B.C.
ACQUISITION 201 B.C. TO 133 B.C.

MILES
100   0   100 200 300 400 500

was provided for expansion into the Near East where Rome was already powerful; even at that time Egypt was virtually a Roman protectorate, the Seleucids were confined to Syria and weakened by dynastic struggles, and only the Hellenized native kingdoms of Bithynia and Pontus enjoyed real independence.

The most striking example of Roman imperialism was provided by the treatment accorded to Carthage. Carthage had become very prosperous after the Second Punic War. Her exports of wine and oil provided serious competition for similar Italian products in the western market. A desire to eliminate this competition and to gain control of the rich land around Carthage led the Romans to seek the termination of Carthaginian independence. A cause for hostilities was discovered by the Romans in 149. The case is an interesting one:

During the Second Punic War the Romans had enlisted the aid of fierce Numidian tribes whose territory bordered on that of Carthage. After the war the Romans had encouraged the Numidians to continue their raids on Carthaginian land. Under the terms of the treaty of 201 the Carthaginians had been forbidden to make war without the consent of Rome. When at last the Carthaginians could endure Numidian depredations no longer, they asked permission to engage in reprisals. The Roman reply was an ultimatum to the Carthaginians to abandon Carthage and move ten miles inland. Carthage closed its gates and prepared to defend itself against the inevitable Roman attack. For three years the Romans besieged Carthage, and in 146 the city was finally taken. Its walls and buildings were destroyed, the site was plowed up, cursed, and sown with salt, and the Carthaginians were sold into slavery. Their territory became the Roman province of Africa.

By 133 B.C. the Roman Empire was already large with a province in Sicily, a combined province of Sardinia and Corsica, two provinces in Spain, and others in Macedonia and Africa as well as one about to be formed in Asia (Minor). When Rome first acquired her empire outside of Italy, her administration of it left much to be desired. The great Roman imperial system so much admired by later generations was the product of a long evolution; in its beginnings it was very crude. The Romans always felt that their empire owed them a living; although their methods of provincial administration were eventually softened and humanized, the ruthless exploitation of the provinces during the republican period cannot be glossed over.

In order to understand the genesis of Roman provincial administration one must first consider the means by which Roman control was extended over Italy. In 265 B.C. the land of Italy could be divided into two categories: (1) the territory which belonged to Rome, and (2) that which belonged to Rome's allies.

1. Within the Roman domain lived the citizens and the subjects of Rome. Among the citizens were those who had full civic rights and those who enjoyed private rights; the latter group lacked the right to vote and to hold office. The full citizens lived in or near Rome or else in the so-called Roman colonies, small garrison communities established at strategic points throughout the peninsula. The second class of citizens (those with private rights) were the inhabitants of the communities of the old Latin League or other communities that had been incorporated into the Roman state under special terms.

2. The allies of Rome were divided into two groups: (a) the Latin allies, and (b) the Italian allies.

(a) The Latin allies were, in part, the people of the few towns of the Latin League that had been spared subjection at the end of the fourth-century conflict between Rome and the league. The rest of the Latin allies were the inhabitants of the so-called Latin colonies. Some of these colonies had been established before the war with the league; they consisted of settlers furnished partly by Rome and partly by the league. After the league lost its independence to Rome, colonies classed as Latin continued to be established by the Romans. The Latin colonies had local self-government, and the colonists could trade and intermarry with the Romans; they were bound to furnish military contingents to aid Rome, and their foreign relations were handled by the Roman government.

(b) The other communities of Italy were the Italian allies of Rome. Each community had a treaty of alliance with Rome by which it was bound to furnish military aid and to give its foreign relations into Roman hands. Local self-government was retained; trade (and often intermarriage) with Romans was allowed.

The political patchwork which the Romans fostered in Italy—the policy of "divide and rule"—was also to be found in the Roman provinces outside the Italian peninsula, although in the provinces it was of a somewhat different character. Each province was an aggregate of three classes of communities: (1) free and federate, (2) free and non-tributary, and (3) tributary.

1. The free and federate communities were the allies of Rome. They retained their own forms of government, paid no tribute, and were bound to aid Rome only in time of war.

2. The free and non-tributary communities paid no tribute, enjoyed local self-government, and were limited only by having surrendered their foreign relations to Rome. It was true, however, that the privileges extended to these communities might be revoked and that the Roman authorities might interfere with their local affairs.

3. The tributary provincial communities were the most common. The inhabitants were Roman subjects; they kept their local governmental institutions, but they were subject to direction by Rome and also had to pay tribute.

The early Roman provincial governors were called *praetors*. It will be recalled that a praetor was a Roman magistrate who ranked just below the consuls. Originally the praetorship was essentially a municipal office at Rome. The first praetorship was that of the *praetor urbanus* (city praetor), a judicial official who might also assume the duties and powers of a consul if both consuls happened to be absent from Rome or incapacitated. Somewhat later appeared the *praetor peregrinus* who handled cases involving both Roman citizens and foreigners. When Rome acquired her first provinces about the middle of the third century B.C., new praetorships were established in order to provide provincial governors. After 146 B.C., however, when the number of provinces continued to grow, it was not felt advisable to add to the number of praetors—there were already six. Instead, all the praetors became judicial officials, and men who had served one-year terms as consuls or praetors at Rome were sent to the provinces as proconsuls and propraetors.[2]

---

[2] As early as 325 B.C. the Romans had discovered the inconvenience of one-year terms for their chief executives. A consul was supposed to relinquish his authority promptly at the expiration of his year of office. In the case of a crucial military campaign, the Romans might thus find themselves in the proverbial position of changing horses in the middle of a stream if they had to withdraw a successful commander and replace him with one whose ability was an unknown quantity. Therefore, they instituted promagistracies; in other words, the successful commander's term of office might be extended for a definite period beyond the one-year limit. The provincial governorships of the proconsuls and the propraetors established after 146 B.C. represented an elaboration of this principle.

The provincial governor, whether a praetor or a promagistrate of the type described above, was charged with the defense and the civil and judicial administration of his province; he also had to see that the provincial tribute (*stipendium*) was sent to Rome. The actual collection of the tribute was usually performed by the equestrian *publicani* who then turned it over to the governor.[3]

The Roman provincial system had many faults. In the first place, the governors ordinarily served only one-year terms. This meant that a governor would barely have time to acquaint himself with the problems of his province before his term came to an end; consequently, few advances could be made and few abuses corrected even if he were conscientious. More often than not, however, the governor was not conscientious. He looked upon his governorship as a great opportunity to reimburse himself for the heavy expenses which he had incurred in gaining his election to office, or he hoped to accumulate enough money to run for a higher post. The governor's expenses were paid by the state, but he received no salary. Nevertheless, there were abundant opportunities for making a fortune in the provinces. The governor might accept presents or bribes; he might resort to extortion and confiscation; or he might close his eyes to the rapacity of the *publicani* and be well paid for doing so.

It was difficult for the senate to restrain the governors. They were too far away to be carefully watched, and they might wilfully disregard the instructions issued by the senate. As a matter of fact, the senators were inclined to overlook provincial abuses. Some of the senators might themselves have been provincial governors, and hence they would hesitate to condemn one of their colleagues for following precedents which they had already set; or perhaps some of them hoped to become governors in the future, and they would not want to abolish practices that might some day prove lucrative to themselves. Moreover, they felt no great sympathy for the downtrodden provincials, mere foreigners whose discomfort really did not matter.

The provincials had little hope of redress for their grievances. They could send deputations to Rome, but there was only a small chance for reform in such cases. The best course was to find some powerful senator who would act as the patron of their province, some man who had a grudge against the governor and would be glad of the opportunity to prosecute him for maladministration. Occasionally a wayward governor would be tried by the comitia tributa, but the percentage of convictions was small. After 149 B.C. a senatorial court was set up at Rome to try cases of extortion; when a governor was tried by a court of his senatorial colleagues, however, the weight of sympathy was bound to be on his side.

In addition to the maladministration current in the provinces, there was also complaint regarding the system of taxation and tax collecting. Taxes

---

[3] For a definition of the equestrians as a class, see below p. 349.

were collected in kind or in money. A fixed sum might be levied upon a province, or the tribute might consist of ten per cent of the annual yield. The former system was hard on the provincials in that a bad harvest might cause great suffering. The *publicani,* moreover, tried to secure as much revenue from a province as was possible, and a compliant governor might allow them to extort fabulous sums. When a province was unable to meet the demands of the *publicani,* these astute businessmen might then advance loans to the provincials which were to be repaid at exorbitant rates of interest. All in all, the lot of the subjects of Rome in the early period was not enviable.

It has already been mentioned that the Punic Wars affected the politics, lives, and culture of the Romans. The expansion into the eastern Mediterranean intensified changes brought about by the earlier conflict in the west. One very serious consequence of continued warfare and imperial expansion was the lamentable demise of the Roman democracy which had been at least incipient in 287 B.C. This phenomenon merits careful analysis.

It is not easy to explain the failure of Roman democracy in simple terms. Important factors in its lack of success were the long foreign wars which Rome undertook in the period 282–146 B.C., the social changes occurring during the same period, and the course followed by Italian economic history after 287 B.C. These factors all contributed to the decline of the old plebeian element (the only group which had the interests of the democracy at heart) and the rise of a new element, a senatorial aristocracy of large landholders (both patrician and plebeian), that wanted to monopolize the government.

Between 282 and 146 B.C. Rome was almost constantly at war with foreign powers. As a result, the attention of the majority of the citizens was concentrated upon external rather than internal affairs, and little attempt was made to consolidate the democratic advance of 287 B.C. More important, perhaps, was the fact that the foreign relations of Rome were handled by the senate; the chronic state of war helped to increase the prestige of the senate, and there was a corresponding decline of the popular assemblies.

The supremacy of the senate might not have had serious results, however, if this body had not been monopolized by a particular social and economic class: the great landholders. A senatorial class, limited in size and hereditary in membership, was built up by these great landholders during the third century B.C. There were several reasons for the growth of a senatorial class. In the first place, a man became a senator by virtue of election to one of the higher governmental offices. Competition for these posts was strong, and the successful candidate was usually the one who could buy the most votes—either by direct bribery, or by winning the good will of the poor citizens by staging magnificent public games or distributing cheap grain. A poor man had little chance of winning an election unless he found a rich backer. From this it will be seen that one important qualification for the senate was the possession of considerable wealth. In the second place, senators were forbidden by law to engage in trade or industry. Since one needed wealth to run for office, few but the wealthy landholders could afford to go into politics; rich traders or manufacturers could not neglect their business enterprises for politics. It was very seldom that any person other than one of the landed gentry made his way into the senate.[4]

Naturally, the senatorial class did not favor democratic government, nor did their general interests harmonize with those of the other citizens of Rome. Democracy might have advanced, however, if it had not been for circumstances which produced the decline and partial extinction of the old plebeian families. The backbone of plebeian resistance to oligarchy had been provided by the sturdy Roman peasants, the small farmers. Unfortunately, during the Second Punic War much of the agricultural land of Italy was laid waste by Hannibal. Moreover, the Roman farmers were called away from their fields to serve in the army, and the land deteriorated in their absence. After the war many of those who returned to their small farms discovered that they could no longer make a living from agriculture. This was partly due to the condition of the soil, but it was also difficult for the Italian farmers to compete with the low-priced grains which now came from Sicily. Not only was Sicily within the Roman economic sphere, but the island was also a Roman province that paid a tribute of grain to the Roman government, and this grain was sold at Rome much below the market price. The small farmers therefore tended to desert their lands or to sell out to large landholders. The large landholders, on the other hand, found it profitable to plant olive orchards and vineyards or to establish great ranches, whereas the small farmers did not have the capital necessary for these operations. Italy became a land of large estates worked by tenants and slaves, and in some areas the peasant almost disappeared from the scene.

It is altogether possible that even if the small farmers had not been wiped out by war and economic changes, the Roman democracy might not have functioned properly, for in order to exercise their political rights of suffrage and legislation, citizens had to be present at Rome, and the lower-class group that was best able to attend the meetings of the assemblies was the urban proletariat of Rome itself. The urban proletariat, as we shall see, became an important political and social group in Rome after 287 B.C., but its devotion to its own peculiar and selfish interests prevented it from accomplishing anything worth while. Actually, it helped to destroy the democracy.

The proletarian class was composed of the poor citizens and the lower-income groups which might be called a lower middle class (but not a bour-

---

[4] Between 233 and 133 B.C. Rome had 200 consuls; a mere 20 senatorial families provided 159 of these officials.

geoisie). These people lived at Rome, and their ranks were swelled by the bankrupt farmers who deserted their lands and came to the capital where they might eke out a precarious existence by selling their votes to the Roman politicians and perhaps finding a day's labor here and there. Added to these (particularly after 200 B.C.) were the new citizens, emancipated slaves and aliens, many of whom were bound to senatorial families as clients. This last group of the proletariat was loyal to the senatorial class rather than to its own, and its vote might be cast in opposition to proletarian interest.

The real interest of the proletarians, however, was not in the welfare of the state or in democracy, but in food and entertainment. As a group they were unpredictable, restless, often riotous, and always hungry for grain and clamorous for amusement at state expense. They constituted a serious problem; and to keep them in some kind of order the policy of "bread and circuses," cheap grain and free entertainment, was introduced. Free grain came later, and the games which accompanied the Roman festivals became more and more elaborate—and more frequent.[5] The proletarians came to feel that the government owed them a living; the power of their votes elected the magistrates and decided legislation, and they felt that they should be paid in some way for performing their civic duty of voting. Naturally, they opposed the extension of Roman citizenship to Rome's subjects and allies because they did not wish to share with others the material blessings of Roman suffrage. If more people were admitted into the state as citizens, the votes of the proletarians would have less cash value.

The senatorial class tolerated, yet despised, the proletariat. It was easy enough to buy the proletarian vote in most cases; if matters came to a showdown, the loyal vote of the senatorial clients among the proletariat could be relied upon. Moreover, the tribunes, who were supposed to represent the masses, no longer served their original purpose. Members of the wealthy group, as well as poor citizens, could now hold the tribuneship, and one tribune hostile to the interests of the "people" could block an action by the use of his veto.

It might be thought that the increase in the volume of trade and commerce and the growth of industry which Italy experienced after 287 B.C. might have afforded some relief to the small Roman farmers who were forced out of agriculture. Unfortunately, trade and industry were monopolized by Greeks and Italians who were not Roman citizens; although the expansion of industry demanded many more skilled workers, few Romans were qualified for such activities and the new jobs were filled by imported slaves.

---

[5] The early games had consisted of horse and chariot races. In the third century, however, gladiatorial contests were introduced. The gladiators were especially trained slaves; the Romans seem to have borrowed the idea from the Etruscans. A variation of the gladiatorial combat was the wild beast hunt which also took place in the arena.

Reference to the new trade and industry brings us to a consideration of a third social and economic class of Roman citizens which appeared after 287 B.C.: the equestrians. The equestrians were wealthy men not of the senatorial class; their census ranking was very high, but they were not office-holders. For the most part, this class grew up during the Punic Wars when enterprising men amassed great fortunes through contracts to supply the Roman armies with food and munitions. Public works contracts also proved lucrative. Later, when Rome acquired her empire outside of Italy, groups of equestrians called *publicani* formed companies which bid for the right to collect provincial taxes; the equestrians would guarantee the state a certain amount, and whatever else they might collect was clear profit. Other equestrian companies obtained contracts to work state mines and to exploit other imperial resources. Once the equestrians were able to build up reserves of capital through these ventures, they could invest in trade and industry. Because the equestrian class fed upon state contracts, the class itself was necessarily interested in politics. The equestrians came to resent the senatorial monopoly of the government, and particularly after 133 B.C., they embarked upon a fierce struggle with the senatorial class for control of the state. As a matter of fact, both the Romans and modern authorities agree in stating that the real turning point in the history of the equestrian class came with the acquisition by Rome of rich territory in the Near East, beginning with the organization of the Kingdom of Pergamum into the province of Asia.

Turning to the cultural changes of the period in question, it may be observed that before 300 B.C. the Romans were largely a simple, hardy nation of farmers whose cultural level was far below that of the more sophisticated Greeks and Carthaginians. The social organization of the Romans closely resembled that of the Greeks of the Dark Ages. The family and the clan were the main elements, and the patriarchal system was even more fully developed than in Greece. The Roman ideal was dignified, austere behavior coupled with great piety. Stress was laid upon devotion to the state. The Romans were tremendously conservative: ancestral custom guided them in everything, and any departure from the norm was regarded as in bad taste. The essentially agrarian character of Roman psychology was shown by the fact that they particularly stressed the virtue of economy, endurance, and hard-headed practicality.

The early religion of the Romans included magical, totemistic, and animistic elements. Great attention was paid to ritual; the Romans did not beg favors of their gods; instead, they made contracts with them. It was not long, however, before the Romans began to borrow from the religions of their neighbors. The Etruscans were early and important contributors: the practice of divination, the idea of the sacred boundary (pomerium), and ideas about the gods were borrowed from them by the Romans. The first

Roman temples, set on high podia, and early cult images were of Etruscan origin. Etruscan gods were included in the Roman pantheon. Later, another element was added when Greek influences began to invade the religious life of Rome. Greek mythology was important, and the mystery religions were introduced.

The Greek influences came into Rome with greatest force after 300 B.C., when contact with the Greeks of the south and in Sicily began to have its effect. When the Romans extended their sway into the eastern Mediterranean region, Rome became thoroughly Hellenized. Not only Greek religion and mythology but also Greek habits and customs, art, literature, and philosophy were adopted, especially by the senatorial and equestrian classes. The old Roman simplicity of life was exchanged for a new luxury and sophistication. Conservative Romans of the old school, like Cato the Censor, tried to stem the rising tide of Hellenism; they inaugurated sumptuary legislation limiting the display of wealth, and they loudly condemned Greek culture in all its social and intellectual aspects, but to no avail. Educated Romans began to learn to read and write Greek, and even Cato took up Greek in his old age.

It should not be forgotten that the composition of the Roman people was also undergoing great changes in this period. The old plebeian stock had been dying out, and the new citizens were non-Romans—Greeks, Etruscans, Italians, Semites, and others—many of whom were the descendants of slaves and conquered peoples who had been brought to Rome. By 150 B.C. it might be said with some justification that the Romans were no longer Romans; hence it is not surprising that under such conditions we should find great cultural changes taking place.

The effect of Greek cultural penetration is shown most clearly in the case of Latin literature. Before 240 B.C. the Romans could hardly have been said to have a literature. There were uses to which writing was put, to be sure, for there were laws, treaties, and other governmental documents as well as religious and business records. Each great clan had pseudohistorical writings in which were recorded the deeds of the ancestors of the clansmen; epitaphs were inscribed on tombs, but there was little else that might be classed as literary composition. The Romans did have poetry and impromptu plays, and oratory was of great importance; nevertheless, this type of expression was transmitted orally and was not ordinarily committed to writing.

In the second half of the third century B.C. the Romans began to create a literature based upon Greek models. In 240 B.C. Livius Andronicus, who had been brought to Rome as a slave from Tarentum many years before, produced a play of the Greek type written in Latin for the Roman games which celebrated the end of the First Punic War. Andronicus' major accomplishment, however, came later when he translated the *Odyssey* into Latin. A young contemporary of his was Cnaeus Naevius, a native of Capua, who wrote tragedies, comedies, and historical plays; he is best known for his epic poem on the First Punic War. At the end of the century came Plautus and Ennius. Plautus wrote over one hundred comedies; his plots were drawn largely from the works of the famous Greek comedy writer, Menander. Ennius wrote plays based upon Greek models, and also a great epic dealing with Roman history down to the end of the Second Punic War. Ennius and Plautus were by far the most distinguished of these early writers. The comedies of Plautus were very popular and are still read and sometimes performed today; it is not unusual to see Plautus' *Menaechmae* and its derivative, Shakespeare's *Comedy of Errors,* as a twin bill. The epic poem of Ennius, though now lost except for some fragments, apparently possessed great literary qualities.

In the second century B.C. flourished the tragedians Pacuvius and Lucius Accius and the comic writer Statius Caecilius. The works of these later writers were more polished and sophisticated than those of their predecessors, but the use—one might say the plundering—of Greek plays was characteristic even of them. The climax of this development of drama in Latin literature was reached in the works of P. Terentius Afer (Terence) whose excellence was such that it could not be surpassed by his contemporaries or successors, or appreciated except by a select group of intellectuals.

One of the most significant writers in the first half of the second century was Cato the Censor, often called the "Father of Latin Prose," who wrote on Roman history, on agriculture, and on oratory. Cato was not the first to write Roman history; before him (about 215 B.C.) Quintus Fabius Pictor and others had compiled brief chronicles or annals written in Greek. Cato, however, wrote in Latin, an example which was followed by his successors.

Cato's *De Agricultura* is informative as to the methods of Italian agriculture after the Punic Wars; it also tells much about Cato himself. Cato's interest was in farming for profit; he stressed the importance of diversification, and he was full of suggestions about new and productive methods. Efficiency was an obsession. He proclaimed that the master should have the selling rather than the buying habit: old slaves and old animals should be disposed of when their usefulness was over. "Though work stops, expenses go on," was one of his favorite maxims, exceeded in popularity only by the more famous "Delenda est Carthago."

Cato, like many later important literary figures, was prominent in politics. He held all the curule offices, from the quaestorship through the consulship, and even attained the censorship, a difficult feat, in 184. It is amusing that Cato as censor abandoned the principles of integrity and thrift which he had so loudly preached through the years: he used his office to play politics, and he spent six million denarii (of government money, of course) on public works. Cato hated the Carthaginians, because their oil and wine were in competition with his, and he hated the Greeks and the new Hellenism which was invading Roman culture. Athough he was a thorough reactionary, he might have felt a little more kindly toward the Greeks if his political rivals, the Scipio family, had not been completely philhellenic. Most especially he hated Scipio Africanus for both personal and political reasons. Scipio had humiliated Cato, with good reason, when the latter was quaestor, and Scipio had taken Ennius away from Cato after Cato had been Ennius' first patron. Cato had his revenge, for he later found ways to persecute Scipio politically, and the great hero died of a broken heart.

The Scipionic circle, in reality an invention of nineteenth-century German scholarship, is the name given to a group of intellectuals associated with Africanus and Scipio Aemilianus, the victor in the Third Punic War. The group included at various times Lucilius, Terence, the orator Laelius, and others, among whom was the Achaean hostage, Polybius, who wrote a great history of Rome in Greek (see above, p. 313). Not only literary but also philosophic interests were represented among these men. Almost the first public interest in Greek philosophy was stimulated by one of the Stoics who came to Rome on a diplomatic mission and was forced to remain in the city longer than he had anticipated because he fell into a Roman sewer and broke his leg.

In the broadest sense, the cultural developments which took place in Rome after 300 B.C., especially after 200, may be characterized simply as the extension of the frontiers of Hellenistic civilization to include the Romans. As creators of civilization the Romans were far less important than the peoples of the ancient Near East and the eastern Mediterranean. The role of the Romans in cultural history was chiefly that of borrowers, adapters, and (later) carriers of culture. From the Etruscans the Romans borrowed some of their religion, art, and political institutions as well as architecture in stone and the use of the arch. From the Greeks came more culture traits in the field of religion and an introduction to literature, the fine arts, philosophy, and science. Greek sculpture and painting exerted an increasing influence upon the Romans after the plundering of Greece (171–146 B.C.), when the conquerors brought home Greek art treasures as part of the spoils. About the same time the Romans began to be attracted by the ethical Greek philosophies, Stoicism and Epicureanism.

It would be most unfair, however, to criticize the Romans for their apparent failure as creators of culture. The major part of this task had been accomplished by others before the Romans had managed to emerge from their Age of Agriculture. In addition, it is only just to point out that, basing their efforts upon the foundations provided by the Greco-Oriental (Hellenistic) civilization, the Romans later made significant contributions, especially to literature and philosophy.

Nevertheless, one ordinarily associates the Romans with the more practical phases of culture, phases in which they made great advances. We shall see later that the Roman forms of municipal government and Roman law were of permanent importance. Roman military organization and science were superior to those of the Hellenistic peoples, and Roman engineering skill, even today, is proverbial. The first of the great Roman roads, the Appian Way (which ran southward from Rome), was built about 312 B.C., and in the years that followed many other highways were constructed. The modern traveller in Italy, France, or Spain can still observe the remains of Roman roads, bridges, aqueducts, and drains; many of these structures have fared well in their struggle with time and are still in use.

Chapter 21

THE LAST CENTURY
OF THE ROMAN REPUBLIC

I N 133 B.C. Rome possessed a considerable empire with a large subject population. During the century that followed, additional territory was obtained; the principal acquisitions were in Asia Minor, Syria, Palestine, Cyprus, Egypt, Cyrene, southern France (Narbonese Gaul), central and northern France (Gallia Comata), and Spain. Since most of the territory held by the Romans bordered upon the Mediterranean Sea, that body of water was important to the empire as a unifying factor, for it provided a means of swift and comparatively easy access to all the provinces. One might say that the Roman holdings in this period constituted a maritime empire; the Romans were later to discover—as the Athenians had discovered in the fifth century B.C.—that a maritime empire was less difficult to hold in subjection than a land empire.

Between 133 and 63 B.C. the Romans were fortunate in that they encountered no really powerful competitors. In this period their only possible rivals were the Seleucids, the Ptolemies, and the kings of Pontus. But the Seleucids were impotent because of dynastic and internal factional strife and the threat of the Parthians on their eastern frontiers, and the Ptolemies had been forced to forswear their imperialism as a result of exhaustion from the Syrian wars of the third century. The kings of Pontus proved vigorous enough, and they were able to stir the Roman provincials in Asia Minor and Greece to revolt; but they were really no match for the military might of Rome.

After 63 B.C., however, when Rome had crushed Pontus and conquered the Seleucids, the Romans found themselves face to face with the Parthians. The Parthians were much more worthy of Roman steel. For nearly three hundred years they threatened the Roman east; if the governmental system of the Roman republic had not been reorganized by Augustus into that of the principate, it is questionable whether the Romans could have continued to hold their eastern provinces.

This brings us to our main subject: the fall of the Roman Republic. As far as the administration of an empire was concerned, the republican system of Rome was unsatisfactory. The Romans were trying to govern an empire by means of a system devised originally for a small city-state. This make-shift arrangement would probably have failed almost immediately if the early Roman Empire had been a land empire and if the Parthians and the Romans had come face to face a hundred years earlier. Fortunately, by the time the Romans began to acquire a land empire and to fight the Parthians, the republican system had ceased to exist except in name.

We have already seen how the acquisition of an empire corrupted the Romans and their government, how imperialism worked havoc upon the old Roman morality and idealism, and how the struggle to gain territory outside of Italy ruined the Roman peasantry. The Roman proletariat, the equestrians, and the senatorial class were, in a sense, the by-products of imperialism. These three classes were now to engage in a struggle for the spoils of empire, a conflict that was to bring the republic to an ignominious end.

In the century of conflict which followed 133 B.C., the participants included not only the three citizen classes, but also two other groups: the Italian allies and the Roman army. The Italian allies sought citizenship and equality with the Romans, while shortly after 100 B.C. the Roman army, which had become a distinct professional group, entered politics in order to seek its best interests.

The army, like the proletariat, was ready to sell itself to the highest bidder. This was a development fraught with great political significance, for whereas before the creation of a professional army a politician might gain certain ends by bargaining with the proletariat to secure votes, much more spectacular results could now be obtained by securing the good will of the army. In dealing with the proletariat one had to keep fairly close to the constitutional forms and work through established governmental channels. By employing the army, on the other hand, might became right, and it was possible to march straight toward one's goal unhampered by constitutional limitations. When a military leader with political aspirations was thus able to make his own rules of the game, the republican constitution had little chance of survival.

After considering the specific aims of all the groups engaged in the struggle for supremacy in Rome, one is surprised that the republic survived as long as it did. The senators grimly defended their monopoly of the high state offices and the senate; in this way they could hold the vast estates that were the source of their wealth, and they could acquire more land. The senators were greatly embarrassed, however, by their financial indebtedness to

355

the equestrians, for many of them had gone to equestrian capitalists to borrow money for political campaigns and other expenses. The equestrians wanted a free hand in exploiting the provinces, and in order to secure this leeway they had to attack the governmental monopoly held by the senators. The proletariat wanted a living; there was some agitation for land, but many proletarians would have been satisfied to have been supported by the state in some way. At any rate, the proletariat always responded to a promise of cheap or free grain or a colonization project. In addition, this group was consistently opposed to any extension of citizenship to Rome's allies or subjects; the Roman masses did not want to share their few privileges with anyone. The Italian allies, as we have already observed, would not be content until they had been given equality and citizenship. Last of all, the army desired not only the plunder of conquest, but also pensions; the veteran soldier usually wanted land so that he could retire comfortably when his term of service was over.

These conflicting aims of the various factions were productive of a series of conflicts that began in 133 B.C. with riots in Rome itself and grew in 90 B.C. to civil war in Italy; soon afterward the whole empire became the battleground of the opposing factions. The almost continuous tumult impressed people with the need for reform. It was obvious that something was fundamentally wrong with the Roman system, and various panaceas were suggested for its ills. There were reactionaries who favored a return to senatorial oligarchy; the equestrians sought timocracy; the proletariat, complete democracy (but no enlargement of the citizen body). A few people like Cicero wanted a coalition of senators and equestrians—timocratic or aristocratic (?) government. Julius Caesar, on the other hand, favored autocracy— a dictatorship, or perhaps an absolute monarchy.

The whole period (133–30 B.C.) is fascinating not only because of its problems and the remedies suggested for them, but also because of the abundance of striking personalities which the age produced. It is interesting to see, however, that in the midst of the political and social confusion, when wars and civil strife interfered with agriculture, commerce, and industry, the frontiers of civilization continued to advance at a slow pace; in the western Mediterranean new peripheral areas were penetrated by Hellenistic culture. At Rome itself, in the heart of the maelstrom, significant and lasting contributions were made to literature and intellectual life.

The most striking features of Roman history in the period from 287 to 133 B.C. are the great wars with the Carthaginians and the Hellenistic kingdoms. As a result, the attention of the student of Roman history is often diverted from the contemporary economic developments which were taking place in Rome itself, and the recurrence of domestic strife in Rome in 133 B.C. appears to come entirely without warning. As a matter of fact, trouble at home had been brewing ever since the Second Punic War, a conflict that

RELIEF SHOWING THE IMPERIAL FAMILY

Courtesy of the Museo Della Civiltà Romana

AUGUSTUS

VESPASIAN

NERO

TRAJAN

HADRIAN

MARCUS AURELIUS

Courtesy of the Glyptothek, Muenchen

THEATER IN AFRICA

Bettman

ARENA IN GAUL

Bettman

HADRIAN'S WALL

Courtesy of the Cambridge University Press

Bettman   *Bettman*

ARCH OF HADRIAN IN ATHENS   GATE AT EPHESUS

Doerner and Goell   *Courtesy of M. I. Rostovtzeff and*
the Yale Dura Expedition

AQUEDUCT OF PISIDIAN ANTIOCH   MAIN GATE OF DURA EUROPUS

had wrought great hardships upon the peasantry. Moreover, in the first half of the second century B.C. the increasing avarice of the equestrians endangered the governmental monopoly of the senatorial class to such an extent that a struggle between these two groups was inevitable. The series of long and expensive wars which preceded 146 B.C. was bound to have an effect upon Roman economic life, and it seems likely that after 146 there was a postwar slump that brought matters to a crisis. Undoubtedly this economic depression reacted as unfavorably upon the senators and equestrians as upon the proletariat, but the masses were also resentful of the severe conscription which the widespread conflicts of 149–146 B.C. had necessitated. Moreover, the passage of a law in 139 B.C. establishing the secret ballot might indicate that the senators, if not the equestrians also, had attempted to intimidate the voters. Therefore, in 133 B.C. when the proletariat found a vigorous leader in Tiberius Gracchus, domestic issues were brought into the foreground.

Tiberius Gracchus was a young nobleman whose mother, Cornelia, was the daughter of Scipio Africanus. Cornelia was a brilliant, well-educated woman who was ambitious for her sons, Tiberius and Gaius, and had devoted much attention to their upbringing. Tiberius, the elder, had embraced the Stoic philosophy with its emphasis upon the brotherhood of man. Despite his close association with the conservative younger Scipio—his brother-in-law and the recent victor over Carthage in the Third Punic War —Tiberius entertained liberal views and had great sympathy for the common people. He feared the possible results of the increase of slavery, and he wished to find some way to restore the free peasantry, the backbone of the Roman army.

In 133 B.C. Tiberius became a tribune. He immediately proposed a plan for the distribution of land to poor Roman citizens with the object of getting the proletarians out of Rome and back on the farms. The land which he proposed to use for this purpose belonged to the state; some of it had been confiscated from Italian communities that had surrendered to Hannibal during the Second Punic War, and some of it had come from other sources, but for many years these resources had been neglected by the government. Much of this state land was in use, however, for many large landholders of senatorial rank whose estates adjoined the government property had been grazing their animals on it and had even brought some of the land under cultivation. After several generations of use these people had come to regard the land as their own. Tiberius could sympathize with the views of these senatorial squatters, and he was ready to deal more than fairly with them. Under the terms of his bill a certain amount of the occupied land could be retained by its users without cost, but the rest was to be made available to the government for redistribution in small plots to new settlers. Proletarian homesteaders would be offered modest holdings; they were to pay rent on the land for a few years, and then they would receive title to it.

At first, the prospects for the plan seemed bright. The senators were inclined to smile indulgently at this enterprising young aristocrat who was so fired with idealistic enthusiasm. But this good feeling was soon lost when Tiberius failed to consult the senate to secure its formal approval of his project; instead, he behaved as if the senators were his enemies and tried to push the land act through the tribal assembly. Now thoroughly angered, the senators arranged to have a conservative tribune named Octavius veto the bill. Tiberius, however, was equal to the occasion; he persuaded the assembly to depose Octavius on the grounds that Octavius had betrayed his trust since he, a tribune, had opposed a measure intended to benefit the people whom he was supposed to represent. When Octavius was thus impeached and removed from office, the land bill was passed and became a law. A judicial board of three—consisting of Tiberius, his brother Gaius, and another relative—was established to carry out a survey of the land and to decide disputes over ownership which might arise. The appropriation to finance the work of the board, however, had to come from the senate which was not in a mood to be co-operative. Tiberius countered by threatening to use money from the treasury of Pergamum, since that rich state had just been willed to Rome. This brought the senators to terms, and the land commission, or board, actually began its work—as we know from inscribed boundary stones which have been found.

Unfortunately for Tiberius, his year of office was nearly over, and the senators had become implacable enemies. They maintained that his deposition of Octavius was unconstitutional—it was, at least, without precedent—and they planned to prosecute Tiberius after the expiration of his tribuneship. This prosecution Tiberius hoped to avoid by seeking re-election, a procedure which was also of undetermined legality. The senate then resorted to violence; bands of rioters, the partisans of the senate and those of Tiberius, fought in the streets of Rome. Tiberius and a large number of his followers were slain in the melee.

For the next decade the senate held the upper hand; but the equestrians, the proletariat, and also the Italian allies were becoming restive. In 123 B.C. Gaius Gracchus, the younger brother of Tiberius and a much more astute politician, became tribune. Gaius obtained the support of the proletariat by reviving Tiberius' land scheme and by securing the passage of bills providing for cheap grain and less severe conscription. He won the equestrians to his side by sponsoring a bill to substitute equestrian for senatorial jurors in the courts which tried provincial officials for extortion; such a change, of course, would give the *publicani* almost a free hand in the provinces, since few senatorial governors would dare to oppose them in the face of almost certain trial and conviction before an equestrian jury. Three other bills endeared Gaius to the equestrians: the first gave them the opportunity to collect the taxes of the rich new province of Asia (the former Pergamene kingdom); the second provided for the establishment of two colonies in Italy and one on the site of Carthage in Africa; the third proposed the construction of new roads in Italy. The commercially minded equestrians were happy at the prospect of a Roman colony on the advantageous site of Carthage, and the contractors anticipated fat contracts for materials to be used in the new roads.

For two years Gaius was the "uncrowned king of Rome." His popularity with the equestrians and the proletariat was so great that the senators did not dare to attack him openly. In 122 B.C. he was re-elected to the tribunate—a law permitting re-election to this office had been passed a few years before. Then Gaius made his mistake: he antagonized his supporters by advocating citizenship for the Italian allies. About the same time he left for Africa to be present at the founding of the Carthaginian colony. During his absence his popularity waned, and the senate began to outbid him for proletarian favor. A senatorial land bill of wider scope and greater liberality than that of Gaius was proposed. Moreover, the senate offered to establish not two, but twelve, colonies in Italy. The senators would not consider giving citizenship to the allies, but they offered to modify the conditions of allied military service.

When Gaius returned to Rome he found that his cause had lost ground. He was not re-elected to the tribuneship for a third term, and gang warfare broke out between his remaining supporters and the senatorial faction. The greater part of the proletariat had been alienated by his plan to enfranchise the allies and had been won over to the opposition by senatorial promises. The equestrians felt that Gaius could do them no more favors, and they too abandoned him. The riots in Rome became so violent that the senate was given an excuse to declare martial law. Gaius and his friends were hunted down by a senatorial posse. Several thousand were killed, and Gaius himself committed suicide. A reward had been offered for the head of Gaius: its weight in gold. The first man to find his body decapitated it, scooped out the brains, and filled the cavity with lead; it weighed almost eighteen Roman pounds.

For more than ten years after the death of Gaius Gracchus the senate ruled unchallenged, until senatorial prestige suffered a severe blow as the result of scandals growing out of a war against Jugurtha, the African king of Numidia. The story began in 118 B.C. when Micipsa, the former king, died. Much against his will, Micipsa had been forced to leave his kingdom to three heirs: two sons and a nephew, Jugurtha. The last could not be omitted from the inheritance because he was extremely popular with the people. Jugurtha was dissatisfied with a threefold division of power; he wanted the whole kingdom. Therefore he killed one of his cousins, and the other fled to Rome where the senate ordered his restoration to Numidia. Shortly after this Jugurtha penned up his surviving cousin in the town of

Cirta where there were also a number of Italian traders. When Cirta fell, these men and Jugurtha's cousin were put to the sword, and in 111 B.C. the Romans sent a force to Africa to punish Jugurtha. Since the Numidians were mounted and the Romans had to march through the desert in heavy armor on foot, Jugurtha proved difficult to catch. At last when he tired of the game and feigned surrender, he bribed the Roman commanders and escaped any real punishment. This caused a great scandal at Rome. There was a senatorial investigation; when Jugurtha was brought to Rome under a promise of safe conduct to testify against the Roman officers, he took advantage of this opportunity to murder a possible rival for his throne while he sojourned in Rome itself. Jugurtha was returned to Africa, and the comedy was resumed; new Roman defeats led to new scandals, new investigations, and the exile of the senatorial commanders involved. In 109 the consul Metellus, a good soldier and a strict disciplinarian, was sent against Jugurtha. Metellus found the army in Africa somewhat lacking in military smartness; this he remedied by long drills, insisting that camp should be made each night in the old Roman manner, and forbidding the legionaries to employ natives to carry their weapons and armor for them. Jugurtha now offered to "surrender," but Metellus could play this game, too; while pretending that peace was in effect, the Romans continued their fighting, at the same time laying waste the land between Numidia and the province of Africa so that Numidian attacks would be made more difficult.

In time the policy of Metellus might have led to victory, but one of his legates, or subordinates, was Gaius Marius, a tough, able, experienced soldier of equestrian status who had already held the praetorship and now aspired to higher office. Marius requested permission to return to Rome in order that he might run for the consulship. Metellus acceded, and Marius sailed for Rome where, with extreme ingratitude, he began to criticize Metellus' conduct of the war intimating that he (Marius) could do much better. As a result, Marius was elected consul for 107 B.C. and appointed to supersede Metellus. He soon made good his promises, despite the fact that the angry Metellus had let the African forces go to pieces; Jugurtha fled into the neighboring kingdom of Mauretania where he sought the aid of its king, Bocchus. Bocchus neither wanted to fight Rome nor to have the popular Jugurtha in his realm, so he conspired with Marius to betray the Numidian. In true cloak-and-dagger style the aristocratic quaestor of Marius, Lucius Cornelius Sulla, penetrated Mauretania in disguise, seized Jugurtha, and brought him out alive. The war was over; Marius returned to Rome in triumph in 105 with Jugurtha as his prisoner.

The triumph of Marius was also a triumph for his class, the equestrian. The senatorial faction was soon pushed further into the background by the new successes of Marius, for he was not long in finding a new field for his talents.

X

While Marius had been in Africa, the Romans had been thrown into a panic by reports of the movements of barbarian tribes, the Cimbri and Teutones, into Narbonese Gaul (southern France) which had been a Roman province since 119 B.C. Ever since the Gauls had sacked Rome in 390 B.C., the Romans had feared a repetition of barbarian invasion from the north. When Marius came back from the Jugurthine War, he was re-elected to the consulship and sent to Narbonese Gaul to repel the expected attack. In preparation, he reorganized the army and also transformed it into a professional body by allowing men to enlist for a sixteen-year period, thus substituting enlistment for conscription. By training his troops well, he inflicted severe defeats upon the barbarians in 102 and 101 B.C. In 100 the hero returned to Rome to enter upon his sixth consulship.

Marius was primarily a military man; he had no talent for political leadership and had to rely upon Roman politicians for aid. He became connected with two demagogues, Saturninus and Glaucia, whose favorite methods were those of mob violence. The activities of these two men became so outrageous that the senate was given an excuse to declare martial law. This maneuvered Marius, who was none too clever about such things, into an impossible position: he was forced to lead a senatorial posse against his own supporters. Saturninus and Glaucia were killed, Marius had to retire from politics, and the senate regained its prestige.

Although Marius proved a miserable failure in the political arena and was not able to consolidate the advances which he had made for his party, he himself was not without significance in the history of Roman constitutional evolution. We have already seen that it was Marius who created the professional Roman army, the group which was later to become a potent force in politics. In addition, he was the first to break the traditional rule against successive consulships. Because he seemed to be the only man who could save Rome, Marius had been allowed to hold the consulship six times in the period between 107 and 99 B.C. This set a precedent to which later aspirants for supreme power were able to appeal. The successive consulships of Marius provide some of the earliest indications of the dissolution of a tradition that had kept the republican constitution intact for several centuries.

Although the senators, equestrians, and proletarians were bitter enemies and each group had its own peculiar aims, there was one point on which all three were agreed: they did not want to extend citizenship to the Italian allies. Ever since the time of Gaius Gracchus the question of Italian enfranchisement had been avoided; the Romans had concentrated their attention upon domestic politics. A few years after Marius' disgrace, however, there appeared a reformer named Marcus Livius Drusus who reopened discussion on the forbidden topic. Drusus was a tribune who had won the favor of the senators by his opposition to the equestrians; he also courted the good will of the proletariat with legislation providing for cheap grain and new colonization. Then, apparently overestimating his popularity and influence, Drusus sponsored a bill to enfranchise the allies. It is not surprising to learn that he was assassinated almost immediately.

The Romans were soon to discover, however, that times had changed. Whereas thirty years before the death of Gaius Gracchus had closed discussion of the question of Italian citizenship, now the murder of Drusus had just the opposite effect. The allies were thoroughly aroused, and they were determined to obtain some kind of a settlement. Even before Drusus had introduced his legislation in their behalf, they had secretly organized their forces. It seems likely that they held little hope that Drusus would succeed; at any rate, as soon as he was murdered, they revolted and set up a government independent of Rome. The war between Rome and the allies (the Social War) was fought in the period between 90 and 88 B.C. As far as the military operations were concerned, the Romans were the victors; but when the war was over, all the allies had been given citizenship —some had been offered civic rights to keep them from joining the revolt, and others had accepted citizenship as the price for laying down their arms. As a consequence of this war, the Roman citizen body was probably more than quadrupled in size.

Both Marius and his former quaestor, Sulla, had been called back into service in the crisis, but Sulla, the most successful general in the Social War and the acknowledged leader of the now dominant senatorial party, was made consul in 88 B.C. Because of his ability and position it was only natural that Sulla should be chosen to take the field against Mithridates, the king of Pontus, who had been quietly gaining influence over the dissatisfied Roman provincials in Asia Minor and Greece. In 88 B.C. Mithridates engineered a general uprising of the provincials in Asia Minor in which eighty thousand Romans were killed. Emboldened by his success, the mainland Greeks invited Mithridates to cross over into Europe to effect their liberation from Roman rule. Despite the opposition of Marius and the equestrians, which was accompanied by a brief civil war in Italy, Sulla managed to retain the upper hand and subsequently left Italy in 87 B.C. to expel Mithridates from Greece. Pontic forces were driven out of Europe, defeated in Asia Minor, and Mithridates was confined to his own kingdom by 84 B.C.

In the meantime, as soon as Sulla had departed from Italy, Marius' party had gained control of the Roman government. Marius himself soon died, but his followers continued in power, instituting a reign of terror in which the senatorial partisans of Sulla in Italy were killed or exiled and their property confiscated. In 83 B.C. Sulla returned to Italy with his veterans of the Mithridatic War. The Marians were driven from the peninsula; some fled to Africa and Sicily, and others to Spain. Only those in Spain escaped immediate punishment; the rest were pursued and destroyed. In Spain, however, the brilliant Marian general Sertorius held the senatorial forces at bay for over a decade.

In Italy Sulla was made dictator and given supreme power to enact laws and reconstitute the republic. He devoted much time to the extermination of his enemies. Wholesale massacres of Marians, or of those suspected of being in sympathy with the party, now took place. Long lists of proscriptions were issued which confiscated the estates of Sulla's opponents and set a price upon the heads of fugitive Marians. Then Sulla embarked upon a reactionary program of legislation calculated to establish the supremacy of the senate in the Roman government. The senate was given the veto power over all legislation, and senators were restored to the jury courts. The powers of the tribunes were curtailed; moreover, it was decreed that if a man held the office of tribune, he should be ineligible for election to any higher post. The distribution of cheap grain was forbidden. His work completed, Sulla retired from public life in 79 B.C. and died the following year.

Sulla had tried to turn back the clock of political evolution, but actually he only arrested it momentarily. Too many groups were opposed to his reforms for any chance of permanence in the arrangements he had made. Numerous adherents of Marius were still alive; equestrians who had not been Marians were much dissatisfied with what Sulla had done; and the proletariat was angered by its loss of political power and cheap grain. Just as soon as Sulla died, there were movements to set aside his reforms. By the end of 70 B.C. few vestiges of his legislation remained.

Nevertheless, Sulla, like Marius, has an important place in Roman constitutional history. Sulla's lengthy dictatorship (82–79 B.C.) provides another illustration of the gradual disintegration of the Roman constitutional tradition. It set a new precedent, and it paved the way for the later absolutism of Julius Caesar. Moreover, Sulla's reforms represented the conservative interpretation of the ills of the Roman government and how they might be remedied.

In the half century after the death of Sulla the Roman Republic came to an end. In this, the last act of the drama, the leading role was played not so much by parties and factions as by individuals. Whereas Tiberius Gracchus, Marius, and Sulla had really been little more than the spearheads of the proletarian, equestrian, and senatorial parties respectively, in the period after 78 B.C. ambitious individuals used the factions as a means to gain personal ends. This statement would not apply to Cicero, but it would certainly be true of Pompey, Crassus, Julius Caesar, Antony, and Octavian. It was not that the various parties were lacking in specific aims, but rather that they lacked the strength to engage in purposeful action. The senatorial party alone possessed sufficient cohesiveness and power to formulate a program and force political leaders to pay some attention to its demands.

As a result, this particular half century is interesting because it is the only period in ancient history in which individuals rather than groups or non-human forces had great power to influence the course of history. A peculiar and unprecedented combination of circumstances was responsible for this phenomenon. The precise point of development that the Roman constitution had now reached, the temper of the proletariat and the other classes, the potential power of the professional army, and a series of external crises were factors which delivered the state into the hands of the ambitious politicians.

After Sulla the first strong man to appear was Cnaeus Pompey. As one of Sulla's supporters, Pompey had helped to drive the Marians from Italy and Africa. In 77 B.C. he was sent to Spain to fight the surviving Marians who had joined Sertorius. This was no easy task, for Pompey was at his best against inferior generals, and Sertorius was anything but second-rate. Pompey had to wait until Sertorius was murdered in 72; after that it was easy enough to triumph over the Marians in Spain.

Just before Pompey returned to Italy, a serious revolt of slaves and gladiators broke out in the vicinity of Naples. Taking refuge on the slopes of Mount Vesuvius, the insurrectionists defeated several Roman armies until one of the praetors for 71, a wealthy equestrian named Crassus, finally broke the back of the rebellion. Pompey entered Italy just in time to intercept a body of the defeated slaves who were trying to escape northward from the peninsula. This was displeasing to Crassus, who had long envied the military prestige of Pompey and had hoped to be able to earn some glory for himself, but this was neither the first nor the last time that Crassus was to find himself in this position.

The low state into which Roman political morals and practice had fallen is well illustrated by what happened next. Pompey and Crassus had been enthusiastic supporters of Sulla when he returned to Italy in 83, yet when they became consuls in the year 70 B.C. they worked together to destroy the last vestiges of Sulla's legislation. In 71 when the elections for the consulship were held, neither Pompey nor Crassus was eligible to run for the office: Pompey had never held any of the offices which led up to the consulship, and Crassus, having been praetor in 71, could not legally be a candidate for the consulship for at least another year. By refusing to disband their armies, however, Pompey and Crassus were able to silence any objection to their candidacy. As an illustration of a certain lack of strong political conviction which was to be characteristic of the later period of the republic, it might be noted that at this time Crassus was the supporter of the senatorial party, while Pompey was supposed to represent the popular faction; within a few years both had changed sides.

Pompey and Crassus had both promised that the power of the tribunes would be restored and the legislative veto of the senate repealed. These promises were fulfilled. In addition, a great scandal paved the way for a reorganization of the jury courts. A man named Verres, who had served three years as a propraetor in the rich province of Sicily, had openly used his position to amass a fortune valued at more than two million dollars. He was reported to have said that his ill-gotten gains of the first year were for himself, those of the second year for his friends, and those of the third year for his jurors. His Sicilian subjects, however, mustered up their courage and brought suit against him for extortion. They made a wise choice in securing a rising young lawyer named Cicero to prosecute their case. Verres was defended by Quintus Hortensius, who had a great reputation in the courts, but Cicero's brilliant conduct of the trial was too much for his opponents. Verres admitted defeat before the trial was over and went into exile. Cicero's reputation was made, and the whole question of the reform of the courts came before the public. In the subsequent reorganization it was decided that the juries would henceforth be composed of equal numbers of senators, equestrians, and *tribuni aerarii* (the next lowest census class).

Shortly afterward the Romans had to find a solution for two pressing problems: piracy had become a serious menace to trade in the eastern Mediterranean, and Mithridates of Pontus had begun to meddle once more in the affairs of the Near East. Both the pirates and Mithridates had been allies of Sertorius, the late opponent of Pompey in Spain. Since their victories over the Seleucids in the first half of the second century B.C. the Romans had allowed their fleet to decline with the result that piracy had increased. For a long time the Romans had been rather complacent about the pirates, since their activities had provided slaves for the public markets in Delos and elsewhere, but when the pirates became so bold as to menace the grain supply of Rome, the proletarian voters felt real concern. Some attempts had been made to restrict the pirates, but none had been successful. Roman operations against Mithridates had been in the hands of Lucullus, who had served as quaestor to Sulla in the earlier war with Mithridates and who was now the governor of Asia. Between 74 and 68 B.C. Lucullus had repelled Mithridates from western Asia Minor and even driven him from Pontus into Armenia, but then Lucullus' soldiers had mutinied, and Mithridates had been able to renew the war with vigor. The real secret of Lucullus' troubles was not that he was a poor general, but that he had earned the hatred of the equestrian investors in Rome by attempting to protect the provincials in Asia from their depredations. It was equestrian agents who had agitated against Lucullus in his military camps and brought about the mutiny.

At Rome people began to say that if the pirates were to be driven from the seas and Mithridates humiliated, the Romans must send out their most outstanding general, Pompey. The senators, however, mistrusted Pompey because he was allied with the equestrians and the proletariat, a coalition known as the *Populares*. Nevertheless, there was no choice, and Pompey became the recipient of a special command against the pirates. His power derived from a bill sponsored by a tribune named Gabinius; the measure, known as the Gabinian Law, was passed in 67 B.C., and it conferred upon a general of consular rank supreme power over the Mediterranean Sea and all Roman territory surrounding it to a distance of fifty miles inland. The appointment was to run for three years, but Pompey proceeded against the pirates with great skill and vigor and broke their power within three months.

The defeat of the pirates pleased the Romans, although they were not so happy about some of the other consequences of Pompey's swift victory. He had a huge fleet and army at his disposal, and his authority would not expire for more than two and a half years. Right at this juncture, however, Lucullus failed in his war with Mithridates, and Pompey's supporters demanded that he should replace Lucullus in Asia Minor. In 66 B.C. a bill was put forward by the tribune Manilius which proposed a command for Pompey in the Mithridatic War. This Manilian Law was backed by Cicero in one of his most famous orations. In a cleverly constructed speech Cicero recalled to his audience the massacre of 88 B.C. which Mithridates had engineered in Asia; then he dwelt upon the losses to the equestrian capitalists which the present war had occasioned; finally, Cicero reviewed the qualifications of Pompey for this new command. The unlucky Lucullus was not mentioned, but when Cicero pointed out that Pompey was a successful commander who was brave and who had control over his troops, he was inferring that Lucullus lacked these qualities.

Within a year's time Pompey had defeated Mithridates and his ally, the king of Armenia. In 64 and 63 B.C. Pompey attacked and annexed the nearly defunct Seleucid kingdom. Its principal territory was soon organized as the Roman province of Syria. A vast amount of plunder was accumulated in these campaigns in the East; the Roman treasury was filled to overflowing, and Pompey's own share of the booty made him the richest man in Rome.

While Pompey covered himself with military glory in the Near East, rich and ambitious Crassus, who had remained in Rome, became more and more envious of the success of his erstwhile colleague. Crassus, fearing that he himself would suffer a political eclipse when Pompey returned, attempted in several ways to secure undisputed control in the politics of the capital. His wealth enabled him to procure the assistance and services of a number of young men who seemed to have political promise; one of his henchmen was Julius Caesar, and another was the infamous Catiline. Among Crassus' schemes was a plan for the annexation of Egypt. The richest country in the Near East, Egypt as a Roman province would provide cheap grain for the proletarians and fabulous profits for the equestrian *publicani*. The proletarians and the equestrians were now the allies of Crassus, since he had abandoned the senatorial for the popular party. But Crassus was more interested in another aspect of his scheme: the annexation would necessitate the employment of a big army which, according to Crassus' plan, would be commanded by his henchman Julius Caesar. This would give Crassus a force equal to the army of Pompey. Ingenious as the scheme was, it was defeated by the opposition of the senate, and Crassus was forced to develop some of his other plans. He hoped, for example, that Catiline could gain the consulship. Several times Crassus supported the candidacy of Catiline but without success. In the campaign of 64 B.C., when the victory of Catiline seemed finally assured, he was beaten by the senatorial candidate, Cicero.

Marcus Tullius Cicero was an equestrian from Arpinum in eastern Latium, the home town of Marius; Cicero had been born there while Marius was campaigning against Jugurtha. Educated in Rome in the nineties, Cicero was trained in the law and also well acquainted with Greek and Latin literature. He showed an early aptitude as a trial lawyer, and before he was twenty-five he had begun his literary career by translating some of the works of Xenophon, producing a textbook on oratory, and writing a poem in praise of Marius. During the latter part of Sulla's dictatorship, Cicero had been absent from Rome studying oratory in Athens and enjoying ill health; needless to say, with the poem about Marius on his record, he would have been less healthy in Rome. In 77 Cicero married Terentia, a wealthy (but unfortunately parsimonious) heiress, who bore him a daughter, Tullia, whom he dearly loved, and a son who was something of a problem. Quaestor in Sicily in 75, prosecutor of Verres in 70, praetor in 66, Cicero had now risen to the consulship in 63.

What Cicero had done was unusual, for he was a "new man," the first of his family to rise to political importance and exchange equestrian for senatorial rank. His success was due to his ability as an orator and lawyer and various shrewdly calculated moves. In 65, for example, when Catiline had been charged with extortion, Cicero thought about defending him in court in order to win the political support of Crassus. On another occasion he undertook to prosecute a friend, whom he thought innocent of an extortion charge, merely in order to win popular acclaim; convicted, his friend died of a broken heart.

Catiline, like Crassus and Pompey, had been a partisan of Sulla, but even that man of iron had been repelled by Catiline's bloodthirstiness and had rejected him. It was said in Rome that Catiline had killed his own brother, seduced a Vestal Virgin (Cicero's sister-in-law), and engaged in other types of unconventional behavior. Though he had become a creature of Crassus, he nevertheless seems to have had a political following of his own.

The three principal candidates for the consulship of 63 B.C. had been Cicero, representing the senatorial group, and Catiline and Antonius, both supported by Crassus. Cicero and Antonius emerged victorious, and the year of their consulship proved to be a very lively one. Cicero, who had long been determined to support Pompey because of his conviction that Pompey had a great future in store for him (and Cicero), found much to do in Pompey's interest. Crassus, equally determined to ruin Pompey, had devised a new scheme: he directed one of his supporters among the tribunes to propose a land act; this would involve disposing of the remaining public land in Italy in order to give farms to proletarians, always a popular move, but the hidden aim of the bill was to raise land prices in Italy so that Pompey would have difficulty in rewarding his veterans when he returned from the war against Mithridates. Fortunately for Pompey, Cicero managed to defeat the bill.

In this year Julius Caesar became *pontifex maximus*. This was an office held for life which gave its holder the headship of the state religion and great political prestige. Caesar managed this through election by the comitia tributa, an unconventional and possibly unconstitutional procedure. In the same year he was a successful candidate for the praetorship of 62.

At this time Caesar was acting as a political strategist for Crassus, but he, like Catiline, had a program and a following of his own. More consistent in his politics than any of the others, Caesar was always a Marian and a champion of the *Populares*. Slightly younger than Cicero, he belonged to the aristocratic Julian clan to which Marius had become allied by marriage to Caesar's aunt. Caesar was as well educated as Cicero, and some people thought him a better orator. Like Cicero, he had first married an heiress, but (unlike Cicero) he managed to divorce her and keep the dowry. His second wife was the daughter of a prominent Marian; she bore him his only legitimate child, Julia, and his refusal to divorce her at Sulla's order had led to his proscription and near execution at the hands of the dictator. Through the importunities of aristocratic friends, Caesar had been pardoned by Sulla, although Sulla had some misgivings, saying that he saw in this young man "many a Marius." After a quaestorship in Spain in 68 Caesar became aedile in 65, when he gained great popular favor by decorating the forum at his own (really at Crassus') expense and providing magnificent gladiatorial shows.

Caesar had paraded his connection with Marius on several occasions before 63, but when he became pontifex maximus he used his power to bring to trial an elderly senator whom he accused of having murdered Saturninus. Before a court of two, consisting of Julius and Lucius Caesar (the brother of Julius), the poor old man was tried and condemned to be tied to a cross and suspended head down from the "unlucky tree." Only the intervention of the consul, Cicero, saved him from a horrible death.

The major event of the year 63, however, was the conspiracy of Catiline. Now almost a perennial candidate for the consulship, Catiline campaigned again in 63, promising a cancellation of debts if elected. Once more unsuccessful, he planned a revolution for late in October. Cicero informed the senate of the conspiracy, martial law was declared, and armies were raised to defend the state. Early in November a plot to murder Cicero was foiled, and Cicero attacked Catiline (who was still in Rome and attending meetings of the senate) in a fiery speech, the "First Oration Against Catiline." The conspirator now left Rome to join his forces which were mustering in Etruria. Other supporters of Catiline, however, remained in the city; early in December Cicero managed to intercept documents which left no uncertainty as to the identity and guilt of these persons. They were arrested, condemned to death without trial, and strangled. In the opening months of 62 government forces met and defeated Catiline's army in the north; Catiline died in the battle, and the danger was over.

Though in his own mind Cicero believed that he had saved the state, other people took a less serious view of the conspiracy. Cicero continued to boast about his achievement for the rest of his life: he polished up and published the four Catilinarian orations, wrote an account of his consulship in both Greek and Latin, and capped the climax with a poem which contained neither truth nor poetry but was notable for the inclusion of what was considered the worst line in all Latin verse: "O happy fate for the Roman state was the date of my consulate!" The judgement of professional poets was anything but kind: Catullus said that Cicero was the best lawyer in Rome—and the worst poet—while Martial noted sadly that no Muse, no Apollo, aided Cicero.

Though Cicero bored people with his endless talk of *his* consulship (though it was a collegiate office), what he had done was to have more serious consequences for him than what he persisted in saying, for in the hysteria of the moment when the conspirators had been arrested, Cicero had been responsible for putting Roman citizens to death without trial. Caesar had argued against the constitutionality of the act, but Cicero had had the support of Cato the Younger, the virtual reincarnation of old Cato the Censor, whose authority and prestige were very great in Rome, and thus the deed had been done. Cicero's crime was employed against him by his enemies to secure his banishment in 58 as well as his execution in 43; his hasty action was to haunt him through life and even provide cause for vilification when he was in his grave.

Despite the failure of Crassus' schemes and despite the continued support of Cicero, when Pompey returned home in 62 he found that he was not universally popular. No politician, Pompey made the mistake of disbanding his army before he discovered that the senate was not disposed to grant pensions to his veterans or ratify the settlement which he had made in the Near East. Crassus and his party were determined to make trouble, but the senatorial party was equally unco-operative. Lucullus, the real conqueror of Mithridates, was bent on revenge; he had the support of Cato, his brother-in-law, whose opposition to Pompey, he said, was based on the fact that Pompey's whole public career had been conducted through offices held by unconstitutional means. Cato was a man of such ostentatious probity that few ever questioned his motives, but he did have the serious fault of always doing the right thing at the wrong time.

The result was a stalemate in politics for two years. Crassus, the senatorial party, and Cicero and Pompey were all about equal in strength so that nothing could be accomplished by any of the three groups except to block one another. Pompey as a politician disappointed even his admirer Cicero. Of his first speech in public after returning to Rome, Cicero reported of Pompey: "Non iucunda miseris, inanis improbis, beatis non grata, bonis non gravis, itaque frigebat." Translating into the vernacular, we should say: "The poor were unhappy, the *Populares* thought it stupid, the rich were displeased, the senatorial party was dissatisfied, and so he laid an egg."

Passing over for the moment the hilarious affair of the scandal which gave Caesar an opportunity to divorce his third wife saying, "Caesar's wife must be above suspicion," we may note that Caesar left Rome at the end of 62 for his propraetorship in Spain. Heavily in debt to Crassus, Caesar was heard to say that he needed "a million and a quarter to have nothing at all." When Caesar returned from Spain in 60 B.C. in somewhat better financial condition, the political stalemate still prevailed in Rome. The astute Julius surveyed the situation and evolved a plan of action:

He clearly saw that, as individuals, neither he nor Pompey nor Crassus could accomplish anything in the face of senatorial opposition. Therefore, he proposed that they should pool their political resources. His logic prevailed; Pompey and Crassus became reconciled, and a political marriage was arranged between Julia and Pompey. The alliance of Caesar, Pompey, and Crassus thus formed is known to history as the First Triumvirate. It should be emphasized that although a political monopoly was secured by the triumvirs, their coalition was a purely private affair—a gentleman's agreement—and had no constitutional basis. Cicero was invited to join with the triumvirs, but he regarded himself as too important to require their support.

The first act of the united leaders was to gain for Caesar the election to the consulship for 59 B.C. Caesar had a colleague in the office, an opposition candidate called Bibulus, but Bibulus was so completely outmaneuvered and relegated to the background that people began to speak of the "consulship of Julius and Caesar." As consul, Caesar was able to obtain the ratification of the settlements made by Pompey in the Near East and pensions for his veterans. To the equestrian friends of Crassus were remitted sums amounting to one-third of the total tribute which they had contracted, but had not been able to extract from the province of Asia. For himself, after some anxious moments, Caesar managed to obtain an appointment for five years as proconsul in Cisalpine Gaul (the Po Valley) and Narbonese Gaul.

Omitting an account of the well known conquest of Gaul which Caesar began in the years 58–56 B.C., we may follow the events in Rome. Crassus and Pompey had been left behind with the task of insuring a continuation of triumviral control. In order to do this, they had to get rid of Cato and Cicero. Cato was easy to handle: he was sent to Cyprus to organize the new Roman government there. Cato knew very well that this was an excuse to get him out of Rome, but his code of ethics demanded that he obey the command of the government.

Cicero, on the other hand, would have to be blasted out of Rome. He had wriggled out of accepting a proconsular command after 63 and had no intention of leaving the capital to struggle along without him. Yet the thing was managed by his banishment.

Back in 62 the main figure in the scandal involving Caesar's third wife had been a dissolute nobleman named Clodius, who was also one of Crassus' henchmen. As pontifex maximus, Caesar was supposed to celebrate in his own house the festival of the Good Goddess, Bona Dea, which was attended only by women. Clodius, who was having an affair with Caesar's wife, had dressed up in female garments and attempted to gain admission. He was detected and recognized, and a suit for sacrilege was brought against him. Caesar, though he divorced Pompeia, had refused to testify against Clodius, and Crassus, by bribing the jurors, got Clodius acquitted. Cicero had taken no real part in the prosecution, but he had gained the undying enmity of Clodius by twitting him about the affair: he called Clodius the "priestess of the Bona Dea" and subjected him to further ridicule. Clodius, promising revenge, was elected to the tribunate at the end of 59; he sponsored legislation pleasing to the proletariat and Crassus, and then proposed a bill to outlaw anyone who had put to death Roman citizens without a trial. Cicero was not worried about the actions of Clodius at first, because he was sure his great and good friend, Pompey, would support and protect him; but after he called on Pompey several times and failed to find him at home, he realized that he had been deserted. The proletarians began to throw rocks at Cicero when he appeared in the street; when the bill for his banishment passed in the spring of 58, Cicero left Rome for an unhappy exile in Macedonia.

In the meantime the triumvirs made further plans for the future. A meeting of the three leaders was held at Lucca in northern Italy in 56 B.C. in which new projects were mapped out. Caesar's command in Gaul was to be extended for another five years; Crassus and Pompey were to hold the consulship in 55 B.C., after which Crassus was to go to Syria to undertake a war with the Parthians and Pompey was to have a free hand in Spain and Africa. In the following years Caesar was able to consolidate his conquest

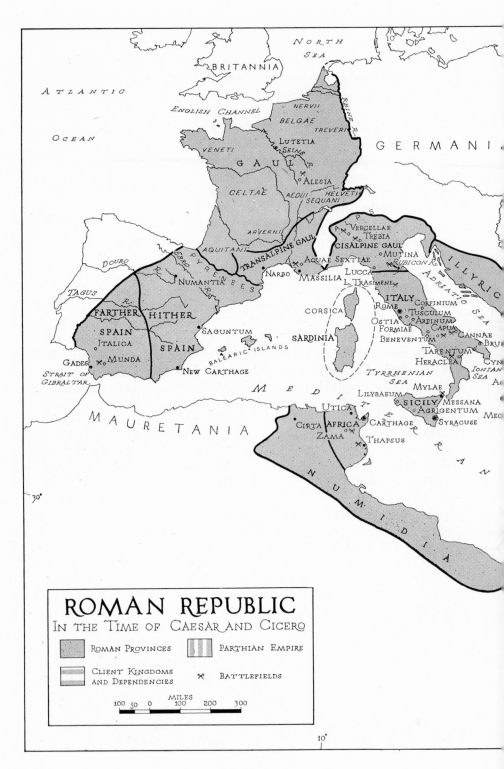

ROMAN REPUBLIC

In the Time of Caesar and Cicero

Roman Provinces

Parthian Empire

Client Kingdoms and Dependencies

× Battlefields

MILES
100 50 0   100   200   300

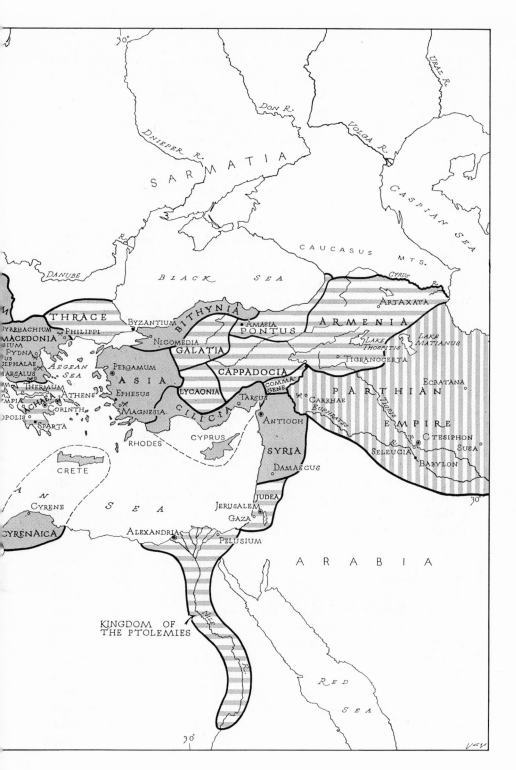

SARMATIA

DNIEPER R.

DON R.

VOLGA R.

URAL R.

CASPIAN SEA

CAUCASUS MTS.

CYRUS R.

DANUBE

BLACK SEA

THRACE

DYRRHACHIUM
PHILIPPI

MACEDONIA
GSIUM
PYDNA
US
EPHALAE
TARSALUS

THERMAUM
MPIA
ACHAEA
CORINTH
OPOLIS
SPARTA

Aegean
SEA

ATHENS

BYZANTIUM

BITHYNIA

NICOMEDIA

Amasia

PONTUS

GALATIA

ARMENIA

ARTAXATA

LAKE
THOSPITIS

TIGRANOCERTA

LAKE
MATIANUS

PERGAMUM

ASIA

EPHESUS

MAGNESIA

LYCAONIA

CAPPADOCIA

CILICIA

TARSUS

COMMA-
GENE

CARRHAE

PARTHIAN

ECBATANA

EUPHRATES

TIGRIS

EMPIRE

CTESIPHON

SUSA

RHODES

CYPRUS

ANTIOCH

SYRIA

DAMASCUS

SELEUCIA

BABYLON

CRETE

A
N
CYRENE

SEA

JERUSALEM

JUDEA

GAZA

CYRENAICA

ALEXANDRIA

PELUSIUM

ARABIA

KINGDOM OF
THE PTOLEMIES

NILE

RED

SEA

373

of Gaul and make a punitive expedition into Germany; in 55 and 54 B.C. he also made two unsuccessful attempts to gain a foothold in Britain. Crassus, who had always hoped for military glory, embarked upon his Parthian campaign with great enthusiasm, but he was no general; he was defeated and killed by the Parthians in 53 B.C.

The death of Crassus brought the First Triumvirate to an end, but it had ceased to work efficiently as an arrangement even before 53. Pompey and Crassus had not been able to co-operate in Rome. Pompey had acquired a tribune named Milo to counteract the activities of Clodius, Milo had secured the recall of Cicero in 57, and Cicero had been doing his best to reconcile Pompey with the senate against Crassus and Clodius. Julia had died in 54; thus a close tie between Caesar and Pompey was severed. After 55 affairs in Rome had been in an uproar. The rival factions of Clodius and Milo fought openly in the streets; Clodius was finally killed in 52, and Milo was exiled despite his defense by Cicero which was something less than halfhearted. Conditions had become so chaotic in Rome that elections could not be held. To restore order, Pompey was made sole consul and given extraordinary powers.

Caesar's second five-year command in Gaul was now drawing to a close. Unless he could be elected to the consulship and assume the office before his command terminated, he would become a private citizen without power and at the mercy of his political enemies. Pompey promised to aid Caesar by allowing him to stand for the consulship *in absentia* but then went back on his word. At length, with the encouragement and support of the senate, Pompey broke with Caesar, and in 49 B.C. Caesar "crossed the Rubicon," the boundary between his province and Italy, to begin a civil war. The senatorial forces, even with Pompey's leadership, could not withstand the attack of Caesar's well trained Gallic veterans. Pompey retired to the Balkans where he was finally defeated by Caesar at Pharsalus in Thessaly in 48; his flight to Egypt ended in assassination there as soon as he arrived.

The years 48–45 B.C. were spent by Caesar in stamping out the resistance of the remaining members of the Pompeian party. Caesar followed Pompey to Egypt in 48; there he met the famous Cleopatra and set her upon the Ptolemaic throne in the face of the rival claims of her brothers. The rest of the Near East was pacified in 47 B.C.; the Pompeian forces in Africa were destroyed in 46, and those in Spain in 45.

With these tasks completed, Caesar settled down in Rome to reorganize the Roman government. His intention was to discard the republic and set up a dictatorship—and perhaps, eventually, an absolute monarchy of the Hellenistic type. The powers he received at this time made him the supreme authority in the Roman state. In 46 B.C. he was given the dictatorship for ten years; at the same time he held the consulship. As pontifex maximus he controlled the state religion. He did not hold the office of tribune, but he was given the *power* of that office which allowed him to veto the actions of magistrates and assemblies and made his person sacrosanct. Special laws gave him the right to make war and peace, to nominate and appoint magistrates, to command all the military forces of Rome, and to supervise the coinage. The sum total of these powers placed Caesar above any other official or government body; he could even legislate at his pleasure.

In addition to establishing a dictatorship, Caesar made certain reforms. He tried to bring about uniformity in the municipal governments of Italy by giving the Italian towns city-state constitutions modeled upon that of the city of Rome. He introduced a new calendar, later known as the Julian calendar, which was used by the Western world until the sixteenth century A.D.; and he planned the codification of Roman law. The size of the senate was increased, the pay of the army was raised, and provincial taxes were reduced. Caesar was particularly interested in colonization: Corinth and Carthage, two advantageous commercial sites, were reoccupied by Roman colonists. His good judgment in choosing likely sites is shown by the fact that the present cities of Seville, Lisbon, Arles, and Toulouse were either colonized or given municipal charters at his order.

It is true that Caesar was ambitious for power, but his policies may be defended on the ground that something had to be done to end factional strife. The republican system had been unable to do this, and things had gone from bad to worse. Perhaps if the economic situation had been more favorable, democracy or timocracy might have been restored; but only peace could remedy the economic situation, and, under the circumstances then prevailing, only a dictatorship could bring peace.

If Caesar had lived, his reforms might have been more beneficial than his contemporaries realized. His attempt to secure uniformity in Italy certainly aided the "Romanization" of the peninsula, and his extension of Roman and Latin citizenship to some provincial communities was an initial step toward raising the provinces to equality with Italy. Even if he had established a monarchy, the continued "Romanization" of the provinces might have led back to the restoration of republican government.

Whatever else one may think of Caesar, the fact remains that he was probably even a greater genius than Alexander. His military ability equalled that of the great Macedonian; his powers of organization are established by his deeds, whereas those of Alexander remain problematical. Brilliant, well educated, a fine orator and writer, Caesar left an indelible impression upon the memory of mankind. His private life and his general moral attitudes are less deserving of praise.

It was Caesar's intention to establish a monarchy, or the fear that he would do so, that proved his undoing. There were two things that always aroused and united the Romans: the fear of a Gallic invasion and the threat of monarchy. When it became rumored that Caesar wanted to be king, his opponents of the old senatorial party began to gain ground. On the fifteenth of March, 44 B.C., just before he was to set out on a campaign against the Parthians, Caesar was assassinated by a group of conspirators led by Caius Cassius, a Pompeian whom Caesar had pardoned and honored with the praetorship, and Marcus Junius Brutus, the son-in-law of Cato[1] and rumored to be one of Caesar's illegitimate progeny.

Caesar's assassins had planned nothing beyond his death. One might almost say that they expected the republic to restore itself. True, the senatorial class as a whole approved their action, and the proletarians had rioted in joy. Nevertheless, there was still the army to be reckoned with in addition to two strong military men: Mark Antony, Caesar's devoted follower who was his colleague in the consulship in 44, and Marcus Aemilius Lepidus, Caesar's assistant as dictator, who bore the title of *magister equitum,* master of the horse. When Antony discovered that he was not to be assassinated, as surviving consul he called the senate into session and explained to the befuddled senators that if they condemned Caesar's government and repudiated it, they would be condemning and repudiating him (Antony) and so would have no government at all. The senators then decided to pretend that Caesar had died a natural death; they ratified his acts and ordained a public funeral for him. At the funeral Antony gave the oration in honor of the dictator and publicly read Caesar's will which disclosed that Caesar had bequeathed a sum of money to each Roman citizen and had ordered some of his property to be made into a public park. This convinced the proletariat that Caesar had been their friend, and they howled for vengeance on the conspirators.

Cicero had been cognizant of the plot against Caesar. He was not present at the assassination, probably for the same reason he was ill on the day of the Battle of Pharsalus, although he later lamented that he had not been invited to "that gorgeous banquet on the Ides of March." Nevertheless, he at last began to play the part of a brave man. Disappointed in the conspirators—"I see it was folly to be consoled by the Ides of March" and "I found a ship breaking up—no plan—no reason"—he began to take the initiative against Antony. In a series of more than a dozen scathing orations, the Philippics, he lashed and derided Antony on the floor of the senate.

Caesar's will had also revealed the adoption of his grandnephew Gaius Octavius (Octavian) as his son and heir. Octavian came to Rome in 44 B.C. to claim his inheritance, but Antony, who had already spent Caesar's fortune, ignored him, for Octavian was only eighteen at this time and had shown no promise of his future greatness. As a result, when Antony at last

---

[1] Cato had fought on the side of Pompey in the civil wars. He committed suicide in 46 at Utica in Africa while besieged by Caesarian forces.

came to an open break with Caesar's murderers late in 44 B.C., he found arrayed against him the power of the senate and also that of Octavian, around whom many of Caesar's veterans had gathered.

Against such opposition Antony could make little headway. Then the senate made its great mistake: it antagonized Octavian by failing properly to acknowledge his aid—Cicero angered him by saying that he was a young man to be praised, honored, and immortalized; the last word might also mean "to have one's throat cut." As a consequence, Octavian, Antony, and Lepidus joined forces. They soon came into the possession of Rome, Italy, and all the western half of the empire, while the conspirators under Brutus and Cassius held the eastern provinces.

Octavian, Antony, and Lepidus forced the senate to appoint them a "committee of three for the reconstitution of the republic" (*triumviri reipublicae constituendae*), and thus the Second Triumvirate came into existence (43 B.C.). This triumvirate differed from the first in that it was an official body, established by law, whereas the First Triumvirate had been only a private arrangement among Pompey, Caesar, and Crassus. The new triumvirs were to hold their supreme office for five years.

The triumvirs now embarked upon a program of proscription, partly out of revenge and partly because they needed money for their troops. One of the first victims was Cicero who was, of course, bitterly hated by Antony. The great orator met death with courage. It might be said that with him died the republic which he had tried to save in his own way by vainly attempting to form a coalition of senators and equestrians in a "concord of the orders." Cicero's head and hands were cut off and exhibited upon the rostra at Rome from which he had so many times spoken. Fulvia, the fury who was the ex-wife of Antony, thrust a dagger through Cicero's tongue when his head was presented to her. It was truly an age of violence and passion.

In 42 B.C. Antony and Octavian took the field against Brutus and Cassius, who held the Roman East. After a double battle at Macedonian Philippi, Brutus and Cassius committed suicide. This left the triumvirs supreme, except for the resistance provided by Sextus Pompey, the son of Pompey the Great, who had supported the senatorial faction with a strong navy.

Between 42 and 36 B.C. Antony was engaged in settling the affairs of the East, Octavian held the West, and Lepidus was placed in charge of Africa. Lepidus was gradually pushed further and further into the background during this period, for he was no match for Antony and Octavian. He was useful, however, as a balance wheel, and therefore he was again included in the triumvirate when its powers were renewed for another five years at the end of 38 B.C. The major problem of these years was the disposal of Sextus Pompey; he was finally defeated by Octavian's close friend and general, Agrippa (36 B.C.).

377

After 36 B.C. affairs resolved themselves into a struggle between Octavian and Antony for possession of the empire. Octavian had never forgiven Antony for what had happened at Rome in 44 B.C. when Antony had squandered Octavian's patrimony and treated him with contempt. This was not all of the difficulty, however, for the fact remained that there was no room in the empire for two supreme rulers. While Sextus Pompey was alive, Antony and Octavian had to remain on friendly terms, but afterward they found themselves natural opponents, and neither was willing to submit or defer to the other.

Antony's popularity with the Romans steadily declined after an unsuccessful Parthian campaign in 36 B.C. Moreover, Antony had fallen under the influence of the Ptolemaic queen, Cleopatra. He married her in 36, casting off his earlier bride, Octavia, the sister of Octavian. In 34 at Alexandria Antony announced the so-called Donations of Alexandria, in which he proclaimed Cleopatra queen of Egypt, Cyprus, Crete, and one of the Syrian provinces; Caesarion, the son of Cleopatra and Julius Caesar, was named joint ruler with her. The two sons she had borne Antony were named kings of other portions of the Near East.

Finally, in 32 B.C. Octavian, representing the Roman government, declared war upon Cleopatra—Antony was not named. Antony and Cleopatra assembled troops in Greece for an attack on Italy, but Agrippa defeated the Egyptian fleet in a naval battle at Actium just off the west coast of Greece in 31 B.C. Antony and Cleopatra sought refuge in Egypt. When Octavian came to Alexandria in pursuit of the culprits in the following year, they committed suicide, and Egypt was at last annexed by Rome (30 B.C.).

Octavian, now master of the whole empire, returned to Rome in 29 B.C. to begin the task of reorganizing a government and a realm that had been reduced to chaos by a century of civil conflict. He was only thirty-four years old when he began this Herculean labor, but the undertaking was to consume the rest of his life. He died forty-three years later—just over the threshold of success.

Chapter 22

CIVILIZATION

IN THE CICERONIAN AGE

LTHOUGH OUR SOURCES of information about Roman society, economics, and culture in the first century B.C. are by no means as full as those for the beginning centuries of the Christian era, they nevertheless permit more than the occasional glimpse of Roman life to which we are limited in earlier periods. In the first century B.C., which is well named the Ciceronian Age, the Roman phase of Hellenistic civilization was fully launched, and we should not allow the lively and fascinating political activities of the period to divert our attention entirely from its other important aspects. This was a great age in literature and thought which exerted a very considerable influence on posterity. In this period also, the city of Rome attained a primacy that went beyond its functions as the political heart of a great empire; in the first century B.C., and for many centuries to come, there were innumerable kinds of roads that led to Rome.

After 133 B.C. Rome tended more and more to become the financial capital of the ancient world. Tribute from the far corners of the Mediterranean basin poured into the imperial coffers, and the equestrian capitalists had investments in even the most remote provinces. Despite the presence of pirates in the East, trade seems to have lost little ground; in Italy there was a growth of industry in the first century B.C.

The chief sources of equestrian revenue were moneylending and the state contracts for public works, the exploitation of natural resources in the provinces, and the collection of provincial taxes. Syndicates or stock companies were often formed in which the equestrians and also the senators (working through private agents) might participate. Capital was supplied by the major partners in the company and by small investors who became stockholders. This was truly "big business"; the *publicani* and the *negotia-*

tores (moneylenders) constituted one of the most powerful "pressure groups" in Roman politics.

Although a few equestrians might invest in trade and industry or enter the banking field, these activities were largely in the hands of Greeks, south Italians, and Semites (Jews, Phoenicians, and Syrians). These people might be Roman citizens; the Italians and Italian Greeks were made citizens after the Social War, and many who were brought to Italy as slaves later were manumitted and became citizen freedmen, but they could not be classed as truly "Roman."

Most of the manufacturing in Italy was done in small shops that employed only a few slaves or free workers. There existed a modest number of larger establishments—those which manufactured pottery, for example—but these were not numerous enough to say that there was mass production in Italian industry. The chief manufactures of Italy were for the home market; they consisted of clothing, furniture, implements, tiles, metalwork, pottery, and other necessities; tanning, milling, and baking were also common industries.

Italy's imports far exceeded her exports. The most valuable exports were agricultural (wine and olive oil), but pottery, metalwork, and Campanian ointments were also exported. Italian imports of grain, slaves, textiles, and luxuries of various kinds overbalanced exports in quantity and value. The chief imported luxuries were wine, spices, precious stones, silks, and glassware, as well as special foods. It is clear that it was not commerce, but the imperial tribute, that helped to keep the economy of Italy on an even keel.

The civil wars and slave rebellions of the first century B.C. interfered with Italian agriculture. The small farms continued to decrease in number, whereas the large estates (*latifundia*) increased; the senatorial class usually invested a large share of its imperial earnings in Italian land. Nevertheless, agricultural production was disrupted by the actual military operations of the period and by the frequent changes in land ownership resulting from the wholesale confiscations authorized by Sulla, Marius, Caesar, Antony, and Octavian. Grazing fared better than agriculture, as one might expect, since the political disturbances would not affect it to such a great extent. Around the Italian cities truck gardening became a profitable occupation.

In some of the provinces the economic situation was distinctly unfavorable. In the East, although trade and industry had not seriously declined, the ravages of the Mithridatic and civil wars had left their mark. The destruction of Corinth in 146 B.C. had been a severe blow in Greece, but even worse was the paralyzing effect of the campaigns of Sulla, Pompey, and Caesar. Sulla had ruined Athens in 86 B.C., and the civil wars of Pompey and Caesar had injured Greek agriculture and grazing. In Asia Minor the provincials groaned under the burden of tribute imposed by the victorious Roman parties; it was necessary to borrow money from the equestrians at excessive interest rates in order to meet the payments demanded. Conditions in Africa, Spain, and Gaul in the West were almost as bad.

In Roman society there was a great gap between the rich and the poor. We know most about the wealthy senators and equestrians who formed only a small group at the top of the social pyramid. Rome had her millionaires and near millionaires who lived in a luxurious manner in their great town houses in Rome and their numerous villas in the country. The houses of the rich were show places which cost fortunes to build or rent. They were filled with sculpture and painting. Many works of art had been brought to Rome by the conquerors of Greece; when the supply of original art works was exhausted, Greek sculptors and painters were hired to produce imitations.

Politics and business engrossed the minds of the majority of wealthy Romans, although there were intellectuals who were interested in philosophy and literature. The typical upper-class education was now of the Greek type with its training in rhetoric, literature, and music, and it was not unusual for men to study oratory and philosophy in the Greek centers of learning— Athens, Rhodes, and others. Some rich men amused themselves by posing as the patrons of artists, literary men, and scholars.

Roman women had always enjoyed considerable freedom, but in the period we are now discussing they were even more emancipated. Divorces and multiple marriages were common; men often married for money or to consolidate political alliances. The old Roman morality among both men and women was so infrequently found in high society that its rare appearance excited comment. Some of the Roman women were well educated and could meet the men on common intellectual ground. Moreover, the influence of women in politics was often important. Certainly, Julia, the daughter of Caesar and the wife of Pompey, helped to make the two men political allies as long as she lived. Antony's wife, the vicious Fulvia, did not hesitate to head an attack upon Octavian.

Not all the Romans of this age were vigorous and purposeful. There were wastrels and spendthrifts who passed their time in search of pleasure. Many people looked upon politics as a great and amusing game. It was expensive, too. Rising politicians incurred heavy debts; the borrowing of Caesar, Antony, and others ran into the millions.

The first century B.C. for the Roman senators and equestrians was an age of easy money, financial insecurity, and rising prices. People borrowed heavily and spent freely, always hoping that "something would turn up." Rich men like Lucullus or Hortensius could spend thousands of dollars (or its Roman equivalent) on a painting or a statue, and others like Cicero did their best to keep up with them. Cicero had what most of us would consider adequate means even today. He was able to buy a house that was worth over one hundred thousand dollars; he owned three tenements in the slums, eight country villas, and ten rest houses, the point of the last being that there were no suitable hotels, and when a rich man journeyed from the city to his country house, he had his own overnight stopping places along the way. Cicero's landed property was worth perhaps four million: in a single day he had thirty thousand in cash on hand, yet he was always in debt. He was always borrowing from his friend Atticus; he borrowed from Caesar and others. He was always buying something—statues, manuscripts, twenty thousand dollars for a dining room table, three thousand just to travel from Italy to Greece. Roman lawyers were not paid for their services, but they might receive gifts and bequests. When Cicero talked about his "outstanding accounts," he was referring to his elderly clients who were on the point of dying and leaving something to him in their wills. One of the great disappointments of his life was his spouse, Terentia, who was a rich woman but refused to share her wealth with him; she was obviously a very sensible woman.

Far different from the luxury and ease of the upper classes was the life of the Roman poor, who led a precarious existence in the slums of the great city. Crowded together in shabby wooden tenements where cleanliness and sanitation were unheard of, the masses lived in almost unspeakable conditions. Often the ill-built tenement structures collapsed or were gutted by fire, catastrophes in which many of the inmates would perish, and the remainder would be left homeless. Always they were undernourished; work was hard to find, and wages were low. Cheap or free grain, water or a little wine, perhaps fish and a few vegetables, served to keep them from complete starvation. About the middle of the first century B.C. the population of Rome hovered near the one-million mark. At this time 320,000 people (one-third of the population) were receiving free grain. The small shopkeepers and the craftsmen managed to struggle along, but the condition of the ordinary skilled and unskilled workers was one of great insecurity. It is best to leave to the imagination the sordid lives of the wives and children of these men.

In the last century of the republic the slave population of Italy reached a new high point. Large numbers of slaves were brought from the territories conquered by the Romans; other people were reduced to slavery when they fought on the losing side in the civil wars. Even these abundant sources were not able to supply the demand. Pirates and slave traders carried off countless thousands every year, and small children might be abducted almost within sight of their parents. Of the Italian population of fourteen million in the first century B.C., four million were slaves.

Slaves were employed in domestic service, industry, agriculture, mining, and ranching. In Roman law the slave was considered not a person but a chattel; he might be sold or transferred like a horse or cow. His master had absolute power over his life. All free men were his potential enemies; he was allowed greater or less freedom of movement depending upon the type of work in which he was employed, but escape was not feasible because no free man would shelter him if he fled from his master. Many of the slaves had once been respected citizens of their home communities in far-off lands; often they were well educated, and in that case they might serve their owners as teachers, secretaries, physicians, or artists. An intelligent and tractable slave might be treated like "one of the family"; he might possibly look forward to manumission at some future date, but even then he would be bound to his former owner by the ties of clientship.

The rural slave population was always restless; out in the country in Italy and Sicily slave revolts were not infrequent. The savagery of these slaves when they broke out in rebellion is a good indication of their feeling toward their condition of servitude and the kind of treatment they received from their owners. The free population consequently feared the slave uprisings and always put them down with great severity. After all, in the ancient world slavery was a basic element of organized society, and people feared that if the slaves were allowed too much leeway, society itself might crumble. Sometimes an unscrupulous political leader would, in desperation, promote a slave rebellion, promising the slaves freedom in return for their support.

The addition of foreign elements to the Roman population continued to bring about a corresponding change in Roman culture. The various peoples who came or were brought to Italy carried thither the customs, habits, and religions of their own countries. On the whole, we may say that the Roman culture of the first century B.C. could not easily be distinguished from that of other people in the Hellenistic world. Cultural change is clearly shown in Roman religion: in the outlying rural areas the old religions of agricultural Italy might still be found, but in the urban centers Greek, Egyptian, and Oriental cults flourished at the expense of traditional beliefs. The educated Romans turned to philosophy as a substitute for religion—particularly to Stoicism and Epicureanism—whereas the lower classes adopted the imported religions. The state cult of Rome survived because it was so closely bound up with the whole system of government. Few, however, considered the state cult as a religion; it was rather an essential formality.

The chief point to remember about the Roman adoption of Hellenistic culture is the eclectic character of this borrowing; the Romans chose what they wanted and made combinations of different elements. This is well illustrated in Roman art and architecture, in which the main influences were Etruscan, classical Greek, and Hellenistic. The Romans employed all three orders of Greek architecture, either separately or in composite forms; their favorite style, however, was Corinthian. They retained the high temple podium of the Etruscans and made considerable use of the arch. Marble, concrete, and stucco were favorite building materials. The first stone theater was built in Rome in 55 B.C. The typical Roman theater differed from similar Greek structures in that it had a stage.

Roman sculpture had both Etruscan and Greek roots. There was much imitation of classical Greek and Hellenistic styles, of course; the main Roman contribution was a continuation and development of the Etruscan use of portraiture in sculpture. Painting continued the Greek tradition; as a matter of fact, it is from Roman painting of the next century (from the frescoes of Pompeii and Herculaneum) that we get our best conception of the character of Hellenistic painting, although one should hasten to add that much of the work has a distinctive Roman quality.

We cannot leave the subject of the last century of the republic without noting the literary production for which it is justly famous. The chief poet of the age was a young man named Catullus, who lived in the first half of the first century B.C. Catullus wrote under the influence of the great Alexandrian poets, particularly Callimachus, and he was able to make his Latin as graceful as their Greek. He wrote much in his short life: a wedding hymn, some lyric poems, a short epic in the style of Callimachus, and a series of love poems addressed to Lesbia, in reality Clodia, the infamous sister of the equally infamous Clodius. These poems to Lesbia are justly admired and well worth reading, though Clodia was an unworthy object of Catullus' affection who toyed with him and then devoted herself to more interesting older men. Clodia had a bad temper and a bad reputation; Cicero called her a "two-bit Clytemnestra."

Philosopher, and great poet, too, was Lucretius (99–55 B.C.), who combined his philosophy and poetry in a long work in which he expounded the ethical and scientific doctrines of Epicurus. His mission, he felt, was to free men from superstition and the fear of death. Although many of his ideas regarding the causes of physical phenomena were fantastic, we do find in his work (*De rerum natura*) embryonic ideas which seem strikingly modern: the atomic theory, the evolution of species, and an explanation of cultural evolution. Lucretius decried the declining morality of the age and the bad effects of imperial wealth upon the Romans. Since many Romans were more attracted to Stoicism than Epicureanism, the poem of Lucretius was not universally applauded. Cicero was condescending; he said that the work of Lucretius was marked by flashes of genius and skill.

Modern students are familiar with Julius Caesar's account of his campaigns in Gaul and Britain, although, unfortunately, these are seldom appreciated by high-school Latin classes. A mature reading of the *Commentaries,* however, may well lead to a reversal of opinion, for the story is fully as fascinating as Xenophon's *Anabasis*—and better written. Caesar did not intend his work to be a history or a chronicle of the events in Gaul, and he was not a journalist like the author of the *Anabasis*. Perhaps it is a political pamphlet, written to publicize and justify Caesar, but whatever it is or was intended to be, it possesses undeniable historical and literary merits. The descriptions of the Gauls and Germans, for example, are invaluable; the narrative of the Gallic revolts is gripping; there are graphic delineations of character; but we are often conscious of the presence of Caesar, who is just a little above the human plane, observing, appraising, deciding.

Sallust, a contemporary and partisan of Caesar, wrote histories of the Jugurthine War, the conspiracy of Catiline, and the decade following the death of Sulla. The first two works have survived intact and are extremely valuable as sources; it is to be regretted that only fragments of the third exist, since it is a period about which we lack first-rate information. Sallust was a well educated man with philosophic tendencies who, like many other Roman historians after his time, had political and military experience. The high moral tone of Sallust and the manner in which he criticizes the degeneracy of his age are hardly fitting for a man who was twice expelled from the senate for immoral behavior. Sallust was not impartial; his works were as much political pamphlets as histories, for he was ardent in his support of the popular party and chose to deal with periods of history in which the senatorial group had not covered itself with glory. It is not surprising, therefore, to find Sallust disparaging of Cicero's role in the conspiracy of Catiline. Nevertheless, Sallust makes good reading, and he is certainly one of the major historians of Rome.

In a somewhat crabbed style Cornelius Nepos produced a series of embryonic biographies, principally of famous Greeks, although the lives of Hamilcar and Hannibal were included. A very learned man who wrote more than seventy books was Marcus Terentius Varro, a first-century encyclopedist. Primarily an antiquarian, Varro's most outstanding works dealt with the Latin language and also with agriculture.

Cicero, the major literary figure of this age, was much more than an orator. True, we have all or parts of more than seventy-five of his orations, but we also have his treatises on rhetoric, political institutions and theory, legal subjects, and philosophy. Most interesting of all Cicero's writings are his letters, of which nearly eight hundred are extant; this figure does not include almost one hundred letters written to Cicero which are usually included in editions of his correspondence. The letters are invaluable for the reconstruction of the life, manners, and history of his age. This correspondence tells too much about Cicero, for he often wrote without reserve to his family and friends, especially to his brother Quintus and his friend and banker, Atticus. So much of the material presents Cicero in an unfavorable light that modern scholars have suspected that the letters which have survived were carefully collected and edited after Cicero's death for the purpose of damaging his reputation. However this may be, Cicero established the letter as a respectable literary form, and his letters were imitated for centuries.

In his works called the *Republic* and the *Laws* Cicero disclosed his theories about the ideal state. He believed firmly in the Roman Republic, but he wished to free it from what he thought were its obvious imperfections and abuses. His attitude was generally conservative. The establishment of a coalition of equestrians and senators as a governing class, with little opportunity for democratic government, was the main theme of his program for reconstruction.

Cicero's philosophy represented a combination of the practical elements of Greek philosophy. He inclined toward Stoicism and the doctrines of the later Platonic school, but he did not like Epicureanism. In philosophy Cicero contributed little that was new; his main significance was that he helped to popularize Greek philosophical concepts.

In oratory and in prose Cicero was outstanding for his distinctive style. His vigorous, rhythmic, carefully balanced periodic sentences with their close attention to sense and sound were admired by his contemporaries and his successors. He managed to combine two contemporary trends in style: the Asianic which was rather florid and the Attic which was severe. Cicero carefully studied the writings of Isocrates and Demosthenes, and he learned something from each.

In the first century B.C. the Roman Republic died—not from the wounds suffered in the civil wars, but from a disease that had struck at the hearts, minds, and souls of the oligarchs who dominated government and society. We have discussed the political ills of the state; we have seen that people recognized the existence of trouble and tried to find a remedy for it. Each reformer had his own panacea: democracy, oligarchy, or autocracy, but no cure had been found. The cloak of city-state government, patched and threadbare, could not cover the nakedness of an empire. This was part of the story, but the rest of it was that the game of government could not be played unless the players adhered to the rules.

The social ills of the oligarchs were recognized, too. It is possible that the behavior of a Clodius or a Clodia was symptomatic rather than typical. There were other women like Clodia, but Terentia, who held Cicero at bay where her purse was concerned, or Pomponia, Quintus' wife, who was always fretting and complaining, or Porcia, Cato's daughter, who was a female Cato in every way, may have been just as symbolic of social chaos as Clodia or Fulvia. The new woman of the first century, with her equality and freedom outside the home, may have been just a bit uncertain and lost without the definition of function in the home and great respect which had been accorded a matron of the old type like Cornelia, mother of the Gracchi.

It was not only the women but also the men who had lost their frame of reference with the decline of the older culture. For the upper classes it was a society in chaos, although the lower classes, if their sepulchral epitaphs are any indication, were unaffected; the proletarians went on in normal, unpretentious ways with the family—husband, wife, and children— devoted and cohesive to the end.

Livy, Sallust, Lucretius, and others blamed the new luxury which was financed by the spoils of empire, but it was more than that. The impact of the full-blown Hellenistic civilization was more than Roman culture could withstand. Some people sought solace in philosophy; they admitted a yearning to withdraw to the "serene fortified sanctuaries built by the teachings of the wise." Others found escape in the mystery religions which came from Greece and the Near East.

Desperate and bewildered as they were, their confidence badly shaken by the civil wars, some Romans nevertheless sensed that a new era was about to dawn. A kind of relief or salvation seemed to be expected either in the next world or here on earth. Cicero cried, "O glorious day when I shall set out to join the assembled hosts of souls and leave the world of sin and strife," while about 40 B.C. in the *Fourth Eclogue* of Virgil one finds the famous lines, "Now comes the virgin. . . .new born babe. . .thou shalt be our prince." We know, of course, that Virgil was referring to a specific little Roman child who was already born, but no Roman or Greek poet of a century earlier would have written a poem predicting a millennium. Anticipation and prophecy were in the air. The stage was set for the acceptance of the paternalism provided by the Roman emperor and the assurance of a future life which Christianity was to promise.

Chapter 23

THE REIGN OF AUGUSTUS

THE DEFEAT AND DEATH of Mark Antony left only one major political figure upon the stage—Octavian. In control of the army and without any immediate rivals, Octavian's predominance was such that he was able to maintain peace and restore order to a world which had been torn by war and civil strife for over a century. Governmental readjustments were made which insured a political stability that lasted, with only a few interruptions, for the next two hundred years.

The period of the *Pax Romana,* the Roman Peace, may be said to begin in 29 B.C. with the return of Octavian to Rome; it came to an end with the assassination of Emperor Commodus in 192 A.D. As a result of the generally peaceful conditions prevailing during these two centuries, ancient civilization reached its climax. The largest political unit known to antiquity, the Roman Empire, ultimately stretched from the British Isles to Mesopotamia, and from the Rhine and Danube frontiers to the edge of the African deserts. At the same time the ancient world came to enjoy an economic and cultural unity which included not only the Roman Empire but also the ancient Near East and India. Urbanization reached its peak in the second century of the Christian era, and ancient civilization attained its greatest complexity.

In considering this great cultural epoch, we shall need a description of its social, economic, intellectual, literary, and artistic life, but perhaps it will be most convenient to discuss first the political developments which occurred. Certainly, the subject of the establishment of the Roman imperial system of government and its subsequent evolution is interesting and important, although it should not be overemphasized at the expense of the non-political features of the age.

Octavian is usually considered the founder of the Roman Empire, *i.e.,* the new system of government which now replaced that of the republic.

Courtesy of the Musei Comunali, Rome

PALACE OF DIOCLETIAN AT SPALATO

THE TETRARCHY

Bettman

Alinari

This should not be understood to mean, however, that he discarded the republican system entirely or that the change was made overnight. We shall presently see that Octavian, for the most part, simply followed certain lines of development in the Roman governmental system that had already been clearly marked out since the time of Sulla, or perhaps even earlier. In the second place, it is probably incorrect to assume that Octavian had any definite idea of his final course of action as early as 29 B.C. Unlike Sulla, who wished to go back to the primitive republic, or Caesar, who wished to establish an autocracy, Octavian did not have a fixed program of reform or innovation. It seems more likely that his actions were dictated by circumstances beyond his control, and that certain political settlements which he made as temporary or compromise arrangements subsequently became permanent. Thus, a new system evolved which became further and further removed from the republican tradition and ultimately, three hundred years later, attained the Oriental theocratic form of the Hellenistic monarchy of Alexander and his successors.

It is doubtful whether the change from the republican to the imperial form of government was immediately apparent to Octavian's contemporaries. Let us review the course of events as they may have appeared to the average Roman of the period.

Ever since the time of Marius a succession of internal and external crises had seemed to necessitate temporary departures from the established constitutional traditions of the republic. A series of extraordinary magistracies—the multiple consulships of Marius, the long dictatorship of Sulla, the commands of Pompey against the pirates and Mithridates, the perpetual dictatorship of Julius Caesar, and other political expedients of a similar kind—had been employed to meet difficult situations. The Second Triumvirate was another special bit of machinery devised to tide the republic over the difficulties of the civil war that followed the assassination of Julius Caesar. When Octavian fought with Antony, he possessed some extraordinary powers the exact nature of which is not clear, for it is believed that the triumvirate was terminated after 33 B.C. with the expiration of the second five-year grant of triumviral powers. Perhaps Octavian retained his authority as triumvir; we do know that the senate, the Roman people, and the army swore an oath of loyalty to him.[1]

Octavian continued to hold extraordinary powers until 27 B.C. It was manifestly impossible to return to ordinary republican practice immediately after Antony was defeated in 30 B.C., for reconstruction was needed after the end of the civil war. The army had to be partially demobilized, rewarded for its services, and some veterans absorbed into civilian life. The

---

[1] Moreover, Octavian held the consulship in 33 B.C., probably proconsular power in 32, and the consulship again in successive years from 31 to 23 B.C.

senate had to be reorganized; Octavian purged it of its non-aristocratic members in 28 B.C. and set the number of the senators at six hundred.

At last, in 27 B.C., Octavian formally returned his extraordinary powers to the senate and the people. In other words, he offered to restore the republican form of government. We shall never know whether this action on his part was sincere, or whether it was merely a political gesture. After all, Octavian still held the consulship and had the loyalty of the army, and his strong position in the state was in little danger of being diminished. Moreover, we can be sure that when he had reorganized the senate in the preceding year, he had been careful to see that no one extremely hostile to himself was included in the reformed body.

In 27 B.C. it must have been clear that the work of reconstruction was not yet complete and that, of all prominent Romans, Octavian was best fitted to finish what he had himself begun. Quite naturally, therefore, he was invested with new powers. The most serious and pressing problems were connected with the revision of provincial administration and the defense of the imperial frontiers. As a result, Octavian was given a special proconsular power over Egypt and certain other provinces, mostly on the frontiers, in which the major portion of the Roman army was stationed; older and more settled interior provinces, ten or eleven in number, were to be administered by the senate. Octavian's proconsular power was originally granted for a period of ten years; it was subsequently renewed in varying grants of ten- and five-year terms.

The settlement of 27 B.C. provided the basis of Octavian's power for the next four years. His proconsular command in the provinces gave him virtual control of the army, and his position as consul (even though he had a succession of colleagues) gave him great authority in Rome and Italy. Moreover, since 28 B.C. he had been *princeps senatus*,[2] and thus he was able to guide the deliberations of the senators. Octavian also had the enthusiastic backing of the rank and file of Roman citizens. His popularity gave him more actual power and authority than his constitutional position could ever confer upon him. Already people in many quarters had begun to think of him as being something more than human. This is well illustrated by the fact that as early as 27 B.C. he was given the title of Augustus (the Revered). After this he was rarely called Octavian, and even now it is customary to refer to him as Augustus, a practice which we also shall follow.

In 23 B.C. Augustus resigned his consulship; he held this office again only at intervals. It has often been suggested that he found certain disadvantages in basing part of his power on the consulship because of the fact

---

[2] *Princeps senatus* was the title bestowed upon the most distinguished member of the senate. The *princeps senatus* had the right to speak first of all the senators when the senate was discussing any measure.

that it was necessary to have a colleague in this office. Nevertheless, it might also be pointed out that if it were his intention to preserve cordial relations with the senatorial group and to share the government of the empire with the senate, it would not be politic of him to monopolize this important senatorial office. As a substitute for the consulship, Augustus was given the full power of a tribune; this had already been done in the case of Julius Caesar. Neither Caesar nor Augustus became tribunes; they merely held the tribunician power. The recipient of this power had all the powers of a tribune (the right to call the Assembly of the Tribes, the veto power, and personal inviolability—*sacrosanctitas*), but he was freed of the disadvantage of having the other tribunes as his colleagues.

With his proconsular imperium in the provinces and his tribunician power at home, Augustus possessed enough power to dominate any ordinary situation in which he might find himself involved; but circumstances arose almost immediately which resulted in an extension of his authority. In 23 B.C., in order that he might deal with an important Parthian embassy, Augustus was given the special right to make war and peace in the name of the Roman state. In 22 B.C. the threat of famine in Rome caused the Romans to place the control of the grain supply in Augustus' hands, and he was also empowered to convene the senate at his discretion. Subsequently, he became a member of each of the four great priesthoods, and in 12 B.C. he was made pontifex maximus, the high priest of the Roman state. These religious offices were extremely important because of the close connection of "church and state" in the Roman political organization.

It is not easy to find a name for the new system of government which gradually evolved in Augustus' time. Did Augustus restore the republic? Many of his contemporaries thought so, for they regarded his position and powers as only temporary. Actually, it was impossible to return to the republican system without the recurrence of civil war. At the same time, it had been shown in the case of Julius Caesar that it was equally impossible to break completely with the republican tradition. "Compromise" and "temporize" must necessarily be the watchwords of Augustus.

It has been maintained by some that Augustus established a new form of government—a dyarchy. The dyarchy would consist of the joint rule of Augustus and the senate. The senate was the very backbone of the republican system of organization; moreover, its responsibility for Roman foreign policy and provincial government rested upon ancient foundations. The senators also constituted the oldest, the most cohesive, and the most influential class within the Roman citizenry. Augustus himself, under a dyarchy, would represent the interests of the equestrians, proletarians, and the army. His proconsular imperium emphasized his relationship to the army, whereas his tribunician power made him the representative of the non-senatorial groups, the equestrians and the proletariat. The division of the provinces into two groups—those administered by the senate and those under the control of Augustus—might be looked upon as another example of the joint rule of Augustus and the senate.

On the other hand, it might be said with considerable justification that the Augustan settlement was a modification of the republic in which the executive branch of the government was strengthened by placing a president at its head, a single executive who was not limited, as the consuls were, by dependence upon the senate or by the difficulties inherent in the existence of a colleague who had equal powers. Augustus was often called the *princeps* (first citizen), and we might well call the modified republic the *principate*.

The delicate and precise balance necessary for the continued existence of the modified republic or the dyarchy was difficult to maintain because it presupposed an essentially static condition. New internal or external crises would naturally result in the amplification of the powers of the princeps, who was already very strong. Moreover, too much depended upon the personality of the princeps himself. He must always exercise restraint in order to keep within the bounds of his expressed authority, for his actual authority was much greater than his theoretical constitutional powers indicated. A brief survey of the position of Augustus will demonstrate this point clearly.

As long as Augustus held his proconsular imperium, he was really the commander-in-chief of the army, and if he retained the loyalty of the soldiers, the senators could not depose him. Even if they had not been cowed by the army, the senators were still impotent. Augustus could convene the senate at his pleasure; as princeps senatus he could speak first on any subject; by virtue of his tribunician power he could veto the action of the senate or any magistrate. As pontifex maximus he could employ his religious powers to influence the conduct of public business. The very composition of the senate itself could be determined by Augustus; he could raise equestrians to senatorial rank; senatorial candidates for the magistracies had to obtain his permission to run for office; if necessary, he could assume the consulship and revise the rolls of the senate by virtue of the consular power of the *lectio senatus.*

Although theoretically the consuls and other high officials possessed powers which might have enabled them to hamper Augustus' actions, it was unlikely that they would attempt to do so, since few men who did not have the approval of the princeps would ever attain high offices. Last of all, the princeps was a long-term magistrate, whereas few of the other officials held office for more than a year at a time.

Another foundation for the predominance of the princeps was provided by the growth of the imperial bureaucracy. The Roman Empire was now a big affair which needed the consistent direction of a permanent executive; it was a task beyond the capacity of amateurs. Many responsibilities had devolved upon Augustus: the command of the army, the government of the provinces which had been assigned to him, the care of the city of Rome, control of the grain supply, the supervision of public works in Rome and the empire, the control of the gold and silver coinage, the conduct of foreign affairs, and great judicial responsibilities. Augustus could not personally attend to each small detail; he needed assistants to whom he could delegate authority. The old machinery of government was used as far as possible, but many of the great personal responsibilities of Augustus could not be entrusted to senators; some of the tasks the senators would have refused to assume, and in other cases Augustus could not be sure of their loyalty. What he needed was obedient, trustworthy assistance; he required people who would take orders, and such persons would be those who had something to gain by serving him. Like the government of the provinces in republican times, the imperial government of the principate began as a household affair with the emperors employing their own personal servants, freedmen and even slaves. On the other hand, there were major tasks which needed to be directed by persons of some social standing; thus, Augustus turned to the equestrians, who were natural allies in the potential struggle for power between the princeps and the senators. As a result, while in provincial administration, in the administration of the city of Rome, and in the care of public works, high posts were accorded to senators, the real work was done by equestrians and freedmen. In more sensitive areas of administration the senators were not used, and the princeps appointed equestrians instead. An outstanding example of this is to be seen in the case of the imperial prefectures, offices filled only by equestrians. The bodyguard of the princeps (the praetorian guard), a small army of nine thousand men commanded by equestrian prefects, was stationed just outside Rome. The important province of Egypt was governed by another equestrian prefect. In Rome itself the police and fire brigade was commanded by the Prefect of the Watch, and the grain supply was administered by another prefect; both these officials were equestrians. From this it will be seen that the bureaucracy was not only dominated by, but also really belonged to, the princeps and not the senate. As the empire increased in size, so did the bureaucracy, and the power of the princeps was thus amplified.

Those who thought that the principate of Augustus was to be only a period of transition which would lead back to the real restoration of the republic should have received some warning from what is called the "problem of the succession." This provides another example of a temporary arrangement that grew into a permanent one. The developments connected with it may be summarized as follows:

Augustus was seldom in good health; one of his most serious illnesses occurred in 23 B.C. and he was near death. Even before 23 he had realized that his life might be cut short at any time. In those early days, while the

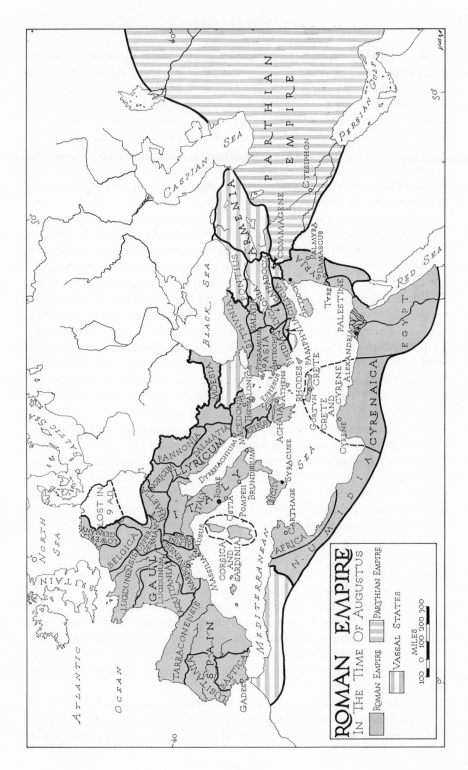

ROMAN EMPIRE
IN THE TIME OF AUGUSTUS

ROMAN EMPIRE
VASSAL STATES
PARTHIAN EMPIRE

MILES
100 0 100 200 300

peace of the empire still rested upon insecure foundations, Augustus felt that chaos might result if he were to die and leave no one to step into his place. His logical understudy must be one who bore the name of Caesar or who was connected with the imperial family in some way.

Marcellus, Augustus' nephew, was his first choice for a successor. Marcellus was given Julia, Augustus' daughter, in marriage, and he was allowed to hold high state offices. In 23 B.C., however, when Augustus was ill, Marcellus was obviously too young and inexperienced to take command if Augustus should die. Therefore, the signet ring of the princeps, a symbol of authority, was given to Agrippa, the trusted friend and principal general of Augustus. Augustus recovered, but Marcellus soon died, and Agrippa became more than ever the chief reliance of the emperor. Julia was now given in marriage to Agrippa, who also became virtually the colleague of Augustus by grants of the proconsular imperium and tribunician power.

In 12 B.C. Agrippa died. His successor was Augustus' stepson, Tiberius, who consequently received Julia, the proconsular imperium, and the tribunician power. Although Augustus later turned away from Tiberius and began to push forward Gaius and Lucius Caesar, the two sons of Agrippa and Julia, the early deaths of the two young men forced Augustus to rely once more upon Tiberius. When Augustus himself finally died at a ripe old age, it was Tiberius who bore the name of Caesar, held the proconsular and tribunician powers, and stood ready to carry on the work of the first princeps.

It is possible to see, in this series of events, the growth of an idea. It is altogether probable that, in the case of Marcellus and again of Agrippa, Augustus felt that the danger of civil war had not passed. Before Agrippa died, however, we may suspect that Augustus had decided that the principate must endure as a governmental form. His subsequent understudies were therefore regarded as heirs to his position.

Once firmly established, the principate could proceed only in one direction—toward autocracy. The power of the princeps increased, and that of the senate waned. Three centuries after the time of Augustus, the principate reached its final and logical form in the Oriental monarchy of Diocletian.

The generally unsettled conditions of the first century B.C. had given the Romans little opportunity to consolidate the territory which they had acquired principally through the campaigns of Pompey and Julius Caesar. Thus, it became the task of Augustus to organize the empire and to find defensible frontiers which would help to eliminate the necessity of maintaining a large army, for a large army was expensive and also dangerous to the state.

In addition to adding Egypt to the empire, Augustus completed the conquest of northwestern Spain and the organization of Caesar's Gaul, but he made no attempt to retain Britain since Caesar had never really secured a foothold there. Augustus believed in employing natural boundaries as frontiers, but in the Near East it was difficult to find any line to separate the Roman and Parthian empires. This problem was solved by using the vassal kingdoms of Armenia, Cappadocia, and Commagene as buffer states; the same thing was done in northwestern Africa, where the vassal kingdom of Mauretania protected the Romans from desert tribes.

In the north Augustus found the entire length of the Danube useful as a boundary, and he incorporated all the territory south of it into the empire—with the exception of Thrace which was not made a province until 46 A.D. For the frontier line running from the north down to the Danube, the Romans had a choice between the Rhine and the Elbe. The Romans already possessed the Rhine boundary, but it was clear that an Elbe-Danube line would make a shorter frontier to defend. Therefore, Augustus resolved to obtain the Elbe line by the conquest of the German territory between the Rhine and the Elbe. The advance into Germany was made, and Augustus was almost on the point of success in 9 A.D. when his general, Varus, and three legions were ambushed and cut to pieces by the Germans in the Teutoberg Forest. This serious loss brought the abandonment of the Elbe line; henceforth, the Rhine was the boundary.

Augustus had not only to reconstruct the Roman government but also the Roman people. The army was brought under discipline and made to realize that it served Rome and not its generals; the men were not addressed as comrades, as had been the custom of the ambitious politicians of the late republic, for when Augustus spoke to the troops he called them soldiers. Roman morale, however, was more difficult to restore. It had been weakened by the civil wars and then completely shaken in the final struggle between Octavian and Antony, particularly since before the victory at Actium it had appeared that Rome might be buried under an avalanche from the Near East. The old Roman spirit must be revived; the morals and patriotism that had made Rome great must be reborn. Augustus deliberately fostered a program of nationalism with the object of restoring the self-respect and confidence of his people. His method was reconstruction through propaganda, aural and visual; through literature, the beautification of Rome, an emphasis upon nationalism in art, a revival of old religious ceremonies, and a series of new coin types the points that Augustus wanted to drive home were suggested and emphasized.

By the end of his reign Augustus could substantiate his boast that he had found Rome a city of brick and left it one of marble. More than fourscore temples were built or restored; from his time dated the Theater of Marcellus, the Baths of Agrippa, a great triumphal arch, a new forum, and two libraries. The Pantheon was built by Agrippa, and Augustus himself ordered the building of a mausoleum. Many statues, including several of Augustus, are known from this age, including the most familiar of all, found in the villa of Livia (Augustus' wife), which portrays the emperor in full armor in a truly majestic pose. Another famous monument of the period was the Altar of Peace (Ara Pacis), which not only emphasized the concept of peace itself but also called the attention of the Romans to their past and present: Aeneas, Romulus and Remus, Mother Earth were shown in separate reliefs, and there was also a frieze representing a procession in which Augustus, the members of the imperial family, priests, senators, and the people of Rome were displayed. Another propaganda device was the huge map of the empire with its roads and cities painted on the wall of the Porticus Vipsania.

Peace and the glory of Rome were themes stressed everywhere. Moreover, Augustus tried to impress upon the mind of his people that a new age had dawned. The Romans had borrowed from the Etruscans the idea of the *saeculum,* era or epoch, which was not a period fixed in terms of years but perceived through signs and portents. A new saeculum should have begun in 43 B.C.; it was heralded by the appearance of a comet, but 43 was not an auspicious time for the beginning of anything. Therefore, when the comet returned in 17 B.C., a new era was proclaimed and celebrated by elaborate ceremonies which lasted the better part of a week. A great hymn, the *Carmen Saeculare,* was composed by the poet Horace for the occasion; Virgil might have done better and would certainly have been chosen, but he had died two years before.

Social reform was also attempted through legislation as well as by persuasion. Sumptuary laws were devised to cut down excessive luxury and ostentation. The institution of marriage, which had come to be regarded rather lightly by the upper classes, was encouraged if not restored to its old Roman position by laws which penalized bachelors, gave special preference to those with large families, and made adultery a criminal offence. People were inclined to laugh a little behind the emperor's back, however, since he himself had been married more than once and had only one child, Julia, who was a notorious adultress.

The principate of Augustus was a great period in Roman literary history, a Golden Age. It was a period not only important in itself but also because it was a culmination of the literary developments of the republic and a point of departure for Roman imperial literature.

Virgil (70–19 B.C.), the author of the *Aeneid,* is the best known of the Augustan poets. The *Aeneid,* although written in imitation of Homer, is more sophisticated than the *Iliad* and *Odyssey* and more artificial; unlike them, it breathes the spirit of nationalism, the very thing that Augustus was trying to foster. Virgil also was indebted to the Alexandrian poets. The *Aeneid* was influenced by Apollonius as well as Homer, and Virgil's *Eclogues* were pastoral poems in the style of Theocritus. The *Georgics,* a didactic poem intended to encourage agriculture and to glorify Italy, received its inspiration from Hesiod, but it stressed the ideas which Augustus was to emphasize in the Ara Pacis.

Horace (65–8 B.C.), a writer of refined and sophisticated poetry, is remembered for his *Satires, Epistles, Odes* and *Epodes.* The poetic form, the satire, had been developed in the second century B.C. by Lucilius; in the skillful hands of Horace it now reached its high point. The *Epistles* are moralizing letters in poetic form which extoll virtue, wisdom, restraint, and simplicity, the traditional Greek view of life. The *Odes* employ Greek lyric meters and are based on Alcaeus and Sappho rather than Catullus and the Alexandrians. The *Epodes* represented an experiment with the iambic style of poetry made famous in Greek literature by Archilochus of Paros. We have already mentioned the *Carmen Saeculare,* but special reference should be made to Horace's *Art of Poetry,* a poetic condensation of Aristotle's *Poetics* in a light and amusing vein.

Love elegies in the style of Catullus and the Alexandrians were written by the Augustan poets Tibullus (54–19 B.C.), Propertius (50–15 B.C.), and Ovid (43 B.C.–17 A.D.). Ovid, the greatest poet of this triumvirate, published his love poetry in two books, the *Amores* and the *Heroides.* He was subsequently banished from Rome because his highly provocative and immoral *Ars Amatoria* (Art of Love) was offensive to Augustus. After this Ovid composed his calendar of Roman festivals, called the *Fasti.* Before his banishment he completed what some consider his best work, the *Metamorphoses,* a series of poems on Greek myths.

The voluminous history of Rome by Livy (59 B.C.–17 A.D.) was also a product of the Augustan period. In one hundred and forty-two books Livy covered the period from Romulus and Remus to 9 B.C.; about one-fourth of this tremendous work remains. Forty years in the writing, it would have to be printed as a ten- or twelve-volume set today. Livy was perhaps the greatest of all the historians who wrote in Latin. He was no Polybius, but he was skillful in narrative, and the literary aspects of his history are its strongest feature. Like Virgil, Livy was a patriot, and his work provided a prose complement to the *Aeneid.*

Roughly contemporary with Livy were Pompeius Trogus, who wrote on Philip of Macedon and Alexander the Great, Dionysius of Halicarnassus whose *Roman Antiquities* (in Greek) covered Roman history, and Diodorus of Sicily who wrote (also in Greek) a universal history which combined the histories of the Greeks and Romans and dealt somewhat with the Near East as well. As a professional historian, Diodorus had definite ideas about the aims and methods of historical writing; he, himself, considering the great task which he had undertaken, is deserving of more recognition than he has received.

Other writers of note were Seneca the Elder, a teacher of oratory and rhetoric, Verrius Flaccus, who dealt with Roman antiquities and the early

Latin language, and Vitruvius, the author of an important work on architecture. Vitruvius had served Augustus as an engineer, surveyor, and architect. His work, divided into ten books, dealt primarily with architecture and the training of architects, but he also included much interesting material on machines of various kinds and engines of war. One of his observations was that the training of an architect must combine a knowledge of craftsmanship with book learning. An architect, said Vitruvius, must be a man of letters, a draftsman, a mathematician, a scientist, a philosopher, a lawyer, and he must know something also about music, medicine, and astronomy. Building materials, methods of construction, and various types of public and private buildings were also discussed in Vitruvius' book.

The central figure of this age is, of course, Augustus himself, the "Architect of the Roman Empire." Augustus, originally called Gaius Octavius, had been born in 63 B.C. during the famous consulship of Cicero and just about a month before the conspiracy of Catiline was hatched in Rome. He died in 14 A.D., having outlived all the friends and enemies of his own generation. At his death there were few individuals in Rome who could remember a time when Augustus was not their emperor. In many ways we are forced to the conclusion that the principate which Augustus founded was a historical accident resulting from the long life of the first princeps.

It is not easy to reconcile the apparent character of Augustus before and after he became emperor; it is almost as if we are dealing with two different people. The hard, callous young man who was willing to proscribe Cicero seems quite unlike the kindly, sympathetic, lovable old man whose birthday was celebrated by the equestrians and for whom the people devotedly brought gifts at the beginning of each new year. The titles of Augustus and *pater patriae* were spontaneously bestowed upon the great ruler as a mark of respect and deep affection. All the world had been yearning for a savior, and one had appeared in human form.

Modest, democratic, and unassuming as a mature man, Augustus refused to follow the autocratic lead of the deified Julius, his adopted father, whose name of Caesar he proudly bore. He declined the dictatorship and the office of prefect of morals, a perpetual censorship, which had been accorded Caesar. He also rejected the custom of being addressed as *Dominus* (Lord) on the ground that slaves used this term in speaking to their masters. Never quick to take offense as princeps, he condoned abusive remarks by the senators, probably feeling that their oratory was a kind of safety valve which allowed them to blow off steam without causing any real harm.

The original of the *Res Gestae,* which might be called the apology or the last will and testament of Augustus, inscribed on a bronze tablet at Rome has long since disappeared, but copies of the text in both Greek and Latin were displayed on stone in the provincial capitals of the Roman Empire. The largest surviving portion of the inscription (in Greek) was found at Ankara in Turkey, but subsequently other copies in Latin as well as Greek were found—a piece here, a piece there, some stones lying on the ground, others built into houses or serving as paving stones—until it has been possible to reconstruct almost the whole text. In the *Res Gestae* Augustus reviewed his career and accomplishments from his appointment as Caesar's heir through his principate. It constitutes our principal source for the long period of his public life; without it we should know very little of the way in which the principate was formed. The fascinating document ends with the words, "When I wrote this, I was in my seventy-sixth year."

Shortly after this the old emperor died. The principate which he founded endured for nearly three centuries, but the Romans retained their affection for Augustus for a much longer time.

Chapter 24

THE ROMAN EMPIRE

(14-192 A.D.)

LTHOUGH THE PERSONALITIES of the emperors who succeeded Augustus are interesting, our real concern must be with the general political developments of the period from 14 to 192 A.D. These developments may be explained in terms of two factors: the struggle of factions within the empire, and the natural evolution of the principate toward autocracy. Thus, we may treat the political history of the imperial period as we did that of the republic.

During the republican era—at least, down to the death of Sulla—we found that various parties or factions were largely responsible for the political vicissitudes of the Romans. The senatorial class, the equestrians, the proletariat, the army, and the allies all had special aims which they tried to achieve or special privileges which they sought to protect. The Social War, of course, eliminated the allies from the picture, and the growing political importance of the army gradually decreased the power of the proletariat. The other factions survived and continued to be significant in determining the course of imperial history. In addition to the senatorial class, the equestrians, and the army, there were new groups of importance on the scene: the praetorian guard and (at a late date) the provincials.

One of the reforms of Augustus was to draw a sharp line between the senatorial and equestrian classes. A senator had to have property valued at one million sesterces ($50,000). Membership in the order was hereditary provided the property qualification could be filled. If it could not, the prospective senator would be demoted to equestrian status. On the other hand, a rich equestrian might hope to gain admission to the senatorial class by a promotion from the princeps. The senators were not only members of the senate; they also served as provincial governors, consuls, and other high state officials in civil and military life.

Equestrians had to possess property valued at four hundred thousand sesterces ($20,000). Free birth and good character were also qualifications for membership in the order. Admission was controlled by the princeps. The equestrians filled minor state offices, and they were the holders of the great prefectures which the princeps never intrusted to senators.

The government of the empire was thus placed on what was, in a way, a timocratic basis. It was largely wealth, rather than ability, which determined class membership. Unfortunately, the division of the classes on the basis of wealth did not help much in breaking the unity of feeling and purpose within the senatorial class itself. The equestrians who were promoted to the senatorial group soon forgot their equestrian sympathies and adopted the point of view of their new colleagues. The senatorial class continued to have a program; it wished to retain its governmental powers and resented any arrogation of authority by the princeps. As late as the second century A.D., many of the senators were still vigorous in their opposition to the principate, which they maintained was almost irreconcilable with liberty.

The equestrians resented the high position of the senators and still hoped for equality with them. Consequently, the equestrians were the natural allies of the princeps in his continuous, though rarely open, struggle with the senate. As time passed, the equestrians made steady gains, especially as a result of the growth of the imperial bureaucracy.

The potentially most powerful faction under the empire was the army; but the fact that the princeps was its commander-in-chief, and the high military offices were held by the senators naturally made the army, on most occasions, the tool of either the princeps or the senators. There were, however, other occasions on which the army chose its own leaders, and then civil war resulted. Ordinarily, the emperors were careful to see that the army was well disciplined—and also well paid. Thus, it was seldom a disturbing element before 192 A.D.

The praetorian guard was a picked group of Italian soldiers. The men had little sympathy for the regular army, and when they entered any situation at all, it was for the selfish interests of themselves as a group. The close connection of the praetorian guard with the princeps meant that the attitude of the guardsmen was sometimes antisenatorial, especially since their commander was an equestrian.

In the early republican period, the city-state Rome had conquered Italy and the citizens of Rome had ruled the Italians. After the Social War, when the Italians were made citizens, it was the Italians (all the Roman citizens of Italy) who ruled the great empire bordering on the Mediterranean. In other words, Italy was a distinct area which enjoyed privileges not accorded to the provinces. During the first century A.D., however, many Romans migrated to the provinces, and numerous communities in the provinces were given Roman citizenship. Naturally, the Roman citizens who dwelt in the provinces acquired regional interests. They began to resent the favored position of Italy; they wanted their own provinces to be placed on an equal footing with the peninsula. As the provinces increased in economic strength (see below, p. 418), their political influence became stronger, and eventually they stood on the same level with Italy. This rise was only gradual, however. It was quite apparent in the second century A.D., although regionalism and decentralization did not attain their greatest importance in politics until the third century.

Keeping in mind the aims of the various factions and the natural tendencies of the system of government known as the principate, we may now turn to a summary of the events and developments of the period from 14 to 192 A.D. This period may be divided chronologically as follows: (1) the Julio-Claudian period (14–68 A.D.), (2) the period of the first civil war (68–69 A.D.), (3) the Flavian period (69–96 A.D.), and (4) the era of the Good Emperors (96–192 A.D.).

At the death of Augustus his stepson Tiberius held the proconsular imperium and the tribunician power. Tiberius convened the senate, and the senate ratified the acts of Augustus, deified him, and after some hesitation, asked Tiberius to continue as princeps in the place of Augustus. With a precedent thus established, a succession of emperors then followed: Tiberius (14–37 A.D.), Gaius (37–41 A.D.), Claudius (41–54 A.D.), and Nero (54–68 A.D.). All these men belonged to the closely related Julian and Claudian clans; their dynasty is therefore known as the Julio-Claudian.

The Julio-Claudian emperors were generally popular with the common people and the army because they were related to Julius Caesar and Augustus. Moreover, their administration was such that the provincials found little reason to complain. The senators, on the other hand, came to hate the Julio-Claudians bitterly. This animosity was caused partly by the friction inevitable in the dyarchal system but mostly by the personal faults of the emperors themselves. Most of our literary sources for the first century A.D. date from the following century when there was at least a fiction of cooperation between the senators and the emperor and when it was fashionable to vilify the Julio-Claudians and their successors, the Flavians. Tacitus and Suetonius, particularly, tried to put the Julio-Claudians in the worst possible light.

Tiberius was a member of the aristocratic Claudian family; his father had served both Caesar and Antony, but it is doubtful whether, under other circumstances, Tiberius would have been a supporter of the principate. As it was, he had spent most of his life in the household of Augustus, and his mother, Livia, was the dowager empress. Tiberius had not had a happy life. He had been forced to divorce his first wife, the daughter of Agrippa, in order to marry Julia whom he detested. Then, after being groomed as Augustus' successor, he had been shoved aside for Gaius and Lucius; worse than that, after they had both died, he had been called back into service again. At the time of his accession he was already fifty-six years old and not at all anxious to be emperor.

Tiberius realized the delicacy of his position, and he was very careful to follow to the letter the policies already laid down by Augustus, especially those relating to the imperial frontiers, where Augustus had rejected any further attempt to conquer Germany and Britain. Many people favored further conquest, however, and this tended to make Tiberius unpopular. One of his first problems was to make his mother, Livia, understand that she did not occupy the throne; this was difficult, but Tiberius managed very well by making Livia appear to be above politics as the wife of the deified Augustus and a kind of high priestess of the imperial cult. Since Tiberius was not a young man, the people of the court did not expect him to reign very long; they began to form parties or factions around the two young men who seemed most likely to succeed him: his son, Drusus, and his nephew and adopted son, Germanicus. Germanicus was the abler and more popular of the two, but he died about 19 A.D. under suspicious circumstances which gave rise to rumors that Tiberius had had him put out of the way. Drusus died four years later, and no obvious successor to Tiberius was to be seen.

With advancing age Tiberius became morose and suspicious. He began to rely heavily upon his praetorian prefect, Sejanus, who played upon Tiberius' fears and suspicions and eventually persuaded him to withdraw to the safety of the island of Capri. This aggravated the dissatisfaction of the senators who were already beginning to chafe at the restrictions imposed upon them by the principate. When several plots against Tiberius were discovered, he began to make use of spies and informers who warned him of real and also imaginary conspiracies. Treason trials were held with increasing frequency, and many senators were convicted and put to death. Sejanus, however, constituted the real danger to Tiberius, since he planned to overthrow him and seize the throne. The aims of Sejanus were finally disclosed to Tiberius by his sister-in-law Antonia; Tiberius managed to have Sejanus arrested and executed in 31, but he had had a narrow escape.

Despite some unrest in the army and a little fighting on the frontiers, the reign of Tiberius was fairly peaceful. One consequence of his long absence from Rome was that the post of prefect of the city (used as a substitute governor of Rome when the emperor was absent under Augustus) now became permanent. Tiberius also transferred the election of the magistrates of senatorial rank from the assembly to the senate. People complained of Tiberius' frugality, but it is possible that he did not have much to spend; the heavy military expenses and building costs of Augustus' reign may have depleted the imperial treasury.

When Tiberius died in 37 A.D., the Romans, including the senators and the army, turned hopefully to his young and popular grandnephew (the son of Germanicus) Gaius, nicknamed Caligula. Gaius, however, soon became insane. In the ensuing reign of terror many were executed or murdered at the command of the mad emperor, who bestowed the consulship upon his favorite horse, shovelled gold dust off the roof of the capitol, proclaimed himself a god, experimented with new poisons on live subjects, made faces at himself in a mirror for light amusement, and bewailed the fact that no great fires, earthquakes, or other catastrophes ever occurred to brighten his dull existence.

In 41 A.D. Caligula was murdered as the result of a senatorial conspiracy. In jubilation the senators proclaimed the restoration of the republic, but the praetorian guard had other plans, since they were vitally interested in the continuation of the principate. While ransacking the palace they came upon Claudius, the uncle of Caligula, hiding in a closet. They dragged him out, proclaimed him emperor, and sent word to the senate which had little choice but to accept.

Claudius, who was crippled and had once been considered by his own family to be mentally deficient, proved himself a careful and conscientious administrator. He was never very popular with the senators, and he did not increase his slight hold on their affections when he chose to rely on the only friends and confidants of his unhappy youth, his freedmen. These Claudius installed as heads of the new government departments of finance, correspondence, petitions, investigation, and records. These key positions in the nascent bureaucratic system were to evolve into important ministries and secretariats by the second century A.D.

Claudius also systematized the government in other ways, revised the courts, provided Rome with a new aqueduct, and improved the harbor at Ostia. Other improvements which he advocated, including three new letters for the Roman alphabet and a new remedy for snake bites, were not universally adopted. A major accomplishment of his reign was the acquisition of new territory, for until the accession of Claudius, there were no important changes in the empire except that Cappadocia and Commagene were reduced to provincial status by Tiberius, and Caligula annexed the kingdom of Mauretania. Claudius, however, not only made Thrace a province but also undertook the conquest of Britain.

It is doubtful whether the conquest of Britain was a necessary step. From the military point of view the English Channel was a much better frontier than any the Romans found in Britain. Furthermore, the cost of conquest and occupation could never be paid from British tribute. On the other hand, any emperor who conquered Britain was likely to be popular, because he would appear to be completing the work of Julius Caesar. Moreover, many argued that the reduction of Britain was the final logical step in the conquest of Gaul. Numerous Gallic malcontents, especially the Druid priests, had taken refuge in Britain, and they were constantly stirring

405

up the Gauls who were Roman subjects. At any rate, Claudius sent Roman forces into Britain in 43 A.D. A foothold was gained in the south, and the Romans expanded their holdings during the next half century.

Claudius was a historian and an antiquarian; he may have been the last person in Rome who knew Etruscan. Among his other distinctions might be included the fact that he was a drunkard and very absent-minded. After he was forced to execute his wife Messalina and her lover, who wished to depose him, he made the fatal mistake of marrying again. His new wife, his fourth, was Agrippina, the sister of Caligula, who was a widow with a teenaged child named Nero. After Claudius had been persuaded to adopt Nero as his son, he died of a gastric disturbance induced, it was said, by one of Agrippina's poisons.

Nero thus became emperor in 54 A.D. The new ruler was young, popular, affable, and highly regarded by the senate during the early years of his reign. For five years he allowed himself to be guided by his mother, by Seneca the Younger, a philosopher, and by Burrus, the praetorian prefect. After this, however, Nero asserted himself. He disposed of his mother, Seneca, and Burrus and became autocratic, extravagant, and antagonistic toward the senate. He devoted much of his time (and that of other people as well) to music and the theater and allowed his new praetorian prefect, Tigellinus, and his freedmen to run the government. There was a revolt in Britain, and the embittered senators began to conspire against Nero. After the great fire in Rome in 64 A.D., for which the Christians were blamed, the heavy taxes imposed by Nero for the rebuilding of the city and the financing of his other expenditures aroused widespread opposition. A revolt broke out in Gaul which spread to Spain where the governor, a senator named Galba, was proclaimed emperor by the troops. In a panic, Nero committed suicide, lamenting "What a great artist the world is losing!"

Galba, who was favored by the senate and the praetorian guard, was brought to Rome and installed as princeps. In the confusion, however, the army got out of hand. The legions on the lower Rhine hailed their commander, Vitellius, as emperor. Galba's strict discipline and parsimoniousness cost him the support of the praetorians, who now murdered him and set Otho, another senator, on the throne (January, 69). Vitellius advanced on Italy. Otho was defeated and committed suicide; Vitellius then became princeps by force of arms (April, 69). Within a short time the Danubian legions and those in the Near East revolted from Vitellius and declared for Vespasian, the principal commander in the war against the Jews which had begun in 66. At the end of 69 Vitellius was overthrown, and Vespasian became master of the empire.

Vespasian was the founder of a new dynasty, the Flavian. He himself ruled from the end of 69 to 79 A.D. He was followed by his elder son, Titus (79–81 A.D.), and his younger son, Domitian (81–96 A.D.).

Ƴ Vespasian came from a long line of publicans. The senate hated him because of his equestrian origin and despised him because he looked like a peasant and acted like one. Unappreciative of the arts, he had once fallen asleep in the theater while Nero was singing. Yet the new emperor had already had much experience in government and a long record of military service. This was the man, people said, who fulfilled the current prophecy that a ruler for the whole world would come out of Judaea.

Leaving his son Titus to finish the Jewish War, Vespasian arrived in Rome early in 70 A.D. A fragmentary inscription, a decree of the senate which was ratified by the popular assembly, records the powers which were given to Vespasian as emperor; it is specified that he shall have the same powers as Augustus, Tiberius, and Claudius, and the incomplete list includes the treaty-making power, the right to convene the senate, freedom from certain laws, as well as the right to nominate candidates for curule posts.

Vespasian was a businessman and a good administrator. By means of rigid economy and higher taxes he wiped out the billion-dollar deficit accumulated by Nero. He also completed the rebuilding of Rome and the pacification of the provinces. The praetorian guard was punished by being reduced in size. It is also interesting to note that under the Flavians the name Caesar, which had been borne as a family name by the Julio-Claudians, now became a title, since the Flavians were not even remotely related to the great Julius. Caesar thus became the origin of the modern titles Tsar and Kaiser.

A great, but simple, man, Vespasian was not fully appreciated by his contemporaries, especially those in the senate who were repelled by his bad manners and Lincolnesque humor. Many of his remarks will not bear repeating, yet he could joke even on his deathbed. As he lay dying, he referred to his imminent deification, saying that he felt he was turning into a god.

Titus was a popular spendthrift and a good soldier who was about thirty-eight years old when he succeeded his father in 79 A.D. Handsome, strong, and possessed of a great memory, he wrote poetry and sang; he was so talented that people began to fear they were about to have a second Nero. Some were worried also about his affection for the Jewish princess Berenice, thinking that she might become another Cleopatra. Something of a Boy Scout, who counted the day lost in which he did not do a good deed, Titus probably deserved a longer and happier reign. He ruled only two years, yet during that time Italy suffered two great catastrophes that would have delighted Caligula: the eruption of Vesuvius in 79 that buried Pompeii and Herculaneum, and a great fire in Rome the following year.

Domitian, the most autocratic and most unpopular of the Flavians, was about thirty when he succeeded Titus in 81 A.D. He made little attempt to co-operate with the senate and insisted upon being addressed as *Dominus et Deus* (Lord and God). His poor generalship cost him the support of the army, while the expense of his military activities and the cost of rebuilding Rome after Titus' fire produced financial difficulties. The Christians and Jews had a bad time under Domitian, and he also expelled philosophers and astrologers from Rome. As a result, practically all those who wrote about his reign at a later time—senators, intellectuals, Christians—could find nothing good to say. He may have been a fairly competent ruler. The target of several senatorial plots, Domitian was finally slain in 96 A.D. as a consequence of a conspiracy that had the co-operation of the praetorian guard.

The Flavian emperors had continued the search for defensible frontiers. The famous general Agricola, the father-in-law of the historian Tacitus, campaigned in northern Britain, pushing the frontier up to the Tyne-Solway line. The most successful move of the Flavians, however, was the shortening of the northern European frontier by drawing a diagonal line from Mainz on the Rhine almost over to Vienna on the Danube. This eliminated a deep salient which cut down into present-day Switzerland.

Domitian's wars against the Dacians, people who lived north of the Danube in what is now Romania, were unsuccessful. The Dacians had been raiding Roman territory, but Domitian could not punish them. When he ended by paying protection money to the enemy, the Romans were scandalized and found another reason for disliking their emperor.

From 14 to 96 A.D., as we have seen, there was constant friction between the princeps and the senators. The senators themselves were never quite powerful enough to overthrow the emperor, but they could always as a last resort gain the support of the praetorians or the army. The so-called Year of the Four Emperors, the period when Galba, Otho, Vitellius, and Vespasian were elevated to the throne in rapid succession, revealed what Tacitus called the "fatal secret": that the army could make and unmake the emperors. Henceforth, the army had to be carefully watched, and, in general, the successful emperors were those whom the soldiers respected or feared.

In the succeeding age, that of the Good Emperors (96–180 A.D.), the Romans enjoyed many years of prosperity and confidence in the future. A certain political equilibrium was attained after the death of Domitian as a better understanding developed between the emperors and the senate and the army was brought under control. It was not until the reign of Commodus (180–192 A.D.) that the spell was broken and times reminiscent of those of Nero and Domitian returned.

The assassination of Domitian caught the army by surprise, nor did the praetorian guard have a candidate for the throne. By default, therefore, the senate was allowed to nominate the princeps. Its choice fell upon an elderly senator named Nerva who was to reign from 96 to 98 A.D. Nerva took an oath never to put a senator to death; he also recalled the political exiles of the Flavian period and punished the informers who had flourished under Domitian. Many people, however, were disposed to worry about the age and infirmity of the new emperor. The restlessness of the army and the praetorians aroused forebodings of a civil war like that which had followed after the death of Nero. Furthermore, no arrangements had been made for the succession. All these problems were solved early in 97 A.D. when Trajan, a Spaniard and a competent general, was adopted by Nerva and given the proconsular imperium and the tribunician power. When Nerva died in 98 A.D., after a brief reign of less than two years, Trajan succeeded him without opposition.

Trajan was the first Roman emperor to be born outside the peninsula of Italy; both he and his father, also a distinguished general, were natives of the Roman colony of Italica in Spain. Trajan (98–117 A.D.) enjoyed great popularity with both the senate and the army. He, like Nerva, took an oath never to put a senator to death; in return, he received strong senatorial support. The army continued to favor Trajan because of his vigorous policies of foreign conquest. In his middle forties at the time of his accession, Trajan was well fitted for the task at hand.

The new reign opened auspiciously with two brilliant campaigns against the Dacians. It was felt that the disgrace incurred by Domitian must be wiped out. Moreover, although the conquest of Dacia would give Rome a province across the Danube which would be hard to defend, the fertile land of Dacia and its gold looked well worth the effort. The Romans needed the precious metal to bolster their sagging currency, and the campaigns would occupy the soldiers and gain popularity for Trajan with the Roman citizens as a whole. By 106 the conquest of the Dacians and the annexation of their country had been completed.

The next step was the rehabilitation of Italy. The Italian economy had been slipping for some time due to the commercial and industrial competition of the western provinces. Trajan inaugurated a big public works program which included much building in Rome and the construction of roads and port facilities in Italy.

Under Trajan the Roman Empire reached its greatest territorial extent. Trajan not only conquered Dacia, but he also annexed an Arabian kingdom that lay to the east of Syria and Palestine (106 A.D.) and almost acquired the Parthian Empire. War between the Romans and Parthians began in 114 A.D. when the Parthians took possession of Armenia. Trajan reconquered Armenia, overran Mesopotamia and Assyria, and penetrated Babylonia to the Persian Gulf. A Jewish revolt in the Near East, however, forced Trajan to retrace his steps from Parthia in 116 A.D., and his death in the following year prevented the consolidation of his Parthian conquests.

Just before Trajan died, he adopted his cousin Hadrian. Hadrian was acclaimed emperor by the army, and his appointment was ratified by the senate. His reign (117–138 A.D.) was generally peaceful, although growing tension between the princeps and the senate might be observed. Hadrian treated the senate with outward respect, but a number of his reforms reduced this body to a subordinate position. His division of Italy into four judicial districts presided over by imperial nominees (*juridici*) struck directly at the traditional senatorial control over the peninsula and also had the effect of reducing Italy to the level of the provinces. Moreover, Hadrian began to rely more heavily upon the equestrians to assist him in governmental administration, and opportunities for civil service careers for those of equestrian rank were increased. Hadrian also replaced the freedmen in the great imperial secretariats with equestrians. These offices, which had originated in the reign of Claudius, now acquired greater prestige.

Hadrian abandoned the Parthian territory which Trajan had gained, and he returned Armenia to its former position as a vassal kingdom. He probably felt that in military and financial strength the empire was incapable of controlling such extensive regions in the east. Hadrian's general policy was one of strengthening the frontiers by adequate fortifications. He fortified the Flavian Rhine-Danube sector, and during his reign the famous wall was built across northern England from the Tyne to Solway Firth.

Hadrian made a great effort to know his empire and its problems. During his reign he managed to visit virtually every province; he was several times in Greece and Asia. Everywhere he encouraged building projects; virtually a whole new suburb was added in southeast Athens, the emperor's favorite city. His fondness for Greece and the Greeks irked some people, and they criticized the emperor's adoption of Hellenic costume and his Greek beard.

Shortly before Hadrian died, he adopted a middle-aged senator who became the next emperor, Antoninus Pius (138–161 A.D.). The reign of Antoninus was notable for its internal peace and freedom from foreign conflicts, and the Romans could celebrate with joy and confidence the nine hundredth anniversary of their city's birth. As a concession to the senate, Antoninus abolished the Italian judicial system that Hadrian had established.

The two adopted sons of Antoninus, Marcus Aurelius and Lucius Verus, succeeded him in 161 A.D. as co-emperors. Marcus Aurelius, the elder princeps, was much more competent than Verus and assumed the major responsibility for imperial government. Hence, Verus' death in 169 A.D. did not lead to any significant changes in the administration of the empire.

There was no conflict between Marcus Aurelius and the senate, even though the emperor did not take the customary oath regarding the senators, and even though he did restore Hadrian's *juridici* in Italy. It was his misfortune to have to engage in a series of foreign wars with the Parthians and with the barbarians who were pressing upon the Danubian frontier. The wars were very expensive; at one time the barren condition of the treasury forced the emperor to sell many of his personal belongings at public auction in order to carry on the war against the barbarians. Earlier, the army upon its return from the Parthian campaigns had brought back a plague which swept over the empire and left thousands dead in its wake.

Marcus Aurelius was the last of the so-called Good Emperors, the line of rulers which had begun with Nerva. The Good Emperors had on the whole kept peace with the senate and given the empire the benefit of careful, conscientious government. The army and the praetorian guard had been kept under strict discipline. Down to the time of Marcus Aurelius, prosperity had been evident throughout the empire except in Italy and Egypt. An increasing number of provincial communities had received grants of Roman citizenship.

The saintly and conscientious Marcus Aurelius deserved a happy reign, but it was a troublesome one instead. This philosopher-emperor, who called himself a citizen of the world, did his best to be a good man and a good emperor. In his *Meditations* and in his letters to his teacher, Fronto, we see him as a well-intentioned, likeable person, devoted to his family, his friends, and his duty. Marcus Aurelius' fault was that he refused to see the faults of others, particularly the faults of the members of his family. He apparently never knew of the infidelities of his empress and never suspected the viciousness and incapacity of his son, Commodus, who was made co-emperor in 177 and succeeded his father in 180.

A nearly empty treasury, a dissatisfied army, and an incompetent emperor soon brought disaster. The senate was antagonized, and the praetorians were alienated. To cap the climax, Commodus seems to have become insane. Among other things, he identified himself with Hercules and insisted on renaming Rome the "Colony of Commodus." He was well on his way toward equalling the exploits of Caligula or Nero when a palace conspiracy accomplished his death by strangulation at the very end of 192.

Although the principate was to survive Commodus by nearly a century, the Augustan system had seen its best days. Future emperors were to take more and more power into their own hands in a more open fashion while the senate continued to decline. The equestrians and the soldiers would soon dominate the bureaucracy, and Italy would cease to enjoy its favored role as regional and provincial interest began to make itself felt.

Historians from time to time have affected to see a difference in principle governing the succession at various periods during the early principate, but such views do not seem to be well founded in fact. It is true that (1) under the Julio-Claudians the throne was kept in the family, that (2) the Flavians passed it from father to son, and that (3) under the Good Emperors the successors were adopted and were mature and experienced men, but it takes very little reflection to see that the principle of hereditary succession was the ideal; the apparent deviations from it were occasioned by expediency. Augustus did not have a son, so he proposed to elevate Julia's children, Gaius and Lucius; when they died, he had to fall back on Tiberius. The rest of the Julio-Claudians lacked heirs, so they did the next best thing which was to select an eligible member of the family. Vespasian had two sons, and the Romans did not question their rights to the throne. From Nerva to Marcus Aurelius there was no emperor who had a son to survive him; the "best man" was designated for the succession because there was nothing else to do. Certainly Marcus Aurelius, who did have a son, did not hesitate to make him the next emperor. "Family" was very important to the Romans; Octavian's prestige was based at first on the fact that he bore the name of Caesar. After Julius Caesar was deified, Augustus had the additional prestige of being the adopted son of a god. In the case of future emperors, the apotheosis of the rulers continued to invest their successors, whether adopted or blood relatives, with this advantage over other possible claimants to the throne.

As time passed and the principate became well established, its organization naturally tended to become more sophisticated. An imperial court with a staff and ceremonial and set ritual developed, responsibilities in certain posts became fixed, and routine affairs began to be handled more smoothly and efficiently. In the time of Augustus many functions had been handed over to members of his household and personal servants. Claudius, who liked things neat and orderly, had organized an embryonic bureaucracy within the palace by establishing secretaryships which were held by his freedmen. He appointed a secretary to handle petitions, another for the imperial records, a secretary of the treasury, two secretaries for the royal correspondence, and so on. This was hardly new in Roman history; Sulla had used his freedmen in much the same manner. Nevertheless, managing the empire was a big business, and the imperial secretaryships grew in importance until these posts came to be regarded as desirable by people of higher social status. In the time of Hadrian the freedmen were removed and replaced by equestrians. New prefectures of somewhat lesser importance than those of the praetorian guard, Egypt, the watch, the city, and the grain supply were created. The fleet, which was used to hold down piracy and for transport and communication, was commanded by prefects, and when Hadrian established an imperial communications system on land, it was also headed by a prefect. On the lower levels there was a growing tendency to multiply the number of imperial agents who functioned as investigators, spies, fiscal officers, legal assistants, and represented the emperor in other ways.

The Roman Empire was an aggregation of urban and rural communities which enjoyed a large measure of local self-government; these communities were grouped into provinces and bound to Rome by varying relationships. At the beginning of the principate there were thirteen provinces; by the death of Augustus, twenty-eight; and in the time of Hadrian, forty-five. Imperial expansion was partly responsible for this increase in number; but many provinces were divided and subdivided to form new provinces so that the task of the governors would be easier and the danger of large-scale revolts lessened.

The administration of the provinces was divided between the princeps and the senate. The eleven provinces under the care of the senate were headed by senatorial governors (former consuls and former praetors) all of whom had proconsular powers. The general arrangements were much as they had been under the republic, and the revenues from these provinces went into the senatorial treasury at Rome, the *aerarium Saturni.*

The provinces that were administered by the princeps were, in general, those most recently acquired and those in which military forces were stationed. These so-called imperial provinces were governed by different types of officials. Egypt, for example, had an equestrian prefect. Small provinces might be under an equestrian procurator, but most of the imperial provinces were governed by imperial legates with propraetorian powers. The legates were assisted by fiscal and military officials. Revenues from the imperial provinces eventually found their way into the central treasury at Rome, the *fiscus.*

The direct taxes in the provinces consisted mainly of a poll tax paid by those who were not Roman citizens, and land and property taxes which were assessed on the basis of a census taken periodically. A fixed sum might be levied annually upon the senatorial provinces, but in the imperial provinces the tribute was a percentage of the annual yield. Indirect taxes consisted of customs duties, a tax on the manumission of slaves, and possibly a sales tax. Food, supplies, and materials might be requestioned from the provincials for the support of the military forces within a given province; this was called the *annona.* The *publicani,* or sometimes individual contractors called *conductores,* collected the indirect taxes. Direct taxes in the senatorial provinces were collected by the *publicani* until about the time of Hadrian, but in the imperial provinces the agents of the emperor were responsible for tax collection from the beginning of the principate.

On the whole, the administration of the provinces was on a much higher plane in the imperial period than it had been during the republican era. Although there continued to be some graft and extortion, the attitude of the government was well expressed by Tiberius, when he warned a governor that it was the duty of a good ruler "to shear his flock, not to skin it."

The old classification of communities within the provinces—free and federate, free and non-tributary, and tributary—persisted. In addition, Roman and Latin colonies were planted in the provinces, and many of the older urban centers in the west were granted Roman or Latin citizenship. Those communities which were urbanized enough to have some form of municipal government were the key points in the provinces. Eventually, the Roman government hoped to attach all rural areas to nearby municipalities, and therefore the growth of towns and cities was encouraged in outlying regions; in the more settled areas, rural territory was turned over to the cities for administration.

Municipal organization varied throughout the empire. In the east the Greek polis with its magistrates, council, and assembly was the prevailing type. In the west the Italian municipal system as reorganized by Julius Caesar provided the model. The western municipalities each had a local senate (*curia*) whose members, the *decuriones,* were men of considerable property. The magistrates were the *duoviri* (two men whose functions somewhat resembled those of the consuls at Rome) and the *aediles,* two other officials who were chiefly treasurers and market commissioners. In both the east and the west municipal government was on a timocratic basis; it was the rich who held the high offices and had the responsibility of government, whereas the poorer citizens had less and less opportunity to express themselves politically. During the second century A.D. the municipalities lost much opportunity for self-government because their financial inefficiency necessitated the interference of the emperor, either through the provincial governor or through special appointees called *curators.*

The municipalities were extremely important as centers of cultural diffusion. Their growth greatly aided the "Romanization" of Spain, Gaul, and Britain as well as northern Africa. The municipalities are interesting to the cultural historian not only because of this particular function but also because of the survival of their governmental form down to the modern period; this survival was especially marked in Spain, and the Spaniards subsequently transplanted their municipal organization to the New World.

An even more outstanding instance of survival is provided by Roman law, which became the basis for medieval canon law, and, in the modern period, for international law and various European legal systems. In early Rome, before the middle of the fifth century B.C., the patrician priests had the guardianship of customs and laws, and the patrician magistrates dispensed justice. After the codification of the Law of the Twelve Tables about 450 B.C. a basis for future expansion was provided. The ancient laws were put into definite form, and new laws could be added as the occasion arose. There was also the important question of the interpretation of the law.

During the republican period, the laws (*leges*) were made by the *comitia centuriata.* At first the plebiscites of the plebeian assembly were binding upon the whole citizen body only when approved by the senate; but after 287 B.C. this approval was no longer needed, and plebiscites passed by the *Comitia Tributa* had the force of law. The decrees (*senatus consulta*) of the senate did not produce much in the way of legislation in the republican period because they dealt chiefly with constitutional matters.

The real development of Roman law came through its interpretation; it is one of the most striking features of the law that it was created not so much by legislation as by jurisprudence. From the very beginning the Law of the Twelve Tables and other Roman laws created problems of interpretation. In the early days the Roman pontiffs had expounded the law to magistrates and private individuals, but by the third century B.C. a class of legal specialists (*iuris prudentes*) had come into existence. The *prudentes* first gave their opinions orally; gradually, however, they began to write books and monographs on legal subjects: elementary handbooks, treatises on procedure and interpretation, and so on. These experts did not practice law or accept money for their services, but their advice was eagerly sought, and they came to be accepted as an integral part of the legal system.

Another important source of change and modification was provided by the praetor's edict. The city praetor, the *praetor peregrinus,* and provincial governors were the principal officers who contributed to the growth of the praetor's edict. When a praetor took office, it was customary for him to issue a statement or edict in which he laid down the principles which he planned to observe in enforcing the laws and allowing redress. Slanted in the direction of increasing equity, the praetor's edict led to the formulation of new legal principles and new remedies at law. Although each praetor issued his own edict, it was naturally customary for him to incorporate into it many precedents established by those who had gone before him in the office. The city praetor was primarily responsible for the development of civil law, but the *praetor peregrinus* and the provincial governors, who dealt with cases involving both Romans and foreigners, had to take into account existing laws and customs which were non-Roman in origin and firmly established. Thus was evolved the concept of the *ius gentium* (Law of Nations), law which applied equally to Romans and foreigners. This, in turn, was bound to effect and enrich the common law. In time a Law of Nature came to be recognized by the jurists also; this was thought to be a pattern of universal law which depended upon "right reason." There is no question that from the second century B.C. onward Roman law was subject to modification by contact with Greek law and Greek philosophical concepts.

The sources of republican law had been, then, statute, interpretation, and edict. In the imperial period, of course, the assemblies declined; by the second century A.D. they no longer made laws. The decrees of the senate, on the other hand, increased in importance because it was through them that the princeps frequently expressed his will. More significant, however, were the edicts, responses, judicial verdicts, and mandates of the emperors. All these came to have the force of law. The mandates were orders to officials, edicts were proclamations, and the responses or rescripts were replies emanating from the palace in answer to questions submitted by magistrates and governors regarding specific points of judicial administration. The emperors themselves were probably not responsible for most decisions; rather, these came from experts on jurisprudence attached to the imperial staff. One of the two praetorian prefects was usually an eminent jurist. In the second and early third centuries A.D. a long series of great authorities served at the court.

The codification of Roman law was a necessity; it had been one of the dreams of Julius Caesar. The process of codification, however, went very slowly. In the second century, under Hadrian, the praetor's edict was codified, and the imperial edicts were codified two centuries later in the time of Theodosius (438 A.D.). The final codification in the *Corpus Juris Civilis* of Justinian was carried out between 529 and 535 A.D. Of the four parts into which the *Corpus* was divided, the first (Institutes) dealt with the principles of law, the second (Digest) contained written opinions of the great jurists, the third (the Code) included the decrees of the emperors, and the fourth (*Novellae*) was reserved for new laws.

Chapter 25

THE CLIMAX
OF ANCIENT CIVILIZATION

THE PERIOD of the Pax Romana was characterized by the most widespread prosperity and most flourishing economic activity the ancient world had ever known. Except in a few scattered regions agriculture, trade, and industry reached new levels of production. The increased volume of trade everywhere led to the growth of new cities as well as an increase of population in the older urban areas; commercial advances were likewise paralleled by an amplification of industrial production. The progress of urbanization naturally brought with it a more complex and more widely diffused civilization.

This was the Roman phase of Hellenistic civilization. To the Hellenistic base were added the contributions which the western Mediterranean had to make, principally the Roman adaptations and elaborations of culture traits that had been borrowed from the peoples of the eastern Mediterranean. New contacts with the Near East, India, and even the Far East were productive of cultural borrowings which were added to the general store of culture traits, and much of this borrowed finery was modified and adapted to meet the needs of the Occident.

The civilization of the first two centuries of the Christian era possessed all the characteristics that we have already associated with Hellenistic civilization. We shall have occasion to observe specific examples of the universalism, individualism, syncretism, eclecticism, and specialization which were present in this age. We have already mentioned urbanization as a characteristic, and it will also be shown that a movement of peoples occurred which might be characterized as colonization.

It is probably a fair question to ask whether the Pax Romana was responsible for the economic prosperity of the first two centuries A.D., or whether the economic prosperity of that period produced the Pax Romana. The answer may be that the peace which the reign of Augustus gave the Roman world provided the necessary impetus and opportunity for economic growth, and that the favorable economic conditions that immediately resulted gave the empire a stability which for many years could not be upset by mere political ruptures and changes.

Looking at the economic life of this period as a whole, we may note certain developments as being especially important. In the first century A.D. Italy reached its commercial and industrial peak. In the meantime the western provinces gradually built up their trade, industry, and agricultural production to a point where, even before 100 A.D., they were fast becoming economically independent of Italy. In the second century these provinces freed themselves from Italian dominance, with the result that Italy fell into a subordinate position in world economic affairs. In the second century, too, the eastern provinces (even including Greece) became more prosperous than they had been since perhaps 100 B.C. The one exception to this rule in the east was Egypt which began to feel the full effects of the ruthless economic exploitation practiced there by the Roman government; the Egyptian situation was also aggravated by a succession of "low Niles" which curtailed agricultural production. Conditions during this period of two centuries were anything but static. On the contrary, there was a gradual, but very definite, change in almost every aspect of economic life and activity; the general situation which prevailed at the end of the period was far different from that in the time of Augustus.

The trade of the Roman Empire had two aspects: internal and external. The internal trade grew by leaps and bounds in the early period of the Pax Romana. The suppression of piracy by the imperial fleet, the reduction of customs barriers, the uniform system of imperial coinage, and the general improvement of communications and facilities for transportation all contributed to this development. The Roman army was employed for widespread road building in all the provinces, harbors were improved, and much use was made of inland waterways, especially in Gaul and Britain.

During the first century A.D. Italy was the chief distributor of manufactured goods to the western provinces. Italy herself produced wine, olive oil, pottery, glassware, and metalwork which she exchanged for the grain, hides, metals, foodstuffs, and raw materials of Spain, Britain, Gaul, and Africa. The Italians were also the middlemen in the trade between the provinces of western Europe and the Near East.

Toward the end of the century, however, there was a growth of domestic manufacturing in Gaul, Britain, and Spain that seriously curtailed Italy's exports to the west. The Gauls and the Britons, in particular, began to make their own pottery, glass, woolens, and metal products. Italy soon felt the effects of an unfavorable balance of trade, a condition further aggravated by the fact that Italian wine and olive oil had to face the increasing competition of similar products from Gaul, Spain, and Africa.

Gaul, Britain, and Spain were all noted for their cattle, horses, sheep, and wheat; metals, too, were important. The British exports included also slaves, dogs, oysters, pearls, and woolen cloth. Among the special products of Spain were flax, honey, fish, oranges, lemons, and figs; the steel of Toledo was already famous. North Africa was mainly an agricultural and pastoral area which exported fruits, vegetables, horses, and cattle as well as wheat, olive oil, and wine.

In the Roman East economic conditions gradually improved and became very favorable during the second century A.D. Greece produced wine and olive oil; the Greek city of Patras was known for its linens; Corinth regained its old prosperity as a trading center and was also a leading manufacturer of terra cotta lamps. Trade and manufacturing were highly significant in the coastal cities of Asia Minor, whereas in the interior agriculture and grazing flourished. The exports of Asia Minor were metal and textile products, parchment, timber, and stone. As the middlemen in the trade between the Parthians and Arabs on the one hand and the Roman Empire on the other, the merchants of Syria continued to find trade profitable. The steel of Damascus and the glassware, dyes, woolens, and linen of Phoenicia were also valuable exports.

We know most about economic conditions in Egypt because of the thousands of papyrus documents that have been recovered from the ruins of Egyptian cities and villages of the Roman period. It has been estimated that the Roman government extracted from Egypt a revenue of about twenty million dollars a year in addition to the five million bushels of wheat annually sent from that country to Rome. Egypt was, of course, a tremendously rich country which produced grains, vegetables, legumes, and fruits of various kinds. Moreover, the Egyptians manufactured vegetable oils, textiles, papyrus, glass, pottery, jewelry, perfumes, and cosmetics. Finally, Alexandria was a commercial center which served as a terminus for the major portion of the great external trade that was built up between the Roman Empire and Arabia, India, and east Africa.

Unfortunately, Roman greed and mismanagement ruined Egypt, the most valuable of all the Roman possessions. Most of the carefully planned state capitalism of the Ptolemies was abandoned for a policy which allowed Roman citizens as well as the Roman government to plunder the country. In Egypt the Roman government levied more than fifty different agricultural taxes which were paid in kind as well as taxes on trades and professions paid in money. There were internal and external customs duties and numerous special levies and assessments. Last of all, more than two hundred miscellaneous taxes are known to have been levied in Egypt.

Returning once more to the subject of trade, we may consider the ex-

WALL OF ANTONINUS
WALL OF HADRIAN

IRELAND

BRITAIN

NORTH SEA

BALTIC

ATLANTIC

OCEAN

ENGLISH CHANNEL

EBURACUM
DEVA o LINDUM
BRITAIN
CAMULODUNUM
LONDINIUM

LUGDUNUM
BATAVORUM
(LOST IN 9 A.D.)
COLONIA
AGRIPPINA

LOWER
GERMANY

GERMAN

BELGICA

LUTETIA

MOGUNTIACUM
AUGUSTA TREVERORUM

CANTABRIAN
SEA

BURDIGALA

LUGDUNENSIS

AQUITANIA

AUGUSTODUNUM

GAUL

UPPER
GERMANY

AUGUSTA VINDELICO
VINDOBO
CARN

CARP

LUGDUNUM

RHAETIA
VINDONISSA

NORICUM

ALPINE
PROVINCES

ALPS

COMUM AQUILEIA
MEDIOLANUM
VERONA PATAVIUM
o BONONIA
RAVENNA
FLORENTIA

SISCIA

ILLYRICUM
PANNONI

40° PORTUS CALE

ASTURICA

SALMANTICA

NUMANTIA

TARRACONENSIS

S P A I N

PYRENEES

TOLOSA

NARBONENSIS

NEMAUSUS
ARELATE
NARBO
MASSILIA

GENUA

LIGURIAN
SEA

ITALY

DALMA
NARO

ADRIATIC
SEA

OLISIPO
LUSITANIA

EMERITA AUGUSTA

CAESAR AUGUSTA

TOLETUM

CASTULO

TARRACO

CORSICA
AND
SARDINIA

ROME
OSTIA

ITALY

CORDUBA
BAETICA

VALENTIA

POMPEII

BRUNDISIUM

TARENTUM

HISPALIS

MALACA

GADES

NEW CARTHAGE

BALEARIC IS.

MEDITE

CARALES

TYRRHENIAN
SEA

CORCYF
IONIA
SEA

TINGIS

HIPPO
REGIUS

UTICA

MESSANA

SICILY

RHEGIUM
AGRIGENTUM
SYRACUSE

MAURETANIA

SITIFIS
CIRTA
LAMBAESIS
THAMUGADI

THEVESTE
AFRICA

CARTHAGE

ATLAS MTS.

GAETULIA

THAPSUS

LESSER
SYRTIS

NUMIDA

OEA
LEPTIS

NEAN

GREATER
SYRTIS

A F R

ROMAN EMPIRE
ABOUT 120 A.D.

| | ROMAN EMPIRE | | PARTHIAN EMPIRE |
| | TEMPORARILY HELD BY ROME | | ARMENIA |

MILES
100 50 0   100 200   300

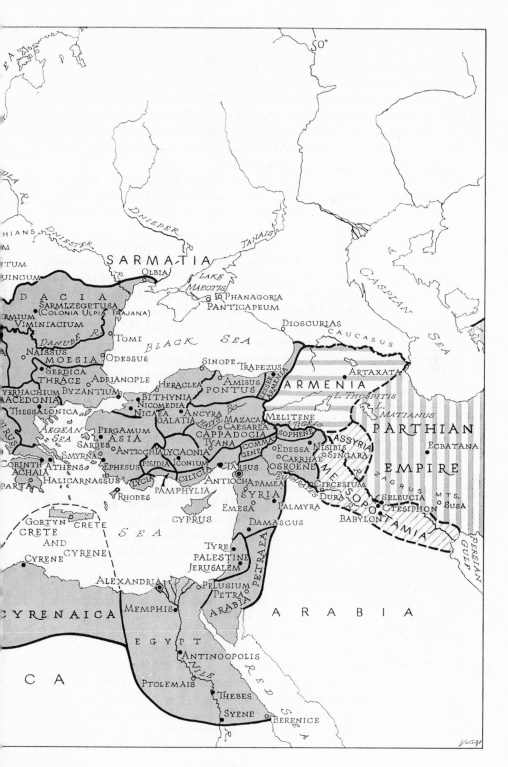

SARMATIA

DACIA
SARMIZEGETUSA
(COLONIA ULPIA TRAJANA)
VIMINIACIUM
DANUBE R.
MOESIA
NAISSUS
SERDICA
THRACE
ADRIANOPLE
YRRHACHIUM BYZANTIUM
MACEDONIA
THESSALONICA
RUS
AEGEAN
SEA
CORINTH ATHENS
ACHAIA
PARTA HALICARNASSUS
PERGAMUM
ASIA
SARDES
SMYRNA
EPHESUS
RHODES

OLBIA
LAKE
MAEOTIS
PHANAGORIA
PANTICAPEUM

DNIEPER
DNIESTER
TANAIS
50°

BLACK   SEA
TOMI
ODESSUS
SINOPE
TRAPEZUS
HERACLEA
PONTUS
AMISUS
BITHYNIA
NICOMEDIA
NICAEA
ANCYRA
GALATIA
MAZACA
CAESAREA
CAPPADOCIA
TYANA
LYCAONIA
ANTIOCHIA
PISIDIA ICONIUM
LYCIA
CILICIA
TARSUS
PAMPHYLIA
ANTIOCHAPAMEA
CYPRUS
EMESA
DAMASCUS
PALMYRA
TYRE
PALESTINE
JERUSALEM

DIOSCURIAS
CAUCASUS
ARTAXATA
ARMENIA
L. THOSPITIS
L. MATIANUS
PARTHIAN
EMPIRE
ECBATANA
MELITENE
SOPHENE
COMMA
GENE
EDESSA
CARRHAE
OSROENE
NISIBIS
SINGARA
ASSYRIA
ZAGRUS
CIRCESIUM
DURA
SELEUCIA
SUSA
CTESIPHON
MTS.
BABYLON
MESOPOTAMIA
PERSIAN GULF

CASPIAN   SEA

GORTYN CRETE
CRETE
AND
CYRENE
CYRENE
CYRENAICA
CA
MEMPHIS
PTOLEMAIS
SYENE

SEA
ALEXANDRIA
PELUSIUM
PETRA
ARABIA
EGYPT
ANTINOOPOLIS
NILE
THEBES
BERENICE
RED SEA

PETRAEA
ARABIA

ternal commercial relations of the Roman Empire. This external trade formed part of a great body of commerce that was carried on over a vast area stretching from the British Isles to the China Sea. In the West Britain and Gaul traded with Ireland, Scotland, Scandinavia, and Germany. Roman merchants crossed the Danube to carry their wares into central Europe; the conquest of Dacia by Trajan had been preceded by Roman economic penetration. The Black Sea region and southern Russia had been in commercial contact with the Mediterranean world since the sixth century B.C. From the cities of northern Africa, caravan routes ran southward into the Sahara, and traders and explorers from Egypt went up the Nile past the cataracts and into Nubia and equatorial Africa.

Most interesting, perhaps, is the subject of trade between the Romans and the East. The commercial relations between the eastern Mediterranean and India had, of course, attained great significance during the Hellenistic period. Up to the time of Augustus most of the Indian trade passed through the hands of Arabian middlemen who transported goods overland to Syria. Augustus, however, by his annexation of Egypt opened the African Red Sea ports to Roman merchants so that they might sail to the cities of southeastern Arabia. Subsequently, an all-water route from the Red Sea to India replaced the early one; the geographer Strabo reported that about 120 ships a year made this voyage.

The Roman government at various times entered into commercial treaties with the Parthians with the idea of furthering trade not only with Mesopotamia but also with the Far East, particularly China. This was because one of the main routes from Syria to China passed through Mesopotamia, across Iran to Bactria, and thence through Turkestan to China itself. Another route ran from Bactria to the Caspian and from there to the Black Sea. In the trade between Syria and Mesopotamia the great caravan city of Palmyra on the edge of the Arabian desert was highly important. We shall later see that Palmyra became rich and powerful enough to take advantage of Roman weakness in the third century A.D. and to maintain an independent political existence for a brief period.

From India the Romans imported cotton, spices, precious stones, ivory, rare woods, indigo, rice, and sugar; from Arabia came spices, frankincense, and myrrh; from China, principally silk and furs. In return, the Romans exported metals, amber, textiles, and glass. Thus, it is clear that one may draw a parallel between the trade relations of the Orient and Occident as they existed in (1) the first two centuries A.D. and (2) the period between the Crusades and the voyages of Columbus and Vasco da Gama. In both cases the trade between Orient and Occident was essentially a luxury trade; the high cost of transportation, the substantial profits demanded by the middlemen of the Near East, and the numerous customs barriers erected between the East and the West all helped to make goods which were relatively cheap in the countries of their origin very expensive when they reached their final destination. Moreover, the balance of trade distinctly favored the East. Oriental exports were mostly of light weight and small bulk, whereas Occidental exports were, in general, both heavy and bulky; the advantage of the Orientals in overland trade is therefore quite plain. The fact that the Orientals wanted most of all the metals of the West, especially gold and silver, meant that the West was being gradually drained of its media of exchange; it has been estimated that five million dollars in gold and silver were lost by the Romans to the Orientals every year. Consequently, the Oriental-Occidental trade was doomed to temporary extinction, and the loss of the precious metals not only made it increasingly difficult for the Romans to trade with the Far East, but also became a contributing factor in the economic decline within the Roman Empire itself.

The only solution to this commercial problem was the discovery of all-water routes to the Far East. The Romans did open an all-water route from Egypt to India; this was probably one reason for the decline of the Parthian Empire. On the other hand, the trade with China continued to be an overland trade, and it was not until the time of Columbus and Vasco da Gama that the Europeans were able to provide a satisfactory answer to this question.

Large companies or corporations for either commercial or manufacturing ventures were rare among the Romans and their subjects. Individuals or families and their employees or slaves handled the majority of business projects. Most manufacturing was done in small shops, although there were some large establishments which produced pottery, metalwork, glassware, or bricks and tiles. The growth of large commercial and industrial firms was to a great extent discouraged by the developments of the second century when, for example, domestic manufacturing increased in the western provinces. This provincial industry existed mainly to satisfy the demands of the local markets, and the bulk of the trade also became regional. Each city and its surrounding agricultural area tended to become an economic unit, a situation which was to be found in the eastern as well as the western provinces.

The large fortunes of the age were made either in trade or in money-lending. The banking practices of the Hellenistic Age were adopted in the West, and as trade and industry grew, banking operations expanded and became more complex. Roman capital was invested not only in Italy but also in the provinces. Land investments in the provinces were favored by the senatorial class, whereas the equestrians put their money into provincial industry and trade. Many Roman families abandoned Italy and settled in the provinces. In fact, the Roman migration from Italy was so great that we may be justified in calling the period a new age of colonization.

Everywhere, with the exception of Italy and Egypt (and possibly Greece), agriculture was in a flourishing condition. In the Near East agricultural serfdom was retained. In Europe, however, serfdom had not yet appeared. Free men worked small farms in the western provinces, and the large estates were cultivated by tenants. The imperial lands (the personal property of the emperor) were managed by overseers (*conductores*) who rented small plots to free tenants (*coloni*).

In Italy toward the end of the first century A.D. the effects of the agricultural competition of the western provinces began to be felt. The government found it necessary to aid the small farmers with loans, and the owners of large estates had to change their methods. Slave labor in Italian agriculture declined. The cessation of civil war and the comparatively few imperial conquests of the principate cut off an important source of slaves. As a result, the prices for agricultural slaves became almost prohibitive, and tenants had to be substituted for slaves on the great landholdings.

In some ways the society of imperial Rome resembled that of the Hellenistic period; in other ways there were marked dissimilarities. For example, both periods saw the rise of an opulent and powerful bourgeoisie which gloried in luxury and ostentation; at the same time the condition of the proletariat became more and more desperate. On the other hand, the Hellenistic period had no group to parallel the Roman senatorial class; the Hellenistic aristocracy was a class of newcomers which lacked the confidence that blue-blooded ancestors imparted to the Roman senators. Moreover, in imperial Roman society the freedmen were more numerous and more influential than they had been in the Hellenistic Age.

At the peak of the Roman social pyramid was the imperial court, composed of the relatives and close friends of the emperor, the influential senators, and the high-ranking equestrian officials. Very near to the princeps were the members of his household, his freedmen, and, occasionally, his slaves. The habits and customs of the court varied with the personalities of the emperors and their wives; the austerity of Augustus, the debauchery of Caligula, or the vulgarity of Vespasian certainly had some influence upon the behavior of those who surrounded them.

As members of an ancient ruling class and a very wealthy one, most of the senators were extremely conscious of the social responsibilities which tradition laid upon them. They guarded their prerogatives jealously and met with biting sarcasm the attempts of the newly rich businessmen of equestrian and freedman status to acquire "culture" in one generation. Surrounding the senators were their clients, impecunious, fawning, sycophantic. Early in the morning the clients assembled at the house of their patron— the struggling artists or poets, the poor relations, the freedmen, the decadent gentility. There the great man received them and their pitiful compliments with a gracious word or a cold stare, depending upon his own personal reaction to the state of the weather or the adequacy of his breakfast. The clients accompanied their patron as he went about his business in the city, breaking a path for him through the crowds and applauding his speeches (if he made any) on art, literature, or public policy. Later, they returned home with him, and each received a small gift of food or money. In addition to providing economic support to his clients, the patron also acted as their legal representative.

The equestrians were the businessmen, the merchants, the industrialists, the bankers, and the contractors. As we have seen, posts were open to them in the imperial civil service, and an equestrian might hope to be made a senator. Many freedmen rose to equestrian status. Like the members of any bourgeois society, the equestrians tried to copy the manners and customs of those above them on the social scale, often with ludicrous results.

The city masses were composed of the small traders, artisans, workers, slaves, and the unemployed. Living conditions in the great urban areas might be described as unattractive; this would be putting it very mildly, considering the crowded tenements, the poor food, and the lack of sanitation which were only the minor discomforts of those accustomed from infancy to a proletarian existence. Nevertheless, many people preferred life in the city to life in the country, for urban life could be exciting and amusing. The gladiatorial combats and beast hunts in the amphitheater, the chariot races in the circus or stadium, the triumphal processions and religious festivals, the fires, riots, and street fights far surpassed any entertainment available in the rural areas. As in the Hellenistic period, clubs and societies were important. There were associations of traders, artisans, and other professional men; these organizations were known as *collegia*—they were not guilds or unions, for their aims were only social. The majority of these organizations —whether collegia, religious clubs, or burial societies—were extremely democratic: free men, freedmen, and slaves all mingled together on equal terms.

The new cities of the West were miniature Romes. They had their temples, theaters, amphitheaters, public baths, and municipal games and festivals. In prosperous times the rich citizens vied with one another for civic offices. In almost every city there were state-supported schools, libraries, and hospitals. The older cities of the East retained their Hellenistic way of life and their Greek city-state customs and organization. Great cities like Alexandria and Antioch changed very little. Corinth grew into a commercial metropolis, whereas Athens became a rather quiet university town.

An outstanding characteristic of the period was its increasing humanitarianism and social consciousness. The state and the municipalities provided money for schools and hospitals, fed the poor, and tried to care for underprivileged children. In Rome at least a quarter of the population received free grain, and the emperors made periodic donations of money to the populace. In the time of Nerva the so-called alimenta was instituted in Italy; the government loaned money to small farmers, and the interest on these loans was given to the Italian municipalities to be used for the support of needy children. Private philanthropy was probably even more extensive than that carried on by the state. Also interesting is the fact that slavery became less harsh; the slaves seem to have been treated with greater consideration, and manumission was made easier to secure. The difficulty of obtaining slaves and their resultant high cost may have had something to do with this changed attitude.

We have already noted the exodus of Romans from Italy to the provinces. There was also considerable movement among the non-Roman elements in the empire; traders and artisans from the Near East and the eastern Mediterranean moved into the west; Greeks, Syrians, and Phoenicians were to be found everywhere. Last of all, since it was relatively easy to journey by land or sea to almost any point in the Roman Empire, travel increased in volume. Certain areas enjoyed a fine tourist trade; everyone who could afford it wanted to see Athens, Corinth, Delphi, and "Troy." In Egypt people visited the pyramids, the Colossus of Memnon, and the temples of Karnak and Luxor; few ever forgot the sight of the priests feeding the tame crocodiles of the Fayum.

The first two centuries A.D. show clearly the effects of universalism, individualism, syncretism, and eclecticism upon religion and philosophy. All these forces contributed to the evolution of Christian doctrine, and they also influenced the major developments in Stoicism. Individualism, in particular, was especially important in decreasing the attention paid to state and municipal cults which could not offer the personal satisfactions that could be gained from the mystery religions, Christianity, or philosophy.

The strongest and most tenacious of the official religions was the imperial cult. During the republican period the conquered peoples in Greece and the Near East had instituted the worship of the goddess Roma. At various times in the first century B.C. this cult included the worship of prominent Romans—Sulla, Pompey, and Julius Caesar. In the time of Augustus, the cult of Roma and Augustus became popular in the East and later spread to the western provinces; in a modified form, it existed in Italy also. Thus, the basis was laid for the evolution of a ruler cult of the Hellenistic type. When Augustus died, he was proclaimed a god by the senate, and Tiberius, as his successor and adopted son, was regarded by the provincials as more than human. Later emperors, particularly Caligula, Domitian, and Commodus, desired deification in their own lifetimes, but they only outraged Roman public opinion. In large part the worship of the living emperor in the provinces was a political fiction, a means of demonstrating loyalty to the ruler by the adoration of his statue and the performance of a sacrifice or by pouring a libation to him.

The most popular religions were the mystery cults with their elaborate rituals and their promises of immortality. The Egyptian cult of Isis continued to gain converts; about 100 A.D. a new competitor, Mithraism, an outgrowth of Zoroastrianism, entered the field. Mithra, the chief deity, was the god of light, the chief general of Ahuramazda in the war against the powers of darkness and falsehood. Because of its militant nature Mithraism was popular with the Roman army where it gained the majority of its converts. Mithraism and Christianity became rivals, and they had much in common.[1]

The period as a whole witnessed a return to superstition. At least this is the impression which is given by the popularity of astrology, oracles, and fakirs who professed to work miracles. Perhaps, however, it is only that we have more information about this age than its predecessor. On the other hand, if we may accept the available evidence, it is possible to explain the reversion to superstition as a reaction to rationalism. People wanted desperately to believe something. Moreover, the world as it appeared through the eyes of a rationalist was not a pleasant place; most people did not want to see the world in its naked reality, and therefore they preferred to blind themselves with emotion and turn to faith in something unseen but infinitely better than what the rationalist could see.

Even philosophy had to surrender to and compromise with these escapist tendencies. The mysteries of Pythagoreanism were revived, and the most successful of the Neo-Pythagorean teachers were mystics and miracle workers. Stoicism became more and more a monotheistic religion, and the materialistic Epicurean philosophy continually lost ground.

The principal philosophical teachings of the age, as advanced by the Stoics and Cynics, aimed at moral regeneration. Stoicism emphasized self-control, self-examination, rational conduct, and the social obligations of the individual. One must seek to follow the "will of God." The most influential of the Stoics was Epictetus (50–120 A.D.), who had many followers. Marcus Aurelius, emperor and philosopher, recorded his own thoughts in his *Meditations,* a valuable source for the intellectual trends of the period. Eclecticism is clearly shown in the elements of Epicureanism which appear among the Stoic doctrines of the *Meditations,* and universalism is demonstrated more than once, particularly when Marcus Aurelius calls himself "a citizen of the world."

We have still to speak of the most important religious phenomenon of the age—the origin and development of Christianity. The beginnings of the Christian faith may be dated, of course, in the reign of Tiberius. The faith subsequently gained many converts; by the middle of the second century A.D. there were thousands of Christians scattered throughout the Roman Empire. Most of them lived in the cities, and they were to be found in largest numbers in the Near East.

Perhaps the clearest perspective of the position of Christianity in the ancient world may be gained if we consider it as it must appear to some hypothetical modern scholar who is not himself a Christian. From such a point of view certain things are apparent. Christianity was a mystery reli-

---

[1] A list of the common elements may be found conveniently in A. A. Trever, *History of Ancient Civilization* (New York: Harcourt, 1939), Vol. II, pp. 596–97.

gion based upon Judaism, but its theology contained a number of basic ideas that were also to be found in Oriental religions which were contemporary with it and likewise in Stoic philosophy. In other words, Christianity appears as the product of a special time and place, a development that was conditioned by a particular social, economic, and intellectual environment.

Christianity originated as a reform movement within Judaism itself. The Jews of that day were divided into a number of sects which maintained differing interpretations of Judaism. Moreover, thousands of Jews had left Palestine during the Hellenistic Age and their descendants were living in many cities of the Roman Empire, especially in Antioch, Alexandria, Ephesus, Corinth, Athens, and Rome. These Jews who lived away from Palestine had been exposed to much Greek, Oriental, and Roman influence, and they naturally incorporated many non-Jewish ideas into their religion. These ideas were not in harmony with the theology that had been developed by the priest class at Jerusalem, for official Judaism had become a rigid and formalized religion. In their program of reform Jesus and his followers attacked this formalism; they stressed the fact that mere formalism was barren, that it was the spirit rather than the letter of the laws which was important. This was the principal reason for the hostility of the priest class toward Jesus; in addition to this, the fact that Jesus made certain criticisms of the rich and openly favored the masses aroused the antagonism of the propertied classes.

After the death of Jesus his followers were forced to abandon their plans to reform Judaism. Orthodox Jews not only resented Christian criticism, but they also accused Jesus of violating the Mosaic code by practicing magic (because of the miracles) and they cast off the Christians as polytheists (because the Christians proclaimed Jesus a god). As a result, the Christian missionaries began to teach among the Gentiles and the Hellenized Jews, where they met with great success.

As soon as the Christian faith spread beyond the borders of Palestine, it was exposed to the influence of religious and philosophic ideas prevalent in the Roman world as a whole, and Christian doctrine was enhanced and modified by the inevitable processes of syncretism and eclecticism. This is another way of saying that the Hellenized Jews and the Gentiles who were converted to Christianity brought into the faith many of their own beliefs.

The success of Christianity was due to several factors. In the first place, it was not a new and radical religion at all; instead, it represented a restatement of many attractive ideas of the past. The idea of a savior god who died, yet lived again, and made possible the redemption of his followers was common to the earlier Oriental fertility cults and the Greek mystery religions. Brotherly love, forbearance, and disregard for temporal matters had been preached by the Stoics for centuries. The Messianic prophecy, Mosaic law, and monotheism formed the principal Jewish heritage of Christianity.

Secondly, while the inspiring mythology of the Christians and the great imaginative appeal of their religion attracted converts, the very amorphous character of early Christian theology allowed the faith to adapt itself to its environment. In addition, the lack of positive dogma in the early years gave the opponents of Christianity little basis for attacks based on theological grounds.

We have noted previously, in discussing Hellenistic philosophy (p. 306), that men had come to feel that they were fighting a losing battle against the overwhelming strength of the forces of nature and the crushing weight of civilization in its social and economic aspects. The philosophers had finally advised people "to make the best of it." The Christians went a step further. They said, "What happens here on earth really does not matter. Live a Christian life, and you shall find your just reward in heaven."

With its simplicity, its emotional appeal, and its promise of a better life to come, Christianity was better fitted than any other faith or philosophy to satisfy the needs of the weary millions of a decaying civilization. It is highly significant that the majority of the first Christian converts came from the lower ranks of society, the slaves and the proletarians, groups among which increasing hopelessness engendered by the harsh economic system had been prevalent since Hellenistic times. As the economic decline of the ancient world became more apparent, particularly in the third century A.D., the bourgeoisie and the aristocracy, too, sought the refuge which Christianity offered.

For three centuries the Christians were persecuted by the Roman government and by private individuals. This was largely because the Christians were misunderstood. As members of a secret society, they were naturally suspect. They were accused of practicing human sacrifice, incest, and atheism. The charge of atheism arose from the fact that the Christians refused to worship pagan gods and had no cult statues. Non-Christians regarded some of Jesus' doctrines or utterances as subversive and aiming at the destruction of private property and the family; certain well known pronouncements of Jesus regarding the family and the rich were interpreted by pagans as being anarchistic and communistic. Moreover, the Christians were confused with the Jews; the pagans could see little, if any, difference between the two groups. Anti-Semitism had been present in the ancient world since the Hellenistic period, and the Christians, as well as the Jews, suffered because of it.

In the eyes of the government the Christians were neither good nor loyal citizens. Their disregard for the affairs of this world aroused the hostility of the state, and the fact that they refused to perform the ceremonies of the imperial cult brought down upon them the suspicion that they were not loyal to the emperor.

The generation of Christians which lived after the death of Jesus felt little need of planning for the future, for they expected his second coming at any moment. As time went on, however, and it was apparent that the millennium would not arrive immediately, definite organization and planning began to take place.

The various Christian communities, especially in the urban areas, soon took the form of religious societies modeled on the collegia. For financial and administrative purposes each community elected boards of officials from the members of their respective congregations: there were the overseers (bishops), the elders (presbyters) who had spiritual duties, and the deacons who looked after the material welfare of the congregation.

During the second century A.D. there were further changes. The board of overseers gave way to a single bishop who was the president of the board of elders. The bishop presided at religious ceremonies and, with the assistance of the deacons, managed the finances of the community. It was also his task to impose discipline and to settle disputes that might arise between members of the congregation. Naturally, the bishops of important metropolitan centers—Antioch, Alexandria, and Rome, for example—were more influential than those of other communities.

At the same time the elders gradually evolved into a definite priest class with special functions and prerogatives. As the ceremonies of worship were elaborated and a fixed ritual developed, the business of the priests became more and more specialized, and a dividing line was drawn between clergy and laity. The laity were called upon to provide financial support for the clergy; when, about 150 A.D., a man named Montanus spoke out against the growth of a priest class, he was promptly branded as a heretic.

The Roman phase of Hellenistic civilization was characterized, like the Hellenistic Age proper, by an increasing literacy. Two developments, the rise of the bourgeoisie and the establishment of numerous state-supported and privately endowed schools, were responsible for the widespread knowledge of reading and writing. Thus, more people engaged in literary production, and they were encouraged in this by the growth of a large reading public. Of special interest is the productiveness of those of equestrian and freedman status, the members of groups which rose to new economic and social heights in the late republican and early imperial periods.

The literature of the great age of ancient civilization was bilingual (people wrote either in Greek or Latin or both), and it was basically Hellenistic. In Latin literature there was a continuation of forms developed in the republican period, but, after all, the republican literature was also basically Hellenistic. As we shall presently see, however, a few new forms appeared.

The character of Roman imperial literature was somewhat limited or influenced by two factors: the power and prestige of the princeps and the necessity for subsidization. Political oratory and the writing of political pamphlets and contemporary history—literary activities which had flourished in the latter days of the republic—now declined simply because it was not wise to offend the government by offering political criticism or by writing or talking too freely about current issues. Even under comparatively liberal regimes, such as those of Augustus, Nerva, Trajan, and the other Good Emperors, writing on political subjects was much restrained.

The difficulties of manuscript production, of marketing literary works, and the lack of copyrights made it hard for authors to make a living despite the large audiences which popular writers might have. Most authors, therefore, unless they were financially independent, had to find a rich patron. Subsidization inevitably affected the character of the literature produced. An author would have to be careful not to offend his patron, and many times he would have to turn out work at the latter's order; under such conditions it was not easy for an author to do the best work of which he was capable.

During the half-century after the death of Augustus, the production of Greek and Roman literary works seems to have remained at the same level as far as volume is concerned, although the quality of the writing is often inferior. From the time of Vespasian down into the second century A.D., however, there is an increase in production (particularly under the liberal second-century emperors and as a result of the prosperity of the period), and many great poets, historians, biographers, and other writers appear on the scene; this is the period known as the Silver Age of Latin literature.

With this chronological background in mind, we may now survey the literary developments which took place in various fields from the death of Augustus down to the reign of Commodus.

Virgil had given great impetus to the writing of epic, and he had numerous followers and imitators. A Spaniard named Lucan (39–65 A.D.) was the author of an epic, the *Pharsalia,* which dealt with the civil war between Julius Caesar and Pompey. In the Flavian period Silius Italicus composed an epic poem on the Second Punic War; the epics of Statius were based upon the ancient myths of Thebes and the Trojan War; and Valerius Flaccus wrote an *Argonautica* (in Latin) in imitation of Apollonius of Rhodes.

The satires of Horace provided inspiration for those of Persius (34–62 A.D.), and in the reign of Trajan the brilliant satirist of the Silver Age, Juvenal, attained his greatest popularity. The Spaniard Martial, who wrote during the Flavian period, is well known for his satirical epigrams which present social life in Rome in a most unfavorable light.

Seneca the Younger, philosopher, dramatist, and the tutor of Nero, was a major figure during the reigns of Claudius and Nero. His philosophical works, based upon Stoic philosophy, were widely read in his own and later times. He also wrote nine tragedies for which Euripides was his chief model; his plays were not suitable for stage presentation, although they could be recited or read with some profit. Seneca, who was considerably indebted to Claudius for numerous favors, showed his true character after Claudius' death; in order to curry favor with Nero and Agrippina, he wrote the *Apocolocyntosis* which ridiculed his former patron. His remarks about Claudius' physical deformity were in the worst possible taste. The wittiest part of the whole composition was its title, which was a play on the Greek word *apotheosis* which meant "to become a god," whereas Seneca's title signified that Claudius had become a pumpkin (colocynth).

Of considerable interest is the development of prose fiction during this age. The *Satyricon,* the story of the adventures of three lively and unscrupulous gentlemen who traveled in south Italy, was written during the reign of Nero. One of its best known episodes is the Dinner of Trimalchio, a description of a banquet given by a newly rich freedman who sought to put on airs. Highly salacious, the *Satyricon* had great appeal for Oscar Wilde, one of its most famous translators. It is generally believed, though actual proof is lacking, that the *Satyricon* was written by Petronius, the elegant and aristocratic arbiter of fashion in Neronian society.

Lucius Apuleius, who came from a Roman colony in Numidia, wrote a fantastic mystical and satirical novel called the *Metamorphoses,* or the *Golden Ass.* It deals with the adventures of a young would-be magician, who wished to transform himself into a bird but changed himself into a donkey by mistake. In the *Metamorphoses* Apuleius included a number of incidental stories of Greek origin.

Though we know of Greek novels as early as the first century B.C., the earliest complete work of this kind which has survived is the *Chaireas and Callirrhoe* of Chariton, which dates from about 150 A.D. The plot of the novel might be called compound rather than complex. The story moves rapidly and contains enough melodrama and romance for several novels. In this respect it was typical, for later Greek works of a similar kind shared its characteristics. Clearly written for people who wanted light entertainment rather than serious reading, the ancient novel belongs in the category we call "escape literature."

An ancient author whose work is timeless in its ability to interest and amuse is Lucian, a Greek who lived in the second century A.D. Lucian wrote satirical dialogues in which he poked fun at philosophers, rhetoricians, miracle workers, sophists, historians, and many others. The story which appears in the Old Testament as "Jonah and the Whale" was a very old one and well known to the people of the ancient world. Lucian told the biggest fish story of all; the whale in his story was so large that it swallowed a whole vessel. The crew sailed around inside the whale for days, discovering all sorts of strange countries and tribes, and finally escaped by cutting down the trees and starting a forest fire in the whale's stomach which caused him to open his mouth and allowed them to sail out again. Lucian is so amusing that people sometimes overlook the fact that he was also a sound literary critic.

One of the greatest works of literary criticism of antiquity is a treatise entitled *On the Sublime,* which was written in the first century A.D. and is usually, though probably inaccurately, attributed to an author named Longinus. Inspiring rather than penetrating, the work is well worth reading for a number of reasons, not the least of which is that it gives an idea of what the Greeks and Romans thought of their literary men. Edward Gibbon said that he had never really understood Greek literature until he read "Longinus."

The Silver Age was notable for its historical writing. A contemporary of Vespasian was Josephus, the Jewish historian, who wrote in Greek the history of his people. Josephus was neither accurate nor critical in his writing, but his works are nevertheless interesting and valuable.

The outstanding historian of the age was, of course, Tacitus. Born during the reign of Nero, Tacitus survived Trajan, though most of his writing was done during that emperor's reign. In two works, the *Annals* and the *Histories,* Tacitus covered the history of the principate from the death of Augustus to that of Domitian. Ironic and embittered, he presented a most unfavorable picture of the Julio-Claudian and Flavian emperors. His sympathies were entirely with the senators, his own class. In addition to his historical works, Tacitus wrote a dialogue on oratory, a description of the people of Germany, and a biography (really a panegyric) of his father-in-law, the general Agricola. Tacitus was possessed of great narrative skill and epigrammatic powers, but he was more of a literary person than a historian; parenthetically, we might note that this was true of all those who are called great Roman historians: Sallust, Livy, and Tacitus. The works of Tacitus contain many famous narrative and descriptive passages: the great fire in Nero's reign, the character sketches of Petronius, Tiberius, and Claudius, and the description of the death of Vitellius. Tacitus was so popular in his own generation as a historian that he planned to continue his history of the principate through the reigns of Nerva and Trajan; we do not have this work, and it is not known whether it was ever completed, but one may suspect that since Tacitus either could not or would not have been able to indulge in his usual vituperation, he might have had little to say.

Next to Tacitus stands Arrian (*c.* 95–175 A.D.), who wrote in Greek the best extant history of the campaigns of Alexander the Great; he entitled it the *Anabasis of Alexander.* Arrian also committed to writing the teachings of the philosopher Epictetus.

The great biographers of the second century A.D. were Suetonius (*fl.* 120 A.D.) and Plutarch (46–120 A.D.). Suetonius wrote in Latin the scandalous and interesting *Lives of the Twelve Caesars,* the biographies of Julius Caesar, Augustus, and the succeeding emperors down to Domitian. He wrote with his public in mind and never sacrificed a good story to the cause of accuracy. Suetonius was also the author of the *Lives of Illustrious Men,* short biographies of Roman literary figures.

The *Parallel Lives* of the Boeotian Plutarch is probably the best-known biographical work of antiquity. Plutarch made comparisons of the lives of

Contributors to the Civilization of the Roman Empire

Roman numerals indicate century in which individual flourished

AGYRIUM
History
Diodorus *I* B.C.

ALEXANDRIA
Geography
Ptolemy *II*
History
Appian *II*
Theology
Philo *I*
Clement *II*
Origen *II*
Athanasius *IV*

AMASIA
Geography
Strabo *I*

AMITERNUM
History
Sallust *I* B.C.

ANTIOCH
History
Ammianus *IV*
Oratory
Libanius *IV*

AQUINUM
Poetry
Juvenal *I*

ARPINUM
Oratory
Cicero *I* B.C.

ASISIUM
Poetry
Propertius *I* B.C.

ATHENS
Rhetoric
Longinus *III*

AUGUSTA TREVERORUM
Theology
Ambrose *IV*

BILBILIS
Poetry
Martial *I*

BURDIGALA
Poetry
Ausonius *IV*

CAESAREA
Theology
Eusebius *IV*

CALAGURRIS
Oratory
Quintilian *I*

CAPUA
Poetry and Drama
Naevius *III* B.C.

CARTHAGE
Comedy
Terence *II* B.C.
Poetry
Nemesian *III*
Theology
Tertullian *II*

CHAERONEA
Biography
Plutarch *II*

CIRTA
Rhetoric
Fronto *II*

COMUM
Oratory
Pliny the Younger *II*

CORDUBA
Philosophy
Seneca the Younger *I*
Poetry
Lucan *I*
Rhetoric
Seneca the Elder *I* B.C.

DALMATIA
Theology
Jerome *IV*

DAMASCUS
History
Nicolaus *I* B.C.

GADES
Agriculture
Columella *I*

GAUL
Comedy
Statius Caecilius *II* B.C.

HALICARNASSUS
History
Dionysius *I* B.C.

HIERAPOLIS
Philosophy
Epictetus *II*

HIPPO
Theology
Augustine *IV*

JERUSALEM
History
Josephus *I*

LESBOS
Fiction
Longus *III*

LUGDUNUM
Poetry
Sidonius *V*

LYDIA
Geography
Pausanias *II*

MADAURA
Fiction
Apuleius *II*

MANTUA
Poetry
Virgil *I* B.C.

NAUCRATIS
Grammar
Athenaeus *III*
Pollux *III*

NEAPOLIS
Poetry
Statius *I*

NICAEA
History
Dio Cassius *III*

NICOMEDIA
History
Arrian *II*

PATAVIUM
History
Livy *I* B.C.
Poetry
Flaccus *I*
Silius *I*

PERGAMUM
Medicine
Galen *II*

PRUSA
Oratory
Dio Chrysostom *II*

ROME (some conjectured)
Agriculture
Cato *II* B.C.

Architecture
Vitruvius *I*
Biography
Cornelius Nepos *I* B.C.
Suetonius *II*
Grammar
Gellius *II*
History
Fabius Pictor *III* B.C.
Julius Caesar *I* B.C.
Pompeius Trogus
I B.C.
Tacitus *I*
Literature
Varro *I* B.C.
Medicine
Celsus *I*
Oratory
Laelius *II* B.C.
Philosophy
Lucretius *I* B.C.
Marcus Aurelius *II*
Poetry
Ennius *III* B.C.
Tibullus *I* B.C.
Satire
Lucilius *II* B.C.
Petronius *I*
Science
Frontinus *I*
Tragedy
Accius *II* B.C.
Pacuvius *II* B.C.

SAMOSATA
Satire
Lucian *II*

SARSINA
Comedy
Plautus *II* B.C.

SICCA
Theology
Arnobius *IV*

SMYRNA
Oratory
Aristides *II*

SULMO
Poetry
Ovid *I*

TARENTUM
Poetry
Livius Andronicus
III B.C.

TARSUS
Theology
Paul *I*

THRACE
Poetry
Phaedrus *I*

TINGENTERA
Geography
Pomponius Mela *I*

TYRE
Philosophy
Porphyry *III*

VENUSIA
Poetry
Horace *I* B.C.

VERONA
Poetry
Catullus *I* B.C.
Science
Pliny the Elder *I*

VOLATERRAE
Poetry
Persius *I*

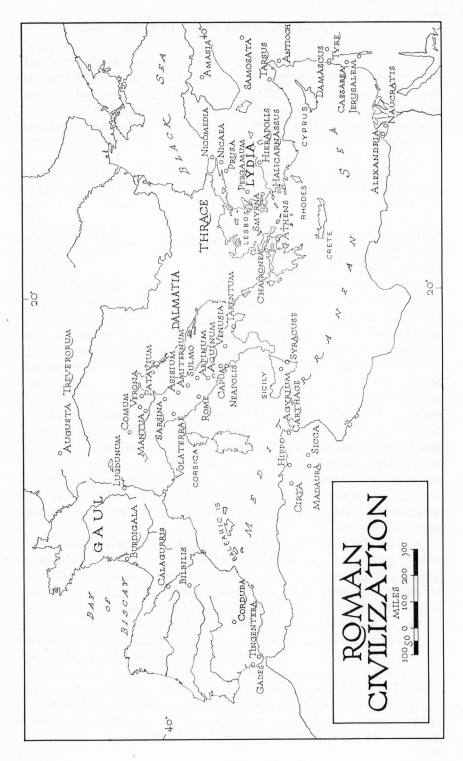

ROMAN CIVILIZATION

MILES
100 50 0   100   200   300

BAY OF BISCAY

GAUL

AUGUSTA TREVERORUM

LUGDUNUM

BURDIGALA

CALAGURRIS

BILBILIS

CORDUBA

GADES
TINGENTERA

BALEARIC IS

CORSICA

VOLATERRAE
SARSINA
MANTUA
COMUM
VERONA
PATAVIUM

ASISIUM
AMITERNUM
DALMATIA
ARPINUM
AQUINUM
VENUSIA
TARENTUM
SULMO
CAPUA
ROME
NEAPOLIS

SICILY
AGYRIUM
SYRACUSE

M E D I T E R R A N E A N   S E A

HIPPO
CIRTA
MADAURA
SICCA
CARTHAGE

BLACK   SEA

THRACE

NICOMEDIA
NICAEA
PRUSA
PERGAMUM
LYDIA
HIERAPOLIS
HALICARNASSUS
SMYRNA
LESBOS
CHAERONEA
ATHENS
RHODES
CRETE

AMASIA
SAMOSATA
TARSUS
ANTIOCH
DAMASCUS
TYRE
CAESAREA
JERUSALEM
CYPRUS

ALEXANDRIA
NAUCRATIS

20°

40°

20°

435

famous Greeks and Romans—Alexander and Caesar, Demosthenes and Cicero, and other similar figures—and so produced a series of biographies that make fascinating reading. His ability to tell a good story and his sense of humor help one to overlook his moralizing and his inaccuracies. Plutarch was also the author of the *Moralia,* a group of essays on diverse subjects: literary, philosophical, humorous. On occasion, the amiable Sage of Chaeronea, as he has been called, could be almost as amusing as Lucian.

Oratory and rhetoric received the overwhelming attention of the writers of the Silver Age. It was a concern of Tacitus, Lucian, and Plutarch, and in the Flavian period lived Quintilian, a Spaniard, who wrote the famous *Education of the Orator* which dealt not only with oratory and education but also with literary history and criticism. While Quintilian gave the Greeks their due, he was inclined to overstate the case for the Latin writers; his judgments are interesting, although it is not possible to agree with him that Sallust was a match for Thucydides, or Livy for Herodotus. The famous Greek orator and moralist, Dio Chrysostom, was a contemporary of Quintilian and Plutarch, and another well known Greek orator, Aristides, flourished in the succeeding generation. Fronto, orator, rhetorician, and tutor of Marcus Aurelius, graced the courts of Hadrian and Antoninus Pius.

Pliny the Younger, the friend of Tacitus and Suetonius, is one of the literary figures about whom we are best informed. He composed a panegyric, a laudatory oration, in honor of Trajan, but his real fame rests upon the many letters that he wrote for publication in the manner of Cicero. The letters were addressed to close friends and to men prominent in public life. Two of these, addressed to Tacitus, describe the eruption of Vesuvius in 79 A.D. Another famous letter, written to Trajan when Pliny was governor in Bithynia, deals with the Christians. Other communications from Pliny addressed to Trajan give important information about provincial government in this period, and Trajan's replies to Pliny are equally interesting.

Scholarship in the imperial period aimed chiefly at preserving and making known the knowledge amassed in previous ages. In the second century A.D., for example, appeared the *Attic Nights* of Aulus Gellius, a hodgepodge of short essays on learning, literature, philology, law, and natural history. At the same time a number of lexicographers were compiling lists of rare Greek and Latin words and their definitions.

The first Christian writing appeared in the Flavian period. The letters of the apostle Paul were collected, and the gospels of Mark, Matthew, Luke, and John were composed between 70 and 100 A.D. Many books later relegated to the Apocrypha were written by Christians during the second century. Moreover, Christian apologists began to defend their religion against pagan attacks in essays and dialogues. The New Testament itself, of course, did not attain its final form until about 370 A.D.

The Romans inherited their scientific knowledge from the Greeks, but Roman science is distinguished by its application to practical things. The utilitarian aspects of Roman science derived from Roman preoccupation with imperial administration, business, and war. The military interests of the Romans often led to developments which were as useful and beneficial to civilians as to soldiers. The military hospital (*valetudinarium*) became the model for hospitals located in many towns, and solicitude for the health of the soldiers brought a growth of medical knowledge which was in turn applied to the general field of public health. The army and the empire were responsible for the development of the magnificent Roman roads and the network of highways that covered the empire. The practical knowledge displayed by the Romans in architecture was demonstrated also in major drainage projects and the construction of aqueducts. The whole field of hydrostatics was one in which the Romans excelled. Roman knowledge of stockbreeding and veterinary medicine was unequalled until modern times.

The extent of Roman science may be seen from an enumeration of the names of the major writers on science who flourished under the empire:

The first half of the first century A.D. witnessed the appearance of two works on geography: one in Greek by Strabo, and the other in Latin by Pomponius Mela. Strabo's work is the most complete treatise on geography that has survived from ancient times. It is a description of the entire known world of his day; much of his information was drawn from older writers, but he himself travelled in some of the regions which he described. The geography by Pomponius Mela is chiefly important for its description of the western Roman Empire and because it is the first book on the subject written in Latin.

Pliny the Elder (23–79 A.D.), the uncle of Pliny the Younger, was an enthusiastic scholar and scientist who not only combed earlier writings for information but also liked to acquire knowledge by actual observation and experiment. As a matter of fact, his intellectual curiosity was the cause of his death, for he attempted to observe too closely the eruption of Vesuvius in 79 A.D. The demise of this great scholar is described in one of his nephew's most famous letters. Pliny the Elder was the author of the *Natural History,* a huge compendium of facts about the natural world which included geography, astronomy, the physical sciences, and even the history of Greek art.

In the second century Ptolemy and Galen flourished. Ptolemy was an astronomer and geographer whose works had great influence upon his contemporaries and the scholars of the Middle Ages. Galen was the author of a medical encyclopaedia which summarized the medical knowledge of the past and provided a useful source of knowledge for later generations.

Brief mention might be made of a few other writers of the imperial period. In the Julio-Claudian age Columella of Spain wrote a treatise on agriculture, and Celsus wrote in Latin on medicine. Under Domitian the soldier and administrator Frontinus composed his *Strategems* on military science and his *Aqueducts* which described the system of the Roman water supply. Last of all, the Greek Pausanias, in the latter half of the second century A.D., produced his *Tour of Greece,* a guidebook to the interesting monuments and buildings in the various Greek cities.

The Roman architect was always hampered by inability to obtain an adequate supply of the best building materials. Italian marble, for example, was very good, and marble could be imported from Greece; but the expense of transportation and the heavy demand for materials made it necessary for the Romans to use their best stone sparingly. As a result, they placed considerable dependence upon brick, concrete, and inferior kinds of stone, using fine marbles only in the most conspicuous places; sometimes a building was covered with a veneer of thin marble slabs. Because of the problem of materials, the Roman architects had to develop their engineering skill to a high point and to exercise the greatest ingenuity.

The Romans continued to use columns and half-columns for façades and exterior decoration, but they came to rely heavily upon the arch, the barrel vault, and the dome, mainly because these structures did not necessitate the use of high grades of stone. Roman architecture was also distinguished by its monumental character, its use of composite styles, and its predilection for lavish decorative relief sculpture.

Although the Romans built temples, stoae, libraries, and theaters, they also introduced new structural types: basilicas, baths, amphitheaters, and triumphal arches. The basilica was an elaboration of the stoa; it was a colonnaded hall covered by vaulting and was used primarily as a law court. This was the architectural form out of which the Christian church evolved. The baths were huge buildings with a complex of rooms; a bath usually contained a large court for exercise, a dressing room, a room which was kept very warm to induce perspiration, a hot bath, and a cold plunge. The larger baths might include libraries, lounging rooms, and lecture halls. The amphitheaters were oval in shape, like our football stadia, and they contained tier upon tier of seats with ramps and stairways rising to a height of several stories. Triumphal arches were decorated with sculptured reliefs and panels as well as columns.

Almost every emperor sponsored a comprehensive building program in Rome, and quite often, especially in the second century, these programs were paralleled by public works projects in the provinces. It was the reigns of Augustus, Nero, the Flavians, Trajan, and Hadrian, however, that saw the greatest activity in construction. Famous imperial buildings were the Pantheon of Augustus' friend, Agrippa, the Colosseum of Vespasian, the Tomb of Hadrian, and the baths constructed by Nero and Titus. It will be remembered that, under Hadrian, the city of Athens experienced a building boom: the temple of Olympian Zeus was finally completed, and the Arch and Library of Hadrian were constructed. It was not only the desire for ostentation and display that encouraged the emperors in their public works projects, but also their concern over unemployment. The story of how Vespasian rejected a labor-saving device for erecting columns because there were already too many people out of work well illustrates the latter point.

The achievement of the Romans in the field of decorative sculpture is not to be despised. The reliefs on the Ara Pacis, on the Arch of Titus, and on the Column of Trajan and that of Marcus Aurelius are often considered superior to Hellenistic reliefs. The spiral bands of relief on the Column of Trajan present graphic episodes from that emperor's Dacian campaigns, and they provide us with a useful source for a period which is deficient in literary sources.

The substantive sculpture of the Romans met with its greatest success in the field of portraiture. On the whole, the sculptured portraits of the Roman imperial period are not idealized; rather they are realistic and seldom complimentary. This is also true of the portraits of the emperors which appear on the coins—we see these rulers as they actually appeared to contemporaries: the debauched Nero, the matter-of-fact Vespasian, the warlike Trajan, the elegant Hadrian, and the harried Marcus Aurelius.

The paintings and mosaics, particularly those found in the ruins of Pompeii and Herculaneum, show the technical skill with which the Roman artists were able to handle these Hellenistic media.

Out of the sculpture and painting of the imperial era grew an art which was to be carried by the Romans to the farthest corners of their empire and which was to be diffused by trade to the Indus. This resulted in the creation of a vast art province which extended from the Atlantic to India and from the Sahara to the Baltic and the Caspian; influences may be discerned as far east as China.

In the minor arts the skilled workers of the imperial era produced fine pottery in addition to handsome metalwork in gold, silver, and bronze. The sophisticated Arretine pottery of the late republic had been a significant export of Italy, but in the first century A.D. it was successfully imitated by the potters of the western provinces. Wherever the Romans lived, one is likely to find the beautiful mosaic work which adorned equally the floors of British and African villas and the houses of faraway Dura-Europus on the Mesopotamian frontier.

This was the climax of ancient civilization, a civilization which had been more than three thousand years in the making, a civilization which was chronologically old and was also aged in many other respects. The road to the top had been long and hard; the way down proved short but painful.

Chapter 26

THE ROAD TO AUTOCRACY

T HE ASSASSINATION of Commodus late in 192 was followed by a second war of the legions which paralleled closely the earlier troubles that had occurred after the death of Nero. The nominee of the praetorian guard was an elderly senator named Pertinax who was acceptable to the senate because it was hoped he might prove a second Nerva. Pertinax, however, disappointed his supporters: he managed to antagonize the senate, and he failed to pay the praetorians the large donative which they had been led to expect. After Pertinax had been assassinated in March, 193, the praetorians held an auction in which an eager and elderly senator named Julianus purchased the throne by paying the praetorians about one thousand dollars apiece. At this point the legions took a hand; both Niger, the Roman governor of Syria, and Septimius Severus, commander of the troops in Pannonia, professed a desire to avenge the murder of Pertinax. Septimius was nearer to Rome; his arrival there in June, 193 was the signal for the murder of Julianus.

In this manner Septimius Severus, who had been born in the Roman province of Africa in 146 and who had a Syrian wife, became the new Roman emperor and the founder of a dynasty which was to rule the empire until 235. At his accession he had two powerful rivals for the throne: Niger, who was finally defeated at Issus in 194, and Albinus, the Roman commander in Britain whose soldiers had proclaimed him emperor after the murder of Pertinax. Albinus had at first been pacified by Septimius with the offer of the post of Caesar (junior emperor), but he became dissatisfied and invaded Gaul where he was defeated in 197 A.D.

Septimius Severus was to reign until his death at York in Britain early in 211. He had campaigned in the Near East with moderate success against the Parthians, who had taken advantage of Niger's withdrawal of troops to cross the frontier, and he also had to fight in Britain against the Scotch

440

highlanders who had been emboldened by Albinus' withdrawal of troops from Britain. Between 202 and 207, however, Septimius had been free to reorganize the Roman government and to make important reforms.

The power of Septimius was frankly based upon army support. The soldiers were given good pay and special privileges, and the senate was pushed into the background. Moreover, the civil service was opened to retired army officers. The praetorian guard, which had been composed exclusively of Italians, was henceforth recruited from provincials. New opportunities were afforded the equestrian class in the army, provincial administration, and the civil service. The senate lost its control over Italy when judicial affairs in Rome and within a radius of one hundred miles of the city were placed in the hands of the city prefect and the rest of Italy made the responsibility of the praetorian prefect. All provincial revenues were combined and went into a single treasury; the distinction between senatorial and imperial provinces thus ceased to exist at least in this respect. The general tendency therefore was to exalt the army and equestrians at the expense of the senate and to debase Italy to the level of the provinces. Militarization and regionalism were beginning to make significant inroads upon the older system of the principate.

Septimius had two sons: Caracalla and Geta. Caracalla, the elder son, had been made co-emperor with his father in 198; Geta was made a Caesar. Septimius may have intended that his sons should rule together after his death, but Caracalla murdered Geta in 212 and took the throne for himself. Caracalla, who fancied himself a second Alexander the Great, spent much time away from Rome fighting expensive wars. He played up to the army, but his popularity even with the soldiers declined when he began to dress like Alexander and to adopt the outmoded phalanx formation; at the same time his costly campaigns against the barbarians in the north and the Parthians in the east necessitated heavy taxes and an inflation of the currency that aroused economic discontent. His most lasting contribution was the famous decree, the Antonine Constitution, which extended Roman citizenship to all but one minor class of free men within the empire (212 A.D.). This was not a philanthropic gesture, but a carefully considered move to increase the number of those subject to certain taxes and municipal services.

In the spring of 217 Caracalla was murdered by his praetorian prefect, a Moorish lawyer named Macrinus. Within a short time, however, Macrinus was deposed by a revolt led by the family of Septimius' Syrian wife, Julia Domna. The former empress had committed suicide at Macrinus' accession, but her sister, Julia Maesa, was more determined. Julia Maesa had two grandsons, Avitus or Bassianus and Alexianus. Bassianus, the elder boy, looked very much like Caracalla who was believed by some to have been his father. Trading on this resemblance and the consternation caused

441

by an eclipse of the sun in 218, Julia Maesa engineered a revolution against Macrinus and placed Bassianus on the throne. Bassianus, better known as Elagabalus, was a religious fanatic and a pervert whose main interest was in the Syrian *baal* which he worshipped in the form of a black stone. By 222 A.D. his excesses and naughty pranks had scandalized the Romans and exhausted the patience of his grandmother, who procured his assassination and put his more tractable cousin, Alexianus, on the throne.

Alexianus, whose throne name was Alexander Severus, was a mere child in 222, and his mother Julia Mammaea ruled as regent. Lacking the enthusiastic support of the army, Julia came to depend upon the senate with which she was willing to co-operate. This was all too good to be true, however, for a woman, a weakling, and the senate could scarcely hope to withstand the desires of the army. After some military reverses Alexander and his mother were killed in 235, and the soldiers proclaimed Maximinus, a general of barbarian Thracian origin, as their emperor.

The murder of Alexander Severus was followed by a half-century of near chaos. In these fifty years there were no less than twenty-six different emperors; only one of them died a natural death. Civil and foreign wars, invasions, revolts, usurpations, and conspiracies were almost without number in this tumultuous period. The army could not be disciplined; the barbarians crossed the frontiers at will. In 227 A.D. the Parthian Empire had gone down into oblivion before the onslaught of a Persian revival which elevated a new dynasty, that of the Sassanids. Zoroastrianism became the national Persian religion; it provided a powerful unifying force within the new empire and also served as a prop for the authority of the Persian king. Naturally, the new Persian nationalism demanded the restoration of the ancient boundaries of the empire of Cyrus and Darius, and this led to attacks upon Roman territory in the Near East. About the middle of the third century A.D. the general confusion was increased by a new plague from the east that swept westward over the Roman Empire.

Political anarchy was productive of economic disruption. Internal and external warfare, accompanied by a revival of piracy and brigandage, hampered trade, cut down the industrial output, and injured agriculture. The imperial treasury was always empty. High pay and frequent donatives to the soldiers to keep them from revolting or to encourage them to it, the cost of foreign wars, and poor financial management prevented any accumulation of government funds. This situation was met by increasing taxation and inflation of the currency. High taxes and inflation were bad enough for business, but there was also the steady withdrawal of the precious metals from the empire through Oriental trade and the hoarding of gold and silver because of inflation. The decrease of the amount of gold and silver in circulation was in itself sufficient to paralyze trade.

As the power of the central government became weak, the political unity of the empire broke up. The low point was reached in the middle of the third century during the reign of Valerian and his son, Gallienus. Valerian was defeated and captured by the Persians in 258, and the empire broke up into three parts: an independent Gallic empire existed between 258 and 274 A.D., and in the east the vassal kingdom of Palmyra was, for all practical purposes, free of Roman control from 260 to 272 A.D. At one time, the Palmyrenes had Egypt and all the Asiatic provinces. Gallienus, however, managed to hold the central part of the empire even though barbarians crossed the European and African frontiers at will.

The threefold division of the empire, while bad for morale, was in many ways a good thing. It gave the emperors at Rome a chance to reorganize their forces and rebuild their power. They were temporarily relieved of the problems and expense of defending Gaul and the east; it was a much-needed breathing spell.

From the time of Claudius Gothicus (268–270) onward, the tide began to turn in favor of Rome. Claudius defeated the Goths who had overrun Greece and Asia. He was followed by a series of equally warlike emperors beginning with Aurelian (270–275 A.D.), a capable soldier and a good administrator. Aurelian enjoyed the respect of the army and was thus able to re-establish discipline. By 274 he had managed to overthrow Palmyra and restore Gaul to the empire. His reform of the currency helped to improve the economic situation. Two reforms that Aurelian might have been able to effect if he had lived longer foreshadowed the developments of the future: first, he apparently intended to make the cult of Mithra, the Unconquerable Sun, the state religion; and second, he seems to have planned to foster the worship of himself as the earthly manifestation of the god, since he took the title *Deus et Dominus Natus,* Born Lord and God. Mithraism was the favorite cult of the soldiers and the principal competitor of Christianity at this time; it was a mystery religion that promised salvation, and the birthday of Mithra was said to be December 25. By making himself a god-king and identifying himself with the popular Mithra, Aurelian might have been able to establish a theocracy which would possess autocratic strength. Within twenty years Diocletian was to proclaim himself a god-king and establish an autocracy, and Constantine was to toy with the idea of combining Mithraism and the state, although he later rejected it to win Christian support. The final solution later in the fourth century was to make Christianity the state religion and establish an autocracy in which the emperor ruled by divine right as the divinely appointed earthly representative of the Christian god.

Aurelian, however, was assassinated unexpectedly in 275, and the senate was given an equally unexpected opportunity to appoint a new princeps, the elderly Tacitus who strove to identify himself with Nerva; but he died before he could find a Trajan. Two more soldier emperors, Probus and Carus (with his two sons), filled the gap between Tacitus and the great Diocletian, who came to the throne in the autumn of 284 and exchanged the principate for the autocracy.

The chaos of the third century had brought the principate to an end, just as the civil wars of the first century B.C. had destroyed the republic. A new order arose upon the ruins of the old, and the whole fiction of the dyarchy was abandoned for an openly autocratic government in which the emperor was the sole source of authority. The concentration of all power in the hands of one man, the dream of Julius Caesar, finally became a reality.

It is one of the paradoxes of Roman political history that the more widely citizenship and political privileges were extended, the less the Romans as a whole were able to participate in their government. After 287 B.C., when the theoretically democratic system had been established, the simultaneous growth of an empire had increased the power of the senate and the equestrians at the expense of that of the masses, and the extension of citizenship to the allies in Italy was really the death sentence of the popular assemblies at Rome. The principate, of course, saw the emperor and the senate sharing a theoretical division of powers. As long as the senators were Italians, this form of government came fairly close to achieving its professed aims; but when citizenship was extended to provincials and provincial senators appeared, the senate began to lose ground to the princeps. The establishment of an autocracy was the final and logical step. In other words, the city-state Rome could govern Italy, and Italy could rule an empire, but when all the subjects of Rome were made citizens they had to be ruled by an emperor.

Two emperors, Diocletian (284–305 A.D.) and Constantine (310–337 A.D.), gave the new autocratic system its form. Diocletian, through the numerous changes which he instituted during his reign, contributed more to the building of the autocracy than Augustus to that of the principate, but even Diocletian did not disdain to use materials provided by his third-century predecessors. His political and economic reforms represent the natural culmination and crystallization of third-century developments. It was then the function of Constantine to modify, adapt, and elaborate Diocletian's work.

Gaius Aurelius Valerius Diocletianus was one of the greatest of the Roman emperors, but very little is known about him as a person. He was born about 245 A.D. in Illyria; his father was said to have been either a scribe or a freedman. Diocletian joined the army where he served under Aurelian and Probus; he rose to the post of commander of the imperial bodyguard, and he accompanied the emperor Carus on the Persian campaign of 283. When Carus died in Ctesiphon, his son, Numerian, led the troops back into Roman territory. As the army marched across Asia Minor, it was discovered that Numerian had been murdered. An investigation was held. Diocletian, commanding the imperial bodyguard and having failed to protect the emperor, was in an unenviable position. He solved his problem very neatly by accusing the praetorian prefect of the murder of Numerian and running the prefect through with his sword before that officer could deny the charge of regicide. The soldiers then acclaimed Diocletian emperor; by the spring of 285 the surviving son of Carus (Carinus) had been over-come, and Diocletian reigned supreme.

By this time the empire was in disorder: revolt had broken out in Gaul, and the Persians were pressing on the eastern frontier; the western legions were not completely satisfied with Diocletian as their leader. Diocle-tian therefore took a colleague, a general named Maximian, who at first had the rank of Caesar and was then promoted to co-Augustus (286). Diocletian took charge of affairs in the East, while Maximian was respon-sible for the West. Troubles continued to multiply: revolt in Egypt, an in-vasion along the Danube, raids in Africa, a new Persian threat. In 293 A.D. two additional but subordinate rulers called Caesars were appointed. The empire was then divided into four parts. Constantius (the father of Con-stantine), the Caesar subordinate to Maximian, ruled Gaul and Britain; Maximian, the co-Augustus, had Italy, Spain, and Africa; Galerius, the Caesar subordinate to Diocletian, watched over the Danubian provinces and the Balkans, and Diocletian took the East as his special region. The em-pire now had four capitals: Diocletian centered his administration at Nico-media; Galerius, Sirmium; Constantius, Lugdunum (Lyons); and Max-imian had his headquarters at Milan. In this manner Rome ceased to be the capital of the empire, and the senate was reduced to the position of a municipal council.

Diocletian continued to be the supreme ruler; he was always regarded as the senior Augustus, and Maximian never questioned his pre-eminence. The authority of the Caesars was based upon grants of the imperium and the tribunician power; Maximian adopted Constantius, and Diocletian Galerius. Moreover, Constantius married Theodora, the daughter of Max-imian, and Galerius married Valeria, Diocletian's daughter. All proclama-tions, decrees, and laws were issued in the name of all four rulers and were supposed to be enforced in all parts of the empire.

Diocletian, Maximian, Galerius, and Constantius each had a praetorian prefect. As a result, the four divisions of the empire were called prefectures. The prefectures were eventually subdivided into thirteen groups of prov-inces called dioceses, each of which was headed by an official called a *vicarius*. Under Diocletian the provinces were broken up into smaller units in order to lessen the danger of revolt and increase the efficiency of adminis-tration. Where there had been only 45 provinces in the time of Hadrian, there were 101 under Diocletian. Moreover, the provincial governors had only civil powers, and the command of military forces was turned over to special officers.

The creation of the tetrarchy, or fourfold division of the empire, led to a rapid restoration of order. Diocletian defeated the Persians and put down the Egyptian revolt with great bloodshed; Galerius stabilized the Danube frontier; Maximian calmed the disturbances in Africa; and Constantius drove Germanic invaders back across the Rhine and reconquered Britain. By 298 unity and peace prevailed everywhere.

It was one thing to re-establish order and unity and still another to insure its permanence. Radical changes in the old system were necessary before this could be done, and this involved the solution of a number of other problems. A new basis must be provided for the power of the emperor, and some arrangement must be made for peaceful succession to the throne. The army must be reorganized for the preservation of internal order and suitable provision made for frontier defense. The whole economy must be reorganized and rejuvenated: this called for a new system of taxation, a halt to inflation, and a revival of agriculture, trade, and industry; it also involved finding a solution for a growing shortage of manpower. Finally, a way must be found to deal with minority groups regarded as subversive, Jews, Christians, and others.

The philosophy of the new kind of government devised by Diocletian was simple. The state must take precedence over any faction or individual, and the state was now identified with the emperor. The emperor stood alone at the head of the government; he directed the administration through the bureaucracy; he made the laws and dispensed justice; he was the commander-in-chief of the army and represented the state in its dealings with foreign powers; he even had the authority to regulate economic life.

An autocrat could not conveniently base his rule upon the consent of those whom he governed or receive his authority from any human agency, the senate or the army. Diocletian therefore proclaimed himself a god. He was thus bound by no human laws, and his subjects addressed him as Lord (*Dominus*), as slaves addressed their master. Constantine was also worshipped as a god by his pagan subjects, but his political alliance with the Christians necessitated a different basis for authority. For the Christians he was the ruler whom God had ordained. Thus, when Christianity came to be the state religion, the emperor was thought to rule by divine right. This was a much better solution for the problem of autocratic authority than that of Diocletian. The idea of a god-king was merely a political fiction which the governed might accept as a *modus vivendi,* but the concept of the ruler as the chosen of God was one that was truly credible.

Neither of these new governmental theories was especially novel. The ensis of the Sumerian city-states had been earthly representatives of the gods, and the Egyptian pharaohs had been gods on earth; the Ptolemies and the Seleucids had continued to use these ideas, and in the new Persian monarchy (established in 227 A.D.) the emperor ruled by divine right. When Diocletian proclaimed himself a god, he borrowed much from the Oriental monarchy of his Persian contemporaries in the way of kingly vestments and jewels, ceremonies and court etiquette, and the establishment of a hierarchy of palace dignitaries.

While the army could not be controlled in any way except by a strong emperor who had its respect and who was not lax in discipline, its effectiveness as an instrument of defense was improved by Diocletian and Constantine through the establishment of a permanent frontier garrison system supported by mobile striking forces. The control of the senate, the ancient enemy of the emperor, was easier to attain. The senate had been nearly defunct even before Diocletian came to the throne. During the course of the third century equestrians had gradually replaced senators in military posts and provincial governorships. Carus, the emperor who preceded Diocletian, had not even asked the senate to ratify his acclamation as emperor by the army. Diocletian himself staged the ceremonies of his own accession at Nicomedia. By moving the capital of the West from Rome to Milan, Diocletian reduced the senate to the position of a municipal council in Rome. The senate remained in Rome in later times, too, when the western capital was moved from Milan to Ravenna, but a second senate was set up in Constantinople (Byzantium) when Constantine transferred his government thither in 330 A.D. The senatorial class did not go out of existence, but it was redefined as a landholding aristocracy and modified by the admission of a number of persons who would have been equestrians under the principate. From this class of new nobles were to come the high officials of the bureaucracy and the advisors of the emperor. The real point was, however, that the senatorial class was henceforth utterly dependent upon the emperor for its position; its traditional prestige and authority no longer had any meaning.

The centralization of government, the revision of provincial administration, and the changes in the economic order under Diocletian produced an increase in the size and complexity of the imperial bureaucracy. The departments of government were headed by great ministers, each of whom worked through a host of subordinate officials. The bureaucracy offered fine positions and opportunities for great careers. Naturally, graft and corruption accompanied the growth of the bureaucracy. As might be expected, contemporaries who were not in the imperial service complained bitterly about the evils of bureaucracy.

In addition to making his political reforms, Diocletian also found it necessary to attack certain economic problems which had arisen during the third century. His stabilization of political life and his victories over the barbarians and the Persians had done much to improve economic conditions, but other more direct steps seemed to be advisable if the economic life of the empire were to be kept on an even keel. Diocletian's reform of the currency and the building program which he instituted were not without precedent, but his revision of the system of taxation was an innovation. Whereas money taxes were now levied upon senators, the propertied classes of the municipalities, and tradesmen, the taxes on land were paid in kind. Land, cattle, and agricultural labor throughout the empire were divided into units of equal tax value. The land unit was called the *iugum,* and varied in size according to the quality of the soil and the type of crops it produced. A certain number of cattle also constituted a *iugum,* and the tax was levied at the same rate as on a *iugum* of land. Labor was taxed by the *caput;* one man or two women became the basic unit of reckoning in this case.

Partly as a result of third-century developments and partly because of these reforms, legal restrictions came to be placed both upon the economic freedom of Roman citizens and even upon their personal freedom. A rigid system of economic castes developed. Henceforth, membership in these castes became hereditary; a man could not change his status even if he wanted to.

In agriculture we have already had occasion to note the growth of large estates which were worked by tenant farmers. The scarcity of agricultural labor led both the government (on the imperial estates) and the large landholders to bring pressure upon the tenants to remain on the land. Diocletian's taxation system made such steps even more necessary. Finally, it was Constantine who legally reduced the agricultural workers to serfdom and bound them to the soil. This system, which was ultimately derived from Egypt, was thus extended to the whole empire.

Traders and artisans suffered the same fate as the agricultural workers. As early as the second century A.D. it had been customary for the government to make use of the associations of merchants and the trade guilds. The collegia of merchants had been intrusted with state contracts to supply their native cities with foodstuffs. In the course of the third century such services were made compulsory. Likewise, the craft guilds had been responsible for certain civic duties; one guild might constitute a fire brigade, another might have other responsibilities, and so on. At any rate, by the fourth century membership in these organizations was made hereditary; the merchants and artisans and their sons not only were bound to enter their ancestral professions but were also forbidden to leave their native towns and cities.

Even the wealthy class of the municipalities now suffered regimentation. The officeholders in the municipalities had always been drawn from the men of property who were also liable for the public services that the Greeks called liturgies (the Roman *munera*). Under Diocletian and Constantine, this municipal aristocracy was transformed into a caste, the *curiales*. The *curiales* of each municipality were then made responsible for the collection of taxes within their city and its surrounding countryside. If they could not collect the amount assessed, they had to make up the difference themselves. They were forced to remain in their native cities, and they enjoyed no more freedom of movement than the serfs or the members of the collegia.

One of the problems with which Diocletian had had to struggle early in his reign was that of establishing a sound currency. His solution was to repudiate the debased issues and issue a new coinage. Without going into the details of this matter, we may note that the real difficulty lay in setting a workable ratio between gold and silver. This is a point which most historians and numismatists seem to have misunderstood completely. People have talked glibly about the progressive debasement of the silver coinage of the empire from the time of Nero onward as if it represented some sort of diabolical scheme of the government to defraud the citizens. The real trouble was that there was a shortage of silver which resulted in an increase in its value. Coins became more valuable as bullion than as currency; if the face value of a coin was, for example, twenty cents, and the silver in it became worth twenty-five cents, it was certainly not to the advantage of its holder to use it as a coin. If gold was reasonably plentiful, its value in relation to silver would decline; if the actual silver in ten coins had the same value as a gold piece, no one could expect to get twenty-five silver coins in exchange for a gold coin even though the government might have set this as the official ratio. Silver would simply disappear from circulation, and there would not be enough gold coins to keep the economy going.

Diocletian, in issuing his new currency, undervalued his silver in relation to gold. This mistake, combined with the fact that many new coins were issued within a short time, very soon led to a rapid price rise and a new shortage of silver. By 301 the situation was so grave that the emperor tried to halt the price rise by an edict which set maximum prices for goods, wages, and services. Many fragments of inscriptions bearing this famous Edict of Prices have been found; we can reconstruct its preamble and a large number of its many provisions. The wages and prices thus disclosed are interesting and important for the study of ancient economics, but the edict itself was a failure because the government lacked the machinery to enforce it effectively. The law soon became inoperative, and the whole problem of the currency was later solved by Constantine who altered the gold-silver ratio but even so had to rely mostly on gold and bronze, since silver continued to be hard to acquire.

In 303 A.D. Diocletian attacked one of his remaining problems, that of controlling or eliminating the subversive elements in the empire. The Christians had always been regarded as bad citizens because many of them were not anxious to serve in the army, but the main objection to the Christians was that their religious beliefs forbade them worshipping the emperor as a god or participating in the ceremonies of the imperial cult. The refusal to worship the emperor's statue was like declining to take an oath of loyalty, and this was enough to make the Christians suspect. Of course, there were other reasons for the enthusiasm with which the persecutions of the Christians were conducted: they were confused by the pagans with the Jews, and there was a great deal of anti-Semitism in the ancient world; the Christians appeared to belong to a secret society, something always feared by the government and against the law; the Christians were suspected not only of political disloyalty but also of being anticapitalist, and it was well known that some Christians opposed the sacred institution of slavery. In bad times, when people were hysterical and confused, they were apt to vent their spleen on others who could not or would not fight back, and the Christians provided an excellent target. The persecution of the Christains was, in short, the ancient version of the witch hunt; it seems hardly necessary to draw any of the obvious twentieth-century parallels.

The Christians were not the first minority group to be attacked by Diocletian's government. During the Persian War the Manichaeans, whose religion combined Christianity and Zoroastrianism, had been harshly treated. This was because there were Manichaeans in both the Roman and Persian empires, and those in Roman territory had been suspected of conspiring with Persia against Rome. With Diocletian's government experiencing some economic difficulties added to the fact that the Egyptian Christians had proved troublesome, an attack on the Christians as a whole was almost inevitable.

The immediate cause of the last great persecution which began in 303 is uncertain. The Christians blamed Galerius who was open in his hostility, but there were also rumors of a Christian plot against Diocletian. At any rate, Diocletian issued an edict that the Christians must conform and worship the gods of the state or they would not be permitted to hold government offices, they would lose the right of judicial appeal, and they would be subjected to torture; Christian slaves were forbidden emancipation, and the churches and sacred books were ordered destroyed. This was followed by other orders by which the clergy were arrested, imprisoned, and tortured, and finally the persecution was extended to all Christians. The persecution was most severe in the East, but its only effect was to produce a new crop of martyrs; the Christians were too numerous and too strong to be eradicated.

In the same year that the persecution was instituted Diocletian was the victim of an illness, perhaps a mental breakdown, which incapacitated him for many months and left him old and broken. As a result, he turned to his final problem, that of the succession. In the spring of 305 Diocletian abdicated and forced his colleague, Maximian, to retire at the same time. Constantius and Galerius were raised to the rank of Augusti, and two new Caesars were chosen. This may have been intended as a blueprint for the future, as some people believe, but the plan failed. Constantius died in 306 before adequate arrangements for future successions could be made. Civil war ensued; by 310 there were five rival Augusti and no Caesars.

Without going into the details of the period after 305 A.D., we may note that finally Constantine, the son of Constantius, became sole Augustus in 324 A.D. He adopted most of the political reforms of Diocletian, but he also made some changes. Although the four prefectures were retained, the prefects lost their military functions and became civil administrative officers. Constantine solved the problem of the succession by making his sons Caesars and thus returned to the principle of hereditary succession.

In addition to amplifying the military and economic program of Diocletian, Constantine made two major decisions. The first was to move the capital of the empire from the West to the more self-sufficient and defensible East at Constantinople; this really amounted to a decision to abandon the West, although Constantine may not have realized it. The second decision was to ally the state with Christianity; the effect of this decision on both the state and the Christians was far-reaching.

The political and economic stabilization that Diocletian and Constantine managed to bring about through the creation of the autocracy and economic regimentation delayed the collapse of the Roman Empire for about a century. The whole theory of the new system was that conditions would remain, or would be forced to remain, static. This, of course, was an impossibility.

In the years that followed, the economic decline continued. Perhaps the increasing cost of government and national defense was more than the empire could bear. Perhaps the inefficiency of the great bureaucracy was one of the chief faults of the system.

At any rate, the political unity that had been the Roman Empire disintegrated. In 395 A.D. the empire was formally split into two parts, and the two sons of the Emperor Theodosius became rulers of independent kingdoms, one in the West and the other in the East. The western empire went down before the barbarian assaults of the fifth century, but the Greek-speaking Byzantine Empire in the East, centered at Constantinople, remained in existence until 1453 A.D.

It was ironic that ancient history was to end in the Near East, where it had begun thirty-five hundred years before. It ended with the movement of the political, cultural, and economic center of the ancient world back to the East; it ended with the triumph of the theocratic system of government and the economic regimentation which had been characteristic of the first primary civilizations; it ended, too, with the adoption of an Oriental religion, Christianity.

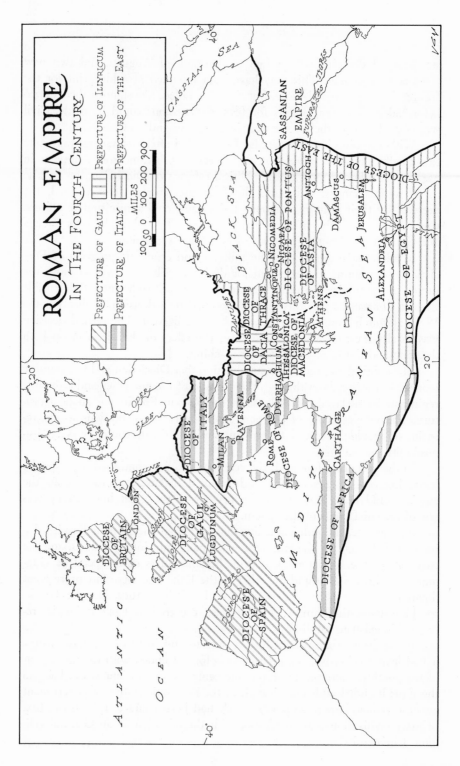

ROMAN EMPIRE
IN THE FOURTH CENTURY

PREFECTURE OF GAUL
PREFECTURE OF ITALY
PREFECTURE OF ILLYRICUM
PREFECTURE OF THE EAST

MILES
100 50 0 100 200 300

DIOCESE OF BRITAIN
LONDON

DIOCESE OF GAUL
LUGDUNUM

DIOCESE OF SPAIN

DIOCESE OF ITALY
MILAN
RAVENNA
ROME

DIOCESE OF AFRICA
CARTHAGE

DIOCESE OF DACIA
DIOCESE OF THRACE
CONSTANTINOPLE
NICOMEDIA

DIOCESE OF PONTUS
NICAEA

DIOCESE OF ASIA

DIOCESE OF MACEDONIA
THESSALONICA
DYRRHACHIUM
ATHENS

DIOCESE OF THE EAST
ANTIOCH
DAMASCUS
JERUSALEM

DIOCESE OF EGYPT
ALEXANDRIA

SASSANIAN EMPIRE

ATLANTIC OCEAN
MEDITERRANEAN SEA
BLACK SEA
CASPIAN SEA

RHINE
ELBE
ODER
LOIRE
SEINE
EBRO
DOURO
DANUBE
NILE
EUPHRATES
TIGRIS

Chapter 27

THE DECLINE
OF ANCIENT CIVILIZATION

T HE CLIMAX REACHED by ancient civilization in the second century
A.D. was followed by a gradual decline in which the political,
economic, and cultural unity of the ancient world slowly disintegrated until it ceased to exist. Western Europe reverted to
what was almost a new Age of Agriculture, although in the eastern Mediterranean the Byzantine Empire managed to keep alight the flickering torch
of ancient culture. We speak of the fall of Rome, but it was more than that:
it was the end of ancient civilization.

There was no sudden collapse. Ancient civilization, a complex structure
reared to a great height by the toil of ages, subsided slowly, almost imper-
ceptibly, like the ruins of some deserted mud-brick city. Contemporaries saw
a changing world, full of invasion and civil war, far different from the
quietude and security of the Pax Romana. People were conscious of the
economic decline, the intellectual sterility, and the artistic stagnation. The
pagans sighed wistfully for the "good old days," but the Christians were
more optimistic and looked ahead for something that was "just around the
corner."

In modern times there have been numerous attempts to explain the
"fall of Rome." In the strictest sense this phrase would apply only to the
collapse of Roman world dominion which was but one aspect of the decline
of ancient civilization; it might even be called a manifestation of it.
Throughout ancient history empires had appeared and disappeared many
times before, yet civilization had either been unaffected or had picked itself
up and risen to new heights. Thus, while the political and military failure
of Rome presents a problem worthy of attention, it must not be allowed to
take precedence over the more important question of the decline of ancient

453

civilization. This fact has been recognized by some, but not all, of those who have wrestled with the problem. In addition, many of the explanations which scholars have offered thus far have confused cause and effect, although it is true that an effect that results from one cause may in turn become the cause of another effect. There is also the danger of selecting a single cause as being responsible for the whole decline; mature consideration will show that a number of factors, rather than a single one, were important.

It is safe to say that theories attributing the decline of ancient civilization to moral degeneracy, race suicide, "failure of nerve," and miscegenation are patently absurd and may be dismissed without further comment. The barbarian invasions, it is true, administered the *coup de grâce* to the Roman Empire, but it is now recognized that the barbarians were able to cross the frontiers because of the internal weakness of the empire and because the barbarians had attained technological equality with the Romans in the art of war. Some have sought the reason for the decline in political or military factors—the lack of democracy, the development of the autocracy, the great political influence which the army acquired—but these things are superficial, or, at best, results rather than causes of decline. The argument that the fall of Rome was due to social conflict or class warfare is plausible, but the evidence is insufficient to supply adequate proof for a theory that has the additional disadvantage of attributing the decline to a single cause. The blame cannot be laid on the rise of Christianity, since the Christian attitude was prompted by the causes which were also responsible for the decline; one might even say that Christianity provided an answer to problems presented by the decline, but it was a palliative and not an antidote. Soil exhaustion, malaria, capitalism, communism, state socialism, overexpansion, underexpansion, the destruction of Greek initiative (whatever that was!), failure to extend prosperity and culture to the masses scarcely exhaust the long and dreary list of superficial, lunatic, or puerile "explanations" for the decline that have found their way into print. Grandiose and intricate theories evolved by great thinkers on the basis of very little fact are also to be rejected. Many of these theories are intellectually stimulating as exercises in logic and provide a sense of achievement for those who fashion them and those who have the time and patience to follow the argument to its conclusion, but they usually leave both creator and admirer too exhausted to realize that the problem has not been solved. One should be on his guard especially against the theory which employs a false analogy; it is a particularly seductive idea that civilizations, like species of plants or animals, have a life cycle.

No one theory of the reasons for the decline of ancient civilization has gained universal acceptance, and probably there will never be one that will satisfy everybody. What we have observed of the process of cultural evolution, however, suggests one or two ideas that may have some bearing on the problem.

The whole question of the latter days of ancient civilization has two main aspects. First of all, it is necessary to explain why a tendency toward stagnation and a lack of creativeness should appear in the art, literature, science, and philosophy of the ancient world before the beginnings of the actual decline in political and economic complexity. Secondly, one must con-sider the possible causes of the decline itself.

The stagnation of art, literature, and philosophy seems to arise from the fact that, as far as certain lines of development were concerned, ter-minal points had been reached. Perfection of some techniques in sculpture, for example, had been attained as early as the time of Praxiteles; the climax of painting came with Apelles. The same thing happened in philosophy and literature. One could not out-Plato Plato or write better satires than Horace had written. There was only one Homer, and one Virgil. Apparently, when development in any field reached a certain point, men did not have the ability to go further, and they had to content themselves with imita-tion and repetition.

Even though certain lines of development might reach terminal points, there was still the possibility of escape from blind alleys through the ex-ploration of side avenues, or, what was less likely, the discovery of new lines to follow. Thus, terminal barriers were avoided again and again in the period before 200 A.D., but in the process new "dead ends" were reached, and the number of possible escapes was constantly being diminished.

Creativeness, however, is largely dependent upon stimulation received from outside contacts. It was no accident that the civilization of antiquity suffered a decline in its creativeness when a cultural unit of great extent came into existence in the second century A.D. As we have seen, this culture area spread from the British Isles to India. It was surrounded by peripheral cultures of lesser degrees of complexity. These peripheral cultures had little to contribute to the civilization of the larger area; they could only borrow from it. The only possible source of stimulus for ancient civilization was China, and that was too far away to provide many fruitful contacts.

On the other hand, ancient civilization itself was of such complexity that there were innumerable opportunities for the combination and elabora-tion of its culture traits. Thus, for a time, one might say that the civilization could feed upon itself. Eventually, however, two factors closed this door. They were: (1) the necessity for specialization of activity, and (2) the overwhelming complexity of the civilization itself.

It is clear that the more complex civilization became, the greater became the necessity for specialization. The inevitable result was that when a man attempted to master one field, he had to limit his contacts with other fields. If he did manage to master his field, there still remained the problem of making a contribution to it. Contributions could be made only with the greatest difficulty unless stimulus could be derived from other fields, but the demands of specialization made this almost impossible.

Let us suppose that an exceptional person did master his field and had time left for outside contacts. He must then, consciously or unconsciously, resort to syncretism and eclecticism in order to glean something useful from the complexity that surrounded him. This complexity had attained such proportions, however, that it defied human understanding. Intelligent selection of ideas from the mass of material available was beyond the power of most individuals, and the whole process of selection assumed the character of a lottery.

The suggestions offered above may provide an explanation for the lack of "progress" or "evolution" in the philosophy, literature, and art of the second century of the Christian era. It partially explains why scientific research of a creative character was retarded, but in the case of science we must remember that the incentive provided by the practical application of knowledge was lacking in the ancient world. Ancient science, which was almost entirely theoretical, was only a form of "scholarship." Consequently, like philosophy and literary scholarship, it tended to become static.

The most promising line of development which was opened up was Christianity. Christianity was, of course, the result of the combination and elaboration, the syncretism and the adroit selection, of older ideas. Under its stimulus art, literature, scholarship, and philosophy were eventually diverted into new channels. Science, however, did not benefit from the new religion, since the Christians had no use for it.

The attainment of "dead ends" and the stifling of the creative impulse halted progress, but there was not necessarily a cultural retreat simply because the forward movement had stopped. On the contrary, if the political and economic situation remained favorable, all existing culture traits could be retained. It is not surprising that respect for the past and an interest in the preservation of culture should be characteristic of the first and second centuries A.D. Compilations of ancient knowledge, commentaries, and summaries began to occupy the attention of those who in earlier periods might have been creators of culture.

The actual decline of culture, on the other hand, came with political and economic disruption. As the cities began to melt away in the West, culture became less complex, and many culture traits were discarded because they were useless in an agricultural society. Moreover, when Christianity supplanted paganism, the trappings of paganism were cast aside. Thus, even within the Byzantine Empire of the East, which was far more urbanized than the West in the medieval period, much of the culture of classical antiquity was rejected because no place could be found for it in the Christian scheme of things.

It has been emphasized throughout this book that the complexity of a civilization depends upon (1) the extent of its urbanization, and (2) what it may have inherited from its predecessors. We have also seen that the lifeblood of a city is its trade; in turn, trade usually fosters industry. From this it is clear that if we wish to learn why ancient civilization declined, we must learn what happened to its trade and industry.

Looking backward over the path we have travelled, we may observe an interesting economic phenomenon. In the beginning the Near East was the commercial and industrial center of the ancient world. There was a flourishing trade within the area of the Near East itself, and also there was trade with the peripheral areas.

The external trade of the Near East merits our consideration because it presents an economic situation which was typical in the ancient world. This trade of the Near East and its peripheral areas consisted largely of the export of manufactured goods to the peripheral areas in return for raw products. As a result of this trade, cities began to appear in the peripheral areas. Industrial production developed in these cities. Ultimately, the cities of the periphery became commercial and industrial centers which supplied new peripheral areas.

The Aegean region was one of the peripheral areas of the Near East. We have seen how the Greeks became traders and manufacturers and how they exchanged their industrial products for the raw products of their colonists and the barbarians who lived around the Mediterranean and the Black Sea. After a time the colonies of the Greeks and the towns of the barbarians grew into cities which became centers of production and distribution for more remote areas.

The whole process was repeated in the case of Italy. Italy, developed mainly through trade with the Greeks, became the economic center of the western Mediterranean in the first century B.C. Through trade with Italy, Gaul and Britain were stimulated to economic advance. Toward the end of the first century A.D. they were rapidly becoming urbanized and were building up their industries. The climax was reached in the second century.

This, however, was the end of the long series of developments that had begun hundreds of years before in the Near East. Except for Scandinavia, Germany, and the New World (which was unknown), there was no peripheral area with which the West could trade. Germany and Scandinavia had little that the western provinces desired, and there were transportation difficulties as well. The result was that the western provinces became largely self-sufficient. They could supply their own agricultural and pastoral products; their industries, because of the lack of a large foreign market, were geared to the needs of the domestic market. Ultimately, this fostered an economic decentralization which led naturally to political separatism.

Although the western provinces might be able to hold their own because of their self-sufficiency, Italy and Greece were less fortunate. The city-states of mainland Greece which had grown to economic maturity through trade with their colonies were not agriculturally self-sufficient. When the colonies attained industrial independence, the Greek city-states lost their sources of prosperity, and economic and political decline resulted. Italy suffered the same fate when the western provinces became industrially self-sufficient and began to raise their own grapes and olives.

The situation in the Near East was much different. The Near East was agriculturally self-sufficient, and its total area, though more or less naturally unified, was large enough to make possible a profitable internal trade. In addition, there was the trade with the Far East and India in which the peoples of the Near East continued to act as middlemen in the distribution of Oriental products to the West. It is therefore clear that, even though the economic structure of the West might collapse, the Near East would still retain a measure of its prosperity. This explains, of course, why the Byzantine Empire survived long after the fall of the West.

The collapse of Roman world dominion had as its underlying causes the economic developments described above. Roman political power was centered in Italy; it cannot be a coincidence that Italy's economic decline which was accompanied by the attainment of self-sufficiency in the western provinces was followed in the third century A.D. by the temporary establishment of an independent Gallic empire and the rise of the kingdom of Palmyra in the self-sufficient Near East.

The restoration of imperial unity by Aurelian shows that the third-century manifestations of separatism were premature, but the chaos of the period accelerated the economic regression that naturally followed the end of commercial and industrial expansion in the West. The attempt of Diocletian and Constantine to maintain an economic *status quo* might have delayed the collapse even longer than it did if the bureaucracy had functioned efficiently, but the final result was inevitable.

The emperors of the period of the autocracy had to defend the frontiers and keep internal order. This necessitated a costly military force. Funds for the army had to be raised by increased taxation. The collection of taxes called for the expansion of the bureaucracy, which in turn increased the cost of government. The major portion of the taxes had to be raised in the prosperous sections of the empire: the western provinces and the Near East. The rest of the empire could contribute very little. Moreover, it was only in the Near East that there existed what might be called a real taxable surplus. In other words, it was only in the Near East that profits were made in amounts large enough to bear the burden of heavy taxation.

The western provinces could "break even," but an additional tax burden would destroy their profits, and then decline would follow. In effect, what happened was that the government took not only the interest (the taxable surplus) but also part of the principal (the working capital of trade, industry, and agriculture). We may therefore conclude that the cost of keeping out the barbarians and maintaining internal unity was more than the Roman Empire could afford to pay. The Near East (the Byzantine Empire) had the resources to defend itself, and thus it survived and retained its independence.

Perhaps we have thought too much about decline and not enough about survival. We should recognize that man's potential ability and urge to create had been diverted into new channels by Christianity, which provided the inspiration for a new culture that was limited mainly by its lack of economic complexity from attaining the status of a civilization. We should recognize also the attractive and instructive parallel that can be drawn between the Dark Ages that ensued in the Aegean between 1200 and 750 B.C. and those that followed the fall of Rome in the West. In both cases the West, though a larger area was involved in the second case, reverted to an Age of Agriculture while civilization survived and revived in the Near East. Although much of ancient civilization was preserved by the Byzantines, something in the nature of a revival was accomplished by the followers of Mohammed, who not only had the advantage of the inspiration and new frame of reference provided by a new religion, but also possessed the economic complexity of the self-sufficient Near East to a far greater extent than the Byzantines. The cultural function of Christianity and the religion of Islam was identical in that both afforded an escape from the dead ends and blind alleys of paganism, but the environmental and economic advantages of the Islamic peoples allowed them to retain more of ancient civilization and to build more rapidly upon its foundations. Through their economic and cultural activities these direct heirs of the ancient Near East were able to contribute a revival of civilization in the West.

Despite the survivals in the eastern portion of what had been the ancient world, the day of ancient civilization had ended, and it is not pleasant to linger in the sad twilight of antiquity amid the ruins of a past which had seemed full of promise for the future. Yet the survivors of the catastrophe in the West spent little time in wailing and lamentation. Encouraged by the promises of their new Christian faith, they set about building a new world, and most of them were happy in their work.

Even though the men of the medieval period in Europe drew heavily upon certain resources provided by their pagan forefathers, it was truly a new world that they created. Within the Mediterranean basin itself the murmur of Greek and Latin was heard but faintly through the clamor of

459

strange barbarian tongues. The old landmarks stood in their accustomed places, but they seemed strangely unfamiliar. The walls of Athena's Parthenon echoed but hollowly the praises of the Virgin Mary, and the gibbering "saints" who fasted atop the ruinous columns of other pagan temples must have angered the ghosts of the now dead "immortals" of Olympus. The real tragedy, however, was that beneath the sands of Egypt and in the dark recesses of the monasteries much of the accumulated wisdom of the Near East, Greece, and Rome lay for centuries unused, neglected, and forgotten.

BIBLIOGRAPHY

The following bibliography is in no sense complete. It is simply intended to provide the student with a list of readable and easily accessible books in English. The titles marked by asterisks are paperbacks which may be purchased at a moderate price.

Atlases and General Works

Cambridge Ancient History. Ed. by J. B. Bury *et al.* 12 vols. Cambridge, Eng.: Cambridge, 1923–39.

Kraeling, E. G. *Bible Atlas*. Chicago: Rand McNally, 1956.

Palmer, R. R., ed. *Atlas of World History*. Chicago: Rand McNally, 1957.

Toynbee, A. J. *Study of History*. Abridged by D. C. Somervell. 2 vols. Oxford: Oxford, 1948–57.

Westminster Historical Atlas to the Bible. Ed. by G. E. Wright and F. V. Filson. Philadelphia: Westminster, 1945.

Near East and the Beginnings of Civilization

*Albright, W. F. *Archaeology of Palestine*. Harmondsworth, Eng.: Pelican (A199), 1949.

*——. *From the Stone Age to Christianity*. New York: Doubleday Anchor (A100), 1957.

*Braidwood, R. J. *Prehistoric Men*. Chicago: Chicago Natural History Museum, Popular Series, Anthropology, No. 37, 1948.

——. *The Near East and the Foundations for Civilization*. Eugene: Oregon, 1952.

Breasted, J. H. *Ancient Records of Egypt*. 5 vols. Chicago: Chicago, 1906–07.

——. *History of Egypt*. 2nd rev. ed. New York: Scribner, 1909.

——. *The Dawn of Conscience*. New York: Scribner, 1934.

*Burrows, M. *What Mean These Stones?* New York: Living Age Books (LA7), 1957.

Capart, J. *Egyptian Art*. Tr. by W. R. Dawson. London: Allen & Unwin, 1923.

Černý, J. *Ancient Egyptian Religion*. London: Hutchinson, 1952.

*Chiera, E. *They Wrote on Clay*. Chicago: Phoenix Books (P2), 1956.

461

*Childe, V. G. *New Light on the Most Ancient Near East*. New York: Evergreen Books (E72), 1957.

Contenau, G. *Everyday Life in Babylon and Assyria*. Tr. by K. R. and A. R. Maxwell-Hyslop. New York: St. Martins, 1954.

*Cook, S. J. *Introduction to the Bible*. Harmondsworth, Eng.: Pelican (A144), 1950.

Curwen, E. C., and Hatt, G. *Plough and Pasture*. New York: Schuman, 1953.

Diringer, D. *The Alphabet*. New York: Philosophical Library, 1947.

*Driver, S. R. *Introduction to the Literature of the Old Testament*. New York: Meridian Books (ML3), 1956.

*Edwards, I. E. S. *The Pyramids of Egypt*. Harmondsworth, Eng.: Pelican (A168), 1952.

Erman, A. *The Literature of the Ancient Egyptians*. London: Methuen, 1927.

*Frankfort, H. *Before Philosophy*. Harmondsworth, Eng.: Pelican (A198), 1949. Out of print.

*———. *The Birth of Civilization in the Near East*. New York: Doubleday Anchor (A89), 1956.

Gaster, T. H. *The Oldest Stories in the World*. New York: Viking, 1952.

Gelb, I. J. *The Study of Writing*. Chicago: Chicago, 1952.

*Ghirshman, R. *Iran*. Harmondsworth, Eng.: Pelican (A239), 1955.

Glanville, S. R. K., ed. *The Legacy of Egypt*. Oxford: Oxford, 1942.

*Gurney, O. R. *The Hittites*. Harmondsworth, Eng.: Pelican (A259), 1952.

Hall, H. R. *Ancient History of the Near East*. 10th ed. London: Methuen, 1947.

Hooke, S. H. *Babylonian and Assyrian Religion*. London: Hutchinson, 1953.

Kenyon, K. *Digging Up Jericho*. New York: Praeger, 1957.

Kramer, S. N. *From the Tablets of Sumer*. Indian Hills, Colo.: Falcons Wing, 1956.

———. *Sumerian Mythology*. Philadelphia: American Philosophical Society, 1944.

Kroeber, A. L. *Anthropology*. Rev. ed. New York: Harcourt, 1948.

Lloyd, S. *Early Anatolia*. Harmondsworth, Eng.: Pelican (A354), 1956.

Luckenbill, D. D. *Ancient Records of Assyria and Babylonia*. 2 vols. Chicago: Chicago, 1926.

Mercer, S. A. B. *Religion of Ancient Egypt*. London: Luzak, 1950.

Neugebauer, O. *The Exact Sciences in Antiquity*. Princeton: Princeton, 1952.

Olmstead, A. T. *History of Assyria*. New York: Scribner, 1923.

———. *History of Palestine and Syria*. New York: Scribner, 1931.

———. *History of the Persian Empire*. Chicago: Chicago, 1948.

*Orlinsky, H. *Ancient Israel*. Ithaca: Cornell, 1954.

Pendlebury, J. D. S. *Tell-el-Amarna*. London: Dickson, 1935.

Perkins, A. L. *Comparative Archaeology of Early Mesopotamia*. Chicago: Chicago, 1949.

*Piggott, S. *Prehistoric India*. Harmondsworth, Eng.: Pelican (A205). Out of print.

Polanyi, K., *et al. Trade and Market in the Early Empires*. Glencoe, Ill.: Free Press, 1957.

Pritchard, J. B. *Ancient Near Eastern Texts Relating to the Old Testament*. Princeton: Princeton, 1950.

Sauer, C. O. *Agricultural Origins and Dispersals*. New York: American Geographical Society, 1952.

Shorter, A. W. *The Egyptian Gods*. London: Routledge, 1937.

*Simpson, G. G. *The Meaning of Evolution*. New York: New American Library of World Literature (MD66), 1952.

Speiser, E. A. *The United States and the Near East*. Cambridge, Mass.: Harvard, 1950.

Steindorff, G., and Seele, K. C. *When Egypt Ruled the East*. Chicago: Chicago, 1942.

Turner, R. E. *The Great Cultural Traditions*. Vol. I. New York: McGraw, 1941.

*Wilson, J. A. *The Culture of Egypt*. Chicago: Phoenix Books (P11), 1956.

Winlock, H. E. *The Rise and Fall of the Middle Kingdom*. New York: Macmillan, 1947.

Woolley, C. L. *The Development of Sumerian Art*. London: Faber, 1935.

*————. *A Forgotten Kingdom*. Harmondsworth, Eng.: Pelican (A261), 1953.

Zeuner, F. E. *Dating the Past*. London: Methuen, 1950.

Greece and the Eastern Mediterranean to 362 B.C.

Andrewes, A. *The Greek Tyrants*. London: Hutchinson, 1956.

Burn, A. R. *The World of Hesiod*. London: Routledge, 1936.

*Burnet, J. *Early Greek Philosophy*. New York: Meridian Books (ML5), 1957.

Buschor, E. *Greek Vase Painting*. Tr. by G. C. Richards. London: Chatto, 1921.

Calhoun, G. M. *The Business Life of Ancient Athens*. Chicago: Chicago, 1926.

Casson, S. *Ancient Cyprus*. London: Methuen, 1937.

Cohen, M. R., and Drabkin, I. E. *A Source Book in Greek Science*. New York: McGraw, 1948.

Dinsmoor, W. B. *The Architecture of Ancient Greece*. New York: Clarke, Irwin, 1950.

Dunbabin, T. J. *The Western Greeks*. Oxford: Oxford, 1948.

*Farrington, B. *Greek Science*. Harmondsworth, Eng.: Pelican (A142), 1949.

Ferguson, W. S. *Greek Imperialism*. New York: Houghton, 1913.

Fowler, H. N., Wheeler, J. R., and Stevens, G. P. *A Handbook of Greek Archaeology*. New York: American Book, 1909.

Freeman, K. *The Work and Life of Solon*. London: Oxford, 1926.

Glotz, G. *Ancient Greece at Work*. Tr. by M. R. Dobie. New York: Knopf, 1926.

Glotz, G. *The Greek City and Its Institutions.* Tr. by N. Mallinson. New York: Knopf, 1930.

Hadas, M. *A History of Greek Literature.* New York: Columbia, 1950.

Hasebroek, J. *Trade and Politics in Ancient Greece.* Tr. by L. M. Fraser and D. C. Macgregor. London: G. Bell, 1933.

Hignett, C. *The Athenian Constitution.* Oxford: Oxford, 1952.

Hill, I. T. *The Ancient City of Athens.* Cambridge, Mass.: Harvard, 1953.

*Kitto, H. D. F. *Greek Tragedy.* New York: Doubleday Anchor (A38), 1954.

Laistner, M. L. W. *A History of the Greek World from 479 to 323 B.C.* London: Methuen, 1936.

Linforth, I. M. *Solon the Athenian.* Berkeley: California, 1919.

Michell, H. *The Economics of Ancient Greece.* New York: Macmillan, 1940.

Mylonas, G. *Ancient Mycenae.* Princeton: Princeton, 1957.

Nilsson, M. P. *Homer and Mycenae.* London: Methuen, 1933.

Pendlebury, J. D. S. *The Archaeology of Crete.* London: Methuen, 1939.

Pickard-Cambridge, A. W. *The Dramatic Festivals of Athens.* Oxford: Oxford, 1953.

Richter, G. M. A. *Archaic Greek Art.* New York: Oxford, 1949.

———. *The Sculpture and Sculptors of the Greeks.* New Haven: Yale, 1950.

Robertson, D. S. *A Handbook of Greek and Roman Architecture.* 2nd ed. Cambridge, Eng.: Cambridge, 1943.

Swindler, M. H. *Ancient Painting.* New Haven: Yale, 1929.

*Taylor, A. E. *Socrates.* New York: Doubleday Anchor (A9), 1953.

Ventris, M., and Chadwick, J. *Documents in Mycenaean Greek.* Cambridge, Eng.: Cambridge, 1956.

Wace, A. J. B. *Mycenae.* Princeton: Princeton, 1949.

Webster, T. B. L. *Art and Literature in Fourth Century Athens.* London: Athlone, 1956.

Woodhouse, W. J. *Solon the Liberator.* Oxford: Oxford, 1938.

*Zeller, E. *Outlines of the History of Greek Philosophy.* New York: Meridian Books (M9), 1955.

Zimmern, A. E. *The Greek Commonwealth.* 5th ed. rev. Oxford: Oxford, 1931.

The Hellenistic Age

Bevan, E. R. *A History of Egypt Under the Ptolemaic Dynasty.* London: Methuen, 1927.

———. *The House of Seleucus.* 4 vols. London: Longmans, 1902.

Bieber, M. *The Sculpture of the Hellenistic Age.* New York: Columbia, 1955.

Bury, J. B., ed. *The Hellenistic Age.* London: Cambridge, 1923.

Cary, M. *The Legacy of Alexander: A History of the Greek World from 323 to 146 B.C.* London: Methuen, 1932.

Dickins, G. *Hellenistic Sculpture.* Oxford: Oxford, 1920.

Jouguet, P. *Macedonian Imperialism and the Hellenization of the East.* Tr. by M. R. Dobie. New York: Knopf, 1928.

Körte, A. *Hellenistic Poetry.* Tr. by J. Hammer and M. Hadas. New York: Knopf, 1929.

Macurdy, G. H. *Hellenistic Queens.* Baltimore: Johns Hopkins, 1932.

More, P. E. *Hellenistic Philosophies.* Princeton: Princeton, 1923.

Robinson, C. A. *Alexander the Great.* New York: Dutton, 1947.

Rostovtzeff, M. I. *The Social and Economic History of the Hellenistic World.* 3 vols. Oxford: Oxford, 1941.

Tarn, W. W. *Alexander the Great.* 2 vols. Cambridge, Eng.: Cambridge, 1948.

———. *The Greeks in Bactria and India.* Cambridge, Eng.: Cambridge, 1938.

———. *Hellenistic Civilization.* London: Arnold, 1930.

Wilcken, U. *Alexander the Great.* Tr. by G. C. Richards. New York: Dial, 1932.

Rome and the Western Mediterranean to 27 B.C.

Abbott, F. F. *History and Description of Roman Political Institutions.* New York: Ginn, 1911.

Altheim, F. *A History of Roman Religion.* Tr. by H. Mattingly. New York: Dutton, 1938.

Anderson, W. J., and Spiers, R. P. *The Architecture of Ancient Rome.* Vol. I. New York: Scribner, 1927.

Bailey, C. *The Legacy of Rome.* London: Milford, 1923.

Broughton, T. R. S. *The Magistrates of the Roman Republic.* 2 vols. New York: American Philosophical Association, 1951–52.

Carcopino, J. *Daily Life in Ancient Rome.* Ed. by H. T. Rowell. Tr. by E. O. Lorimer. New Haven: Yale, 1940.

*Cowell, F. R. *Cicero and the Roman Republic.* Harmondsworth, Eng.: Pelican (A320), 1956.

Debevoise, N. *A Political History of Parthia.* Chicago: Chicago, 1938.

Duff, J. W. *A Literary History of Rome.* 2 vols. London: Benn, 1927.

*Frank, T. *Life and Literature in the Roman Republic.* Berkeley: California, 1956.

———, et al. *Economic Survey of Ancient Rome.* 5 vols. Baltimore: Johns Hopkins, 1933–40.

Hadas, M. *History of Latin Literature.* New York: Columbia, 1952.

———. *Sextus Pompey.* New York: Columbia, 1930.

Hill, H. *The Roman Middle Class.* New York: Macmillan, 1952.

Holmes, T. R. *The Roman Republic and the Founder of the Empire.* 3 vols. Oxford: Milford, 1923.

Homo, L. *Primitive Italy and the Beginnings of Roman Imperialism.* Tr. by V. G. Childe. New York: Knopf, 1926.

Homo, L. *Roman Political Institutions from City to State.* Tr. by M. R. Dobie. New York: Knopf, 1929.

Laistner, M. L. W. *The Greater Roman Historians.* Berkeley: California, 1947.

Marsh, F. B. *A History of the Roman World from 146 to 30 B.C.* London: Methuen, 1935.

*Pallottino, M. *The Etruscans.* Harmondsworth, Eng.: Pelican (A310), 1955.

Platner, S. B., and Ashby, T. *A Topographical Dictionary of Ancient Rome.* Oxford: Oxford, 1929.

Sandys, J. E. *Companion to Latin Studies.* Cambridge, Eng.: Cambridge, 1926.

Scullard, H. H. *A History of the Roman World from 753 to 146 B.C.* London: Methuen, 1935.

————. *Roman Politics, 220–150 B.C.* Oxford: Oxford, 1951.

Syme, R. *The Roman Revolution.* Oxford: Oxford, 1939.

Taylor, L. R. *Party Politics in the Age of Caesar.* Berkeley: California, 1949.

The Roman Empire

Abbott, F. F., and Johnson, A. C. *Municipal Administration in the Roman Empire.* Princeton: Princeton, 1926.

Boak, A. E. R. *Manpower Shortage and the Fall of the Roman Empire in the West.* Ann Arbor: Michigan, 1955.

Bouchier, E. S. *Life and Letters in Roman Africa.* London: Oxford, 1913.

————. *Spain Under the Roman Empire.* London: Oxford, 1914.

Buchan, J. *Augustus.* New York: Houghton, 1937.

Charlesworth, M. P. *The Roman Empire.* Oxford: Oxford, 1951.

————. *Trade Routes and Commerce of the Roman Empire.* Cambridge, Eng.: Cambridge, 1926.

Collingwood, R. G. *Roman Britain.* Oxford: Oxford, 1932.

Cumont, F. *Oriental Religions in Roman Paganism.* London: Cecil Chambers, 1911.

*Dill, S. *Roman Society from Nero to Marcus Aurelius.* New York: Meridian Books (ML1), 1956.

Friedländer, L. *Roman Life and Manners, the Early Empire.* Tr. by J. H. Freese and L. A. Magnus. 4 vols. Oxford: Oxford, 1908–13.

Gibbon, E. *The History of the Decline and Fall of the Roman Empire.* Ed. by J. B. Bury. 7 vols. London: Macmillan, 1900–1902.

Halliday, W. R. *The Pagan Background of Early Christianity.* Liverpool, 1925.

Hammond, M. *The Augustan Principate in Theory and Practice During the Julio-Claudian Period.* Cambridge, Mass.: Harvard, 1933.

Holmes, T. R. *The Architect of the Roman Empire.* 2 vols. Oxford: Oxford, 1928–31.

Jones, A. H. M. *The Cities of the Eastern Roman Provinces.* Oxford: Oxford, 1937.

*Katz, S. *The Decline of Rome and the Rise of Medieval Europe.* Ithaca: Cornell, 1955.

Lot, F. *The End of the Ancient World.* Tr. by P. and M. Leon. New York: Knopf, 1931.

Magie, D. *Roman Rule in Asia Minor.* Princeton: Princeton, 1950.

Mattingly, H. *Roman Imperial Civilization.* London: Arnold, 1957.

Parker, H. M. D. *A History of the Roman World from* A.D. *138 to 337.* London: Methuen, 1935.

Robathan, D. M. *The Monuments of Ancient Rome.* Rome: M. Bretschneider, 1950.

Rostovtzeff, M. I. *The Social and Economic History of the Roman Empire.* Oxford: Oxford, 1926.

Salmon, E. T. *A History of the Roman World 30* B.C.–*138* A.D. 2nd rev. ed. London: Methuen, 1950.

Scramuzza, V. *The Emperor Claudius.* Cambridge, Mass.: Harvard, 1940.

Starr, C. G. *Civilization and the Caesars.* Ithaca: Cornell, 1954.

———. *The Roman Imperial Navy.* Ithaca: Cornell, 1941.

*Walbank, F. W. *The Decline of the Roman Empire in the West.* New York: Abelard-Schuman, 1953.

Warmington, E. H. *The Commerce Between the Roman Empire and India.* Cambridge, Eng.: Cambridge, 1928.

*Wheeler, M. *Rome Beyond the Imperial Frontiers.* Harmondsworth, Eng.: Pelican (A335), 1955.

Winspear, A. D., and Geweke, L. K. *Augustus and the Reconstruction of Roman Government and Society.* Madison: Wisconsin, 1935.

Index

Index

Index

Index

Index